# THE LAW AND ECONOMICS

## OF

# IRRATIONAL BEHAVIOR

# THE LAW AND ECONOMICS

## OF

# IRRATIONAL BEHAVIOR

EDITED BY FRANCESCO PARISI

AND VERNON L. SMITH

STANFORD ECONOMICS AND FINANCE
*An imprint of Stanford University Press*
*Stanford, California 2005*

Stanford University Press
Stanford, California

"Threatening an 'Irrational' Breach of Contract" by Oren Bar-Gill and Omri Ben-Shahar was originally published in *Supreme Court Economic Review 11* © 2003, University of Chicago Press. "The Free Radicals of Tort" by Mark Grady was originally published in *Supreme Court Economic Review 11* © 2003, University of Chicago Press. "Probability Errors: Some Positive and Normative Implications for Tort and Contract Law" by Eric Posner was originally published in *Supreme Court Economic Review 11* © 2003, University of Chicago Press. "On the Psychology of Punishment" by Cass Sunstein was originally published in *Supreme Court Economic Review 11* © 2003, University of Chicago Press. Reprinted with permission.

Printed in the United States of America on acid-free, archival-quality paper

Library of Congress Cataloging-in-Publication Data

The law and economics of irrational behavior / edited by Francesco Parisi and Vernon L. Smith.
   p. cm.
  Includes bibliographical references and index.
  ISBN 0-8047-5143-9 (cloth : alk. paper)—ISBN 0-8047-5144-7 (pbk. : alk. paper)
   1. Law and economics.   2. Rational choice theory.   3. Deviant behavior.   4. Law—Economic aspects—United States.   I. Parisi, Francesco, 1962–   II. Smith, Vernon L.

K487.E3L3875 2005
330'.01'156—dc22                  2004021322

Original Printing 2005

Last figure below indicates year of this printing:
14  13  12  11  10  09  08  07  06  05

Typeset by G&S Book Services in 10.5/13.5 Minion

# CONTENTS

# TABLES AND FIGURES

## Tables

## Figures

# ACKNOWLEDGMENTS

The editors of this volume owe a debt of gratitude to many friends and colleagues that have contributed to this project at different stages of its development. Most notably, we would like to thank Dan Polsby and Paul Stavis for encouraging research on the law and economics of irrational behavior. The Stanley Medical Research Institute and the George Mason University Law and Psychiatry Center provided generous funding for the project. Some of the papers contained in this volume were presented at a conference held at George Mason University on November 1–2, 2002. Additional papers were commissioned by the editors. Terry and Elisabeth Chorvat provided invaluable help in coordinating this initiative. David Lord scrupulously assisted the editors in preparing the manuscript for publication and drafting of the introduction. Without their help this project would not have been possible. Finally, we would like to thank University of Chicago Press for granting the permission to publish the papers by Eric A. Posner, Cass Sunstein, Mark F. Grady, and the paper jointly authored by Oren Bar-Gill and Omri Ben-Shahar, which have appeared in volume 11 of the *Supreme Court Economic Review* (2003).

# LIST OF CONTRIBUTORS

OREN BAR-GILL is John M. Olin Fellow in Law and Economics, The Society of Fellows, Harvard University.

OMRI BEN-SHAHAR is Professor of Law and Economics, University of Michigan School of Law.

F. H. BUCKLEY is Professor of Law and Director, Law and Economics Program, George Mason University School of Law.

JONATHAN CAULKINS is Professor of Operations Research and Public Policy, H. John Heinz III School of Public Policy and Management, Carnegie Mellon University.

TERRENCE CHORVAT is Associate Professor of Law, George Mason University.

ROBERT COOTER is Herman F. Selvin Professor of Law, University of California, Berkeley School of Law (Boalt Hall).

YUVAL FELDMAN is Lecturer, Faculty of Law, Bar-Ilan University, Israel.

VINCY FON is Assistant Professor, Department of Economics, George Washington University.

ROBERT H. FRANK is Goldwin Smith Professor of Economics, Ethics, and Public Policy, Johnson Graduate School of Management and Department of Economics, Cornell University.

GERD GIGERENZER is Director, Max Planck Institute for Human Development, Berlin.

MARK F. GRADY is Professor of Law, UCLA School of Law.

ELIZABETH HOFFMAN is President, University of Colorado.

PETER H. HUANG is Associate Professor of Law, University of Minnesota Law School.

CHRISTINE JOLLS is Professor of Law, Harvard Law School.

GREGORY LA BLANC is Adjunct Professor, Department of Economics, University of Virginia.

ROBERT MACCOUN is Professor of Law and Public Policy, University of California, Berkeley School of Law (Boalt Hall) and Goldman School of Public Policy.

KEVIN MCCABE is Professor of Economics and Law, George Mason University.

STEPHEN J. MORSE is Ferdinand Wakeman Hubbell Professor of Law, University of Pennsylvania School of Law, and Professor of Psychology and Law in Psychiatry, University of Pennsylvania School of Medicine.

MARCO NOVARESE is Lecturer in Economics, Faculty of Law, University of Piemonte Orientale, and Researcher, Centre for Cognitive Economics, University of Piemonte Orientale.

MICHAEL E. O'NEILL is Associate Professor of Law, George Mason University School of Law, and Commissioner, U.S. Sentencing Commission.

FRANCESCO PARISI is Professor of Law and Director, Law and Economics Program, George Mason University School of Law.

ERIC A. POSNER is Professor of Law, University of Chicago School of Law.

JEFFREY J. RACHLINSKI is Professor of Law, Cornell University School of Law, Visiting University of Pennsylvania School of Law.

SALVATORE RIZZELLO is Professor of Economics and History of Economic Thought, Faculty of Law, University of Piemonte Orientale, and Coordinator, Centre for Cognitive Economics, University of Piemonte Orientale.

OLE-JØRGEN SKOG is Professor of Sociology, University of Oslo.

VERNON SMITH is Professor of Economics and Law, George Mason University, and Nobel Laureate in Economics, 2002.

CASS R. SUNSTEIN is Karl Llewellyn Distinguished Service Professor of Jurisprudence, University of Chicago School of Law and Department of Political Science.

THOMAS S. ULEN is Swanlund Chair, University of Illinois at Urbana-Champaign, and Professor of Law, University of Illinois College of Law.

THE LAW AND ECONOMICS

OF

IRRATIONAL BEHAVIOR

# INTRODUCTION

*Francesco Parisi and Vernon Smith*

Friedrich Nietzsche (1878) once wrote, "The irrationality of a thing is no argument against its existence, rather a condition of it." Since the inception of Adam Smith's invisible hand, economics has largely been guided by rational choice theorists who advance the notion that the logical pursuit of self-interest drives human choice in a free society and leads to prosperity. However, although proponents of rational choice are quick to remember the notions of empirical economics that have sprung forth from Smith's *Wealth of Nations*, it is often forgotten that Smith's work was predicated on a philosophy that justice and other moral virtues limit the pursuit of self-interest (Kilcullen 1996a). In his other great work, *The Theory of Moral Sentiments*, Smith provides an analysis of various feelings and psychological dispositions relating to morality and invites the reader to test his ideas against their own experience of these feelings (Kilcullen 1996b). This reliance on psychology by the greatest economic mind of our times might lead a person to believe that the field historically would have been more influenced by a broader set of social theories. However, until recently, economic thought has largely focused on the empirical study of self-interest that leads to utility functions, supply and demand curves, and Pareto optimal solutions. It is only more recently that the findings of behavioral economists have raised some doubts on the previously unquestioned assumptions of human rationality and have made large inroads into this discipline.

Behavioral economists accept many of the premises of traditional economic thought, for example, that situational outcomes are the result of individual decisions, taking place in a particular economic environment. But behavioral economists go a step further, arguing that the human action not only is shaped by relevant economic constraints but is highly affected by people's endogenous preferences, knowledge, skills, endowments, and a variety of psychological and physical constraints (Smith 1991, 2000). Incentives matter and incentives drive human behavior, but incentives are often more than simple monetary gain. Thus, forms of experimentation more penetrating than traditional game theoretic analyses are needed to truly understand human choice and behavior.

Behavioral thought has come to play a large role in economic theory. One could just look at Alan Greenspan blaming "irrational exuberance" for unduly escalating market values to realize the relevance of behavioral analyses in policy and political discourse. In academic analyses, the relevance of these tools spans from the understanding of microbehavior to general equilibrium theory. For example, no longer could the value of assets be determined simply by the financial equations of the market. Rather, a combination of emotions and heightened attention to the market, fed by the optimistic cheerleading of pundits, led to an excessive desire to "get into the game" (Shiller 2000). But behavioral and experimental economics' unique blend of psychology, economics, and neuroscience can explain more than the overvaluing of stocks. In many ways it offers an analytical opening where mainstream economic models have failed. The former theory may help explain questions such as why Americans save too little, acquire too much debt, and manage their investment portfolios in a self-destructive fashion (Dubner 2003).

The rise of behavioral economics and the findings of experimental economics, however, have led to a clash between the rational choice theory and the belief that this idea does not properly account for the montage of human emotions, biology, and attitudes. One anonymous economist has been quoted as saying, "What you have to understand is that behavioral economics is attacking the foundation of what welfare economics is built on."

However, it may be possible to end the intellectual tug-of-war between rational choice theorists and behavioralists without turning it into a zero-sum game. In the present text, twenty-eight authors have joined together to present such a possibility. Covering a wide range of fields from neuroscience to economics to law and sociology, these distinguished academics have presented an array of valuable contributions that, aware in their own application that rational choice theory can no longer be bought in a wholesale fashion, aim at revisiting its basic premises in such a way as to ensure a more rigorous analytical model. These authors then proceed to offer a practical application of this modified theory to a variety of economic and legal problems that have bedeviled traditional economic thought.

These chapters offer an important contribution to the ongoing research program, incorporating the findings of psychology and other behavioral sciences, to reevaluate more systematically the process of human choice and the structure of human judgment and well-being. These sciences, while revealing important differences between traditional economic assumptions and the process of human choice, unveil important facts about human nature, allowing a more realistic and complete economic representation of the true form of human preferences and choice.

## IRRATIONALITY AND BOUNDED RATIONALITY IN LAW, PSYCHOLOGY, AND ECONOMICS

In the first set of chapters, the authors provide the intellectual foundation for a behavioral theory that questions many of the assumptions of rational choice. Contributions range from reviews of mainstream research on biases in judgment under uncertainty to more radical challenges to the economic model of human choice, such as critiques of the familiar assumptions about preference and choice. Relying on the idea of bounded rationality, these authors argue that rational choice theory fails to account for everyday experiences. Why, for example, are millions of dollars given away anonymously if people are only driven by rational, self-interested impulses? Why do some humans find themselves incapable of controlling self-destructive impulses that lead them to choices they know are not in their own best interest? These questions can be answered in a variety of ways. Psychology instructs us that the needs of human reality impose cognitive limits on humankind that restrict inputs into the decision-making process, leading to seemingly irrational choices. Neuroscience teaches us that the structure and activity of the brain influence human choices and that physiological damage can radically alter decisions and perceptions of rationality. Other ideas, such as prospect theory and optimism bias that result in the misperception of odds and risks, are evaluated as factors that likewise limit the process of rational choice.

The chapters in this section lay the analytical groundwork that is needed to understand from an economic perspective why humans frequently behave in an irrational fashion. Rather than simply dismiss rational choice theory as an intellectual failure, these authors explain some of the weaknesses that have confronted traditional economic analysis and offer theoretical models that will help rectify some of these inconsistencies.

Robert Frank argues that the analytical power of pure rational choice theory is compromised, because it fails to adequately address the cognitive errors that are part of everyday human experience, it does not address the impulse-control problem of many individuals that will drive a person to make a seemingly irrational choice, and its premise that humans always make self-interested choices does not explain the voluminous number of anonymous charitable donations that are made each year. Frank puts forth the adaptive rationality standard, that is, a person chooses efficient means to achieve an end, but the person's goals are not a preordained objective such as self-interest. Frank argues that the more flexible adaptive rationality standard offers a better tool than rational choice theory does for understanding everyday issues such as savings rates and the failure to reach efficient agreement in contract negotiations.

Gerd Gigerenzer offers a more refined focus of Frank's first criticism of rational choice theory. Focusing on the existence of cognitive and memory failures, Gigerenzer argues that the methodology of human choice must be understood within the constraints on reason that our own minds impose on us. In order to truly understand the heuristics or decision-making processes utilized by individuals, one must consider not only the cognitive process of people but the environmental constraints and limitations in which the decision-making process occurs. Gigerenzer examines several different heuristic devices that individuals use to limit the cognitive information that goes into reaching decisions, including one-reason-based decisions, a preference for recognizable outcomes, and so forth. Gigerenzer concludes that these devices, which take into account humanity's cognitive limits, have strong predictive ability in regard to human choice.

Kevin McCabe, Vernon Smith, and Terrence Chorvat argue that the law and economics field would be intellectually strengthened if more consideration were given to the arising field of neuroeconomics. Neuroeconomics is defined by the authors as the use of technology such as functional magnetic resonance imaging (fMRI) scans to determine which area of the human brain is used when making economic decisions. The authors maintain that there is a great deal of heterogeneity among humans in terms of their perception and cognition of different circumstances. Thus, if one gains a solid understanding of which parts of the brain are used to make particular decisions, a predictive function can be achieved. The chapter concludes by surveying the field of potential practical applications of neuroeconomics to the law, including contract law, property law, choice of law, business associations, and the study of juries.

The authors of the first three chapters in this section attempt to examine how human psychology affects outcome choices. Robert Cooter rounds out this section by examining the reverse question: How do the choices we make, such as the laws we abide by, change our values? Cooter argues that we choose laws to achieve certain ends, but the eventual result is that those very laws change who we are as people and what values we hold.

## THE ECONOMICS OF IRRATIONAL BEHAVIOR

In the second section, the analysis extends to a broader examination of how irrational behavior affects our everyday economic decisions. Contributions focus on the economic implications of modifying traditionally accepted norms of rational choice. What do ideas such as bounded rationality, prospect theory, and optimism bias have to teach us about the choices of individuals when they must face decisions about resource consumption, revenge and retaliation in negotiation and economic activity, or cooperation and laughter?

Looking at the issue of addiction, author Ole-Jørgen Skog rejects the classical notion that alcoholism is a biological disease triggered by consumption. Skog takes something of an economic approach, maintaining that addiction must be understood as choice, though not necessarily a rational one. Skog argues that addicts show several components of irrational thinking and decision making, including unstable preferences and inconsistencies between short-term and long-term motives. Skog reasons that choice is best understood in the area of addiction if we reject rational choice's insistence on stable preferences and accept that preferences vary based on environmental factors.

Just as addiction can lead to irrational behavior, so can other factors and emotions, such as a desire for revenge and retaliation. Authors Vincy Fon and Francesco Parisi posit that norms of negative reciprocity have been present in all civilizations and have played an important evolutionary role in human development. Humans are guided by an innate sense of fairness that drives their actions, attitudes, and behaviors. By constraining the actions of revenge that are born out of this sense of fairness, a net social benefit can be achieved.

Building on the framework of negative reciprocity such as retaliation, Elizabeth Hoffman, Kevin McCabe, and Vernon Smith endeavor to provide an analytical foundation for understanding how reciprocity allows for trade. The authors posit that in situations where trading partners are familiar to each other, the actors will use techniques of positive reciprocity to ensure fair behavior and to achieve the desired outcome. However, in trading environments characterized by unfamiliar players, the actors will rely on the option of punishing a defector to ensure fairness in negotiations and adherence to agreements.

The authors of the first three chapters in this section began the process of taking the larger thematic notions of behavioral economics and applying them to everyday choices, human interactions, and so forth. Marco Novarese and Salvatore Rizzello offer a methodological approach to examining these theories in practice. The authors set forth an experiment that investigates the interaction between individual aspirations and decision making in an environment characterized by uncertainty and limited information.

F. H. Buckley concludes this section by taking the very light subject of laughter and showing how it too can be analyzed with the economic tools employed by other authors in this book. Buckley presents as an economic market the silent negotiation between the audience and the jester, leading to the development of communities of interest and comic norms.

## THE JURISPRUDENCE OF IRRATIONAL BEHAVIOR: RETHINKING LAW AS A BEHAVIORAL INSTRUMENT

The third section of the book builds on the contributions of the previous sections to consider how the understanding of human choice and the departures from the assumptions of rational choice affect the idea of law as a behavioral instrument and the design of legal and judicial institutions.

Contributions examine the implications that irrationality and limited rationality have for our jurisprudential system. How should courts confront the cases of the mentally ill given that the assumption of rationality cannot always hold? What alterations must be made to the criminal justice system in light of this theory? Should the premise of the criminal sanction be altered to account for the fact that not all choices are the product of well thought out, rational decision making?

Stephen Morse begins the section with a broad overview of mental health law, finding a common thread in the notion that some people with mental disorders are treated specially by our legal system because they appear to lack the capacity for reason. Morse begins by examining the notion of the individual and legal responsibility, with particular emphasis on how people who are mentally ill are treated in the legal system. Morse argues that instead of adopting a new body of law that deals specifically with mental health, mental disorders should instead be used as evidentiary tools that bear on the question of whether an individual in a given situation possessed the capacity to reason.

The next three chapters expand the role that irrationality plays in shaping jurisprudence beyond the bounds of mental health law, to cover its applicability to criminal sanctions for the community at large. Christine Jolls examines the cognitive failures of humans, such as the optimism bias, and reasons that these must be considered when drafting law enforcement policies, or they will not result in maximum detection and deterrence at minimum cost. These failures help explain why policies such as prohibitions against employment discrimination have failed to always change societal and human behavior. Michael O'Neill continues the examination of the interaction between cognitive limits and criminal sanction by reasoning that perfectly rational decisions are inhibited because individuals do not have access to all information necessary to make the fully rational choice. Accordingly, O'Neill concludes that policy makers must take irrationality into consideration, because typical methods of punishment will often not deter misbehavior.

Jonathan Caulkins and Robert MacCoun offer a very practical application of the principles laid out by Jolls and O'Neill. Caulkins and MacCoun argue that the reason many drug dealers do not respond to typical deterrence policies is that rational decisions are inhibited. This may help explain why retail cocaine and heroin prices have fallen sharply despite very large increases in drug enforcement, targeted primarily at suppliers.

Moving from the perspective of the criminal to that of the sanctioner, Cass Sunstein argues that strong emotions such as outrage often result in inconsistent and irrational punishments and jury awards, because it is hard to translate outrage into coherent legal terms and norms. Once policy makers are armed with a better understanding of this, rules can be structured for maximum deterrence. Continuing the endeavor to shape a proper system of sanctions, Yuval Feldman and Robert MacCoun endeavor to answer the question of how and when norms arise and how the process of individual internalization of norms occurs. The authors conclude that norms cannot be viewed as arising from a single source and that policy makers hoping to use norms to affect behavior must understand the multiplicity of the origin of norms as well as the factors that moderate the application of norms in a particular individual's life.

## IRRATIONAL BEHAVIOR AND THE DESIGN OF LAW

The final section of the book offers specific policy applications of the theories of bounded rationality. The analytical framework presented by the authors provides insights into a diverse range of human problems, such as traffic safety, torts, contract law, and securities regulation.

Thomas Ulen reviews the literature and arguments of both rational choice theorists and behavioral economists and how these ideas would present potential solutions to reduce the social costs of traffic accidents. Ulen maintains that society must accept the limited rationality of its citizens. As a result, policy makers and regulators should favor technological innovations over approaches such as tort law in achieving enhanced traffic safety.

Mark Grady examines a legal oddity that states that irrational and rational people should be treated the same in terms of liability for their own actions, but the same does not hold true for persons who are accused of prompting a third party to act dangerously. Grady reconciles this apparent discrepancy by explaining that tort law must be understood not as promoting corrective justice in a moral sense but as focusing liability where it will have the greatest impact, on responsible people. Understanding the rules that are used to encourage responsible persons to curb the excesses of irresponsible persons is necessary to having a full understanding of the tort system.

Several chapters in this volume have established the fact that people frequently do not approach decision making with an accurate estimation of the probability of positive or negative events happening to themselves. This begs the question of how legal rules should be properly developed to ensure optimal social behavior, taking into consideration the fact that people do not properly estimate the probability of relevant events. Posner presents an explanation of how altering tort rules can affect behavior if individuals are either optimistic or insensitive to actual probabilities. Posner reasons that when rules such as negligence and strict liability are used to correct inaccurate perceptions of probability, they will result in levels of care that exceed the socially optimal outcome. Posner concludes the chapter by briefly expanding the reach of his discussion to include its potential application to other areas, such as contract law.

Oren Bar-Gill and Omri Ben-Shahar argue that in the realm of contract law, courts should alter the traditional rules of contract modification and uphold any modification as long as the threat that led to their adoption was credible. The authors maintain that this should be the case, even if the credible threat seems irrational, as there are a wide variety of situations in which an economic actor would want to threaten an irrational breach of contract. By failing to uphold modifications under these circumstances, the authors believe courts would not lessen the occurrence of irrational conduct but would only hamper the choice of threatened parties, forcing them to accept breach instead of modification.

The last two chapters examine the role that irrationality plays in the regulation of the securities markets and investing. Peter Huang maintains that emotions play a strong role in investing decisions. Frequently, emotions diverge from cognition, and it is the former that often drives behavior. Emotional responses by investors have particular salience because of a line of securities regulations that mandate a broad swath of public disclosure by companies. Emotional reactions to these disclosures can lead investors to make unsound decisions. Understanding the role of emotions in investing and, in particular, the emotional reaction to mandated disclosure is vital in creating appropriate securities regulation.

Jeffrey Rachlinski and Gregory La Blanc believe that investors need more than what cognition alone provides in order to make the decisions that result in an efficient market. The authors maintain that if investors acted solely in a rational, cognitive way, they would withhold noncognitive information that the market desperately needs and would hamper the market's liquidity. As a result, the authors believe that many reforms aimed at protecting investors from the cost of their own cognitive mistakes (that is, structuring the tax code to favor pooled investing over individual accounts, curbing Internet investing, and so forth) must be weighed in light of the potential negative effects they could have on the market, not just in terms of their protection of the individual investor.

## CONCLUSION

The design of legal rules often rests on predictions about how people will respond to legal rules and institutional constraints. Much of the early work in law and economics has been deeply influenced by models of rational choice and behavioral theories of human action, which have traditionally provided the theoretical basis for such predictions. In recent years, mainstream economics has begun to take notice of the intellectual and practical relevance of departures from rational and informed choice. In 2001, George Akerloff, Michael Spence, and Joseph Stiglitz won the Nobel Prize in economics for arguing that markets don't always act efficiently because buyers and sellers don't always have access to the information they need to make optimal choices (Hillsenrath 2003). The same year, Matthew Rabin won the John Bates Clark Medal for his efforts to expand the realm of economics through psychology (Maclay 2001). In 2002, Daniel Kahneman and Vernon Smith won the Nobel Prize in economics for their respective contributions to behavioral and experimental economics. This mainstreaming of behavioral theory and the ongoing process of incorporation of psychological findings in the process of economic modeling show the intellectual power of these ideas.

This intellectual undertaking is unavoidably destined to engage several generations of scholars, given the complexity of real-world human choice relative to the simplifications of early rational choice approaches. It will be a fascinating undertaking, which has the potential of generating a vast array of policy implications in the fields of law and institutional design. This volume takes a step in this direction, bringing together the contribution of scholars who are pioneering in this area, with a presentation of some of the most exciting developments and relevant implications for legal and economic theory.

This volume explores the most relevant developments at the interface of economics and psychology. With special attention to models of irrational behavior, it draws the relevant implications of such models for the design of legal rules and institutions. It is hoped that this will offer a starting point for how this discussion can continue in the applied field of law and economics. The findings of this volume reveal that the application of economic models of irrational behavior to law is especially challenging because specific departures from rational behavior differ markedly from one another. Furthermore, the analytical and deductive instruments of economic theory have to be reshaped to deal with the fragmented and heterogeneous findings of psychological research, turning toward a more experimental and inductive methodology.

Dubner, S. 2003. Calculating the irrational in economics. *New York Times,* June 28.

Hilsenrath, J. 2003. Three Americans win Nobel for economics for challenging theory of efficient markets. http://classes.igpa.uiuc.edu/jgiertz/Nobel-asymmetric-information.htm.

Kilcullen, R. 1996a. Adam Smith: The moral sentiments. Teaching Materials on the History of Political Thought, Macquarie University. http://www.humanities.mq.edu.au/Ockham/y64l01.html.

———. 1996b. Tape 1: Adam Smith, The theory of moral sentiments. Teaching Materials on the History of Political Thought, Macquarie University. http://www.humanities.mq.edu.au/Ockham/y6401.html.

Maclay, K. 2001. Berkeley economist wins John Bates Clark Medal. *Berkeleyan,* May 2. http://www.berkeley.edu/news/berkeleyan/2001/05/02_rabin.html.

Nietzsche, F. 1878. *Human, all too human.* Leipzig: C. G. Naumann.

Shiller, R. 2000. *Irrational exuberance.* Princeton, NJ: Princeton University Press.

Smith, V. 1991. *Papers in experimental economics.* Cambridge: Cambridge University Press.

———. 2000. *Bargaining and market behavior: Essays in experimental economics.* Cambridge: Cambridge University Press.

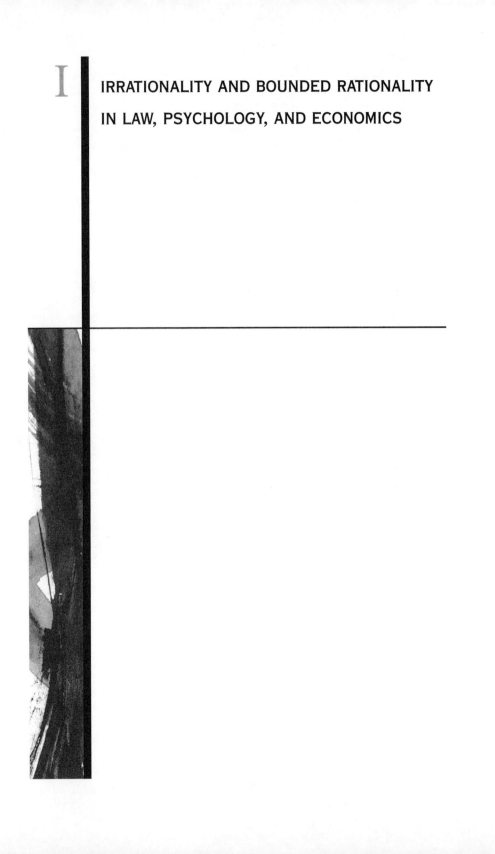

# I

# IRRATIONALITY AND BOUNDED RATIONALITY
# IN LAW, PSYCHOLOGY, AND ECONOMICS

# 1

## DEPARTURES FROM RATIONAL CHOICE: WITH AND WITHOUT REGRET

*Robert H. Frank*

Among interdisciplinary marriages, the contemporary law and economics movement has clearly been one of the most fruitful on record. As the following passage from Richard Posner's (1983) foreword to *The Encyclopedia of Law and Economics* suggests, the movement's tireless practitioners have left few significant areas of legal scholarship untouched by economic analysis: "Apart from the obvious examples—areas such as taxation and antitrust and securities regulation and (other) regulated industries and commercial law, all areas where the law is explicitly engaged in regulating economic activity—recent decades have seen a broadening of interest to include tort, contract, family, intellectual property, constitutional, criminal, admiralty, labor, arbitration, and antidiscrimination law, among others" (http://allserv.rug.ac.be/~gdegeest/foreword.htm).

Although the movement has become more methodologically diverse in recent years, its analytical core remains the Chicago-style price theory approach outlined in the first edition of Posner's (1973) pioneering text. Scholars in this tradition almost invariably assume that individuals are narrowly self-interested, well informed, well disciplined, and possessed of sufficient cognitive capacity to solve relatively simple optimization problems.

During recent decades, however, theoretical and empirical developments in economics and psychology have challenged each of these core assumptions. The challenges fall into three broad categories: (1) we often make systematic cognitive errors that prevent us from discovering which choices will best promote our interests; (2) even when we can discern which choices would be best, we often have difficulty summoning the willpower to execute them; and (3) we often pursue goals that appear inconsistent with self-interest, narrowly understood. I will consider each challenge in turn.

## 1.1 BOUNDED RATIONALITY

The late Nobel laureate Herbert Simon (1984) was the first to impress upon economists that human beings are incapable of behaving like the rational beings portrayed in standard rational choice models. Simon, a pioneer in the field of artificial intelligence, stumbled upon this realization in the process of trying to instruct a computer to "reason" about a problem. He discovered that when we ourselves confront a puzzle, we rarely reach a solution in a neat, linear fashion. Rather, we search in a haphazard way for potentially relevant facts and information and usually quit once our understanding reaches a certain threshold. Our conclusions are often inconsistent, even flatly incorrect. But much of the time, we come up with serviceable, if imperfect, solutions. In Simon's terms, we are "satisficers," not maximizers.

Subsequent economists have taken Simon's lead and have developed a very sophisticated literature on decision making under incomplete information. We now realize that when information is costly to gather and cognitive processing ability is limited, it is not even rational to make fully informed choices of the sort portrayed in traditional models. Paradoxically, it is irrational to be completely well informed! The literature on decision making under incomplete information, far from being a challenge to the traditional model, has actually bolstered our confidence in it.

But there is another offshoot of Simon's work, one that is less friendly to the traditional model. This research, which has been strongly influenced by cognitive psychologists Daniel Kahneman and the late Amos Tversky, demonstrates that even with transparently simple problems, people often violate the most fundamental axioms of rational choice. One of the most cherished tenets of the rational choice model, for example, is that wealth is fungible. Fungibility implies, among other things, that our total wealth, not the amount we have in any particular account, determines what we buy. Tversky and Kahneman (1974), however, provided a vivid experimental demonstration to the contrary. They told one group of people to imagine that having earlier purchased tickets for ten dollars, they arrive at the theater to discover they have lost them. Members of a second group were told to picture themselves arriving just before the performance to buy their tickets when they find that they have each lost ten dollars from their wallets. People in both groups were then asked whether they would continue with their plans to attend the performance. In the rational choice model, the forces governing this decision are the same for both groups. Losing a ten-dollar ticket should have precisely the same effect as losing a ten-dollar bill. And yet, in repeated trials, most people in the lost-ticket group said they would not attend the performance, whereas an overwhelming majority—88 percent—in the lost-bill group said they would.

Kahneman and Tversky explained that people apparently organize their spending into separate "mental accounts" for food, housing, entertainment, general expenses, and so on. People who lose their tickets act as if they are debiting ten dollars from their mental entertainment accounts, whereas those who lose ten dollars debit their general expense account. For people in the former group, the loss makes the apparent cost of seeing the show rise from ten dollars to twenty dollars, whereas for those in the second it remains ten dollars. The rational choice model makes clear that the second group's assessment is the correct one. And on reflection, most people do, in fact, agree that losing a ticket is no better reason not to see the performance than losing a ten-dollar bill.

Kahneman and Tversky identified a large catalog of systematic departures from rational choice, most of which stem from the application of judgment and decision heuristics. For instance, we often estimate the frequency of an event, or class of events, by the ease with which we can summon relevant examples from memory (Tversky and Kahneman 1981). On balance, this availability heuristic is an effective rule of thumb, because it is generally easier to recall examples of things that happen frequently. The problem is that frequency is not the only factor that influences ease of recall. If people are asked, for example, whether there are more murders than suicides in New York State each year, most answer confidently in the affirmative, yet there are always more suicides than murders. Murders are easier to recall not because they are more frequent but because they are more salient.

Cognitive errors stemming from the use of judgment and decision heuristics often lead to departures from the predictions of standard rational choice models. I call such examples "departures from rational choice with regret," the idea being that once people are made aware of the cognitive errors they have made, they seem motivated to avoid those errors in the future.

Many proponents of the traditional law and economics model appear reluctant to amend the model to take account of systematic cognitive errors. Some argue, for example, that in competitive environments, the penalties associated with such errors will reduce their frequency, enabling us to safely neglect them. Yet the mere fact that people make systematic cognitive errors does not imply that that reliance on heuristics is maladaptive in any global sense. The important question is whether following some alternative strategy would lead to better results on average. Rules such as the availability heuristic are extremely easy to apply and work well much of the time. The costs of an occasional wrong decision must be weighed against the obvious advantages of reliance on simple decision and judgment rules.

In any event, there is clear evidence that systematic cognitive errors exist and are widespread. Absent a clear showing that reliance on heuristics is a losing strategy on balance, there is a strong methodological case for taking explicit account of cognitive errors in descriptive models of individual behavior.

## 1.2 IMPULSE-CONTROL PROBLEMS

A second troubling feature of the traditional law and economics model is that it appears to rule out the possibility that people might regret having chosen behaviors whose consequences were perfectly predictable at the outset. Yet such expressions of regret are common. Many people wake up wishing they had drunk less the night before, but few wake up wishing they had drunk more.

It is likewise a puzzle within the traditional law and economics model that people often incur great expense and inconvenience to prevent behaviors they would otherwise freely choose. For example, the model has difficulty explaining why some people pay thousands of dollars to attend weight-loss camps that will feed them only fifteen hundred calories per day.

Welfare analysis based on the traditional law and economics model assigns considerable importance, as it should, to people's own judgments about what makes them better off. In this framework, it is not clear how one could ever conclude that a risk freely chosen by a well-informed person was a wrong choice. By itself, the fact that the choice led to a bad outcome is clearly not decisive. If someone is unlucky enough to be killed crossing the street, for example, we would not conclude that the person's decision to cross the street was necessarily a bad one. The traditional model thus suggests that criticizing someone's decision to have an unprotected sexual encounter that resulted in AIDS would be similarly problematic. If the person knew the risks and yet freely chose to ignore them, this model makes it hard to say more than that the person was just unlucky.

Compelling evidence from psychology suggests, however, why expressions of regret may often be genuine, why people might impose constraints on their own behavior, and why risks freely chosen by a well-informed person may not be optimal from his or her own point of view. This evidence concerns behavior in the realm of intertemporal choice.

The rational choice model says that people will discount future costs and benefits exponentially at their respective rates of time preference. With exponential discounting, the choice between two alternatives will be the same no matter when the choice is made. Consider, for example, the pair of choices A and B:

A: $100 tomorrow versus $110 a week from tomorrow

B: $100 after fifty-two weeks versus $110 after fifty-three weeks

If future receipts are discounted exponentially, people will always make the same choice under alternative A as they do under alternative B. Because the larger payoff comes a week later in each case, the ordering of the present values of the two alternatives must be the same in A as in B, irrespective of the rate at which people discount. When people confront such choices in practice, however, there is a pronounced tendency to choose differently under the two scenarios: most pick the $100 option in A, whereas most choose the $110 option in B.

Richard Herrnstein, George Ainslie, George Loewenstein, and others who have studied intertemporal choices experimentally have amassed substantial evidence that individuals tend to discount future costs and benefits not exponentially, as assumed by the rational choice model, but hyperbolically.[1] Under hyperbolic discounting, the psychological impact of a cost or benefit falls much more sharply with delay than it does under exponential discounting. One consequence is that preference reversals of the kind just observed are all but inevitable under hyperbolic discounting. The classic reversal involves choosing the larger, later reward when both alternatives occur with substantial delay, then switching to the smaller, earlier reward when its delay falls below some threshold. Thus, from the pair of alternatives labeled B, in which both rewards come only after a relatively long delay, most subjects chose the larger, later reward; whereas from the pair labeled A, most chose the earlier, smaller reward.

So why would people pay thousands of dollars to attend a weight-loss camp that will feed them only fifteen hundred calories per day? If they tend to discount future costs and benefits hyperbolically, the answer is clear: they really *want* to eat less, but they know that without imposing constraints on themselves they will lack the willpower to do so.

The tendency to discount future costs and benefits hyperbolically gives rise to a variety of familiar impulse-control problems and, in turn, to a variety of strategies for solving them. Anticipating their temptation to overeat, people often try to limit the quantities of sweets, salted nuts, and other delicacies they keep on hand. Anticipating their temptation to spend cash in their checking accounts, people enroll in payroll-deduction savings plans. Foreseeing the difficulty of putting down a good mystery novel in midstream, many people know better than to start one on the evening before an important meeting. Reformed smokers seek the company of nonsmokers when they first try to kick the habit and are more likely than others to favor laws that limit smoking in public places. The recovering alcoholic avoids cocktail lounges.

Effective as these bootstrap self-control techniques may often be, they are far from perfect. Many people continue to express regret about having overeaten, having drunk and smoked too much, having saved too little, having stayed up too late, having watched too much television, and so on. The exponential discounting model urges us to dismiss these expressions as sour grapes. But from the perspective of the hyperbolic discounting model, these same expressions are coherent. In each case, the actor chose an inferior option when a better one was available and later feels genuinely sorry about it. As with behaviors that stem from systematic cognitive errors, those that stem from impulse-control problems may be described as "departures from rational choice with regret."

In view of the obvious difficulties to which hyperbolic discounting gives rise, it might seem puzzling that this particular feature of human motivation is so widespread. As with cognitive errors that stem from reliance on judgmental heuristics, however, here too it is important to stress that the fact that hyperbolic discounting leads to bad outcomes some of the time does not imply that it is maladaptive in a global sense. Hyperbolic discounting forcefully directs the organism's attention to immediate costs and benefits. If forced to choose between a motivational structure that gave heavy weight to current payoffs and an alternative that gave relatively greater weight to future payoffs, it is easy to imagine why natural selection might have favored the former. After all, in highly competitive and uncertain environments, immediate threats to survival were numerous, and there must always have been compelling advantage in directing most of one's energies toward meeting them.

In any case, there is clear evidence here too that hyperbolic discounting exists and is widespread. Absent a clear showing that this motivational structure is disadvantageous on balance, there is a persuasive methodological case for taking explicit account of it in descriptive models of individual behavior.

### 1.3 NON—SELF-INTERESTED MOTIVES

The traditional law and economics model excludes other-regarding motives. It concedes, for example, that *homo economicus* might volunteer in a United Way campaign in order to reap the benefits of an expanded network of business or social contacts, but insists that she would never make anonymous donations to charity. Yet such donations exceed $100 billion a year in the United States. The traditional model acknowledges that *homo economicus* might tip in a local restaurant to ensure good service on his next visit, but predicts that he would not tip when dining alone in a restaurant far from home. Yet tipping rates are essentially the same in these two situations. The traditional model also concedes that *homo economicus* might go to the polls in a local ward election, in which a single vote might be decisive, but predicts universal abstention in presidential elections. Yet tens of millions of people regularly vote in presidential elections. In short, the traditional self-interest model is simple and elegant, but it also predicts incorrectly much of the time.

The most widely employed alternative to the self-interest model is the present-aim model (Parfit 1984), which holds that people are efficient in the pursuit of whatever objectives they happen to hold at the moment of action. The obvious appeal of the present-aim model is that it enables us to accommodate the plurality of goals that many people actually seem to hold, thus permitting us to account for behaviors that are anomalous within the self-interest framework. Someone donates anonymously to charity not because she hopes to receive indirect material benefits but because she gets a warm glow from helping others in need. Someone tips in a restaurant away from home not to ensure good service on his next visit but because he feels sympathy for the waitperson's interests. Someone votes in a presidential election not because his vote might tip the balance but because he feels it his civic duty to do so. And so on.

But the present-aim model's flexibility also turns out to be its biggest liability. The problem is that virtually any bizarre behavior can be "explained" after the fact simply by assuming that the individual had a sufficiently strong taste for it. I call this the "crankcase-oil problem": If someone drinks a gallon of used automobile crankcase oil, then writhes in agony, and dies, a present-aim theorist has a ready explanation: the person must have *really* liked crankcase oil. The Chicago school thus has sound reasons for its methodological skepticism about the present-aim model. As they correctly point out, a model that can explain virtually everything is not really a scientific model at all.

We are confronted, then, with a choice between two flawed alternatives. The self-interest standard of rationality generates refutable predictions about behavior, but these predictions often turn out to be flatly incorrect. The present-aim standard accommodates a much broader range of observed behavior but remains vulnerable to the charge of excessive flexibility. In place of these two, I propose a third standard, which I call "adaptive rationality." As I will argue, this standard is significantly more flexible than the self-interest standard, but it achieves that flexibility in a way that sidesteps the present-aim standard's unconstrained flexibility.

## 1.4 THE ADAPTIVE RATIONALITY STANDARD

Like both the self-interest and present-aim standards, the adaptive rationality standard assumes that people choose efficient means to achieve their ends. But unlike the other conceptions, which take goals as given, adaptive rationality regards goals as objects of choice themselves and, as such, subject to a similar efficiency requirement.

By what criterion might we evaluate the efficiency of an individual's choice of goals? Because the problem that plagues the present-aim standard is excessive flexibility, the efficiency standard we employ for evaluating alternatives to this model should be both objective and strict. On both counts, Darwin's theory of natural selection, enriched to allow for the influence of cultural and other environmental forces during development, is an attractive candidate. In this framework, the design criterion for a goal or taste is the same as for an arm or a leg or an eye—namely, the extent to which it assists the individual in the struggle to acquire the resources required for survival and reproduction. If it works better than the available alternatives, selection pressure will favor it. Otherwise, selection pressure will work against it. My proposal, in brief, is that analysts be free to add a taste to the utility function, but only upon showing that an individual motivated by that taste need not be handicapped in the competition to acquire the resources needed for survival and reproduction.

This standard passes the simple test of ruling out a taste for drinking crankcase oil. Indeed, it might seem such a stringent standard as to rule out any other conception of rationality other than narrow self-interest. After all, if natural selection favors the traits and behaviors that maximize individual reproductive fitness, and if we *define* behaviors that enhance personal fitness as selfish, then self-interest becomes the only viable human motive by definition. This tautology was a central message of much of the sociobiological literature of the 1970s and 1980s.

On a closer look, however, the issues are less simple. For there are many situations in which individuals whose only goal is self-interest are likely to fare worse than others who pursue a richer mix of goals. Such is the case, for example, when individuals confront commitment problems, of which the one-shot prisoner's dilemma provides a clear illustration. If both players in this game cooperate, each does better than if both defect, and yet each gets a higher payoff by defecting no matter which strategy the other player chooses. If both players could commit themselves to a strategy of mutual cooperation, they would have a clear incentive to do so. Yet mere promises issued by narrowly self-interested persons would not seem to suffice, for each person would have no incentive to keep such a promise.

Suppose, however, that some people have a (perhaps context-specific) taste for cooperating in one-shot prisoner's dilemmas. If two players knew one another to have this taste, they could interact selectively, thereby reaping the gains of mutual cooperation. It is important to stress that merely having the taste is by itself insufficient to solve the problem. One must also be able to communicate its presence credibly to others and be able to identify its presence in them.

Can the presence of a taste for cooperation be reliably discerned by outsiders? In a series of experiments, Frank, Gilovich, and Regan (1993b) found that subjects were surprisingly accurate at predicting who would cooperate and who would defect in one-shot prisoner's dilemmas played with near strangers. In these experiments, the base rate of cooperation was 73.7 percent, and the base rate of defection only 26.3 percent.[2] A random prediction of cooperation would thus have been accurate 73.7 percent of the time, and a random prediction of defection accurate only 26.3 percent of the time. The actual accuracy rates for these two kinds of prediction were 80.7 percent and 56.8 percent, respectively. The likelihood of such high accuracy rates occurring by chance is less than one in one thousand.

Subjects in this experiment were strangers at the outset and were able to interact with one another for only thirty minutes before making their predictions. It is plausible to suppose that predictions would be considerably more accurate for people we have known for a long time. For example, consider a thought experiment based on the following scenario: An individual has a gallon jug of unwanted pesticide. To protect the environment, the law requires that she turn in unused pesticide to a government disposal facility located thirty minutes' drive from her home. She knows, however, that she could simply pour the pesticide down her basement drain with no chance of being caught and punished. She also knows that her one gallon of pesticide, by itself, will cause only negligible harm if disposed of in this fashion.

Can you think of anyone who you feel certain would dispose of the pesticide properly? Most people say they can. Usually they have in mind friends they have known for a long time. If you feel you can identify such a person, then you, too, accept the central premise of the adaptive rationality account—namely, that it is possible to identify non–self-interested motives in at least some other people.

The presence of such motives, coupled with the ability of outsiders to discern them, makes it possible to solve a broad range of important commitment problems. Knowing this, even a rational, self-interested individual would have every reason to choose preferences that were not narrowly self-interested. Of course, people do not choose their preferences in any literal sense. The point is that if moral sentiments can be reliably discerned by others, then the complex interaction of genes and culture that yields human preferences can sustain preferences that lead people to subordinate narrow self-interest to the pursuit of other goals. To be endowed with such preferences creates the possibility of solving a variety of commitment problems.

For example, although *homo economicus* might want to deter a potential aggressor by threatening to retaliate, his threat would not be credible if the cost of retaliation exceeded the value of what he stood to recover. By contrast, someone known to care strongly about honor for its own sake could credibly threaten to retaliate, even in such cases. Such a person would thus be much less vulnerable to aggression than someone believed to be narrowly self-interested.

Similarly, although *homo economicus* might want to deter a one-sided offer from a potential trading partner by threatening to reject it, his threat would not be credible if his incentives clearly favored accepting the offer. By contrast, someone known to care strongly about equity for its own sake could credibly threaten to refuse such offers. Such a person would thus be a more effective bargainer than someone believed to be narrowly self-interested. It is clear, in any event, that people often reject one-sided offers even when their material incentives strongly favor accepting them (Guth, Schmittberger, and Schwarze 1982).

A second potential pathway whereby moral sentiments might be adaptive at the individual level is by helping people solve a variety of impulse-control problems (Frank 1988). Consider, for example, the iterated prisoner's dilemma. As Rapoport and Chammah (1965), Axelrod (1984), and others have shown, the tit-for-tat strategy fares well against alternative strategies in the repeated prisoner's dilemma. Self-interested persons thus have good reasons to play tit for tat, yet to do so they must first solve an impulse-control problem. Playing tit for tat means cooperating on the first interaction, which in turn implies a lower payoff on that move than could have been had by defecting. The reward for playing tit for tat lies in the prospect of a string of mutually beneficial interactions in the future. The rational choice model with exponential discounting says that if the present value of the current plus future benefits is larger by cooperating now, the actor will cooperate. But if a person discounts hyperbolically, this does not follow. Because the gain from defecting comes now, whereas its cost comes in the future, the hyperbolic discounter confronts an impulse-control problem.

The moral sentiment of sympathy, which figured so prominently in Adam Smith's early writings, helps to solve this problem. Someone who feels sympathy for the interests of his trading partner faces an additional cost of defecting, one that occurs at the same time as the gain from defecting. Because of this cost, the person who sympathizes with his trading partners is less likely to defect and is thus more likely to reap the long-run gains of cooperation.

Moral sentiments and other non–self-interested motives figure prominently in economic and social life. The traditional law and economic model ignores such motives. In its framework, the behaviors they provoke are viewed as irrational. But I find it more descriptive to call them "departures from rational choice without regret," because when people are told that they are behaving irrationally under the self-interest standard, they typically do not seem to want to alter their behavior. The attraction of the adaptive rationality standard is that it provides a methodologically rigorous framework within which to expand the narrow range of motives considered in traditional models. In the same fashion, it provides a coherent framework within which to take explicit account of systematic cognitive errors and impulse-control problems.

## 1.5  SOME LEGAL APPLICATIONS

Although the cognitive errors literature spawned by Kahneman and Tversky has important implications for the law and economics movement,[3] my focus in this section will be on departures from rational choice associated with impulse-control problems and the pursuit of non–self-interested goals.

### 1.5.1  Impulse-Control Problems and the Law

#### 1.5.1.1  Regulating Crimes of Passion, Gambling, and Entrapment

Statutory law itself implicitly recognizes the force of impulse-control problems in some contexts. For instance, the law of homicide is relatively lenient in the case of a husband who has murdered his wife's lover upon encountering them together in bed. Most countries impose at least some restrictions on gambling. Entrapment law implicitly acknowledges the injustice of tempting a normally law-abiding citizen to break the law, and in many jurisdictions it is illegal to leave one's keys in a parked car. Legal sanctions against addictive drugs are also common in countries around the world.

#### 1.5.1.2  Regulating Marriage and Sexual Behavior

Impulse-control problems arise with particular force—and often with severe consequences—in the domain of sexual behavior, and here too an understanding of the relevant motivational forces has important implications for the law. Someone who eats too much will gain a few pounds, but sexual indiscretions have become a life-and-death matter. Most people know by now that "safe sex" is the most sensible option for sexually active single persons. Yet many ignore this knowledge in the moment of decision. People who confront life-threatening and relationship-threatening impulse-control problems have an interest in the regulation of sexual behavior—their own as well as others'—that is fundamentally different from the one suggested by the dispassionate focus of the traditional law and economics model.

The traditional law and economics model leaves little room even to acknowledge impulse-control problems in mature adults. For example, the single, fleeting reference to impulsivity in Richard Posner's 442-page *Sex and Reason* comes in reference to teenagers, and even here he adds a parenthetical remark that downplays its significance: "Teenagers are on average more impulsive, hence on average less responsive to incentives, than adults are (although Chapter 10 presented evidence of rational behavior by teenagers toward abortion)" (1992, 331).

The traditional law and economics model cannot accommodate the notion that people might improve their lives by deliberately restricting their own options. Yet many of the laws and social norms that define acceptable behavior simply cannot be understood without reference to the fact that people confront powerful temptations to engage in sexual activity that is contrary to their long-run interests.

Consider, for example, the laws and norms regarding adultery. Spouses may strongly wish to remain in their marriages and realize that their prospects for doing so will be higher if they remain sexually faithful. And yet they may also recognize the potential lure of extramarital romance. Anticipating this conflict, most wedding ceremonies attempt to strengthen the partners' resolve by having them make public vows of fidelity. And in most societies, these vows are backed up by legal and social sanctions against adultery.

Posner appears puzzled by such practices, which he regards as having arisen from arbitrary religious beliefs: "[O]ur sexual attitudes and the customs and laws that grow out of them and perhaps reinforce or even alter them by some feedback process, are the product of moral attitudes rooted in religious beliefs rather than in the sort of functional considerations examined in the preceding chapter" (1992, 236).

But why not use the same functionalist perspective to examine the content of morality? The adaptive rationality standard draws our attention to potential gains available in many situations from steering clear of options that might later seem compellingly attractive. Systems of morality may be viewed as simply yet another means by which we attempt to achieve the desired commitments.

### 1.5.1.3 Regulating Savings

Higher savings rates support dramatically higher lifetime consumption. Suppose, for example, that two people start with the same income and that the first saves 20 percent and the second saves 5 percent of each year's earnings, including interest from savings. If the rate of return is 10 percent, only eleven years will elapse before the high saver's consumption overtakes the low saver's. After twenty years, the high saver's consumption is 16 percent greater; after thirty years, 35 percent greater.

The high-savings trajectory might seem the compelling choice, yet even the low-savings trajectory overstates the actual rate of savings in the United States. People with low savings often voice regret about not having saved more. But the rational choice model with exponential discounting insists that the difference between these two life histories is merely a reflection of differing preferences and hence not a proper subject for welfare comparisons or regulatory intervention. On this view, government programs aimed at stimulating personal savings rates are unambiguously welfare reducing.

Once we acknowledge hyperbolic discounting, however, we are more inclined to take the low saver's expressions of regret at face value and to trust the intuition that the thrifty person really has done better. After all, the decision to save confronts the individual with a standard impulse-control problem. A given amount of consumption must be sacrificed today so that a larger amount of consumption may take place in the future. The hyperbolic discounter may know she should save for the future yet be sorely tempted by the rewards of immediate consumption.

These observations suggest the utility of viewing thrift as a moral virtue, because persons who hold that view will be better able to resist the temptation to consume. Explicit recognition of the impulse-control problem confronting savers also suggests that collective action to promote savings may be welfare enhancing.

### 1.5.2 Moral Sentiments and the Law

The traditional law and economics model asks us to interpret laws and regulations as means that enable narrowly self-serving actors to better achieve their ends. Yet numerous details of legal custom and practice appear inconsistent with this interpretation. Some examples follow.

#### 1.5.2.1 Remorse as a Factor in Sentencing

Consider the role of expressions of remorse in criminal sentencing (Eisenberg, Garvey, and Wells 1998). In self-interest models, such expressions are viewed as cheap talk. If saying one feels sorry about the crime one has committed is known to result in a lower sentence, then the inevitable expressions of remorse should contribute no relevant information for sentencing purposes. On this interpretation, a sentence should depend on the severity of the offense alone.

Yet in jurisdictions around the globe, the average length of a convicted defendant's sentence varies inversely with the amount of remorse displayed. Although the self-interest framework correctly highlights defendants' powerful incentives to feign remorse, most legal systems have apparently decided that courts have at least some capacity to distinguish feigned expressions from those that are heartfelt. In several specific ways, the adaptive rationality framework helps underscore the logic of this position. It explains why legitimate feelings of remorse might be adaptive at the individual level and predicts that the strength of such feelings may vary sharply across individuals. In addition, it sheds light on the specific mechanisms by which we make inferences about both the nature and strength of such feelings (Frank 1988, chap. 6). On the plausible view that genuinely remorseful defendants are less likely to become repeat offenders, shorter sentences for such defendants are justified.

Closely related to the role of expressions of remorse in criminal sentencing is the role of apology in tort cases. Because an apology can be interpreted as evidence of guilt in the American legal system, many attorneys strongly caution their clients against apology in damage lawsuits. Although this advice is intelligible, it ignores the critical emotional role of apology in dispute resolution. Evidence suggests that "plaintiffs are more likely to sue when they do not get an apology, and more likely to forgo compensation when they receive one" (O'Hara and Yarn 2002, 4).

### 1.5.2.2 Failure to Reach Efficient Agreements

The traditional law and economics framework predicts that when someone is named as a defendant in a lawsuit, the expected outcome is a pretrial settlement. After all, each side is in a position to estimate the expected settlement if the case were to go to trial, and each side stands to avoid substantial costs of litigation by agreeing to a pretrial settlement on the basis of those expectations. Although such settlements are in fact common, they occur with far lower frequency than predicted by the self-interest model. Accounts of failure to settle stress the importance of feelings of animosity and vindictiveness between disputing parties (Huang 1992). The adaptive rationality standard accommodates such feelings, noting that although they motivate people to incur avoidable costs on some occasions, they generate benefits as well, by helping to deter potential aggressors.

In the same vein, self-interest models predict that when two affected parties can negotiate with one another at negligible cost, they will agree to waive any inefficient injunction issued by a court. Yet such agreements are much rarer than predicted, and here too vindictive feelings appear to explain why. In a recent study of twenty nuisance cases, for example, Farnsworth found

> no bargaining after judgment in any of them; nor did the parties' lawyers believe that bargaining would have occurred if judgment had been given to the loser. The lawyers said that the possibility of such bargaining was foreclosed not by the sorts of transaction costs that usually are the subject of economic models, but by animosity between the parties and by their distaste for cash bargaining over the rights at issue. (1999, 373)

A similar disconnect is observed with respect to the American legal system's treatment of breach of contract. The law and economics movement has spawned numerous studies that advocate ratification of breach of contract whenever it can be shown that the cost to the promisor of fulfilling the contract would exceed the resulting benefits to the promisee (Warkol 1998). Yet the courts have routinely failed to follow this recommendation, perhaps because "the theory of efficient breach fails to account for intangible human reactions such as someone's desire to be declared the winner or to see the other party declared the loser" (Warkol 1998,

345). Because the "emotional distress caused by a breach, which does not in itself constitute a tort, ordinarily is not recoverable in damages" (Schwartz 1979, 276), efficient breach may not be efficient after all.

Traditional models in law and economics either ignore the emotional responses of litigants in such cases or tacitly assume that those responses will closely track expected monetary outcomes. By contrast, the adaptive rationality standard highlights the central role of the emotions and helps us understand why they are often little related to expected monetary outcomes.

### 1.5.3 Laws and Regulations Motivated by Concerns About Relative Consumption

The utility function most widely used in the law and economics literature assumes that well-being depends on current and future levels of absolute consumption. Considerable evidence suggests, however, that well-being depends as much or more on current and future levels of relative consumption.[4] The adaptive rationality standard holds that a taste for relative consumption can be introduced into the utility function if being thus motivated need not compromise resource acquisition in competitive environments. If people known to care about relative consumption are indeed better bargainers than those thought to care only about absolute consumption, this test is met.

Adding a taste for relative consumption alters the descriptive and normative message of the rational choice model about many issues of interest in the law and economics movement. Workplace safety regulation provides a representative illustration. Traditional models hold that the optimal amount of workplace safety will be provided as long as labor markets are competitive and workers are well informed about the potential health and safety risks they face. When these conditions are satisfied, workers can survey their options and choose the job with the wage-safety combination that best satisfies their preferences. The traditional law and economics framework thus predicts unequivocally that regulations mandating higher safety levels in competitive labor markets will reduce welfare.

Marxists and other critics of the market system have long countered that labor markets are not effectively competitive and that safety regulation is needed to prevent employers from exploiting workers. The puzzle for both camps is to explain why safety regulations are most binding in those labor markets that on traditional measures are the most highly competitive. Once we acknowledge that people care not only about absolute consumption but about relative consumption as well, an explanation is at hand.

For example, consider a representative "community" composed of two such individuals, A and B, each of whom faces a choice between working in a safe job at a salary of $400 per month or an "unsafe" job at a salary of $500 per month. The safe job pays less only because of the costs of maintaining higher safety. The lone adverse consequence of working in the unsafe job is a modest reduction in life expectancy. A and B choose independently, and each picks the job that promises the highest utility. The satisfaction each gets from a particular job depends on three factors: (1) absolute consumption, (2) relative consumption, and (3) job safety. A's utility function has the form $U = X + R + S$, where

$X$ = A's monthly consumption in dollars;

$R$ = A's satisfaction from relative consumption

200 if A's consumption exceeds B's,

0 if the two have equal consumption, and

200 if A's consumption is less than B's;

and

$S = 200$ if A has a safe job, 0 if an unsafe job.

B's utility function is symmetrically defined.

Given these opportunities and preferences, the utilities of the four possible combinations of choices are as summarized in Figure 1.1.

The utility functions used to generate Figure 1.1 tell us that having the safer job is worth $200 per month to each worker. Because the cost of providing the extra safety is only $100 per month, it might seem that the safer job would be the obvious best choice for each. Yet the payoffs in Figure 1.1 confront A and B with a prisoner's dilemma, so there is no reason to feel confident that a socially optimal combination of choices will emerge. On the contrary, the choice of the unsafe job is a dominant strategy for both players, even though each does worse under that combination of choices than if each were to have chosen the safe job. Under these circumstances, there is little mystery about why A and B might favor regulations that mandate greater levels of workplace safety, even in perfectly competitive markets.

Analogous reasoning suggests the possible attraction of a variety of similar restrictions on other individual choices. Consider, for example, the widespread restrictions against the sale of babies and sex, which have been challenged forcefully in the law and economics literature by Posner (1992) and others. From an individual seller's perspective, the income gained from participating in such transactions is advantageous for two reasons: because of the utility of the additional consumption it will support and because of the improvement to the seller's position in

**B's choice**

|  | Safe job @ $400/mo | Unsafe job @ $500/mo |
|---|---|---|
| **Safe job @ $400/mo** | U = 600 each<br><br>(second best for each) | U = 700 for B, 400 for A<br><br>(best for B, worst for A) |
| **Unsafe job @ $500/mo** | U = 400 for B, 700 for A<br><br>(best for A, worst for B) | U = 500 each<br><br>(third best for each) |

**A's choice** (label to the left of the table rows)

**Figure 1.1** Job safety choices when relative consumption matters

purely relative terms. From the collective vantage point, the second payoff is spurious, because any one person's advance in relative terms necessarily entails a relative decline for others.

Of course, merely to observe that positional concerns render the sale of sex and babies misleadingly attractive to individuals is not to say that these activities should be proscribed completely. On the contrary, the relative position argument says individual incentives are misleadingly high for virtually *everything* we might sell for money—not just safety, babies, and sex but also our leisure time, future job security, and a host of other environmental amenities. The problem is not that we exchange these items for money but that we sell them too cheaply. In the case of workplace safety, the solution is not to ban risk but to make it less attractive to individuals. Regarding the length of the workweek, the best solution is not strict limits on hours worked but rather a change in incentives (such as overtime laws) that make long hours less attractive. Analogously, the best response in the sexual domain may not be to ban prostitution or the sale of babies but rather to make these activities less attractive to potential sellers.

The same logic suggests a clear rationale for laws favoring monogamy over polygyny. In polygynous species in the animal kingdom—which is to say most species—dominant males enjoy enormous reproductive payoffs. In one colony of seals, for example, 4 percent of the adult males sired almost 90 percent of all offspring (Dawkins 1976). Not surprisingly, payoffs of this magnitude stimulate intensive competition among males for access to fertile females. This competition manifests itself variously in the form of physical combat and elaborate forms of displays and courtship rituals. Although this competition does often lead to genetic innovations that serve the interests of the species as a whole, for the most part it is profoundly wasteful.

Peacocks as a species, for example, would be better off if each individual's tail feathers were to shrink by a significant proportion. But these feathers are an important form of courtship display, and the gain to any individual bird from having shorter tail feathers would be more than offset by the reproductive penalty.

In polygynous human societies, males who rank high in the wealth distribution tend to have disproportionately many wives. Here, too, the struggle for position is often costly. Laws favoring monogamy might thus be viewed as an arms-control agreement of sorts. By preventing the concentration of reproductive success in the hands of a small minority of men, they reduce the incentive to engage in costliest aspects of the struggle to move forward in the relative wealth distribution.

In the self-interest models that dominate the law and economics literature, people care about absolute consumption but not about relative consumption. In these models, the individual pursuit of maximum utility leads to an efficient allocation of resources. Thus, it is natural for someone such as Posner to say, in reference to a woman's right to hire another woman to bear a child for her, "I do not see how regulation of that right could be inimical to women's interests as a whole" (1992, 424).

There is abundant evidence, however, that concerns about relative consumption also loom large for most people. Under this broader and more realistic view of preferences, there is no presumption that individual decisions yield socially optimal allocations. Because one person's forward movement in any consumption hierarchy entails backward moves for others, income-generating activities are misleadingly attractive to individuals. The logic of the broader model thus suggests the possible attraction of policies that make the pursuit of additional wealth less attractive. Taxes on income, workplace safety regulation, and a variety of restrictions on commercial sexual activity fall into this category.

## 1.6 SUSTAINING LAWFUL BEHAVIOR

Material incentives clearly matter. Ultimately, however, the law can do only so much to constrain individual behavior. To achieve a well-ordered society, we must rely at least in part on people's willingness to subordinate personal interests for the common good. Although the adaptive rationality standard embraces the possibility of voluntary self-restraint in such cases, the self-interest standard all but denies that possibility.

It is troubling, therefore, that at least some evidence suggests that exposure to self-interest models tends to inhibit self-restraint. For example, Frank, Gilovich, and Regan (1993a) found that economics majors were more than twice as likely as nonmajors to defect when playing one-shot prisoner's dilemmas with strangers, a difference that was not merely a reflection of the fact that people who chose to major in economics were more opportunistic to begin with.[5] We also found that academic economists were more than twice as likely as the members of other disciplines to report giving no money at all to any private charity.[6]

These findings suggest that our choice among standards of rationality may be important not just because of our attempts to predict and explain behavior but also because of its potential impact on our willingness to engage in self-restraint. If so, the law and economics movement has even greater reason to reconsider its exclusive commitment to the self-interest standard.

## 1.7 CONCLUSIONS

In the end, theories of human behavior depend critically on their assumptions about people's capacities and goals. Some individuals are well characterized by the high levels of cognitive capacity and self-discipline and the egoistic goals assumed in traditional rational choice models. Yet many others are clearly prone to systematic cognitive errors, lacking in self-discipline and willing to make significant financial sacrifices in pursuit of a variety of non–self-interested goals.[7]

As Milton Friedman was fond of saying, the test of a theory is not whether its assumptions can be shown to be true, but rather the extent to which it helps us to explain and predict behavior. Fair enough. But by that test, the self-interest model's record has been fairly spotty.

Methodological purists rightly object that an unconstrained ability to introduce ad hoc assumptions about capacities and tastes would deny the traditional model its status as an empirically refutable scientific theory. As I have argued, however, the adaptive rationality standard provides a principled basis for broadening the traditional model, one that does not entail abandonment of the methodological high ground.

In practical legal and regulatory policy terms, the greatest shortcomings of the traditional model stem from its inability to accommodate what I have called departures from rational choice without regret. The most compelling rationale for a law or regulation that constrains behavior is to prevent harm to others. Although cognitive errors are systematic and widespread, they generally cause no harm to other people. Nor is there evidence that such errors are associated with large welfare losses. More important, any damage caused by cognitive errors is at least in principle subject to remedial action by the very persons who are prone to those errors. Even though taking account systematic cognitive errors is indisputably important for generating more accurate predictions of behavior in many domains, it is not clear that these errors meet the threshold for enacting laws that constrain individual behavior.

In the case of impulse-control problems, the scale of the associated welfare losses—including those associated with diet-related illnesses, insufficient savings, and drug and alcohol abuse—is considerably larger than in the case of cognitive errors. But here, too, many of the relevant injuries are self-inflicted and hence, at least in principle, subject to remedial action by affected parties. Taking impulse-control problems into account is important for understanding patterns of human behavior, and in exceptional cases may even justify the enactment of laws that restrain individual choice.

The welfare losses associated with departures from rational choice without regret are often dramatically larger than those associated with departures from rational choice with regret. Because the former losses are much less susceptible to individual remedial action, they present a far more compelling case for collective action. Consider, in particular, the welfare losses associated the contest for relative position in the distributions of income and consumption. These losses run to hundreds of millions, perhaps even several trillions, of dollars each year in the U.S. economy.[8] Stemming as they do from a multiperson prisoner's dilemma, these losses cannot be curtailed by unilateral individual action. It is thus in this domain that broadening the traditional law and economics model promises to help identify laws, regulations, and other collective steps with the potential to generate truly significant welfare enhancements.

1. Two of the most important earlier papers on this issue are by Chung and Herrnstein (1967) and Ainslie (1975). The most detailed and current summary of the relevant evidence appears in Ainslie (1992). See also Elster (1979), Schelling (1980), Thaler and Shefrin (1981), and Winston (1980). For a series of papers that discuss economic applications of the hyperbolic discounting model, see Elster and Loewenstein (1992).

2. In an extensive meta-analysis of empirical studies of the one-shot dilemma, Sally (1995) finds that such high rates of cooperation are not uncommon.

3. For a discussion, see Sunstein, Jolls, and Thaler (2000).

4. The points developed in this section are developed in greater detail in Frank (1985a, 1985b).

5. We found, for example, that the difference in defection rates grew larger the longer a student had studied economics. Questionnaire responses also indicated that freshmen in their first microeconomics course were more likely at the end of the term to expect opportunistic behavior from others than they were at the beginning.

6. For more on the issue of whether exposure to the self-interest model inhibits cooperation, see Marwell and Ames (1981); Carter and Irons (1990, 1991); Yezer, Goldfarb, and Poppen (1996); and Frank, Gilovich, and Regan (1996).

7. For a discussion of evidence on this point drawn from the labor market, see Frank (1996).

8. For a discussion of these losses, see Frank (1999).

Ainslie, G. 1975. Specious reward: A behavioral theory of impulsiveness and impulse control. *Psychological Bulletin* 82:463–96.

———. 1992. *Picoeconomics: The strategic interaction of successive motivational states within the person.* New York: Cambridge University Press.

Akerlof, G. 1983. Loyalty filters. *American Economic Review* 73:54–63.

Axelrod, R. 1984. *The evolution of cooperation.* New York: Basic Books.

Carter, J., and M. Irons. 1990. *Are economists different and if so why?* [longer unpublished version of the 1991 paper]. Worcester, MA: College of the Holy Cross.

———. 1991. Are economists different and if so why? *Journal of Economic Perspectives* 5:171–77.

Chung, S., and R. Herrnstein. 1967. Choice and delay of reinforcement. *Journal of the Experimental Analysis of Behavior* 10:67–74.

Dawkins, R. 1976. *The selfish gene.* New York: Oxford University Press.

Eisenberg, T., S. Garvey, and M. Wells. 1998. But was he sorry? The role of remorse in capital sentencing. *Cornell Law Review* 6 (83): 1599–1697.

Elster, J. 1979. *Ulysses and the Sirens.* Cambridge: Cambridge University Press.

Elster, J., and G. Loewenstein, eds. 1992. *Choice over time.* New York: Russell Sage.

Farnsworth, W. 1999. Do parties to nuisance cases bargain after judgment? A glimpse inside the cathedral. *University of Chicago Law Review* 66:373–436.

Frank, R. 1985a. The demand for unobservable and other nonpositional goods. *American Economic Review* 75:101–16.

———. 1985b. *Choosing the right pond.* Oxford: Oxford University Press.

———. 1987. If *homo economicus* could choose his own utility function, would he want one with a conscience? *American Economic Review* 77:593–604.

———. 1988. *Passions within reason.* New York: Norton.

———. 1999. *Luxury Fever.* New York: The Free Press.

Frank, R., T. Gilovich, and D. Regan. 1993a. Does studying economics inhibit cooperation? *Journal of Economic Perspectives* 7:159–71.

———. 1993b. The evolution of one-shot cooperation. *Ethology and Sociobiology* 14:247–56.

———. 1996. Do economists make bad citizens? *Journal of Economic Perspectives* (Winter): 187–92.

Gauthier, D. 1985. *Morals by agreement.* Oxford: Clarendon.

Gibbard, A. 1990. *Wise choices, apt feelings: A theory of normative judgment.* Cambridge, MA: Harvard University Press, and Oxford: Oxford University Press.

Guth, W., R. Schmittberger, and B. Schwarze. 1982. An experimental analysis of ultimatum bargaining. *Journal of Economic Behavior and Organization* 3:367–88.

Hirshleifer, J. 1987. On the emotions as guarantors of threats and promises. In *The latest and the best: Essays on evolution and optimality*, ed. J. Dupre. Cambridge MA: MIT Press: 308–326.

Huang, P. 1992. Emotional responses in litigation. *International Economic Review* 12:31.

Marwell, G., and R. Ames. 1981. Economists free ride, does anyone else? *Journal of Public Economics* 15:295–310.

McClennen, E. 1990. *Rationality and dynamic choice: Foundational explorations*. New York: Cambridge University Press.

Nesse, R., ed. 2001. *Evolution and the capacity for commitment*. New York: Russell Sage.

O'Hara, E., and D. Yarn. 2002. On apology and consilience. *Washington Law Review* 77:1121–92.

Parfit, D. 1984. *Reasons and persons*. Oxford: Clarendon Press.

Posner, R. 1983. *Economic analysis of law*. Boston: Little, Brown.

———. 1992. *Sex and reason*. Cambridge, MA: Harvard University Press.

Rapoport, A., and A. Chammah. 1966. *Prisoner's dilemma*. Ann Arbor: University of Michigan Press.

Sally, D. 1995. Conversation and cooperation in social dilemmas: A meta-analysis of experiments from 1958 to 1972. *Rationality and Society* 7:58–92.

Schelling, T. 1960. *The strategy of conflict*. New York: Oxford University Press.

———. 1978. Altruism, meanness and other potentially strategic behaviors. *American Economic Review* 68:229–30.

———. 1980. The intimate contest for self-command. *Public Interest* (Summer): 94–118.

Schwartz, A. 1979. The case for specific performance. *Yale Law Journal* 89: 65–100.

Sen, A. 1985. Goals commitment and identity. *Journal of Law Economics and Organization* 1:341–55.

Sunstein, C., C. Jolls, and R. Thaler, eds. 2000. *Behavioral law and economics*. New York: Cambridge University Press.

Thaler, R., and H. Shefrin. 1981. An economic theory of self-control. *Journal of Political Economy* 89:392–405.

Tversky, A., and D. Kahneman. 1974. Judgment under uncertainty: Heuristics and biases. *Science* 185:1124–31.

———. 1981. The framing of decisions and the psychology of choice. *Science* 211:453–58.

Warkol, C. 1998. Resolving the paradox between legal theory and legal fact: The judicial breach of the theory of efficient breach. *Cardozo Law Review* 20:321–53.

Winston, G. 1980. Addiction and backsliding: A theory of compulsive consumption. *Journal of Economic Behavior and Organization* 1:295–394.

Yezer, A., R. Goldfarb, and P. Poppen. 1996. Does studying economics discourage cooperation? Watch what we do, not what we say. *Journal of Economic Perspectives* (Winter): 177–86.

# 2 IS THE MIND IRRATIONAL OR ECOLOGICALLY RATIONAL?

*Gerd Gigerenzer*

When I left a restaurant in a charming town in Tuscany one night, I looked for my yellow green rented Renault 4 in the parking lot. It wasn't there. Instead, there was a blue Renault 4 sitting in the lot, the same model, but the wrong color. I can still feel my fingers hesitating to put my key into the lock of this car, but the door opened. I drove the car home. When I looked out the window the next morning, there was a yellow green Renault 4 standing in bright sunlight outside. What had happened? My color constancy system had failed in the artificial light of the parking lot. Color constancy, an impressive adaptation of the human perceptual system, allows us to see the same color under changing conditions of illumination: under the bluish light of day as well as the reddish light of the setting sun. Color constancy, however, fails in certain artificial lights, such as sodium or mercury vapor lamps, which were not present in the environment when mammals evolved (Shepard 1992).

Human color vision is adapted to the spectral properties of natural sunlight. In other words, our perceptual system assumes that there is a certain structure of information in our environment and, on this basis, draws a conclusion or an "unconscious inference," as Helmholtz (1856–66/1962) aptly termed it. Similarly, visual illusions such as the Müller-Lyer illusion and Shepard's (1990) "turning tables" are based on an assumption about the world (here, that objects are three-dimensional) that the cognitive system uses to infer length and shape from a two-dimensional drawing. The mind makes us see the properties of a three-dimensional object, which can differ systematically from the two-dimensional picture on paper. Like color constancy, however, these smart perceptual systems can be fooled and may break down when stable, long-term properties of the environment to which they were adapted are changed. Every intelligent system makes errors. Otherwise, it could not go beyond the information given, make ambitious guesses, and be creative.

Just like a perceptual system that makes uncertain bets, a good memory system must risk error in order to function well. But hasn't Mother Nature committed colossal blunders in burdening us with such a dysfunctional system that makes us forget events as time passes by, attribute memories to the wrong sources, and block when producing a name to accompany a familiar face? Some of the most prominent memory researchers argue that this is not the case (e.g., Anderson and Schooler 2000; Schacter 2001). In their view, the sins of memory are by-products ("spandrels") of a system adapted to the structure of the environment. An unlimited memory, for instance, could be disastrous: The sheer mass of details stored could critically slow down and inhibit the retrieval of the few important experiences when they are needed. And too much memory in storage would impair the mind's ability to abstract, infer, and learn. Autistic persons, for instance, discriminate more accurately between true and false memories than others do and can have spectacular rote memory abilities. But they can remember the gist of these events less well (Schacter 2001, 193). A human brain or an artificial neural network that starts with an overabundant memory capacity may never be able to learn a language (Elman 1993). In contrast, a working memory that starts small (and then grows) can act as a filter on environmental input, enabling learning of important linguistic scaffolding first (Hertwig and Todd, 2003). Less can be more.

These examples illustrate the interplay between a cognitive process, such as a color constancy mechanism, and the structure of an environment, such as the spectral properties of sunlight. In this chapter, I apply this ecological perspective to the study of bounded rationality and draw some consequences for legal research. I endorse the goal expressed by legal scholars to arrive at "a more nuanced understanding of human behavior that draws on cognitive psychology, sociology, and other behavioral sciences" (Korobkin and Ulen 2000, 1053). However, legal scholars have not always been presented with a nuanced understanding, but with a lopsided view of cognitive psychology.

## 2.1 WHAT IS BOUNDED RATIONALITY?

The traditional view is that there are two unrelated sets of bounds to the human mind: purely external constraints, such as the costs of searching for information in the world; and purely internal constraints, such as limits on the amount of information we can hold in working memory. Given the view that these constraints are unrelated, bounded rationality has been understood in two opposing ways. First, it has been seen as the attempt to make optimal choices given the demands of the world, which has led to the notion of optimization under constraints (e.g., Conlisk

1996; Sargent 1993). Second, bounded rationality has been interpreted as the sub-optimal outcome of a limited cognitive system, leading to a list of cognitive illusions. It is the second interpretation that behavioral economists have in mind when they portray bounded rationality as the study of cognitive illusions and decision anomalies (e.g., Camerer 1998; Rabin 1998). Jolls, Sunstein, and Thaler write: "Bounded rationality, an idea first introduced by Herbert Simon, refers to the obvious fact that human cognitive abilities are not infinite. We have limited computational skills and seriously flawed memories" (1998, 1477). In a footnote, the authors reference an article by Simon from 1955.

There is a third view, the one that Simon has actually proposed. Rather than the external and internal bounds being regarded as separate and unrelated, the two sets of bounds may actually be linked. This third view is known as the study of ecological rationality (Gigerenzer, Todd, and the ABC Research Group 1999). Simon's ecological conception is best illustrated by his analogy between bounded rationality and a pair of scissors. One blade is human cognition; the other is its environment. If one looks only at cognition and its limitations, one can hardly understand why and how cognition works so well when it does, just as looking at one blade alone does not explain how scissors cut. The view Jolls, Sunstein, and Thaler refer to is not Simon's but Kahneman and Tversky's. In the cited 1955 paper, Simon had already emphasized that there are two sides to his new conception of rationality: cognition and the structure of the environment. "Broadly stated, the task is to replace the global rationality of economic man with a kind of rational behavior that is compatible with the access to information and the computational capacities that are actually possessed by organisms, including man, in the kinds of environments in which such organisms exist" (99). One year later, in his *Psychological Review* article "Rational Choice and the Structure of Environments," Simon (1956) put the ecological aspect of bounded rationality into the title.

Thus, Simon's bounded rationality is not the study of cognitive limitations. It is not a collection of irrationalities that need to be added to rational choice theory. In Simon's view, as well as in Reinhard Selten's (another Nobel laureate who has made major contributions to models of heuristics) and my view, bounded rationality is the study of the match between cognitive heuristics and structures of environments (Gigerenzer and Selten 2001a, 2001b). The goal of the study of bounded rationality, as we conceive it, is threefold:

- Design and test models of the heuristics that people use to make decisions in an uncertain world. These heuristics do not involve optimization calculations and, for the most part, do not compute probabilities and utilities. The building blocks of these heuristics—such as rules for search, stopping, and decision—are the elements of the adaptive toolbox, which allows us to generate new heuristics by recombining building blocks or by nesting extant heuristics.

- Describe the environments that a given heuristic can exploit. This study of the match between heuristic and environmental structure allows us to predict success and failure, that is, the ecological rationality of heuristics.

- Use these results for the prescriptive operation of heuristics. That is, design and teach heuristic procedures in situations where an optimizing model is unknown, it is inferior to a heuristic, it is dangerous because it is too slow, or it is overly information-greedy and expensive. For instance, tit for tat is a fast and frugal heuristic that has three simple building blocks: cooperate first; memorize only your partner's last move; and reciprocate, that is, cooperate if your partner does and defect if your partner does. Nevertheless, it can outperform rational choice strategies as well as sophisticated computational models in a class of environments (e.g., when interacting with cooperative players). In these situations, the prescription is not rational choice or computational power, but a simple and smart heuristic.

In summary, there exist three interpretations of bounded rationality. The focus on the constraints in the world has allowed economists to equate bounded rationality with optimization under constraints. Simon has vehemently protested against this reduction. The focus on constraints in the mind has led many behavioral economists to equate bounded rationality with an assembly of cognitive illusions. But this again means looking at only one of the two blades. The third interpretation, Simon's view, is neither optimization in the world nor irrationality in the mind. It concerns models of heuristics and environments, and their match. The rationality of the heuristics in the adaptive toolbox is not logical but ecological.

## 2.2  WHAT IS A HEURISTIC?

The term *heuristic* is of Greek origin, meaning "serving to find out or discover." In his Nobel prize–winning paper, Einstein (1905; taken from Holton 1988) used the term *heuristic* in its title to indicate an idea that he considered incomplete, given the limits of our knowledge, but useful. The mathematician Polya (1954) thought of heuristic thinking as a high form of mathematical thinking for problems that cannot be solved by logic or probability theory. For instance, even for games such as chess and Go, which have few and clear rules, there is no optimal strategy known: they are NP-hard (that is, the solution cannot be calculated in polynomial time). Chess masters and chess computers have to rely on heuristics in order to win. From the Gestalt psychologists to Herbert Simon, and from machine learning to decision making (Payne, Bettman, and Johnson 1993), heuristics have been seen as positive tools that help when uncertainty is high, optimization out of reach, and deadlines pending.

Heuristic refers to the cognitive process that generates a decision. A model of a heuristic describes the steps of this process. In the simplest case, these include a search rule (what information is searched for in what order, inside or outside of memory), a stopping rule (when search is stopped and further information ignored), and a decision rule (how a decision is derived from the information found). For instance, models of "satisficing" (e.g., Selten 2001) specify a rule of search (search sequentially through alternatives), a stopping rule (stop search when the first object is encountered that meets an aspiration level, which may be lowered as a function of search time), and a decision rule (choose the first object that meets the aspiration level).

The adaptive toolbox is, in two respects, a Darwinian metaphor for decision making. First, evolution does not follow a grand plan but results in a patchwork of solutions for specific problems. The same goes for the toolbox: First, its heuristics are domain specific, not general. Second, the heuristics in the adaptive toolbox are not good or bad, rational or irrational, per se, only relative to an environment, just as adaptations are context bound. The structure of an environment, also called the problem structure, includes the statistical structure of the environment and the goals of the decision maker.

When the term *heuristic* became used in the cognitive illusions program around 1970, its meaning was changed in several respects. It was now used in problems that could be solved by probability theory. In these problems, a heuristic could per definition only result in bad judgments, and every single demonstration was negative. In fact, the terms *heuristic* and *bias* became almost synonymous and were used interchangeably. For instance, Jolls, Sunstein, and Thaler (1998) list both biases and the availability heuristic under the rubric "judgmental errors." Rachlinski (2000) calls both the hindsight bias and the representativeness heuristic "cognitive phenomena" (93) and "cognitive processes" (96). This causes confusion in terminology: A heuristic is an explanation for a bias or error, not another error. A bias is the outcome of a cognitive process, not the process itself. More important, there is a serious and unresolved problem for legal scholars: the vagueness of the heuristics proposed, which invites creative storytelling.

## 2.3 THE PROBLEM WITH VAGUE LABELS

As I see it, there are two ways in which a theory can fail: by being wrong or being indeterminate. The latter may be worse for scientific progress, because indeterminate theories resist attempts to prove, disprove, or even improve them. Theories assuming the maximization of subjective expected utility have been criticized for being indeterminate, because of the many degrees of freedom for determining the utilities and utility functions. This flexibility would allow a person to account, after the fact, for almost all observations. Importing psychology has been proposed as a remedy. "We believe the behavioral approach imposes discipline on economic theorizing because assumptions cannot be imported at will" (Jolls, Sunstein, and Thaler 1998, 1489). The problem, however, has been treated with the same ailment. Vague utilities have been substituted with vague heuristics. The fault does not lie with psychology but with the kind of psychology imported.

The main goal of the cognitive illusions program was "to understand the cognitive processes that produce both valid and invalid judgments" (Kahneman and Tversky 1996, 583). It is understandable that when heuristics were first proposed as the underlying cognitive processes in the early 1970s, they were only loosely characterized. Yet more than thirty years and many experiments later, explanatory notions such as "representativeness" remain vague and undefined, unspecified with respect both to the antecedent conditions that elicit (or suppress) them and to the cognitive processes that underlie them. My fear is that legal decision theory will be stuck with plausible yet nebulous proposals of the same type, such as that judgments of probability or frequency are sometimes influenced by what is similar (representativeness), what comes easily to mind (availability), and what comes first (anchoring). These "heuristics" are mere verbal labels, or one-word explanations. There is no process model or specification of search, stopping, and decision rules. There is no explication of the characteristics of the situations in which a heuristic is successful and in which it would fail (see the exchange between Gigerenzer [1996] and Kahneman and Tversky [1996]). The problem with these heuristics is that they at once explain too little and too much. Too little, because we do not know when and how they work; too much, because, post hoc, one of them can be fitted to almost any experimental result.

### 2.3.1 Representativeness

The representativeness heuristic is invoked when judgments do not conform to some norm, such as Bayes' rule, but seem to be based on a form of similarity judgment. However, psychological research has long since proposed and tested precise models of similarity, including Euclidean distance, City Block distance, likelihood ratio, and feature-matching models. In light of these precise theories, the new preference for vague labels such as *representativeness* reflects a step backward, which is in itself an interesting phenomenon. Legal scholars are quick to explain the behavior of judges, jurors, or ordinary criminals whose behavior seems to deviate from rational choice theory by invoking representativeness. Assertions such as that most courts have fallen victim to "a profound misunderstanding of the laws of probability in precisely the way that the representativeness heuristic predicts" have become explanatory rhetoric in the legal context (e.g., Rachlinski 2000, 90). The good news is that this term can be invoked to account for many behaviors inconsistent with rational choice theory; the bad news is that it is so vague that it can account both for "A" and "not-A." Note that if a concept can explain both A and its logical contradiction, then its predictive value is nil. Following are a few illustrations.

### 2.3.1.1 How to "Explain" A and Not-A

*2.3.1.1.1 Hot-hand fallacy.* The hot-hand fallacy in basketball refers to the intuition of fans and coaches that players tend to get "hot" after having scored a few times in a series. The intuition is that after a series of $n$ hits, the player's probability of another hit will increase (and that of a miss will decrease), whereas the statistical evidence suggests that nothing changes. This fallacy was attributed to the representativeness heuristic. The reason given was that "even short random sequences are thought to be highly representative of their generating processes" (Gilovich, Vallone, and Tversky 1985, 295). People predict another hit because a hit is representative of the previous series of $n$ hits.

*2.3.1.1.2 Gambler's fallacy.* The gambler's fallacy is an intuition that was discussed by Laplace and refers to playing the roulette wheel. The intuition is that after a series of $n$ "reds," the probability of another "red" will decrease (and that of a "black" will increase). The gambler's fallacy was also attributed to the representativeness heuristic. The reason given was that "the occurrence of black will result in a more representative sequence than the occurrence of an additional red" (Tversky and Kahneman 1974, 1125). People do not predict another "red" because "black" will make the resulting series of $n + 1$ events look more representative to a series with the true probability of .5.

Note that these two phenomena are exactly opposite. In the hot-hand fallacy, the intuition is that after a series of $n$ equal outcomes, the same outcome will occur again; in the gambler's fallacy, the intuition is that after a series of $n$ equal outcomes, the opposite outcome will occur. Nevertheless, the notion of the representativeness heuristic is flexible enough to account for both logical possibilities (Ayton and Fischer, 2004). In the hot-hand fallacy, the similarity is taken to be between the new outcome and the series of $n$ outcomes; and in the gambler's fallacy, the meaning of similarity is switched to that between the series of $n + 1$ outcomes and the underlying probability of the outcome. If at any time a basketball coach can be found who exhibits a cold-hand fallacy, then the version of the representativeness heuristic used for the gambler's fallacy will also be able to explain this phenomenon.

A second way to explain both A and not-A is to invoke representativeness if A is observed and another heuristic if not-A is observed. Freudian psychoanalysis is indeterminate in this sense. If the patient reports that he dreamt of having sex with his mother, this proves the Oedipal hypothesis of the theory. If he does not report so, this proves the repression hypothesis of the theory. This problem can be illustrated by the base-rate fallacy and conservatism.

*2.3.1.1.3 Base-rate fallacy.* In Bayesian-type problems, people typically estimate the posterior probability of an event (such as that a person is a lawyer or has a disease, given some evidence) from the base rate, the hit rate (sensitivity), and the false positive rate. The conclusion of many studies has been that people neglect or underweight the base-rate information, that is, they commit the base-rate fallacy. This phenomenon has also been attributed to the representativeness heuristic: People ignore the base rates because they rely solely on the hit rate. The hit rate can often be seen as a form of similarity, such as the probability from a description given that the person is a lawyer. Note that we now have a third meaning of representativeness: to infer the posterior probability by the hit rate, that is, to confuse a conditional probability with its inverse probability.

*2.3.1.1.4 Conservatism.* The base-rate fallacy refers to ignoring or underweighting base rates. The opposite error would be to rely only on base rates or to overweight base rates. In fact, overweighting base rates counted as an established fact in the 1960s and was called *conservatism* (e.g., Edwards 1968). It has never been determined why people seemed to be conservative in the 1960s but neglected base rates in the 1970s, when Kahneman and Tversky's research began. Whatever the reason, conservatism can be just as easily "explained" by invoking one of the other two heuristics, anchoring and adjustment: people anchor on the base rate and adjust a bit. The notion of anchoring is indeterminate in the sense that it is left open what the anchor might be. For instance, nothing would prevent one from taking the hit rate as the anchor and "explaining" the base-rate fallacy by proposing that people anchor on the hit rate and adjust a bit toward the base rate.

Labels that can account, after the fact, for almost everything are unable to predict people's future behavior. This undesirable state of affairs has not gone unnoticed by legal scholars: "Availability may account for overreaction to a catastrophe, anchoring may explain underreaction (Noll and Krier, 2000, 351). The general point is that behavioral law and economics will make little progress by relying on vague notions such as representativeness to "explain" the thinking of jurors or judges or to design legal institutions that can counteract cognitive illusions. At first glance, this may be disappointing news for those who have started to see the world through "representativeness," but this sour insight is a necessary step for proceeding from one-word explanations to theories of human behavior.

### 2.3.2 Availability

The term *availability* has been used to explain distorted frequency or probability judgments. Beginning with the original work (Tversky and Kahneman 1973), this term has had various meanings, such as the number of instances that come to mind and the ease with which the operations of retrieval can be performed. Despite, or possibly because of, its vagueness, availability has been invoked to explain various phenomena—for instance, why the purchase of earthquake insurance rises after a quake, why personal experience distorts crime risk perception, or more generally, why "people disproportionately weigh salient, memorable, or vivid evidence even when they have better sources of information" (Rabin 1998, 30). Similarly, legal scholars have invoked availability as after-the-fact accounts of legal phenomena, including underregulation and overregulation (Jolls, Sunstein, and Thaler 1998), and "collective availability errors," such as residents' worry about the health effects of Love Canal (Kuran and Sunstein, 2000). For instance, in Sunstein's (2000) reader on behavioral law and economics, the term "availability" changes its meaning from chapter to chapter. A person overestimates one risk over another, so we are told, because "an incident is readily called to mind or 'available'" 5), or "simply because many of his acquaintances have the disease" 381), or because people "have recently witnessed an occurrence of that event" 15). The first use of the term "availability" refers to ease of retrieval, the second to the number of instances retrieved, and the third to recency. Ease of retrieval of one instance and the number of instances retrieved, however, can lead to *opposite* conclusions (Schwarz and Vaughn, 2000; Sedlmeier, Hertwig and Gigerenzer, 1998), and furthermore, recency does not imply that a large number of instances is recalled, nor vice versa. These concepts are not the same. In other places, we are told that availability is "just another name for the 'salience' of standard political theory" 353), or that it does not refer to the actual ease of retrieval but to "judging how easy it is to recall other instances of this type (how 'available' such instances are)" 15).

Given how little specification there is on what availability does and does not mean, the weight of the argument rests on the experimental evidence. In a widely cited study designed to demonstrate how people's judgments are biased due to availability, Tversky and Kahneman (1973) had people estimate whether each of five consonants ($K, L, N, R, V$) appears more frequently in the first or the third position in English words. Each of these five selected consonants occurs more frequently in the third position, which is atypical because the majority of consonants occur more frequently in the first position. Two-thirds of the participants judged the first position as being more likely for a majority of the five consonants. This result was interpreted as a demonstration of a cognitive illusion and attributed to the availability heuristic: Words with a particular letter in the first position come to mind more easily. However, there was no independent measure of availability in this study, nor has there been a successful replication in the literature.

Sedlmeier, Hertwig, and Gigerenzer (1998) defined the two most common meanings of availability, measured them independently of people's frequency judgments, and tested whether availability can actually predict them. The number of instances that come to mind was measured by the number of retrieved words within a constant time period (availability-by-number), and ease of retrieval was measured by the speed of the retrieval of the first word for each letter (availability-by-speed). The test involved a large sample of letters rather than the five consonants, which, as described previously, were atypical. The result was that neither of the two definitions of availability could predict people's actual frequency judgments, inconsistent with Tversky and Kahneman's speculation. Instead, the judgments were roughly a monotonic function of the actual proportions, with a regression toward the mean, that is, an overestimation of low and an underestimation of high proportions.

The general point is that if one does not define the process to which the term *availability* refers, one cannot prove, disprove, or improve this notion. The letter study, which is probably the most cited evidence for availability, did not provide such a test, and when we defined *availability* in two different ways, neither could predict people's estimates.

What is the alternative? Jurors and judges certainly do use heuristics, and there in fact exist models of heuristics that describe the steps of the process (e.g., Dhami, 2003; Dhami and Ayton 2001). As mentioned previously, a model of a heuristic is about the process that underlies a decision, such as specifying a search rule, a stopping rule, and a decision rule. It can be descriptive or put to prescriptive use. Consider a case that illustrates both uses and raises legal issues.

## 2.4 A HEURISTIC FOR EMERGENCY ROOM DECISIONS

A man is rushed to the hospital with serious chest pains. The doctors suspect acute ischemic heart disease (myocardial infarction or unstable angina) and need to make a decision, and they need to make it quickly: Should the patient be assigned to the coronary care unit or to a regular nursing bed with ECG telemetry? How does, and how should, a doctor make such a decision? In a Michigan hospital, doctors sent some 90 percent of the patients to the coronary care unit. The physicians were concerned with being sued if they mistakenly sent a patient to a regular bed and the person subsequently had a heart attack and died. The other possible error, wrongly sending a patient into the care unit, seemed fairly safe and socially acceptable, even if the patient were to die as a consequence of this decision. From the point of view of the hospital and the patients, however, this defensive decision making led to unnecessary costs (too many people in the coronary care unit), decreased the quality of care provided (the unit was overcrowded), and became a health risk for patients who should not have been in the unit (it is one of the most dangerous places in a hospital due to the risk of secondary infections, which can be fatal).

Researchers at the University of Michigan Hospital tried to solve this overcrowding problem by training the physicians instead to use a decision-support system (Green and Mehr 1997). The heart disease predictive instrument (Pozen et al. 1984) consists of a chart with some fifty probabilities and a logistic regression formula programmed into a pocket calculator with which the physician can compute the probability that a patient has acute ischemic heart disease and therefore requires the coronary care unit. A quick glance at the chart makes it clear why physicians were generally not happy using this and similar systems (Corey and Merenstein 1987; Pearson et al. 1994). It is difficult to understand, and the calculations are not obvious. The hospital then faced the following dilemma: Should patients in life-and-death situations be classified by physicians' intuitions that are natural but suboptimal or by complex calculations that are alien but possibly more accurate?

There is, however, a third alternative: smart heuristics that correspond to the structure of natural intuitions but can have the accuracy of fancy statistical models. Green and Mehr (1997) constructed a decision heuristic by using three of the building blocks developed by my research group: ordered search, a fast stopping rule, and one-reason decision making (Gigerenzer and Goldstein, 1996; Gigerenze, Todd, and the ABC Research Group 1999). The resulting heuristic is shown in Figure 2.1 in the form of a fast and frugal decision tree. It ignores all fifty probabilities and asks only a few yes-or-no questions. If a certain anomaly appears in a patient's electrocardiogram (the so-called ST segment change), the patient is immediately admitted to the coronary care unit. No other information is searched for. If that is not the case, a second question is asked: Is chest pain the patient's primary complaint? If not, the patient is immediately classified as low risk and assigned to a regular nursing bed. No further information is considered. If the answer is yes, then a third and final question concerning other factors is asked to classify the patient.

This decision tree employs fast and frugal rules of searching, stopping, and decision making. First, it searches sequentially through predictors according to a

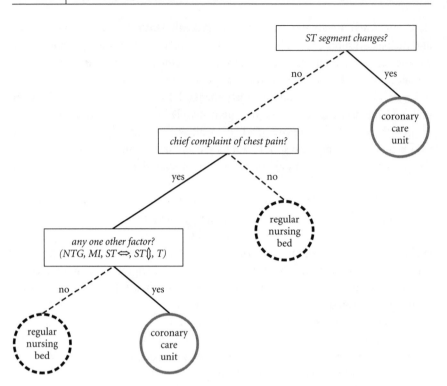

**Figure 2.1** A fast and frugal decision tree for coronary care unit allocation. The third question is a composite one, and the answer is yes if at least one of the following factors is present. *NTG*: Patient reports a history of PRN use of nitroglycerin for relief of chest pain; not necessary to have used NTG for this episode. *MI*: Patient reports a history of definite myocardial infarction. *ST* ⟺: Initial EKG shows ST segment "barring," "straightening," or "flattening" in at least two leads excluding aVR. *ST* ⇕: Initial EKG shows ST segment elevation or depression of at least 1 mm in at least two leads excluding avR. *T*: Initial EKG shows T waves that are "hyperacute" (at least 50% of R-wave amplitude) or inverted at least 1 mm in at least two leads excluding aVR.

SOURCE: For details, see Green and Mehr 1997.

simple order (predictor with the highest sensitivity first, predictor with the highest specificity second, and so on). Second, search can stop after each predictor; the rest is ignored. Third, the strategy does not combine—weight and add—the predictors; for instance, a change in the ST segment cannot be compensated for by any of the other predictors. Only one predictor determines each decision. This decision rule is an instance of one-reason decision making. The entire heuristic is a realization of a fast and frugal tree, which is defined as a decision tree with a small number of binary predictors that allow for a decision at each branch of the tree.

### 2.4.1 How Accurate Is the Fast and Frugal Tree?

Emergency room decisions, like most important choices, need to satisfy multiple performance criteria. Making a decision fast is crucial in situations where hesitation can cost a life. A second and related criterion is frugality, that is, the ability to make a good decision with only limited information. A third criterion is transparency—an accurate system is worth little when it is not accepted by the physicians. Unlike logistic regression, the steps of the fast and frugal tree are transparent and easy to teach. Making decisions in a fast, frugal, and transparent way is the general advantage of heuristics. But how accurate is the fast and frugal tree compared to the logistic regression?

On the y-axis, Figure 2.2 shows the proportion of patients correctly assigned to the coronary care unit, as measured by a subsequent heart attack. On the x-axis is shown the proportion of incorrectly assigned patients. The diagonal line represents chance performance. A perfect strategy would be represented by a point in the upper left-hand corner, but no such performance exists, given our limited knowledge about heart attacks.

The predictive accuracy of the physicians at the Michigan hospital turned out to be at the chance level, even slightly below. They sent about 90 percent of the patients into the care unit but could not discriminate between those who should and should not have been there. The heart disease predictive instrument did much better than the physicians' intuition. Its performance is shown by a series of open squares, which represent various trade-offs between the two possible errors. The counterintuitive result is that the fast and frugal tree was more accurate in classifying actual heart attack patients than both the physicians' intuition and the heart disease predictive instrument. It correctly assigned the largest proportion of patients who subsequently had a myocardial infarction into the coronary care unit. At the same time, it had a comparatively low false-alarm rate. Note that the expert system had more information than the smart heuristic and could make use of sophisticated statistical calculations. Nevertheless, in this complex situation, less is more. Simplicity can pay off.

Fast and frugal decision making is currently discussed in medicine as an alternative to rational choice (Elwyn et al. 2001). The legal aspect is illustrated by a patient who was not sent into the coronary care unit but subsequently died of a heart attack. Figure 2.2 shows that the heuristic leads to some of these types of cases, although fewer than the decision-support system does. For instance, the patient who

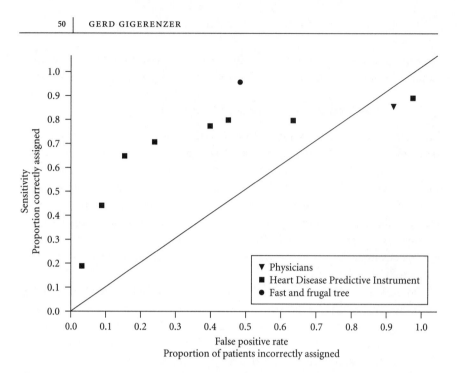

**Figure 2.2** Coronary care unit decisions by physicians, the Heart Disease Predictive Instrument (HDPI), and the fast and frugal tree. Accuracy is measured by the proportion of patients correctly assigned to the coronary care unit, and the proportion of patients incorrectly sent to the unit. Correct assignment is measured by the occurrence of myocardial infarction. An ideal diagnostic instrument would be represented by a point in the upper left-hand corner, but in the real world, no such performance exists. SOURCE: After Green and Mehr 1997.

died might have had no ST segment change and the primary complaints were not chest pain, so the patient was sent to a regular bed. The patient's relatives sue the hospital for malpractice because the doctors did not check the other variables further down the tree or those that the decision-support system measures and integrates. Does the hospital have a chance of winning? The answer depends on the standard of health care (Engel 2000). Time pressure, coronary care unit space, and cost-benefit calculations might count, and formal rules of consent and relying on state-of-the-art treatment might play a role. But the state of the art in medicine and other fields is still shaped by the misleading ideal of full information. Collecting all pieces of information and combining them in an "optimal" way, such as in logistic regression, are assumed to always be the best thing to do. The wisdom in simplicity is news to many.

## 2.4.2 Robustness

For which problem structures will a fast and frugal tree be accurate? This question of ecological rationality is treated in detail by Martignon and Hoffrage (1999, 2002) and Martignon et al. (2003). I will briefly discuss here two features of the environmental structure faced by the hospital: a large degree of noise and the task of predicting new patients whose characteristics are not yet known.

Assume first an ideal world with the opposite structure. First, there is omniscience: The fate of each patient (heart attack or not) is completely predictable, that is, there is no form of noise in the environment. Second, there is no novelty: We aim only at a model that fits the known data of a population of patients and do not aim at a model that predicts the fate of new patients, which may differ in unknown ways from the ones we have investigated. In this safe world, a logistic regression is always as accurate as or better than the fast and frugal tree. More is better. This, however, is no longer true when we look at the actual situation of the Michigan hospital.

The decision support system was validated on several thousand patients in a large hospital (the training set). But it was subsequently applied in different hospitals, such as the Michigan hospital, to new groups of patients who deviated in unknown ways from the original sample (the test set). In this situation, the support system that may have been "optimal" in the original population need no longer be the best. This is the case when there is noise in the environment, that is, when the fate of the patient is difficult to predict. When one has to predict (as opposed to fit a model to extant patients) and there is noise, a model that relies on many pieces of information may then suffer from overfitting.

In general, a model $A$ overfits the training set if there exists an alternative model $B$ such that $A$ has higher or equal accuracy than $B$ in the training set but lower accuracy in the test set. Models with many free parameters, such as logistic regression or Bayesian methods, tend to overfit in environments in which information is noisy or fluctuating, particularly when forced to make predictions from small samples. This relation between degree of noise, number of free parameters, and fitting and predictive accuracy is mathematically formulated by various theorems. One version is Akaike's (1973) theorem, which asserts the following: Assume two models that belong to a nested family in which one has fewer adjustable parameters than the other. If both have, on average, the same number of correct inferences on the training set, then the simpler model (that is, the one with fewer adjustable parameters) will have greater (or at least the same) predictive accuracy on the test set.

The theorem illustrates that simplicity can mean not only beauty but also predictive accuracy. There are various mathematical methods to search for robust heuristics, but these are of little help in situations in which the parameters of the population are unknown. The "true" problem of inductive inference is in generalizing to new situations, such as new groups of patients, whose features are not yet known. Here, one can compute the best robust method only after the fact. Fast and frugal heuristics have a built-in feature that can generate robustness in these situations—their focus on the few most important variables helps them avoid overfitting and perform robustly.

The treatment allocation heuristic illustrates the continuum between a descriptive and a prescriptive heuristic. The model in Figure 2.1 is descriptive for doctors who use this heuristic intuitively. It can also be used prescriptively by teaching physicians for treatment allocation. A systematic treatment of models of heuristics, both descriptive and prescriptive, is beyond the scope of this chapter. I refer to Gigerenzer, Todd, and the ABC Research Group (1999), Gigerenzer and Selten (2001b), Todd and Gigerenzer (2000; with comments) and Payne, Bettman, and Johnson (1993).

## 2.5 HOW TO HELP PEOPLE REASON THE BAYESIAN WAY

Sunstein (1997, 1187) notes that "juries are likely to make many mistakes in terms of probability assessments and that correction of those mistakes is a large task of the legal system." How can the legal system solve this task? Sunstein proceeds by introducing availability, anchoring, and representativeness as the typical suspects that might cause jurors' clouded minds. As the reader may infer, I do not believe that this game of imagination will provide a cure for jurors' clouded minds, nor does Sunstein come up with a solution. In this section, I will show how the view of ecological rationality can provide such a solution. Recall that the cure for the breakdown of color constancy is not in debiasing the mind but in changing the environment. One has to restore the original spectral properties of the ambient light. The same holds true if one wants to free jurors and judges from innumeracy. The problem is not dispositional, that is, in the mind or in its cognitive limitations. Rather, it is contextual, that is, in an interplay between mind and environment.

### 2.5.1 Physicians

Consider breast cancer screening with mammography, which incurs costs of about $2 billion every year in the United States. Given how much money is spent for this technology, physicians and patients should understand what its outcome means. A woman tests positive and asks her physician how likely it is that she has breast cancer. The relevant statistical information for the woman's age group is as follows:

> The probability that a woman has breast cancer is 1% [base rate]. If she has breast cancer, the probability of a positive screening test is 80% [sensitivity]. If she does not have breast cancer, the probability of a positive screening test is 10% [false positive rate].

The posterior probability $p(H \mid D)$ that a woman who tests positive actually has breast cancer can be calculated by Bayes' rule. Here, $H$ stands for hypothesis, such as cancer, and $D$ for data, such as a positive test result:

$$p(H \mid D) = \frac{p(H)p(D \mid H)}{p(H)p(D \mid H) + p(\text{not-}H)p(D \mid \text{not-}H)}$$

$$= \frac{(.01)(.80)}{(.01)(.80) + (.99)(.10)} \approx .07. \tag{1}$$

That is, most women who test positive in screening do not have breast cancer. Figure 2.3 (left) shows the estimates of twenty-four physicians, including radiologists, gynecologists, and internists, with an average professional experience of fourteen years (Gigerenzer 2002; Hoffrage and Gigerenzer 1998). Each point corresponds to one physician. There was alarmingly little consensus: Estimates ranged between 1% and 90%. One-third of the physicians (eight) concluded that the probability of breast cancer given a positive mammogram is 90%. Another third of the physicians estimated the chances to be between 50% and 80%. Another eight thought the chance was 10% or less, and half of these estimated the probability as 1%, which corresponds to the base rate. The median estimate was 70%. If you were a patient, you would be justly alarmed by this diversity of medical opinion. Only two of the physicians reasoned correctly, giving estimates of about 7%. Another two estimated the chances to be near this value, but for the wrong reasons. For instance, one physician confused the false positive rate with the probability that the patient has breast cancer, given that she has a positive mammogram.

We know from protocol analysis and interviews how the majority of the physicians reasoned. Those who estimated the probability to be 90%, for instance, did so for two reasons. They either mistook the sensitivity for the posterior probability or, alternatively, subtracted the false positive rate from 100%, which results in the same estimate. In both cases, the base rate is ignored—an instance of the base-rate fallacy. This analysis illustrates that the confusion of the posterior probability with the sensitivity of the test (which is the third meaning of representativeness;

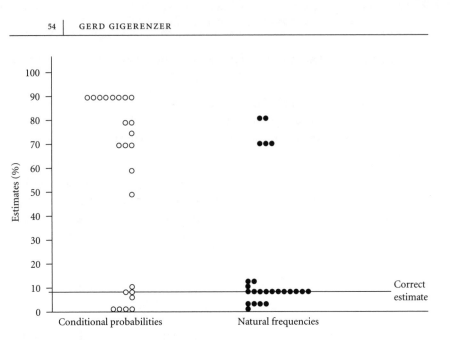

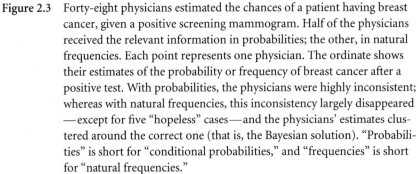

**Figure 2.3** Forty-eight physicians estimated the chances of a patient having breast cancer, given a positive screening mammogram. Half of the physicians received the relevant information in probabilities; the other, in natural frequencies. Each point represents one physician. The ordinate shows their estimates of the probability or frequency of breast cancer after a positive test. With probabilities, the physicians were highly inconsistent; whereas with natural frequencies, this inconsistency largely disappeared — except for five "hopeless" cases — and the physicians' estimates clustered around the correct one (that is, the Bayesian solution). "Probabilities" is short for "conditional probabilities," and "frequencies" is short for "natural frequencies."

see previous discussion)—is only one of several explanations for base-rate neglect, and in the present case, an infrequent one. Only two physicians estimated 80%, which is the value of the sensitivity (Figure 2.3, left).

Overestimating the chance of breast cancer after a positive screening test exacts unnecessary physical, psychological, and monetary costs. For instance, every year more than three hundred thousand American women who do not have breast cancer undergo a biopsy as a consequence of false positives, and for every one hundred dollars spent on screening, an additional thirty-three dollars is spent on following up on false positive results (Gigerenzer 2002).

Is there a solution? Let us now switch the external representation from conditional probabilities to natural frequencies. For most of the time during which the human mind evolved, information was encountered in the form of natural frequencies, that is, counts that have not been normalized with respect to base rates. Following is an example of a representation in terms of natural frequencies:

Ten of every 1,000 women have breast cancer. Of these 10 women with breast cancer, 8 will test positive. Of the 990 women without breast cancer, 99 will also test positive.

How many of those who test positive actually have breast cancer? Natural frequencies help people to see the answer: 8 out of the 107 women who tested positive actually have cancer. Natural frequencies facilitate Bayesian computations because they carry information about base rates, whereas normalized frequencies and probabilities do not. Let $a$ represent the frequency of $D$ and $H$ (for example, positive test and disease), and let $b$ represent the frequency of $D$ and not-$H$. The posterior probability can be calculated as follows:

$$p(H|D) = \frac{a}{a + b} = \frac{8}{8 + 99} \approx .07. \tag{2}$$

Note that with natural frequencies, base rates need not be directly paid attention to. In contrast, if natural frequencies have been normalized with respect to the base rates, resulting in conditional probabilities or relative frequencies, one has to multiply the normalized values by the base rates in order to bring the base rates "back in" (compare Equations 1 and 2).[1] Unlike conditional probabilities, natural frequencies are an efficient representation for Bayesian reasoning because the representation does part of the computation (Gigerenzer and Hoffrage 1999).

Would the same simple method work with physicians who make diagnostic inferences in daily practice? Figure 2.3 (right) shows that when the information was presented in natural frequencies, the physicians' estimates clustered around the correct answer. There were only five physicians left who still estimated the chances at greater than 50%. The same positive effect of an efficient representation was obtained from physicians, medical students, and laypeople for colorectal cancer screening and other standard diseases (Gigerenzer 2002; Gigerenzer and Hoffrage 1995; Hoffrage, Lindsey et al. 2000).

### 2.5.2 Legal Professionals

In the counseling room as well as in the courtroom, choosing an efficient representation can make the difference between life and death. Like medical tests, DNA fingerprinting requires reasoning about base rates, false positives, and false negatives. Even so, out of some 175 accredited U.S. law schools, only one requires a course in basic statistics. Lindsey, Hertwig, and Gigerenzer (2003) asked advanced law students and legal professionals (including law school professors) to evaluate two criminal case files based upon two actual rape and murder cases. In both cases, a match was reported between the DNA of the defendant and a trace on the victim. One case involved additional eyewitness identification, whereas the other case was based solely on a data-bank match.

When the statistical information was expressed as conditional probabilities, only 13% of the professionals and less than 1% of the law students correctly inferred the probability that the defendant was actually the source of the trace, given a match (Figure 2.4a). When the identical information was stated in terms of natural frequencies, the correct inferences increased to 68% and 44%, respectively. Did the representation also matter for the verdict? Yes. More professionals and students voted "guilty" when the evidence was presented in terms of probabilities, that is, when their minds were clouded (Figure 2.4b). Note that the effect of external representation on guilty verdicts shown in Figure 2.4b was stronger than the effect of the presence or absence of an eyewitness identification.

In conclusion, as in the case of color constancy, the solution for difficulties in statistical reasoning is choosing a proper way to present the information. The effect shown in Figures 2.3 and 2.4 can be further enhanced by explicit training in how to translate conditional probabilities into natural frequencies (Sedlmeier and Gigerenzer 2001). Some physicians and legal scholars have told me that one reason to study medicine or law was to avoid statistics and psychology. The interplay between statistics and psychology, however, shows how innumeracy can be turned into insight. Reasoning does not occur only inside the head; choosing the right representation is part of problem solving. As Herbert Simon wrote in *The Sciences of the Artificial*, "Solving a problem simply means to represent it so as to make the solution transparent" (1969, 77).

### 2.5.3  Guidelines for Communicating Statistical Information in Court

Conditional probabilities are not the only kind of probabilities that confuse people. Single-event probabilities are another source of confusion. Consider first a case in which the defendant is accused of committing a rape and subsequent murder. His DNA matches a trace found on the victim. Otherwise, there is little evidence against him. What does this match imply? The court calls an expert witness, and the jury hears this testimony:

> The probability that this match has occurred by chance is one in one hundred thousand.

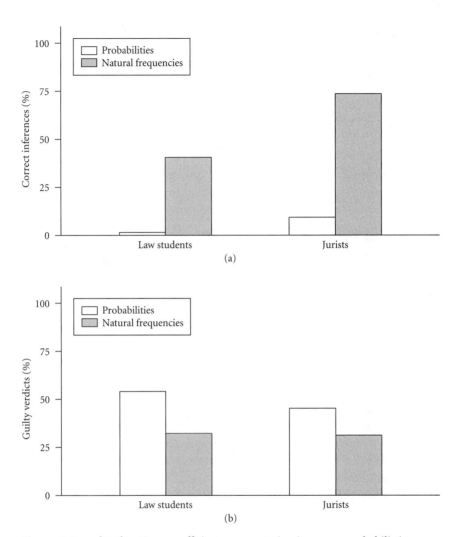

**Figures 2.4a and 2.4b**  How an efficient representation improves probabilistic reasoning and influences verdicts in legal professionals and law students.
When 27 legal professionals and 127 law students responded to DNA
evidence presented in terms of conditional probabilities, few could correctly infer the probability that the defendant was actually the source
of the trace, given a DNA match. With natural frequencies, more than
40 percent of the students and the majority of the professionals "saw"
the correct answer (Figure 2.4a). Representation also influenced participants' ultimate verdict (Figure 2.4b). With conditional probabilities,
more students and professionals voted "guilty."

SOURCE: Hoffrage, Lindsey et al. 2000; Lindsey, Hertwig, and Gigerenzer 2003.

You can already see the defendant behind bars. However, imagine that the expert had phrased the same information differently:

Out of every one hundred thousand people, one will show a match.

How many people are there who could have committed this murder? If the murder occurred in a city with 1 million adult inhabitants, then there should be ten inhabitants whose DNA would match the sample on the victim. On its own, this fact seems very unlikely to land the defendant behind bars.

In the first statement, the uncertainty is represented as a single-event probability ("that this match occurred by chance"); in the second, as a frequency in a class of people. There is broad evidence in the experimental literature that jurors, attorneys, and even expert witnesses are confused, or confuse themselves, by using the form of conditional probabilities or single-event probabilities (e.g., Koehler 1997). The courts could counter this problem by insisting that DNA evidence, or other statistical evidence, be presented in court in natural frequencies rather than in conditional probabilities or single-event probabilities. However, few courts have recognized the relevance of how statistical information is presented in trials. A British court of appeal recently recommended that DNA evidence be presented in frequency formats (see Redmayne 1998, 451; 2001, 71–72).

## 2.6 THE ADAPTIVE TOOLBOX

### 2.6.1 Heuristics and Their Building Blocks

The three building blocks of the fast and frugal tree in Figure 2.1—sequential search through the most valid cues, fast stopping rule, and one-reason decision making—have been observed in human and animal behavior. For instance, mate choice in female guppies follows the Take The Best heuristic, which uses the same building blocks (Gigerenzer and Goldstein 1999). If a female has a choice between two males, one of which is much more orange than the other, she will choose the more orange one. The stopping rule for the orangeness cue is that one male must be much (about 40 percent) more orange than the other. If the males are close in orangeness, she prefers the one she has seen mating with another female, and so on (Dugatkin 1996). Mate choice in female guppies illustrates sequential and limited search, stopping rules, and one-reason decision making. In humans, experiments have shown that in proper environments in 60 percent to 90 percent of all cases, search through cues follows exactly the order that Take The Best predicts: people stop searching exactly when the first discrimination cue is found and base their decision on only one cue (e.g., Bröder 2000, 2003; Bröder and Schiffer, 2003; Newell and Shanks, 2003; Newell, Weston, and Shanks, 2003).

Heuristics can provide process models for phenomena for which there has previously been no good explanation. The hindsight bias, which is a by-product (not an adaptation itself) of an adaptive memory updating mechanism, is a case in point. Until recently, there was no process model, only verbal suggestions, such as memory traces, that would merge. The first process model, the RAFT model, was able to predict when a person would show a hindsight bias, a reversed hindsight bias, or no hindsight bias in 75 percent of cases (Hoffrage, Hertwig, and Gigerenzer 2000). This makes clear that hindsight bias is not a disposition but a product of the interaction between a cognitive system and its environment, which in some cases can even produce a reversed hindsight bias.

The recognition heuristic is a second example of a heuristic present in both animals and humans. Norway rats prefer foods they recognize from having tasted them or from having smelled them on the breath of other rats (Galef 1987; Galef, McQuoid, and Whiskin 1990). This heuristic for food choice is followed even if the rat whose breath is smelled happens to be sick at the time. That is, recognition dominates illness information. Humans rely on name recognition in a variety of situations. For instance, when a consumer has the choice between a product whose name she recognizes and one she does not, she is likely to pick the recognized one. In other words, the recognition heuristic can be applied only when one is partially ignorant, that is, has heard of one but not of the other brand name. It is ecologically rational in situations where name recognition correlates with the criterion one wants to infer (such as quality), which is often the case in competitive situations, but can be exploited by firms that count on increasing name recognition through advertisement. In experiments, people follow the recognition heuristic in some 90 percent of the cases in ecologically rational situations (Goldstein and Gigerenzer 2002). For an overview of heuristics and their building blocks, see Gigerenzer, Todd, and the ABC Research Group (1999), Gigerenzer and Selten (2001b), and Payne, Bettman, and Johnson (1993).

## 2.6.2 Ecological Rationality

The study of the match between heuristics and the structure of environments is essential to understanding when and why heuristics are successful. For instance, one can prove that in environments with a noncompensatory cue structure (Martignon and Hoffrage 1999), fast and frugal trees (such as the treatment allocation heuristic) and the Take The Best heuristic are as accurate as or more so than any "optimal" linear model, such as multiple regression. Looking at both bounds of the mind, internal and external, also helps to understand the role of so-called cognitive limitations. Against the background of full rationality, behavioral economists and legal scholars tend to present limited capacities as a general deficiency.

The Take The Best heuristic, for instance, works for a mind that has limited memory, ignores dependencies between cues, and does not add and weight information into a decision. Nevertheless, it has been shown that in a noisy world, its predictive accuracy can be as good as or better than multiple regression, (Czerlinski, Gigerenzer, and Goldstein 1999). One of the best-known memory limitations is the working memory capacity of "seven plus or minus two" (Miller 1956). There is no reason why evolution should not have produced a larger capacity, and memory artists are proof that the potential is actually there. Kareev (2000) has argued that this limitation has an adaptive function, allowing a person to detect substantive correlations in the environment, such as a correlation between a symptom and a disease. The reason is that the sampling distribution of the correlation coefficient is highly skewed with small sample size, and skewness means that substantially more than 50 percent of the observed correlations are larger than the true correlation, which in turn increases the chance of noticing such a correlation in a noisy environment.

Looking at both blades of Simon's scissors can also reveal that not everything that looks like a fallacy is one. For instance, in the behavioral economics literature, overconfidence bias is still presented as a human disposition. "[S]ome basic tendency toward overconfidence appears to be a robust human character trait" (Shiller 2000, 142). This conclusion has been justified by reference to more than one hundred experiments in which confidence is studied with general knowledge questions. Two biases were reported, insufficient calibration and overconfidence bias. However, Erev, Wallsten, and Budescu (1994) showed that in a situation where two variables (confidence and proportion correct) are imperfectly correlated, regression to the mean is a sufficient condition for imperfect calibration to arise. They showed that if one had analyzed the data the other way round, one would have erroneously concluded that the same data suggest underconfidence, which is consistent with the regression phenomenon. Gigerenzer, Hoffrage, and Kleinbölting (1991) pointed to a second aspect of the environment, the sampling process, and showed that the overconfidence bias is present with selected questions but disappears with random samples. Griffin and Tversky (1992) disputed this effect of sampling. However, a meta-analysis of 135 studies has finally shown that overconfidence consistently disappears when questions are randomly sampled and that this finding cannot be attributed to a hard-easy effect (Juslin, Winman, and Olsson 2000). To summarize, in the experimental environments, an ideal statistical device would generate phenomena similar to those observed by humans, which have been mistaken as cognitive illusions.

## 2.7 CONCLUSIONS

Behavioral economics has been criticized for merely listing anomalies without providing a theory. A conception of bounded rationality in the line of Herbert Simon's two bounds can, I believe, help to overcome this state of affairs. You can only beat a theory with a theory. Name is destiny, and the term *behavioral* has the connotation of an input-output theory that treats the mind as a black box. B. F. Skinner and other behaviorists would have congratulated behavioral economists for their hesitation to open that black box and for refraining from models of heuristics. Perhaps a change in name could act as a signal.

Neoclassical economics has conventionally assumed that individuals have stable preferences, and behavioral economists' new assumption seems to be that individuals have stable cognitive illusions. Neither is true. The concept of the adaptive toolbox and the building blocks for heuristics can provide an alternative in order to build a bridge between psychology on the one hand and economics and the law on the other.

1. Note that the reason why natural frequencies facilitate insight and conditional probabilities create clouded minds is that the former do part of the computation (see the difference between Equations 1 and 2). The reason is not—to use a popular dichotomy introduced into behavioral law and economics—the difference between an "inside" and "outside" view (Kahneman and Tversky 1996). This distinction has been used to refer to the difference between a single case and a frequency, but it does not grasp the ecological factor here. For instance, changing the probability version of the mammography problem to relative frequencies, which would then be an "outside" view, makes no difference to the clouded minds. Relative frequencies do not facilitate Bayesian computations, whereas natural frequencies do (Gigerenzer and Hoffrage 1999).

REFERENCES

Akaike, H. 1973. Information theory and an extension of the maximum likelihood principle. In *2nd International Symposium on Information Theory*, ed. B. N. Petrov and F. Csaki, 267–81. Budapest: Akademiai Kiado.

Anderson, J. R., and Schooler, L. J. 2000. The adaptive nature of memory. In *Handbook of memory*, ed. E. Tulving and F. I. M. Craik, 557–70. New York: Oxford University Press.

Ayton, P., and I. Fischer. 2004. The Hot-Hand Fallacy and the Gambler's Fallacy: Two Faces of Subjective Randonmness? *Memory and Cognition*.

Bröder, A. 2000. Assessing the empirical validity of the "Take the Best" heuristic as a model of human probabilistic inference. *Journal of Experimental Psychology: Learning, Memory, and Cognition* 26:1332–46.

Bröder, A. 2003. Decision making with the "adaptive toolbox": Influence of environmental structure, intelligence, and working memory load. *Journal of Experimental Psychology* 29:611–25.

Bröder, A., & Schiffer, S. 2003. Take The Best versus simultaneous feature matching: Probabilistic inferences from memory and effects of representation format. *Journal of Experimental Psychology: General* 132:277–93.

Camerer, C. F. 1998. Bounded rationality in individual decision making. *Experimental Economics*, 1:163–83. Conlisk, J. 1996. Why bounded rationality? *Journal of Economic Literature* 34:669–700.

Corey, G. A., and J. H. Merenstein. 1987. Applying the acute ischemic heart disease predictive instrument. *Journal of Family Practice* 25:127–33.

Czerlinski, J., G. Gigerenzer, and D. G. Goldstein. 1999. How good are simple heuristics? In *Simple heuristics that make us smart*, G. Gigerenzer, P. M. Todd, and the ABC Research Group, 97–118. New York: Oxford University Press.

Dhami, M. K. 2003. Psychological models of professional decision-making. *Psychological Science* 14:175–80.

Dhami, M. K., and P. Ayton. 2001. Bailing and jailing the fast and frugal way. *Journal of Behavioral Decision Making* 14:141–68.

Dugatkin, L. A. 1996. Interface between culturally based preferences and genetic preferences: Female mate choice in *Poecilia reticulata*. *Proceedings of the National Academy of Sciences* 93:2770–73.

Edwards, W. 1968. Conservatism in human information processing. In *Formal representation of human judgment*, ed. B. Kleinmuntz, 17–52. New York: Wiley.

Elman, J. 1993. Learning and development in neural networks: The importance of starting small. *Cognition* 48:71–99.

Elwyn, G., A. Edwards, M. Eccles, and D. Rovner. 2001. Decision analysis in patient care. *Lancet* 358:571–74.

Engel, C. 2000. Psychological research on heuristics meets the law. *Behavioral and Brain Sciences* 23:747.

Erev, I., T. S. Wallsten, and D. V. Budescu. 1994. Simultaneous over- and under-confidence: The role of error in judgment processes. *Psychological Review* 101: 519–27.

Galef, B. G., Jr. 1987. Social influences on the identification of toxic foods by Norway rats. *Animal Learning and Behavior* 18:199–205.

Galef, B. G., Jr., L. M. McQuoid, and E. E. Whiskin. 1990. Further evidence that Norway rats do not socially transmit learned aversions to toxic baits. *Animal Learning and Behavior* 18:199–205.

Gigerenzer, G. 1996. On narrow norms and vague heuristics: A rebuttal to Kahneman and Tversky. *Psychological Review* 103:592–96.

Gigerenzer, G. 2002. *Calculated risks: How to know when numbers deceive you.* New York: Simon and Schuster. Published in the UK by Penguin as *Reckoning with risk: Learning to live with uncertainty.*

Gigerenzer, G., and D. G. Goldstein. 1996. Reasoning the fast and frugal way: Models of bounded rationality. *Psychological Review* 103:684–704.

———. 1999. Betting on one good reason: The Take The Best heuristic. In *Simple heuristics that make us smart,* G. Gigerenzer, P. M. Todd, and the ABC Research Group, 75–95. New York: Oxford University Press.

Gigerenzer, G., and U. Hoffrage. 1999. Overcoming difficulties in Bayesian reasoning: A reply to Keren and Mellers & McGraw. *Psychological Review* 106:425–30.

———. 1995. How to improve Bayesian reasoning without instruction: Frequency formats. *Psychological Review* 102:684–704.

Gigerenzer, G., U. Hoffrage, and H. Kleinbölting. 1991. Probabilistic mental models: A Brunswikian theory of confidence. *Psychological Review* 98: 506–28.

Gigerenzer, G., and R. Selten. 2001a. Rethinking rationality. In *Bounded rationality: The adaptive toolbox,* ed. G. Gigerenzer and R. Selten, 1–12. Cambridge, MA: MIT Press.

———. 2001b. *Bounded rationality: The adaptive toolbox.* Cambridge, MA: MIT Press.

Gigerenzer, G., P.M. Todd, and the ABC Research Group. 1999. *Simple heuristics that make us smart.* New York: Oxford University Press.

Gilovich, T., R. Vallone, and A. Tversky. 1985. The hot hand in basketball: On the misconception of random sequences. *Cognitive Psychology* 17:295–314.

Goldstein, D. G., and G. Gigerenzer. 2002. Models of ecological rationality: The recognition heuristic. *Psychological Review* 109:75–90.

Green, L., and D. R. Mehr. 1997. What alters physicians' decisions to admit to the coronary care unit? *Journal of Family Practice* 45:219–26.

Griffin, D., and A. Tversky. 1992. The weighing of evidence and the determinants of confidence. *Cognitive Psychology* 24:411–35.

Helmholtz, H. von. 1856–66/1962. *Treatise on psychological optics*. 3 vols. Repr. New York: Dover.

Hertwig, R., and P. M. Todd. 2003. More is not always better: The benefits of cognitive limits. In *The psychology of reasoning and decision making: A handbook*, ed. L. Macchi and D. Hardman. 213–31. Chichester, UK: Wiley.

Hoffrage, U., and G. Gigerenzer. 1998. Using natural frequencies to improve diagnostic inferences. *Academic Medicine* 73:538–40.

Hoffrage, U., R. Hertwig, and G. Gigerenzer. 2000. Hindsight bias: A by-product of knowledge updating? *Journal of Experimental Psychology: Learning, Memory, and Cognition* 26:566–81.

Hoffrage, U., S. Lindsey, R. Hertwig, and G. Gigerenzer. 2000. Communicating statistical information. *Science* 290:2261–62.

Holton, G. 1988. Thematic origins of scientific thought. 2nd ed. Cambridge, MA: Harvard University Press.

Jolls, C., C. R. Sunstein, and R. Thaler. 1998. A behavioral approach to law and economics. *Stanford Law Review* 50:1471–1550.

Juslin, P., A. Winman, and H. Olsson. 2000. Naive empiricism and dogmatism in confidence research: A critical examination of the hard-easy effect. *Psychological Review* 107:384–96.

Kahneman, D., & Tversky, A. 1996. On the reality of cognitive illusions. A reply to Gigerenzer's critique. *Psychological Review* 103:582–91.

Kareev, Y. 2000. Seven indeed, plus or minus two and the detection of correlations. *Psychological Review* 107:397–402.

Koehler, J. J. 1997. One in millions, brillions, and trillions: Lessons from People vs. Collins (1968) for People vs. Simpson (1995). *Journal of Legal Education* 47:214–23.

Korobkin, R. B., and T. S. Ulen. 2000. Law and behavioral science: Removing the rationality assumption from law and economics. *California Law Review* 88:1051–1144.

Kuran, T., and Sunstein, C. R. 2000. Controlling availability cascades. In *Behavioral law and economics*, ed. Sunstein, C. R., 374–97). Cambridge: Cambridge University Press.

Lindsey, S., R. Hertwig, and G. Gigerenzer. 2003. Communicating statistical evidence. *Jurimetrics* 43:147-63.

Martignon, L., and U. Hoffrage. 1999. Why does one-reason decision making work? A case study in ecological rationality. In *Simple heuristics that make us smart*, G. Gigerenzer, P. M. Todd, and the ABC Research Group, 119–40. New York: Oxford University Press.

———. 2002. Fast, frugal and fit: Lexicographic heuristics for paired comparison. *Theory and Decision* 52:29–71.

Martignon, L., O. Vitouch, M. Takezawa, and M. Forster.2003. Naive and yet enlightened: From natural frequencies to fast and frugal decision trees. In *The psychology of reasoning and decision making: A handbook*, ed. L. Macchi and D. Hardmann, 189–211. Chichester, UK: Wiley.

Miller, G. A. 1956. The magical number seven, plus or minus two: Some limits on our capacity of processing information. *Psychological Review* 63:81–97.

Newell, B. R., and D. R. Shanks. 2003. Take the best or look at the rest? Factors influencing 'one-reason' decision-making. *Journal of Experimental Psychology: Memory, Learning, and Cognition* 29:53–65.

Newell, B. R., Weston, N., and Shanks, D. R. 2003. Empirical tests of a fast and frugal heuristic: Not everyone "takes-the-best." *Organizational Behavior and Human Decision Processes* 91:82–96.

Noll, R. G. and Krier, J. E. 2000. Some implications of cognitive psychology for risk regulation. In *Behavioral law and economics*, ed. C. R. Sunstein, 325–343. Cambridge: Cambridge University Press.

Payne, J. W., J. R. Bettman, and E. J. Johnson. 1993. *The adaptive decision maker*. New York: Cambridge University Press.

Pearson, S. D., L. Goldman, T. B. Garcia, E. F. Cook, and T. H. Lee. 1994. Physician response to a prediction rule for the triage of emergency department patients with chest pain. *Journal of General Internal Medicine* 9:241–47.

Polya, G. 1954. *Mathematics and plausible reasoning*, vol. 1, *Induction and analogy in mathematics*. Princeton, NJ: Princeton University Press.

Pozen, M. W., R. B. D'Agostino, H. P. Selker, P. A. Sytkowski, and W. B. Hood. 1984. A predictive instrument to improve coronary-care-unit admission practices in acute ischemic heart disease. *New England Journal of Medicine* 310:1273–78.

Rabin, M. 1998. Psychology and economics. *Journal of Economic Literature* 36:11–46.

Rachlinski, J. J. 2000. Heuristics and biases in the courts: Ignorance or adaptation? *Oregon Law Review* 79:61–102.

Redmayne, M. 1998. The DNA database: Civil liberty and evidentiary issues. *Criminal Law Review* (July): 437–54.

———. 2001. *Expert evidence and criminal justice*. New York: Oxford University Press.

Sargent, T. J. 1993. *Bounded rationality in macroeconomics*. Oxford: Oxford University Press.

Schacter, D. 2001. *The seven sins of memory: How the mind forgets and remembers*. New York: Houghton Mifflin.

Schwarz, N., & Vaughn, L. A. 2002. The availability heuristic revisited: Ease of recall and content of recall as distinct sources of information. In *Heuristics and biases: The psychology of intuitive judgment*, ed. T. Gilovich, D. Griffin & D. Kahneman, 103–19. New York: Cambridge University Press.

Sedlmeier, P., and G. Gigerenzer. 2001. Teaching Bayesian reasoning in less than two hours. *Journal of Experimental Psychology: General* 130:380–400.

Sedlmeier, P., R. Hertwig, and G. Gigerenzer. 1998. Are judgments of the positional frequencies of letters systematically biased due to availability? *Journal of Experimental Psychology: Learning, Memory, and Cognition* 24:1–17.

Selten, R. 2001. What is bounded rationality? In *Bounded rationality: The adaptive toolbox*, ed. G. Gigerenzer and R. Selten, 13–36. Cambridge, MA: MIT Press.

Shepard, R. N. 1992. The perceptual organization of colors: An adaptation to regularities of the terrestrial world? In *The adapted mind: Evolutionary psychology and the generation of culture*, ed. J. H. Barkow, L. Cosmides & J. Tooby, 495–532. New York: Oxford University Press.

Shiller, R. J. 2000. *Irrational exuberance*. Princeton, NJ: Princeton University Press.

Simon, H. A. 1955. A behavioral model of rational choice. *Quarterly Journal of Economics* 69:99–118.

———. 1956. Rational choice and the structure of environments. *Psychological Review* 63:129–38.

———. 1969. *The sciences of the artificial*. Cambridge, MA: MIT Press.

Sunstein, C. R. 1997. Behavioral analysis of law. *University of Chicago Law Review* 64:1175–95.

Sunstein, C. R. (ed.), 2000. *Behavioral law and economics*. Cambridge: Cambridge University Press.

Todd, P. M., & Gigerenzer, G. 2000. Precis of *Simple heuristics that make us smart. Behavioral and Brain Sciences* 23:727–80.

Tversky, A., and D. Kahneman. 1973. Availability: A heuristic for judging frequency and probability. *Cognitive Psychology* 5:207–32.

———. 1974. Judgment under uncertainty: Heuristics and biases. *Science* 185:1124–31.

# 3 LESSONS FROM NEUROECONOMICS FOR THE LAW

*Kevin McCabe, Vernon Smith, and Terrence Chorvat*

In the last few decades, one of the major developments in the study of law has been the application of social sciences to legal problems. The necessity of this application is obvious. Laws are made by humans, and hence the study of human behavior is clearly pertinent to the study of law.[1] Economics, which is the study of how individuals and society choose to allocate scarce resources to satisfy their wants, clearly should have implications for understanding legal problems (Posner 1998). The study of human behavior can tell us a great deal about how humans will react to rules and hopefully allows us to generate better regulations. One of the key problems with the application of economics to legal problems has been the seeming unreasonableness of these assumptions of modern economics.[2] Some have argued that the assumptions that humans always follow their rational self-interest or that preferences can necessarily be stated in a coherent way are incorrect, and therefore the conclusions that follow from them are questionable (Ulen 2000).

In the last few years, medical imaging technology has developed sufficiently to enable us to examine human brains as the subjects perform cognitive activities. The application of these technologies to study the brains of individuals as they make decisions relevant to economic problems is known as neuroeconomics. This chapter argues that this subdiscipline is likely to have profound effects on the way we view many, if not all, legal problems. In introducing an additional win-

Terrence Chorvat would like to thank the Law and Economics Center for its financial support.

dow to the study of human behavior, it not only will provide new insights but will also help us feel more confident in some of the conclusions we have already drawn.

Part 3.1 of the chapter discusses the current schools of law and economics scholarship. It discusses how both traditional law and economics scholarship, as well as behavioral law and economics, have had a significant impact on legal scholarship. It also discusses some other schools of economics that have not yet had as much impact on legal scholarship, specifically Austrian economics, experimental economics, and New Institutional economics. Part 3.2 discusses the new discipline of neuroeconomics. It discusses the methods used in this field and some of the major results already discovered. In particular, it shows that individuals appear to be very heterogeneous in their manner of cognitive processing, and this heterogeneity can, to a fair degree, explain differences in behavior. Part 3.3 discusses the ways in which neuroeconomics is likely to have a significant impact on the law and economic analysis. It examines the potential application of neuroeconomics to five major areas of the law: contract law, property law, choice of law, the laws of business association, and the study of juries.

The field of neuroeconomics is only just emerging.[3] The conclusions to be derived from this field of research are far from certain. However, even the preliminary results are interesting, both because they shed new light on earlier findings from other schools of economics and because they are giving a glimpse as to the promise of this method. The impact on law and economics scholarship from neuroeconomics is likely to be enormous.

## 3.1 LAW AND ECONOMICS SCHOLARSHIP

### 3.1.1 Traditional Law and Economics Scholarship

Law and economics scholarship has begun to dominate legal academia.[4] This discipline has sought to bring the insights of economics into the understanding of legal problems. This research has helped both to better understand legal issues and to aid in drafting "better" laws. Law and economics has clearly gone beyond legal fad to become one of the key tools in legal analysis. There is scarcely a single area of legal scholarship that is untouched by law and economics. It has significantly affected disciplines from contract law (Craswell and Scwartz 1980) to tax law (Aaron and Boskin 1980) to legal history (Bernstein 1998) to family law (Brinig and Buckley 1996).

Traditional law and economics scholarship is almost entirely based on what is generally referred to as neoclassical economics. This school derives its conclusions from certain assumptions about human behavior, such as consistent preferences and rational behavior (Varian 1993). These assumptions and conclusions are generally stated in mathematical terms in order to ensure rigor and to reduce potential ambiguity of result.

The area of neoclassical economics most commonly invoked by scholars of traditional law and economics is price theory. This particular area examines questions involving the behavior of utility-maximizing individuals and profit-maximizing firms. Because it is a neoclassical theory, it also assumes that individuals act to rationally maximize their "utility" from their opportunity set (Varian 1993). From these assumptions, price theory derives conclusions about how economic actors will behave if the price of goods, services, or behaviors increases. Because this form of analysis is generally quite mathematically rigorous, the conclusions of any particular model are entirely dependent on the assumptions made. The most famous and most generally applicable conclusion of price theory is that one's own price demand curve slopes downward (Silberberg 1992).[5]

Traditional law and economics has largely been the application of price theory to legal problems.[6] Just as price theory has helped to explicate an enormous amount of human behavior, traditional law and economics scholarship has been able to aid in the analysis of an enormous number of legal problems in a fairly parsimonious way. The success of this school of thought is undeniable. One of the most prominent conclusions of the law and economics literature seems to be that interference in the market needs some type of special justification (Posner 1998). Although this is clearly not the conclusion of all who practice traditional law and economics, it is clearly the view of many such practitioners (Calabresi and Melamed 1972).[7]

Law and economics has been so successful that even some of the more advanced areas of neoclassical economics, such as game theory, have begun to be applied to legal issues. The subdiscipline of game theory and the law is beginning to attract a fair number of adherents (Baird, Gertner, and Picker, 1992). However, the seeming hyperrationality of game theory has not yet received quite the same degree of acclaim in the legal academy as price theory has (Posner 1998).

In addition, just as neoclassical economics has led to quantitative empirical work to test the parameters of the neoclassical models, econometric methods are also fast becoming a common mode of analysis in the legal academy. As this particular mode of analysis has reached law schools, it has led to a significant increase in the number of empirical studies published in law reviews,[8] a phenomenon that for the most part should be welcomed.

### 3.1.2 Behavioral Law and Economics

Traditional law and economics scholarship has been so successful that it has helped to create its own counterrevolution in behavioral law and economics. The behavioral law and economics movement has tried to incorporate research that runs counter to traditional law and economics. Just as traditional law and economics is based on neoclassical price theory, behavioral law and economics is based on behavioral economics. Behavioral economics has attempted to undermine some of the assumptions upon which neoclassical economics is based and replace them with what are viewed as more realistic assumptions about human behavior. In particular, behavioral economics is based on results of experiments in which individuals have not, in general, exhibited rational utility-maximizing behavior. These experiments generally involved asking individuals questions about how they would react to a particular situation (Kahneman , Knetsch and Thaler1990). The results have often been used to argue against some of the conclusions about the abilities of markets to function well (Langevoort 2001). Many of these experiments have been quite controversial (Plott and Zeiler 2002). Some argue that these findings do not apply to real market situations (Ulen 2000). Such critics point out that the findings are very sensitive to the experimental techniques and the particular techniques are not similar to the kinds of conditions one would find in real economic situations (Ulen 2000).

As mentioned previously, behavioral economics relies on studies of actual human behavior in experiments. These studies often show that individuals behave quite differently than predicted by neoclassical models, particularly with regard to thinking about how to deal with risk and uncertainty (Kahneman and Tversky 1998) and about how to discount for future value.[9] Some studies have also shown that how a question is framed will often affect the outcome, which would seem to run counter to traditional neoclassical theory (Camerer, Loewenstein, and Prelec 2004).

The most prominent theory that has emerged from behavioral economics is prospect theory. Under prospect theory, although individuals still behave as utility maximizers, as they do under neoclassical models, the utility function is much more complicated (see Figure 3.1) than traditional expected-utility maximization (Camerer, Loewenstein, and Prelec 2004). Under this theory, individuals are not trying to maximize wealth but improvements to wealth, and the individuals are risk averse regarding gains and are risk preferring regarding losses (Kahneman and Tversky 1998).

Behavioral economics is beginning to be quite popular in the legal academy.[10]

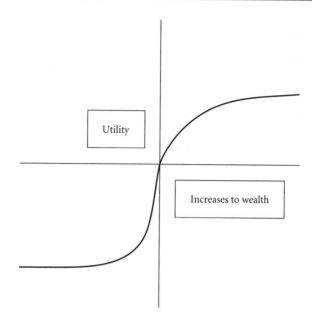

**Figure 3.1**    Under prospect theory, the curve of utility function has a kink in it
instead of the usual smooth curve. For positive increases to wealth, the
utility function is concave; for decreases to wealth, it is convex.

Not only is the amount of behavioral literature growing (Kahneman and Tversky
1998) but there are also more conferences and classes on behavioral law and economics.[11] Behavioral law and economics is itself beginning to significantly influence legal academy.

### 3.1.3  Other Schools of Economic Thought

Although neoclassical economics and behavioral economics have had the greatest
impact on the legal academy (Posner 1998; Jolls, Sunstein and Thaler, 2001), there
are other schools of economic thought that view economic problems from different perspectives. The three schools discussed here are Austrian economics, experimental economics, and New Institutional economics.

#### 3.1.3.1  Austrian Economics

The typical methodology of Austrian economics is to deduce economic principles logically from the axiom that humans are attempting to improve their circumstances. Although the methods and the assumptions sound very similar to the
first principles of neoclassical economics, the practitioners of Austrian economics

are more skeptical that theory can be derived and tested empirically in the manner of modern neoclassical economics and its associated econometrics. There is less emphasis on mathematical models and rigorous proof and more emphasis on insight. Some of the adherents of this school have often used historical data to prove their points, but without the rigor of modern econometrics (Rothbard 2000).

Austrian economics is at odds with both neoclassical economics and behavioral economics in this methodology. Austrian economics questions the coherence of many of the results of both of these schools (Caplan 2003). Its methods are more akin to history and other social sciences than neoclassical economics is (which has adopted hard sciences such as physics as its model).

Some profound insights have been gained by "Austrian" methods. The particular strengths of this school are ideas concerning large-scale systemwide issues, such as the business cycle and the usefulness of the market (Hayek 1989, 1994). For example, Hayek and the other prominent Austrian economists argue that impersonal bargaining, such as what occurs in financial markets, is different from personal bargaining, such as what may happen within a family. Impersonal bargaining may be required in many situations in which individuals do not have time to have personal relationships with all of those with whom they transact business. This distinction is inherent in human behavior and sometimes causes people to treat impersonal situations as personal, causing impersonal exchange to fail (Hayek 1989, 1994). Austrian economics argues that markets are the best method to integrate the information held by individuals in impersonal bargaining situations (Smith 2002).

### 3.1.3.2 Experimental Economics

An area related to behavioral economics that has not yet had as much impact on legal scholarship is experimental economics. Whereas the methods used by experimental economics and behavioral economics may superficially appear the same in that both place emphasis on the way humans behave in experiments, experimental economics examines economic problems from a perspective different from that of behavioral economics. Behavioral economics focuses on the reasoning process of individual actors. Experimental economics focuses more on the ways in which individuals interact in exchange situations rather than on particular reasoning problems.[12] Experimental economics focuses on actual economic activities rather than the particular assumptions of the neoclassical model.

Experimental economics has produced some particularly striking findings. For example, game theory would predict that cooperative behavior should break down in games with finite periods (Varian 1993). However, when actual experiments are conducted, this behavior does not result except in the most extreme experiments

(Hoffman, McCabe, and Smith 1998). The experiments show that individuals are both more cooperative and trusting than predicted by game theory. These experiments also show that where trust is possible, it leads to more optimal outcomes than if all are operating as traditional game theory actors (Hoffman, McCabe, and Smith 1998).

One can analogize the difference between experimental economics and behavioral economics to the difference between economics and psychology.[13] Behavioral economics focuses on individual rationality, whereas experimental economics is looking at how individuals interact in somewhat simplified economic situations.[14]

### 3.1.3.3 New Institutional Economics

New Institutional economics (NIE) describes efforts to explain how institutions such as government, markets, firms, and so on behave by using analytical methods that are similar to those used in neoclassical theory. That is, those individuals associated with NIE tend to study how rational individuals create institutions and attempt to solve or exploit agency problems. This idea contrasts with that used in price theory, which posits that efficient actors, such as firms or individuals, will automatically result from competitive pressures (Alchian and Demsetz 1972). Of course, the extent to which firms are not profit maximizers or government does not maximize social welfare can impact our understanding of these actors and aid in crafting legal rules that relate to them.[15] NIE has had a significant effect on fields such as antitrust law, the law of business associations, and related fields. The focus of the analysis of this school is on the transactions costs. NIE is clearly related to fields such as public choice (Posner 1998) and social choice (Arrow 1963). One can argue that traditional law and economics is itself a form of NIE, because the focus of law and economics is on the efficiency of an institution (laws or government) and often uses the common tools of NIE, transactions costs, and agency costs (Buchanan and Tullock 1961). However, this connection is not normally made. Traditional law and economics is normally considered to be a direct descendant of price theory rather than of NIE (Posner 1998).

These three schools of thought have led to many powerful conclusions that have often not been fully appreciated in the legal academy. Of course, some in the legal academy are skeptical of any or all schools of economic thought (Ulen 2000) and seem to have assumptions about the behavior of people that contradict each other.

## 3.2 NEUROECONOMICS

Each of these schools seems to have significant differences in their basic assumptions about the fundamental unit of economics, the individual. Neoclassical economics seems to assume that we are ruthlessly rational. Behavioral economics assumes that we make systematic reasoning mistakes. Austrian economics seems to assume rationality, but not so rigorously as neoclassical economics. Therefore, a natural area of focus should be the cognitive processes individuals use to perceive different economic and legal situations. Directing our study to what is occurring in the brains of individuals as they make economic decisions can help us decide when each of these schools is correct and when each is wrong; additionally, it can help us develop new theories of economic behavior.

### 3.2.1 Description of the Research and Its Methodologies

Neuroeconomics is the study of how the embodied brain interacts with its external environment to produce economic behavior.[16] Technology has now advanced to the point where we can obtain information about the areas of the brain that are activated as individuals are performing different activities. By studying these results, we can gain new insights into why the particular behaviors result from specific stimuli.

Studies of the brain and its effects on behavior have been conducted for quite some time. Among the earliest neurology research were studies of patients with brain lesions.[17] Although there has been a wealth of information derived from these studies, the clarity of the information obtained is less obvious. That a patient who incurs brain damage can no longer perform a particular function does not necessarily mean that the damaged region of the brain was where that function "resided." There are various things that might be required to perform an action: recording sensation, processing responses, binding the action with other information, and so forth. It may not be clear exactly which of these functions has been impaired by the damage. However, these types of studies have indicated that there appears to be some localization of functions of the brain.

More recently, technology has advanced to the point where we can begin to examine brains in vivo as they perform functions. For these investigations, the two most important technologies are positron-emission tomography (Camerer, Loewenstein, and Prelec 2004), commonly known as PET scans, and functional magnetic resonance imaging, or fMRI.[18] Both methods detect changes in metabolism or blood flow in the brain while the subject is engaged in cognitive tasks. For neuroeconomics studies, fMRI is becoming the method of choice. The spatial resolution is superior with fMRI, with current scanners able to resolve volumetric area of 3 mm$^3$, and there is the potential to have even greater degrees of resolution as more powerful magnets become available (Gazzaniga, Ivry, and Mangun 2002). Because fMRI does not involve the injection of radioactive tracers as required for

PET scans, the same individual can be tested repeatedly, either in a single or multiple sessions. Multiple tests permit the observation of many more data points, which can allow for more advanced statistical analysis.

Temporal resolution is also much better with fMRI. In PET scans, the subject must be continuously engaged in a given experimental task for at least forty seconds in order to obtain useful results (Gazzaniga, Ivry, and Mangun 2002). One particular type of fMRI, called event-related fMRI, can be used to study changes in the brain that occur over one to two seconds (Gazzaniga, Ivry, and Mangun. 2002, 142–143). Because of this short time period, experimenters can more readily relate the effects to specific events with fMRI.

Another new technology that is gaining popularity is transcranial stimulation, which involves stimulating a region of the brain by use of magnets that are located outside the patient. Because magnetic force can act at a distance, actual contact is unnecessary. There are problems with this methodology in that it is not clear how much the effects are related to the actual processing that occurred within the region stimulated or to a response of other areas of the brain as a result of the stimulation to one area.[19]

In some sense, neuroeconomic studies are the precise point where psychology and economics meet. This research allows to us observe what is happening within individuals as they engage in economic behavior. Researchers can now both observe how the individual reacts to particular stimuli and note at the same time how that individual actually behaves. This methodology therefore joins behavioral economics, with its focus on individual reasoning, and experimental economics, with its focus on interactive behavior.

### 3.2.2 Experimental Results

There have been a number of studies using neuroimaging technology to examine how people perceive economic problems. One needs to stress that the full implications of this work is only beginning to be understood. However, the preliminary results are quite interesting. One of the most prominent findings involves the heterogeneity of perception and reasoning. To some extent, heterogeneity of brain structure is obvious. Left- or right-handedness is clearly a difference in the way brains are organized (Gazzaniga, Ivry, and Mangun 2002). More important, neuroimaging studies have shown that individuals will often use different parts of the brain for the same or similar problems. Interestingly, knowing which parts of the brain are used can help us predict how the particular individuals will behave.

Neuroeconomic studies show that the way in which we process information can have a significant impact on the opportunities we perceive and how we evaluate them. If we can determine where a particular individual processes information, we are closer to predicting how that individual will behave. Some of the studies have verified key conclusions of earlier schools, and others have challenged their conclusions.[20]

This section discusses three intriguing areas of study: reciprocity, perceptions of risk and uncertainty, and addiction. Some of the experimental results have confirmed neoclassical conclusions; some, behavioral; and some, neither.

### 3.2.2.1 Reciprocity

Among the most interesting neuroeconomic research already conducted is that related to reciprocity. As discussed earlier in connection with experimental economics, a key conclusion of many studies in experimental economics is that individuals often cooperate more frequently than game theory would predict. In addition, these studies show that individuals who cooperate actually do better overall than they would if they were completely self-interested individuals. Many people expect that others will opt for cooperative solutions, even when the other actor may have to make a choice against self-interest. Importantly, these people who assume cooperation by others are generally correct; people act cooperatively much more than would be predicted in a rational analysis. However, there is also a substantial percentage of the population that does not trust nor reward trust (McCabe et al. 2001).

Given this heterogeneity, a natural question concerns what neuroimaging can tell us about the differences between cooperators and noncooperators. Studying where the activity in the brain is occurring during these experiments yields interesting results. An experiment was conducted in which subjects engaged in various games. As an example of these experiments, in the trust game, the first decision maker decided between the following choices: (1) to give both players a payoff of 45 tokens or to let the second decision maker choose between giving the first player a payoff of 180 and the second a payoff of 225;[21] and (2) to have the first player receive a zero payoff and the second, a payoff of 405 (see Figure 3.2). In order to trust the second player, the first must believe the second will cooperate against self-interest. Subjects sometimes would deal with a computer and sometimes with another human. In each case, this was disclosed to the subject. In addition, the computer's strategy (a 75% probability of choosing the [180, 225] payoff and 25% probability of choosing the [0, 405] payoff) was disclosed to the subjects.[22] The experiment was conducted while the subject was in the fMRI machine. The neuroimage of the subject was taken 1.5 seconds before the decision was reported and compared between subjects. Of the twelve subjects, seven were classified as cooperators and five as noncooperators.

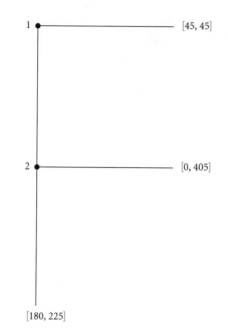

**Figure 3.2**   Visual representation of the trust game

The neuroimages of the subjects show that cooperators and noncooperators have different patterns of brain activity. Cooperators had a common pattern on BOLD activation. Subjects who cooperated had activity in many parts of the brain. The areas activated are commonly associated with calculation, visual recognition, and social situations. This suggests that cooperation requires individuals to use a mechanism in the brain that allows them to focus on mutual gains and allows inhibition of immediate gain to permit a cooperative decision.[23] One of the key areas of difference between cooperators and noncooperators was in Brodmann's area 8.[24] This area is commonly associated with visualization and social situations. Cooperators have more activity in this region than noncooperators do. Interestingly, the brain activity of noncooperators resembled the brain activity of those who are simply playing against a computer. This evidence tells us that there are likely fundamental differences in the ways in which the two groups perceive the trust problem facing them (at least in this game). These subjects did not seem to merely place a different level or value on cooperation or even to simply make different guesses about what others were doing. Neuroimaging evidence tends to indicate that the two groups were using a different mechanism to perceive the problem.

### 3.2.2.2 Risk and Uncertainty

As discussed earlier, in connection with behavioral economics, one of the areas of conflict between neoclassical economics and behavioral economics is the way in which individuals perceive risk and uncertainty.[25] One study looking at the ways in which individuals perceive risky gains, risky losses, and ambiguity in both losses and gains found interesting results (Smith et al. 2002). To understand these results, we need to first distinguish between risk and ambiguity. Under risk, the likelihoods of alternative outcomes are fully known. Under ambiguity, the likelihoods are unknown. In this experiment, subjects were asked to choose from which urn they would prefer to select balls. They were given higher rewards if the balls of particular colors were drawn.[26] In one urn, the contents were disclosed to the subject, meaning they could calculate the probability of drawing a particular color. The subjects did not know the contents of the other urn. These choice activities were conducted while brain activity was measured with PET scans (Smith, et al. 2002). This study reveals that the brains of these subjects did not behave according to a prevalent assumption of economics, the independence of the evaluations of payoffs and outcomes. With respect to risky choices, they behaved in accordance the basic notion of prospect theory, in that individuals appear to be risk-averse for gains and risk preferring for losses (Smith, et al. 2002). On the other hand, subjects were always ambiguity averse.[27] The neurological evidence gives some clues as to why this might be the case. Risky gains activated an area in the ventromedial region, and risky losses stimulated an area in the dorsomedial region. The ventromedial area is connected with emotional response, whereas the dorsomedial area is connected more with higher cognitive function.

### 3.2.2.3 Addiction

A key discovery of neuroeconomic research is that individuals who have addictions actually have higher discount rates (Grant 2002). This research found that while individuals are addicted to a substance, they demonstrate a higher discount rate not only for the substance to which they are addicted but other substances as well (Corradin and Perali 2002). However, when the addiction is ended, the discount rate returns to what it was before the addiction started (Corradin and Perali 2002). Therefore, the different discount rates can, to some degree, be explained by neurological-chemical features such as addiction.[28]

### 3.2.3 Preliminary Implications

Understanding how human brains process information can facilitate the building of economic and legal institutions that better serve as extensions of our ability to enter into social exchange. It may help us both to structure institutions that aid in reciprocal or trusting behavior and to productively deal with risk and ambiguity (Chorvat 2002). The previous findings show that individuals have different ways of perceiving and reacting to the same stimuli. Knowing the mechanisms used to process stimuli can help us predict actions taken by individuals and thereby help us structure rules to encourage optimal behavior. The next section discusses how these findings might apply to legal problems.

## 3.3 APPLICATIONS TO LAW

This section discusses five areas to which the findings of neuroeconomics can be applied. Of course, this research is very preliminary, and conclusions based on it must be taken with caution. This section is intended to give a flavor of the work to which neuroeconomics could apply. The five areas discussed are contract law, property law, choice of law, the laws of business association, and the study of juries. Neuroeconomics can have an impact both on positive theories of what is occurring and on normative theories of how we should structure the law. For each of these areas, the section will first examine the basics of the traditional law and economic analysis and examine the behavioral critique. It will then proceed to discuss how neuroeconomics could impact the study of the area of the law.

### 3.3.1 Contract Law

As it relates to the law of contracts, traditional law and economic scholarship has focused on how the law improves efficiency. Commercial activity could exist in a world without contracts because it could be based on reputational effects (Posner 1998). However, as Akerlof (1970) and others have pointed out, such markets may break down. It may be less costly for society to create an ability to make promises that will be enforced and prevent opportunistic behavior (or at least make it more difficult). This allows people to be able to rely on a promise and base their behavior on it. This theory helps explain the development of much of contract law. For example, it can help to explain the notion of consideration, which means that both sides have to perform some beneficial action to the other party for the agreement to be enforceable (Posner 1998). This shows the efficiency of the law, because we want to use resources to encourage productive behavior; so rather than make all promises enforceable, we enforce only promises that lead to productive behavior.

The behavioral account of contract law agrees with much of this description but is skeptical of some the applications of the theory. Many authors have discussed how the endowment effect and the status quo bias can have effects on the negotiation of contract terms (Korobkin 1998a, 1998b). This scholarship focuses on the notion that individuals are not likely to behave efficiently from either an individual or societal perspective (Rachlinski 2001). This might give society an incentive to limit freedom of contract to the extent individuals cannot behave optimally on their own (Ulen 2000).

As discussed in Part II, the neuroeconomic evidence shows that perception and analysis are heterogeneous in the population and that some individuals are more likely to behave according to game theory predictions, whereas others will cooperate more (McCabe et al. 2001). This might argue in favor of different types of rules for different types of contracts. For example, if the group or society is characterized by a high level of trust, a greater degree of ambiguity in a contract may still result in a reasonable understanding. In such cases, some of the results from behavioral economics (such as not really checking the terms or understanding them and signing the agreement anyway) may be due to rational time allocation. In other situations, where the parties are more skeptical of the cooperating behavior of the other party, the actors may behave more as game theory would predict. In such a lower trust situation, greater specificity maybe required.[29] The optimal rules might therefore be different for different types of contracts. Neuroeconomic research could help inform us about how these relationships are perceived and how this affects behavior.

If people have different ways of perceiving or behaving, then we may want the law to acknowledge this. The way in which a contract is perceived by the parties involved and the way they are likely to behave given that perception should inform our view of the efficiency of any set of rules.

This research can help us to better craft legal rules. One focus of neuroeconomic research should be to understand what type of legal rules would foster higher-trust relationships. Such relationships tend to be less costly, because they are cheaper to both the participants and society.[30] Of course, we need to be mindful of Hayek's point that it is difficult, if not impossible, to generally turn impersonal contacts into personal ones and we should not expect a perfect ability to accomplish this. However, if laws can, on the margin, attempt to foster trust rather than distrust, we should strive toward this goal.

### 3.3.2 Property Law

Traditional law and economics analysis assumes that property simply enters into the utility function of actors, perhaps with other items as well.[31] Traditional law and economics analysis makes the same assumptions as neoclassical economics, such as the more of a good, the better. Of course, within this paradigm, there is still a great deal of freedom for creating models.[32]

The neoclassical assumptions lead in the area of property law to results such as those in the Coase theorem, which implies that if transactions costs are kept low enough, it does not matter if property rights are not awarded to the most efficient user of the property; the property will eventually end up in the hands of the most efficient user (Coase 1960). If this is so, the lesson is that we should attempt to keep transactions costs low rather than try to find the most efficient party, which may be more difficult.[33]

The behavioral law and economics analysis looks at these questions differently. It adds ideas such as the endowment effect. Under this anomaly, the value of a piece of property to an individual increases as soon as the individual is actually given the property. That is, before someone is given a mug, the person might value it at two dollars, but after it is given, the person values it at four dollars (Plott and Zeiler 2002). From this perspective, the Coase theorem may not hold anymore. If simply giving one party the property causes the person to value it more than before, the original allocation becomes important. The party who would have derived more value from it (Kahneman, Knetsch, and Thaler 2000) might not value it enough to acquire it from the person who in fact received it, so that even if transactions costs are zero, it is possible that property can be awarded inefficiently.[34]

Neuroeconomics can help us understand how individuals actually view property and how that perception of property affects behavior. The heterogeneity already observed indicates not only that people place different values on the same piece of property (as neoclassical analysis would agree) or that the value may change dependent upon circumstances (as behavioral economics assumes) but also that the way in which the notion of ownership is processed by different people may be quite different. This is not merely a difference in the amount of utility assigned to a piece of property; instead, the entire concept may be different. This can help explain why property may have different values in different contexts, because it may also mean different things to the same person in different contexts. Some may view it as a resource to be shared, and others may view it entirely in a noncooperative way. Understanding this may help explain the anomalies normally thought of with behavioral economics and help provide a solution to one of the greatest problems of behavioral economics as viewed by its critics—a central theory from which one can deduce the particular behaviors observed.[35]

The heterogeneity discovered by neuroeconomics may also help explain the variance of results between neoclassical and behavioral economics. The Coase theorem may be likely to work better in some situations than in others because property may be viewed differently by different individuals and in different situations. Therefore, neuroeconomics may help generate better property rules to maximize efficiency.

The efficiency can also apply to intellectual property. Different types of intellectual property may be viewed differently by different actors. Individual artists may view copyright law differently than the owners of a business do. This may imply that the rules applying to copyrights, patents, and so forth owned by corporations may be different than those for individuals, but of course this may not be correct. Perhaps they are perceived differently. The neuroeconomics of corporate officers may also be helpful in making these determinations.[36]

### 3.3.3 Choice of Law

Very often, it is not clear which legal regime should apply to a particular problem. If an Illinois company makes a product that is purchased by a New York resident in Virginia, which injures the purchaser while in Pennsylvania, which jurisdiction's law should apply? A similar question involves which legal regime should apply to a particular question within a jurisdiction: tort laws, contract laws, securities laws, or some other laws.

The traditional analysis of choice of law was based on governmental interest analysis (Currie 1959).[37] This inquiry focused on which government had a greater interest in the question. The law and economics analysis of choice of law has tended to eschew this somewhat vague analysis, although largely agreeing with its conclusions in most cases (O'Hara and Ribstein 2000). Only relatively recently has economics analysis been brought to bear on the choice of law analysis. The law and economics scholarship of choice of law questions has been largely of three types: game theory, empirical analysis, and maximization of individual utility.

Kramer (1990) has applied game theory to the choice of law problem. He views choice of law as a positive-sum game, where each state faces a prisoner's dilemma with infinite repetition, so the folk theorems apply, yielding cooperation (see also Solimine 1989). He looks at domestic problems (for example, is it a torts law problem or a contract law problem?) as a choice of law problem as well.

Another type of analysis has been to attempt to empirically predict which choice of law rules will be chosen by various states (Solimine 1989). The conclusions here have been subject to much debate, because it has proven difficult to determine firm results. The reason is that only decided cases can be analyzed, and it is unclear what effect the decided cases have on controversies that are settled without a court opinion. These analyses, and those that apply game theory, seem to be positive theories rather than normative theories of how the law should be. In addition, because these are decisions made by institutions, concepts such as Arrow's theorem and public choice problems need to figure significantly in the analysis.

More recently, the analysis has shifted to normative analysis of optimal rules from the individual perspective (O'Hara and Ribstein 2000). The primary model has been the contract model: what the parties agreed upon, or what they might agree to *ex ante,* because this is believed to be the efficient paradigm (O'Hara and Ribstein 2000). When the contract model cannot be used, the models that are used are generally based on economy of judicial resources.[38]

Because this analysis is largely based on a freedom of contract analysis, the behavioral critiques of freedom of contract would also apply to this analysis. The rules should deal with transactions between cooperators and noncooperators. Behavioral economics would argue whether choice of law clauses are examined or even understood (Rachlinski 2001). If assent is not truly given, one should not base too much on it. Other considerations, such as fairness, might become more important. Indeed, the behavioral critique is that choice of law rules do not really affect individual behavior much because they are not really noticed (Sterk 1994).

The behavioral account argues that such laws might not have a great effect on behavior and so instead focuses on the individual. Because behavior is misplaced, concerns such as fairness and protection of the less-aware plaintiffs, become more important.[39] Future neuroeconomic research can potentially aid the analysis of these problems.

Understanding the heterogeneity that neuroeconomics informs us exists within and between populations should alter our perspective on this problem. Different legal regimes develop in different environments. Low-trust environments may create one set of social norms and laws, and high-trust cultures may have a different set of social norms. This will not necessarily cause a problem, but when they interact, members of a low-trust culture will try to use the rules of the high-trust culture strategically, or vice versa. The study of the interaction between cooperators and noncooperators and which rules are the most efficient between them is a future avenue of neuroeconomic research.

### 3.3.4 Laws of Business Association

The key questions in the economic analysis of the laws of business association concern what individuals are trying to optimize and what methods they use.[40] The particular analysis of why specific entities are chosen to conduct business is based on the Jensen-Meckling hypothesis that agency costs in the environment are the primary fact in making this decision.[41] The agents will choose a corporate form if the business requires formal structure with separation of ownership and management. If flexibility is needed and the owners essentially need to be the managers, a partnership will be chosen (Jensen and Meckling 1976).

The behavioral economics accounts agree with these descriptions, but they introduce cognitive biases such as overconfidence into the analysis and conclude that individuals may choose the wrong entity because they do not realistically evaluate the prospects (Bankman 1994; Fleischer 2003).[42] This would lead us to think that we should limit the ability of individuals to choose particular forms of entities for particular kinds of businesses.

The application of neuroeconomics to these transactions again relates heterogeneity to the analysis. These types of organizations may also have embedded in them different levels of trust. The entity is related not only to the business environment but also to the particular relations between the owner-managers. Hence, the degree of trust will influence the choice of entity. If different individuals, families, and cultures have different levels of trust, it may help explain the choice of entities, not just the environment. In order to understand the selection of an entity as well as the particular agreements reached, one has to understand the dynamic between individuals who cooperate and those who defect and between those individuals who may have better information and those who do not.[43]

### 3.3.5 Study of Juries

The traditional law and economics scholarship that analyzes juries focuses on questions such as the decisions of the optimal makeup of the jury, the economics of the decision of whether to seek a jury, the number of jurors, whether verdicts should be unanimous or merely a majority, and whether jury service should be voluntary or conscripted (Posner 1998). Traditional law and economics theory of the jury also examines the efficacy of the jury system itself (Posner 1998). This is done within the context of all actors rationally pursuing their own self-interest.

The behavioral critique of this account is based on cognitive biases demonstrated in experiments. In particular, it argues that issues such as framing of the questions can have a significant outcome on the decision of the jury (McCaffrey, Kahneman, and Spitzer 2001). In particular, understanding that the difference between framing the question the jury decides as an *ex ante* question or an *ex post* question can make a significant difference in the decision that is rendered. This calls into question many of the rules for dealing with the jury. Some behavioral scholars discuss how other cognitive biases, such as hindsight bias (which makes it seem as if events that actually did occur were more likely to have occurred *ex ante* than they in fact did), can have a significant impact on the jury (McCaffrey, Kahneman, and Spitzer 2001; Rachlinski 2001; Sunstein, Kahneman, and Schkade 2001). Behavioral scholars also discuss problems such as the inability of jury members to calculate probabilities in a Bayesian manner and the effects it can have on decisions.

Neuroeconomics can advance the study of juries by examining what mechanisms jurors use to process the information given to them and how these methods differ in the population. Evidentiary rules could be drafted to comport better with the way individuals actually perceive evidence. In addition, this field of research can allow us to begin to examine the benefits of the size of the jury and other traditional law and economics questions by examining the advantage of having different types of individuals giving their perspective on a decision of liability.

## 3.4 CONCLUSIONS

This chapter has discussed how the emerging results from neuroeconomics might have profound effects on the way we view legal problems. The research already conducted seems to both agree and disagree with all of the schools of economics. By understanding the cognitive processes used by individuals, we can achieve significant progress in our understanding of legal and economic problems. Neurological and psychological evidence shows that the brain is not a Universal Turing machine, swiftly solving partial differential equations, which neoclassical economics seems to sometimes assume.[44] It is designed to do certain things. Evolution did not waste energy allowing the brain to do largely irrelevant operations. On the other hand, modeling the brain in such a way has led to significant ability to predict behavior.

Now that medical technology has advanced to the point where we can actually examine the brain while it is performing functions, we can move from the simpler models of neoclassical economics, or even behavioral economics, to examine what is casually occurring at the deeper level of the brain. This research will result in better models of human behavior and consequently a better understanding of legal problems.

1. Although many who follow schools of thought such as the natural tradition may argue that law derives from objective universal principles, it is clear that the actual laws we have are created by humans. Arguable exceptions include Islamic Law, the laws found in Leviticus, etc. These legal systems are beyond the scope of this chapter.

2. Friedman (1953) argues that the unreasonableness of the assumptions of a model is not as important as the empirical value of the predictions (also see Ulen 2000).

3. The first major book discussing this discipline is by Glimcher (2003).

4. Posner's (1998) *Economic Analysis of Law* is one the most cited works in history.

5. However, this can also be derived from irrational actors (Becker 1962).

6. Friedman (1996) even defines *economics* as "the study of rational behavior," which is almost certainly too restrictive.

7. Because of these results, traditional law and economics scholarship has been viewed by many in the legal academy as having a conservative bias. Perhaps this is a result of the impact of the Chicago school economics and certainly of the law and economics movement.

8. This is in contrast to Austrian economics, which normally eschews such types of methods. See the discussion of Austrian economics later in this chapter.

9. Discounting future benefits relative to current benefits often does exhibit dynamic consistency (Kahneman and Tversky 1998).

10. Kahneman and Tversky are now also among the most-cited authors in law reviews. One might denominate the conference at which the information in this chapter was presented as such a conference.

11. An Internet search on Yahoo! discovered about twenty such courses. One of the authors of this chapter (McCabe) teaches a class in behavioral law and economics.

12. This methodology is more in line with the behavioral analysis of researchers such as Gigerenzer and Selten (1996), who argue that one cannot simply look at particular reasoning methods in isolation. When they are examined in simple (and sometimes complex) economic behavior, if there are offsetting misconceptions that operate to generate optimal behavior, the misconceptions are likely to show up in experimental economic studies rather than in behavioral studies.

13. Evidence for this is found in the fact that both Tversky and Kahneman were trained as psychologists, not economists.

14. The difference between psychology and economics can be analogized to the difference between the study of atomic structure as a branch of both physics and chemistry that studies how molecules form and how they interact. In some sense chemistry is derivative of physics, but at this point we cannot simply derive the behavior of people when they interact from their behavior when they are reacting alone.

15. That governments may not be able to behave rationally (that is, have consistent preferences) was demonstrated by Arrow (1963).

16. This term was invented in 1996 by one the authors of this chapter (Kevin McCabe) when trying to name a course on neurology and economics. One could also apply the term to the method in which the brain allocates its own scarce resources and the effect it has on behavior.

17. The case of Phineas Gage is described by Macmillan (2002).

18. This technology is based on Linus Pauling's discovery in the field of chemistry that the amount of oxygen carried by hemoglobin changes the degree to which it disturbs a magnetic field. The signal is known as blood oxygen level dependent, or BOLD, and it is used for most brain-imaging studies (Gazzaniga, Ivry, and Mangun 2002).

19. There may some increase in the incidence of epilepsy from this method. It is always difficult to understand something that is counterfactual (Camerer, Loewenstein, and Prelec 2004).

20. Studies on the ways in which money operates indicate that relative values are important as well as values (Tremblay and Schultz 1999). For an analysis of neuroeconomics, see Smith (2003).

21. This payoff involved receiving tokens that were exchanged for money at the end of the experiment.

22. In the first payoff, 180 relates to the payoff for the first decision maker and 225, to the payoff for the second decision maker.

23. The areas activated when the subject was cooperating included Brodmann's areas 17 and 18 and areas in the parietal lobe. Brodmann's area 7 is the place in a primate's vision pathway that helps to place things. Also activated were the middle frontal gyrus and the frontal pole, Brodmann's areas 9 and 10. Half the subjects in the experiment consistently attempted to cooperate. The non-cooperators showed no difference between working with a computer and a human.

24. Brodmann analyzed the cellular structure of the cortex and described it as being composed of fifty-two separate regions. Later research has shown that these regions are often correlated with different functions performed by the brain (Gazzaniga, Ivry, and Mangun 2002).

25. For arguments that ambiguity aversion can be placed into a neoclassical framework, see Chorvat (2002).

26. This is the classic Ellsberg urn situation (Chorvat 2002).

27. For a discussion of the prevalence of ambiguity versus risk see Chorvat (2002).

28. This research ties into the hot-cold reasoning wherein addiction can be thought of as continually increasing the "heat" of the reasoning process (Loewenstein 1996).

29. In *Pennzoil v. Texaco*, the litigants disagreed over whether there was a valid contract. Joseph Jamail, the lawyer for Texaco, argued that in Texas, a handshake formed a contract. The jury agreed and held there was a valid contract.

30. Of course, some contracts, such as those derived by the Mafia, may be high trust but should not be enforced.

31. This can be described as $U(p, \ldots)$ where $p$ is the property.

32. Such models include the utility curve, preferences, etc.

33. This is related to NIE, as discussed earlier.

34. The idea can be illustrated by way of an example. There are two individuals, A and B, who could be awarded the good. Before the good is awarded, they value it ten dollars and twelve dollars, respectively; afterward, they value it at seventeen dollars and nineteen dollars, respectively. Although B always values the asset more, if we give it to A, A will never sell it to B, even though transactions costs are zero. In some sense, this has the effect of having very large transactions costs. However, these transactions costs are built in to humans, not just our institutions.

Thus, one needs to have some notion of a social welfare function, which relates to the addition of the welfare of all members of the society. For example, one could use a Samuelson-Bergson social welfare function (Bergson 1938).

35. Behavioral economics is sometimes referred to by its critics as the anomalies literature (Fama 1991).

36. Operant conditioning when the two things are closely related (i.e., personal and corporate gain) then may be perceived simply as individual gain (Camerer, Loewenstein, and Prelec 2004).

37. This was a replacement of the place of injury, etc., analysis found in the First Restatement.

38. These models consider how can we improve the efficiency of legal regimes by allowing parties to avoid particularly bad sets of laws.

39. Leflar (1977) argues that the key normative standard is getting to the "right" decision. Sterk (1994) argues that this is in effect what judges are currently doing.

40. Are they maximizing profit, minimizing cost, sacrificing?

41. This is similar to NIE.

42. Limited liability is no longer much of a concern because limited liability companies can be taxed as a partnership and still have limited liability, as corporations do. Bankman (1994) indicates that the government may be profiting from such companies, because entrepreneurs do not make sufficient use of tax losses.

43. Certain types of people, known as high Machs (after Machiavellian), are willing not to reciprocate when it is not in their interest. Low Machs reciprocate even when it is not in their own interest.

44. Interestingly, robots are really not very intelligent and are unable to do things that many insects can do (Camerer, Loewenstein, and Prelec 2004).

Aaron, H., and M. Boskin, eds. 1980. *The economics of taxation*. Washington, DC: Brookings Institution.

Akerlof, G. 1970. The market for lemons: Quality, uncertainty and the market mechanism. *Quarterly Journal of Economics* 84:488.

Alchian, A., and H. Demsetz. 1972. Production, information costs and economic organization. *American Economic Review* 62:777.

Arrow, K. 1963. *Social choice and individual values*. 2nd ed. New Haven, CT: Yale University Press.

Baird, D., R. H. Gertner, and R. C. Picker. 1992. *Game theory and the law*. Cambridge, MA: Harvard University Press.

Bankman, J. 1994. The structure of Silicon Valley startups. *University of California Los Angeles Law Review* 41:1734.

Becker, G. 1962. Irrational behavior and economic theory. *Journal of Political Economy* 70:1.

Bergson, A. 1938. A reformulation of certain aspects of welfare economics. *Quarterly Journal of Economics* 68:233.

Bernstein, D. 1998. The law and economics of post–Civil War restrictions on interstate migrations by African-Americans. *Texas Law Review* 74:781.

Brinig, M., and F. Buckley. 1996. The market for deadbeats. *Journal of Legal Studies* 25:207.

Buchanan, J., and G. Tullock. 1961. *The calculus of consent*. Ann Arbor: University of Michigan Press.

Calabresi, G., and A. Melamed. 1972. Property, liability rules and inalienability: One view of the cathedral. *Harvard Law Review* 85:1089.

Camerer, C., G. Loewenstein, and D. Prelec. 2004. Neuroeconomics: How neuroscience can inform economics. *Journal of Economic Literature* (forthcoming).

Caplan, B. 2003. Why I am not an Austrian economist. Unpublished manuscript. http://www.gmu.edu/departments/economics/bcaplan/whyaust.htm.

Chorvat, T. 2002. Ambiguity and income taxation. *Cardozo Law Review* 23:635.

Coase, R. 1960. The problem of social cost. *Journal of Law and Economics* 3:1.

Corradin, S., and F. Perali. 2002. Dynamic analysis of addiction: Impatience and heterogeneity. University of Verona, Italy, working paper. dipeco.economia.unimib.it/happiness/accepted_papers/corradin_perali.pdf.

Crawell, R., and A. Schwartz, eds. 1980. *Foundations of contract law*. Oxford: Oxford University Press.

Currie, B. 1959. Notes on methods and objectives in the conflict of laws. *Duke Law Journal* 1959:171.

Fama, E. 1991. Efficient capital markets II. *Journal of Finance* 46:1575.

Fleischer, V. 2003. The rational exuberance of structuring venture capital start-ups. 57 Tax L. Rev. 137.

Friedman, D. 1996. *Price theory.* Mason, OH: South-Western.

Friedman, M. 1953. *Essays in positive economics.* Chicago: University of Chicago Press.

Gazzaniga, M., R. B. Ivry, and G. R. Mangun. 2002. *Cognitive neuroscience: The biology of the mind.* New York: Norton.

Gigerenzer, G., and R. Selten. 1996. Rethinking rationality. In *Bounded rationality: The adaptive toolbox,* ed. G. Gigerenzer and R. Selten, 1–12. Cambridge, MA: MIT Press.

Glimcher, P. 2003. *Decisions, uncertainty, and the brain: The science of neuroeconomics.* Cambridge, MA: MIT Press.

Grant, S. 2002. Impaired decision-making in substance abusers: Brain imaging and cognitive models. National Institute on Drug Abuse working paper, Bethesda, MD.

Hayek, F. 1989. *The fatal conceit.* Chicago: University of Chicago Press.

———. 1994. *The road to serfdom.* Chicago: University of Chicago Press.

Hoffman, E., K. McCabe, and V. Smith. 1998. Behavioral foundations of reciprocity: Experimental economics and evolutionary psychology. *Economic Inquiry* 36:335.

Jensen, M., and W. Meckling. 1976. Theory of the firm: Managerial behavior, agency costs, and ownership structure. *Journal of Financial Economics* 3:305.

Jolls, C., C. Sunstein, and R. Thaler. 2001. A behavioral approach to law and economics. In *Behavioral law and economics,* ed. C. Sunstein. Cambridge: Cambridge University Press.

Kahneman, D., J. Knetsch, and R. Thaler. 1990. Experimental tests of the endowment effect and the Coase theorem. *Journal of Political Economy* 98:1325.

———. 2000. Experimental test of the endowment effect and the Coase theorem. In *Behavioral law and economics,* ed. C. Sunstein. Cambridge: Cambridge University Press.

Kahneman, D., and A. Tversky. 1998. Choices, values and frames. In *Choices, values and frames,* ed. D. Kahneman and A. Tversky. Cambridge: Cambridge University Press.

Korobkin, R. 1998a. Inertia and perception in contract negotiation: The psychological power of default rules and form terms. *Vanderbilt Law Review* 51:1583.

———. 1998b. The status quo bias and contract default rules. *Cornell Law Review* 83:608.

Kramer, L. 1990. Rethinking choice of law. *Columbia Law Review* 90:277.

Langevoort, D. 2001. Organized illusions: A behavioral theory of why corporations mislead stock market investors (and cause other social harms). In *Behavioral law and economics*, ed. C. Sunstein. Cambridge: Cambridge University Press.

Leflar, R. 1977. Choice of law: A well-watered plateau. *Law and Contemporary Problems* 41:10.

Loewenstein, G. 1996. Out of control: Visceral influences on behavior. *Organizational Behavior and Human Decision Processes* 65:272.

Macmillan, M. 2002. *An odd kind of fame*. Cambridge, MA: MIT Press.

McCabe, K., D. Houser, L. Ryan, V. Smith, and T. Trouard. 2001. A functional imaging study of cooperation in two-person reciprocal exchange. *Proceedings of the National Academy of Sciences* 98 (20): 11832.

McCaffrey, E., D. Kahneman, and M. Spitzer. 2001. Framing the jury: Cognitive perspective on pain and suffering awards. In *Behavioral law and economics*, ed. C. Sunstein. Cambridge: Cambridge University Press.

O'Hara, E., and L. Ribstein. 2000. Conflict of laws and choice of law. In *Encyclopedia of law and economics*, ed. B. Boukert and G. de Geest. Cheltenham, UK: Elgar.

Plott, C., and K. Zeiler. 2002. The willingness to pay/willingness to accept gap, the "Endowment Effect" and experimental procedures for eliciting valuation. Caltech social science working paper no. 1732.

Posner, R. 1998. *The economic analysis of law*. 5th ed. New York: Aspen.

Rachlinski, J. 2001. A positive psychological theory of judgment in hindsight. In *Behavioral law and economics*, ed. C. Sunstein. Cambridge: Cambridge University Press.

Rothbard, M. 2000. America's great depression. Auburn, AL: Ludwig von Mises Institute.

Silbeberg, E. 1992. *The structure of economics: A mathematical approach*. New York: McGraw-Hill.

Smith, K., J. Dickhaut, K. McCabe, and J. V. Pardo. 2002. Neuronal substrates for choice under ambiguity, risk, gains and losses. *Management Science* 48:77.

Smith, V. 2002. Constructivist and ecological rationality in economics: Nobel Prize lecture. http://www.gmu.edu/departments/law/currnews/smith-lecture.pdf.

———. 2003. Experimental methods in (neuro)economics. In *The encyclopedia of cognitive science*, ed. L. Nadel. New York: Nature.

Solimine, M. 1989. An economic and empirical analysis of choice of law. *Georgia Law Review* 24:49.

Sterk, S. 1994. The marginal relevance of choice of law theory. *University of Pennsylvania Law Review* 142:949.

Sunstein, C., D. Kahneman, and D. Schkade. 2001. Assessing punitive damages (notes on cognition and valuation in law). In *Behavioral law and economics*, ed. C. Sunstein. Cambridge: Cambridge University Press.

Tremblay, L., and W. Schultz. 1999. Relative reward preference in primate orbito-frontal cortex. *Nature* 398:704.

Ulen, T. 2000. Rational choice in law and economics. In *Encyclopedia of law and economics*, ed. B. Boukert and G. de Geest, 790. Cheltenham, UK: Elgar.

Varian, H. 1993. *Microeconomic analysis*. New York: Norton.

# 4 | TREATING YOURSELF INSTRUMENTALLY: INTERNALIZATION, RATIONALITY, AND THE LAW

*Robert Cooter*

The Puritans came to Massachusetts seeking a life of greater restrictions.
*Garrison Keillor*

---

Effective law appeals to good people and deters bad people. Deterrence theory has improved greatly in recent years through the application of economics and psychology. In contrast, the theory of internalized values has improved modestly, partly because of the failure of economics to progress in this area. Economists typically assume that people pursue self-interest as they perceive it. Perceived self-interest presupposes personal goals, including the central values by which people define themselves. Instead of explaining how people acquire their goals, economics conventionally "takes preferences as given." Economics thus offers no account of how a person becomes the self in which he or she is interested.

To solve this problem, economics needs a theory of self-development, including a theory of endogenous preferences. The fluorescence of behavioral economics in the 1990s brought economics into intimate contact with cognitive psychology. The contact, however, involves only a small part of psychology. Whereas cognitive psychology concerns beliefs, much of the rest of psychology concerns values and motives. A more complete interaction between economics and psychology that brings economics in touch with values and motives will contribute to the development of an economic theory of endogenous preferences.

I will sketch a way to make the connection. A moral principle holds that we should treat others as ends. This chapter concerns the opposite problem: treating ourselves as means. We treat ourselves as means when we shape ourselves to achieve our ends. Rational self-development involves commitment to a discipline that changes a person's skills and values. As Garrison Keillor's droll quotation on the New England Puritans suggests, we choose the constraints that change us.

To illustrate the problem of self-development, consider a young person with talent for music and accounting who must choose between conservatory and business school. Business school and conservatory will impart different skills. Accountants and musicians have different opportunities to make money and music. Business school and conservatory will also impart different values. Accountants and musicians disagree systematically about the importance of money and music for a good life. Thus, the student must make choices affecting both skills and values.

To analyze this problem, I combine the economic theory of decision making and the psychological theory of cognitive dissonance. Economic theory characterizes preferences and opportunities, and psychological theory shows their connection. After the foundations for a theory of rational self-development have been sketched, the conclusion briefly discusses some potential applications to law.

## 4.1 EXAMPLE: ACCOUNTANT OR MUSICIAN?

I will analyze the expected changes in a young person choosing between conservatory and business school. Figure 4.1 depicts the expected change in values. Business school will give him a keen appreciation of wealth, as indicated by $U_{1 \text{ accountant}}$. Conservatory will give him a keen appreciation of aesthetic values, as indicated by

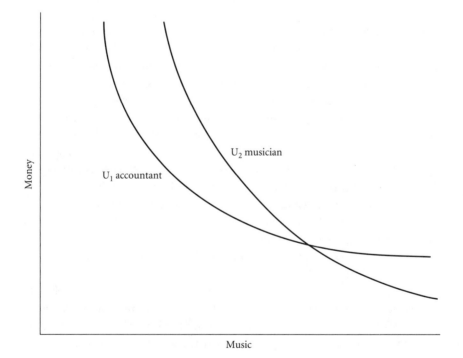

**Figure 4.1** Future preferences of accountant and musician

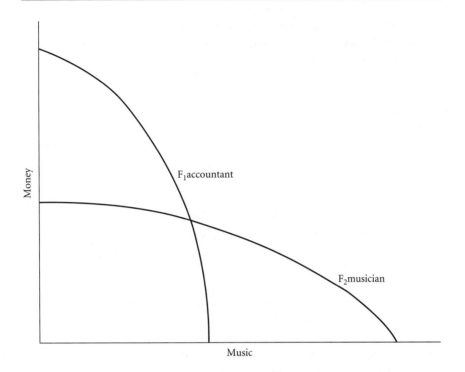

**Figure 4.2**  Opportunities of musician and accountant

$U_{2 \text{ musician}}$. To appreciate the difference in values, consider the slope of the two utility curves at the point where they intersect. His expected preferences as a future musician indicate that he would trade a lot of money for more music, and his expected preferences as a future accountant indicate that he would trade a lot of music for more money.

Having characterized preferences in Figure 4.1, I characterize opportunities in Figure 4.2. A skillful accountant with a personality for business has different opportunities than a skillful musician with a personality for performing. Specifically, an accountant has more opportunities to make money, and a musician has more opportunities to make music. Figure 4.2 depicts this difference, where the accountant has opportunities $F_{1 \text{ accountant}}$ and the musician has opportunities $F_{2 \text{ musician}}$.

## 4.2  COGNITIVE DISSONANCE AND MARKET SIGNALING

Preferences in Figure 4.1 represent subjective trade-offs, and opportunities in Figure 4.2 represent objective trade-offs. Now I turn to their psychological connection in the theory of cognitive dissonance.[1] According to this theory, commitment to an activity that changes opportunities, as in Figure 4.2, will cause a change in values, as in Figure 4.1. Thus, cognitive dissonance theory asserts that actors who change their objective trade-offs will cause their subjective trade-offs to change.

To see why, I briefly relate commitment in economics and dissonance in psychology. In economics, "commitment" especially refers to a decision that raises prices to the decision maker. Consider an illustration from Sun Tzu's *The Art of War*. An army may commit to advance by burning the bridges behind it, thus raising the price of retreat. In notation, an actor commits to x by raising the relative price of not-x. Specifically, let x denote "advance," and let not-x denote "retreat." The army commits to x by burning the bridges it has crossed, which raises the price of not-x. Note that raising the relative price of not-x is materially equivalent to lowering the relative price of x. Thus, we could also say that an actor commits to doing x by lowering its price relative to the price of not-x.

Why commit? Raising the price of retreat proves to the enemy that the advance is no bluff. Once the invading army must advance, retreat may be the defending army's best move. In general, actors in a strategic interaction sometimes gain an advantage by raising their own costs of doing something. My concern here, however, is not with strategy but with values.

Whereas economics is clear about how commitment affects strategy, psychology is clear about how commitment affects values. Cognitive dissonance theory predicts that committing to x makes the actor willing to pay relatively more for it. In other words, cognitive dissonance predicts that an act increasing the *objective* price of not-x causes an increase in the actor's subjective price of x. For example, studying music rather than accounting makes getting money hard relative to playing music, which causes the actor to increase his valuation of music relative to money.

Why does the actor's commitment to something increase its subjective value? Most people want to think of themselves as having good judgment. Good judgment implies good outcomes of choices. Thus, people want to see their world as obeying this syllogism:

I make good choices.
*I chose this.*
Therefore, this is good.

*Cognitive dissonance* is the psychological term for the discomfort produced when my own choice produces bad outcomes.

Actors who make a bad choice must live with the discomfort or else change their evaluation of the outcome. Studies by psychologists and sociologists demonstrate the surprising frequency with which people respond to bad outcomes by changing their beliefs about what counts as bad. An outcome regarded as bad by subjects before choosing may seem good after it results from their choice.

To illustrate cognitive dissonance in self-development, consider the student who hesitates between studying accounting and music. Regardless of which alternative the student chooses, he will probably strain to like it. Assume that the student chooses conservatory over business school. The student might subsequently seek new friends among musicians rather than businesspeople, focus his thoughts on the advantages of music over business, join discussions about the superficial values of the bourgeoisie, and listen to music rather than the stock market report at dinner. Even if the student struggles in conservatory and gets bad results, he may convince himself that his failures are actually good for him.

Now I show how to depict cognitive dissonance graphically. Figures 4.1 and 4.2 represent the difference in preferences and opportunities expected by a graduate of conservatory and business school. Cognitive dissonance theory predicts that commitment to a course of study that produces the opportunities in Figure 4.2 will cause the values in Figure 4.1. Specifically, the student who commits to business school raises the cost of music relative to money and faces opportunities $F_1$, which causes him to acquire preferences $U_1$. Similarly, the student who commits to conservatory raises the cost of money relative to music and faces opportunities $F_2$, which causes him to acquire preferences $U_2$.

This psychological theory connects preferences and opportunities. In economics, the theory of market signaling also connects preferences and opportunities. However, the direction of causation is reversed in the two theories. Whereas cognitive dissonance postulates that opportunities change preferences, market signaling postulates that preferences change opportunities, as I will explain.

In markets where actors rely on signals, changing values can change a person's opportunities. To illustrate, a business prefers to hire a young executive with a keen desire for wealth, whereas an orchestra prefers to hire a young musician dedicated to art. Knowing this fact, a person applying for a job as an executive will represent herself as dedicated to wealth, whereas a person applying for a job as a musician will represent herself as dedicated to art. Many of the signs that indicate motivation by a particular goal are easier to acquire by people who actually have the motivation than by people who lack it. For example, a person who is dedicated to art will spend her leisure time differently than a person dedicated to wealth. Under certain circumstances, how a person spends leisure time can signal the person's motivations.

In general, the ability to signal and detect character is one of the most important skills in social life, as well as in experimental games that involve cooperation (Cooter and Eisenberg 2001). Having noted the connection between cognitive dissonance and market signaling, I will not explore the latter any further in this chapter. (Melvin Eisenberg and I have already written on the connection between character and business opportunity.)

## 4.3 METAVALUES

Choice occurs when preferences meet opportunities. Figure 4.3 combines Figures 4.1 and 4.2 in order to depict the different choices that the student will make, depending on whether he becomes an accountant or musician. As an accountant, his preferred point in Figure 4.3 involves more money than music; and as a musician, his preferred point involves more music than money. The problem addressed in the next section is how to choose between going to business school and reaching the accountant's preferred point in Figure 4.3, or going to conservatory and reaching the musician's preferred point in Figure 4.3.

A rational person who understands psychology recognizes that his commitments will change his values. In particular, the student should foresee that his commitment to accounting or music would result in the outcomes depicted in Figure 4.3. To decide which commitment to make, however, he needs to choose among values. I will suggest how to choose, which involves going beyond conventional economics.

Perhaps the student views money and music as means to something else. For example, the student may want happiness, pleasure, social status, self-fulfillment, moral goodness, or some other general value. Connecting the choice of the particular alternative to metavalues can solve the student's problem.

To illustrate, assume that the student wants to be happy above all. The student might think of happiness as a metavalue or metapreference that lies behind his desire for money and music. He recognizes that studying music will cause him to gain relatively more happiness from music than money, and studying accounting will cause him to gain relatively more happiness from money than music. If he could predict with confidence how much happiness each one will bring him, then he might choose the career that promises more happiness.

The preceding discussion assumes that happiness is the metavalue that the student maximizes. Perhaps some people seek happiness and others seek pleasure, social status, self-fulfillment, moral goodness, and so forth. In this chapter, I will not discuss whether everyone seeks, or ought to seek, happiness. Instead, I want to focus on the fact that young people seldom know what they really want to accomplish or who they really want to be. In my example, the student is probably uncertain about whether he wants happiness more than, say, fame. And even if he is certain that he wants happiness more than fame, he is probably uncertain about

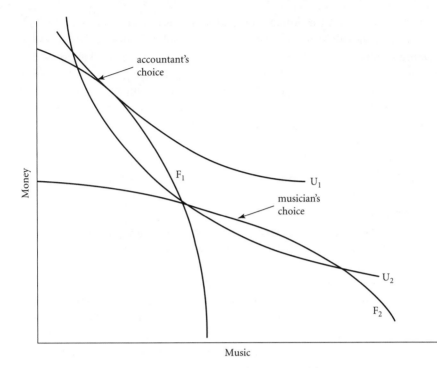

**Figure 4.3**   Choices by accountant and musician

which career path will bring him more of it. In general, self-development involves self-discovery because the effects of choices on metavalues are uncertain.

The problem of uncertainty raises technical questions about how to extend expected utility theory to choices that affect preferences, but I will not pursue these technical questions here. Instead, I turn to a way of choosing that does not involve the calculus of expected utilities.

## 4.4   PARETO SELF-IMPROVEMENT

Economic theorists have intensively studied choice when the decision makers are uncertain about the external world and certain about their values. Economic theorists, however, have devoted much less analysis to decisions when values are uncertain. Although little economic analysis concerns uncertainty about value, something useful can be learned from what has been done. The problem of uncertain values arises especially when economists advise policy makers who face unfamiliar trade-offs. Here is a typical example from decision theory: Assume that a public hospital must choose between adopting two procedures, one of which causes injury with high probability and no deaths, while the other causes death with low probability and no injuries. Depending on its choice, the hospital can anticipate many injuries or few deaths. Most hospital officials are uncertain about their relative valuation of statistical injuries and deaths. (Many similar examples exist.)[2]

A decision maker may be certain about the relative value of extreme alternatives and uncertain about the relative value of close alternatives. For example, the hospital administrator in this case may be confident that statistical injuries above a certain level exceed the cost of a statistical death (say, 50:1 or above) and statistical injuries below a certain level fall short of the cost of a statistical death (say, 10:1 or below). In between these extremes, however, the administrator may be uncertain about relative values.

An important task for decision theory is to identify the critical numbers on which such a decision turns. This approach is sometimes called "sensitivity analysis," because it aims for the minimum information about values to which the actual choice is sensitive. For example, the hospital's choice is insensitive to a tradeoff of statistical injuries to death that exceeds 50:1 or falls short of 10:1. If the actual choice is sufficiently extreme to fall in the insensitive range, the hospital officials can choose without inquiring further into their values. Conversely, if the actual choice is inside the sensitive range, the hospital officials cannot choose without inquiring further into their values.

The hospital's alternatives are lumpy, as watermelons are, and not continuous, as gasoline is. In general, when choices are lumpy, the best alternative may be so much better than the next-best alternative that the choice is insensitive to a range of reasonable values.

Now I will adapt an economic concept in order to perform a sensitivity analysis of the student's choice between accounting and music. The concept of Pareto efficiency provides the basis for a sensitivity analysis of the student's decision. When one alternative is compared to another in conventional welfare economics, a choice is "Pareto superior" if everyone prefers it to the alternative. I have extended this concept to a situation where a person's values can change. When one alternative is compared to another, I describe a choice as "Pareto superior" if it is preferable to the alternative when evaluated using each of the decision maker's possible preferences. In my extension, possible preferences of a single person play the same role as actual preferences of different people in conventional welfare economics. The conventional analysis thus concerns *interpersonal* Pareto superiority, and my unconventional analysis concerns *intrapersonal* Pareto superiority.

Figure 4.3 illustrates intrapersonal Pareto superiority. Recall that the point labeled "musician's choice" indicates the combination of money and music that the student will choose if he becomes a musician. Also recall that the point labeled "accountant's choice" indicates the combination of money and music that the student will choose if he becomes an accountant. Notice that the accountant's utility curve, $U_1$, in Figure 4.3 passes through the accountant's preferred point and above the musician's preferred point. This fact indicates that the accountant likes what he receives better than what he would get as a musician. Also notice that the musician's utility curve, $U_2$, in Figure 4.3 passes through the musician's preferred point and below the accountant's preferred point. This fact indicates that the musician likes what he would get as an accountant better than what he actually receives as a musician. Thus, Figure 4.3 depicts a situation in which the student prefers the combination of money and music that he expects to receive as an accountant rather than a musician, regardless of whether he compares the outcomes with the values of an accountant or a musician. For this student in these circumstances, becoming an accountant is intrapersonally Pareto superior to becoming a musician.

Notation helps to clarify the concept of intrapersonal Pareto superiority. Let $x_1$ and $x_2$ denote two possible outcomes, such as the accountant's choice and the musician's choice in Figure 4.3. Let $U_1$ and $U_2$ represent two possible preference orderings. The outcome $x_1$ is intrapersonally superior to $x_2$ if $U_1(x_1) > U_1(x_2)$ and $U_2(x_1) > U_2(x_2)$.

Figure 4.3 depicts one choice that is intrapersonally Pareto superior to the other. Figure 4.4 depicts all such choices. Specifically, the set of points labeled "Pareto superior" in Figure 4.4 contains all combinations of money and music that yield higher satisfaction than the musician's most preferred point, regardless of whether the actor develops musician's preferences or accountant's preferences.

If one alternative is intrapersonally Pareto superior to the other, this fact provides a strong reason to choose without inquiring any further into values. To see why, return to the example of the student. To make a decision, the student would like to add metavalues to the alternatives, but the student is uncertain about his metavalues. Assume that the accountant and musician's preferences, $U_1$ and $U_2$, respectively, are two extreme possibilities for the rate at which money and music trade off in the student's true system of metavalues, W. Under this assumption, the student who chooses the Pareto superior alternative necessarily makes a choice that is better by his metavalues. Consequently, the student who grows in self-knowledge will not regret his choice.[3]

To illustrate in notation, I assume that the accountant's and musician's preferences, $U_1$ and $U_2$, respectively, are two extreme possibilities for the rate at which money and music trade off in the student's true system of metavalues, W. Consequently, W is a weighted average of $U_1$ and $U_2$, which I write $W = bU_1 + (1 - b)U_2$, where $0 \leq b \leq 1$. The student's uncertainty implies that he does not

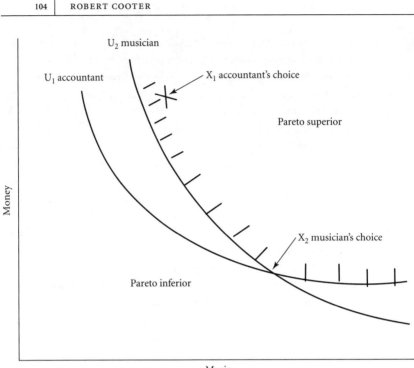

**Figure 4.4** Pareto self-improvement

know the true value of *b*. Fortunately, a Pareto superior alternative yields higher W for all possible values of *b* in the interval $0 \leq b \leq 1$. Consequently, the student who chooses the Pareto superior alternative will not regret his choice later when he understands the true value of *b*.

Intrapersonal Pareto superiority has an important connection to cognitive dissonance. In my example, cognitive dissonance theory predicts that a student who commits to accounting will develop the preferences of an accountant, $U_1$, and a student who commits to music will develop the preferences of a musician, $U_2$. If the student makes the Pareto superior choice and cognitive dissonance operates as predicted, the student will not regret his choice. If, however, the student makes the Pareto inferior choice and cognitive dissonance operates as predicted, the student will regret his choice.

Applied to individuals, the predictions of cognitive dissonance theory are probabilities, not certainties. Over time, individuals may reflect on their choices and preferences, which can undermine and even undo nonrational processes such as cognitive dissonance. In the extreme case, the actual direction of change in values might reverse the prediction of cognitive dissonance theory. In the reverse case, the student who commits to accounting ends up with the musician's values, and the student who commits to music ends up with the accountant's values. If the student makes the Pareto superior choice and his values change in the reverse direction from the prediction of cognitive dissonance theory, the student will not regret his choice. If, however, the student makes the Pareto inferior choice and his values change in the reverse direction from the prediction of cognitive dissonance theory, the student will regret his choice.

## 4.5 CONCLUSION AND POSSIBLE APPLICATION TO LAW

Economic theories of behavior especially concern choosing the best means to an end. Individuals treat themselves as a means when they change themselves to achieve their ends. The theory of cognitive dissonance predicts how commitments, which change objective opportunities, change subjective values. By definition, a commitment to one alternative increases the objective price of the rejected alternative. By cognitive dissonance theory, commitment causes an increase in the subjective value of the chosen alternative.

Cognitive dissonance theory provides a framework to model how law changes values. Laws create obligations backed by sanctions, which raises the price of doing wrong relative to doing right. In a democracy, citizens ideally see themselves as makers of the law. When this ideal is achieved, citizens see themselves as having raised the relative price of wrongdoing. In other words, citizens ideally see their legal obligations as their commitments. When democratic commitments strengthen, the citizens like conforming to the law.

Reasonable people, who recognize that they will probably come to like their commitments, seek a rational basis for them. Because commitments change values, individuals must choose among values in order to make commitments. Rational people may use metavalues such as happiness to choose among values. In many circumstances, however, choosing by metavalues demands more self-knowledge than the decision maker possesses.

In these circumstances, the decision maker can sometimes avoid the problem if the connection between opportunities and values is strong enough. A strong connection can cause one outcome to dominate the others when evaluated with any likely values. I call a choice that is better with respect to any likely preferences of a decision maker "intrapersonally Pareto superior" or, more simply, a "Pareto self-improvement" (Cooter 1998a, 1998b). According to this analysis, people will tend to change their preferences when doing so increases their satisfaction relative to their initial preferences and their final preferences.

In a well-organized democracy, citizens gain advantages from obeying the law and participating in government, relative to disobeying the law and not participating in government. Many people, consequently, commit to being good citizens. The commitment is stable because they have no intrapersonally Pareto superior alternative. Segments of the population who do not gain from obeying the law and participating in government tend not to commit to being good citizens. A well-organized democracy tries to extend the advantages of obeying the law and participating in government to everyone so that everyone has a reason to commit to being a good citizen.

Cognitive psychology, which has influenced law and economics theory, is a small part of psychology. The larger part includes motivational psychology. If successful, the theory that I propose in this chapter could provide a framework for incorporating motivational psychology into law and economics theory.

## NOTES

1. The theory of cognitive dissonance was especially developed by Festinger (1962). A good exposition is in Griffin (1997) and in Mills and Harmon-Jones (1999). For an economist writing on dissonance and morality, see Rabin (1994). For early writing by an economist on the subject, see Akerlof and Dickens (1982).

2. Another example is a choice between two alternative locations for an airport, when the decision maker is uncertain about the relative value of saving time to travelers and reducing noise to residents. Yet another example is a decision about whether to build an atomic energy plant when the decision maker is uncertain about the relative value of electricity and the risk of a nuclear accident.

3. A metapreference feature with this function corresponds to a nondecreasing social welfare function written over the preferences of different individuals.

## REFERENCES

Akerlof, G., and W. Dickens. 1982. The economic consequences of cognitive dissonance. *American Economic Review* 72:307–19.

Cooter, R. 1998a. Expressive law and economics. *Journal of Legal Studies* 27: 585–608.

———. 1998b. Self-control and self-improvement for the "bad man" of Holmes (O. W. Holmes Centenary Lecture Conference). *Boston University Law Review* 78:903–30.

Cooter, R., and M. Eisenberg. 2001. Fairness, character, and efficiency in firms. *University of Pennsylvania Law Review* 149:1717–33.

Festinger, L. 1962. *A theory of cognitive dissonance theory*. Stanford, CA: Stanford University Press.

Griffin, E. 1997. Cognitive dissonance theory of Leon Festinger. In *A first look at communication theory*, 536. New York: McGraw-Hill.

Mills, J., and E. Harmon-Jones. 1999. *Cognitive dissonance: Progress on a pivotal theory in social psychology*. Washington, DC: American Psychological Association.

Rabin, M. 1994. Cognitive dissonance and social change. *Journal of Economic Behavior and Organization* 23:177–94.

# II THE ECONOMICS OF IRRATIONAL BEHAVIOR

# 5 ADDICTION, CHOICE, AND IRRATIONALITY

*Ole-Jørgen Skog*

Addictions are puzzling. Why do people indulge in consumption of a drug to the point of physical and social damage, and why do they continue such behavior, despite contrary statements of intent and negative sanctions from others?

Addictive behavior can be seen from two different perspectives—either as a disease or as choice. The classical disease concept is based on the idea that the agent has lost control of his or her substance consumption. The behavior is in effect not conceived as volitional. On the other hand, advocates of the choice perspective insist that the substance-dependent person controls his or her own behavior. Some of the latter theorists would even claim that so-called dependence is just a vice or a bad habit (Szasz 1972). Others would see it as a result of perverted preferences and ambivalence. Addictive substances are assumed to be unusual commodities with properties that can create malignant motivational conflicts.

The disease concept has its roots in the late eighteenth and early nineteenth centuries. A central agent in this process was Benjamin Rush, who organized the developing medical and commonsense wisdom of the late eighteenth century into a distinctly new paradigm for alcohol dependence (Levine 1978). Prior to this period, drunkenness and inebriety were mostly seen as a sin. With Rush however, habitual drunkenness came to be seen as a disease with an identified causal agent (alcohol), characterized by an inability to choose, (that is, a truly compulsive activity). He designated the condition as a "disease of the will" and gave the following vivid clinical example from the mouth of a dependent drinker: "Were a keg of rum in one corner of a room, and were a cannon constantly discharging balls between me and it, I could not refrain from passing before that cannon, in order to get at the rum" (Rush 1812, 266).

After World War II the "disease model" of alcoholism reached its peak, particularly in the United States, and Jellinek (1960) summarized the basic elements of the theory in his influential monograph "The Disease Concept of Alcoholism." In addition to this academic tradition, the disease view was also, and even more strongly, advocated by a lay "alcoholism movement" with its roots in Alcoholics Anonymous (AA) (see Fingarette 1988, 1991). The main difference between the classical view of Rush and the neoclassical view of Jellinek in the post-Prohibition era is that Rush assumed that everyone could contract the disease if he or she drank enough, but Jellinek considered that only a small subset of the population was vulnerable.

The neoclassical theory can briefly be summarized as follows: Alcoholism is a specific disease triggered by the consumption of alcoholic beverages. Not everyone is susceptible. Some individuals are allergic to alcohol; but most people are not. A susceptible person who starts to drink is on a slippery slope that may end in disaster. The stages are well defined and develop in a fairly regular order. Symptoms accumulate, becoming increasingly disabling and demoralizing. Eventually, loss of control develops. When the agent takes a drink, a chain reaction is triggered, and the alcoholic is unable to control his or her drinking ("one drink, one drunk"). The only recovery from alcoholism comes from complete abstinence.

However, during the last third of the twentieth century, this conception has been challenged. Empirical evidence has accumulated that the alcohol addict is strongly influenced by environmental restraints and opportunities (Heather and Robertson 1981; Marlatt, Demming, and Reid 1973; Mello and Mendelson 1965, 1966, 1972; Pattison, Sobell, and Sobell 1977), and this suggests that they are in fact able to choose (cf. Skog 2000). Furthermore, the stages are much less regular than assumed. Severely alcohol-dependent individuals may have long periods of moderate drinking (Polich, Armor, and Braiker 1980; Skog and Duckert 1993), and a substantial fraction can return to normal drinking (Nordström and Berglund 1987; Vaillant 1983). At a conceptual level it has been pointed out that the argument offered by the advocates of the no-choice interpretation is incoherent. Quite often, it is simply based on the observation that addicts claim that they do not wish to act in a certain way, but they still do at some later stage. However, this is not a compulsion; it is just an example of dynamic inconsistency. In advance, the agent intended to abstain, but at the time of acting has changed his or her mind. The agent may be ambivalent, having good reasons for abstaining, but obviously even stronger reasons for indulging at the critical moment.

These observations suggest that alcoholism, as well as other addictions, should be studied from the point of view of choice. The question then becomes whether and how addiction differs from ordinary habits. Of particular interest is the concept of rationality. To argue that addictions can (and should) be understood as choice does not imply that addictions can be fully understood as *rational* choice. Therefore, a central question is whether addiction can be meaningfully described as rational choice, or if irrationalities of different sorts play an integral role. This will be a main theme on the pages to follow.

In the next section follows a discussion of conceptualizations of addiction, starting with the definition proposed in the *Diagnostic and Statistical Manual of Mental Disorders* (DSM-IV) of the American Psychiatric Association (1994). Most economics papers on addiction from recent years are based on commonsense conceptions of addiction. A more realistic starting point is clearly needed. Then follows a discussion of rationality and addiction, taking as point of departure Gary Becker's theory of rational addiction. I shall argue that most cases of substance dependence harbor different violations of the standard model of rational choice (which includes stable preferences). The two main types are irrational belief formation and inconsistencies in the preferences—in particular, dynamic inconsistency. In the last part of the chapter I shall discuss different mechanisms underlying dynamic inconsistency. Hyperbolic discounting is one mechanism, but I shall argue that this is probably not the most important one.

## 5.1 DEFINING ADDICTION

DSM-IV defines substance dependence—or addiction—in terms of a cluster of cognitive, behavioral, and physiological symptoms indicating that the individual continues use of the substance despite significant substance-related problems. DSM-IV lists seven criteria and suggests that dependence is present when three (or more) have occurred within the last twelve months. The criteria are (1) tolerance; (2) withdrawal; (3) often consuming more than was intended; (4) persistent desire or unsuccessful efforts to cut down; (5) spending a great deal of time with drug-related activities; (6) giving up important social, occupational, or recreational activities; and (7) continuing consumption despite physical or psychological harm.

All the symptoms listed may be present in degrees. Some individuals may experience very high degrees of tolerance, whereas others may have less tolerance to the same substance; some may experience violent withdrawal symptoms, whereas others experience milder symptoms; and the desire and unsuccessful efforts to cut down may vary considerably across individuals, to mention just three examples. Hence, dependence is something that comes in degrees (cf. Edwards 1987). Any cutoff will necessarily be more or less arbitrary. Nevertheless, for practical purposes it may still be convenient to have a label for those who are severely addicted, and practical convenience is probably the motive behind the categorical concept suggested by the authors of DSM-IV. In the following discussion I will use the words *addiction* and *dependence* interchangeably, as a shorthand for "at the high end of the continuum."

In the literature on addiction, including the DSM-IV, one frequently encounters claims to the effect that "compulsive" substance use is characteristic of dependence. This concept should not be taken literally. The term is probably only meant to imply that individuals have very strong appetites that they find difficult to resist, even if their evaluative judgment strongly suggests that they should abstain or cut back. This internal, motivational conflict is something quite different from an external compulsion, as when you are unable to resist the forces of nature or to resist another person whose physical strength exceeds your own. As Watson (1999) points out, "Unlike external obstacles, ... motivational obstacles work in part not by defeating one's best efforts, but by diverting one from effective resistance. One's behavior remains in these cases in an important sense voluntary." And he adds that addictive substances "enslave by appeal, rather than by brute force." Hence, "compulsive substance use" should be understood as a metaphor.

The first two DSM-IV criteria describe physiological effects. Tolerance is defined by either "(a) a need for markedly increased amounts of the substance to achieve intoxication or the desired effect" or "(b) markedly diminished effect with continued use of the same amount of the substance" (181). This implies two different mechanisms, as exemplified in the diagrams of Figure 5.1. In the left-hand diagram, corresponding to (a), the consumer can tolerate a higher intake and obtains more pleasure at high levels than before the onset of tolerance. At lower levels the consumer may or may not obtain the same effects as before. In the right-hand diagram, corresponding to (b), the consumer obtains less pleasure from any given level of intake (at least at moderate levels) and possibly maximal pleasure at a higher level of intake than before the onset of tolerance (although the latter is not explicitly stated in DSM-IV). Tolerance is present if either of these changes is observed.

Withdrawal occurs when blood or tissue concentrations of a substance decline after prolonged heavy use. This generates substance-specific physiological, as well as cognitive and behavioral, symptoms: "distress or impairment in social, occupational or other important areas of functioning" (185). Continued intake of the same (or a closely related) substance relieves withdrawal symptoms.

The remaining five items are said to describe "the pattern of compulsive substance use that is characteristic of Dependence" (178). However, whereas this is true for the third and the fourth items, the last three items describe consequences of prolonged heavy use which do not in themselves have to imply "compulsion" or "enslavement."

The third criterion describes a type of akrasia, or weakness of the will: "the sub-

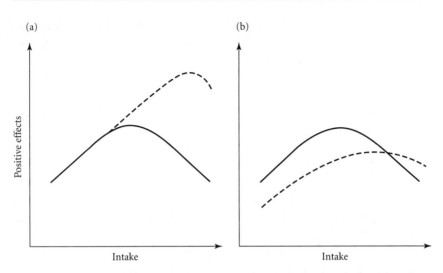

**Figure 5.1**  Effect of different levels of intake before (solid line) and after (dotted line) onset of tolerance, according to the two different mechanisms mentioned in DSM-IV

stance is often taken in larger amounts or over a longer period than was intended" (181). The agent is in effect dynamically inconsistent, being unable to hold on to his or her plan. In the classical alcoholism literature, this was conceived as a physiological effect of the first drink, causing "loss of control" in the alcohol-dependent person (e.g., Jellinek 1960). Experimental evidence, using placebo designs, later demonstrated that the mechanism was of a more psychological nature: drinking alcohol, without knowing it, did not necessarily cause loss of control, whereas (mistakenly) believing that one had consumed alcohol could trigger such symptoms (Marlatt, Demming, and Reid 1973).

What is actually observed in so-called loss of control is that the consumers intend to act in a certain way prior to the consumption event but change their mind after consuming a few units. This might be explained by substance-related physiological and/or psychological cues (Drummon 2000, 2001), visceral motives (Loewenstein 1999), or hyperbolic discounting (Ainslie 1992, 1999). In either case, the observation does not imply that the agents are unable to control their own behavior, only that something has made them change their mind.

The fourth criterion describes ambivalence and motivational conflict: "there is a persistent desire or unsuccessful efforts to cut down or control substance abuse" (181). Addictive substances have both good and bad effects, and these effects generate simultaneous motives for both indulging and abstaining—the former typically being the strongest among active addicts. However, the relative strength of these motives typically varies over time, producing an intermittent consumption pattern. Periods of heavy use are followed by periods of abstention or more controlled use, only to be succeeded by relapse to heavy use again, and so it continues.

The last three criteria are of a different nature. Whereas akrasia and ambivalence refer to cognitive inconsistencies within the agent, the last three criteria describe matter-of-fact consequences of long-term heavy consumption. The fifth criterion says that "a great deal of time is spent in activities necessary to obtain the substance . . . , use the substance . . . , or recover from its effects." The sixth criterion is that "important social, occupational, or recreational activities are given up or reduced because of substance use"; and the last, that "the substance use is continued despite knowledge of having a persistent or recurrent physical or psychological problem that is likely to have been caused or exacerbated by the substance" (181).

The fact that substance use has become time-consuming, displacing other activities and giving rise to recognized harmful effects, will typically be interpreted by bystanders as a sign that something is wrong with this person. However, these consequences may or may not be conceived as unacceptable by the consumer. If they are unacceptable, these consequences will be part of the motivational foundation of akrasia and ambivalence. If they are not, the agent is simply a person who accepts these effects and is willing to pay this price for substance use. For instance, the individual may feel that life is a misery anyway but that it becomes less intolerable with the substance, even if there is a price to pay. A significant change that gave the person's life new meaning (say, a religious rebirth) might bring the abuse to an end without much difficulty. Hence, the last three items need not signify a pattern of compulsive substance use. They could simply be signs of "perverted" preferences, violating extant social norms.

According to DSM-IV, neither tolerance nor withdrawal is necessary or sufficient for dependence. Some individuals "show a pattern of compulsive use without any signs of tolerance or withdrawal. Conversely, some postsurgical patients without Opioid Dependence may develop a tolerance to prescribed opioids and experience withdrawal symptoms without showing any signs of compulsive use" (178).

One could ask if there are any symptoms that should be considered necessary for addiction. A fairly obvious answer is that an addicted person is always characterized by a strong appetite for the substance in question. As noted in DSM-IV, "Although not specifically listed as a criterion item, craving (a strong subjective drive to use the substance) is likely to be experienced by most (if not all) individuals with Substance Dependence" (176). However, having a strong appetite is clearly not sufficient for addiction. A dedicated collector of stamps or antiques may have a very strong subjective taste for her favorite items and spend a lot of time on this activity, even to such an extent that it interferes with her social life. People around her may find her interest rather absurd and think that she spends too much time and money on it. Still, this does not mean that she is addicted. If the circumstances demanded it, she might be both able and willing to cut back; but as long as the circumstances do not demand it, she has no real motive for cutting back.

Heather (1998) has argued that criterion four is a sine qua non of addiction, claiming that the agent's struggle to escape enslavement to a behavior is what sets addiction apart from an ordinary behavior, governed by light or strong appetites. A person who consumes heavily, who has developed tolerance and withdrawal, and who is experiencing health problems due to substance use, would, according to this view, not be conceived as an addict unless there is also a struggle. In Heather's terminology, the no-struggle individuals are simply heavy (excessive) users who prefer to continue doing what they do, even if they have to pay a certain price in the form of health problems.

The struggle is generated by motivational conflict, that is, a combination of a strong appetite and good reasons for abstaining or cutting back. Typical reasons are exemplified by the last three items on the DSM-IV list (too time-consuming, negative consequences for social life, and negative consequences for health). The existence of a struggle clearly signifies the "pattern of compulsive substance use that is characteristic of Dependence" (DSM-IV, 176). However, one could argue that even though the struggle is sufficient, it is not a necessary criterion.

Whether or not a person is struggling to escape enslavement is very much dependent on the circumstances and context. For instance, a person who does not wish to quit consuming drug X under the prevailing circumstances, and who makes no attempt, could both find it difficult to refrain and experience repeated failures if the situation changes. Imagine the same person in two different contexts. In context A, his spouse (reluctantly) accepts his excessive X-ing, it does not destroy the family economy, and users are not stigmatized. He is not struggling to get out of his habit. Then the context changes to B. Users are stigmatized, the prices go up to such an extent that he can no longer deal with his financial obligations, and his wife threatens to leave him. Now he struggles to end his abuse. The person is the same, and only the socioeconomic context has changed. It hardly makes sense to say that this person was addicted under B but not under A. The concept of addiction refers to a state that the person is in. It is not a concept that refers only to events—events of addictive behavior. A person who is in a state of addiction may, under certain circumstances, exhibit addictive behavior (that is, events), whereas the same individual may fail to exhibit this behavior under other circumstances.[1] Consequently, displaying addictive behavior (that is, struggling) cannot be a necessary criterion.

Nevertheless, one could argue that the struggle to control substance use captures an essential aspect of addiction, namely, enslavement, and that it should be incorporated in the definition somehow. The right way of doing this is in the form of a counterfactual conditional. Hence, one could say that a person is addicted if this person has demonstrated failure to refrain, despite having attempted to do so, or would have demonstrated such failures under different environmental conditions. Whether or not the last three symptoms on the DSM-IV list are present obviously depends on the circumstances, and if the circumstances do not at present enforce these symptoms on the addicted person, the person is not motivated to quit. If the circumstances change and these problems are experienced, the person may attempt to refrain and experience great difficulty.

Consider someone who smoked in the 1950s. She developed a strong appetite for cigarettes but did not know that they caused substantial health problems. Therefore, she had no strong motive for quitting. On some occasions she had been forced by the circumstances to abstain (for instance, she had been without tobacco for a while on a camping trip), and she knew that abstention was very unpleasant. Hence, she recognized that she was enslaved but found this unproblematic as long as there were no serious side effects. Undoubtedly, the "pattern of compulsive substance use that is characteristic of dependence" was present, and she was clearly in an addictive state. The absence of a struggle simply signifies that the countermotives were not very strong because of the prevailing circumstances: she did not know the health risks (nor did anyone else, at least not for certain), the social costs were small and acceptable, and the time spent on tobacco-related activities was not unusual. A few years later, this person had good reasons for believing that smoking causes severe health problems and had become motivated to quit. However, she may have found it very difficult and may have relapsed several times, thus fulfilling criterion four.

In sum, there seem to be two factual criteria and one counterfactual criterion for addiction: First, the agent has developed a very strong appetite for the substance. Second, the agent finds it very unpleasant to abstain. Third, if the agent had very strong motives for discontinuing the habit, the person would have to struggle hard and experience great difficulty.

Some consumers may fulfill the DSM-IV criterion for substance dependence without satisfying the criterion outlined here. Typical cases may be consumers who are using the substance as a kind of self-medication for different types of problems. If their underlying problem disappears (for example, the case of religious rebirth mentioned earlier), they might be able to stop without too much difficulty. Perhaps these self-medicating consumers should not be called addicts, but something else—for instance, (symptomatic) heavy consumers. They are obviously not enslaved in the same sense as the addicts fulfilling the criteria outlined previously.

## 5.2 RATIONAL ADDICTION?

Granted that addicts are in fact choosing to do what they are doing, the next question is whether these choices are rational. Can addictive behaviors be understood within the framework of standard rational choice theory? According to Becker and coworkers (Becker 1992; Becker, Grossman, and Murphy 1992; Becker and Murphy 1988), the answer is affirmative. They assume that addicts have consistent preferences, that they act according to these preferences, that they are informed about the future consequences of their behavior, and that they take these consequences into consideration. It is also assumed that the agents always do what is best for them, all things considered and given their own subjective tastes; that they have stable preferences; and that they are dynamically consistent—that is, not suffering from akrasia or weakness of the will. Or in their own words: "we claim that addictions, even strong ones, are usually rational in the sense of involving forward-looking maximization with stable preferences" (Becker and Murphy 1988, 675).

In this theory, addiction is conceived as a kind of habit formation. Present utility is affected by past consumption. Addictive commodities are assumed to have two properties that set them apart from normal commodities. First, high consumption in the past reduces the utility of present consumption. Second, the marginal utility of present consumption increases with past consumption (see Figure 5.2). Both assumptions are realistic. The first is supported by tolerance, but also by delayed harmful effects of past consumption. The second implies that reduced utility caused by past consumption can be compensated by increasing present consumption, at least to some extent. Relief of withdrawal symptoms is of this type and, in general, any suppression of pains caused by past consumption, including the recognition that one has ruined one's life.

It can be demonstrated that the theory predicts two types of heavy consumption (Skog 1999a). Type I are consumers who are only weakly motivated by future consequences. They are not motivated to constrain their consumption. They are heavy consumers simply because they like it (for example, symptomatic heavy consumption), and they do not care much about the long-term problems. If they were somehow forced by the circumstances to refrain from their substance for a while, they would immediately relapse when the circumstances allowed. Type II are more future oriented. They have been trapped at a level of welfare they realize is sub-

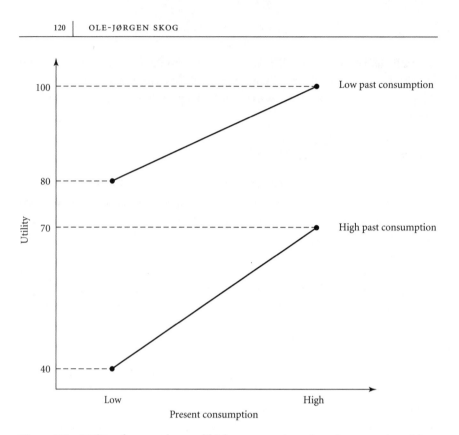

**Figure 5.2** Utility of present low and high consumption when the person has either had a low or high consumption in the past

optimal. If forced to refrain for a while, they would not relapse. However, as long as they are in the high-consumption mode, they are unwilling to cut back. They realize that life would improve in the long run, but only at the price of a temporary setback. And although they are to some extent motivated by future improvements, this motivation is insufficient.

The Type I consumer resembles the heavy consumer (addict?) in Herrnstein and Prelec's primrose path theory. The latter is unaware of the fact that present high consumption decreases the utility of both future consumption and the alternatives to consumption and is in effect following a path of ignorance to heavy and harmful intake (Herrnstein and Prelec 1992). In Becker's theory the consequences are the same, the difference being that the agent knows this to be the case but is not sufficiently motivated by these negative consequences.

Because Type II is the most interesting case, I shall concentrate on this type, as Becker does. First, it should be noted that the original theory is incomplete because it does not offer a satisfactory explanation of how a rational person ends up in the suboptimal state. A rational person of Type II would never start a consumption career that ended in heavy consumption. Becker and Murphy suggest that some exogenous shock (a life crisis) might be responsible but do not explicitly model the entry process. However, life crises would clearly not be an empirically realistic explanation of entry in most cases of addiction. Orphanides and Zervos (1995) have developed the theory a step further by assuming that the rational Type II agent takes a calculated risk. This theory offers at least a formal solution to the entry problem.

However, the whole idea that addicts can be conceived as fully rational, forward-looking utility maximizers with stable preferences is unrealistic. Such agents always do what is best according to their own utility calculus. They have no motive for changing their consumption behavior and should not struggle to cut back. If they think it is best to cut back, they will cut back. And if they do not, they will simply continue. There is no room for ambivalence and struggling with oneself in standard rational choice theory. Yet, the very idea of addiction is intimately tied to these concepts.

In particular, Becker's theory has no room for typical addiction-related phenomena such as repeated remission and relapse. Within the logic of this theory, these phenomena can only occur in response to exogenous shocks. Hence, Becker needs to postulate shocks both to bring the agent into the state of addiction in the first place and to bring about successive stages of remission and relapse. In effect, these phenomena are not integral parts of the theory.

Orphanides and Zervos's modified version faces the same problem. In this model, consumers are supposed to be of two types—vulnerable or not vulnerable. The consumers are assumed not to know initially which type they are. If consumers decide to experiment, they may at some stage realize that they are vulnerable, but it is too late and they end up in a high-consumption state. If, however, such an agent should somehow manage to quit (say, due to external pressure), there would be no second gamble. A rational agent cannot be naive more than once, and relapse should not occur.

The fact that standard rational choice theory is unable to elucidate and explain essential aspects of the phenomenon of addiction may be taken to suggest that these phenomena are driven by nonrational mechanisms, or at least by mechanisms that fall outside the rigid frames of standard theory (that is, rational choice plus stable preferences). Imperfections and irrationalities in information processing are quite obvious mechanisms, as is dynamic inconsistency. I shall briefly review some arguments and evidence regarding the first and will then pursue the second at some length.

Becker and Murphy, as well as Orphanides and Zervos, assume that the rational agent makes a choice on the basis of realistic information about the possible effects of consumption choices. In particular, they assume that the inexperienced agent actually knows how an addictive craving will be experienced and how unpleasant the harmful consequences of excessive use will be. This is obviously unrealistic. As Walt Whitman has put it, "None know—none can know, but they who have felt it—the burning, withering thirst for drink, which habit forms in the appetite of the wretched victim of intoxication" (1842/1929, 148).

The problem an inexperienced person will have in understanding in advance how enslavement feels and, more generally, in understanding how it feels to be a person with different preferences compared to the preferences one actually has at present, is only one side of the issue. Another side is the problem of retaining a fresh and realistic memory of strong motives actually experienced in the past. Loewenstein (1999) has argued that people in general tend to have a biased memory of visceral motives, typically underestimating their strength. If this is correct, it would be quite difficult for a person with strong outbursts of visceral motives to plan ahead, for instance, by setting up realistic defense strategies to avoid giving in to these outbursts.

Furthermore, people in general seem to be the victims of numerous mistakes in belief formation (Kahneman and Tversky 2000). In relation to addictive substances, it has been observed that smokers believe that the risk of lung cancer is lower than nonsmokers believe (Viscusi 1992). (However, both tend to overestimate the actual risk.) This may be due to a selection mechanism, as those who have low estimates are more likely to start smoking, or to a cognitive dissonance (a self-service bias of the type "since I smoke, it cannot be very dangerous"), or both. More direct evidence regarding self-serving bias has been reported by McKenna (1990), demonstrating that individual smokers tend to believe that they are less likely than the average smoker to suffer health problems as a result of smoking.

Studies of compulsive gamblers have also uncovered irrational belief formation. In games where there is a 50 percent chance of winning, some gamblers believe that after a run of five or six losses, the likelihood of winning has increased. Others make the opposite mistake and believe that the likelihood of winning has gone down (Wagenaar 1988). Another mechanism is driven by the "psychology of a near win." Even in games of pure chance, gamblers interpret outcomes similar to the one they had bet on as confirmation that they were on to something (Wagenaar 1988). The tendency to transform losses into "near wins" obviously can produce very biased expectations. A further indication that gamblers are victims of irrational beliefs is, as Elster (1999) notes, the very existence of the *Monte Carlo Revue Scientifique*, which logs successive outcomes at roulette.

In some respects, addicts seem to be slow learners. After several relapses, agents ought to understand that certain social situations are dangerous, that one or two drinks tend to trigger further drinking, and that in certain mental states they are vulnerable to temptations. If fully rational, they should try to avoid these situations and to abstain from the first two drinks. However, addicts who fulfill DSM-IV's third criterion are obviously unable to understand their own pattern. In fact, teaching addicts to monitor and understand what triggers their own substance consumption is an important part of many treatment programs. However, the limited success of treatment bears witness to how difficult this learning process can be.

Besides being unable to learn from past experiences, addicts may suffer from other types of irrationality as well—for instance, wishful thinking, denial, and an inability to anticipate their own future motivational states. Denial is a phenomenon that addiction therapists frequently encounter. Griffith Edwards gives the following case abstract:

> A 50-year-old accountant was brought along to a psychiatric clinic by his partner, who said that unless something was done his colleague would have to be pensioned off. The patient's breath smelled heavily of drink, his liver was mildly enlarged and he had bruises from several recent falls. He charmingly acknowledged his gratitude to the partner for taking this trouble, but said that the poor man was overworked, worried and getting things out of proportion. The patient admitted to having an occasional beer at lunch-time, but that was the limit of his drinking. He was then seen again with his wife, who said that he was permanently intoxicated, that he was frequently incontinent, that he had recently fallen down stairs when drunk and that empty bottles were falling out of every cupboard. He said that his wife was a dear woman but a terrible worrier, that of course he was often tired at the end of the day (who wasn't?), and that as for falling down those steps there had been a loose stair rod. (1987, 345)

Although in pure form, denial is pictured as operating at a subconscious level, it is sometimes difficult to know the extent to which addicts are only trying to manipulate others and to which they also manipulate themselves. However, the client exemplified by Edwards would hardly pass the test of rationality, whether he believes his own interpretation or not. If he believes it himself, he is a victim of irrational belief formation; and if he does not, his beliefs about other agents' rationality are irrational.

Denial can be conceived as a type of wishful thinking. Externalization of the locus of control is another type. Addicts often claim that they are not fully responsible for their own actions. They claim that under certain circumstances they cannot help consuming their substance of choice, because they are sick. They are in effect using the sick role as an "excuse"—an unintended side effect of conceiving addiction as a disease, as it were. They obviously wish to continue consuming their substance of abuse and, believing—or pretending to believe—that they have lost the capacity for self-control, suit these preferences. Once again, if they actually believe that this is the case, they are victims of irrational belief formation; and if they do not, their beliefs about other people's rationality are irrational.

In conclusion, although it seems clear that addicts are in fact capable of choosing, it is equally clear that they are typically less than fully rational. They often fall victim to irrational belief formation, and the capacity for learning from past experiences is limited—at least with respect to the effects and consequences of substance abuse.

## 5.3 ADDICTION AND HYPERBOLIC DISCOUNTING

The clinical addict's struggle to curtail his or her habit is often characterized by intermittent periods of abstention or moderate consumption followed by periods of relapse to the old pattern of abuse. Clearly, this state is not one with a fixed balance between the agent's pro and con motives. The balance fluctuates over time, and sometimes abstention motives have the upper hand, whereas consumption motives are dominant in other periods.

An interpretation of this pattern has been suggested by George Ainslie (1975, 1992, 1999). He claims that people (and animals) are hardwired to discount the future hyperbolically, as opposed to the exponential discounting assumed in standard theory. Whereas exponential discounting implies that people never give in to temptations, hyperbolic discounting implies the opposite. Typically, in the choice between a smaller, earlier reward A and a larger, delayed reward B, the exponential discounter would consistently prefer one or the other and would not change her mind as the actual time of choice came closer. A hyperbolic discounter would behave differently (see Figure 5.3, left-hand diagram). Well in advance of the moment of choice ($t_1$), the agent might find it best to wait for the larger, delayed reward B (her valuation curve for B is higher than the one for A). However, shortly before the moment of choice, the curves intersect, and during the interval $t_0$ to $t_1$ she thinks that A is the better alternative. In effect, she tends to give in to temptations. Hyperbolic discounting therefore predicts temporary preferences.

The same mechanism applies when the agent is choosing between abstention and consumption, where consumption is followed by a delayed, unpleasant side effect (Figure 5.3, right-hand diagram). Prior to $t_0$ the agent thinks that the unpleasant side effect B is larger than the pleasure of consuming A. However, when the reward A is very close, that is, during the time interval $t_0$ to $t_1$, the valuation is

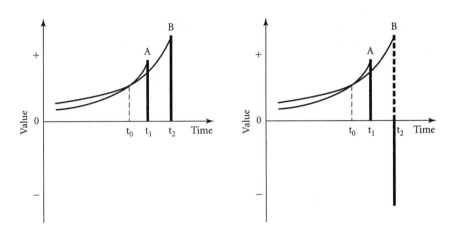

**Figure 5.3**    Hyperbolic discounting of future rewards. The curves describe the sub-
                jective, discounted values of the rewards at different points in time. At
                left, A is an earlier, smaller reward, whereas B is a delayed, larger reward.
                The agent must choose between them. At right, A is an earlier reward,
                followed by a delayed punishment B, which is larger than A. (The
                broken bar is a mirror image of B, inserted for ease of comparison.)

reversed. During this phase she is discounting the future side effects so much that
they do not match up with the instantaneous reward A, and the temptation becomes "irresistible." Hyperbolic discounting does in effect predict relapse.

Hyperbolic discounting is predicted by Herrnstein's matching law (Herrnstein
1961). Experimental evidence, both with animals and humans, confirms that hyperbolic discounting is the normal state of affairs (Mazur 1987). In particular,
Vuchinich and Simpson (1998) have demonstrated that in the case of heavy social
drinkers and problem drinkers, a hyperbolic function describes temporal discounting more accurately than an exponential function does.

An agent who is struggling to overcome addiction is in effect engaged in a battle
between his own long-term and short-term motives. At a distance, he is firmly determined not to consume the drug again, but when the opportunity is near, he
changes his mind. The agent could obtain self-control by setting up a causal mechanism that will prevent him from choosing A at $t_0$ (self-binding, or the Ulysses
strategy).[2] Furthermore, the agent could use a bundling strategy, or personal rules
(Ainslie 1992). The agent realizes that he will be faced with many similar choices
(for example, many drinks or cigarettes) in the future and that he will have no reason to believe that he will be able to resist the temptation in the future if he is unable to resist this time. This changes his mental bookkeeping from many single
events into one series of identical choices, where the alternatives are "always A"

and "always B." Ainslie demonstrates that this change may be sufficient to motivate the agent to overcome the temptation and to wait for the larger, delayed reward. Whether or not these strategies will work in real life depends on, among other things, the person's willpower—the ability to be motivated by distant choices of the same kind.

Ainslie's analyses are mainly concerned with simple choices between an early, smaller reward and a delayed, larger reward. If the agent's willpower is strong enough (that is, if he bundles a sufficiently large number of similar choices), he will be able to resist the temptation, and in the opposite case he will not.

However, addictive substances pose the agent with more complex choices, the structure of which was described in Figure 5.2. The present choice has consequences for present utility, but it also affects the utility obtained from similar choices in the future. An analysis of hyperbolic discounting of this kind of choice problem uncovers a more complex pattern (Skog 1999b). First, there is an asymmetry between addicted states and nonaddicted states. A given person, with a certain level of willpower, may be able to resist the temptation of reentering a high-consumption mode if her present state is abstention or low-consumption. However, if this person is presently in the high-consumption mode, the same level of willpower could be insufficient for resisting the temptation of continued high consumption. (The same asymmetry is predicted by Becker's theory.) Hence, in the case of complex choices, whether or not any given level of willpower will be sufficient to resist temptation is state dependent.

Second, well in advance of the time of choice, the agent may feel confident that she will be able to resist the temptation. She takes a large number of future choices into consideration and evaluates future abstention (or low consumption) higher than future high consumption. However, even if the level of willpower remains unchanged, she may find that her firm intention deteriorates when approaching the actual time of choice. Hence, the dynamic inconsistency problem that is associated with hyperbolic discounting does not completely disappear in an agent who has developed personal rules—it reappears at a higher level.

These phenomena are illustrated in Figure 5.4, which describes how hyperbolic discounters with personal rules evaluate the choice outlined in Figure 5.2 at different points in time prior to the actual time of choice. Their willpower is measured by the number of similar choices in the future that motivate them (that is, their motivational horizon). One can determine how an individual with a fixed level of willpower (say, 10) will change his evaluation over time by following a horizontal line at that level. Well in advance (prior to time 1) he unconditionally evaluates low consumption as the best alternative. If he is currently in the low-consumption

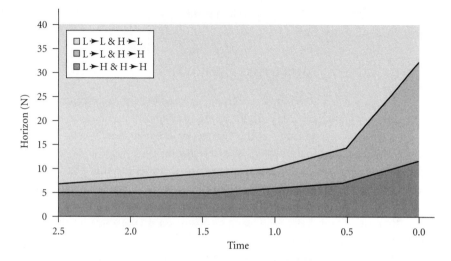

**Figure 5.4**   Preference structures for people with different horizons (willpower) at different times prior to the time of choice. The symbols are read as follows: In region L → L and H → L, an agent in the low-consumption mode (L) will remain in L, and a person in the high-consumption mode (H) will switch to L, and so on.

mode, he plans to continue with low consumption (L → L), and if currently in the high-consumption mode, he intends to switch to low consumption (H → L). However, when he has moved closer to the time of choice (after time 1), his evaluation has changed. If currently in the high-consumption mode, he evaluates continued high consumption as better (H → H), and if in the low-consumption mode, he will still think that continued low consumption is better (L → L). Finally, at the very moment of choice (time 0), his evaluation changes again, and now he evaluates heavy consumption as the better option, even if he is currently in the low-consumption mode (L → H).

Consequently, personal rules do not offer a simple once-and-for-all solution to the problems of akrasia. Even if agents stick to their rules, they face problems. In complex decision problems of the addiction type, agents may firmly believe that they are ahead of the problem, only to find that defenses evaporate at the critical moment. Furthermore, the very existence of personal rules is threatened from within. Agents who see "always abstain" as better than "always indulge" typically will find "indulge now and abstain in the future" the better option. The long-term motivation is therefore constantly threatened by short-term motives, and they are tempted to define the imminent choice as an exception to their personal rule—

"I can smoke today—but just today—because this is my birthday" or "because we have friends to dinner," and so on. Consequently, relapses are to be expected.

## 5.4 THE LIMITATIONS OF HYPERBOLIC DISCOUNTING

Consider a severely addicted smoker who has reached the stage of seriously struggling to end her habit. She has read a lot about quitting, has attended a class about how to quit smoking, and during the last few days has gradually reduced consumption of cigarettes. In the evening she feels that the time is ripe and goes to bed with the firm intention of not smoking tomorrow. Sometime after breakfast the next day she lights a cigarette. This story fits the hyperbolic discounting theory. In the evening, the next morning was far away and the value of smoking less than the larger, but more remote benefits of being a nonsmoker. In the morning, the temptation had moved much closer.

However, although hyperbolic discounting could underlie certain types of dynamic inconsistency, it cannot explain all temporary preferences. Many cases of temporary preferences must be explained by something else. In fact, hyperbolic discounting is a potential mechanism only in decision problems with a fixed temporal structure. Many everyday decision problems do not have this structure.

The observational and experimental evidence for hyperbolic discounting refers to situations where the time distances are outside the agent's personal control. Not only is the extra delay of the large reward B (compared to the small reward A) outside the agent's control—even the location on the time axis is outside the agent's control. Although certain choices—in particular, some economic choices—do in fact have the structure outlined in Figure 5.3, with strict environmental confinements (for example, a bank or an employer) defining the agent's location on the time axis, this is *not* so in relation to many personal choices. In these cases it is up to the agent to decide if the next event A is now, in ten minutes, in one hour, tomorrow, or whenever. And if the decision is made now, to the effect that the next event is in five hours, there is nothing to prevent the agent from deciding ten minutes later that the next event is now. Hence, the temporal structure of personal decision problems is often not well defined.

In the context of decision problems that are not temporally well defined, if the agent on some occasions feels that it is best to abstain and makes the reverse judgment on other occasions, the explanation for the difference cannot be closeness to the time of choice. Other factors must explain the difference. An obvious explanation would be all kinds of fluctuations in the person's motivations. These fluctuations could be due to identifiable environmental stimuli, or they could be related to the agent's physical, cognitive, or emotional state. Certain cues—external or internal—may trigger the appetite for drugs, whereas other cues may trigger the appetite for abstention. Sometimes the first could be dominant; at other times, the latter.

Therefore, explaining the temporary preferences of everyday personal habits by hyperbolic discounting is to put the cart before the horse. When the agent's appetite for the drug is small compared to the motives for abstention, it is easy to decide—and to hold on to this decision—that the next event is remote. When the appetite is strong, the agent may be strongly motivated to decide that the next event is imminent. Consequently, under these circumstances it is the appetite that determines the time distance, and not vice versa.

Below are two addiction examples that clearly cannot be explained by hyperbolic discounting. The first has been described by Thomas Schelling:

> A man gave up smoking three months ago. For the first six or eight weeks he was regularly tormented by a desire not to smoke, but the last three or four weeks have been less uncomfortable and he is becoming optimistic that he has left cigarettes behind him for good. One afternoon a friend drops in for a business chat. The business done, our reformed smoker sees his friend to the door; returning to the living room, he finds, on the coffee table, an opened pack of cigarettes. He snatches up the pack and hurries to the door, only to see his friend's car disappear around the corner. As he will see his friend in the morning and can return the cigarettes, he puts the pack in his jacket pocket and hangs the jacket in the closet. He settles in front of the television with a before-dinner drink to watch network news. Twenty minutes into the news, he walks to the closet where his jacket hangs and takes the cigarettes out of the pocket, studies the pack for a minute, and walks into the bathroom, where he empties the cigarettes into the toilet and flushes it. He returns to his drink and his news. (1999, 265).

Obviously, this reformed smoker does not wish to smoke now, and neither does he wish to smoke later in the evening. Presumably, his present self wishes to prevent his own future self from smoking. Schelling offers a series of different interpretations of what is going on in this example. In most of Schelling's cases, the agent believes that his own valuation may change later in the evening, say, because he knows that he is tempted to smoke after having consumed alcohol, or because the presence of cigarettes tends to trigger craving, or because he always craves cigarettes in the evening, and he is not certain that he will be able to resist the temptation with cigarettes easily available. Whatever the concrete mechanism, there is a change in the agent's preferences, caused by external cues, his own actions, or internal changes in his emotional and cognitive state. This change could take the form of an increased appetite for cigarettes, weakened motives for abstention, and/or changes in his time preferences. Any one of these changes could bring about a change in his future self's choice, and he prevents this by getting rid of the cigarettes—to the satisfaction of his present self, but perhaps to the despair of his future self.

In his "Confessions of an English Opium-Eater," Thomas De Quincey tells the following story, illuminating a similar constraint on one's own future behavior, but this time putting the future self in focus:

[H]e went so far as to hire men—porters, hackney-coachmen, and others—to oppose by force his entrance into any druggist's shop. But, as the authority for stopping him was derived simply from himself, naturally these poor men found themselves in a metaphysical fix, not provided for even by Thomas Aquinas or by the prince of Jesuitical casuists. And in this excruciating dilemma would occur such scenes as the following:

"Oh, sir," would plead the suppliant porter—suppliant, yet semi-imperative (for equally if he did, and if he did not, show fight, the poor man's daily 5s. seemed endangered)—"really you must not; consider, sir, your wife and—"

*Transcendental Philosopher*—"Wife! what wife? I have no wife."

*Porter*—"But, really now, you must not, sir. Didn't you say no longer ago than yesterday—"

*Transcendental Philosopher*—"Pooh, pooh! yesterday is a long time ago. Are you aware, my man, that people are known to have dropped down dead for timely want of opium?"

*Porter*—"Ay, but you tell't me not to hearken—"

*Transcendental Philosopher*—"Oh, nonsense. An emergency, a shocking emergency, has arisen—quite unlooked for. No matter what I told you in times long past. That which I now tell you, is—that, if you don't remove that arm of yours from the doorway of this most respectable druggist, I shall have a good ground of action against you for assault and battery." (1821/1994, 22–23)

The transcendental philosopher's preferences obviously had changed quite a lot because of the alleged "emergency." Whether or not this emergency actually was "quite unlooked for" is difficult to know for sure, but one might suspect that it was not. Exactly what caused the change remains hidden in De Quincey's text. However, it should be clear that neither De Quincey's nor Schelling's cases can be understood as results of hyperbolic discounting, because the time of the (anticipated) consumption event was not fixed but chosen by the agent himself.

In conclusion, hyperbolic discounting cannot be the only mechanism underlying temporary preferences. There must be other and, perhaps even more important, mechanisms. The main mechanism could be that preferences are simply not stable over time but fluctuate. These fluctuations might be the direct result of environmental stimuli, as when someone suddenly experiences a strong appetite for ice cream when she sees it. Or they could be due to changes in the agent's internal state, as when he becomes desperate because of enduring social isolation. Both types could create dynamic inconsistencies.

## 5.5 FLUCTUATIONS IN PREFERENCES

Instabilities in preferences (including time preferences)—triggered either by external stimuli or the agent's internal state—would have at least two effects. First, the agent would sometimes choose to consume and at other times choose to abstain. Relapse and remission would occur, depending on the circumstances. Second, whatever the source of these fluctuations, the agent will gradually understand her own inclination and, after having accumulated sufficient experience, may be expected to develop strategies to control her future self. When she is in preference mode A, she may wish to prevent her future self from acting in certain ways while being in another mode, B. Of course, this could work both ways, and in mode B the person may try to prevent herself from binding herself when returning to mode A. However, in practice there will often be an asymmetry between modes (Skog 1997).

As a first example, let us look at instabilities in appetites. Consider Becker's consumer, faced with the binary consumption choice in Figure 5.2, and let us assume that he is an exponential discounter with a discount factor equal to 0.7. If he is currently in the high-consumption mode, he will continue to consume heavily. If he is in the abstention mode, he will abstain (see Skog 1999a). Assume that he is currently in the latter mode. If his appetite increases, the utility of consumption may increase from 100 to 102. If he believes that the increased value of consumption will prevail even in the future (that is, that the utility of consumption when he has consumed much in the past has also increased by two utils, from 70 to 72), he will start to consume heavily. And when his appetite at some later stage returns to "normal," he is trapped at a high level. However, if he knows from past experience that this sudden increase in appetite is only temporary, he may be able to resist the temptation. A larger increase in his appetite (say, to 105 utils) could be "irresistible," however, even if he knows that it is only a temporary vacillation.

Moreover, knowing that he occasionally experiences sprees of irresistible appetites, the agent in the abstention mode will try to prevent his future self from giving in to these temptations. He will act according to his present valuation, not respecting the valuation of his alter ego (see Skog 2001). By setting up the appropriate causal machinery, the abstinent self may increase the costs of heavy consumption for his future self. In the context of addiction, taking disulfiram (trade name Antabuse) is a highly relevant example. Antabuse produces painful toxic effects if the agent consumes alcohol. It is taken on a daily basis, and its effect lasts for a day or two. Thus, the agent will have to plan ahead a couple of days if he wishes to consume alcohol. This will sometimes give him the time needed to reconsider.

As a second example of unstable preferences, let us consider time discounting. Sometimes people are strongly motivated by future rewards and punishments. At other times they are much less motivated by remote consequences. These things vary, and people are not always equally patient and concerned about their future. What I have in mind are not systematic changes over the life cycle nor systematic changes as one approaches the moment of choice (hyperbolic discounting), but more erratic variations. As in the case of fluctuations in appetites, these may be triggered either by unforeseen environmental changes, or they may be a kind of endogenous noise.

Fluctuations in people's discount functions would create phenomena quite similar to those generated by fluctuations in appetites (see Skog 1997 for a detailed analysis). If the reformed addict should experience a sudden myopia, future problems would no longer have the same motivational power, and she may relapse. And if she is already on a heavy spree, an increase in concern for her own future may be enough to bring her out of the high-consumption mode. If she were of Type II in the aforementioned typology, she would not immediately relapse when her discount rate returned to normal. However, abstention (or low consumption) would not be a permanent state. At some later stage a fluctuation in the opposite direction (myopia) could bring about a new relapse. Hence, fluctuations in people's rate of discounting predict repeated patterns of remission and relapse.

Even fluctuations in time discounting would generate strategic battles within the person, such as those previously exemplified and similar to those analyzed by Ainslie in connection with hyperbolic discounting. For instance, when in the mode of patience, the agent will be motivated to prevent herself from doing stupid things when the next myopic mode arrives. She could do this by binding herself as Ulysses did (or the alcoholic on disulfiram) or with Ainslian personal rules. The recovering smoker may understand that it is not only a question of none versus one cigarette now. The choice is between none now and in the future, versus one now, another in an hour from now, and so on. This bunching of successive choices, based on the conviction that the agent's current choice is a precedent for future choices, can be sufficient for choosing abstention, both if the agent discounts the future hyperbolically and when the agent's discount function fluctuates (Skog 1997).

In conclusion, some sort of dynamic inconsistency would seem to be a necessary ingredient in any theory aimed at explaining the essential features of addiction. These dynamic inconsistencies would generate strategic battles within the person, of more or less the same type, whatever the actual source of the inconsistencies—be it hyperbolic discounting or fluctuations in appetites and time preferences. Given the limited validity of hyperbolic discounting, fluctuations would appear to be a worthwhile study object. So far, fluctuations have not been the subject of broad empirical studies, with the exception of fluctuations caused by environmental cues, but the issue deserves more attention in the future.

## 5.6 RESISTING TEMPTATIONS

The abundance of different precommitment strategies that people use to constrain their own future behavior is perhaps the best evidence that people occasionally experience (unwanted) changes in their own preferences. Why would a perfectly rational agent with stable preferences spend money on a piggy bank, later to be destroyed, unless he or she wishes to prevent becoming a victim of temporary changes in preferences?

The literature on self-control has largely been concerned with cognitive strategies of different sorts. Physically preventing oneself from giving in to temptations, such as Schelling's former smoker, is one example. Letting relapse have painful effects, as in the case of disulfiram, is another. Besides these self-binding strategies, Ainslie (1992) describes three soft techniques. In addition to personal rules, which have already been mentioned, agents may try to divert their own attention away from the temptation (attention control) or prepare their emotions—either negative emotions toward the tempting object or positive emotions toward the alternative.

All of these mechanisms are of the pull type. There is, however, also a push mechanism to be considered. Dynamic inconsistency, either due to hyperbolic discounting or to fluctuations in preferences, could be expected to generate its own countermeasures that might prevent the agent from giving in to temptations. The mechanism is anticipated regrets. Elsewhere, I have demonstrated that this mechanism could outbalance the temptation under certain circumstances (Skog 2003).

The argument is based on the fact that a person with unstable preferences who betrays his firm decision to abstain or to wait for a delayed large reward, and instead goes for the immediate, smaller reward, will regret his decision at some later stage. He could have obtained a larger reward and he intended to wait for it. Or he has broken his promise to abstain and now must suffer the negative consequences. When he has experienced this phenomenon a number of times and comes to understand his own weakness, he will automatically anticipate at the time of choice his own regret. Regrets are unpleasant, and anticipated regrets ought to have motivational power. When the agent knows in advance that he will regret a certain choice, he may be unable to ignore this fact at the time of choice. (It should be noted that this regret is asymmetrical, as opposed to the regrets of standard regret theory.)

The effect of anticipated regrets could be conceived as a reduction of the utility of the early, larger reward. The size of this reduction would depend on how vividly the agent imagines the future pain of regret and his rate of discounting of this pain. (Large inter-individual differences could exist in this respect, and this would obviously produce differences just as large in the ability to resist temptations.)

Cost in the form of anticipated regret may be large enough to prevent a dynamically inconsistent agent from giving in to short-term temptations. If the intensity of an agent's regret is modest, anticipation of regrets will obviously not be of widespread importance, as only agents with very small discount rates will refrain from choosing the earlier, small reward because of anticipated regrets. However, if the motivational power of regrets is substantial, even agents with a large discount rate may be able to refrain after having realized the consequences of their dynamic inconsistency. From an empirical point of view, the important question then becomes the following: How strong are people's regrets, and to what extent are they motivated by anticipated regrets in different life areas?

The importance of this regret mechanism would depend on what kind of choice problem one is facing. For many private economic choices, the loss is very concrete and well defined; strong emotions are not involved. Under these circumstances anticipated regrets may play an important role, ensuring that most agents do in fact behave as if they were dynamically consistent. In the case of strong appetites, such as addictions, gains and losses are more diffuse and harder to compare. For instance, aversive consequences of consumption are less certain, and their exact nature and intensity less predictable. Second, the agent's exact valuation of pleasures and pains is less rigid and more subjective, and possibly variable over time, depending on the agent's emotional state. Under these circumstances, the role played by anticipated regrets may be smaller. However, even in these cases one would expect that anticipated regrets might to some extent counteract temporary preferences.

In the case of addictive substances, the consumer will gradually experience the facts of life, and her valuation of the pains should gradually become more realistic. One would therefore expect that anticipated regrets become increasingly more important as the career develops, and at some stage the consumer's motivation may become strong enough for her to quit or cut back. For some time, the consumer may still be vulnerable to temporary fluctuations in appetite and to acute myopia, but after some time anticipated regrets may become strong enough to prevent these relapses. This mechanism therefore predicts that some addicts will cut back on their consumption, either gradually or more abruptly, and that relapse will tend to occur less often. The prediction corresponds well to empirical observations. Maturing out of addiction is a well-known phenomenon and frequently occurs without treatment (Orford 1985; Vaillant 1983). Some alcoholics stop rather abruptly, and others experience a gradual change from alcohol abuse to social drinking (Nordström and Berglund 1987).

## 5.7 CONCLUSION

Addiction is not simply a strong appetite. It is a strong appetite that continues to have a significant impact on the agents' behavior, even if the circumstances give them (according to their own evaluation) very good reasons for cutting back. This enslavement generates ambivalence, struggle, remission, and relapse.

These central features of addiction cannot be adequately dealt with by theories embedded within the framework of standard rational choice theory. First, there is every reason to think that irrational belief formation plays a central role in the addictions, thus violating the basic premise of rational choice theory. Second, standard theory is based on the assumption that the preferences remain stable. This assumption is clearly incompatible with the empirical facts of addiction. Instability of one sort or another is obviously needed in order to explain what is actually observed.

Hyperbolic discounting is an attractive theory of temporary preferences because they are generated by a systematic, simple, and empirically well supported mechanism. However, I have argued that hyperbolic discounting cannot explain many everyday instances of temporary preferences simply because they do not have the right temporal structure. Other mechanisms must be responsible for the temporary preferences often found in people's private lives.

What do I have to offer instead of hyperbolic discounting? Not much, if you are looking for a single, simple mechanism. My proposal is simply that we have to abandon the assumption of stable preferences in standard theory and admit that preferences fluctuate in response to all sorts of environmental cues, as well as in response to the agent's emotional set—which also fluctuates in ways we do not understand very well. The result is, of course, a less parsimonious theory but also a more realistic theory.

The stable preference assumption of standard theory causes no serious problems as long as one applies rational choice theory on phenomena where small changes in preferences produce only small changes in outcome. This is probably true for many economic phenomena. However, when one turns to nonlinear phenomena, one can no longer ignore instability of preferences. I submit that the addictions belong to the latter type. Instability is a hallmark of addiction, and small changes may sometimes produce dramatic effects.

Finally, a word about empirical tests. So far, empirical tests of the rational addiction theory have focused on the prediction that (anticipated) future price changes affect current consumption (Becker, Grossman, and Murphy 1994; Chaloupka 1991). However, this is not a proper test of this theory, as all theories that conceive addiction as volitional behavior by forward-looking agents predict the same phenomena. In particular, Gruber and Köszegi (2001) demonstrate that hyperbolic discounting has the same implication. In order to test the theory of rational addiction against these other choice theories, one needs to move beyond the econometrics of addictive substances.

## NOTES

1. A similar argument applies to allergies: A person who is allergic to a certain substance does not exhibit symptoms of allergy when not exposed to the substance, but we would nonetheless say that the person is allergic to this substance.

2. The agent may sometimes obtain the same effect simply by promising himself that he will invest in such mechanisms if he should give in to short-term temptations in the future (see Skog 1997).

REFERENCES

Ainslie, G. 1975. Specious rewards: A behavioral theory of impulsiveness and impulse control. *Psychological Bulletin* 82:463–96.
———. 1992. *Picoeconomics*. Cambridge: Cambridge University Press.
———. 1999. The dangers of willpower. In *Getting hooked: Rationality and addiction*, ed. J. Elster and O.-J. Skog, 65–92. Cambridge: Cambridge University Press.
American Psychiatric Association. 1994. *Diagnostic and statistical manual of mental disorders*. 4th ed. Washington DC: American Psychiatric Association.
Becker, G. 1992. Habits, addictions, and traditions. *Kyklos* 45:327–46.
Becker, G., M. Grossman, and K. Murphy. 1992. Rational addiction and the effect of price on consumption. In *Choice over time*, ed. G. Loewenstein and J. Elster, 361–70. New York: Russell Sage.
———. 1994. An empirical analysis of cigarette addiction. *American Economic Review* 84:396–418.
Becker, G., and K. Murphy. 1988. A theory of rational addiction. *Journal of Political Economy* 96:675–700.
Chaloupka, F. 1991. Rational addictive behavior and cigarette smoking. *Journal of Political Economy* 99:722–42.
De Quincey, T. 1821/1994. *Confessions of an English opium eater*. Repr. Hertfordshire, UK: Wordsworth Classics.
Drummon, C. 2000. What does cue reactivity have to offer clinical research? *Addiction* 95 (Suppl. 2): S129–44.
———. 2001. Theories of drug craving, ancient and modern. *Addiction* 96: 33–46.
Edwards, G. 1987. *The treatment of drinking problems*. New York: McGraw-Hill.
Elster, J. 1999. *Strong feelings*. Cambridge, MA: Harvard University Press.
Fingarette, H. 1988. *Heavy drinking: The myth of alcoholism as a disease*. Berkeley: University of California Press.
———. 1991. Alcoholism: The mythical disease. In *Society, culture, and drinking patterns reexamined*, ed. D. Pittman and H. White, 417–38. New Brunswick, NJ: Rutgers Center of Alcohol Studies.
Gruber, J., and B. Köszegi. 2001. Is addiction "rational"? Theory and evidence. *Quarterly Journal of Economics* 116:1261–1303.
Heather, N. 1998. A conceptual framework for explaining drug addiction. *Journal of Psychopharmacology* 12:3–7.
Heather, N., and I. Robertson. 1981. *Controlled drinking*. London: Methuen.

Herrnstein, R. 1961. Relative and absolute strengths of response as a function of frequency of reinforcement. *Journal of Experimental Analysis of Behavior* 4: 267–72.

Herrnstein, R., and D. Prelec. 1992. A theory of addiction. In *Choice over time*, ed. G. Loewenstein and J. Elster, 331–60. New York: Russell Sage.

Jellinek, E. 1960. *The disease concept of alcoholism.* New Brunswick, NJ: Hillhouse.

Kahneman, D., and A. Tversky. 2000. *Choices, values, and frames.* New York: Cambridge University Press/Russell Sage.

Levine, H. 1978 The discovery of addiction. *Journal of Studies on Alcohol* 39: 143–74.

Loewenstein, G. 1999. A visceral account of addiction. In *Getting hooked: Rationality and addiction,* ed. J. Elster and O.-J. Skog, 235–64. Cambridge: Cambridge University Press.

Marlatt, G., B. Demming, and J. Reid. 1973. Loss of control drinking in alcoholics: An experimental analogue. *Journal of Abnormal Psychology* 81:233–41.

Mazur, J. 1987. An adjusting procedure for studying delayed reinforcement. In *Quantitative analyses of behavior V: The effect of delay and of intervening events on reinforcement value,* ed. M. Commons, J. Mazur, J. Nevin, and H. Rachlin, 55–73. Hillsdale, NJ: Erlbaum.

McKenna, F. 1990. Heuristics or cognitive deficits: How should we characterize smoker's decision making? In *Addiction controversies,* ed. D. Warburton, 261–70. Chur, Switzerland: Harwood.

Mello, N., and J. Mendelson. 1965. Operant analysis of drinking patterns of chronic alcoholics. *Nature* 206:43–46.

———. 1966. Experimental analysis of drinking behavior of chronic alcoholics. *Annals of New York Academy of Sciences* 133:828–45.

———. 1972. Drinking patterns during work contingent and non-contingent alcohol acquisition. *Psychosomatic Medicine* 34:139–64.

Nordström, G., and M. Berglund. 1987. A prospective-study of successful long-term adjustment in alcohol dependence—social drinking versus abstinence. *Journal of Studies on Alcohol* 48:95–103.

Orford, J. 1985. *Excessive appetites: A psychological view of addiction.* Chichester, UK: Wiley.

Orphanides, A., and D. Zervos. 1995. Rational addiction with learning and regret. *Journal of Political Economy* 103:739–58.

Pattison, E., M. Sobell, and L. Sobell. 1977. Emerging concepts of alcohol dependence. New York: Springer.

Polich, J., D. Armor, and H. Braiker. 1980. *The course of alcoholism: Four years after treatment.* Santa Monica, CA: Rand.

Rush, B. 1812. *Medical inquiries and observations, on the diseases of the mind.* Philadelphia: Kimber and Richardson.

Schelling, T. 1999. Epilogue: Rationally coping with lapses from rationality. In

*Getting hooked: Rationality and addiction,* ed. J. Elster and O.-J. Skog, 265–84. Cambridge: Cambridge University Press.

Skog, O.-J. 1997. The strength of weak will. *Rationality and Society* 9:245–71.

———. 1999a. Rationality, irrationality, and addiction: Notes on Becker's and Murphy's theory of addiction. In *Getting hooked: Rationality and addiction,* ed. J. Elster and O.-J. Skog, 173–207. Cambridge: Cambridge University Press.

———. 1999b. Hyperbolic discounting, willpower, and addiction. In *Addiction: Entries and exits,* ed. J. Elster, 151–68. New York: Russell Sage.

———. 2000. Addict's choice. *Addiction* 95:1309–14.

———. 2001. Theorizing about patience formation—the necessity of conceptual distinctions. *Economics and Philosophy* 17:207–19.

———. 2003. Hyperbolic discounting, regrets, and anticipation. Unpublished manuscript.

Skog, O.-J., and F. Duckert. 1993. The development of alcoholics' and heavy drinkers' consumption: A longitudinal study. *Journal of Studies on Alcohol* 54:178–88.

Szasz, T. 1972. Bad habits are not diseases: A refutation of the claim that alcoholism is a disease. *Lancet* 2:83–84.

Vaillant, G. 1983. The natural history of alcoholism. Cambridge, MA: Harvard University Press.

Viscusi, K. 1992. *Smoking.* Oxford: Oxford University Press.

Vuchinich, R., and C. Simpson. 1998. Hyperbolic temporal discounting in social drinkers and problem drinkers. *Experimental and Clinical Psychopharmacology* 6:292–305.

Wagenaar, W. 1988. *Paradoxes of gambling behavior.* London: Erlbaum.

Watson, G. 1999. Disordered appetites: Addiction, compulsion, and dependence. In *Addiction: Entries and exits,* ed. J. Elster, 3–28. New York: Russell Sage.

Whitman, W. 1842/1929. *Franklin Evans or the inebriate.* Repr. New York: Random House.

# 6 REVENGE AND RETALIATION

*Vincy Fon and Francesco Parisi*

Humankind operates within a set of constraints. Some constraints have evolutionary origins, others are the result of human design, and still others are the result of sheer accident (Buchanan 1978). Norms of positive and negative reciprocity are important constraints that affect human behavior. Indeed, reciprocity constraints are pervasive among behavioral, social, and legal rules. Although much attention has been devoted to the economics of reciprocity in cooperation (Fehr and Schmidt 2000; Fon and Parisi 2003; Hoffman, McCabe, and Smith 1998), little consideration has been given to the economics of negative reciprocity and retaliation. The present study fills this gap in the literature and looks into an aspect of retaliation. The model attempts to identify the extent to which retaliation norms can be understood as a mechanism to induce more socially desirable behavior among self-interested parties.

This chapter is structured as follows. Section 6.1 starts with the stylized fact that humans have a natural predisposition toward reciprocity and retaliation. Although different theories provide different explanations for the origins of retaliatory norms in human behavior, most evolutionary theories suggest that if reciprocal and retaliatory behaviors pay off, processes of cultural adaptation would generate norms to specify the forms that reciprocity will take. This chapter proceeds to investigate whether reciprocal behavior, in particular retaliatory behavior, pays off, and it fur-

The authors would like to thank Dan Milkove for his comments and Erin Ruane Karsman for her research assistance.

ther identifies the conditions under which retaliatory behavior serves as an instrument for achieving more desirable social outcomes.

In Section 6.2, we develop an economic model of mutual aggression and unregulated revenge in which parties can draw a benefit from attacking others and are subject to attack from other parties. We examine the subgame perfect Nash equilibrium outcome in this game, describing the interaction between independent parties in the absence of norms of retaliation and other legal or social constraints. This section serves as a benchmark case for the subsequent study of retaliation norms.

Sections 6.3 and 6.4 consider the impact of two alternative retaliatory regimes. We compare the mutual aggression outcome to the results induced by such regimes. The first regime of retaliation, presented in Section 6.3, is characterized by *kind-for-kind* retaliation, subject to an *ex post* test of proportionality. In such an environment, victims of a wrong privately carry out in-kind retaliation. The degree of retaliation is chosen by the aggrieved party but is subject to an *ex post* test of proportionality. The aggressor who suffered excessive retaliation is entitled to get even with the retaliator, imposing further harm induced by the excess retaliation. The second regime, presented in Section 6.4, is characterized by a *measure-for-measure* rule of fixed retaliation. Under such a regime, the original victim is allowed to retaliate by duplicating the harm in the same objective measure and modality as the harm suffered initially. Because retaliation is strictly regulated and the retaliatory action cannot exceed the measure of the original harm, no *ex post* test of proportionality follows under such a regime.

Section 6.5 compares the results of our two regimes of retaliation, examining the differential impact of those alternatives when heterogeneous parties are involved in a conflict. Section 6.6 summarizes the results, exploring the extent to which retaliation norms can be viewed as important ingredients of the evolution of peaceful cooperation.

## 6.1 RETALIATION AND NEGATIVE RECIPROCITY

In spite of great variation of ethical values from one culture to another, norms of reciprocity and retaliation stand as universal principles in virtually every human society, both historical and contemporary. No single principle or judgment is as widely and universally accepted as the reciprocity principle, in both its positive and negative versions. The relative importance of the positive and negative components of the reciprocity principle appears to depend on the state of advancement of society and administration of justice. More notably, reciprocity norms first materialize in their negative form in lesser developed societies, whereas norms of positive reciprocity dominate in more developed societies. In early codes of the Babylonian and biblical tradition, the reciprocity principle takes the first form, as a principle of negative reciprocity or retaliation.[1] The talionic principle of "an eye for an eye, a tooth for a tooth," is the most notable illustration of the early principles of negative reciprocity. Similar incarnations of principles of retributive justice emerge in virtually every early legal system for the treatment of wrongdoing, both voluntary and involuntary (Parisi 2001). These rules in turn represent a broader concept of reciprocity, which was subsequently articulated as a positive mandate. The command to "love thy neighbor as thyself" sums up the positive and prescriptive nature of the rule of positive reciprocity.

Economists and behavioral scientists have devoted considerable attention to both positive and negative connotations of reciprocity. In the early 1870s, Charles Darwin had already written in *Descent of Man*: "[A]s the reasoning powers and foresight . . . became improved, each man would soon learn from experience that if he aided his fellow-men, he would commonly receive aid in return. From this low motive he might acquire the habit of aiding his fellows; and the habit of performing benevolent actions certainly strengthens the feelings of sympathy, which gives the first impulse to benevolent actions." (1871)

In recent years, several seminal studies have developed theories of reciprocity and retaliation that provide an evolutionary explanation of such behavior in humans and animals. With this expansion has come debate over what motivates and propagates reciprocity and retaliation. Evolutionary biologists and sociobiologists argue that the species that have successfully evolved over time are those that have incorporated some form of positive and negative reciprocity into their preference profiles and behavioral patterns. In particular, evolutionary forces have led individuals to acquire a taste for retaliatory justice, which generates a private benefit by imposing retaliation on a wrongdoer. Conversely, evolutionary psychologists and Darwinian anthropologists suggest that reciprocity requires a more complex explanation than simple genetics provides.[2] This school of thought focuses on conscious (rather than subconscious) motivations for human behavior, suggesting that environmental factors greatly influence how and why humans act as they do.[3]

The common ground of understanding between these schools of thought is that as a result of evolution, be it genetic or cultural, humans have developed an innate sense of fairness. This sense of fairness is the foundation for both positive and negative reciprocity attitudes. Research has shown that in conjunction with positive and negative reciprocity attitudes, human actors are particularly skilled at detecting cooperators and cheaters in social interactions. Interestingly, current research shows that people are in many ways better at solving problems that require cheater detection (deciding whether a social contract had been violated) than problems that involve detecting cooperators (Cosmides and Tooby 1989). This suggests that human psychology developed in such a way as to give a greater role to negative reciprocity than to positive reciprocity, facilitating the second-party enforcement of such norms.

Research in behavioral and experimental economics recognizes the stylized fact that humans are predisposed toward negative reciprocity (Hoffman, McCabe, and Smith 1998). Whether they are genetic, cultural, or institutional, retaliatory attitudes often characterize human action. Actual circumstances and experiences may lead to retaliatory behavior by many people. Experimental and behavioral evidence shows that people exhibit a strong tendency toward reciprocity. This suggests that there are punitive and retaliatory motives that lead humans to retaliate even when it is privately suboptimal to carry out punishment. Humans demonstrate a willingness to punish defectors, even when punishment is personally costly and there are no plausible future benefits from so behaving (Gintis 2000). The presence of a taste for negative reciprocity has been confirmed by experimental evidence showing that although payoff consequences are important, other motives that are not captured by the objective payoffs of the game constitute the driving force of retaliatory behavior. These retaliatory attitudes are triggered when humans interact with other humans but are not present when the game is played against impersonal entities. For example, people react differently when playing against a computer (to which they cannot attribute defection intentions) and when playing against other humans. Conversely, harm suffered from the action of other humans justifies a retaliatory response, even in one-shot interactions in which reputational incentives are not at work. No such retaliation is generally observed when playing against a mindless computer. Likewise, if the harm was occasioned by subjects who had no alternative behavioral choice, blame is absent and the victims' natural instinct for retaliation is less likely to be present.[4]

Current theories and experimental evidence thus concur in suggesting that an instinct for negative reciprocity is deeply rooted in human nature.[5] As Friedman and Singh (1999) put it, "vengeance or a taste for negative reciprocity is an important part of the human emotional repertoire."[6] These findings raise the fundamental question of whether revengeful and retaliatory behavior pays off. This study centers its focus on this question and identifies the environments under which retaliatory behavior may be explained as instrumental to achieve more desirable outcomes. In the following sections, we develop an economic model of unregulated revenge under which parties benefit from unilaterally attacking others and where individuals benefit from retaliation when suffering wrongdoing from others. Subsequent sections consider alternative regimes of retaliation and their impact on outcomes in case of conflict.

## 6.2 VIOLENCE IN THE STATE OF NATURE

When conflicts arise in the absence of a commonly recognized rule of conduct, interaction between individuals is governed by the most elementary law of nature: what one party can do to another, the other can do as well. Subject to their relative strength, parties engage in a relationship of mutual aggression. Relationships based on force likely permeated interaction between individuals and groups for a great part of human history.

We consider a stylized setting where aggressors obtain a unilateral benefit by attacking other parties and where victims are allowed to indulge in like behavior. After considering the subgame perfect Nash equilibrium, we derive the social optimum in such a mutual aggression. These results serve as a benchmark for evaluating subsequent regimes of regulated retaliation.

### 6.2.1 Asymmetric Parties

Consider two parties with different relative strengths. Both parties are potential aggressors or victims of aggression. Regardless of their strength, aggressors can draw a unilateral benefit when attacking another party. One party's attack imposes a cost on the other party. Individuals differ in their subjective propensity to attack and retaliate. The subjective net benefits from aggression are assumed to differ between parties according to their strength, whereas costs imposed on the victims are assumed equal.

The aggression strategy adopted by each party is $s_1 \in [0, 1]$. Each party's payoff function depends on the level of aggression exercised against others and the level of harm suffered due to others' aggression. We assume that the marginal benefit of aggression is constant and there is increasing marginal cost from the harm suffered due to others' aggression.

Parties have different predispositions toward aggression, represented by different net marginal benefits of harm and retaliation for the two parties. For any given level of aggression, the losses imposed on the respective opponents are assumed equal. Thus, the payoffs for the parties are given by:

$$P_1(s_1, s_2) = -as_2^2 + bs_1,$$
$$P_2(s_1, s_2) = -as_1^2 + cs_2.$$

We assume that $0 < b < a$ and $0 < c < a$ to ensure that the highest levels of mutual aggression ($s_1 = s_2 = 1$) generate negative payoffs for both parties. Further, without loss of generality, consider the case in which party 1 enjoys a higher net marginal benefit from harming the other party: $c < b$. This implies that party 1 has a greater predisposition toward aggression than party 2 does. The reason may be that there is a stronger subjective preference for aggression and retaliation or that there is greater strength and lower costs to aggression. We thus generally refer to party 1 as the stronger or more aggressive party and party 2 as the weaker or less aggressive party. Combining these assumptions, the parameters $a$, $b$, $c$ satisfy the requirement $0 < c < b < a$.

### 6.2.2 The Subgame Perfect Nash Equilibrium

Aggressors can benefit from unilaterally attacking others, and potential victims can undertake similar strategies against their aggressors. Parties choose the level of aggression according to their subjective strength and predisposition. In stage 1, one party (party 1) chooses a strategy, $s_1 \in [0, 1]$. In stage 2, the other party (party 2) chooses a strategy, $s_2 \in [0, 1]$. Information is complete. That is, the structure of the game and the rationality of the parties is common knowledge.

Now consider the subgame perfect Nash equilibrium of the game by backward induction. In stage 2, as $\dfrac{\partial P_2}{\partial s_2} = c > 0$, party 2 chooses $s_2 = 1$ for any given $s_1$. In stage 1, given that party 2 will choose $s_2 = 1$, party 1 chooses $s_1 = 1$ because $\dfrac{\partial P_1}{\partial s_1} = b > 0$. Thus, the subgame perfect Nash equilibrium outcome is $(s_1^N, s_2^N) = (1, 1)$ with full mutual harm for both parties. The subgame perfect Nash equilibrium payoff for parties 1 and 2 are $b - a$ and $c - a$, respectively. These payoffs are both negative.

### 6.2.3 The Social Optimum

In order to evaluate the outcomes of mutual aggression in the state of nature and of the alternative regimes of retaliation considered in the following sections, we identify the socially optimal levels of mutual aggression as those that maximize aggregate payoffs for the parties. The social outcome that fulfills the Kaldor-Hicks criterion is given by:

$$\arg\max_{s_1, s_2} \ (-as_2^2 + bs_1) + (-as_1^2 + cs_2).$$

Thus, the efficient outcome consists of strategies $(s_1^S, s_2^S) = \left( \dfrac{b}{2a}, \dfrac{c}{2a} \right)$. Note that this outcome is characterized by a positive level of mutual aggression—a level, however, that falls short of the subgame perfect Nash equilibrium level that would dominate in the state of nature.[7]

The payoffs for parties 1 and 2 under the socially efficient outcome are

$\dfrac{2b^2 - c^2}{4a}$ and $\dfrac{2c^2 - b^2}{4a}$, respectively, whereas the total social payoff equals $\dfrac{b^2 + c^2}{4a}$. Note that although the payoff in a social optimum for the stronger party, party 1, is always positive, the payoff for the weaker party, party 2, may not be. For the weaker party's payoff to be positive, its level of aggressiveness must be fairly high compared to the more aggressive counterpart.[8] However, the parties' total payoff in a social optimum will always be positive.

Because the parties cannot effectively bind their strategies to one another, each party faces a dominant strategy of aggression. As a result, greater overall violence than is socially optimal will obtain in the subgame perfect Nash equilibrium. This highlights the problems associated with unregulated revenge, as anthropologists and historians have often suggested. We finally note that in the mutual aggression case examined previously, the subgame perfect Nash equilibrium is not order dependent. The same outcome, characterized by maximum harm and maximum retaliation, $(s_1^N, s_2^N) = (1, 1)$, would obtain regardless of the order of moves and in both simultaneous and sequential games. Likewise, the socially optimal outcome is independent of the order of moves and equal in both simultaneous and sequential games: $(s_1^S, s_2^S) = \left(\dfrac{b}{2a}, \dfrac{c}{2a}\right)$.

### 6.2.4 From Mutual Aggression to Revenge and Retaliation

All human societies practiced retaliation at one stage or another. Practices of retaliation evolved over time. In the early phase of discretionary retaliation, there were no formal or legal controls on the victim's behavior. Early customs of retaliation granted victims some degree of discretion over the severity of punishment imposed on wrongdoers. The early conceptions of retaliatory justice, however, often imposed qualitative limits on punishment. Retaliation contained the idea of punishment in kind—captured by the etymology of the word *talio* (retaliation), which comes from the word *talis* (equal in kind)—without imposing any limit on the measure of punishment. In other words, early norms of retaliatory justice embedded the notion of "kind-for-kind" punishment without imposing the additional constraint of "measure-for-measure" (Blau 1916; Parisi 2001).[9]

Although no rational departure from the peaceful equilibrium would be expected under a kind-for-kind regime, given that a disturbance of the peaceful equilibrium could prove very costly, an involuntary shock could trigger a medium-term feud with considerable dissipation of wealth.[10] These problems were subsequently mitigated by the emergence of norms of proportional retribution, which led to an *ex post* scrutiny of the private retaliation carried out by the original victim. At this stage, retaliation was still privately carried out and thus was influenced by the victim's subjective instinct for revenge, but in case of blatantly disproportionate retaliation, the unequal harm done to the parties could be brought into balance by imposing in-kind punishment on the overreacting party.[11] We refer to this regime as kind-for-kind retaliation.

The subsequent evolution of norms of retaliation led to the articulation of fixed retaliatory penalties, imposing a measure-for-measure constraint on the parties' retaliatory strategies. The Biblical *lex talionis* and the comparable provisions found in ancient codifications introduced an *ex ante* constraint on private retaliation by the victim, with an upper limit of 1:1 to the measure of legitimate retaliation.

Historically, the administration of retaliatory justice proceeded from privately carried out revenge to forms of supervised retaliation. In this context, it should be noted that the two regimes of retaliation impose different monitoring requirements for their implementation. The kind-for-kind retaliation regime allows parties to carry out retaliation without any adjudication and only requires a system for the *ex post* correction of excessive retaliation. As the development of the law progressed, the restrictions regulating vengeance were extended. The injured party, who was originally allowed to carry out the execution himself (subject to a constraint of proportionality), later was only allowed to do so under the supervision of authority and eventually was only permitted to attend the execution. The second regime of measure-for-measure retaliation utilized third-party supervision of the talionic punishment to prevent excesses. Under this phase of supervised retaliation, the talion was carried out by the victim (or the victim's family) in the presence of witnesses and under the direct supervision of an official executioner.[12]

It is interesting to note that the historical illustrations of retaliation considered in this chapter were instrumental to both promoting and constraining practices of retaliation.[13]

In some situations the human instinct for revenge provides the natural impetus for carrying out retaliation even when it is privately costly and may appear *ex post* irrational. In those situations, the natural instinct for revenge may extend beyond proportional retaliation and the measure-for-measure limit to retaliation serves to constrain such human impetus.[14] Yet in other situations, retaliation norms emerge to encourage retaliatory practices. This second function of norms of retaliation can be understood, considering that retaliation often imposes a private cost on the retaliator as well as on the wrongdoer.[15] Revenge duplicates the loss rather than effectuates a compensatory transfer and, as such, is incapable of undoing the original harm. Given the sunk nature of the original loss, carrying out costly retaliation is often irrational *ex post*. Further, retaliation creates a public benefit to society at large in terms of maintained deterrence for future wrongdoing, while imposing a private cost on those who enforce talionic penalties. Similarly, when members of the victim's family need to carry out retaliation in the absence of a central enforcement authority, a second-order collective action problem may arise, with free riding in retaliation. These factors may generate a suboptimal participation incentive to carry out the retaliatory action. In this sense, social and religious norms and other retaliatory institutions can be viewed as instruments to maintain an optimal level of private enforcement of retaliatory punishment.[16]

The following two sections examine the effect of these retaliation norms in promoting a more desirable social coexistence. Section 3 analyzes norms of kind-for-kind retribution, and Section 4 considers rules of measure-for-measure retaliation, studying the effects of such constraints on the parties' interaction.

## 6.3 KIND-FOR-KIND REVENGE WITH *EX POST* TEST OF PROPORTIONALITY

The first regime of regulated retaliation is characterized by retaliation subject to an *ex post* test of proportionality. Victims of a wrong carry out in-kind retaliation. The degree of retaliation is chosen by the aggrieved party but is subsequently subject to a test of proportionality. In case of excessive retaliation, the party suffering excessive retaliation can seek relief and impose further harm on the overreacting retaliator. Norms of proportional retribution render excessive retaliation a wrong in and of itself and justify action by the victim of retaliation to reestablish the balance of reciprocal harm with its retaliator.

In order to consider the outcome of retaliatory interaction in the presence of a proportionality test, we modify the previous game by introducing a test of proportionality after the first exchange of harm and retaliation by the parties. Given the possibility of excessive retaliation by the second mover, we extend the simple game to a three-stage game to allow for the getting-even round. In particular, in stage 1 we assume that the first party chooses its initial level of aggression. We refer to this as the *aggression stage*, in which the first party harms the other party. In stage 2, the *retaliation stage*, the second party retaliates. The extent of this retaliation may trespass into the region of excessive retaliation. In stage 3, the behavior of the second party is evaluated in light of a test of proportionality. Punitive actions greater than the socially accepted level of retaliation would be considered excessive.

Although the extent of acceptable retaliation changes over time, the following model considers the case in which imposing punishment equal in severity to the original harm constitutes the limit of acceptable retaliation. If the retaliation carried out by the victim or the victim's clan exceeds such a limit, the first party may get even with its retaliator under the criterion of proportional retribution. We refer to this as the *getting-even stage*.

Note that in the following models, tests of proportionality and rules of fixed retaliation focus on objective harm caused by the parties rather than subjective loss suffered by the parties. Thus, for example, the loss of an arm justifies an equal mutilation of the wrongdoer's limb, regardless of the parties' subjective valuation of their respective bodily integrity. This objective application of retaliatory norms is consistent with historical examples of retaliation, which often called for a mechanical duplication of harm regardless of the subjective circumstances of the case.[17]

We assume that an aggressor can draw a unilateral benefit when attacking another party, similar to the case of mutual aggression in the state of nature. Victims benefit from engaging in vindictive behavior when suffering an unjustified attack from another. This benefit may result from an evolved taste for revenge or from compliance with existing social norms, requiring victims to retaliate in order to preserve their honor and reputation. The harmful activity imposed by one party imposes a cost to the other party subject to attack. Individuals differ in their subjective propensity to attack and retaliate. Each party's payoff function depends on the level of aggression exercised against others and the level of harm suffered from others. We assume that there are bounds to the levels of aggression and retaliation: $s_i \in [0, 1]$. Without loss of generality, we consider the case in which party 1 enjoys a higher net marginal benefit from harming the other party: $c < b$. This means that party 1 has either a greater predisposition toward aggression or a greater instinct for revenge.

To better understand the features of this regime of retaliation with an *ex post* test of proportionality, we consider two scenarios. In the first scenario, the more aggressive party (party 1) moves first, undertaking an aggression on the other, less aggressive party (party 2). We refer to this scenario as the *MLM* game to signify the sequence of moves: *more* aggressive first, *less* aggressive second, and *more* aggressive third. In the second scenario, the order of moves is reversed. We shall refer to this alternative scenario as the *LML* game to signify the reversed sequence of moves: *less* aggressive first, *more* aggressive second, and *less* aggressive third.

### 6.3.1 The *MLM* Case

In the *MLM* game the more aggressive party (party 1) moves first, harming the other, less aggressive party (party 2). The less aggressive party retaliates in the second stage, and the more aggressive first party imposes an eventual getting-even punishment in the third stage.

Recall that under this regime of retaliation, parties' choices in stages 1 and 2 are unconstrained and are subject to a subsequent test of proportionality such that, if the measure of retaliation in stage 2 exceeded the measure of harm occasioned by the original aggression in stage 1, a getting-even stage 3 provides the occasion to reestablish the balance of harm suffered by the parties. Excessive retaliation is possible because retaliation is carried out in the absence of a monitoring authority, and the second party's instinctive preference for revenge may occasionally lead to excessive retaliatory action. Parties know that third-stage behavior will be evaluated in light of a test of proportionality and subject to possible correction.

Backward induction will help us identify the parties' strategies and the equilibrium outcome of this game. In stage 3, given the retaliatory action of the less aggressive party in stage 2 ($s_2$), and recalling the original level of aggression in stage 1 ($s_1$), the allowed getting-even reaction of party 1 is the following:[18]

$$\tilde{s}_1^R = \begin{cases} s_2 - s_1 & if \quad s_2 > s_1 \\ 0 & if \quad s_2 \le s_1 \end{cases}.$$

In stage 2, given the choice of party 1 in stage 1 ($s_1$) and knowing the feasible reaction of party 1 in stage 3 ($\tilde{s}_1^R$), party 2 confronts the following problem:

$$\underset{s_2}{Max} \quad P_2 = -a(s_1 + \tilde{s}_1^R)^2 + cs_2.$$

This is equivalent to:

$$\underset{s_2}{Max} \quad P_2 = \begin{cases} -as_2^2 + cs_2 & if \quad s_2 > s_1 \\ -as_1^2 + cs_2 & if \quad s_2 \le s_1 \end{cases}.$$

The first branch represents *excessive retaliation*. Here, the maximization problem captures the effect of the reciprocity constraint in the retaliation game, showing the expected cost of the getting-even stage as a result of excessive retaliation in stage 2. The second branch shows *fair retaliation*, in which the retaliatory action does not exceed the original harm. In this latter case, since retaliation $s_2$ does not exceed the boundary $s_1$, the retaliator faces no expected cost from stage 3 in terms of punishment for disproportionate reaction. Thus, if carried out within the confines of proportionality, retaliation in stage 2 can create benefits without imposing any cost on the retaliator (party 2).

If $s_2 > s_1$, $\underset{s_2}{\arg \max} P_2 = \dfrac{c}{2a}$. If $s_2 \le s_1$, $\underset{s_2}{\arg \max} P_2 = s_1$. Hence, the reaction function of party 2 is:

$$s_2^R = \begin{cases} \dfrac{c}{2a} & if \quad \dfrac{c}{2a} > s_1 \\ s_1 & if \quad \dfrac{c}{2a} \le s_1 \end{cases}.$$

In stage 1, knowing the reaction of party 2 ($s_2^R$) and the possibility to get even in stage 3, party 1 confronts the problem:[19]

$$\underset{s_1, \tilde{s}_1}{Max} \quad P_1 = -a s_2^{R^2} + b(s_1 + \tilde{s}_1)$$

$$= \begin{cases} -a\left(\dfrac{c}{2a}\right)^2 + b(s_1 + \tilde{s}_1) & s.t. \ s_1 + \tilde{s}_1 = \dfrac{c}{2a} & if \ \dfrac{c}{2a} > s_1 \\[3mm] -a s_1^2 + b s_1 & s.t. \ \tilde{s}_1 = 0 & if \ \dfrac{c}{2a} \le s_1 \end{cases}.$$

In the first branch, representing the choice of excessive retaliation $\left(\dfrac{c}{2a} > s_1\right)$, party 1 chooses a small harmful activity in stage 1, expects a disproportionate retaliation from party 2 in the following stage, and is allowed to get even in stage 3 to reestablish the overall balance between respective harms suffered by the parties. In this case, there is an infinite number of solutions to $s_1$ and $\tilde{s}_1$, subject to the conditions $s_1 + \tilde{s}_1 = \dfrac{c}{2a}$ and $s_1 < \dfrac{c}{2a}$. Whatever the choices of $s_1$ and $\tilde{s}_1$, the payoff for party 1 is $\dfrac{c(2b - c)}{4a}$.

In the second fair retaliation branch $\left(\dfrac{c}{2a} \le s_1\right)$, party 2 matches the harmful activity imposed by party 1. In this case, $\arg\max\limits_{s_1} -a s_1^2 + b s_1 = \dfrac{b}{2a}$, and the best payoff for party 1 is $\dfrac{b^2}{4a}$. Because $\dfrac{b^2}{4a} > \dfrac{c(2b - c)}{4a}$ is equivalent to $(b - c)^2 > 0$ and the latter inequality always holds, the payoff from fair retaliation always exceeds the payoff from engaging in excessive retaliation. This leads party 1 to opt for $s_1^R = \dfrac{b}{2a}$. Consequently, this regime of retaliation induces equilibrium strategies $(s_1^R, s_2^R, \tilde{s}_1^R) = \left(\dfrac{b}{2a}, \dfrac{b}{2a}, 0\right)$. The payoffs for parties 1 and 2 are $\dfrac{b^2}{4a}$ and $\dfrac{b(2c - b)}{4a}$, respectively.

### 6.3.2 The *LML* Case

In this scenario, the less aggressive party (party 2) moves first, harming the other, more aggressive party (party 1). The more aggressive party retaliates next, and the less aggressive party moves again in the third stage to impose the getting-even punishment.

In stage 3, the getting-even stage, party 2 chooses its strategy given the previous choice of the more aggressive party in stage 2 ($s_1$), and recalling its own choice in stage 1 ($s_2$), according to the following reaction function:

$$\tilde{s}_2^R = \begin{cases} s_1 - s_2 & if \quad s_1 > s_2 \\ 0 & if \quad s_1 \leq s_2 \end{cases}.$$

In the retaliation stage 2, given the choice of party 2 in stage 1 ($s_2$) and knowing the expected reaction of party 2 in stage 3 ($\tilde{s}_2^R$), party 1 confronts the problem:

$$\underset{s_1}{Max} \quad P_1 = -a(s_2 + \tilde{s}_2^R)^2 + bs_1.$$

This is equivalent to:

$$\underset{s_1}{Max} \quad P_1 = \begin{cases} -as_1^2 + bs_1 & if \quad s_1 > s_2 \\ -as_2^2 + bs_1 & if \quad s_1 \leq s_2 \end{cases}.$$

Recall that the first branch represents excessive retaliation and the second branch represents fair retaliation. In this latter case, the retaliator faces no expected cost from the getting-even stage.

If $s_1 > s_2$, $\underset{s_1}{arg\ max}\ P_1 = \dfrac{b}{2a}$. If $s_1 \leq s_2$, $\underset{s_1}{arg\ max}\ P_1 = s_2$. Hence, the reaction function of party 1 is:

$$s_1^R = \begin{cases} \dfrac{b}{2a} & if \quad \dfrac{b}{2a} > s_2 \\ s_2 & if \quad \dfrac{b}{2a} \leq s_2 \end{cases}.$$

This allows us to consider party 2's strategy in stage 1, the aggression stage. Knowing the expected retaliation of party 1 ($s_1^R$) and the possibility to get even in stage 3, party 2 is confronted with the problem:

$$\underset{s_2, \tilde{s}_2}{Max} \quad P_2 = -as_1^{R^2} + c(s_2 + \tilde{s}_2)$$

$$= \begin{cases} -a\left(\dfrac{b}{2a}\right)^2 + c(s_2 + \tilde{s}_2) \quad s.t.\ s_2 + \tilde{s}_2 = \dfrac{b}{2a} & if \quad \dfrac{b}{2a} > s_2 \\ -as_2^2 + cs_2 \qquad\qquad\qquad\quad s.t.\ \tilde{s}_2 = 0 & if \quad \dfrac{b}{2a} \leq s_2 \end{cases}.$$

In the first branch, characterized by excessive retaliation $\left(\dfrac{b}{2a} > s_2\right)$, a small harmful activity by party 2 in stage 1 would trigger excessive retaliation from party

1 in the following stage. The less aggressive original wrongdoer would be allowed to get even in stage 3, and this would lead to a level of mutual harm that exceeds the wrongdoer's private optimum. As in the previous case in which the order of moves was reversed, an infinite number of possible solutions $s_2$ and $\tilde{s}_2$ satisfy

$$s_2 + \tilde{s}_2 = \frac{b}{2a} \text{ and } s_2 < \frac{b}{2a}.$$

A particularly interesting possibility is $s_2 = \dfrac{c}{2a}$ and $\tilde{s}_2 = \dfrac{b-c}{2a}$, with payoff equal to $\dfrac{b(2c - b)}{4a}$. This case is interesting because $s_2 = \dfrac{c}{2a}$ constitutes party 2's best choice of action if it was the stronger party. Then the retaliation-induced equilibrium outcome is $(s_2^R, s_1^R, \tilde{s}_2^R) = \left( \dfrac{c}{2a}, \dfrac{b}{2a}, \dfrac{b-c}{2a} \right)$. At the retaliation-induced equilibrium, payoffs for parties 1 and 2 are $\dfrac{b^2}{4a}$ and $\dfrac{b(2c - b)}{4a}$, respectively.

The second branch is characterized by fair retaliation $\left( \dfrac{b}{2a} \le s_2 \right)$. Party 1, victim of the original wrong, imposes retaliation on party 2 in the same degree as the harm suffered. Given proportionality in retaliation, no getting-even punishment in stage 3 follows. In this case, since $\arg\max_{s_2} -as_2^2 + cs_2 = \dfrac{c}{2a}$, the unconstrained choice for party 2 is $s_2 = \dfrac{c}{2a}$. Recall that party 2 is the less aggressive party as $c < b$ is assumed. Hence, $s_2 = \dfrac{c}{2a} < \dfrac{b}{2a}$ is implied. But this violates the upper bound constraint for the fair retaliation branch. Thus, the upper bound constraint must be binding and $s_2^R = \dfrac{b}{2a}$. With this choice, the less aggressive party (party 2) preempts excessive retaliatory action by party 1 by adopting a level of initial aggression consistent with the expected level of reaction by the other party. The induced equilibrium outcome takes the form $(s_2^R, s_1^R, \tilde{s}_2^R) = \left( \dfrac{b}{2a}, \dfrac{b}{2a}, 0 \right)$. The same potential payoff for party 2, $\dfrac{b(2c - b)}{4a}$, obtains in the fair retaliation and excessive retaliation scenarios.

This result rests on the fact that even though the weaker party undertakes the initial aggression, it is the stronger party who ultimately determines the harm level from the retaliatory interaction. The less aggressive party has a multitude of options, all yielding identical payoff. When confronting party 1, the less aggressive first mover (party 2) can expect a level of retaliation consistent with the more aggressive predisposition of the opponent, regardless of the actual gravity of the initial offence. Party 2 can allocate $s_2$ and $\tilde{s}_2$ in different ways, but all alternative allocations yield the same payoff.[20]

A second observation concerns the parties' participation in the retaliatory exchange. Because the retaliatory game is started by an initial aggression, the participation constraint to this interaction should be considered. Whereas initial aggression by the strong party is always feasible, initial aggression by a weaker party requires special conditions. A less aggressive party will engage in such violent interaction only when the expected payoff of the game is positive. The weaker party will not engage in initial aggression if $\dfrac{b(2c - b)}{4a}$ is negative. For this participation constraint to be met, $c$ must be greater than $b/2$ (recall that $c$ is smaller than $b$ by assumption). This further means that the difference in the strength and predisposition to violence between the parties should not be too large for the participation constraint to be met.

### 6.3.3 Comparing *MLM* and *LML* Games

Table 6.1 summarizes payoffs for the kind-for-kind retaliation, in which excessive or disproportionate retaliation is subsequently sanctioned with a punishment aimed at reestablishing the balance of harm inflicted on the two parties. The payoffs for the two cases of *MLM* and *LML* retaliation are as follows.

A few conclusions should be drawn from this table. First, the total payoffs for both parties are the same, independent of the sequence of moves between more aggressive and less aggressive parties. Neither the *MLM* game nor the *LML* game is efficient, as the total payoffs for these games $\left( \dfrac{bc}{2a} \right)$ are less than the total payoff under social optimum $\left( \dfrac{b^2 + c^2}{4a} \right)$. The possibility of retaliatory action by the second mover subject to *ex post* scrutiny of proportionality improves upon the scenario of unregulated revenge considered in Section 2. Recall that the subgame perfect Nash equilibrium with unregulated revenge generates total negative payoffs for the parties, $(b - a) + (c - a) < 0$. The payoffs under this game thus represent a Pareto improvement over the case of unregulated revenge.

Second, regardless of the order of moves, the payoff for the more aggressive party is higher than the payoff for the less aggressive party. Hence, there is a more-aggressive-party advantage. This is quite intuitive because this regime of retaliation allows the more aggressive party to influence the total level of reciprocal violence, either directly by means of initial aggression or subsequently by means of

TABLE 6.1
*Kind-for-kind retaliation*

|  | Payoff for party 1 (M) |  | Payoff for party 2 (L) | Total payoff |
|---|:---:|:---:|:---:|:---:|
| MLM game | $\dfrac{b^2}{4a}$ | > | $\dfrac{b(2c-b)}{4a}$ | $\dfrac{bc}{2a}$ |
| LML game | $\dfrac{b^2}{4a}$ | > | $\dfrac{b(2c-b)}{4a}$ | $\dfrac{bc}{2a}$ |

excessive retaliation. If confronted by a more aggressive party, the weak first mover expects retaliatory action of the other party to maximize the optimal level of revenge for the more aggressive party, regardless of the gravity of the initial offense. It is therefore rational for the weaker party to preempt the more aggressive party by adopting the more aggressive party's desired level of harm as its own or to wait and get even at a later stage.

The only instance in which the more-aggressive-party advantage is not present is when the weaker party, being the first mover, can control participation in this game and abstain from an aggression on its stronger opponent. This relates to the final observation that for substantial differences between predispositions to violence of the parties, the less aggressive party rationally refrains from imposing an initial harm on a more aggressive party. In particular, when the less aggressive party controls participation, the retaliatory exchange can only be observed if $0 < b/2 < c < b$.

## 6.4 FIXED RETALIATION AND THE MEASURE-FOR-MEASURE PRINCIPLE

In this section, we consider a second regime of retaliation, characterized by a more direct rule of fixed measure-for-measure retribution. Under such a regime the original victim is allowed to impose retaliation duplicating the harm in the same objective measure and modality as the originally suffered harm. Because retaliation is strictly regulated and imposition of talionic penalties is constrained *ex ante*, retaliation cannot exceed the original harm, rendering an *ex post* test of proportionality unnecessary under such a regime.

This regime of retaliatory justice also has historical analogues. Anthropologists and legal historians have amply documented the transition from discretionary revenge to norms of proportional retribution. Across different cultures and legal traditions, practices of unregulated revenge and mutual aggression are initially constrained by norms of kind-for-kind retribution and subsequent rules of measure-for-measure retaliation. These norms were eventually codified, establishing a single talionic multiplier for almost all cases of wrongdoing. The establishment of sanctions based on fixed 1 : 1 retaliation characterizes this regime.[21] The incorporation of retaliatory practices into bodies of written law during the ninth and eighth centuries B.C.E. is best exemplified by the biblical *lex talionis*.[22] The talionic rules of this period serve two main purposes. First, they create an upper limit to retaliatory justice: only one life for a life can be vindicated, no more. Second, they serve as minimum punishment for the criminal: no less than the law requires.[23] In later times, upper and lower limits began to diverge, with legitimate criminal penalties falling somewhere between those two boundaries.

We proceed to consider this form of retaliatory punishment, modifying our previous game by including a fixed retaliation constraint. As for the previous cases, in stage 1 the first party chooses its level of initial aggression. In stage 2, the second party chooses its level of retaliation, subject to a fixed retaliation constraint allowing the initial victim to impose measure-for-measure harm on its aggressor. The measure of retaliation cannot exceed the measure of the original harm.

As before, to understand the mechanics of this retaliation game, we consider two alternative situations. In the first scenario, the more aggressive party (party 1) moves first, undertaking an aggression on the other, less aggressive party (party 2). We refer to these alternative scenarios as the *ML* game. In the second scenario, the order of moves is reversed. We shall refer to this alternative scenarios as the *LM* game to signify the sequence of a *less* aggressive first mover and a *more* aggressive second retaliator.

In both scenarios the first mover's choice (initial aggression choice) is unconstrained, but the second party's reaction is directly constrained by the rule of fixed retaliation, imposing a maximum ceiling to the measure of retaliatory harm. Note that the rule of fixed retaliation is germane to the principle of proportional retribution that governed stage 3 in the previously considered group of games. In the present scenario, however, proportionality has *ex ante* effects, operating as a constraint on the retaliatory reaction of the second mover, rather than operating *ex post*, as a test of proportionality to reestablish the balance between the harmful behaviors of the parties.

### 6.4.1 The *ML* Game

In the ML scenario the more aggressive party (party 1) moves first, harming the other, less aggressive party (party 2). After suffering aggression from party 1, party 2 can retaliate and impose in-kind harm up to the level of the harm originally imposed by the other party. We investigate the *ML* retaliation-induced equilibrium by backward induction.

In stage 2, given any choice of party 1 in stage 1 ($s_1$), party 2 is allowed to choose at most $s_1$ and is confronted with the following problem:

$$\underset{s_2}{Max}\quad P_2 = -as_1^2 + cs_2 \quad s.t. \quad s_2 \le s_1.$$

Because $\dfrac{\partial P_2}{\partial s_2} = c > 0$, $P_2$ is increasing in $[0, s_1]$. Hence $s_2^R = s_1$ and the less aggressive party matches the more aggressive party's harmful behavior.

In stage 1, knowing $s_2^R$, party 1 faces the following problem:

$$\underset{s_1}{Max}\quad P_1 = -as_2^{R^2} + bs_1 = -as_1^2 + bs_1.$$

Hence, $s_1^R = \dfrac{b}{2a}$ is chosen. The retaliation-induced equilibrium outcome is $(s_1^R, s_2^R) = \left(\dfrac{b}{2a}, \dfrac{b}{2a}\right)$. The retaliation-induced equilibrium payoffs are $P_1^R = \dfrac{b^2}{4a}$ and $P_2^R = \dfrac{b(2c - b)}{4a}$. Note that the sum of the payoffs for the two parties is $\dfrac{bc}{2a}$.

### 6.4.2 The *LM* Game

In the *LM* scenario the less aggressive party (party 2) moves first, harming the other, more aggressive party (party 1). Also in this case, once the initial harm is inflicted, the victim is allowed to impose retaliatory harm, not to exceed the harm originally suffered. Again, we investigate the *LM* retaliation-induced equilibrium by backward induction.

In stage 2, given an initial aggression by party 2 in stage 1 ($s_2$), party 1 is allowed to retaliate at most $s_2$ and is confronted with the following problem:

$$\underset{s_1}{Max}\quad P_1 = -as_2^2 + bs_1 \quad s.t. \quad s_1 \le s_2.$$

Because $\dfrac{\partial P_1}{\partial s_1} = b > 0$, $s_1^R = s_2$. Hence, the more aggressive party always retaliates at the maximum allowable level, matching the harm level originally imposed by the less aggressive party in stage 1.

In stage 1, knowing $s_1^R$, party 2 faces the following problem:

$$\underset{s_2}{Max}\quad P_2 = -as_1^{R^2} + cs_2 = -as_2^2 + cs_2.$$

Hence, $s_2^R = \dfrac{c}{2a}$ is chosen. The retaliation-induced equilibrium outcome is $(s_2^R, s_1^R) = \left( \dfrac{c}{2a}, \dfrac{c}{2a} \right)$. The payoffs in such equilibrium are $P_2^R = \dfrac{c^2}{4a}$ and $P_1^R = \dfrac{c(2b - c)}{4a}$. Note that the sum of the payoffs is again $\dfrac{bc}{2a}$.

### 6.4.3  Comparing the *ML* and *LM* Games

Table 6.2 summarizes payoffs for the *ML* and *LM* situations in which the victim of a wrong can impose retaliation in kind not to exceed the harm initially imposed by the aggressor.

Although neither retaliation game is efficient, the total payoffs for both games are the same. Further, both *ML* and *LM* games generate equilibria that constitute a Pareto improvement over the subgame perfect Nash equilibrium under unregulated revenge.

Second, note that payoffs for the parties depend on the order of their moves. More specifically, the payoff for the more aggressive party is larger when it moves first than when it moves last. Likewise, the payoff for the less aggressive party is larger when it moves first than when it moves last. Hence, the regime of fixed retaliation creates a first-mover advantage.

Third, although the payoff for the more aggressive party is always positive, the payoff for the less aggressive party can be negative. Negative payoffs may be present when the more aggressive party moves first and the less aggressive party engages in a retaliatory exchange when its taste for retaliation is substantially lower than the other party's: $2c < b$. The reason is that the weak and less aggressive party, if subject to an initial aggression, would engage in retaliation and would rationally match the level of harm imposed by the stronger initial aggressor. The resulting

T A B L E   6 . 2
*Measure-for-measure retaliation*

| | Payoff for party 1 (M) | | Payoff for party 2 (L) | Total payoff |
|---|:---:|:---:|:---:|:---:|
| *ML* game | $\dfrac{b^2}{4a}$ | $>$ | $\dfrac{b(2c - b)}{4a}$ | $\dfrac{bc}{2a}$ |
| | $\vee$ | | $\wedge$ | $=$ |
| *LM* game | $\dfrac{c(2b - c)}{4a}$ | $>$ | $\dfrac{c^2}{4a}$ | $\dfrac{bc}{2a}$ |

level of mutual aggression exceeds what the weaker party would have chosen as a first mover.

Further note that when the weaker party is the first mover, it can control the initial level of aggression and indirectly determine the level of retaliation it will endure. Participation in this situation is always assured, regardless of the parties' different predispositions to violence.

## 6.5 UNREGULATED REVENGE AND KIND-FOR-KIND AND MEASURE-FOR-MEASURE RETALIATION

In this section, we sum up our previous findings, comparing the relationship between the regimes' (1) mutual aggression in the state of nature; (2) kind-for-kind retaliation, subject to an *ex post* test of proportionality; and (3) measure-for-measure retaliation.

Both kind-for-kind retaliation and measure-for-measure retaliation regimes are improvements over mutual aggression. Although individual payoffs for strong and weak parties vary under different regimes, total payoffs for the two parties are identical under both kind-for-kind and measure-for-measure regimes. Hence, the two regimes yield an equal improvement in the social aggregate payoff, compared to the benchmark case of mutual aggression in the state of nature. This may suggest that the historical transition from kind-for-kind retaliation to measure-for-measure retaliation was driven by distributional concerns rather than efficiency considerations.[24]

The two regimes of retaliation lead to a socially optimal level of aggression and retaliation if parties are identical. This is consistent with the general result according to which reciprocity constraints lead to optimal levels of cooperation between symmetric players (Fon and Parisi 2003). The optimality result does not hold when our regimes of retaliation are applied to heterogeneous players. When asymmetries are involved, in both cases of kind-for-kind and measure-for-measure retaliation the total payoff falls short of the maximal payoff in a social optimum.

Different regimes of retaliation generate different payoffs for the parties when asymmetries are involved. Regardless of the regime, when there is a conflict, the weaker party is always worse off than the stronger party.

Additionally, depending on the circumstances, some of the differences between the parties' payoffs depend on the order of moves, whereas others depend on the parties' aggressiveness and relative strength. In the measure-for-measure regime the payoffs for the parties depend on the order of their moves. More specifically, the payoff for the more aggressive party is larger when it moves first than when it moves last. Likewise, the payoff for the less aggressive party is larger when it moves

TABLE 6.3
*Comparing retaliation regimes*

| | Payoff for party 1 (M) | | Payoff for party 2 (L) | Total payoff |
|---|---|---|---|---|
| *LML* game (kind-for-kind) | $\dfrac{b^2}{4a}$ | $>$ | $\dfrac{b(2c - b)}{4a} (> 0 \text{ or} < 0)$ | $\dfrac{bc}{2a}$ |
| | $\vee$ | | $\wedge$ | $=$ |
| *LM* game (measure-for-measure) | $\dfrac{c(2b - c)}{4a}$ | $>$ | $\dfrac{c^2}{4a} (> 0)$ | $\dfrac{bc}{2a}$ |

first than when it moves last. Hence, the regime of fixed retaliation creates a first-mover advantage, in contrast to the more-aggressive-party advantage observed under the kind-for-kind regime.

One corollary follows from this difference. Given the first-mover advantage, the participation constraint for the weaker party is always fulfilled when it is the first mover in a measure-for-measure retaliation regime. This is not so in the kind-for-kind regime. As shown in Table 6.3, the participation constraint for the weaker party in such a system may not be satisfied, even when the weaker party moves first.[25] This means that fewer instances of retaliatory conflict may emerge under the kind-for-kind regime than for the measure-for-measure alternative.

Table 6.3 compares individual and total payoffs under the two regimes of retaliation when the weak or less aggressive party moves first. We limit the comparison to this subset of situations because, as indicated previously, no differences between the two regimes are ascertainable when the stronger or more aggressive party moves first (that is, the individual payoffs are the same under the *MLM* and the *ML* games).

As mentioned before, in the kind-for-kind *LML* retaliation game, the payoff for the weaker or less aggressive party may be negative. This implies that under the kind-for-kind regime, the weaker party may abstain from undertaking an initial aggression, whereas initial aggression may always be rational in a measure-for measure regime. This difference is justified by the fact that in the two-stage *LM* game, the weaker party chooses the level of harm and indirectly controls the level of retaliation, thus being able to choose the privately optimal level of initial aggression. In the kind-for-kind regime, the weaker party lacks control over the level of mutual harm because the equilibrium level of harm is determined by the preference of the stronger party. Thus, under such a regime, the weaker party may find it rational to abstain from engaging in an initial aggression, even when aggression would have been rational in a measure-for-measure regime. Further, the weaker party can achieve a better payoff in the *LM* game than in the *LML* game. This suggests that the transition from kind-for-kind to measure-for-measure retaliation benefits the less aggressive and weaker members in the group.

Differences in participation constraints among the various cases are also quite instructive. First, recall that neither party voluntarily chooses to engage in a game of mutual aggression, because negative payoffs are expected. However, in the state of nature, parties control only their strategies, and neither party single-handedly controls the outcome. Thus, in spite of the negative expected payoffs, mutual aggression dominates in equilibrium. The remaining cases of regulated retaliation between asymmetric parties provide mixed participation incentives. The participation constraint is always satisfied under both regimes of retaliation when symmetric parties are involved. This is consistent with the intuition that if aggression yields a net benefit to one party, it would also be beneficial to its opponent, given the parties' identical preferences. Specifically, because the first regime of proportional retribution creates a more-aggressive-party advantage, the less aggressive party, if substantially weaker, may avoid participation, if given an opportunity to do so. Likewise, under the second regime of fixed retaliation, the first mover has a strategic advantage. This may create incentives for the disadvantaged second mover to avoid being attacked by a more aggressive party, if given an opportunity to escape the conflict.

## 6.6 CONCLUSIONS

Vindictiveness and retaliation may be as important as honesty for the evolution of cooperation. Negative reciprocity can achieve results that cannot be achieved with positive reciprocity alone. For example, the presence of positive reciprocity norms could not easily correct unilateral aggression problems. In our analysis, this can be seen by the fact that players without a taste for retaliation would be quite ineffective at constraining other players' unilateral aggression. Put differently, positive reciprocity and negative reciprocity have different domains of application. In the presence of cooperative first movers, positive reciprocation would provide an effective response; but in the face of an aggressive first mover, positive reciprocity would provide a quite inadequate response. Retaliation with like aggression becomes necessary. Positive reciprocity will not help in case of aggression by others, just as negative reciprocity cannot do much to reward positive cooperation from others. This indicates that positive and negative reciprocity are complementary strategies that provide best strategic attitudes in different sets of social interactions.

This leads us to suggest that there may be an important relationship between the evolution of vindictiveness and the sustainability of peaceful cooperation in human societies. A population endowed with attitudes of positive reciprocity but not ready for negative reciprocity could easily fall prey to invaders with unilateral aggression strategies. In evolutionary terms, positive reciprocity without a complementary attitude for negative reciprocity would not be evolutionarily stable.

In this chapter, after considering a simplified model of mutual aggression and unregulated revenge, we examined two alternative regimes of retaliation. Under the first regime of kind-for-kind retaliation, individuals engage in private retaliation, subject to an *ex post* test of proportionality. The measure of retaliation is discretionary and depends on subjective circumstances and vindictive predisposition of the parties. Excessive retaliation is corrected *ex post*. Whenever appeasement between the parties is not achieved at the retaliation stage, balance in the relationship between the parties is reestablished at a third stage. In this stage, excessive retaliation by the original victim is sanctioned with the imposition of a getting-even punishment on the overly vindictive party. Under the second regime of measure-for-measure retaliation, a victim's reaction is directly constrained by a rule of fixed retaliation, which limits punishment to the measure of the harm originally suffered. Under this regime, excessive retaliation is prevented, rendering the getting-even stage unnecessary.

Our economic model identified the attributes of these regimes of retaliation. Both regimes of retaliation represent improvement over the alternative regime of mutual aggression in the state of nature. Interesting differences between the two regimes of retaliation emerge in the case of asymmetric parties. In the kind-for-kind regime with an *ex post* test of proportionality, the overall level of reciprocal violence is ultimately determined by the preference of the more aggressive party. This creates a more-aggressive-party advantage. No such advantage is found under the second regime of retaliation, characterized by fixed measure-for-measure punishment. In this regime, the equilibrium level of reciprocal harm is unilaterally determined by the initial aggressor, because the victim can replicate only the harm that it originally suffered. Thus, with asymmetric parties the preference of the active aggressor rather than the retaliator will be satisfied. This creates a first-mover advantage. These differences vanish in two sets of circumstances. First, the two regimes yield no differences in the retaliation-induced outcomes when symmetric parties are involved. Second, no advantage will be present if the disadvantaged party can exit the game, for example, by refraining from attacking a more aggressive opponent. The model further shows the limits of the various retaliatory regimes when heterogeneous parties are involved. This may explain the success and diffusion of norms of retaliation among homogeneous groups and the gradual abandonment of such retaliatory regimes when differences among groups and individuals over time became more sizable.

These results reveal that norms of proportional retribution and practices of fixed retaliation can increase social value by avoiding the subgame perfect Nash equilibrium of mutual aggression and by encouraging parties to converge toward a more desirable level of peaceful coexistence. Given a vengeance motive and preference for retribution in human nature, peaceful and cooperative behavior is no longer dominated by strategies of unilateral aggression and can become part of a Nash equilibrium even when there is no repeat interaction. The fear of proportional retaliation can support better social outcomes, effectively constraining the levels of mutual aggression that would otherwise dominate in equilibrium. These results support recent theories providing an evolutionary explanation of negative reciprocity in human behavior. These theories suggest that retaliatory attitudes develop because they pay off. Human attitudes for revenge and retaliation operate as a trigger device that allows players credibly to precommit to carry out retaliation in case of unjust harm. These human traits allow players to avoid the undesirable outcome of mutual aggression and unregulated revenge that dominates in the absence of such emotional or cultural constraints.

1. Early notions of punitive justice are embedded in the ancient practices of indiscriminate personal revenge. In this sense, biblical scholars describe practices of retaliation as a form of "revenge traveling toward justice (Blau 1916, 4).

2. Evolutionary psychologists and Darwinian anthropologists do not view reciprocal and retaliatory behavior as the result of a gene that subconsciously motivates its host to act in particular ways. Evolutionary psychologists hypothesize that our minds are predisposed to learn behavioral responses that promote cooperative outcomes. Although humans are not born with fair, cooperative, or reciprocal responses, they learn such responses developmentally from social exposure.

3. Friedman and Singh (1999) show that positive or negative regard for others is not an innate and unconditional sentiment but rather is contingent on others' behavior.

4. Intention-based theories predict an absence of punishment in games in which no intention can be expressed. The motive to punish unfair intentions plays an important role in negative reciprocity. Fehr and Schmidt (2000) provide evidence suggesting that many subjects who reduce the payoff of other players lack the desire to change the equitability of the payoff allocation. Instead, many subjects seem driven by the desire to punish. The desire to hurt other players is consistent with intention-based models of reciprocity.

5. Friedman and Singh (1999) point out viability and credibility problems with vengeance and negative reciprocity. These problems find different answers in the literature. Bowles and Gintis (2001) consider the genetic evolution of vengeance in the context of a voluntary contribution game. They contemplate a direct tie between two discrete traits, a preference for punishing shirkers and a preference for helping a team of cooperators. Friedman and Singh propose a coevolution model to demonstrate the vengeance motive, where coevolution refers to the interaction of individual-level ("gene") selection and group-level ("meme") selection. Bowles and Gintis further note that all known groups of humans maintain social norms, or memes, that prescribe appropriate behavior toward fellow group members and typically prescribe different appropriate behavior toward individuals outside the group. The success of the meme, as with any other adaptive unit, is measured by its ability to displace alternatives, or its fitness. A meme prescribing a particular pattern of vengeful behavior is more fit than existing alternatives when it brings higher average fitness to group members.

6. The authors model the important role of vengeance in sustaining coopera-

tive behavior but highlight an intrinsic free-rider problem: "the fitness benefits of vengeance are dispersed through the entire group but the fitness costs are borne personally" (Friedman and Singh 1999, 19).

7. Because $0 < c < b < a$, $s_1^S = \dfrac{b}{2a} < \dfrac{b}{a} < 1 = s_1^N$ and $s_2^S = \dfrac{c}{2a} < \dfrac{c}{a} < 1 = s_2^N$.

8. That is, $\dfrac{2c^2 - b^2}{4a}$ is positive if $2c^2 > b^2$. Because $c < b$ implies $c^2 < b^2$, the requirement that $2c^2 > b^2$ must hold for the payoff of the weaker party to be positive means that $c$ cannot be too much smaller than $b$.

9. Under a kind-for-kind regime, wrongdoing was vindicated by the victim (or in the case of homicide, by the closest kin within the group). These practices of retaliation initially allowed private revenge with talionic multipliers greater than 1 and gave origin to possible spirals of violence.

10. Parisi (2001) notes that in the event of an involuntary disturbance of the peaceful equilibrium (e.g., involuntary harm, mistakenly attributed wrongdoing, etc.), a costly game of mutual aggression would follow.

11. In the absence of a commonly accepted rule, the measure of revenge was left to the discretion of the victim or his clan. As historians and anthropologists tell us, in-kind punishment often came in multiples of the harm originally suffered by the victim. Parisi (2001) considers the dynamics of retaliation under this early regime of retaliatory punishment.

12. The absence of a police system across different clans may thus explain why the kind-for-kind practices of retaliation historically preceded the institution of measure-for-measure retaliation.

13. Unlike prior practices carried out in the absence of customary or codified rules, the *lex talionis* created an express and well-defined punitive rule. The victim (or the victim's family) was entitled and, at the same time, obligated to perpetrate literal talionis in the measure indicated by the law: "Thou shalt give life for life, eye for eye, tooth for tooth, hand for hand, foot for foot, burning for burning, wound for wound, stripe for stripe" (Exodus 21:23–25).

14. A possible explanation for the higher-than-proportional instinct for revenge is given by the presence of enforcement errors, requiring higher multipliers to maintain effective deterrence.

15. The avengers of blood risked their own lives for the vindication of the group as a whole (Sulzberger 1915).

16. The vindication of an innocent victim is generally carried out by the victim's clan. As pointed out by the rabbinic interpretations, under the older tradition described in Genesis, the blood avenger is not a definite person—any member of the tribe could carry out the retaliation (Sulzberger 1915, 1, 116). The action, however, was ordinarily orchestrated by the chief of the clan, who, acting as a residual claimant, had an interest in minimizing the external losses to his group. Under the later rule of Deuteronomy, we find a more detailed specifica-

tion of the procedure for the talionic punishment. The diffuse punitive entitlement of the earlier customs described in Genesis rendered the administration of justice rather uncertain and unrestrained. The change brought about by the rules of Deuteronomy reduced the risk of coordination errors, avoiding the possibility of multiple reprisals for the same wrong as well as the likelihood of leaving some wrongs unpunished. Under the regime of Deuteronomy, the institution of *Goel*, the nearest of blood, evolves. In the absence of a central law enforcement system, the closest family member of the victim had the right, and more important, the duty to carry out retaliation. Failure to carry out such a gloomy task was considered disgraceful. This further assured the consistent punishment of wrongdoers.

17. Anthropologists and legal historians note that talionic rules always impose harm in the same objective gravity (eye for an eye) regardless of the subjective loss suffered by the victim (Parisi 2001).

18. The notation ~ is used to represent the choice variable of a party in stage 3, the subscript $i$ refers to party $i$, and the superscript $R$ denotes decisions made under the retaliation game.

19. The problem confronting party 1 can be described more compactly by writing the two subproblems with more than one constraint and without an "if" proposition. However, our formulation renders the backward induction more transparent.

20. In fact, an infinite number of choices that party 2 can take all lead to the same payoff.

21. Interestingly, this limit is applicable independently of the level of social undesirability of the crime and the probability of detection of the wrongdoer. The generality of the 1:1 constraint, however, had several advantages over the discretionary imposition of retaliatory penalties. Contrasting the dynamics of the two legal regimes shows that the biblical *lex talionis* introduced a stabilizing constraint in the (otherwise unstable) dynamics of discretionary retaliation (Parisi 2001).

22. Exodus 21:23–25; Leviticus 24:17–22. See note 13.

23. In this way the *lex talionis* provided at the same time for an upper and a lower limit to punishment.

24. Parisi (2001) suggests that kind-for-kind retaliation regimes might lead to explosive spirals of violence when parties have different conceptions of fair retaliation. In this sense, the transition from kind-for-kind retaliation to measure-for-measure retaliation may be explained by the need to avoid such an escalation of violence.

25. This is indicated by the fact that the payoff for party 2, the weaker party, can be positive or negative under kind-for-kind retaliation.

REFERENCES

Blau, A. 1916. Lex talionis. *Yearbook of the Central Conference of American Rabbis* 26:1, 7.

Bowles, S., and H. Gintis. 2001. The evolution of strong reciprocity. www.umass .edu /economics /publications /econ2000_05.pdf.

Buchanan, J. 1978. Markets, states and the extent of morals. *American Economic Review* 68:364 – 68.

Cosmides, L., and J. Tooby. 1989. *Evolutionary psychology: A primer*. Cambridge, MA: MIT Press.

Darwin, C. 1871/1994. The descent of man, and selection in relation to sex. In *The moral animal*, ed. R. Wright, 189. Repr. New York: Vintage.

Fehr, E., and K. Schmidt. 2000. Theories of fairness and reciprocity—evidence and economic applications. In *Advances in economics and econometrics— 8th World Congress, Econometric Society monographs*, ed. M. Dewatripont, L. Hansen, and S. Turnovsky, 208 –257. Cambridge: Cambridge University Press.

Fon, V., and F. Parisi. 2003. Reciprocity-induced cooperation. *Journal of Institutional and Theoretical Economics* 159:76 –92.

Friedman, D., and N. Singh. 1999. On the viability of vengeance. Discussion paper, University of California, Santa Cruz.

Gintis, H. 2000. *Game theory evolving: A problem-centered introduction to modeling strategic behavior*. Princeton, NJ: Princeton University Press.

Hoffman, E., K. McCabe, and V. Smith. 1998. Behavioral foundations of reciprocity: Experimental economics and evolutionary psychology. *Economic Inquiry* 36 (3): 335 –52.

Parisi, F. 2001. The genesis of liability in ancient law. *American Law and Economics Review* 3:82.

Sulzberger, M. 1915. *The ancient Hebrew law of homicide*. Philadelphia: Greenstone.

# 7 | WHAT MAKES TRADE POSSIBLE?

*Elizabeth Hoffman, Kevin McCabe, and Vernon Smith*

Trade is a ubiquitous activity, and yet, like spoken language, we take it for granted, rarely conscious of the complex interactions taking place between others and ourselves. Consequently, our question may seem at first trivial, or maybe unnecessary, because in fact we seem to have no trouble trading. However, the social world in which we live is becoming increasingly complex, and institutions that support trade will likely have to occur more by informed design than by adaptation through spontaneous order from incremental change and selection. For example, with the recent introduction of the Internet, computer and communication technologies allow potential trading partners to be anywhere. Trades can take place at any time, and almost any degree of anonymity can be guaranteed. But this anonymity has increased the potential for opportunistic behavior and has created a public outcry for solutions. In this chapter we provide a framework for understanding the difference between trade that takes place between partners and trade between anonymous strangers.

There is considerable interest in studying the development of institutions that reduce opportunistic behavior, allowing economic agents to maximize potential gains from exchange. Coleman (1990) describes a number of social capital infrastructures that facilitate cooperation, and Putnam (1995) asks, why do traditional organized forms of social capital formation seem to be in decline today? Ostrom (1992) asks, how do in-groups form the social capital that allows them to benefit from mutual exchange? And North (1990) asks, how did northern Europeans in the late medieval and early modern periods develop institutions that allowed the development of relatively anonymous long-distance trade and long-run economic growth?

North makes the case for the development of effective third-party enforcement to allow impersonal exchange between groups. His central hypothesis is that deficiencies in economic growth can be attributed in large part to the failure of exchange institutions to develop mechanisms of third-party enforcement that are necessary to support long-distance (or impersonal) exchange. Drawing on North's insights about the development of long-distance trade, we address the following research questions: Why is third-party enforcement necessary for impersonal exchange, but not for personal exchange? And what makes third-party enforcement effective?

To answer these questions, we must first understand how humans have solved the problem of personal exchange. Evolutionary psychologists (see Barkow, Cosmides, and Tooby 1992) hypothesize that we have evolved mental modules that allow us to readily devise, and enforce, the implicit contracts necessary for personal exchange. These modules include an emotionally regulated response to either the creation of, or the defection from, an implicit contract. They hypothesize that humans have the ability to naturally infer the epistemic states of others, to detect others' intentions, and to autonomically engage in appropriate reciprocity behaviors. Hoffman, McCabe, and Smith (1998) use research from evolutionary psychologists to interpret data on cooperation in two-person bargaining games.

McCabe and Smith (1999) have developed a theory of mental accounting that individuals are postulated to use to solve the problem of social exchange. Goodwill accounting is a reputation scoring mechanism whereby people keep mental accounts of the extent to which potential trading partners can be relied upon to use trust in exchange settings. Subjects then weigh the subjective risk of cooperation against the goodwill of their trading partners to decide whether or not to initiate, or reciprocate, potential exchanges. We hypothesize in this chapter that the subjective risk of trading, as well as the goodwill of potential trading partners, will be updated, but differently, as individuals gain experience in different trading environments. Not only do people keep goodwill accounts but research by cognitive neural psychologists Baron-Cohen (1995) and Brothers (1995) suggests that people are good at reading how much goodwill they have with others in a variety of exchange environments.

However, the modules that govern intentionality detection and reciprocity have been adaptively constructed over evolutionary time to create forms of social capital that support highly personal networks of exchange. See Colson (1974) for an analysis of social networks in tribal societies. Economic history, on the other hand, documents that most of the world's sustained economic growth has occurred in the last thousand years. Given this rapid change in our economic environment, mental modules for personal exchange that developed in evolutionary time are likely to be inadequate for modern exchange. So how is modern trade made possible? Most economists would agree that economic growth is sustained by an ever-widening circular flow of goods and services made available through specialization and technological innovation. Furthermore, to take advantage of the gains from exchange made possible through technological innovation, institutions must be invented to augment the mind's natural capacity for personal exchange and create new forms of social capital.

In this chapter we consider a two-person, extensive-form "assurance" game that offers players two alternatives for achieving a cooperative exchange: the Trust subgame requires mutual trust; whereas the Punish subgame offers a credible assurance that cheaters will be punished when they fail to reciprocate on an exchange. We postulate that individuals first try to use positive reciprocity responses (Trust subgame) that represent adaptations for personal exchange in long-term relationships. If this fails, they then resort to assurances of third-party enforcement (Punish subgame) to achieve the gains from exchange. We predict that the form of the economic environment, either personal exchange or impersonal exchange, will play an important role in determining what kind of social capital is required.

## 7.1 EXPERIMENTAL DESIGN

Our experimental design manipulates two variables. The first variable changes the degree to which goodwill accounting can be used to build social capital that sustains cooperation. This variable takes on two values, same pairing (for personal exchange settings) or distinct pairings (for impersonal exchange settings). The second variable changes the amount of subjective risk subjects are predicted to associate with cooperation and highlights the importance of institutions in building social capital that sustains cooperation. This variable takes on two values that reflect the opportunity cost of offering assurances through third-party enforcement.

### 7.1.1 The Extensive Form Game

The extensive form game studied in this chapter is adapted from McCabe, Rassenti, and Smith (1996) and illustrated in Figure 7.1. The low opportunity cost form of the game (LOC), which we discuss first, has symmetric outcomes of 150 points to each player on both sides of the tree. The game is played as follows. Player 1 moves first at node $x_1$. He or she can either end the game, at a payoff of 0 points to each player, or move down, allowing player 2 to go left or right at node $x_2$. If player 2 goes left, the next option to player 1 is the same as it is on the right side of the tree: stop the game at 100 points to player 1 and 0 points to player 2, or move down at $x_3$. The interesting difference between the left and right sides of the tree comes with the next decision on the left side. If player 1 moves down at $x_3$,

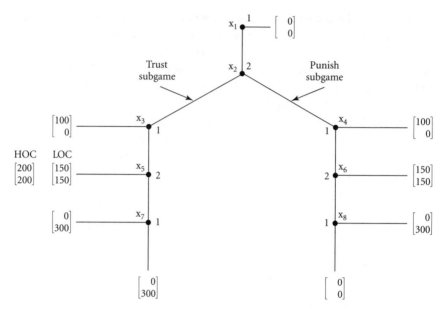

**Figure 7.1** Decision trees for assurance game. The high opportunity cost (HOC) payoff condition makes left-branch cooperation more valuable than left-branch cooperation in the low opportunity cost (LOC) payoff condition. Otherwise, all payoffs remain the same.

player 2 can either end the game at 150 points for each player or move down at $x_5$, thereby guaranteeing himself or herself 300 points. Thus, on the left side of the tree, player 1 should move down at $x_3$ only if he or she can trust that player 2 will move left instead of down at $x_5$.

If player 2 goes right, player 1 then has the option of stopping the game at 100 points to player 1 and 0 points to player 2 or moving down at $x_4$. Player 2 then has the option of stopping the game at 150 points to each player or moving down at $x_6$. If player 2 moves down at $x_6$, player 1 has the option of stopping the game at either 0 points to each player or at 0 points to himself or herself and 300 points to player 2. The punishment option, down at $x_8$, we interpret as being made possible by a third-party enforcement mechanism. If player 1 plays "steal" (down at $x_6$), then player 1 can move to have the surplus confiscated by a third party (the experimenter).

Notice that cooperation to split the total possible payoff of 300 points can be achieved on either side of the game tree. However, cooperation on the left can only be achieved if player 1 is sufficiently *trusting* to move down at $x_3$ and player 2 is sufficiently *trustworthy* to move left at $x_5$. Cooperation on the right can be achieved by threat of punishment. If player 1 moves down at $x_4$ and player 2 does not move right at $x_6$, player 1 can punish player 2 at no cost.

Note, however, that cooperation by trust weakly dominates cooperation by threat of punishment. If the right and left branches of the tree are compared, the payoffs are the same at adjacent nodes except at the bottom, where there are 300 more points available at $x_7$ than at $x_8$. The game involves assurance because a right move by player 2 at $x_2$ assures player 1 that it is not in player 2's interest to move down at $x_6$. No such assurance characterizes defection at $x_5$ on the left.

In the high opportunity cost (HOC) form of the game, we introduce a payoff benefit associated with cooperation on the left. The payoff to each participant increases from 150 to 200 if they cooperate on the left instead of on the right. Alternatively, this benefit to cooperation on the left can be viewed as an opportunity cost associated with using a third-party mechanism to provide assurance that cheaters will be punished. In these treatments, we operationalize the cost associated with maintaining institutions for cooperation through threat of punishment in impersonal trade.

## 7.1.2 Experimental Treatments

We repeat each game in two different ways to vary the degree to which goodwill accounting can be used to build social capital that sustains cooperation. In the personal exchange (PE) environment, players are paired with the same partner for fifteen trials. In the impersonal exchange (IE) environment, each player plays exactly once with every other player. Thus, the game is repeated fifteen times, but on each trial each player plays with a distinct other player. On each trial the role, player 1 or 2, is randomly assigned within each pair. Table 7.1 describes the number of sessions, pairings, and outcomes for each cell of our 2 × 2 design.

TABLE 7.1
*Experimental design*

| | OPPORTUNITY COST OF THIRD-PARTY ENFORCEMENT | |
|---|---|---|
| Exchange environment Type of repeated exchange | Low opportunity cost (LOC) 150 | High opportunity cost (HOC) 200 |
| Personal (PE) Same pairing | 3/24/360* | 3/24/360 |
| Impersonal (IE) Distinct pairing | 3/24/360 | 3/22/352 |

*a/b/c where a = number of sessions, b = number of pairs, and c = number of observations.

### 7.1.3 Hypotheses

We hypothesize that there will be a significant difference in the way bargaining pairs adapt over time, both between the PE and the IE environments and between the LOC and HOC payoff conditions. We further hypothesize that subjects who must move at node $x_2$ will place a higher subjective risk to moving left, that is, trusting their counterparts, in the LOC condition than the risk they will assign to moving left in the HOC condition. Goodwill accounting asserts that subjects will move left at $x_2$ when their counterparts have sufficient goodwill to cover the subjective risks of cooperating. Therefore, for the same initial levels of goodwill we predict that subjects are more likely to begin playing left in the HOC condition than in the LOC condition.

In the IE environment, subjects are distinctly paired in each trial. Based on this meeting experience, we predict they will update their estimates of the subjective risks of cooperation on the left. The less cooperative past counterparts have been, the greater the risks they will assign to playing left with future counterparts. However, in the PE environment, where subjects always meet the same counterparts, they have no new information, and thus we predict will not update the subjective risks of moving left. Moreover, in the PE environment, we predict that subjects will update the goodwill of their counterparts, something they cannot do in the IE environment. The more cooperative counterparts are, the more goodwill they get, whereas defection reduces goodwill.

Because the left branch of the game has greater built-in incentives for defection, we predict that the ability to build goodwill will be important in sustaining cooperation on this side. Thus, we predict greater left-branch cooperation in the PE environment than in the IE environment in both the LOC and HOC conditions. Furthermore, because the reward from left-branch cooperation is higher in the HOC condition, we predict that within the PE environment, left-branch cooperation will be higher in the HOC condition than in the LOC condition. Finally, because the subjective risk of playing left starts out lower in the HOC condition, we predict that left-branch play in the IE environment will deteriorate more slowly in the HOC condition than in the LOC condition.

In the IE environment, there is no opportunity to develop a trust relationship with one person, making the maintenance of personal exchange difficult. Some players 2 may go left at first, but they are likely to encounter players 1 who are not trusting enough to move down at $x_3$, and they will be discouraged from future left-branch play. Players 2 who move left and are paired with players 1 who move down at $x_3$ will increase the subjective risk of playing left and will become less trustworthy with other counterparts when they are player 1. This will further discourage left-branch play. Thus, we expect the IE outcomes to converge to (150, 150) cooperation on the right. The threat of punishment provides assurance to players 1 who are not trusting and punishment for players 2 who are not trustworthy. In the language of exchange institutions, players will use the assurance of being able to punish cheating to build social capital for cooperation on the right branch of the game.

We note that our hypotheses are all extragame theoretical (that is, the hypotheses are generated by assumptions outside those usually made by game theoretical models). Because the game will be repeated only a finite number of times, Nash equilibrium game theory predicts right-branch play for all pairs in both the PE and IE environments and the LOC and HOC conditions. Left-branch play, if it occurs at all, should always result in the outcome (100, 0).

### 7.1.4 Procedures

Experiments were conducted at the University of Arizona's Economic Science Laboratory. Subjects received five dollars upon appearing for the experiment and were paid privately their accumulated earnings after the experiment was completed. The instructions and the game tree were displayed on computers. Subjects indicated their choices by using the computer mouse to click on arrows indicating the direction of move at each node.

Each player was seated at an isolated computer terminal. All players were in the same computer laboratory, but each subject knew only that he or she was paired with another player in the same laboratory. The identity of the pairings was never revealed. In the PE environment, each subject was informed that he or she would be matched once at random with some other subject and would interact with that person repeatedly for the entire experiment. In the IE environment, each subject was told that he or she would be matched exactly once with every other subject in the laboratory, with random assignment of player types on each interaction. In both the PE and IE environments, no subject was told the identity of any other subject with whom he or she was paired.

### 7.2 RESULTS

Figures 7.2 and 7.3 display the experimental results by treatment, game, and groups of decision trials. The numbers along the sides of the figures represent the outcomes in each of the two treatments' successive groups of trials. Notice that in the (PE, LOC) experiments (Figure 7.2), left play declines at first but then stabilizes at approximately one-third of total outcomes in trials 6–15. Moreover, whether subjects play right or left, they are likely to end at one of the cooperative outcomes.

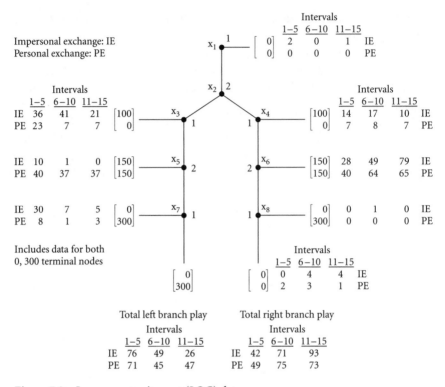

**Figure 7.2**   Low opportunity cost (LOC) data

In the (PE, HOC) experiments (Figure 7.3), left play starts out high and remains high for the entire experiment. As in the LOC experiments, the outcome is generally cooperative. But, as predicted, increasing the benefit associated with cooperation on the left increases left cooperative play.

Left play in the (IE, LOC) experiments (Figure 7.2) declines across trial blocks. Of those pairs that do play left, most of the PE pairs end at (150, 150). In contrast, most of the IE pairs end at (100, 0). Those of the IE pairs who do venture beyond (100, 0) generally go to (0, 300) instead of (150, 150). Thus, for those going left, trust can be maintained in the PE pairings but not in the IE pairings.

There is a similar, although less pronounced, difference between the PE and the IE environments on the right branch in the LOC condition. A small, but consistent number of IE pairs continue to stop at (100, 0), even on the right, whereas an increasing number do find the cooperative outcome of (150, 150). Those that cheat on a move down at (100, 0) almost always get punished and end up at (0, 0). Comparing by trial block, fewer PE pairings stop at (100, 0). Almost all those that move right end up at (150, 150). Of the few who try to cheat, all get punished.

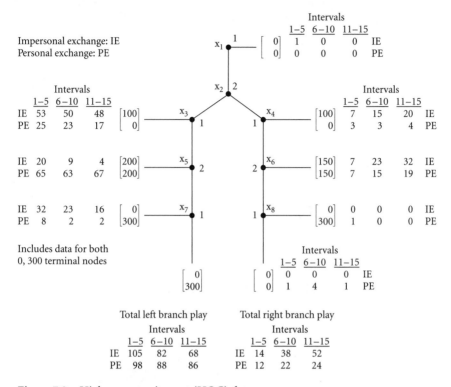

**Figure 7.3**   High opportunity cost (HOC) data

As predicted, raising the opportunity cost associated with cooperation through threat of punishment in the HOC experiment (Figure 7.3) makes the development of cooperation particularly difficult in the IE experiments. Although left play declines over the course of the experiments, it is not extinguished, as it is in the LOC experiment. Even though players continue to play left, however, cooperation on the left declines throughout the experiment. An increasing proportion of left play results in either a (100, 0) or a (0, 300) outcome. The difficulty associated with continued attempts to cooperate on the left also affects the attempts to cooperate on the right. Those that do move right continue to get stopped at (100, 0), even though every move down ends at (150, 150). Thus, history matters, and the resulting dynamics affects the path to a new stationary equilibrium (North 1990).

Tables 7.2–7.5 display the data in the form of node and branch conditional probabilities for each outcome. They are read as follows. Looking at row 1 for (IE, LOC) (Table 7.2) in trial 1, of the twenty-three pairs that got to the top of the tree (one stopped at 0, 0), eleven went left and twelve went right. Thus, conditional on getting to the top of the tree, the probability of going left was 0.48 and of going

## TABLE 7.2

Low Opportunity Cost (LOC) Payoff Condition, Impersonal Exchange (IE) Environment, Node (Branch) Conditional Outcome Frequencies

| Trials | Left branch | $E(\pi_2\mid$ left) | 100 / 0 | $E(\pi_1\mid$ down) | 150 / 150 | 0 / 300 | Right branch | $E(\pi_2\mid$ right) | 100 / 0 | $E(\pi_1\mid$ down) | 150 / 150 | 0 / 300 | 0 / 0 |
|---|---|---|---|---|---|---|---|---|---|---|---|---|---|
| 1 | 11/23 = .478 | 136 | 5/11 = .455 (.455) | 50 | 2/6 = .333 (.182) | 4/4 = 1 (.364) | 12/23 = .522 | 138 | 1/12 = .083 (.083) | 150 | 11/11 = 1 (.917) | 0 | 0 |
| 1–5 | 76/118 = .644 | 138 | 36/76 = .474 (.474) | 37 | 10/40 = .25 (.132) | 30/30 = 1 (.395) | 42/118 = .356 | 100 | 14/42 = .333 (.333) | 150 | 28/28 = 1 (.667) | 0 | 0 |
| 6–10 | 49/120 = .408 | 46 | 41/49 = .837 (.837) | 19 | 1/8 = .125 (.020) | 7/7 = 1 (.143) | 71/120 = .592 | 108 | 17/71 = .239 (.230) | 136 | 49/54 = .907 (.690) | 1/5 = .20 (.014) | 4/5 = .80 (.056) |
| 11–15 | 26/119 = .218 | 58 | 21/26 = .808 (.008) | 0 | 0 | 5/5 = 1 (.192) | 93/119 = .782 | 127 | 10/93 = .108 (.108) | 143 | 79/83 = .952 (.849) | 0 | 4/4 = 1 (.043) |
| 15 | 2/24 = .083 | 0 | 2/2 = 1 (1) | 0 | 0 | 0 | 22/24 = .917 | 136 | 2/22 = .091 (.091) | 150 | 20/20 = 1 (.909) | 0 | 0 |

right was 0.52. Of the eleven that went left, five stopped at (100, 0) and six went down, for conditional probabilities of 0.45 left and 0.55 down. Of the six that went down, only two stopped at (150, 150); the rest went down, cheating on their partners' trust. As the (IE, LOC) experiments progress, the conditional probability of left play at the top of the tree declines from 0.64 in trials 1–5 (0.48 in trial 1) to 0.22 in trials 11–15 (0.08 in trial 15). For those pairs that do go left, the conditional probability of stopping at (100, 0) rises from 0.47 in trials 1–5 to 0.84 in trials 6–10 and 0.81 in trials 11–15. For those who try to go beyond (100, 0), the trusting partner almost always loses.

On the right-hand side of the tree, the conditional probability of stopping at (100, 0) falls from 0.33 in trials 1–5 to 0.24 in trials 6–10 to 0.11 in trials 11–15. For those pairs who do go past (100, 0), the conditional probability of achieving (150, 150) is consistently better than 0.90, with almost all deviations punished with a (0, 0) payoff. Thus, (IE, LOC) pairs can learn to cooperate. But they must first find the right side of the tree and then be willing to move down at (100, 0). Finding (150, 150) requires trial and error. First, they may stop at (100, 0) on either the left or the right, or one player may cheat at (0, 300) on the left. If they tried left first, they may eventually move right. Once they have moved right, either at the beginning or later, they may find (150, 150). However, some must stop first at (100, 0). Those that do venture past (100, 0) on the right almost always find (150, 150).

In contrast with the (IE, LOC) results, the conditional probability of left play declines at first (Table 7.3) but then stabilizes at 0.38–0.39 in the (PE, LOC) pairings. Of those that go left, only 0.15–0.16 stop at (100, 0). The rest go down, with a conditional probability of 0.92–0.97 of achieving (150, 150) in the last ten trials. For those who go right, the conditional probability of stopping at (100, 0) stabilizes quickly at 0.10–0.15, and the conditional probability of achieving (150, 150) also stabilizes quickly at better than 0.95. Thus, for PE pairings, left and right play quickly becomes equally profitable.

Tables 7.4 and 7.5 show the impact of increasing the payoff to cooperation on the left to (200, 200) in the conditional probabilities framework. For PE pairs, increasing the payoff makes left play consistently more likely. The conditional probability of left play is 91% in the first trial and 77% in the last trial, with an average probability more than 80%. Moreover, the conditional probability of getting to (200, 200), once play has proceeded left and down, is about 90%, with about 60% of all the trials ending in a (200, 200) outcome. This outcome suggests that in a world of personal exchange and mutual trust and trustworthiness, trading partners are quite adept at maximizing and equally distributing the gains from exchange.

As Table 7.5 shows, however, increasing the opportunity cost of using punishment to enforce cooperation through impersonal exchange makes the development

## TABLE 7.3

Low Opportunity Cost (LOC) Payoff Condition, Personal Exchange (PE) Environment, Node (Branch) Conditional Outcome Frequencies

| Trials | Left branch | $E(\pi_2\mid$ left) | 100 0 | $E(\pi_1\mid$ down) | 150 150 | 0 300 | Right branch | $E(\pi_2\mid$ right) | 100 0 | $E(\pi_1\mid$ down) | 150 150 | 0 300 | 0 0 |
|---|---|---|---|---|---|---|---|---|---|---|---|---|---|
| 1 | 17/24 = .708 | 79 | 8/17 = .471 (.471) | 150 | 9/9 = 1 (.529) | 0 | 7/24 = .292 | 129 | 1/7 = .143 (.143) | 150 | 6/6 = 1 (.857) | 0 | 0 0 |
| 1–5 | 71/120 = .592 | 118 | 23/71 = .324 (.324) | 125 | 40/48 = .833 (.563) | 8/8 = 1 (.113) | 49/120 = .408 | 122 | 7/49 = .143 (.143) | 143 | 40/42 = .952 (.816) | 0 | 2/2 = 1 (.041) |
| 6–10 | 45/120 = .375 | 139 | 7/45 = .156 (.156) | 146 | 37/38 = .974 (.882) | 1/1 = 1 (.022) | 75/120 = .625 | 128 | 8/75 = .107 (.107) | 143 | 64/67 = .955 (.853) | 0 | 3/3 = 1 (.040) |
| 11–15 | 47/120 = .392 | 137 | 7/47 = .149 (.149) | 139 | 37/40 = .925 (.787) | 3/3 = 1 (.064) | 73/120 = .608 | 134 | 7/73 = .096 (.096) | 148 | 65/66 = .985 (.890) | 0 | 1/1 = 1 (.014) |
| 15 | 8/24 = .333 | 150 | 1/8 = .125 (.125) | 129 | 6/7 = .857 (.755) | 1/1 = 1 (.125) | 16/24 = .667 | 141 | 1/16 = .063 (.063) | 150 | 15/15 = 1 (.938) | 0 | 0 0 |

TABLE 7.4

Table 7.4
High Opportunity Cost (HOC) Payoff Condition, Personal Exchange (PE) Environment, Conditional (Unconditional) Outcome Frequencies

| Trials | Left branch | $E(\pi_2\|$ left) | 100 / 0 | $E(\pi_1\|$ down) | 200 / 200 | 0 / 300 | Right branch | $E(\pi_2\|$ right) | 100 / 0 | $E(\pi_1\|$ down) | 150 / 150 | 0 / 300 | 0 / 0 |
|---|---|---|---|---|---|---|---|---|---|---|---|---|---|
| 1 | 20/22 = .91 | 140 | 7/20 = .35 (.318) | 169 | 11/13 = .846 (.50) | 2/2 = 1 (.091) | 2/22 = .091 | 150 | 0 | 150 | 2/2 = 1 (.091) | 0 | 0 |
| 1–5 | 98/110 = .891 | 157 | 25/98 = .255 (.227) | 178 | 65/73 = .89 (.591) | 8/8 = 1 (.073) | 12/110 = 0.11 | 112 | 3/12 = .25 (.027) | 117 | 7/9 = .778 (.064) | 1/2 = .5 (.01) | 1/2 = .5 (.01) |
| 6–10 | 88/110 = .80 | 150 | 23/88 = .261 (.209) | 194 | 63/65 = .969 (.573) | 2/2 = 1 (.018) | 22/110 = .20 | 102 | 3/22 = .136 (.027) | 118 | 15/19 = .789 (.136) | 0 | 4/4 = 1 (.036) |
| 11–16 | 103/132 = .780 | 166 | 19/103 = .184 (.144) | 193 | 81/84 = .964 (.614) | 3/3 = 1 (.025) | 29/132 = .220 | 124 | 4/29 = .138 (.033) | 144 | 24/25 = .960 (.182) | 0 | 1/1 = 1 (.001) |
| 15 | 17/22 = .773 | 182 | 2/17 = .118 (.091) | 187 | 14/15 = .933 (.636) | 1/1 = 1 (.045) | 5/22 = .227 | 150 | 0 | 150 | 5/5 = 1 (.227) | 0 | 0 |

TABLE 7.5

High Opportunity Cost (HOC) Condition, Impersonal Exchange (IE) Environment, Conditional (Unconditional) Outcome Frequencies

| Trials | Left branch | $E(\pi_2\mid \text{left})$ | 100 / 0 | $E(\pi_1\mid \text{down})$ | 200 / 200 | 0 / 300 | Right branch | $E(\pi_2\mid \text{right})$ | 100 / 0 | $E(\pi_1\mid \text{down})$ | 150 / 150 | 0 / 300 | 0 / 0 |
|---|---|---|---|---|---|---|---|---|---|---|---|---|---|
| 1 | 22/24 = .917 | 163 | 10/22 = .455 (.417) | 100 | 6/12 = .50 (.25) | 6/6 = 1 (.25) | 2/24 = .083 | 75 | 1/2 = .5 (.041) | 150 | 1/1 = 1 (.041) | 0 | 0 |
| 1–5 | 105/119 = .882 | 129 | 53/105 = .505 (.445) | 77 | 20/52 = .385 (.168) | 32/32 = 1 (.269) | 14/119 = .118 | 75 | 7/14 = .50 (.059) | 150 | 7/7 = 1 (.059) | 0 | 0 |
| 6–10 | 82/120 = .683 | 106 | 50/82 = .610 (.417) | 56 | 9/32 = .281 (.075) | 23/23 = 1 (.192) | 38/120 = .317 | 91 | 15/38 = .395 (.125) | 150 | 23/23 = 1 (.192) | 0 | 0 |
| 11–15 | 68/120 = .567 | 82 | 48/68 = .706 (.40) | 40 | 4/20 = .20 (.033) | 16/16 = 1 (.133) | 52/120 = .433 | 92 | 20/52 = .385 (.167) | 150 | 32/32 = 1 (.267) | 0 | 0 |
| 15 | 11/24 = .458 | 127 | 6/11 = .545 (.25) | 40 | 1/5 = .20 (.042) | 4/4 = 1 (.167) | 13/24 = .541 | 104 | 4/13 = .308 (.167) | 150 | 9/9 = 1 (.375) | 0 | 0 |

of cooperation much harder to achieve. In contrast to the (IE, LOC) experiments, in which less than half went left on the first trial, more than 91% try left play on the first trial. Although left play declines, it still averages more than 50% for the last five trials. Thus, at the end of the (IE, HOC) experiments, subjects are just getting to the point where they start in the (IE, LOC) condition. Despite continued attempts to go left and a better than 50% conditional probability of going down after going left, they never achieve cooperation to any great extent. Conditional on going left and down, only about 30% cooperate. The rest cheat. Yet they keep trying, frustrating the development of mechanisms for enforcing cooperation through threat of punishment. The higher payoff on the left is simply too tempting. Averaged over the last five trials, less than 30% of the outcomes can be characterized as cooperative on either the left or the right. This illustrates how difficult it is to develop mechanisms to support impersonal trade when maintaining those mechanisms requires that traders forgo gains that could be captured through personal trade or through cheating on attempts to develop personal trading relationships.

If we look at the decision in terms of the expected value of moving left or right and then out or down, we can see how the incentives drive the outcomes. In the (IE, LOC) experiments, shown in Table 7.2, the expected value of left play declines from 136 in trial 1 to 0 in trial 15. Once players have gone right, the expected value of playing down is consistently higher than the expected value of any other action, averaging more than 140 throughout the experiment.

In contrast, in the (IE, HOC) experiments shown in Table 7.5, the expected value of left play is 163 in trial 1 and is still high, 127, in trial 15. Similarly, once players have gone right, the expected value of playing down is 150 throughout the experiment. Thus, despite continued cheating on the left and a high conditional expected value associated with cooperation on the right, the expected value of playing left stays sufficiently high to keep players from moving to the right branch of the game.

In the PE environment shown in Tables 7.3 and 7.4, the expected value of left play starts high and rises throughout the trials in both the LOC and HOC payoff conditions.

## 7.3 CONCLUSIONS

The complex organization of the human mind is known to be the product of at least a few million years of evolutionary adaptation to solve the problems of hunting and gathering. The ability to infer other players' mental states, reciprocity, and the ability to detect and punish cheaters are important elements of a mind adapted to personal exchange in hunter-gatherer environments. The experiments discussed in this chapter illustrate how humans use these skills to their advantage in two different environments in which cooperation is possible. In one case, achieving cooperation is relatively easy; in the other, it is considerably more difficult.

The personal exchange cases illustrate how even anonymous members of a group can form stable pairs, communicate with signals, develop relationships of trust, learn to read one another's minds, and achieve consistent cooperation. Moreover, when the stakes associated with one kind of cooperation increase relative to another, each easily infers that the other would prefer the higher payoff.

The impersonal exchange cases illustrate how individuals who are trying to cooperate must warily test each new individual. Cooperation through trust is almost impossible in such an environment because no individual has the opportunity to build a reputation for trust. If player 2 wants to cooperate, he or she must move right at the top of the tree. That provides "assurance" to player 1 that player 2 is willing to submit to punishment for cheating. On the left, player 2 can cheat with impunity. Player 1 may still be wary of players 2's intentions and go right at (100, 0). But some players 1 will take the chance and go down at (100, 0), allowing players 2 to go right at (150, 150) or to cheat (0, 300). Moreover, both players must go through this elaborate dance each period because each one meets a new "friend" or "foe" each time.

Over time, as a variety of different players in the population interact with one another in the (IE, LOC) treatment, cooperation with assurance becomes more widespread and the institutional seeds to support impersonal, long-distance trade are planted. What is particularly interesting about this example is that cooperation does develop, despite the strong incentive for player 1 to take the (100, 0) and not run the risk of player 2 cheating. This provides one more example of the powerful importance of cooperation in social exchange. This propensity is so strong in humans that it emerges even with anonymous same pairings.

It is also interesting, however, that cooperation on either the right or the left does not develop in the (IE, HOC) treatment. The continued higher return to cooperation on the left encourages enough players 2 to go left, players 1 to go down, and players 2 to cheat. This keeps the left-play returns from opportunistic behavior by players 2 higher than the right-play returns from cooperation with assurance. This suggests that the development of impersonal trading institutions that provide third-party enforcement depends critically on creating an environment in which the returns to cooperation with threat of punishment exceed the returns from cheating.

## REFERENCES

Barkow, J., L. Cosmides, and J. Tooby, eds. 1992. *The adapted mind: Evolutionary psychology and the generation of culture*. New York: Oxford University Press.

Baron-Cohen, S. 1995. *Mindblindness: An essay on autism and theory of the mind*. Cambridge, MA: MIT Press.

Brothers, L. 1995. Neurophysiology of the perception of intentions by primates. In *The cognitive neurosciences*, ed. Michael Gazzaniga, 1107–15. Cambridge, MA: MIT Press.

Coleman, J. 1990. *Foundations of social theory*. Cambridge, MA: Harvard University Press.

Colson, Elizabeth. 1974. *Traditions and contract: The problem of order*. Chicago: Adeline.

Cosmides, L., and J. Tooby. 1994. Better than rational: Evolutionary psychology and the invisible hand. *American Economic Review* 2:327–32.

Hoffman, E., K. McCabe, and V. Smith.1998. Behavioral foundations of reciprocity: Experimental economics and evolutionary psychology. *Economic Inquiry* 36:335–52.

McCabe, K., S. Rassenti, and V. Smith. 1996. Game theory and reciprocity in some extensive form experimental games. *Proceedings of the National Academy of Sciences* 93:13421–28.

McCabe, K., and V. Smith. 1999. Goodwill accounting in economic exchange. In *Bounded rationality: The adaptive toolbox*, ed. G. Gigerenzer and R. Selten, 305–26. Cambridge, MA: MIT Press.

North, D. 1990. Institutions, institutional change and economic performance. Cambridge, MA: Cambridge University Press.

Ostrom, E. 1992. Community and the endogenous solution of common problems. *Journal of Theoretical Politics* 4 (3): 343–51.

Putnam, R. 1995. Bowling alone: America's declining social capital. *Journal of Democracy* 6 (1): 65–78.

# 8 | SATISFACTION AND LEARNING:
## AN EXPERIMENTAL GAME TO
## MEASURE HAPPINESS

*Marco Novarese and Salvatore Rizzello*

It is well known that the concept of "satisficing behavior " developed and described by Herbert Simon (1976) is the core of a decision-making model that is an alternative to the one used in standard economics. According to the standard economics model, economic agents, in their actions, exclusively apply criteria aimed at maximizing their own utility or, with reference to firms, their own profit. Maximization behavior is at the basis of the idea that a system can, in this way, reach an efficient and optimum allocation of the available resources, an allocation that guarantees the maximum level of satisfaction for all the agents and is compatible with the system's resources.

Yet according to the severe criticism that has been leveled at its foundations by extensive literature (Egidi and Rizzello 2004), this approach is on the whole unrealistic, and it is not consistent with any feedback arising from the sciences studying human behavior. Such criticism has disputed the maximization approach in favor of a more realistic approach, consistent with these sciences: the satisficing approach. According to this approach, in Simon's view, human behavior in decision-making and problem-solving processes aims at satisfying individual levels of aspiration. On the one hand, these arise from individual psycho-neurobiological

The experiment presented in the paper was carried out at the Alex Laboratory in Alessandria. We wish to thank Guido Ortona and Marie Edith Bissey for their cooperation The software used, SWIEE, was developed by Riccardo Boero. Other people participated in the organization of the experiment: Paolo Parodi, Maria Teresa Servello, Alessandra Sterpone, and Cesare Tibaldeschi. A preliminary version of this experiment was presented at the conference "The Paradoxes of Happiness," held in Milan on March 21–23, 2003. We thank Robert Sugden and Robert Frank for their useful comments.

characteristics. On the other hand, these adjust to the individual experience. Because experience is ever changing, the individual levels of aspiration become dynamic and interindividual levels of aspiration become variable.

It is evident that this kind of perspective radically changes the standard economic approach, which is based on the idea that maximization, efficiency, individual satisfaction, and social coordination are directly and automatically linked to each other. Thus, economics tends to focus attention on the necessary means to "reach efficiency" rather than on the ends. The satisficing approach, however, describes a world in which agents act in a situation of uncertainty, with limited information. These agents develop partially unstable routines and make (sometimes systematic) errors but reach effective solutions. The agents' ends cannot be precisely predetermined, and they are often unexpected and undefined because they are directly interrelated to the behavior and choices of other agents. These other agents act in a situation of uncertainty and limited information, make systematic errors, and may have differentiated levels of aspiration. Nevertheless, a relevant aspect of this approach is that the relationship between means and ends is overturned, and ends become more important than means.

In the span of five decades, the remarkable developments of Simon's studies and of the extensive literature that directly draws on his contributions to decision making have combined into the procedural rationality model, which synthesizes individual and organizational decision making. In the last decade, a new discipline known as cognitive economics has emerged (Egidi and Rizzello 2004). Additionally, a very recent branch of experimental economics has developed that deals with the experimental analysis of differentiated learning processes, of the processes of coordination in conditions of uncertainty, and of the emergence of shared rules (Egidi and Narduzzo 1997; Novarese 2003, 2004; Novarese and Rizzello 2003). Thus, the research based on Simon's work focuses on a few very specific but relevant aspects of decision making. It has highlighted the partially dynamic and partially stable nature of the individual levels of aspiration and is now trying to verify whether it is possible to gather empirical data on the level of satisfaction reached by individuals in decision-making processes.

This aspect has not been sufficiently researched, and one of the main purposes of this chapter is to suggest a possible, though fraught with difficulties, path of experimental research. As to the dynamics and the stability of the levels of aspiration, the literature offers interesting contributions (Gigerenzer 2003; Kahneman, Slovic, and Tversky 1982; Kahneman and Tversky 1979, 1984; Posch, Pichler, and Sigmund 1999; Selten 1999; Tversky and Kahneman 1974, 1986; Witt 1993). In order to explain the partially stable nature of the levels of aspiration, we may assume that two different processes occur, both of which are connected to the human perceptive characteristics. The first process is a typical path-dependent mechanism. As stated elsewhere (Rizzello 1997, 1999) and on the basis of the tradition of Hayek's contributions on perception and on the nature and role of knowledge—contributions that are complementary to Simon's works on rationality and decision making—individual perceptive mechanisms are typically path dependent and depend on both individual experience and mental and neurobiological characteristics with a highly innate component. The second mechanism, concerning the partially stable nature of the individual levels of aspiration, was developed above all by Kahneman and Tversky (1974) through the anchoring effect (the first alternative deeply affects the decision-making process; here the affinity to path dependence is evident). This mechanism was also developed by Tietz (1997), who highlighted the adaptation mechanism of the levels of aspiration following Selten's contributions on the aspiration adaptation theory, which was developed in the 1960s and only recently translated into English (Selten 1998).

Regarding the partially dynamic dimension, the recent literature offers extremely interesting contributions. Among them we wish to point out the model based on the win-stay, lose-shift principle developed by Nowak and Sigmund (1993). They draw on Thorndike's (1911) behavioral tradition, according to which an individual (or an animal in the behavioral tradition) is likely to repeat an action if it has proved successful and to change it if it has not. Although this idea is mainly applied in game theory, it explicitly stresses the problem of the change, which has also been discussed with interesting results by the cognitive theory (Witt 1993). On the basis of this theory, the following assumption takes shape: in a decision-making dimension in which alternative actions are assessed, the levels of aspiration may actually lower or rise within a given range; but if the individual were to go beyond this range, his or her actions would turn into an innovative behavior, arising from possibly incoherent high levels of dissatisfaction, which can be explained by means of the theory of cognitive dissonance (Akerlof and Dickens 1982; Festinger 1957).

In this analytical framework, this chapter aims at indicating a path of research that may offer a contribution for measuring the levels of satisfaction in decision-making processes. To this end, within an experiment designed to reach other results, we decided to try to analyze the levels of satisfaction and their evolution for the subjects involved, their connection with the shaping and the stability of the levels of aspiration, or their tendency toward change. This was carried out during another experiment whose main goal was to analyze the learning processes and the processes of coordination of individuals who were asked to decide in conditions of uncertainty and limited information. We deemed it important to extend the analysis to the levels of satisfaction, not only because it is a central aspect in Simon's model but also because this could be a relevant element per se. In fact, the subject might carry out a given action just because it is satisfying per se, independent of the economic payoff in the strict sense of the word.

Finally, it is necessary to state that a survey of the literature in this field showed that this is one of the first experiments aimed at measuring satisfaction.[1] Therefore, a number of methodological issues arise (one of the few similar experiments available in the literature is that of Charness and Haruvy [2000]). One of the purposes of this chapter is to stir a methodological discussion on these aspects.

In the next section we will first briefly illustrate the experiment and then discuss the results in detail. We hope that we can show that although the results concerning the analysis of the levels of satisfaction and their evolution are neither definitive nor consolidated, they are still significant. We are aware of these limits; nevertheless, we hope that we have pointed out a promising path that will allow us to reach more robust results in the near future by means of the tools of cognitive economics and of experimental economics.

## 8.1 EXPERIMENTAL ANALYSIS

In this section we illustrate the results of an experimental analysis in which, along with organizational coordination, the participants' level of satisfaction was measured by explicitly asking them to evaluate it themselves. This is the same method used to measure individual happiness with reference to one's own standards of living: by means of surveys, the subjects are asked to give a mark to their "life satisfaction" (see, for instance, Ferrer-i-Carbonell and Frijters 2004; Hayo and Seifert 2003).

For the experiment described here, it is necessary to take some aspects into account and to explain a few points in detail. This analysis was carried out within a broader research project aimed at studying, from a cognitive perspective, individual and organizational learning processes and the emergence of shared institutions and behaviors. In the experimental analyses based on this approach, the environment and the game proposed do not usually refer to standard situations or models of economics, because the situations are usually more complex (with reference to the kinds of variables or possible choices rather than to the task to be performed). The purpose of the research program is to understand how organizational or individual learning and decision-making processes actually work rather than to simply analyze the results. To do this, we need to enter the "black box" of the decision-making processes and understand its mechanisms. This purpose has a strong influence on the experimental approach used, as described in detail in Novarese (2003).

The analysis of satisfaction is not the specific purpose of the experiment. In fact, it is an additional analysis in an environment set up with broader purposes. This brings about a few problems and constraints concerning variables we can observe (and it does not comply with experimentalists' usual methods). Still, it allows us to assess the subjects in a less limited environment, guarantees economies of scale with other analyses, and provides interesting—though preliminary—results, which are well worth studying because they are a new kind of data.

The main purpose of this chapter is to focus on what emerges in terms of the levels of satisfaction. We will present tables that need confirmation from other studies, but they suggest important ideas that in the future might be compared with data from other similar experiments.

## 8.2 THE SUM 10 EXPERIMENT

A team of three players is anonymously and randomly built among participants. The game has 36 rounds. Each of the players has a set of numbers. This set remains unchanged in every round and is composed of the values 0, 1, 3, 4, and 10. In every round each player has to declare one of the numbers in his or her set. The numbers of the three people playing together are then summed. Based on the sum, each player receives a payoff, following this rule:

- if $S(i) = 10$, $I(i) = 40 - D(i)$
- if $S(i) > 10$, $I(i) = 30 - D(i)$
- if $S(i) < 10$, individual payoff $= 0 -$ declared number

where

- $S(i) =$ sum of the team I, of which player i is a member
- $I(i) =$ player i: individual payoff
- $D(i) =$ number declared by player i

The game is divided into two parts. In the first part (rounds 1–26) the players are coupled with artificial agents. In the second part the groups consist of permanently coupled human beings. The players do not know that they are playing with artificial agents. They are told that they will be coupled with two players in the first part and with two new players in the second part. The players do not know the number of rounds.

There are the following three kinds of artificial agents:

1. Group 1: One agent always plays 3. One agent always plays 3 (first choice) and repeats this number if in the preceding round the human player chooses 4; otherwise, it plays 0. Thus, in order to always obtain 10, the human player should choose 4.

2. Group 2: One agent always plays 4. One agent plays 3 (first choice) and repeats this number if in the preceding turn the human player chooses 3; otherwise, it chooses the necessary number to reach 10 (for example, if the player chooses 2, this agent chooses $10 - 2 - 3 = 5$; if the player chooses 4, this agent chooses 3). This way, the human player is presumably urged to always choose 3.

3. Group 3: Both artificial agents always choose 0 (in round 1 only, for technical reasons, they play a different number: 3 or 4). Therefore, in order to obtain sum 10, the players should play 10.

The experiment was carried out by means of the specific software SWIEE (Boero 2001). The appendix discusses the instructions received by the participants and the computer screens shown to the players. In each round the players are asked to choose a number, state what sum they expect to obtain in the following rounds, and estimate (with a number from 0 to 10) the level of satisfaction for the result obtained in the preceding round (in round 36 the satisfaction is missing; therefore, it will be excluded from the analysis).

The experiment was carried out in November 2002 at the Centro Alex Laboratory of the Università del Piemonte Orientale in Alessandria. The experiment was organized by the Centre for Cognitive Economics. Twenty-four first-year law students, who were attending an introductory course on economics, participated in this experiment. On the basis of the score obtained, they were granted credits for their exam. At the end of the game the participants were asked to fill in a questionnaire commenting upon the game. A note on terminology is useful here. "Total score" refers to the sum of the scores obtained in the first or second part or in the whole game. "Score" refers to the sum obtained in each round.

## 8.3 CORRELATION BETWEEN POINTS AND SATISFACTION AT AN INDIVIDUAL LEVEL

The reliability and the meaning of the data pertaining to the player's satisfaction are the first aspects of the experiment that we need to understand. The participants had no concrete motivation to disclose their actual satisfaction. Therefore, they might declare values at random. Moreover, generally speaking, a person might find it difficult to express his or her own level of satisfaction with a number, as there may be several aspects affecting that level. In order to verify the data reliability, it would be necessary to know the actual model of each player's answers, or we should decide at the least to verify a given model. In other words, data reliability might depend upon the variables we choose to verify it. But this work's aims are mainly descriptive. Therefore, the analysis does not follow strong assumptions concerning the players' behavior. Certainly, satisfaction depends upon the evolution of the game, but the variables to be taken into account may vary (and might be different for different players).

The hypothesis most likely to prove true is that the subjects first take the scores into account. Nevertheless, it is also possible that other aspects are taken into consideration along with, or as an alternative to, the scores. Moreover, the relation between result and satisfaction might be not homogeneous.

The following indicators are proposed (Table 8.1): the correlation coefficient between score obtained and satisfaction expressed in a given round, reckoned on the basis of each player's individual data;[2] and the correlation coefficient between satisfaction expressed and one variable in a given round, reckoned on the basis of each player's individual data.

This is certainly an imperfect indicator (the relation between scores and satisfaction might not be linear; a player, for example, might attribute a different level of satisfaction to two alternatives, even if they lead to a quite similar score, such as gaining a score of 36 declaring 4, thus paying more than the other two team members, or 37). Nonetheless, this is significant and offers a preliminary view.

Table 8.1 presents the joined distribution of the values of the correlation coefficients: between individual scores and satisfaction and between the team's mean score and individual satisfaction. The two values are generally quite close to each other. In most cases (20 out of 24) the highest value is the first one. Thus, satisfaction seems to be more strictly connected to the individual's than to the team's score (the two values are not necessarily coincident). For three players, both coefficients are not significantly different from 0 (according to Pearson's test at a level of confidence of 99 percent). In one case both coefficients are negative; in another case they both exactly equal 1.

This is a first index of the data reliability, because data are correlated with two significant indicators of the evolution of the game. Table 8.1 also highlights a sharp heterogeneity among players and presents the most significant correlations.[3]

Table 8.2 allows us to assess, from a different perspective, the connection between sums obtained by the team, individual score, and mean satisfaction stated. The sums obtained by the team and the possible individual score are associated. For example, player 1 obtains sum 10 in three different ways (that is, by means of three combinations of his or her own choices or other partners' choices), thus gaining three different (for him or her) scores. In other words, a player may obtain 10 by stating different numbers: 10, 3, 4, 2, or 0 (depending on what the other team members declare).

Therefore, we can understand the extent to which individual satisfaction is associated with the scores rather than with the sum obtained by the team (consid-

TABLE 8.1

*Distribution of individual values of the correlation
between scores and satisfaction in each turn*

| | | CORRELATION ON TEAM SCORE | | | | | | |
|---|---|---|---|---|---|---|---|---|
| | | < 0 | 0 | 0−0.5 | 0.5−0.8 | 0.8−1 | 1 | Total |
| Correlation on | < 0 | 1 | | | | | | *1* |
| individual score | 0 | | 3 | | | | | *3* |
| | 0−0.5 | | | 5 | | | | *5* |
| | 0.5−0.8 | | | 3 | | | | *3* |
| | 0.8−1 | | | | 5 | 6 | | *11* |
| | 1 | | | | | | 1 | *1* |
| | Total | *1* | *3* | *8* | *5* | *6* | *1* | *24* |

NOTE: Significance: 99%.

ered as an indicator of the ability to obtain 10, which might be perceived as the game's main goal, but also as an indicator of the team's rather than the individual's interests).

Let us take into account, for example, player 2, who obtains sum 10 in three different ways (or, in other words, obtains different scores associated with the sum 10). The mean satisfaction is always the same (equal to 9). It seems, then, that satisfaction is independent of the scores. Player 18's values are similar; player 10 is even more satisfied with 36 than with 37, and with 20 than with 26).

Apparently, for other participants, player 3 for example, the score deeply affects satisfaction, more or less independently of the team performance (at any rate, the two values are strictly connected): player 3 gives value 8 to score 36 and attributes a higher level of satisfaction to 37.

On the basis of Table 8.2, most players seem to consider their individual scores more important than the team performance, but some of them seem to have different ideas. From Table 8.2 we can also infer that a few players (1, 11, 14, 17) attribute a high level of satisfaction—sometimes even higher than the one stated for their highest scores—to 0 and negative values.[4] This seems to be a paradoxical result, but it is consistent with what has emerged in other experiments: players punish their partners when they behave opportunistically, even when this means losing or not obtaining marks. Such behavior produces a very high level of satisfaction, which might compensate for the loss of points. Thus, Table 8.2 further justifies such behavior. It is not just a strategic choice aimed at inducing the others to behave in a more unselfish way.

It is necessary to distinguish the existence of possible trends from other kinds of behavior, which bring about variable coupling between levels of satisfaction and scores but not a well-defined trend. A player might attribute different levels of

## TABLE 8.2
*Mean individual satisfaction attributed by players to different sums and scores in the whole game*

| Player | SUM < 10 | | | | SUM = 10 | | | | | SUM > 10 | | | | |
|---|---|---|---|---|---|---|---|---|---|---|---|---|---|---|
| | -4 | -3 | -2 | 0 | 30 | 36 | 37 | 38 | 40 | 20 | 26 | 27 | 28 | 30 |
| 1 | | 9.00 | 8.60 | 7.17 | | 5.00 | 8.50 | 6.00 | | | 8.00 | 8.50 | 6.75 | 9.00 |
| 2 | 3.75 | 2.50 | 7.00 | 5.57 | | 9.00 | 9.00 | 9.00 | | 5.00 | 9.00 | 9.00 | | |
| 3 | 0.00 | 0.00 | 0.00 | | | 8.00 | 9.00 | | | | 6.58 | 7.00 | | |
| 4 | | 0.00 | 4.00 | 5.25 | | | | | 8.00 | | | 7.00 | 8.00 | 7.00 |
| 5 | 0.00 | 3.33 | | | 5.00 | | | | | 5.00 | | | | |
| 6 | 4.40 | 2.20 | 2.00 | 4.33 | | | | | 10.00 | 8.00 | 6.33 | | 9.00 | 10.00 |
| 7 | | | 0.00 | | | 7.00 | 10.00 | | | 7.25 | | 10.00 | | |
| 8 | 2.50 | 3.33 | 5.00 | 4.14 | | | 10.00 | | | | | | | |
| 9 | | | | | | | | | | | | 1.00 | | |
| 10 | 4.25 | 3.67 | 1.00 | | | 8.75 | 10.00 | | | 7.13 | 5.50 | 8.33 | | |
| 11 | | 0.00 | 10.00 | | | | 8.00 | | | | 9.00 | | | |
| 12 | | 3.00 | 3.00 | 5.81 | | 8.00 | 10.00 | | | 7.50 | 8.00 | | | 7.00 |
| 13 | | 2.00 | 2.00 | 3.17 | 6.20 | | 8.00 | | 10.00 | | | | | |
| 14 | | | 6.50 | 7.00 | 4.08 | | | | | 0.00 | | | | |
| 15 | 1.67 | 3.00 | | 2.00 | 5.31 | | | | 8.80 | 5.50 | 8.00 | | | |
| 16 | 0.00 | 0.00 | | 0.00 | 1.86 | 9.13 | | | | | 8.00 | | | |
| 17 | 0.00 | 0.00 | | 10.00 | 4.29 | | 10.00 | 8.50 | | | | | | |
| 18 | 4.00 | | | 7.50 | 10.00 | 10.00 | 10.00 | | | | | | | |
| 19 | 1.00 | 10.00 | | 1.00 | | | 9.23 | | | | | | | 1.00 |
| 20 | 5.33 | 6.50 | 8.00 | 4.00 | 5.32 | 9.55 | | | | 5.67 | 5.00 | 6.00 | | |
| 21 | 2.67 | 3.50 | 0.00 | 1.20 | | | 8.00 | | | 2.25 | | | | |
| 22 | | | 2.50 | 3.00 | | | 8.00 | 8.00 | 10.00 | | 7.00 | 8.33 | 6.00 | |
| 23 | 3.00 | 3.00 | 3.00 | 6.18 | | | | | 9.00 | 4.50 | | | | 8.00 |
| 24 | 0.00 | 0.00 | 0.00 | 0.20 | 1.00 | | | | | 2.00 | | | | |

satisfaction to the same score for different reasons. It might depend on reactions due to that specific moment of the game. Or the player might not attribute significance to different (and close to each other) levels of satisfaction, which, in the player's opinion, are identical: thus the player might randomly choose one or the other. At the top end we find the player who always chooses random values. On the contrary, the evolution of the level of satisfaction implies that there is a certain stability in close rounds and that the variations should take place as rounds go by.[5]

Tables 8.1 and 8.2 refer to the whole game; therefore, they do not distinguish between the two parts. Therefore, we cannot analyze an aspect that might be important (especially in a cognitive perspective): the possible evolution of the relation between result and satisfaction. The next section deals with this aspect.

## 8.4 THE EVOLUTION OF SATISFACTION

### 8.4.1 Performance and Satisfaction in the First Part of the Experiment

As stressed in the first part of the experiment, players are "trained" in different ways through the interaction with different kinds of artificial agents.[6] Three treatments have been tested. The first one is built to force players to choose 4. The second treatment aims to train players to choose 3. The third treatment is based on agents whose aim is to force human players to declare 10, always choosing 0.

The first aspect to be analyzed is the effect of this treatment on the behavior of the players in the first part and the result on their satisfaction. For this reason we take into account different values as measures of performance and behavior.

The mean individual total score of the treatments differs in a statistically highly significant way (two kinds of tests were carried out: the analysis of the variance and the Wilcoxon Rank sum nonparametric test; they give very similar results in all cases).[7] Group 2 has the highest score, as expected. The lowest score is, a little unexpected, that of group 1 (see Table 8.3).

Consider also the following findings:

- The percentage of 4 played in treatment 1 is higher than in the other treatments, but the difference is not statistically significant.
- The percentage of 4 in treatment 1 is lower than the percentages of 3 and of 10 in treatments 2 and 3, respectively.
- Group 1 declared a higher percentage of 0 than group 3 did.
- Group 1 has the lowest mean number of sums equal to 10 but the highest of sums higher than 10.

TABLE 8.3

*Mean value of indicators in the first part of the experiment by treatment*

|  | Group 1 | Group 2 | Group 3 | p value of F test | p value of Kruscal-Wallis test |
|---|---|---|---|---|---|
| Mean of total score | 205.5 | 854.6 | 407.7 | 0.0001 | 0.0001 |
| Mean of satisfaction | 5.5 | 8.9 | 4.5 | 0.0001 | 0.0001 |
| Mean of rounds in which sum = 10 | 3.2 | 20 | 13.2 | 0.0001 | 0.000 |
| Mean of rounds in which sum > 10 | 5.5 | 3.9 | 0.0 | 0.0001 | 0.03 |
| Mean of rounds in which sum < 10 | 17.7 | 2.3 | 12.3 | 0.0001 | 0.000 |
| Mean number of 0 declared | 11.0 | 0.9 | 9.0 | 0.01 | 0.00 |
| Mean number of 3 declared | 2.3 | 22.0 | 1.4 | 0.0001 | 0.00 |
| Mean number of 4 declared | 6.4 | 1.8 | 2.3 | 0.14 | 0.23 |
| Mean number of 10 declared | 5.5 | 0.0 | 13.3 | 0.001 | 0.00 |
| Mean of DISP1 | −1.4 | 0.78 | −5.1 | 0.001 | 0.0004 |

The game at the basis of the experiment has two dimensions: at least one of the players should accept "paying" more than the others, but the team should also succeed in coordinating their actions. Coordination is easier in treatment 3, as the other two players always choose the same numbers. In treatment 1, there is an artificial agent that changes its behavior, making it more difficult for the human players to understand the right number to choose before having to decide whether to accept it.

The lower score and the lower percentage of sums equal to 10 in treatment 1 are then probably related partly to this coordination problem, as it seems strange that players accept playing 10 but not 4 (and as treatment 1 has a higher percentage of sums higher than 10). As noted earlier, choosing 0 can be a way to punish partners' free riding, but—looking at these data—it can also be considered a kind of self-protecting behavior ("as I'm not able to make a positive score, I save points, declaring 0") or a way to punish partners for not being clear in their strategies.

As expected, treatment 2 has the highest mean satisfaction. Group 1 has a mean satisfaction a little higher than that of group 3 (the difference is not significant: the $p$ value of the $F$ test of the ANOVA $= 0.36$; the $p$ value of the Kruscal-Wallis test $= 0.34$), even if its score is significantly lower ($p$ value of $F$ test of ANOVA $= 0.04$; $p$ value of Kruscal-Wallis test $= 0.04$).

The comparisons of the levels of satisfaction, scores being equal, can be carried out using a regression of the mean satisfaction on the individual total score obtained in the same period (first or second) with a dummy indicating the training treatment. The regression is shown in Table 8.4.

The dependent variable is the mean individual satisfaction in the first part of the experiment. The independent variables are as follows:

- the total individual score in the first part (TOTAL SCORE 1)
- a dummy variable for those who underwent training in group 1 (DUM_1)
- a dummy variable for those who underwent training in group 2 (DUM_2)
- the mean difference, in all rounds of the first part, between a player's score and the score of the other players on the same team (DISP1); a positive value means that the player got a higher score, 0 means that the score is equal, a negative value means that the player got a lower score; individuals in treatment 3 can make points only with negative values of DISP1; the variable can be equal to 0 only if the sum is 0; for group 1 the situation is similar, but human players can get more than the artificial agent when playing 0 (in this case, the artificial agent got a mean negative score); for group 2 the index can assume more values (positive or negative), because there are different possible solutions; players can, in fact, get more or less points than the artificial agents can

The regression confirms that, given the score, the training in treatment 3 leads to a lower satisfaction (about 2 points), whereas there are no significant differences between the other treatments. In fact, when we add the dummies for the treat-

TABLE 8.4

*Main results of a series of regressions with mean satisfaction in the first part as dependent variable (all treatments and treatments 1 and 2)*

| TOTAL SCORE 1 | DUM_1 | DUM_2 | DISPL | $R^2$ | p value of F test |
|---|---|---|---|---|---|
| All treatments ($n = 24$) | | | | | |
| 0.006 (p.v. = 0.00) | — | — | — | 0.52 | 0.0001 |
| 0.005 (p.v. = 0.02) | 2.14 (p.v. = 0.09) | 1.94 (p.v. = 0.04) | — | 0.66 | 0.0001 |
| 0.005 (p.v. = 0.00) | — | — | 0.29 (p.v. = 0.02) | 0.63 | 0.0001 |
| 0.006 (p.v. = 0.06) | (1.45) (p.v. = 0.24) | (0.19) (p.v. = 0.95) | (0.21) (p.v. = 0.55) | 0.67 | 0.0002 |
| Treatments 1 and 2 only ($n = 16$) | | | | | |
| 0.005 (p.v. = 0.0001) | — | — | — | 0.89 | 0.0001 |
| 0.005 (p.v. = 0.0001) | (−0.12) (p.v. = 0.87) | — | — | 0.89 | 0.0001 |

NOTES: A dash indicates a variable not included in the estimation; parameters not significant at a 90% level are in parentheses; and p.v. is the *p* value.

ments, the fit of the model improves, and the variables are significantly different from 0. If we consider only the first two treatments, the dummy is not significant and does not improve the fit. This fact, related to the previous findings, suggests that opportunism could cause more dissatisfaction than problems of coordination. Players of treatment 3 are relatively less satisfied because they should face opportunistic agents. Players in group 1 face a difficult environment, beyond the opportunism of the partners.

This result can be explained with a reference to the theory of procedural rationality, according to which players reduce their levels of aspiration if the environment faced is seen as difficult. But in treatment 3 the environment is simple; players see the others making points and should accept an unfair result.[8]

### 8.4.2 Evolution of Satisfaction and Effects of the Training Period

In this section we try to explain to what extent the players' mean satisfaction changes as a result of the experience in the first part of the game, in which the kinds of partners, and consequently choices and results, are quite different. See Novarese (2004) for a more detailed analysis of the possible effects of the training period on players' behavior in the second part of the game. The attention in this chapter is instead focused on satisfaction and on its relation to score.[9]

Table 8.5 compares many mean values of the three groups.[10] Among the treatments there are no significant differences in mean total score. There are some differences in the number of sums equal to 10, but they are not very significant. Players in treatment 2 play more 3 than in the other treatments.[11]

To compare the levels of satisfaction of the treatments, scores being equal, a new

TABLE 8.5

*Mean value of indicators in the second part of the experiment by treatment*

| | Treatment 1 | Treatment 2 | Treatment 3 | p value of F test (ANOVA) | p value of Kruskal-Wallis test |
|---|---|---|---|---|---|
| Mean of total score | 140.8 | 177.8 | 225.9 | 0.23 | 0.41 |
| Mean of satisfaction | 6.9 | 5.8 | 5.6 | 0.68 | 0.84 |
| Mean of rounds in which sum = 10 | 1.9 | 2.9 | 5.0 | 0.12 | 0.20 |
| Mean of rounds in which sum > 10 | 2.9 | 2.5 | 1.8 | 0.41 | 0.29 |
| Mean of rounds in which sum < 10 | 3.3 | 2.6 | 1.3 | 0.16 | 0.16 |
| Mean number of 0 declared | 3 | 1.6 | 2.6 | 0.69 | 0.48 |
| Mean number of 3 declared | 1.5 | 4.3 | 0.3 | 0.01 | 0.02 |
| Mean number of 4 declared | 6.4 | 1.8 | 2.3 | 0.14 | 0.76 |
| Mean number of 10 declared | 0.9 | 0.9 | 2.4 | 0.32 | 0.39 |
| DISP2 | 0.70 | 0.13 | −0.83 | 0.64 | 0.64 |

TABLE 8.6

*Main results of a series of regressions with mean satisfaction
as dependent variable (treatments 1 and 2)*

| TOTAL SCORE 2 | DUM_1 | DISP2 | SCORE1 | SATIS1 | $R^2$ | $p$ value of $F$ test |
|---|---|---|---|---|---|---|
| 0.02 (p.v. = 0.00) | — | — | — | — | 0.41 | 0.0069 |
| 0.02 (p.v. = 0.00) | 1.74 (p.v. = 0.04) | — | — | — | 0.57 | 0.0044 |
| 0.02 (p.v. = 0.00) | — | — | — | −0.40 (p.v. = 0.07) | 0.54 | 0.0058 |
| 0.02 (p.v. = 0.00) | — | — | −0.003 (p.v. = 0.01) | — | 0.64 | 0.008 |
| 0.02 (p.v. = 0.00) | — | (0.09) (p.v. = 0.66) | — | — | 0.43 | 0.02 |
| 0.02 (p.v. = 0.00) | — | (−0.04) (p.v. = 0.80) | −0.002 (p.v. = 0.02) | — | 0.64 | 0.00 |
| 0.02 (p.v. = 0.00) | 1.72 (p.v. = 0.06) | (−0.04) (p.v. = 0.80) | — | — | 0.57 | 0.00 |

NOTES: A dash indicates a variable not included in the estimation; parameters not significant at a 90% level are in parentheses; and p.v. is the *p* value.

series of OLS regression was performed, using the individual mean satisfaction in the second part as the dependent variable.

The independent variables are as follows:

- the total individual score in the second part (TOTAL SCORE 2)
- dummy variable for those who underwent training in group 1 (DUM_1)
- dummy variable for those who underwent training in group 2 (DUM_2)
- the mean individual differences between the player's score and the scores of his or her partners in the second part (DISP2, built as DISP1 but with the data of the second part)
- total score obtained in the first part of the experiment (SCORE1)
- mean satisfaction obtained in the first part of the experiment (SATIS1)

Different specifications have been estimated on different subsamples. Tables 8.6 and 8.7 show the main results.

### 8.4.3 Treatments 1 and 2

In Table 8.6, group 1 and group 2 can be more easily compared in terms of distribution of the score in the second part, and the greater difference in the first part is

TABLE 8.7

*Main results of a series of regressions with mean satisfaction*
*as dependent variable, considering all treatments*

| TOTAL SCORE | DUM_1 | DUM_2 | SCORE1 | DISP2 | SODD1 | $R^2$ | p value of F test |
|---|---|---|---|---|---|---|---|
| 0.02 (p.v. = 0.00) | — | — | — | — | — | 0.40 | 0.0009 |
| 0.02 (p.v. = 0.00) | 3.26 (p.v. = 0.00) | (1.32) (p.v. = 0.21) | — | — | — | 0.59 | 0.0004 |
| 0.02 (p.v. = 0.00) | — | — | — | 0.37 (p.v. = 0.01) | — | 0.56 | 0.0002 |
| 0.02 (p.v. = 0.00) | 2.59 (p.v. = 0.02) | 0.28 (p.v. = 0.03) | — | 0.28 (p.v. = 0.03) | — | 0.67 | 0.0002 |
| 0.02 (p.v. = 0.00) | — | — | (−0.001) (p.v. = 0.42) | — | — | 0.42 | 0.003 |
| 0.02 (p.v. = 0.00) | — | — | (−0.0009) (p.v. = 0.48) | 0.37 (p.v. = 0.01) | — | 0.57 | 0.0002 |
| 0.02 (p.v. = 0.00) | — | — | — | — | (0.03) (p.v. = 0.89) | 0.40 | 0.0002 |

NOTES: A dash indicates a variable not included in the estimation; parameters not significant at a 90% level are in parentheses; and p.v. is the *p* value.

more clear. In the first part of the experiment, groups' scores are quite different because of the different behaviors of the artificial agents faced. Given the scores, there are no differences in satisfaction. On the contrary, as shown in Table 8.7, in the second part, scores being equal, group 1 has a higher mean score. Group 2 has almost all its highest mean values of satisfaction for high scores.

Regarding the first part of the experiment, we saw that by adding the dummy, referring to the treatment, we did not improve the fit of the base model (which includes only the score as an independent variable). Therefore, it does not look significant. In the second part, by adding that variable, which is fully significant and has a positive value, we improved the fit of the estimate. Thus, it seems that in the first part, for these treatments, there are no significant effects specifically due to training. On the contrary, in the second part the total score is less explicative of the variance of satisfaction. By adding the information on training, we can better understand the mean satisfaction. Those who underwent training in group 1 have significantly lower satisfaction values (at a 95 percent trust level), given the scores.

If instead of the dummy in the training we introduce into the estimate the mean satisfaction obtained in the first part of the experiment (that is, a value that is certainly linked to the kinds of agents faced in the previous part), the capacity to foresee and the significance of the model decrease. Satisfaction in the first part has a negative sign: those who obtained a higher mean satisfaction in the training period have a tendency to be less satisfied in the second part.

However, if we introduce the variable referring to the score in the first part, the model's explaining capacity increases. The variable has a negative sign: higher score corresponds to a lower level of satisfaction in the second part. This might indicate that the effect of training here is mainly linked to the score obtained.

### 8.4.4  Treatment 3

Now we consider treatment 3 in comparison with the others. The regression proposed in Table 8.7 shows that between groups 2 and 3 there are no differences (whereas group 1 maintains its higher intercept). The variable DISP2 seems to be more relevant for this group. In fact, it becomes significant in Table 8.7 when we add the data from this treatment. In the regression on individual groups, DISP2 has the strongest relevance (and significance) for these players. This strongest sensibility to the differences in score with the partners was probably acquired in the first part of the game (in the second part, treatment 3 has no different mean values of DISP2, as shown in Table 8.5).

The score of the first part loses its significance, probably because of the differences between the low scores in groups 1 and 3. As seen in the first part, in one case there are problems of coordination, whereas in the other, players should accept low scores because of the opportunism of artificial agents. This difference seems to have dissimilar effects on the satisfaction in the first part, and it is then also a possible source of these new divergences.

Table 8.7 shows the results of a series of estimations on the data for the second part of each treatment. With the usual problem of the small dimension of the samples, what emerges here confirms and expands some previous findings.

Treatment 1 has the lowest elasticity to score and the highest value of the intercept. The score in the results of the first part is the most significant variable able to explain satisfaction. Treatment 2 has the sharpest inclination, an intercept higher than that of group 3, and is influenced only by the score. Treatment 3 has the lowest intercept and is strongly influenced by the variable DISP2.

## 8.5  SUMMARY OF THE MAIN EMPIRICAL FINDINGS AND CONCLUDING REMARKS

The analysis proposed here suggests a series of ideas and research hypotheses that should be further tested and investigated but that are plausible and, in some cases, can be related to other empirical or theoretical works. The first result, which is not necessarily obvious a priori, is that it is possible to measure satisfaction in an experiment, despite a few problems and limits, which might be better understood or even solved in new experiments.

Apparently, satisfaction is mainly affected by the score. Given this value, there are, nevertheless, other elements affecting satisfaction. The most important is the need for not being subject to others' opportunism. At least a few subjects might also be influenced by the ability of succeeding in carrying out their task within the experiment, and as a consequence, by the general team performance rather than only by their own score.

Experience and learning seem to play a relevant role in affecting the mean satisfaction levels. The empirical evidence here seems to suggest that training in a situation in which coordination is difficult improves the mean levels of satisfaction in the next period. Training in a situation in which players have to interact with strongly opportunistic partners causes players' satisfaction to be penalized by the opportunism of the others. These seem to be important results with manifold valences. On the one hand, this might affect subjects' behavior during the experiments, and it should therefore be given due consideration at a methodological level. More generally, this is a further demonstration of the relevance of learning processes in the way subjects perceive the environment. Finally, this result appears also to be coherent with Simon's model, linking satisfaction, levels of aspiration (which were not measured here), and performance.

The available data did not allow us to directly test the eventual effect of satisfaction on individual behavior. We were also not able to directly test this effect because this kind of analysis is complex and it would be necessary to know the levels of aspiration and the expectations, which are very difficult to measure.[12] We hope that these findings will be useful for further research.

The game is divided into two parts.

Each part is subdivided into a number of rounds.

The computer randomly and anonymously groups 3 players.

In each turn you have the numbers 0, 2, 3, 4, and 10 (included) at your disposal, and you have to declare one of them.

Your number will be added to that of the two other players in your group.

On the basis of the sum obtained, the score will be determined by these rules, identical for the three players:

- If the sum is 10, score = 40 − declared number; for example, if you declare 4, and both other players in your group declare 3, the sum is 10; you gain a score of 40 − 4 = 36, and the other two players gain 40 − 3 = 37.

- If the sum is higher than 10, score = 30 − declared number; for example, if you declared 4, the first player coupled with you declared 4, and the second declared 3, the sum is 11; your score is 30 − 4 = 26; the second player gains 30 − 4 = 26, and the third gains 30 − 3 = 27.

- If the sum is lower than 10, score = 0 − declared number; for example, if you declared 4, the first player coupled with you declared 0, and the second declared 3, the sum is 7; you gain 0 − 4 = −4 (you lose 4); the second player gains 0 − 0 = 0; and the third gains 0 − 3 = −3 (the player loses 3).

All through the first part you will be grouped with the same two players.

In the second part (your computer will inform you when the second part starts) you will be coupled to two other players, who will be the same until the end of the game.

At each round, you will be asked to answer to the following questions:

- On a scale of 0 (unsatisfied) to 10 (satisfied), what is your level of satisfaction for the results you obtained in the preceding round?

- What is the mean sum you expect to gain in the following rounds?

Before going on to the next round, it is necessary to wait until all players (not only the ones coupled with you) have answered. You might have to wait. Be patient! The computer will pass to the new page automatically, as soon as it is possible to continue.

1. The survey we are referring to is based upon the archives JSTOR and NEP—*New Economic Papers* (thus covering the consolidated literature and new or recent articles) and on a number of online economic journals.

2. It is also possible to reckon the correlation coefficient for all players in a given round (or in a given set of rounds). The results, not shown, are coherent with those proposed here.

3. The correlations among other variables were tested but are not presented here because the results were less interesting.

4. This can lead to an individual correlation coefficient with negative or null values.

5. With reference to Tables 8.1 and 8.2, it is necessary to point out that a possible evolution of the satisfaction associated to given scores would bring about less significant values of the individual correlation coefficient.

6. The players don't know that they are playing with artificial agents and are not told of undergoing a "training period."

7. It is evident that the score is always highly correlated with the other possible indicators (such as the sum of the team).

8. This hypothesis will be tested again in another experiment, comparing these results with those of a sum 10 experiment in which the score is equal for all members of a team (where there is no room for opportunism).

9. Score is the variables that are more correlated to satisfaction. Nevertheless, the score is highly correlated to the other values (sum of the team) that might be relevant, and therefore the analysis has a general valence.

10. Although in the first part of the experiment each individual is independently observed, the situation is now changed, and many individual variables of the members of each team are strongly related to those of their partners. The score, for example, is highly related among team members (even if within the group there is a negative correlation) as the number of rounds in which the sum is equal to 10. Other values, such as the distribution of the numbers declared by a player, may or may not be related to that of the other players; a player may be willing to impose his or her strategies or can try to adapt his or her behavior to that of the others. The analysis of this aspect here is focused on the levels of satisfaction, and the other aspects are seen only from this perspective, which avoids facing the problem of dependence.

11. At an individual level there is a significant correlation between the numbers declared in the first and second parts. See also Novarese (2003).

12. In the experiment proposed, we tried to measure levels of aspiration by means of the expected sums, but no significant results emerged, probably because of measurement problems.

## REFERENCES

Akerlof, G., and W. Dickens. 1982. The economic consequences of cognitive dissonance. *American Economic Review* 62:307–19.

Boero, R. 2001. SWIEE: A Swarm Web Interface for Experimental Economics. In *Agent based methods in economic and finance: Simulations in swarm*, ed. F. Luna and A. Perrone, 88–105. Amsterdam: Kluwer Academic.

Charness, G., and E. Haruvy. 2000. Self-serving biases: Evidence from a simulated labor relationship. *Journal of Managerial Psychology* 15:655–67.

Egidi, M., and A. Narduzzo. 1997. The emergence of path-dependent behaviours in cooperative contexts. *International Journal of Industrial Organization* 5: 677–709.

Egidi, M., and S. Rizzello. 2004. *Cognitive economics*. Vol. 169 of The International Library of Critical Writings in Economics. Cheltenham, UK: Elgar.

Ferrer-i-Carbonell, A., and P. Frijters. 2004. How important is methodology for the estimates of the determinants of happiness? *Economic Journal, Royal Economic Society* 114 (127): 641–59.

Festinger, L. 1957. A theory of cognitive dissonance. Stanford, CA: Stanford University Press.

Gigerenzer, G. 2003. Striking a blow for sanity in theories of rationality. In *Essays in honor of Herbert Simon*, ed. M. Augier and J. M. James, 389–409. Cambridge, MA: MIT Press.

Hayo, B., and W. Seifert. 2003. Subjective economic well-being in Eastern Europe. *Journal of Economic Psychology* 24 (3): 329–48.

Kahneman, D., P. Slovic, and A. Tversky, eds. 1982. Judgment under uncertainty: Heuristics and biases. New York: Cambridge University Press.

Kahneman, D., and A. Tversky. 1979. Prospect theory: An analysis of decision under risk. *Econometrica* 47:263–91.

———. 1984. Choices, values and frames. *American Psychologist* 39:341–50.

Novarese, M. 2003. Toward a cognitive experimental economics. In *Cognitive paradigms in economics*, ed. S. Rizzello, 82–106. London: Routledge.

———. 2004. Learning in different social contests. Paper presented to the Sabe/ Iarep Cross Fertilization Between Economics and Psychology conference, Philadelphia, July. www.novarese.org/pub.htm.

Novarese, M., and S. Rizzello. 2003. A cognitive approach to individual learning: Theoretical issues and some experimental results. Working paper, Departimento di Scienze Giuridiche de Economiche, Alessandria, Italy. www.novarese.org/pub.htm.

Nowak, M., and K. Sigmund. 1993. A strategy of win-stay lose-shift that out-performs tit-for-tat in the prisoner's dilemma game. *Nature* 364:56–58.

Posch, M., A. Pichler, and K. Sigmund. 1999. The efficiency of adapting aspiration levels. *Proceedings of the Royal Society*, ser. B (266): 1427–36.

Rizzello, S. 1997. The microfoundations of path-dependency. In *Evolutionary economics and path-dependence*, ed. L. Magnusson and J. Ottosson, 98–118. Cheltenham, UK: Elgar.

———. 1999. *The economics of the mind*. Aldershot, UK: Elgar.

Selten, R. 1998. Aspiration adaptation theory. *Mathematical Psychology* 42: 191–214.

———. 1999: What is bounded rationality? SFB 303 Universität Bonn Discussion Paper No. B-454 prepared for the Dahlem conference, 1999.

Simon, H. 1976. From substantive to procedural rationality. In *Method and appraisal in economics*, ed. S. Latsis. Cambridge, MA.: Cambridge University Press.

Thorndike, E. 1911. *Animal intelligence*. New York: Macmillan.

Tietz, R. 1997. Adaptation of aspiration levels—theory and experiment. In *Understanding strategic interaction—essays in honor of Reinhard Selten*, ed. W. Albers, W. Güth, P. Hammerstein, B. Moldovanu, and E. van Damme, 345–62. Heidelberg: Springer-Verlag.

Tversky, A., and D. Kahneman. 1974. Judgment under uncertainty: Heuristics and biases. *Science* 185:1124–31.

———. 1986. Rational choice and the framing of decisions. *Journal of Business* 59:S251–78.

Witt, U. 1993. Emergence and dissemination of innovations—some problems and principles of evolutionary economics. In *Nonlinear dynamics and evolutionary economics*, ed. R. Day and P. Chen, 91–100. Oxford: Oxford University Press.

# 9 | THE MARKET FOR LAUGHTER

*F. H. Buckley*

One of the strongest cultural signals about how to live comes from laughter, whose sting we can never ignore. We can bear poverty, illness, even shame, but not ridicule, and the strategies we employ to immunize ourselves from it constitute a thick code of conduct. There are moral codes and legal ones, but laughter's code is different, for it teaches us how to extract joy from life.

My claim—not a novel one—is that laughter signals a feeling of superiority to a butt, who is thereby informed of a comic defect in his character or behavior. By highlighting such vices, laughter teaches us a superior life plan, of grace and suppleness, that is immune from ridicule. Laughter has a secondary purpose, which I call sociability: by creating communities with common butts, it serves as a bonding device between jesters and listeners. Listeners who laugh take the jester's side against the butt and cement a relationship of trust between themselves and the teller.

In most laughter, therefore, three persons may be found: jester, listener, and butt. Like Janus, laughter has two faces: one face smiles amiably at a listener and the other smirks at a butt. The teller proposes a joke to the listener, who may either accept it by laughing or reject it by silence. By laughing, the listener accepts a tie of solidarity—a *lien de rire*—with the jester. In this way the laugher's superiority may coexist with a sense of sociability. The *sociability* thesis explains the relationship between jester and listener, whereas the *superiority* thesis explains the relationship between the jester and listener on one side and the butt on the other.

---

This chapter is adapted from *The Morality of Laughter* (Ann Arbor: University of Michigan Press, 2003).

## 9.1 THE SUPERIORITY THESIS

The superiority thesis has been advanced by philosophers who agreed about little else, including Plato, Aristotle, and Descartes. However, the idea that laughter signals superiority is most closely identified with Descartes' contemporary, Thomas Hobbes. Writing in an era of political confusion, Hobbes proposed the simplest and most reductionist account of human action. We are prompted to action by our appetite for pleasure and aversion to pain. Nothing else counts, and good and evil are merely the names we give to things that please or displease us. The ability to procure the good or avoid the bad is "power," and among the passions Hobbes famously accorded priority to was the search for power. "So that in the first place, I put for a general inclination of all mankind, a perpetual and restless striving of power after power, that ceaseth only in death" (Hobbes 1651/1968, 161). By this, what Hobbes had in mind was power over others. "Power simply is no more, but the excess of the power of one above that of another" (Hobbes 1640/1994, 48). The realization that we possess power over other people is glory, and the sudden realization of that power produces laughter. It is a "sudden glory," a cry of triumph that signals our discovery of superiority to a butt "and is caused either by some sudden act of their own, that pleaseth them; or by the apprehension of some deformed thing in another, by comparison whereof they suddenly applaud themselves" (Hobbes 1651/1968).

The Hobbesian account of motivation is thin, as there are a good many things that motivate us besides the desire for relative status—how we rank compared to others. However, status is obviously very important to us. We are concerned not only with how we do absolutely—our wealth, intelligence, and so on—but also with how these compare with other people's endowments. Our sense of contentment may even depend more on relative than absolute status. A man on the dole might live like a prince when compared with fifth-century Merovingian nobles, but as his only reference group is composed of his contemporaries, he may still burn with resentment at his lot.

Relative status is greatly affected by ridicule. Even those who deny that the jester signals his superiority through laughter will admit that the butt is made to feel inferior. Relative to the jester, the butt is degraded; relative to the butt, the jester moves up a notch. The butt knows this, of course, and for this reason resents the joke. Is it then a great stretch to assume that the jester sees it the same way? Speaking for butts everywhere, Hazlitt (1818/1907) said that "our humiliation is their triumph."

The superiority thesis might thus appear uncontroversial. If a man is presumed to intend the natural consequences of his acts, then the jester intends to communicate his superiority to the butt. But do we intend natural consequences in this way? Jests often spring to our lips without premeditation, and the listener's laughter is immediate and unreflective. It might reveal a sense of superiority, in the sense that one who shares the comic vice or is conscious of his inferiority will not laugh along. But while he laughs he is not calculating rankings on a status index. The Hobbesian account of laughter must thus be amended. We laugh because the joke is funny, and not as a move in a status competition.

Nevertheless, laughter may still be said to signal a sense of superiority. We may distinguish two senses in which we signal information. The signal might first reveal private thoughts, as where a blush reveals our embarrassment, and this was laughter's signal of superiority according to Hobbes. But if Hobbes were right, as Addison (1711) noted in *Spectator* no. 47, "when we hear a Man laugh excessively, instead of saying he is very Merry, we ought to tell him he is very Proud." Laughter is therefore more accurately regarded as a second kind of signal, one that reveals beliefs without bringing them to mind. We do not compare ourselves to the butt before we laugh; but were we to do so, we would rank him beneath us, so far as the comic vice is concerned. Unless we consider him our inferior, we could not laugh.

## 9.2 LAUGHTER AS A SIGNAL

The superiority thesis is not the only explanation of laughter. Other theories have been proposed, notably an incongruity theory under which we laugh when we recognize some absurdity or logical error. I do not find incongruity theories persuasive on their own terms. In addition, only the superiority thesis may ascribe a purpose to laughter and explain both when and *why* we laugh. We laugh when we identify an inferior butt; and our laughter signals valuable information to him about how and how not to live. By contrast, what purpose is served by the apprehension of an incongruity?

Signaling theories assume an informational asymmetry, with a butt who is unaware of his folly until the jester points it out to him. Once informed of his comic error, the butt might correct his behavior, but until then he is risible. Plato noted the need for an informational asymmetry in the *Philebus*:

*Socrates.* Taken generally, the ridiculous is a certain kind of folly, specifically a vice. It is that kind of vice which can be described as the opposite of the inscription at Delphi.

*Protarchus.* You mean "Know Thyself," Socrates?

*Socrates.* I do. And the opposite would read "Know not thyself."

This raises the question of why we employ laughter to signal information. Why not simply tell the butt of his error, without ridiculing him? After all, most information can be communicated directly without any fuss. ("You just slipped on a banana.") But laughter does more than disclose a comic vice; it also administers a very sharp sanction. We are taught to navigate through life so as to minimize the possibility of laughter, for few things are less pleasant than to find oneself the object of ridicule.

As instinctive behavior, laughter enjoys other advantages over the rational, moral lecture. Laughter is sudden and unreflective. Deliberation drains it; debate kills it. It is always remembered better than a lecture. Because we take so much delight in shared laughter, humor is also a conduit for transmitting information, with the joke moving quickly throughout society. In quattrocento Italy, a clever epigram traveled up and down the peninsula and made its author famous by the time it returned a month later (Burckhardt 1929/1958).

As laughter requires an informational asymmetry, the jester and listener must be wiser than the butt. One cannot tell a joke without meaning to do so. At Trafalgar, Nelson's dying words to his captain were "Kiss me, Hardy." But as that was a little over the top for the naval hagiographer, the tradition arose that Nelson's last thoughts were on fate and not love and that what he had said was "Kismet, Hardy." One thing is certain: He did not mean both, for if he had, he would have died with a pun on his lips. Absent the intent, he did not jest, for one cannot pun without meaning to do so.

As a signaling device, laughter assumes a normative order from which the butt has deviated. Our laughter enforces social norms—rules or standards that prescribe behavior and direct the butt to mend his ways. Through their laughter, teller and listener reaffirm a shared vision about how life should be lived and proclaim that the butt is guilty of a comic vice. There is no satire without a butt who is satirized, no butt without a message of inferiority, and no message of inferiority without a normative message. Take away the moral criticism, said Northrup Frye (1957), and one is left with irony or fantasy, with Kafka, but not satire.

## 9.3 THE SURVIVAL OF THE WITTIEST

Many of the leading evolutionary theorists were fascinated by laughter and suggested that it might promote a superior society. Through derision, said Darwin (1872/1998), we "show the offending person that he excites only amusement." Our laughter corrects flaws, and people with a sense of humor have a suppleness that marks them as superior candidates to pass on their genes. The instinct to laugh might thus have been selected for survival by the principle of natural selection. Rival explanations that do not ascribe a purpose or benefit to laughter cannot provide an evolutionary account for its survival.

How might evolutionary processes account for the special characteristics of laughter? A single laugh requires a complex series of physical movements that are exceedingly difficult to mimic. Fifteen facial muscles are contracted; the eyes becomes brighter and sparkle; respiratory patterns change and the laugh is emitted (Koestler 1989). And all of this happens in a flash and without conscious effort. The mystery is how such a complicated and automatic response might have evolved for something seemingly so trivial as a joke or witticism.

We also react sharply to other kinds of stimuli. For example, physical injury might also produce a complicated bodily reaction. But there a physical stimulus produces a physical response. What is remarkable about laughter is that the stimulus may take place on a high intellectual plane. Arthur Koestler (1989) noted that "humor is the only domain of creative activity where a stimulus on a high level of complexity produces a massive and sharply defined response on the level of physiological reflexes." Other complex stimuli—fine art, for example—might register and produce an emotional response, but not the physical reaction of laughter, which is wrenched from us like a sneeze. But it is not wholly physical either, because it is preceded by a mental awareness in which we "get" the joke. In no other act is comprehension followed by so immediate a physical response.

For those who, like Arthur Koestler, reject the superiority thesis, laughter is an evolutionary puzzle. Koestler called laughter a *luxury* emotion. Pleasant in itself, it serves no extrinsic purpose that he could see. In that sense, it might be thought intrinsically valuable. Perhaps no deeper purpose is needed, he thought. Doesn't the simple joy of laughing suffice? Or if a more profound explanation is needed, what of its deeper therapeutic benefits? A sense of humor reduces anxiety, anger, and depression and increases tolerance for pain (Weisenberg, Tepper, and Schwarzwald 1995). However, this simply pushes the inquiry back one stage. If laughter is a luxury and intrinsically pleasant, how is it that we became hardwired to laugh *when* we do? After all, we might have been programmed to take pleasure in very different ways, over very different things. So why are pratfalls funny, but not sunsets?

The superiority thesis is uniquely able to account for why we laugh when we do, and as it ascribes a purpose to our laughter, is readily understood in the context of evolutionary theories of behavior. This can most easily be seen in sexual humor. Laughter has always had a close connection to fertility. The origins of comedy may be traced to the Dionysian revel (*komos*), with its phallic masks, riotous laughter, and songs of joy (Cornford 1961; Gurewitch 1975). Western folk revels such as the charivari also celebrate sexual potency. Even today, the intimate connection between fertility and humor explains the savage pleasure we take when transgressing sexual taboos through an obscene joke (Greig 1923). Our laughter signals that we are alive to sexual pleasure and are willing to violate moral norms to enjoy it.

As for nonsexual humor, the comically simple or clumsy may plausibly be regarded as poor genetic vehicles. By contrast, the wit signals a greater ability to extract joy from life and an acuity of judgment in identifying comic vices that mark him as a social leader. As Dutch primatologist Frans de Waal (1989) has noted, the alpha male in a monkey cage needs more than brute strength to dominate his fellows; he also needs alertness and guile, qualities that are plausibly correlated with wit. For both man and monkey, laughter may economize on more violent forms of competition among male pretenders by signaling who the likely winner of the contest will be.

## 9.4 THE SOCIABILITY THESIS

Laughter's bite comes at the butt's expense, and looked at solely from the victim's perspective, might sometimes be cruel. But laughter also establishes or reinforces a bond between the jester and listener that usefully permits them to promote their trust in each other. With the trust comes a greater ability to exploit profitable opportunities for joint gain.

The problem of trust in bargaining arises because of the difficulty in signaling private information about product quality and the promisor's intentions. If bare promises were credible, the promisee could simply ask the promisor whether the goods are merchantable and whether the promisor intends to perform. But as Hobbes (1651/1968) recognized, talk is cheap and therefore unreliable. In a Hobbesian state of nature, a bare promise not supported by the state's legal system is "but words, and breath," with "no force to oblige, contain, constrain, or protect any man."

All is well if the promisor can resolve the problem of trust through a binding legal promise. What happens if the promisor cannot, however? The promise might be too vague to be easily enforced (or to trust to an American jury). Long-term contracts between business parties necessarily leave many details to be decided at a later time. In a joint venture contract, for example, the parties cannot at formation specify how the relationship will be governed years later. There is an implicit promise of good faith, but the parties might not want to see everything made the subject of litigation. Finally, the promise might have been made in a social or family setting in which social sanctions ordinarily suffice and neither party wished to incur legal liability.

In such cases, the problem of trust cannot be solved by contract. Yet the need for trust remains. It is a crucial element in the social norms that Jon Elster calls the cement of society. Without trust our friendships would become affairs of momentary convenience, on which no plans, no projects for future cooperation, could be formed. We rely so often upon friends and associates that we often forget we are doing so. We scatter our promises about, without paying much attention to what we are doing. We make seemingly trivial promises, to meet for lunch or to return a call, on whose performance deep friendships depend. And we make unspoken promises that are the foundation of trust: I will take your side; I will not betray you.

Once the parties begin to cooperate, their relationship may become self-enforcing. A pattern of reciprocal altruism might emerge, through which parties in repeated transactions may confidently adopt cooperative strategies to extract bargaining gains. Before a pattern of reciprocal altruism can begin, however, there is a prior stage during which we choose those with whom we wish to deal. How can promise keeping be signaled at this stage? And how can the promisee detect cheaters before the first round of the game? The answer is written on our faces, the most public part of our body, where our emotions register for all to see. Facial signals reveal our deepest feelings to others and permit them to make reliable inferences about our future behavior.

We may express our sentiments in other ways, of course, but what is special about facial expressions is that they are so hard to mimic. We show our anxiety when lying, for example. When our sins are detected, our blushes and downcast eyes may convict us; when accused falsely, as Hero was in *Much Ado About Nothing*, our innocence shines through. Blushing is thus a useful commitment device. It increases the likelihood of detection and the costs of lying and strengthens the incentive to tell the truth. Others will repose greater confidence in us, and this will permit us to extract increased gains from joint cooperation.

Sudden genuine laughter is also written on our faces, by muscles over which we lack full self-control. The counterfeit laugh, produced for purely strategic purposes, is a pale imitation. Imagine being told an unfunny joke by a boorish superior, where it is politic to affect a laugh. One might bare one's teeth and emit the sound of laughter, but this can ordinarily be distinguished from companionable, uproarious laughter. The subordinate's pretended laugh might usefully communicate subservience to a domineering superior but does not signal a shared mirth and friendship.

When Darwin tested the photos of true and feigned laughter on a small group of subjects, everyone recognized the genuine smile, and no one thought the false smile was sincere (Darwin 1872/1998; Ekman 1985). The difference between the two kinds of smiles is physiological. In the false smile, the corrugator muscle is more contracted, causing a frown. In the true smile, the eyelid muscles are more contracted, and the upper lip is drawn up more. The cheeks are drawn upward, and in older people wrinkles are formed under the eyes. The eyes are bright and sparkling, and the corners of the mouth are retracted.

What is remarkable about all of this is how complicated a thing it is to smile. The facial movements are unconscious and costless when the smile is genuine, of course. But if the smile or laugh is insincere, there are simply too many muscles to move, and it unsurprising that nobody is fooled. On command, we might move one facial muscle, mechanically, as we might lift an arm; but we cannot will *all* of the right muscles to move in the required way. When the smile passes into a laugh, these facial movements intensify. We move fifteen facial muscles in a coordinated manner and alter our breathing patterns (Koestler 1989). EEG studies of brain activity also report that true and false smiles are wholly different mental events (Ekman, Davidson, and Friesen 1990). For virtually all of us, the false smile or laugh is simply too hard to counterfeit.

If the false smile or laugh could be costlessly produced, it would not signal one's private sentiments. A lemons market would develop, and smiles and laughs would soon die out. But the costs of smiling and laughing are differentially borne by true and false signalers. For genuine laughter, the muscular exertion imposes a minimal cost—one calorie, let us say. The costs are far greater for the false signaler, who must contort his muscles in what will seem an unnatural position. Because of this, a separating equilibrium arises in which the differential costs of true and false smiles or laughter make them a credible indicator of private sentiments (Spence 1973).

Yet this might not suffice if a subgroup of the population could invest in honing its ability to signal falsely. Suppose that whereas true laughter requires the movement of fifteen muscles, we may all detect as false a laugh in which only ten muscles are exercised. A particularly skilled flimflammer might then find that feigning an eleven-muscle laugh can reap substantial fraudulent rewards. This development might be countered in one of two ways. The nonfraudulent who stand to be gulled by the flimflammer might invest in the production of better skills in detecting false laughter, such that any laugh in which fewer than twelve muscles are exercised will be identified as false. Alternatively, they might move an extra two muscles in sincere laughter if these cannot easily be duplicated by the fraud artist.

The result is an arms race. One side acquires a weapon, and this is matched by its rivals. Each side builds up its arsenal, even though both would be better off if they could agree on a weapons ban. When the weapons are false laughter and flimflam antennae, however, no test-ban treaty can be written. This may explain how it happened that laughter became such a subtle signal, and why we move fifteen and not ten muscles to laugh. Or why it might take more muscles at a future evolutionary moment, thousands of years from now. Our society might thus be composed of a large majority of honest people and a small minority of sociopaths, with the former investing in lie detection and the latter specializing in cheating and breach. Where the payoffs from the two strategies are the same, the parties are in equilibrium, because no one has an incentive to switch from one strategy to the other (Edelmann 1987).

For laughter to serve as a trust-building device, not only must the laugh reveal private sentiments but these must be durable. If they were wholly plastic, if an expression of feelings today gave no clue about tomorrow's feelings, then facial expressions would not signal anything about promise keeping. We are not made that way, however. We have durable preferences that cannot be abandoned without emotional pain. Such preferences impose a cost, to the extent that they constrain future choices. They might make it painful to betray one's family, for example, and those who have gone through a divorce might have wished that it were easier to do so ("so that the healing process can begin," as liberal clerics put it). But if it were painless to leave one's wife, then divorce rates would be higher and marriage rates would be lower.

Laughter is one of the many private ceremonies through which we demonstrate durable preferences of loyalty or disloyalty to others. Joke telling is a means of sniffing out friends. Sincere friends laugh together in a special way that false friends cannot duplicate. The laughter is open, unreserved, and joyful. The weaker the tie, the more strained the laughter. Where the listener has recently betrayed the teller, the laughter often has a lupine quality: the cheeks are pulled back and the teeth are bared; the listener's gaze rests on the teller, and the general expression is ironic. The emotional cost of hiding the enmity is simply too great for most false listeners, and the appropriate inference will be made. If you cannot laugh with me, how can I trust you? You say you like me, and share my interests? Then come into my bar and laugh at my jokes. Only then will I trust you. And the more risqué the joke, the stronger the signal of friendship.

## 9.5 IS LAUGHTER EFFICIENT?

We have identified two kinds of gains laughter might produce. Because it communicates a sense of superiority to the butt, laughter confers *signaling* gains, informing us of what constitutes a defective life plan. Because it promotes solidarity between teller and listener, laughter also provides the *bonding* gains of increased mutual trust that permit parties to exploit profitable opportunities. In spite of these benefits, laughter might fail to provide an optimum set of signals. First, there might be too little laughter because of free-rider problems. Second, laughter might be excessive rather than inadequate. We might spend too much time at wit-work and too little time at the serious business of life.

### 9.5.1 Too Little Laughter

As a social experience, laughter resembles a market in which the parties bargain for inclusion in competing coalitions of jesters and listeners. No one seeks to be a butt, and joining a jester in laughing at another might be a useful device to deflect laughs at oneself. The selection of butts might thus be seen as a matter of negotiation between jester and listener. The jester proposes a butt for laughter, and this offer may be accepted by the listener through a return of laughter or rejected through silence. In such a laughter exchange, individuals may be seen to trade off butts through implicit agreements about who is risible. These bargains determine what counts as a comic vice, because jokes must have a content to amuse.

How do comic norms arise? Economists assume that bargains are shaped by personal preferences that in turn are shaped by social norms, but until recently had not turned their attention to how such norms are formed. When they did, they were met with what seemed a major obstacle: How can a valuable norm be produced if no one has an incentive to do so? A free-rider problem arises because the costs of producing a public good (that confers a benefit on everyone) exceed the benefit any one individual derives from it. Suppose that in a society of one hundred people, a social norm offers a benefit of 1 to each person but costs 10 to produce for a net benefit of 90 to society. Will the norm be produced? The person who takes the initiative to do so will expend 10 and get 1, for a net loss of 9. Those who hang back and free ride will gain 1 each. Each person has thus an incentive to hang back and wait for someone else to produce the norm. When everyone tries to free ride in this way, the norm will not be created (Coleman 1990).

Free-rider problems might be minimized, and cooperative behavior might emerge, through the patterns of reciprocal altruism. The parties may learn to trust each other when they engage in repeated transactions and a stable relationship develops. In that case one party might be willing to bear personal costs in producing a public good (such as a valuable comic norm) because the party expects the other party to reciprocate. For example, the light banter that accompanies major business transactions often provides the trust-building context needed to support contracting. Nevertheless, reciprocal altruism provides an incomplete explanation of laughter norms, because it does not account for their content. Two associates who seek to build up a pattern of cooperation might choose any person for a butt or any defect for a comic vice. What is needed, however, is an explanation for why we laugh *when* we do. In particular, why do we all find the same sorts of things amusing, even where there is no long-term relationship between us?

The second way in which free-rider problems may be overcome is suggested by the superiority thesis, which also explains when we laugh. Under superiority explanations, laughter always affects status: the jester and listener move up a pace, and the butt steps back. The jester has thus an incentive to exercise wit, as the listener does to laugh along. This gives the parties a private incentive to create laughter norms. Joke entreprenuers—professional comics—will find a ready market for their ability to see the humor in what others pass over without laughter. A Will Rogers or Mort Sahl could convulse audiences by bringing out a newspaper and offering a droll spin on the headlines. "I don't belong to an organized political party," said Rogers. "I'm a Democrat." Even without a monetary reward, the joke entrepreneur will derive the satisfaction that comes from dominating a conversation. During the joke, no one else speaks, and if successful, the jester may move up several notches in our estimation. Through a well-timed sally, the jester might also deflate an argument and move the conversation in his direction. Wit is thus an important tool for opinion leaders.

Because of the private benefits of membership in a coalition of laughers and the loss of status that comes from being identified a butt, people will compete for membership in winning (jester-listener) coalitions. By itself, however, this does not explain how comic norms arise—how one character trait rather than another becomes identified within a society as risible. Assume that when a joke is successful, the status gains for the jester and listener are 1 for both, and the status loss for the butt is $-2$. The gains to the jester and listener equal the butt's costs, so the status changes sum to 0. In such a situation, every winning coalition would be unstable, in the sense that a butt could always offer an equal status gain to listeners by cracking his own joke at the first jester's expense. The first-round jester might thus turn into a second-round butt. Knowing this, why would he initiate the first joke? The incentive to create laughter might thus disappear. Laughter would signal an empty superiority, because the victory would ordinarily be short-lived. Nor would laughter communicate a message about how to live, because the norms would continually change.

Suppose, however, that laughter does signal useful information about comic vices and that some people are natural butts: their character traits are socially undesirable. The game would now have a solution, in the sense that it would produce a single winning coalition and a single butt. Assume again that the status gains and losses of laughter sum to 0. But assume also that in addition to the private status gains at which we have been looking, there are social benefits associated with the enunciation of socially valuable comic norms: the social gain is 2 when the natural butt is ridiculed and 0 otherwise. Here, the status gains and losses cancel out, but not the social gains of laughter. Thus, the natural butt will never be able to compete listeners away to laugh with and not at him, and the process of coalition formation will promote valuable comic norms.

In addition, the costs of wit-work are so low that they may plausibly be thought exceeded by the benefits each individual derives from the norm. Did their wit impose a cost on Shakespeare's Beatrice and Benedict, who took pleasure in mocking each other? It might even be costlier to remain silent. "Not write?" asked Pope. "But then I think";

> And for my soul I cannot sleep a wink.
> I nod in company, I wake at night,
> Fools rush into my head, and so I write.
> *First Satire of the Second Book of Horace Imitated*

One might speak of a cost function for all of this, but it is more like a by-product of being alive than a computational or physical chore.

Finally, laughter solves other problems that hamper norm formation in other realms. Norms are launched in competition with other norms, and before one norm dominates, there is a "milling-about" period in which the different norms are assessed (Coleman 1990). The greater the number of members in the group, the longer the tryout period will be. With laughter, the costs are slight and the try-out group is small. Listeners have it in their power to accept or reject the proposed joke, and acceptance must be instantaneous if it is to count at all. The instinct to retell the joke also ensures that it reaches a wide audience. Thus, the milling-about delays are relatively short.

## 9.6 TOO MUCH LAUGHTER

Free-rider concerns suggest the possibility that we might hear too little laughter. But there is also a possibility of too much laughter, where the costs of laughter outweigh its benefits. In Patrice Leconte's film *Ridicule* the court of Louis XVI ignores substantive policy problems and devotes its energy to deftly delivered barbs. A young nobleman arrives at court from the provinces with a worthy plan to drain some marshes. The plan is filed away, as is every project for improvement. But the nobleman perseveres, after he is given good advice by a courtier: "Be witty, sharp and malicious and you will succeed." No one gets anywhere without stepping on someone first, and the favorite weapon is wit. A rival may be humiliated by a bon mot and even driven to suicide by a court that, six years before the Revolution, literally laughs its head off.

Laughter confers the public benefit of correcting comic vices and the private benefits of increased status. It might then be excessive where the private benefits crowd out the public benefits. For example, suppose that laughter levels are efficient, in the sense that with any more effort at ridicule, the costs of wit-work would exceed all signaling and bonding benefits. Would the mockery cease? Possibly not,

Player 2

|  |  | Cooperate | Defect |
|---|---|---|---|
|  | Cooperate | 5, 5 | −10, 10 |
| Player 1 | Defect | 10, −10 | −5, −5 |

**Figure 9.1**    Excessive laughter

because the parties might continue to have a private incentive to ridicule one another. *Ridicule* described such a world, in which value-increasing work is ignored and the courtiers obsess over wasteful status gains. Apart from devoting too much time on wit-work, the courtiers might also worry excessively about being caught out as butts. The impulse to shield oneself from laughter by practicing the comic virtues is normally benign, but might not be so when the laughter is excessive. Then the courtier might sacrifice the real happiness of originality in pursuit of status gains, and all idiosyncrasy would be lost in a world of dull conformity.

We may model this through an example (see Figure 9.1). Assume that ridicule confers a private status gain of 10 to jesters against a cost of 10 to butts (leaving listeners out in this model). Once again, the combined status gains and costs net to 0. Both parties are better off if they refrain from ridicule and concentrate on improving the drains. Joint cooperation means that both parties abstain from ridicule and offers them a good drains payoff of 5 apiece; joint defection, in which wasteful ridicule continues from both sides and efficient drains remain unbuilt, is associated with a loss of 5 each. The relative status for one party is equal to that of the other with either joint cooperation or joint defection. But where one party cooperates and the other defects (through ridicule), the former gets the sucker's payoff of −10 and the latter sees his status rise by 10.

When each party has the private incentive to laugh excessively, the result is a prisoner's dilemma game in which joint defection is socially wasteful but individually rational for both parties. Whatever strategy party 2 employs, party 1 is always better off by defecting; and the same is true of party 2, relative to party 1's choices. The players will wastefully display their wit because their status and position depend so importantly upon them.

As in an arms race, the courtiers in *Ridicule* might be better off if they could write an effective agreement to ban the use of wit. No such agreement is possible, of course. Nevertheless, there is reason to think that the problem of excessive laughter is self-correcting. The real obstacle to an arms treaty is observability.

Where one party's move in an arms race can be detected by the other side (through measurements of nuclear tests, for example), the parties might coordinate a halt to the competition without a test-ban treaty through strategies of reciprocal altruism. In laughter competitions, one party has only to stop joking and wait for the move to be reciprocated. The tendency to excessive wit might thus be circumvented through simple patterns of cooperation.

In addition, one of our most important and least appreciated predispositions—boredom—dampens excessive laughter. Following Pascal, we may define *boredom* as the inability to be happy alone in a room. We are bored doing nothing and are bored when we repeat the same act over and over. Boredom can be modeled as a damper on the benefits of repeated action. With each new round, the marginal benefit of the act declines. Returning to the example in Figure 9.1, suppose that because of boredom the status gain declines by 1 on each new game. After five games the parties will suspend play, because the status gain would thereafter be exceeded by the costs of excessive ridicule. Before the jokes become excessive, the audience would leave, taking the status gains with them. We are therefore permitted to doubt whether the competition for relative status results in wasteful, excessive laughter.

In sum, we might have too much laughter where the parties have private incentives to ridicule one another and where this serves no useful purpose; or too little laughter where the social gains of laughter remain unexploited because of free-rider problems. We might laugh too often or not often enough. It is difficult to know what to make of theoretical arguments that tug in opposite directions, particularly when each has a tendency to correct itself.

Our laughter might thus be seen as a valuable signaling device. This is not to claim that laughter signals cannot mislead, as some kinds of laughter rest on erroneous beliefs or invidious preferences. But in most cases the butt would be wise to attend to the message of laughter. Not that the butt has much choice in the matter.

REFERENCES

Burckhardt, J. 1929/1958. *The civilization of the Renaissance in Italy*. Vol. 1. Repr., New York: Harper and Row.

Coleman, J. 1990. *Foundations of social theory*. Cambridge, MA: Harvard University Press.

Cornford, F. 1961. *The origins of attic comedy*. Garden City, NJ: Anchor.

Darwin, C. 1872/1998. *The expression of the emotions in man and animals*. Repr., New York: Oxford University Press.

De Waal, F. 1989. *Chimpanzee politics: Power and sex among apes*. Baltimore: Johns Hopkins.

Edelmann, R. 1987. *The psychology of embarrassment*. Chichester, UK: Wiley.

Ekman, P. 1985. *Telling lies: Clues to deceit in the marketplace, politics, and marriage*. New York: Norton.

Ekman, P., R. Davidson, and W. Friesen. 1990. The Duchenne smile: Emotional expression and brain psychology II. *Journal of Personality and Social Psychology* 58:342–53.

Frye, N. 1957. *The anatomy of criticism: Four essays*. Princeton, NJ: Princeton University Press.

Greig, J. 1923. *The psychology of laughter and comedy*. New York: Cooper Square.

Gurewitch, M. 1975. *Comedy: The irrational vision*. Ithaca, NY: Cornell University Press.

Hazlitt, W. 1818/1907. *Lectures on the English comic writers*. Repr., London: Oxford University Press.

Hobbes, T. 1651/1968. *Leviathan*. Repr., London: Penguin.

———. 1640/1994. Human nature. In *Human nature and de corpore politico*. Repr., Oxford: Oxford University Press.

Koestler, A. 1989. *The act of creation*. 2nd ed. London: Penguin.

Spence, M. 1973. Job market signaling. *Quarterly Journal of Economics* 87:355.

Weisenberg, M., I. Tepper, and J. Schwarzwald. 1995. Humor as a cognitive technique for increasing pain tolerance. *Pain* 63:207.

# III

## THE JURISPRUDENCE OF IRRATIONAL BEHAVIOR: RETHINKING LAW AS A BEHAVIORAL INSTRUMENT

# 10 | THE JURISPRUDENCE OF CRAZINESS

*Stephen J. Morse*

Rules throughout criminal and civil law, encompassed within the general rubric "mental health law," treat some people with mental disorders specially. For example, an agent who makes a grossly careless mistake about the need to use deadly self-defense will be guilty of some degree of culpable homicide, but if the belief about the need to use deadly force is delusional, the agent may be found not guilty by reason of insanity. For another example, a businessperson who makes a bad deal because he or she was careless in determining his or her financial capabilities will not be able to avoid the contract, but if a similar bad deal is produced by a delusional belief, the agent may well be found to have been incompetent to contract and may avoid much or all of the contract. For a final example, a person suffering from a serious physical illness may refuse reasonable treatment for any reason he or she wishes. Indeed, the agent is under no duty to give any reason at all; his or her wishes must be respected. But if the refusal is grounded in a delusional belief, the agent may be forced to accept treatment.

The special legal treatment of some people with mental disorders is also endorsed and often required by constitutional law. In our system, with few and highly limited exceptions, we do not preventively detain citizens solely on grounds of dangerousness (*Kansas v. Hendricks*, 521 U.S. 246, 358 (1997)). Agents who present a highly predictable danger to other people must be left alone unless the agent's behavior comes sufficiently close to completion of a crime so that the conduct qualifies for attempt liability. If the danger an agent presents is produced by serious mental disorder, however, the agent may be civilly committed. Although current constitutional law permits capital punishment, it is unconstitutional to execute an agent who is not competent to be executed because the agent's severe mental disorder prevents him or her from understanding what is happening or why (*Ford v. Wainwright*, 477 U.S. 399 (1986)). Additionally, the Eighth Amendment entirely prohibits execution of people with mental retardation (*Atkins v. Virginia*, 536 U.S. 304 (2002)). A person accused of crime cannot be tried if mental disorder or retardation renders the defendant incompetent to stand trial because the defendant cannot understand the nature of the proceedings or cannot assist counsel effectively (*Drope v. Missouri*, 420 U.S. 162 (1975)).

The questions such cases raise are why at least some people with mental disorders are treated specially and what, if anything, mental health law teaches us about jurisprudence generally. Because mental health laws exist throughout civil and criminal law, they have the potential to reveal deeper understanding of the law's usual presumptions. I have argued that the disparate mental health laws have a similar, coherent structure (Morse 1978). In the present chapter, using common-sense folk psychology and philosophical theories of mind, action, and responsibility, I attempt to continue the arguments presented earlier. The core thesis is that understanding the coherence of mental health law and its general implications for jurisprudence depends on the central role that the uniquely human capacity for reason plays in law. The capacity for reason or rationality is the root of our concern for agency and for choice, and it is the foundation for the maximal exercise of liberty. In short, the reason that some people with mental disorder are treated specially is that they appear to lack the capacity for reason in some contexts. Consequently, they are not responsible for their conduct, and the usual legal consequences, including traditional liberties, do not apply.[1]

People with mental disorders, including those who suffer most severely, are not automatons, and their actions are not mechanisms. They are people, and their actions, like the actions of all people, are the products of practical reasoning and not simply the mechanistic outcome of various biological, psychological, or sociological causes. "Craziness" is a property of agents and their actions, not of mechanisms. Thus, proper understanding of mental health law requires an account of personhood.

The chapter begins by presenting a general account of the law's view of the person and responsibility. The account, which is positive and normative, attempts both to explain our system and to defend its basic assumptions. I offer a defense to the metaphysical challenge rooted in determinism that often seems to undermine the possibility of responsibility for people with mental disorders (and perhaps responsibility for anyone) (e.g., Pereboom 2001; Strawson 1989). I conclude that the coherence of the system survives such a challenge and that determinism has nothing to do with why people with mental disorders are treated specially. I also conclude that an alternative, fully consequential system would be coherent. Nonetheless, adopting it would give up too much we value and such a system is unlikely to be adopted.

Then the discussion turns to mental health law. I first consider the structure and justification of mental health law generally, demonstrating that it flows logically from the law's view of the person and the nature of law itself. I then consider how the law should understand and assess the two core questions of mental health law: Who is crazy? and Are crazy people responsible? In particular, I address the role of scientific understanding of psychopathology and the role of experts in adjudicating mental health law cases. I conclude that despite enormous advances in our biological, psychological, and sociological understanding of the causes and consequences of the phenomena termed *mental disorders*, virtually all mental health law doctrines can be understood and cases can be adjudicated primarily using commonsense observations of behavior and traditional moral and legal theory and doctrine. Next I address whether mental abnormalities should provide the basis for an independent body of legal doctrine and conclude that they should not. Instead, I propose that there should be generic criteria for nonresponsibility and that mental abnormality should play solely an evidentiary role in deciding whether an agent lacks the capacity for rationality in a particular context. Finally, I consider various case studies to test the merits of the generic rationality and responsibility criteria this chapter proposes.

## 10.1 RATIONALITY AND RESPONSIBILITY

This section first considers the nature of law and the view of the person that law presupposes and then turns to the theory of responsibility inherent in law and ordinary morality alike.[2] Next, it addresses the excusing conditions entailed by the law's view of responsibility and the most common, erroneous challenges to this account. Finally, it turns briefly to the possibility of a completely consequentialist alternative.

### 10.1.1 Rules, Persons, and Rationality

Most simply, law is a guidance system that structures human interaction by informing people what they may and should do and what the consequences of various courses of conduct will be. Law is, of course, not the only guidance system people use. Morality, manners, and various other noncodified bodies of rules and norms are also meant to guide our behavior, but law is a central, ubiquitous guidance system in our society. To the best of our knowledge, only human beings are capable of using guiding rules to regulate their behavior. Neither inanimate objects and forces nor any infrahuman species has such systems to guide conduct. There are no chimpanzee legislatures, and there is no dolphin Ms. Manners.

The law clearly treats people as intentional agents and not simply as part of the biophysical flotsam and jetsam of the causal universe. It could not be otherwise. Systems of rules at the least are meant to guide or influence behavior and thus to operate as potential causes of behavior. Legal rules are not simply mechanistic causes that produce "reflex" compliance. They operate within the domain of practical reason. Agents are meant to and can only use these rules as potential *reasons for action* as they deliberate about what they should do.[3] Legal rules are thus action guiding primarily because they provide an agent with good moral or prudential reasons for forbearance or action. Unless people were capable of understanding and then using legal rules as premises in deliberation, law would be powerless to affect human behavior.[4] I am not suggesting that human behavior cannot be modified by means other than influencing deliberation or that human beings always deliberate before they act. Of course it can and of course they do not. But law operates through practical reason, even when we most habitually follow the legal rules.

Law can directly and indirectly affect the world we inhabit only by its influence on practical reason.[5] All things being equal, the only aspect of the human condition that is fully "up to us," that is fully "within our control," that can be fully guided by and the product of our reasons, is intentional action or forbearance.[6] In the entire chain of causation that leads to compliance with or breach of a moral or legal obligation, only action is potentially fully determined by reasons. Consequently, law and morality alike are concerned primarily with action and not with thoughts, feelings, character, and other variables that are not fully guidable by reason. In sum, the law's view of the person is a creature whose actions can in principle be explained as the product of reasons, as potentially reason responsive.

Law is thus different from the social sciences, including psychology and psychiatry. The latter, which provide much of the clinical and scientific data that underpin mental health law doctrine and decision making, are uncomfortably wedged between reason-giving and mechanistic accounts of human behavior. Sometimes they treat behavior "objectively," as primarily mechanistic or physical; other times, social science treats behavior "subjectively," as a text to be interpreted. Yet other times, social science engages in an uneasy amalgam of the two. What is always clear, however, is that the domain of the social sciences is human action and not simply the movements of bodies in space. One can attempt to assimilate folk psychology's reason-giving to mechanistic explanation by claiming that desires, beliefs, and intentions are genuine causes. Indeed, folk psychology proceeds on the assumption that reasons for action are genuinely causal. But even if reasons are causal, the type of causation involved is not mechanistic. For now, law and social science must simply accept that human beings are creatures for whom practical reason, including deliberation, plays a potentially action-guiding role.

The claim that reason can guide only human action does not imply that human beings are always guided by reason, including by the reasons legal rules provide. Like all human capacities, the capacity to be guided by reason may or may not be exercised. Much human action is unreasonable, thoughtless, foolish, irrational, nonrational, and the like. Nevertheless, the capacity to guide one's actions by reason develops through childhood and adolescence and is present in most adults. Successful human interaction, not to mention the survival of the species, would be impossible without this capacity. It is the touchstone of moral and legal responsibility. Moreover, when important rights and interests are at stake, we expect each other to use our capacity to be guided by reason, once again including the reasons law provides. The failure of law always to guide action successfully does not undermine the claim that the action-guiding function is crucial to the theoretical and practical importance of law in human interaction.

## 10.1.2 Responsibility

Responsibility is a socially constructed legal and moral ascription to and attribute of agents and their actions that dictates the appropriate interpersonal response, including legal and moral responses. Responsible agents are those who may and should bear the consequences of their conduct in particular contexts. Being responsible is strongly associated in our culture with liberty. In general, the exercise of maximal liberty is reserved for those agents who are fully responsible, and it follows from law's primarily action-guiding function that responsible agents are those who can be guided by the law.[7] It follows implicitly that responsible agents are those with a sufficient capacity to be guided by reason, a capacity usually referred to as rationality. Only agents with rational capacity are in general required to bear the full consequences of their actions. For example, although young children certainly act for reasons and can be guided by reason to some degree, they are not held fully responsible in many contexts until their rational capacity has evolved to adult capacity through maturation.

The general capacity for rationality and what rationality demands in any legal context must inevitably be defined normatively, including politically. Let us begin with the concept of rationality, about which there is no uncontroversial definition in any of the disciplines that address this notion. Nonetheless, a few commonsense, useful observations are possible. At the most basic level, rationality refers to a minimal form of coherence between desires, beliefs, and actions, itself a normative notion, that is constitutive of mind, agency, and coherent personhood. This notion of rationality does not carry us very far, however, because most human beings, including people with severe mental disorders or with mild or moderate developmental disability, meet this basic, normative conception of rationality.

More important is a broader normative meaning that refers to a congeries of cognitive and emotional capacities that make relatively successful human interaction and guidance possible. At the very least, it must include the ability, in Susan Wolf's words, "to be sensitive and responsive to relevant changes in one's situation and environment—that is, to be flexible" (1990, 69). On this account, rationality is the ability to perceive accurately, to get the facts right, and to reason instrumentally, including weighing the facts appropriately and according to a minimally coherent preference ordering. It includes the ability to perceive and appropriately to use emotional considerations, such as empathy, in deciding how to act. In sum, rationality is primarily the general ability to recognize and be responsive to the good reasons that should guide action (Fischer and Ravizza 1998). Put yet another way, it is the ability to act for good reasons. Understood this way, rationality is of course a continuum concept, and individuals differ widely in their ability to get the facts straight, to understand the rules, to reason, and the like. People with fewer endowments and less fortunate life experience will find it harder to be rational; people with more endowments and better experience will find it easier.

The preceding characterization of rationality is normative but abstracted from any concrete context. Although it is possible to speak of minimal rationality that might be required for any imaginable context, it is more helpful to recognize that what rationality demands varies with context and will be defined according to normative social, cultural, historical, moral, and political expectations. Contextual rationality would thus refer to the ability or capacity to understand and to be guided by the legal rules operative in that context. More specifically, the capacity for rationality has three aspects: the agent must be able to perceive and to comprehend the relevant facts; the agent must be able to comprehend and to conform to the applicable legal rules; and the agent must be able to assess the import of the facts and rules, including their relationship to each other. According to this notion, agents might be considered capable of rationality in some contexts but not in others.

What we demand of each other in any context at any time is not self-defining and can thus shift as expectations evolve. In general, the amount of rational capacity the law requires to hold adults fully responsible is not high, because our society prefers to treat people as responsible and thus to grant citizens the right to pursue their projects unencumbered by a parentalistic state. Nonetheless, greater or lesser capacity could be required in general or in specific contexts precisely because the capacity for rationality is normatively defined. Because responsibility is dependent on the capacity for rationality and the latter is arrayed along a continuum, so, too, can responsibility be arrayed along a continuum if the law so desires.

Because I claim that the capacity for rationality is the primary responsibility condition, the concept of rationality must do a great deal of work in the account presented. One might therefore desire a more precise, uncontroversial definition, but such a desire would be unreasonable. The definition I am using, which is always open to normative revision, is grounded in our ordinary, everyday understanding of practical reasoning and its critical role in human interaction, including morality. We are, after all, the only creatures on earth who truly act for reasons. We have always successfully employed the imprecise definition I am using to evaluate the moral and nonmoral conduct of ourselves and others. To require more is to require the impossible and the unnecessary. Moreover, if one wishes to abandon rationality as the core responsibility condition, the burden is then on the agent rejecting rationality to offer and justify a more morally compelling and precise alternative.

## 10.1.3 Nonresponsibility: The Excusing Conditions

This section considers the two conditions that I claim exhaust the realm of excuses for action: lack of the general capacity for rationality and compulsion or coercion.[8]

### 10.1.3.1 Lack of Capacity for Rationality

As a logical corollary of rationality's central role in responsibility, lack of the capacity for rationality is the core nonresponsibility or excusing condition in both law and morality. Thus, our legal culture does not hold responsible an agent who is incapable of being guided by reason in a particular context. Some classes of agents suffer from general deficits in the capacity for rationality. Young children, people with severe dementias, and people with profound developmental disabilities are good examples. Virtually no member of these classes can meet any legal rationality requirement; thus, such people will not be subject to the usual consequences of action, and they will be subject to broad parentalistic intervention. Nonetheless, youth, dementia, and retardation are not excusing conditions per se but are simply proxies in these cases for the lack of a sufficient capacity for rationality that is the genuine nonresponsibility condition.

Other conditions bear a less consistent relation to the capacity for rationality that the law requires for responsibility. People with mental disorders, less severe dementias, and less severe retardation and agents operating under stress, fatigue, or grief are all good examples. To assess the responsibility of agents in such conditions, we must focus on the capacity for rationality, not simply the presence of a condition that can affect rationality. In any case in which the agent acted irrationally, we must always try to answer the counterfactual question: Was the agent capable of acting rationally if he or she had recognized or was given good reason to do so? Although these conditions may compromise the capacity for rationality, they may not do so in all cases sufficiently to warrant a conclusion that the agent was not responsible. Responsibility may nonetheless obtain, or it may be diminished but not obliterated.

How much the capacity for rationality must be compromised to negate or diminish responsibility is a normative political, social, and moral issue that science cannot resolve. Valid data can disclose much about human capacities and how they may be altered, but deciding when agents will be excused from bearing the full legal consequences of their actions or when parentalistic intervention is permissible or required is a legal question.

### 10.1.3.2 Compulsion or Coercion

Compulsion or coercion is a second nonresponsibility condition that excuses agents from bearing the full legal consequences of their actions. The best understanding of compulsion is that the agent is placed through no moral fault of his or her own in a threatening, "do it or else" situation. If the threat is sufficient, the agent will be excused from the consequences of doing "it" because we believe as a moral matter that the choice was too hard to expect the agent to resist. For example, an agent charged with murder for killing an innocent third party may have the excuse of duress if the defendant was coerced to kill by a malefactor who threatened the agent with death unless the agent killed the innocent victim. In these cases, the agent clearly acts intentionally and there is no problem with the agent's capacity for rationality. Although we often say that the agent had no choice, in fact the agent did have a choice, albeit a very hard one. These cases must therefore be distinguished from cases of literal physical compulsion in which there is literally no choice and the agent is not responsible because the agent does not act at all. For example, if the malefactor literally pulled the agent's trigger finger despite the agent's earnest resistance, the trigger pulling would not be the agent's action.

Cases of compulsion, especially those arising from internal psychological states, are often explained using the concept of a volitional, will, or control problem, but this is not the best explanation of why compulsion excuses.[9] If a volition is understood as an intention to execute a basic action, the compelled agent has no volitional problem (Moore 1993). The will or volition operates effectively to permit the agent to act intentionally to avoid the threatened consequence. Once again, the agent is excused because he or she faces an unreasonably hard choice occasioned through no fault of his or her own.

Most potential cases of compulsion involve metaphorical compulsion, and the normative issue is, when does the threat become sufficient to excuse the agent's action? Although choice situations involving offers rather than threats may appear to leave an agent with as little choice as some threatening situations, offers increase freedom. Accepting a genuine offer one cannot rationally refuse is not a case of compulsion. Compulsion is also not based on empirical assumptions about the specific capacities of individual agents to resist compelling conditions. It is a normative, moralized standard. The best interpretation of objective standards for compulsion, such as the "person of reasonable firmness," is that they ask when a choice was too hard to require the agent to resist or face negative legal consequences for yielding. If, objectively, a person of reasonable firmness would resist, the choice is not too hard, and the agent will be held responsible for the conduct in question.

The "person of reasonable firmness" standard does not mean that everyone who does not have a disposition of reasonable firmness will be excused. The defense of duress in criminal law is not available to a defendant allegedly "unable" to resist, if a person of reasonable firmness would have been able to resist. Those who are fortunate enough to be especially firm and those who are of average firmness will be able to meet the standard quite readily. Those who are of less than average dispositional firmness will have more trouble resisting when they should. Still, if we judge that the person had the general capacity to comply with the reasonable firmness standard, then she will be held responsible for yielding when she should not, even if it is harder for her to resist than for most agents. Similarly, if the conditions under which an agent contracted were objectively noncompelling, the agent will be held responsible, even if he subjectively felt entirely compelled and behaved as he did only because he felt this way. Objective legal standards always impose differential costs on agents, depending on the agent's endowments. People with less than average ability to meet them are still held to these standards if they are generally capable of meeting them. This legal result comports with common sense and ordinary morality. When important expectations are involved—for example, be careful; keep your promises; don't harm others—we believe it is fair to expect fellow citizens capable of meeting reasonable standards to comply (Hart 1968).

Compulsion might be assimilated to a rationality problem in the following way. In most cases of compulsion, the agent recognizes that there is good normative reason not to behave as the threat dictates. For example, the hapless killer knows that he or she should not kill the innocent victim because it is wrong to take an equally innocent life to save your own. The threat thus operates to divorce the agent's generally and characteristically motivating normative reasons from the motivating reasons on this occasion. It is surely rational to accede to a sufficient threat rather than to suffer dreadful consequences, but the agent would have no rational reason to act that way independent of the wrongfully applied threat. Thus, the agent's capacity to be motivated by what he or she considers the best reasons for action under baseline normal conditions is substantially diminished. Nonetheless, compulsion is usually considered an excusing condition independent of lack of rational capacity.

External threats are not necessary in all cases that appear to require a compulsion excuse. How should we understand alleged cases of compulsion when there is no external threat, when internal psychological states seem to compel the agent's behavior? This issue vexes theories of action and responsibility generally, and it has specific relevance for mental health law. For example, some claim that allegedly abnormal conditions, such as addictions or aberrant sexual desires, compel conduct. The problem is not limited to abnormal mental conditions, however, and we should remember that an agent allegedly compelled by internal psychological states still acts intentionally in response to those states. Such agents are not literally compelled, and their actions are not pure mechanisms (Morse 2002). They simply act in response to desires experienced subjectively as terribly strong and allegedly overwhelming. Compulsion in such cases is metaphorical rather than literal, but the metaphor of mechanism is often used.

To cash out the mechanistic metaphor, examples of the following kind are given.[10] Assume that an agent needs to urinate but is unable to find an appropriate place to do so. As time passes and the bladder continues to fill, the desire to urinate will become increasingly powerful and unpleasant. At some point, however, the person's bladder will empty because the pressure on the urethral (urinary) sphincter will mechanically force it to open; he or she will no longer be able to "hold it in," no matter what the cost might be for doing so. For example, suppose the agent is threatened with death for permitting his or her bladder to empty. The agent will surely exercise control for a very lengthy period, but the bladders of all agents will finally empty because, ultimately, this will be a product of a literally uncontrollable mechanism. The sphincter "fails" because the physical pressure on it is too great.

Strong abnormal desires are allegedly analogous to the full bladder. Increasing desire is analogized to increasing pressure on the sphincter, and we are supposed to conclude that people are no more responsible for yielding to abnormal desires than they are for emptying their bladders. But abnormal desires are not physical forces, actions are not mechanisms, and people are not sphincters. There are no "desire units" that will finally mechanistically force the "action switch" to flip if enough "desire units" are added. Assuming that a recidivist child molester wants to live, if we threaten him with immediate death for touching a child, he will not touch a child.[11] The analogy to literal mechanism fails, but if the mechanistic picture is in one's head, it is easy to conclude that the sexual predator cannot control himself and is therefore not responsible. Such agents may in fact not be responsible, but this will have to be demonstrated using the criteria for irrationality and compulsion rather than concluded by label.

Consider the following scenario. Imagine an agent with a strong sexual drive for adult members of the opposite sex who finds fantasy and masturbation unsatisfactory and who cannot afford the services of a prostitute. The sexual desire of such an agent might become extremely intense. If the agent engaged in sexual assault to satisfy the desire, the agent surely acts intentionally but might claim that he felt compelled, could not help himself, or the like. How should we understand and evaluate this claim? Two answers suggest themselves: an internal hard choice claim, wherein the internal desire operates like an external threat; and a disability claim, wherein the internal desire somehow disables the agent. Let us consider these in turn.

In internal hard choice cases, the agent faces supremely dysphoric inner states —psychological pain—unless the agent acts to satisfy the desire. The hard choice in this case is either to act wrongfully to satisfy the desire or to suffer psychological pain.[12] A model of hard choice created by the threat of internal dysphoria may be the best explanation of why we believe agents are not responsible in an array of cases that are often thought to require a "volitional" or control excuse, such as our initial example and cases of pedophilia, pyromania, compulsive gambling, drug "addiction," and the like. In all, the predisposition causes intense desires, the frustration of which threatens the agent with great dysphoria. Perhaps a person of reasonable firmness faced with sufficient dysphoria would yield. If so, perhaps the coward or other "subjective" cases should not be held responsible in the absence of irrationality because they satisfy a properly expansive hard choice, nonresponsibility condition.

Although the internal hard choice model is plausible and competing explanations that rely on so-called volitional problems are confused or lack empirical support (Morse 1994), I contend that this model is problematic. First, at the most practical level, it will often be too difficult to assess the degree of threatened dysphoria that creates the hard choice. Second, it is simply not clear that the fear of dysphoria produces a choice sufficiently hard to excuse an agent from the usual legal consequences of his or her action, except in precisely those cases in which we would assume naturally that the agent's rational capacity was essentially disabled. Death and grievous bodily harm are dreadful consequences for virtually any rational person. Other threatened consequences, such as lesser physical, emotional, or economic harms, may also be extremely unpleasant and subjectively feared, but threat of such lesser harms will not warrant a hard choice excuse in most legal contexts. For example, committing crimes is itself considered so wrong that we require people to buck up and obey the law, even if they are very fearful.

Dysphoric mental or emotional states are surely undesirable, but does their threat produce a sufficiently hard choice to warrant nonresponsibility? I do not know the answer to this question, but perhaps at the extreme they do. People suffering from severe depressive disorders, for example, report subjective pain that is as great and enduring as many forms of grievous bodily harm, and sometimes they kill themselves to avoid the psychological pain. But people do not consciously engage in legally relevant behavior to ward off the feared onslaught of severe depression. And people suffering from such severe depression are undeniably irrational. It seems unlikely that most rational agents threatened with dysphoria face a sufficiently hard choice to warrant nonresponsibility. I suspect that the feared dysphoria of unconsummated compulsive cravings is not as severe as the fear of death or grievous bodily harm. If this is right, few sufferers from internal compulsion would succeed with a hard choice excuse, albeit we might feel sympathetic toward their plight. In sum, I am claiming that the person who appears genuinely incapable of resisting when the threats are objectively insufficient to excuse, if any there be, will almost certainly be a person with irrational fears or other irrational beliefs that will satisfy the irrationality criteria for nonresponsibility.

The second possible internal compulsion rationale is that inner cravings or desires can disable an agent's rational capacities. I believe that this is the best explanation of why we excuse in inner compulsion cases. The claim is that when desires become sufficiently intense, the agent can think of nothing else and cannot bring his or her normative competence to bear (Kennett 2001; Morse 2000b). The strength and salience of the desire make it exceedingly difficult and perhaps impossible for the agent to use ordinary self-management techniques, including distracting oneself and employing competing reasons to avoid the undesirable conduct. Fundamental components of rationality, the capacities to think clearly and self-consciously to evaluate one's conduct, are compromised. The agent may not recognize the various options at all or may not be able coherently to weigh and to assess those that are recognized. For moral and legal purposes, the precise mechanisms by which desires can compromise rationality are less important, however, than the clear evidence that they can (Elster 1999). Note that if the desire sufficiently interferes with the agent's ability to grasp and be guided by reason, then a classic irrationality problem arises and there is no need to resort to compulsion as an independent ground for excuse.

A final argument concerning allegedly irresistible desires straightforwardly assimilates such cases to irrationality cases by claiming that some desires are themselves irrational and the agent who suffers from them is therefore irrational. From the radically subjective viewpoint of thinkers from Hume to those of modern rational choice, it is impossible to give an adequate account of the irrationality of desires. They are just brute "givens" that cannot be evaluated in terms of rationality.[13] Moreover, if the desire is weak, however abnormal it may be, it is difficult to imagine why a weak desire should excuse. In the face of weak desires, we can fairly expect agents to exercise self-control if yielding to the desire will cause harm to others or to themselves. Strong desires can of course interfere with our ability to reason well, to bring good reason to bear, but then it is not the content of the desire but the effect of the desire's strength on cognitive abilities that is doing the excusing work. And from this point of view, there is no reason to distinguish allegedly abnormal from normal desires. Wanting something too much can be an affliction and may seem irrational, but once again, it will potentially furnish an excuse only because intense wanting may disable rational capacity.

A potential problem for either explanation of internal compulsion as an excuse—internal hard choice or the assimilation to irrationality—arises from time framing. The source of the hard choice or rational disability is typically a characteristic desire the agent experiences. The agent's conduct may seem excusable when the desire is intense and creates a threat of dysphoria or disables the agent's rationality. During those periods when the desire is more quiescent and the agent can think straight, however, the agent will almost always be aware that periods of nonresponsibility will arise. Intense desires are seldom one-off events that surprise the agent, and both such desires and consequent action can usually be avoided by preparation. If the agent fails to take such steps, then the agent can be held responsible for actions that are excusable at the moment they occur. For example, an agent threatened with death or bodily harm unless the person commits a crime cannot claim a duress excuse if he or she culpably placed himself or herself in a situation in which the threat would be made.[14] Thus, in most cases of internal compulsion, the agent will be held responsible because he or she was capable of taking steps to prevent the internal compulsion situation from occurring.

## 10.1.4 The Challenge to Responsibility

Some people concede that the concept of responsibility that plays such a large role in law, morality, and politics is justifiable, but they provide confused or superficial explanations of the excusing conditions, some of which are inadvertently challenges to the very possibility of responsibility. Others are openly skeptical about the reality of the concept of responsibility. They believe that it is make-believe, an illusion that can be justified, if it can be justified at all, only by the good consequences this mass error creates (Smilansky 2000). I have addressed the former claims at length elsewhere (Morse 1998), so here I shall address only the most persistent error of this type. I shall not address the deeper, more interesting challenge because this chapter assumes the justifiability and importance of some concept of responsibility (see Morse 2000c).

The belief that causation of behavior is per se an excusing position is a common, confused, and, indeed, incoherent claim that I have termed the *fundamental psycholegal error*. The belief is erroneous whether the alleged cause is normal or abnormal, or whether the cause is biological, psychological, sociological, astrological, or a combination of all of the above. Although I and others (Moore 1985) have persistently exposed the error, it continues to arise in the legal literature, and I shall continue to expose the fallacy. Because scientific understanding of behavior increases rapidly and the relation between normal and abnormal biological causes and responsibility is considered particularly relevant to mental health law, I give an especially full account of this relation.[15]

Determinism or universal causation cannot be an excusing or nonresponsibility condition. If either is a true description of causation, it applies to all events in the universe. If either were an excusing condition, all behavior would be excused and no one would be responsible. Perhaps this is the way the world "really" is. If so, our practices of holding some people legally responsible and exempting others from responsibility are perhaps morally suspect, but determinism or universal causation cannot be an excusing condition in a world with responsibility. Of course, excusing conditions such as irrationality or compulsion are themselves caused by something, but they are not excuses because they are caused.

So-called partial or selective causation is an oxymoron that fails to correct the fundamental psycholegal error. Causation is not a matter of degree. If behavior is caused at all, as it surely is, it is fully the product of its jointly sufficient causes.[16] We know more about the causes of some behavioral phenomena than about others, but partial information is different from partial causation. Causation per se is not an excuse and behavior is not excused to the extent it is caused. Responsibility is not inversely proportional to the strength of causation. Young children are not excused because their behavior is more caused or determined than the behavior of adults. They are not fully responsible because they have not yet obtained the full capacity for rationality.

Even an abnormal cause does not excuse or create nonresponsibility per se, including psychopathology or pathology of the brain and nervous system. When agents behave inexplicably irrationally, we frequently believe that underlying pathology produces the lack of capacity for rationality, but it is the irrationality, not the pathology, that produces nonresponsibility. After all, pathology does not always produce an excusing condition, and when it does not, there is no reason to excuse the resulting conduct. To see why, imagine a case in which pathology is a but-for cause of rational behavior. Consider a person with paranoid fears for her personal safety, who is therefore hypervigilant to cues of impending danger. Suppose on a given occasion she accurately perceives such a cue and kills properly to save her life. If she had not been pathologically hypervigilant, she would have missed the cue and been killed. She is perfectly responsible for this rational, justifiable homicide. Or take the case of a hypomanic businessperson, whose manic energy and heightened powers are but-for causes of making an extremely shrewd deal. Assume that business conditions later change unforeseeably and the deal is now a loser. The deal was surely rational and uncompelled when it was made, and no sensible legal system would later void it because the businessperson was incompetent to contract. Even when pathology is an uncontroversial but-for cause of behavior, that conduct will be excused only if an independent excusing condition, such as sufficient irrationality or hard choice, is present. Even a highly abnormal cause will not excuse unless it produces a genuine excusing condition.

In this age of exciting and rapid advances in brain science, the discovery of biological pathology that may be associated with legally relevant behavior lures many people to treat the agent as purely a mechanism and the behavior as simply the movements of a biological organism. Because mechanisms and their movements are not appropriate objects of moral and legal responsibility, the inevitable conclusion seems to be that the agent should not be held legally responsible. Nevertheless, causation is not an excuse nor does it necessarily create nonresponsibility. Even within a more sophisticated theory of nonresponsibility or excuse, brain or nervous system pathology will usually play a limited role in supporting an individual excusing condition.

Biological causation will be only part of the causal determinants of any intentional conduct, which is always mediated by one's culture, language, and the like. Biological variables are not the sole determinants of intentional human action. More fundamentally, biological causation will not excuse per se because people are biological creatures and biology is always part of the causal chain for everything we do. If biological causation excused, no one would be responsible. Intentional human action and neuropathologically produced human movements are both biologically driven, yet they are conceptually, morally, and legally distinguishable. Moreover, if biology were "all" the explanation and everything else, including causal reasons for action, were simply epiphenomenal, as some materialists claim, then our entire notions of ourselves and responsibility would surely alter radically. But eliminative materialism is philosophically controversial, and science furnishes no reason to believe that it is true (Fodor 1987; Searle 1992; Strawson 1989). Indeed, it is not clear conceptually that science could demonstrate that it is true. Moreover, there is a perfectly plausible evolutionary story to explain why we are deliberating creatures that act intentionally for reasons, which is the true basis for responsibility. Thus, until the doctor comes and convinces us that our normative belief in human agency and responsibility is itself pathological, biological causation per se does not excuse.

Abnormal biological causation also does not excuse per se. Human action can be rational or irrational, uncoerced or coerced, whether its causes are "normal" or "abnormal." Whatever the causes of human action may be, they will ultimately be expressed through reasons for action, which are the true objects of responsibility analysis. Suppose, for example, that a confirmed brain lesion, such as a tumor, is a but-for cause of behavior. That is, let us suppose that a particular piece of undesirable behavior would not have occurred if the agent never had the tumor. Make the further, strong assumption that once the tumor is removed, the probability that this agent will behave in the legally relevant manner drops to zero. Although one's strong intuition may be that this agent is not responsible for the undesirable behavior, the given assumptions do not entail the conclusion that the agent should be excused. The undesirable behavior is human action, not a literally irresistible mechanism, and the causal role of the brain tumor does not necessarily mean that the behavior was irrational or compelled. As Fingarette and Hasse (1979) demonstrated, that conclusion requires independent analysis of irrationality and compulsion rather than the question-begging answer that diseases excuse.

Moreover, it is a mistake to assume that specific brain pathology inevitably produces highly specific complex intentional action. Certain areas of the brain do control general functions. For example, Broca's area in the left frontal lobe controls the ability to comprehend and produce appropriate language. A sufficient lesion in this site produces and enables us to predict aphasia. But there is no region or site in the frontal lobes or anywhere else in the brain that controls specific, complex intentional actions. No lesion enables us to explain causally or to predict an agent's reasons and consequent intentional action in the same direct, precise way that a lesion in Broca's area permits the explanation or prediction of aphasia. Neurological lesions can dissociate bodily movements from apparent intentions, producing automatisms and similar "unconscious" states.[17] But such states rarely produce legally relevant behavior, and when they do, the agent is not considered responsible. In these cases we need not even reach the issue of whether the agent's intentional action is rational, however, because action itself is lacking. The story relating brain or nervous system pathology to intentional conduct will be far more complicated and far less direct than the already-complicated correspondence between brain lesions and the reduction or loss of general functions.

The effect of brain or other nervous system pathology will affect the agent more generally. Suppose, for example, the tumor in the previous example makes the agent irritable or emotionally labile, or suppose that brain changes produced by chronic substance use change inhibitory mechanisms. Such conditions surely make it harder for any agent to behave well in the face of variables such as provocation, stress, or the temptations of substances, for example, but per se they do not render an agent irrational. Other agents may be equally irritable, labile, or uninhibited as the result of environmental variables, such as the loss of sleep and stress associated with, say, taking law exams or trying an important, difficult, lengthy case. But these people would not be excused if they offended while in an uncharacteristic state, unless that state sufficiently deprived them of rationality. People with congenital abnormalities or lifelong character traits that predispose them to undesirable legally relevant behavior would have even less excuse for undesirable behavior because they had the time and experience to learn to deal with those aspects of themselves that made behaving well harder.

Consider the case of Charles Whitman, who killed many victims by shooting passersby from the top of the tower on the University of Texas campus. He suffered from a brain tumor, and let us assume that we could demonstrate incontrovertibly that he would not have shot if he had not suffered from the tumor. But whether he is nonetheless responsible depends not on the but-for causation of his homicides but on his reasons for action. If Whitman believed, for example, that mass murder of innocents would produce eternal peace on earth, then he should be excused, whether the delusional belief was a product of brain pathology, childhood trauma, or whatever. But if Whitman was simply an angry person who believed that life had dealt him a raw deal and that he was going to go out in a blaze of glory that would give his miserable life meaning, then he is unfortunate but responsible, whether his anger and beliefs were a product of the tumor, childhood trauma, an unfortunate character, or whatever.

All human action is, in part, the product of but-for causes over which agents have no control and that they are powerless to change, including their genetic endowments and the nature and context of how they were raised. If people had different genes, different parents, and different cultures, they would be different. Moreover, situational determinants over which agents have no control are but-for causes of much behavior. A victim in the wrong place at the wrong time is as much a but-for cause of the mugging as the mugger's genetics and experiences. If no victim is available, no mugging occurs, whatever the would-be mugger's intentions are. Such considerations are treated by philosophers under the rubric "moral luck" (Statman 1993). Our characters, our opportunities, and the outcomes of our actions are in large measure the product of luck, and if luck excused, no one would be responsible. A brain tumor or other neuropathology that increases the probability that the sufferer will engage in irrationally motivated, legally relevant behavior is surely an example of dreadful luck. But unless the agent is in fact irrational or the behavior is compelled, there is no reason to excuse the agent simply because bad luck in the form of biological pathology played a causal role. A cause is just a cause. It is not per se an excuse.

The locutions "free will" or "free choice" are often used as criteria for responsibility and their lack as criteria for excuse. But these are usually just conclusory labels that are placeholders for the genuine responsibility and excusing criteria. There is no uncontroversial philosophical definition of these terms. When employed as the opposites of determinism or universal causation, they are subject to the same problems just explored: everyone or no one will be responsible. Finally, it is sometimes said that lack of control over conduct is the reason we excuse, but this locution obscures more than it clarifies. Determinism or universal causation is not inconsistent with control over one's conduct. If it were, everyone or no one would be responsible, depending on whether determinism or universal causation were true. Thus, understood as the opposite of determinism, control cannot explain the excusing conditions we now have or any coherent system in which some people are excused and most are not. The ability to have control, in the operative sense, has nothing to do with determinism. As we have seen repeatedly, legally relevant behavior involves undoubted human action. In such cases, lack of control is a metaphorical or commonsense notion. Of course, if an agent is irrational or compelled, it will be hard to do the right thing, but then irrationality or compulsion is doing the genuine excusing work. Lack of control is the result, not the cause, of the excusing condition.

### 10.1.5 A Consequentialist Alternative

The argument so far has assumed that responsibility concepts and practices based in the capacity for rationality have independent value. That is, even if we might manipulate behavior more effectively and produce undoubted social goods by abandoning practices rooted in responsibility, we do not and should not always do so. Although consequences are always crucial to any moral or legal regime, even the strictest deontologists usually concede that there are thresholds beyond which a moral agent must consider consequences. Focusing exclusively on consequences seems unjustified, however, because other values, such as justice or liberty, might be unjustifiably sacrificed.

Consider the examples of the insanity defense and autonomous medical decision making. If the insanity defense were abolished, as four states have done, it is possible that there would be a net decrease in crime and an increase in public safety generally. Perhaps crazy potential criminals can be deterred by the threat of punishment, and criminal sentences may be a more secure form of incapacitation than commitment to a hospital, which must cease at any time the patient is either no longer crazy or no longer dangerous.[18] The insanity defense thus may not be an efficient criminal law doctrine if the sole goal of criminal law is optimum crime reduction. Nonetheless, most criminal justice theorists believe that the insanity defense should not be abolished because, according to our jurisprudence, some criminal defendants are so lacking the capacity for rationality that they are not moral agents. As a result, it would be unfair and cruel to punish them. For another example, optimum promotion of health and consequent cost savings might be achieved by permitting the state or health professionals more power to regulate the lives of citizens. This is a perfectly plausible hypothesis, but in the interest of maximal liberty and autonomy, we allow responsible patients to make their own lifestyle and treatment decisions, no matter how foolish or unwise these might be or how much their choices externalize costs to more continent citizens.

Although our jurisprudence rejects pure consequentialism, it would of course be possible to adapt this alternative to our currently mixed system. Such a system might be entirely coherent. Instead of focusing on responsibility, why not simply create a legal regime that gave maximum incentives to crazy people to behave less crazily and thereby to impose fewer costs on society? In each area of mental health law, one would simply identify the consequential goal to be achieved and then adjust the rules to achieve those goals accordingly. If those rules were consistent with rationality and responsibility values, so much the better, but it would not be required. All mental health law rules would be judged solely by their ability to produce socially optimum consequences. In criminal law, for example, hard-nosed law and economics analysis suggests that we should adopt what Hart (1968) has termed the "economy of threats" approach.[19] In such a scheme, one might want to retain the insanity defense and various forms of civil commitment, because crazy people might not be deterred by the threat of punishment.[20] Again, perhaps abolition would be more efficient, but perhaps not. It is an empirical issue. For another example, one might enforce all contracts, even if some agents were unable to understand rationally what they were doing when they contracted.

Even assuming the conceptual coherence of pure consequentialism and the possibility of calibrating the rules successfully and identifying those who could be properly "incentivized," our society is not yet ready to adopt such a moral and legal regime. Responsibility is too crucial to liberty broadly conceived and to our sense of ourselves to be abandoned. Nonetheless, it is certainly true that any rational mental health law should be firmly cognizant of the costs and benefits of particular rules.

## 10.2 THE JURISPRUDENCE OF CRAZINESS

This section begins with a justification of the structure and function of mental health law and an account of how mental disorder affects behavior that is derived from the account of legal personhood, rationality, and responsibility presented in Section 10.1. Next, I consider the two fundamental questions that all mental health laws address: Who is crazy? and Is this crazy person responsible?[21] I suggest the appropriate way that the law should try to address these questions, with special emphasis on the role of the disease concept and evolving understanding of psychopathology.

### 10.2.1 The Structure and Function of Mental Health Law

All mental health laws, all laws that treat some people with mental disorders specially, have three elements: (1) the person must have a mental abnormality, (2) the person must engage in legally relevant behavior, and (3) the mental disorder must cause or produce the legally relevant behavior.

The mental abnormality criterion is necessary but not sufficient. Our law does not treat people specially solely because they may suffer from a mental disorder, no matter how severe and manifest the disorder may be. Also, the U.S. Supreme Court has made it clear that legislatures are free to define mental abnormality as they wish and they are not bound by the diagnostic criteria or terminology of any professional group such as psychiatrists and psychologists.[22] In practice, however, the application of most mental health laws does depend on psychiatric and psychological criteria, and the type of abnormality usually required is severe.[23]

The second criterion, legally relevant behavior, is also necessary but not sufficient. In a liberal polity such as ours, the law is unconcerned with behavior it deems an insufficient public or private problem to occasion regulation. People are generally permitted to pursue their projects and are expected to bear the usual legal consequences. Some behavior does present a prima facie case for regulation, however, such as the threat of substantial danger to others or to oneself. How substantial the problem must be to justify mental health law regulation is of course a normative political, moral, and social question that might be resolved differently as political and social conditions change.

The first two criteria are together necessary but not sufficient. The mental abnormality must produce the legally relevant behavior. Even if the agent is undoubtedly crazy and undoubtedly engaging in legally relevant behavior, a mental health law will not apply unless the causal relation obtains. Note that the causal relation required is not "mechanical" causation. It is causation that operates through practical reason. Mental disorder must disable the agent's rationality concerning the legally relevant behavior. For example, suppose an agent suffers from a paranoid disorder that leads him to believe that certain people pose a threat to him and he is also an armed bank robber by profession. In this case, the agent is crazy and presents a substantial danger, but his mental disorder is independent of his dangerousness. As long as he never threatens the people he delusionally believes are threatening him, he cannot be civilly committed and could be restrained by the criminal justice system only if there were probable cause to believe he had attempted or committed a crime.

Mental abnormality must produce the legally relevant behavior because only then does the agent sufficiently lack the capacity for rationality and is therefore nonresponsible in the context to warrant special legal treatment. This rationale follows inevitably from the law's emphasis on rationality as the precondition for responsibility. The result is what I have termed *desert-disease jurisprudence* (Morse 1999b). The state can intervene to restrict liberty only if a person deserves such restriction based on conduct for which the agent is responsible or if the person suffers from a mental abnormality sufficient to render the agent nonresponsible.

Mental health law depends crucially on the nonresponsibility condition. If an agent lacked or lacks the capacity for rationality, the law's standard presumptions in favor of liberty, autonomy, and bearing the usual legal consequences of one's actions are suspended. Preventive detention is a classic example. No matter how dangerous an agent may be, civil commitment is warranted only if sufficient mental abnormality causes the agent to be dangerous because the agent is not capable of rationality.[24] For another example, a person who does not know right from wrong or does not know what he or she is doing will potentially have an insanity defense only if mental disorder produces those cognitive states. If they arise from ignorance or carelessness, the insanity defense will not be available because we believe the agent was capable of knowing the relevant information or being more careful.

The interesting question is how to understand the nonresponsibility condition for which the legal criterion is the causal relation between mental abnormality and legally relevant behavior. There is substantial debate about the theoretical status of the disease or disorder concept of mental or behavioral abnormalities. Even if the disease concept is valid, however, mental and physical disorders differ in fundamental ways (Wakefield 1992a, 1992b). The causal path from the underlying causes of the signs and symptoms of mental disorder to the ensuing actions that may be legally relevant works through the practical reason of the agents, whereas in almost all cases the consequences of physical disorder are caused entirely mechanistically and do not involve action at all.

Mental disorder plays a causal role in an agent's legally relevant behavior by causing the agent to have crazy but motivating reasons. That is, the mental disorder may interfere with the agent's capacity to grasp and be guided by good reason by creating difficulties at the level of perception, desire, or belief. For example, an agent may act in response to a command hallucination to commit some heinous deed. Or an agent's strong desires, classified as abnormal for these purposes, may cloud the agent's ability to perceive and to weigh the good reasons not to yield to the desire.[25] Or finally, a delusional belief system may motivate by making otherwise unthinkable behavior seem entirely rational in light of the delusional premises. Andrea Yates, the depressed Texan who killed her five children to save them from Satan's torments, represents such a case.

Compare two cases. In the first, an agent's arm strikes another because she suffers from an uncontrollable neurological disorder that unpredictably causes an involuntary arm movement; a sign of the neurological disorder. In the second, the agent intentionally strikes a victim because he suffers from a delusion—a crazy thought symptomatic of mental disorder not based in reality that is impervious to contrary evidence and argument—that the victim is a mortal enemy who is about to attack the agent. Treating these strikings precisely alike for moral and legal purposes would be to reduce human beings solely to mechanisms and would deny the importance of agency and rationality, which are concepts fundamental to the law's view of the person and to the guiding function of law. The first case does not involve action; the second involves potentially excusable action.

### 10.2.2 The Core Questions of Mental Health Law

We are now in a position to demonstrate how to answer the two core questions that all mental health laws pose: Is the person crazy? and Is the person responsible?

As we have seen, the mental abnormality criterion of all mental health laws is expressed in diverse terms, sometimes adopted from psychiatry or psychology and sometimes not, and the responsibility question is addressed by the criterion that requires that mental disorder produce or cause the legally relevant behavior. But the label for abnormality is hardly important, and the causation question misleadingly suggests that the question is one of mechanism. The real question for legal purposes is whether there is ground to believe that the agent's capacity for rationality seems sufficiently compromised to warrant the belief that the nonresponsibility condition is met and that special legal treatment is justified in the context. In other words, were the agent's reasons for action so crazy that we believe the person incapable of rationality and therefore the usual presumptions in favor of liberty, autonomy, and bearing the usual consequences of one's actions should not apply? Each legal test in each doctrinal domain simply tells us which kinds of crazy reasons will engender special legal treatment in that domain.

The law views the person as a practical, reasoning, intentional agent. In other words, the law accepts the folk psychological explanation of human action, which explains action in terms of desires, beliefs, and intentions. Within this account, the crucial question is always, Why did you do that? Mental health law is no exception to this general legal view. When we cannot make sense of an agent's legally relevant behavior, we must always ask, Why is the agent behaving this way? and we must always understand that the answer will be a reason rather than a mechanistic cause. So, if a criminal defendant appears unable to understand the nature of the proceedings or to assist counsel, we need to ask what mental states the defendant seems to be experiencing that produce these difficulties. If we want to know whether we should accept a patient's refusal to accept or to adhere to a seemingly justified medical prescription, we must ask why the patient does so. If we want to know whether a criminal defendant was legally insane, we must ask why the defendant committed the crime. And in all cases, to repeat, even if the reason given is crazy or does not make rational sense, we must still ask whether the agent was capable of being rational. After all, the incapacity to be rational is why some crazy people are treated specially. Thus, the core question in all mental health law cases is whether the agent's reason for the legally relevant behavior was crazy and evidence of a sufficient incapacity for rational behavior. Virtually any other question is a distraction from mental health law's central task.

Psychiatric or psychological diagnosis adds little to this determination (Morse 1978, 604–15; 1982; but see Bonnie and Slobogin 1980). As even the most cursory examination of the most recent edition (and all other editions) of the American Psychiatric Association's (2000) *Diagnostic and Statistical Manual of Mental Disorders* (hereinafter DSM-IV-TR) discloses, the necessary criteria for all diagnoses are behavioral—perceptions, feelings, desires, thoughts, beliefs, and actions. Physical dysfunction or abnormality is almost never required, and when it is, the primary criteria are still behavioral signs and symptoms (e.g., American Psychiatric Association 2000, 136–43). The question is whether a diagnosis produces value added beyond the information conveyed by the behavioral criteria that define the diagnostic category. The fundamental legal issue in mental health law cases is never whether the agent simply suffers from a disease or disorder; rather, it is always whether the agent has a crazy reason for legally relevant conduct. It is difficult to imagine, therefore, what additional information the diagnostic term conveys, es-

pecially because an agent may well be responsible for legally relevant conduct motivated by symptomatic crazy thoughts, perceptions, desires, feelings, and actions.
Moreover, as DSM-IV-TR recognizes, all people whose behavior meets the criteria for the same diagnosis are not alike.[26] Asking whether a particular disorder, say,
schizophrenia, causes the legally relevant behavior is far less efficient and precise
than asking about and assessing the agent's reasons for action directly. Finally, relevant general information can easily be provided without using diagnostic terminology. For example, without using a diagnostic term and speaking only in terms
of behavior, an expert could provide research evidence that indicates that people
who have crazy thoughts similar to those of the agent under consideration also
tend to behave in other, specified ways. It can be extremely difficult in some
cases to determine what the agent's reasons were, but a diagnosis will not clarify
the obscure.

Although a diagnosis may furnish little independent information to the finder
of fact, experts always use such terms in their work, and why should we bar them
from doing so in courts or administrative proceedings if the diagnosis does no
harm? Moreover, serious mental disorder is a gross and verifiable cause of lack of
rational capacity and thus places an allegedly objective, independent constraint on
treating people specially because they are not responsible (*U.S. v. Moore*, 486 F.2d
1139, 1180 (D.C. Cir. 1973)). Without some constraint, the determination allegedly will be subject to arbitrary, relativistic criteria.[27] The presence of diagnosable
mental disorder provides some warrant for the conclusion that there was genuine,
objective impairment of the agent's general capacity for rationality.

These arguments have force, but the presence of a mental disorder has less
constraining value than proponents believe. For the most part, only those agents
grossly out of touch with reality will satisfy the nonresponsibility criterion, and
such a mental state is objectively irrational even without a diagnostic label. Cases
of lesser irrationality will not qualify for special legal treatment, even if the behavior does warrant an official diagnosis. Finally, most diagnoses of mental disorder
are based on subjective, socially constructed criteria that may be manipulated for
social, legal, and political purposes.[28] That is, psychiatric and psychological diagnoses are instinct with normativity. If our society for any reason wishes either to
expand or to contract the class of people with alleged mental disorders for whom
special legal treatment is appropriate, diagnostic categories will not inhibit such
action. I freely concede that the criteria for rationality that I have offered do not
provide a precise, objective guide to the lack of a general capacity for rationality,
but this is a problem inherent in the notion of rational practical reasoning. No
such guide, including diagnosis, can substitute for careful evaluation of reasons for
action.

I contend further that diagnoses have the potential for substantial harm in mental health law adjudication because they tend to encourage the mistaken impression that the conduct of crazy people is just a mechanism rather than action for reasons. In addition, there is often dispute about the appropriate diagnosis, if any, which wastes time and distracts the fact finder from the essential question of crazy reasons. For example, the John Hinckley jury should not have considered whether Hinckley was suffering from schizoid or schizotypal personality disorder or schizophrenia; rather, it should have considered only whether he was out of touch with reality, and if so, to what extent. The answer to the former question cannot produce an answer to the latter. To decide if Hinckley acted for crazy reasons required analysis of his contemporaneous reasons for attempting to assassinate President Reagan, including life historical data relevant to determining what those reasons were.

Focusing on diagnoses and treating legally relevant behavior as a sign or symptom, or as the product of a sign or symptom, risks question begging about the nonresponsibility assumption. If a crazy thought or an "abnormal" desire motivates behavior, we may tend to think that the agent "could not help" it because, seemingly analogously, people cannot prevent most physical symptoms from occurring. But once again, legally relevant actions caused by mental disorder are actions, not pure mechanisms.[29] The question is whether the agent's action was reason responsive: Could the agent's action have been altered by rational considerations, including prudential incentives, moral norms, and other variables that affect our practical reason? Terming a condition or behavior a disease, disorder, sign, or symptom does not per se answer that question. Whether an action meets the criteria for special legal treatment—lack of rational capacity or compulsion—is an empirical question that a diagnostic label cannot provide. Indeed, the American Psychiatric Association (2000, xxxvii) explicitly warns that psychiatric diagnoses and criteria entail no legal conclusions about responsibility or even about whether an agent meets legal criteria for the presence of a mental disorder.

Consider the examples of people with delusions and people with pedophilia. An agent validly diagnosed as manifesting delusions that predispose the agent to behaving legally relevantly may, depending on the agent's clinical condition, have greater or lesser access to reality concerning the crazy belief (Oltmanns 1988). At some times, delusions totally capture the reality of the delusional context, and the person appears unable to recognize that the belief may be false and is impervious to logic and argument. At other times, delusions may be less totalizing, permitting what has been termed "double awareness" (Sacks, Carpenter, and Strauss 1974). Although the agent actually maintains the false belief, the agent is aware that it might not be true and may be affected by logic and argument. How much the delusion "captures" the agent is an empirical question; whether that degree of capture sufficiently deprives the agent of rational capacity to warrant special mental health law treatment is a normative, legal judgment. Accurate characterization of the belief as delusional answers neither question with any degree of precision.

Now consider a person with pedophilia, such as Leroy Hendricks, who claims that his desire for children is overpowering and that he is helpless to avoid yielding to it.[30] If yielding to a strong "abnormal" desire is "just like" a biophysically involuntary bodily movement, then yielding is apparently not responsible action. As we have seen, however, the analogy is flawed. A desire is simply a desire, whether it is caused by biological abnormalities or the alignment of the planets (Feinberg 1970). There is no literal physical compulsion, as there is in cases of reflex, spasm, and the like. It is literally true that an agent cannot help a reflexive bodily movement, but it is not true that an agent literally cannot help acting to satisfy at least some strong desires in some situations.

Thick, contextual descriptions of the agent's reason for action and relevant life historical data are necessary to decide if an agent lacked the capacity for rationality (or any other capacity we may care about). These data may be obtained from the agent, family, friends, coworkers, observers generally, and mental health professionals. Mental health professionals may be trained, efficient observers, if they are good clinicians. In general, however, all people are quite expert at gleaning other agents' reasons for action. Without this expertise, successful human interaction would be impossible. In limited instances, test data, including various biological measures, might help determine the limits of particular cognitive or emotional capacities or if an agent is malingering.[31] But in general, freely available, observational behavioral data will be the best source of information, and if there is a conflict between the test results and inferences from observational data, the latter is far more likely to be valid.

With the fullest possible understanding of the agent's reasons for action, it will typically be possible to decide according to the operative norm of rationality if the person acted crazily, but the question of the general capacity for rationality in the circumstances remains open. How do we know that an agent who has acted crazily is incapable of acting rationally? The standard answer is that the crazy action is the symptom of a disease and symptoms are not "voluntary." There is some truth to this response, but it is ultimately question begging. Mental health law must make the capacity judgment about rationality in the same commonsense fashion that we make all judgments about an individual's capacities. In light of what we know generally about human behavior, we draw inferences about an agent's capacities from the present circumstances and from life historical data.

Let me conclude this section with a realistic example of the foregoing considerations. Some killers convicted of capital murder waive their constitutional right to present mitigating evidence at the capital sentencing stage of the proceedings. In effect, they consent to their own execution. Provided that their waiver is voluntary, that is, rational and uncoerced, the law permits them to waive based on respect for their personhood and autonomy. Now, why would an agent waive the right to present undoubtedly relevant, potentially effective, mitigating evidence? Why would an agent consent to what is in effect state-assisted suicide? One possibility is that he or she feels genuinely morally guilty and believes that he or she deserves to die for the capital crime committed. Assuming, as the vast majority of states do, that some capital killers do deserve to die, such a reason would be perfectly rational. But, to take an easy case, suppose the killer genuinely, delusionally believes that her own death will bring the victim back to life. This would clearly be a crazy reason, without regard to why the killer was delusional.

Now consider a more difficult example. Suppose after substantial evaluation of a killer who killed his own loved ones, a clinician concludes that the killer suffers from an underlying depression that has produced irrational guilt. It is commonplace that losses can predispose to depression and that depression can produce irrational guilt. The question is whether this killer actually suffers from irrational guilt, a question not answered by the diagnosis of depression. Indeed, evidence of irrational guilt will indicate that depression is present, rather than the reverse. And such evidence would have to be behavioral, based on the killer's thoughts, feelings, and perceptions about why he wants to die and why the potential mitigating evidence does not demonstrate that perhaps he does not deserve to die. Further, that such thoughts, feelings, and perceptions may have been the product of depression does not indicate whether the decision to waive the right to present mitigating evidence was based on a sufficiently crazy reason to invalidate the waiver. This decision is normative. In sum, causal explanations will add little to thick, behavioral description and commonsense inferences from such descriptive data (Morse 1999a).

## 10.3 IS MENTAL HEALTH LAW NECESSARY?

In this section I argue that there is no need for independent mental health law. Instead, mental disorder should simply be used as evidence that bears on the more generic question of whether any agent should be treated legally specially because the agent lacks the capacity for rationality in a particular context.

Mental health laws define their criteria functionally. For example, a legally insane agent does not know the nature of his or her conduct; an agent incompetent to contract does not understand the nature of the deal; an agent incompetent to stand trial does not know the nature of the proceedings or cannot assist counsel; a civilly committable agent is dangerous. But again, even if these functional criteria are met, the mental health law will apply only if an agent was incapable of being rational in the circumstances. The issue that then arises is what role psychiatric or psychological abnormality should play in such an assessment. In other words, is the first criterion, the presence of a demonstrable mental disorder, necessary for the application of special legal treatment? After all, an agent's capacity to grasp and be guided by reason might be compromised by a host of other variables, including stress, fatigue, grief, nonculpable involuntary intoxication, poor education, low intelligence, or indoctrination, to name but a few.[32]

Historical and procedural concerns are the most persuasive reason why mental abnormalities should be the basis for an independent substantive body of law rather than simply an evidentiary consideration useful to adjudicate a generic rational incapacity doctrine. The claim is that most people have experience with the many other variables that might compromise rationality, and the law has developed distinct doctrines to deal with them. The provocation-passion doctrine that reduces a culpable intentional homicide from murder to manslaughter is an example. On the other hand, it is alleged, most people do not have experience with mental abnormality, and thus we need a distinct body of doctrine that requires special types of expertise to adjudicate cases. As I have argued, however, for legal purposes there is little that is special about mental disorder, and most issues that it raises can be evaluated using observations and common sense.

Moreover, there is danger in continuing the present regime because it leads to confusion about mental health law and the other doctrines that respond to other rationality-compromising variables. I contend that lack of the capacity for rationality is the overarching nonresponsibility context in our jurisprudence and that the fundamental error that people make about responsibility is to think that causation excuses. Thus, they think that mental disorder or passion or a history of abuse or some other apparently causal variable is the excusing condition instead of focusing on how that variable may have compromised the agent's rational capacity. Such a conceptual error, which the current regime foments, creates both doctrinal and adjudicative confusion.

Another question is whether other variables that might compromise rationality should be encompassed within the domain of mental abnormality. It would be possible, for example, to treat cases of rational incapacity caused by stress or fatigue as cases of temporary insanity. The problem, of course, is that this suggestion could cause confusion about the genuine basis of responsibility just addressed previously, and it would lead to undesirable psychiatric and psychological imperialism. Stress may compromise rationality, but not necessarily because it produces a condition properly characterized as a mental disorder. All untoward mental states, including compromised rationality, are not symptoms of a disorder or a disease, even if they have the same functional properties.

Perhaps the greatest danger of a comprehensive, generic nonresponsibility criterion is that it might sweep too broadly, treating far too many people as nonresponsible. Indeed, one interpretation of this suggestion implies that such a doctrine might entirely undermine the possibility of responsibility. The requirement that there must be a mental disorder at least limits the potential for nonresponsibility. Although there is some merit to this objection, I think that it is not dispositive.

Experience with mental health law suggests that we are able to limit the number of people found nonresponsible. In general, only those suffering from severe, usually psychotic, disorders are found to meet mental health law criteria.[33] These are precisely the people with mental disorders whose rational capacity is sufficiently compromised to warrant the conclusion of nonresponsibility. This limitation within the application of mental health law also implies that the legal system, including lay finders of fact, is able to make distinctions concerning which agents should be found nonresponsible. If there were a generic criterion, judges could certainly prescreen and exclude evidence in cases that presented no plausible claim for nonresponsibility, and judges or juries could be trusted to make sensible judgments in cases presenting a colorable claim.

A more specific worry is that people who are habitually angry, stressed, careless, or the like might claim that they lacked the capacity to be more rational. Therefore, they could not help but be angry, stressed, or careless and thus could not conform to the law's usual requirements. I am willing to concede that there may be a few people with such powerful, ingrained predispositions who are genuinely incapable of meeting normative legal standards. Hart (1968) long ago noted that so-called objective standards should be divided into two components: an invariant standard of conduct and a requirement that the agent is capable of meeting that standard. Although the law now holds all agents to the invariant standard, Hart suggested that this was unfair to those who could not fairly be expected to meet this standard. So, for example, some people simply may not be able in general to meet ordinary standards of care. If so, it would be unfair to hold them responsible for failure to meet these standards. Deciding how hard it must be to meet such a standard before finding an agent nonresponsible is of course a normative issue, but common sense again suggests that most agents will be able to meet the relatively low standards that the law imposes. Again, those with fewer endowments and less fortunate life experiences may find it harder than others, but in most cases they would be capable of meeting the standard with sufficient effort, and finders of fact may be trusted to determine which agents could not do so.

There is a related, potentially more powerful challenge to the proposal for a generic lack of rational capacity issue. Some would claim that the focus on rational capacity or any other general capacity is misguided. That is, people do not possess general capacities and are only capable of doing what they in fact did at a given time. This claim is profound because it further implies the claim that no one is ever responsible because no one could ever have acted differently from how he or she did act at a given time.

I think the challenge to the notion of a general capacity fails because it is empirically false and its metaphysical implication is unjustified. A general capacity is nothing more than an underlying ability to engage in certain behavior (Wallace 1994). English speakers, for example, have the general capacity to speak English, even when they are silent or are speaking a different language. Of course, the general capacity can refer to behavior that may be a continuum. For example, a person of average strength might be able easily to lift a certain amount of weight. As the weight increased, it would become harder for the person and would finally become impossible. As long as the agent is generally capable of certain conduct and there is reason for the agent to do so, it is fair to hold the agent responsible for failing to engage in such conduct. For example, suppose an object fell on and pinned down a victim that the agent had a duty to aid. If the object were light, the average agent might have no difficulty removing it; if it were heavy, removing it would be more difficult, but morality and the law alike would expect the agent to strain to do so and would blame an agent who did not exercise a capacity he or she possessed. People often engage in legally relevant behavior for nonrational, irrational, and foolish reasons, but this does not excuse them or render them nonresponsible if they are generally capable of rationality.

The claim that an agent cannot exercise a general capacity on a specific occasion when the agent did not exercise it is simply a form of the reductio that no one is capable of doing anything other than what he or she did do. This is trivially true in the sense that agents cannot do "p" and "not-p" at the same time. It does not follow, however, that it is impossible for an agent to exercise a general capacity. An English speaker who is silent surely has the general capacity to speak English. A more general and challenging version of the same claim is the argument from determinism, which would suggest that the notion of a general capacity is useless because at a fixed time, given antecedent events and the fixed laws of the physical world, only one outcome is ever possible for both people and the other moving parts of the universe. Such an argument is an external, metaphysical attack on the basic concepts and practices of responsibility. Taken seriously, it would suggest that no one should ever be treated as more or less responsible than anyone else because no one or everyone is responsible. Thus, this argument cannot possibly explain or furnish internal grounds for criticism of current concepts and practices.

The notion of a general capacity is one we use all the time to evaluate the behavior of ourselves and others, and there is no reason to abandon it in the face of an unknowable metaphysical challenge.

I conclude that there is no objection in principle to adopting generic criteria for lack of the capacity for rationality in specific legal contexts. The question in every case would be whether the agent was capable of meeting the responsibility standard. Consider the insanity defense, for example, using the Model Penal Code formulation for the legally relevant behavior: the lack of substantial capacity to appreciate the criminality [wrongfulness] of his conduct or to conform his conduct to the requirements of law (A.L.I. 1985, sec. 4.01(a)).[34] This lack of capacity might be proven by using evidence of mental abnormality *and* any of the host of other variables that might substantially compromise an agent's capacity for rationality at the time of a crime. This would be a far more rational way to determine criminal responsibility than either arbitrarily excluding some cases that should qualify or wedging all sympathetic cases into a psychiatric procrustean bed. Finally, in criminal law there is a powerful argument that the law should adopt a generic "partial responsibility" defense of mitigation that would apply to all crimes and that would be based on diminished capacity for rationality among defendants who might be legally sane (Morse 2003). Such a defense would replace the menage of mitigating doctrines, such as provocation-passion or extreme mental or emotional disturbance, that typically apply only to reduce murder to manslaughter within homicide law and that have no consistent rationale.

## 10.4 CASE STUDIES OF GENERIC NONRESPONSIBILITY

This section addresses how the law should assess the criminal responsibility of three agents who commit atrocious acts but who probably do not meet the usual criteria for legal insanity: Psychopath [hereinafter P], Terrorist [T], and Jeffrey Dahmer. I do not propose to evaluate these cases thoroughly but instead hope suggestively to indicate that the generic rationality approach provides the best tool for assessing them.

As traditionally diagnosed, the psychopath is an egocentric agent who lacks empathy and conscience.[35] For most people, of course, the capacity for empathy and the internal moral compass of conscience furnish the most compelling reasons not to breach moral and legal expectations. Indeed, if the law's threats were the primary prophylactic against criminal behavior, human society would be vastly more dangerous than it is.[36] The psychopath cannot be guided, however, by the reasons that empathy and conscience provide. Psychopaths can be guided only by purely self-regarding prudential reasons, such as the avoidance of pain, but they are morally irrational (Gauthier 1986; Wolf 1990). The law now treats psychopaths as responsible,[37] but there is a plausible normative argument that psychopaths are "morally insane" and not sufficiently guidable by reason to be held morally responsible. The point here is not to resolve this issue but to indicate that the generic rationality approach offers the most sensible framework for resolving such normative debates about culpability. Of course, if the psychopath is held not responsible, then an otherwise unwarranted deprivation of liberty, such as indefinite civil commitment, might be justified to control the danger such an agent poses.

In the case of Terrorist, I wish to distinguish four possible descriptions of his reasons for action, each of which will be treated as a "pure" case, although a mixed case is surely plausible.[38] The first is Angry T, an agent seething with anger and resentment, who simply hates Americans and wishes to harm them but knows that there is no plausible moral or legal justification for his actions. The second is Rationalizing T, who not only hates Americans and wants to harm them, but who also believes that Americans in some sense "deserve" or "have coming to them" the harms that he will inflict.[39] The third, Arrogant T, fully believes that his deeply held religious view justifies his action, but although he is capable of considering whether this belief is justified, he is simply unwilling to entertain this possibility because of his unjustifiable, arrogant belief in his own rectitude.[40] The fourth, Impervious T, also fully believes that his religious view justifies his actions, but unlike Arrogant T, Impervious T is genuinely unable to entertain the possibility that he is mistaken, perhaps because he has been so thoroughly indoctrinated or for other explicable reasons.[41]

The generic rationality criterion suggests that Angry T, Rationalizing T, and Arrogant T are all responsible, although there may be culpability differences among them, but Impervious T might not be responsible.[42] Each of the first three is part of the moral community because each is rationally capable of recognizing the unjustified harmfulness of his behavior, whereas Impervious T is not.[43] Some may deny that Arrogant T is capable of entertaining the possibility that his actions are unjustified. How, after all, can one rationally argue with someone who holds a belief based in unverifiable faith? There is some truth to this claim, but every believer knows that all religious, moral, and political claims are subject to dispute, even among believers, and thus most believers know that they may hold unjustifiable beliefs. Indeed, to fail to hold Arrogant T responsible for his actions would fail to take him seriously as a moral agent. If, contrary to the assumption in the descriptions, Arrogant Ts are indistinguishable from Impervious Ts—that is, the former are genuinely unable, as opposed to unwilling, to challenge their own beliefs before harming others—then all true believers might be nonresponsible. Such agents would be terribly dangerous, however, and various forms of extreme civil confinement might be required to prevent them from causing great harm.

Let us consider two more variants of T, Secular T (ST), who genuinely believes that her actions are justified to serve the greater good of human beings, but the belief is not grounded in religious faith, and Crazy T (CT), whose justification seems based on beliefs that have no contact with reality. ST and CT are similar to Arrogant or Impervious T, but their moral or political justification is idiosyncratic to them or to an ideology unacceptable to the polity at large. In a sense, they are like an agent who makes an actual mistake of law and believes that he or she is acting lawfully and justifiably. We do not allow an excuse for such a mistake, but the justification is entirely consequential. We fear that deterrence or the objective primacy of law will be undermined. Still, there is a powerful moral claim that agents who make such mistakes should not be held culpable *if* the agent was not capable of recognizing the error. After all, an agent who believes that he or she is acting justifiably seems less culpable than those who know their actions are not justified, because the acts of the former appear less indifferent to the rights and interests of others.

In the case of ST, the agent knows that there are disputes, but her justification is coherent and rationally conceivable. Violent political radicals, such as Timothy McVeigh, are good examples. Assume that such agents are firmly committed and deeply believe in the justice of their actions. Unless prior indoctrination, the intensity of their belief, or some other factor renders them unable to consider the possibility that they are not justified, there seems no reason not to hold such people responsible. *They* certainly believe that they are responsible. CT is an easier case. If her idiosyncratic belief lacks contact with reality, then the agent is probably not capable of rationality. Suppose, for example, that the agent has had an auditory hallucination and believes that the Lord has told her to kill because the victim is the devil,[44] or suppose that the agent believes in an entirely idiosyncratic and apparently incoherent religion that justifies killing under circumstances that would not qualify for justification under our law (*State v. Crenshaw*, 659 P. 2d 488 (Wash. 1983)). Such an agent surely lacks the capacity for rationality concerning this belief and the actions it motivates.

There can be difficult cases on the margin of ST and CT. Theodore Kaczynski, the Unabomber, might present such a case. Some may think that Kaczynski was crazy, rather than misguided, but careful reading of his Manifesto suggests that he had a reasonably coherent moral and political view that has clear roots in the history of Western moral and political theory. One might also wonder if Kaczynski was crazy because his choice of means to further his agenda was so instrumentally unsuited to that end, but, that conclusion, too, would be controversial. That he acted alone and not as part of an organized group may seem to imply that he is so idiosyncratic that he is crazy, but his behavior seems equally if not more consistent with the inference that he is simply a misguided "loner." I do not have the answer in Kaczynski's case, but again, I believe the crucial distinction is whether he is arrogant or impervious and not whether he suffers from a diagnosable mental disorder that may have played a causal role in the formation of his motivating beliefs.

Finally, consider Jeffrey Dahmer, the infamous Milwaukee resident who kidnapped and killed young victims in order to have sex with them and eat them after they were dead (Schwartz 1992). Dahmer knew and endorsed the moral and legal rules prohibiting his conduct. He submitted a typed apology to the judge that tried him that indicated Dahmer's genuine remorse, knowing full well that the sincerity of his apology would not prevent him from spending the rest of his life in prison. Although Dahmer carefully planned his crimes and attempted to avoid detection, suggesting a high degree of organization, contact with reality, and instrumental rationality, during the course of his homicidal encounters he was evidently in a state of extraordinary arousal that altered his cognitive and emotional capacities (Masters 1993).[45] Thus, at the time of the homicides, Dahmer's capacity for rationality was clearly impaired. Nonetheless, in the periods between the crimes, Dahmer's rationality was unimpaired, and he was capable of recognizing both the enormity of what he desired to do and the necessity of taking steps to prevent himself from doing it. Dahmer was a moral agent who knew that he would do it again and clearly had sufficient instrumental rationality to determine what steps would be necessary to prevent himself from killing and the capacity to take such steps. Dahmer may deserve pity. As gruesome as his desires and acts may be, however, there appears to be no reason not to hold him fully responsible for his knowing failure to stop himself before he killed.

## 10.5 CONCLUSION

Assuming the validity and desirability of treating human beings as potentially morally responsible agents, mental health law makes coherent sense. At least some people with mental disorders lack the capacity for rationality in some legal contexts, and the usual legal rules applicable to rational agents should not apply. This chapter has argued, however, that there is no need for independent mental health law because the rationality criteria upon which this body of doctrine is based can be generalized to any agent who may nonresponsibly lack rational capacity. The law should potentially treat specially any agent lacking rational capacity for any reason. Moreover, focusing on the genuine nonresponsibility condition, lack of the capacity for rationality, will avoid the conceptual and practical confusions caused by focusing on the causes of the nonresponsibility condition, such as mental disorder.

1. I recognize that a polity need not be concerned with agency, responsibility, and liberty. Such notions are embedded in our culture, law, and Constitution, however, and I will not defend their virtues here. Rather, I shall simply assume their applicability and desirability.

2. This section borrows extensively from two recent treatments of the same issues (Morse 1999a, 2000a).

3. Searle writes,

> Once we have the possibility of explaining particular forms of human behavior as following rules, we have a very rich explanatory apparatus that differs dramatically from the explanatory apparatus of the natural sciences. When we say we are following rules, we are accepting the notion of mental causation and the attendant notions of rationality and existence of norms. . . . The content of the rule does not just describe what is happening, but plays a part in *making it happen*. (2002, 133)

See also Alexander and Sherwin (2001).

4. This view assumes that law (and morality) are sufficiently knowable to guide conduct, but a contrary assumption is largely incoherent. As Shapiro writes, "Legal skepticism is an absurd doctrine. It is absurd because the law cannot be the sort of thing that is unknowable. If a system of norms were unknowable, then that system would not be a legal system. One important reason why the law must be knowable is that its function is to guide conduct" (2000, 131). I do not assume that legal rules are always clear and thus capable of precise action guidance. If most rules in a legal system were not sufficiently clear most of the time, however, the system could not function. This chapter does not address jurisprudential questions concerning law's authority generally and whether legal rules are binding only if they comport with morality.

5. I believe that this view is consistent with virtually any jurisprudential theory about the essential nature of law and that such consistency is an attractive feature of the view.

6. For the sake of simplicity, I will henceforth refer only to the case of action. But the analysis applies equally to the case of forebearance.

7. Rawls writes that

> the principle of responsibility is not founded on the idea that punishment is primarily retributive or denunciatory. Instead it is acknowledged for the sake of liberty itself. Unless citizens are able to know what the law is and are given a fair

opportunity to take its directives into account, penal sanctions should not apply to them. This principle is simply the consequence of regarding a legal system as an order of public rules addressed to rational persons in order to regulate their cooperation, and of giving the appropriate weight to liberty. . . . In particular, the principle of liberty leads to the principle of responsibility. (1999, 212)

Although Rawls is discussing criminal law, the underlying claim applies more generally.

8. Agents whose bodily movements cause harm will also not be considered responsible in most cases if those movements are not actions. Such claims are not about excused action, however. In criminal law, for example, the lack of an action defeats the prima facie case rather then provides an affirmative defense.

9. I discuss "internal" cases infra.

10. The specific example was first suggested by an anonymous participant at a conference. One can endlessly proliferate such examples (Morse 2000b).

11. What reasons would have motivational salience in an individual case is of course an open question, and individual agents will respond to different reasons. The point is simply that the actions of agents responding to strong desires are actions and not mechanisms, and thus they are potentially reason responsive. The example might also suggest that if it takes a gun to one's head to motivate a person not to engage in certain actions, then it must be very hard not to perform those actions. Again, this is true in a colloquial sense best explained in terms of irrationality, but it does not mean that there is anything wrong with the agent's will.

12. I have explored such a model for inner coercion at length elsewhere (Morse 1994).

13. Nozick (1993) argues that we have no adequate theory of the substantive rationality of desires. Some philosophers disagree, but no satisfyingly adequate account has been provided. Some noninstrumental desires may seem entirely incoherent, the sort of want no rational agent could conceivably have. Suppose, for example, an agent had a strong desire simply to count the blades of grass on a large lawn. At such an extreme, judging a desire irrational in itself might be justifiable. But few desires of this sort that have much motivational salience arise and create legal or moral problems. Even those desires that seem most deviant bear close relationship to those that do not. Consider Jeffrey Dahmer, for example, who had intense desire to have sex with and to cannibalize dead people. As gruesome as these desires are, we know that the objects of sexual desire can be extraordinarily diverse and that arguably even "cannibalistic," incorporative urges are not uncommon but take many unexceptionable, redirected, and sublimated forms of expression. Thus, Dahmer may be seen as an extraordinary statistical outlier rather than an agent entirely omitted from the distribution.

14. E.g., Model Penal Code, sec. 2.09.

15. Recently published issues of prestigious journals contain illustrative examples of advances in scientific understanding of the causes of legally relevant behavior. Caspi et al. (2002) found that maltreated male children were more likely to exhibit antisocial behavior if they had a defect in the genotype that confers high levels of the neurotransmitter encoding enzyme, monoamine oxidase A. This enzyme metabolizes various neurotransmitters linked to violence if the levels of those neurotransmitters are low. Goldstein and Volkow (2002) report that addiction involves cortical processes that result in the overvaluation of drug reinforcers, the undervaluation of other reinforcers, and defective inhibitory control of responses to drugs. Stein et al. (2002) discovered that genetic factors can influence the risk of exposure to assaultive trauma and to posttraumatic stress disorder (PTSD) symptoms that may ensue.

16. In the alternative, some behavior may be randomly uncaused. Of course, no one could be responsible for such behavior, nor could it be identified.

17. I thank Norman R. Relkin, M.D., Ph.D., for making this point to me particularly clearly.

18. *Foucha v. Louisiana*, 504 U.S. 71 (1992). As we shall see infra Section 10.2.1, unless the patient is still dangerous because he or she is crazy, the crucial non-responsibility condition that is a predicate for the application of a mental health law—in this case, civil commitment following an acquittal by reason of insanity—is not met.

19. Many people worry about the implications of such an approach, such as the specter of punishing the innocent if crime would be reduced (Rawls 1999). I shall assume that this problem can be solved by consequentialists (see Dennett 1984).

20. See, e.g., *Kansas v. Crane*, 534 U.S. 407, 122 S. Ct. 867, 874 (2002) (Scalia, J., dissenting, and arguing that involuntary civil commitment of mentally abnormal sexual predators is justified because such agents are not deterrable).

21. I first claim that these were the fundamental questions in *Crazy Behavior* (Morse 1978), and I continue to believe they are the core issues. My current justification is different in many respects, some of which are quite substantial. Many mental health laws also ask a predictive question: What will this crazy person do in the future as the result of his or her craziness? I shall not address the predictive question because it is not fundamental, but it is nonetheless important to the application of many mental health laws, especially those that provide for preventive detention.

22. *Kansas v. Hendricks*, 521 U.S. 346, 358–59 (1997); reaffirmed in *Kansas v. Crane*, 534 U.S. 407, 122 S. Ct. 867, 871 (2002).

23. The federal test for legal insanity adopted in 1984 is a good example; 18 U.S.C. sec. 17(a) adopts a cognitive test for legal insanity that requires the presence of a "severe" mental disease or defect.

24. See *Kansas v. Hendricks*, 521 U.S. 346, 358 (1997) (holding that involun-

tary civil commitment of mentally abnormal sexually violent predators is justifiable only if such agents are "unable to control their dangerousness"); reaffirmed in *Kansas v. Crane*, 534 U.S. 407, 122 S. Ct. 867, 870 (2002) (holding that the inability to control oneself that warranted commitment must be "serious"). In *Hendricks* and *Crane*, loss of control was the crucial nonresponsibility criterion, but the meaning of loss of control was never sufficiently explained. Although it sounds like an internal compulsion criterion, I have argued that it is better understood as an irrationality criterion (Morse 2002, 1064–75).

25. Again, many people might wish to characterize this case as one in which the symptom of mental disorder—the strong, abnormal desire—compels the conduct, but these cases are better treated as instances of irrationality.

26. In DSM-IV-TR, there is no assumption that each category of mental disorder is a completely discrete entity with absolute boundaries dividing it from other mental disorders or no mental disorder. There is also no assumption that all individuals described as having the same mental disorder are alike in all important ways. The clinician using DSM-IV-TR should therefore consider that *individuals sharing a diagnosis are likely to be heterogeneous even in regard to the defining feature of the diagnosis* and that boundary cases will be difficult to diagnose in any but a probabilistic fashion (American Psychiatric Association 2000, xxi, emphasis added).

27. Richard Bonnie has pressed this point in conversation.

28. For example, Poussaint (2000) argues that extreme racism [never defined] is a delusional disorder when it leads to violent attacks on other groups [but apparently is not a disorder if it does not lead to violence]. Recall that as recently as the early 1970s, psychiatric orthodoxy held that a sexual preference for an adult member of one's own sex was a symptom of a psychiatric disorder (American Psychiatric Association 1968). In 1973, the association *voted* to exclude homosexuality per se as a recognized disorder. There had been no scientific or clinical advances that supported the change, however. What changed were the values of the majority of psychiatrists (Morse 1978).

29. In rare cases, mental disorder may produce altered states of consciousness that create legal unconsciousness or "automatism." These cases arise primarily within criminal law. Agents in such states appear to behave intentionally, and their movements are clearly guided by realistic feedback from the environment, but the agent's consciousness is partial or divided and the agent's ability to be aware of what he or she is doing is diminished or destroyed entirely. Most jurisdictions treat these cases as claims of no action that defeat the prosecution's prima facie case, but other jurisdictions treat them as a matter of affirmative defense.

30. Indeed, *Hendricks* claimed that not only were the desires compelling, especially when he was stressed, but that only death would prevent him from acting on his predatory desires.

31. For example, scores on standardized tests of intelligence can aid the deter-

mination of whether a capital defendant suffers from retardation and therefore may not be executed.

32. Although defendants with psychotic disorders demonstrate greater impairment than other defendants, psychosis is a poor predictor, because defendants exhibit high rates of legal impairment in the absence of major mental disorders (Viljoen, Roesch, and Zapf 2002).

33. Steadman et al. (1993) found that the decision to acquit by reason of insanity was most strongly affected by clinical factors; more than 80 percent of those acquitted were diagnosed with schizophrenia or another major mental disorder. Berg, Appelbaum, and Grisso (1996) report the results of the MacArthur Treatment Competence Study, which indicated that more than 70 percent of subjects with severe schizophrenia performed in the unimpaired range on each of three measures of legal competence to make a medical treatment decision. For a more complete report of the MacArthur research, see Grisso and Appelbaum (1995).

34. I take no position here concerning whether this is a desirable test for nonresponsibility for crime. I use it simply as an example.

35. Psychopathy must be distinguished from antisocial personality disorder (Hare 1998). The latter is a disorder officially recognized by the American Psychiatric Association (2000) and is defined largely by persistent, serious antisocial behavior. Psychopathy is not so recognized, but there are good data to support the validity of the construct, especially among males, and it is routinely used by clinicians. It is defined in large measure in terms of the underlying psychopathology, such as lack of the capacity for empathy, that may predispose psychopaths to engage in antisocial behavior. The overlap between the two categories is substantial but not perfect. Many people who engage in persistent, serious antisocial behavior are not psychopaths, and all psychopaths do not engage in the type of antisocial behavior that would support the DSM-IV-TR diagnosis of antisocial personality disorder.

36. This is a familiar observation (Hobbes 1968).

37. Section 4.01 (2) of the Model Penal Code exempts from the insanity defense people whose disorder is marked by repetitive criminal or antisocial behavior. This would appear to exempt those with antisocial personality disorder, but potentially to permit the insanity defense for psychopaths. Nonetheless, the provision has been understood and interpreted to exclude psychopaths.

38. I am making the assumption that with sufficient information we could determine which description was accurate. In some cases it might be difficult to do so, but I believe that in virtually all cases we can do so sufficiently accurately to permit a reasonably confident moral and legal evaluation.

39. The use of such rationalizations has been a cornerstone of an influential theory of the causation of delinquent behavior (Sykes and Matza 1957). The empirical support for this theory is unclear, however (Adler, Mueller, and Laufer

1995). Even if rationalization is not a central, unifying explanatory mechanism for delinquent behavior, it is a common defense mechanism people often use to salve their consciences.

40. I borrow the term "arrogant" in this context from Kennett. She describes such agents as follows:

> The ignorance of some agents is to be explained primarily by their lack of humility with regard to their epistemic capacities and their evaluative beliefs. Though they may claim to value truth, their commitment is only to the truth of the particular view they endorse; they simply do not entertain the proposition that this view could be mistaken. An overweening belief in their own infallibility justifies to them their dismissal of anything which might constitute counter evidence to conclusions already reached and entrenches their errors. (2001, 175–77)

41. In the cases of Arrogant and Impervious T, the agent might feel either regret or joy or some combination of such sentiments in response to the harm he causes. I leave open whether this type of reaction should make a difference in our moral response to either or both of these cases.

42. I will not address these potential culpability differences, but the criteria would be the mental states with which these rational agents committed their crimes. Skeptics of various varieties might deny that any religious beliefs are rational and that those who believe them are incapable of rationality in that domain, but rationality is normative and must be judged in part according to cultural expectations and practices. In our culture, of course, religious faith is not considered per se evidence of lack of rational capacity, although in extreme cases, it may be hard to distinguish a rational from a delusional religious belief.

43. Consider the infamous case of the more than nine hundred followers of the Reverend Jim Jones, who died at their Guyanese community, Jonestown. The facts are in dispute, but apparently after consulting with some members of the group, Jones instructed his followers to commit suicide. Although some adults were forced to do so and many children were killed, most adults drank poisoned punch without coercion. Jones and his lieutenants believed that the religious community, usually referred to as a "cult," might be forcibly disbanded and they chose death instead (Hall 1987; Maaga 1998).

44. These are so-called deific decree cases (*State v. Cameron*, 674 P. 2d 650 (Wash. 1983)).

45. For a brilliant but disturbing fictional portrait of the psychology of a person such as Dahmer, see Joyce Carol Oates's *Zombie* (1995). Oates's portrait of Quentin P is profoundly disturbing precisely because it is so believable and makes sense of the agent's motivation. On the other hand, Quentin P appears to be a psychopath, whereas Dahmer allegedly was not.

Adler, F., G. Mueller, and W. Laufer. 1995. *Criminology*. 2nd ed. New York: McGraw-Hill.

Alexander, L., and E. Sherwin. 2001. *The rule of rules: Morality, rules and the dilemmas of law*. Durham, NC: Duke University Press.

American Psychiatric Association. 1968. *Diagnostic and statistical manual of mental disorders*. 2nd ed. Washington, DC: American Psychiatric Association.

———. 2000. *Diagnostic and statistical manual of mental disorders*. 4th ed. and Text Revision (DSM-IV-TR). Washington, DC: American Psychiatric Association.

Berg, J., P. Appelbaum, and T. Grisso. 1996. Constructing competence: Formulating standards of legal competence to make medical decisions. *Rutgers Law Review* 48:345, 373.

Bonnie, R., and C. Slobogin. 1980. The role of mental health professionals in the criminal process: The case for informed speculation. *Virginia Law Review* 66:427.

Caspi, A., J. McClay, T. Moffitt, J. Mill, J. Martin, I. Craig, A. Taylor, and R. Poulton. 2002. Role of genotype in the cycle of violence in maltreated children. *Science* 297:851.

Dennett, D. 1984. *Elbow room: The varieties of free will worth wanting*. Cambridge, MA: MIT Press.

Elster, J. 1999. *Strong emotions: Emotion, addiction and human behavior*. Cambridge, MA: MIT Press.

Feinberg, J. 1970. *Doing and deserving*. Princeton, NJ: Princeton University Press.

Fingarette, H., and A. Hasse. 1979. *Mental disabilities and criminal responsibility*. Berkeley: University of California Press.

Fischer, J., and M. Ravizza. 1998. *Responsibility and control: A theory of moral responsibility*. Cambridge: Cambridge University Press.

Fodor, J. 1987. *Psychosemantics: The problem of meaning in the philosophy of mind*. Cambridge, MA: MIT Press.

Gauthier, D. 1986. *Morals by agreement*. Oxford: Oxford University Press.

Goldstein, R., and N. Volkow. 2002. Drug addiction and its underlying neurobiological basis: Neuroimaging evidence for the involvement of the frontal cortex. *American Journal of Psychiatry* 159:1542.

Grisso, T., and P. Appelbaum. 1995. The MacArthur Treatment Competence Study III: Abilities of patients to consent to psychiatric and medical treatments. *Law and Human Behavior* 19:149.

Hall, J. 1987. *Gone from the promised land: Jonestown in American cultural history.* Somerset, NJ: Transaction.

Hare, R. 1998. Psychopaths and their nature: Implications for the mental health and criminal justice systems. In *Psychopathy: Antisocial, criminal and violent behavior,* ed. T. Milton, E. Simonsen, M. Birket-Smith, and R. Davis, 188–92. New York: Guilford.

Hart, H. 1968. *Punishment and responsibility.* Oxford: Oxford University Press.

Hobbes, T. 1968. *Leviathan.* Ed. C. Macpherson. New York: Viking.

Kennett, J. 2001. *Agency and responsibility: A common-sense moral psychology.* Oxford: Oxford University Press.

Maaga, M. 1998. *Hearing the voices of Jonestown.* Syracuse, NY: Syracuse University Press.

Masters, B. 1993. *The shrine of Jeffrey Dahmer.* London: Hodder and Stoughton.

Moore, M. 1985. Causation and the excuses. *California Law Review* 73:1091, 1112–14.

———. 1993. *Act and crime: The theory of action and its implications for criminal law.* Oxford: Oxford University Press.

Morse, S. 1978. Crazy behavior, morals and science: An analysis of mental health law. *Southern California Law Review* 51:527, 557–58, 604–15.

———. 1982. Failed explanations and criminal responsibility: Experts and the unconscious. *Virginia Law Review* 68:971, 1059–70.

———. 1994. Culpability and control. *University of Pennsylvania Law Review* 142:1587, 1619–34, 1658–59.

———. 1998. Excusing and the new excuse defenses: A legal and conceptual review. In *Crime and justice: A review of research,* ed. M. Tonry, 329, 349–62. Chicago: University of Chicago Press.

———. 1999a. Crazy reasons. *Journal of Contemporary Legal Issues* 10:189, 190–209, 222.

———. 1999b. Neither desert nor disease. *Legal Theory* 5:265.

———. 2000a. Rationality and responsibility. *Southern California Law Review* 74:251, 252, 258.

———. 2000b. Hooked on hype: Addiction and responsibility. *Law and Philosophy* 19:3, 28–29, 38–43.

———. 2000c. The moral metaphysics of causation and results. *California Law Review* 88:870, 881–89.

———. 2002. Uncontrollable urges and irrational people. *Virginia Law Review* 88:1025, 1057–58, 1064–65.

———. 2003. Diminished rationality, diminished responsibility. *Ohio State Journal of Criminal Law* 1:289.

Nozick, R. 1993. *The nature of rationality.* Princeton, NJ: Princeton University Press.

Oates, J. 1995. *Zombie.* New York: Plume.

Oltmanns, T. 1988. Approaches to the definition and study of delusions. In *Delusional beliefs*, ed. T. Oltmanns and B. Maher, 4. New York: Wiley.

Pereboom, D. 2001. *Living without free will*. Cambridge: Cambridge University Press.

Poussaint, A. 2000. What a Rorschach can't gauge. *New York Times*, January 9, sec. 4, p. 19.

Rawls, J. 1999a. *A theory of justice*. Rev. ed. Cambridge, MA: Belknap.

———.1999b. Two concepts of rules. In *Collected papers*, ed. S. Freeman, 20. Cambridge, MA: Harvard University Press.

Sacks, M., W. Carpenter, and J. Strauss. 1974. Recovery from delusions: Three phases documented by patient's interpretation of research procedures. *Archives of General Psychiatry* 30:117, 119–20.

Schwartz, A. 1992. *The man who could not kill enough: The secret murders of Milwaukee's Jeffrey Dahmer*. Secaucus, NJ: Carol.

Searle, J. *The rediscovery of mind*. Cambridge, MA: MIT Press.

———. 2002. End of the revolution. *New York Review of Books*, February 28, 33.

Shapiro, S. 2000. Law, morality and the guidance of conduct. *Legal Theory* 6:127.

Smilansky, S. 2000. *Free will and illusion*. Oxford: Oxford University Press.

Statman, D., ed. 1993. *Moral luck*. Albany: State University of New York Press.

Steadman, H., M. McGreevy, J. Morrissey, L. Callahan, P. Robbins, and C. Cirincione. 1993. *Before and after Hinckley: Evaluating insanity and defense reform*. New York: Guilford.

Stein, M., M. Chartier, M. Lizak, and K. Jang. 2002. Genetic and environmental influences on trauma exposure and posttraumatic stress disorder symptoms: A twin study. *American Journal of Psychiatry* 159:1675.

Strawson, G. 1989. Consciousness, free will and the unimportance of determinism. *Inquiry* 32:3.

Sykes, G., and D. Matza. 1957. Techniques of neutralization: A theory of delinquency. *American Sociological Review* 22:664.

Viljoen, J., R. Roesch, and P. Zapf. 2002. An examination of the relationship between competency to stand trial, competency to waive interrogation rights and psychopathology. *Law and Human Behavior* 26:481, 497–99.

Wakefield, J. 1992a. The concept of mental disorder: On the boundary between biological facts and social values. *American Psychologist* 47:373.

———. 1992b. Disorder as harmful dysfunction: A conceptual critique of DSM-III-R's definition of mental disorder. *Psychological Review* 99:232.

Wallace, R. 1994. *Responsibility and the moral sentiments*. Cambridge, MA: Harvard University Press.

Wolf, S. 1990. *Freedom within reason*. Oxford: Oxford University Press.

# 11 ON LAW ENFORCEMENT WITH BOUNDEDLY RATIONAL ACTORS

*Christine Jolls*

> In deciding whether to double park, a resident of Econville will compare his benefit from double parking to the expected fine. . . . Therefore, to achieve optimal deterrence—that is, deterrence only of those double-parking violations in which the benefits are less than the [previously stipulated] $10 congestion cost—it is necessary for the expected fine to equal $10. . . .
>
> Given each possible expenditure on enforcement and the resulting probability of detection, the fine can be set so that the *expected* fine equals $10. . . . If detection is certain, then the fine should be $10. If the probability of detection is .1, then a $100 fine will result in a $10 expected fine. And if the probability of detection is .001, a fine of $10,000 is necessary to generate an expected fine of $10. Thus, if the fine is set appropriately, the optimal deterrence of double-parking violations can be achieved with each expenditure on enforcement.
>
> This observation immediately suggests what the efficient system of law enforcement is for Econville. Because optimal deterrence can be achieved with each expenditure on enforcement, there is no reason not to spend the least amount possible. In other words, the City Council should hire a part-time inspector for $500 per year [previously stipulated to be the least amount possible], catch one out of every thousand double-parking violators, and fine each violator $10,000. Because [the probability of detection is .001], the expected fine is $10.
>
> A. Mitchell Polinsky (1989, 77–78)

The potential parking violators in the foregoing account by A. Mitchell Polinsky, in his classic law and economics text, are assumed to calculate in a fully rational way the costs—given the probability of detection—and benefits of double parking and then to make fully optimal decisions about how to behave. Bounded rationality, by contrast, refers to the important limits that exist on human cognition (Simon 1955). As emphasized by the burgeoning literature in behavioral economics, "actors often take short cuts in making decisions" and, as a result, make systematic errors in choosing their preferred courses of action (Korobkin and Ulen 2000, 1075).

This research was prepared in the spring of 2003 and reflects sources as they existed at that time. Thanks to Louis Kaplow, Steven Shavell, and Cass Sunstein for helpful discussions and suggestions.

Bounded rationality may be understood as either a challenge or a complement to traditional economic analysis, which typically assumes unbounded rationality (Jolls, Sunstein, and Thaler 1998a, 1476). Generally speaking, bounded rationality—together with other aspects of behavioral economics[1]—is more likely to be understood as a challenge to traditional economic analysis when that analysis produces questionable or implausible predictions or prescriptions, and is more likely to be understood as a complement to traditional economic analysis when that analysis produces predictions or prescriptions that seem sensible. Thus, for instance, behavioral economics is generally viewed as a challenge to traditional economic analysis in contexts in which traditional economic analysis predicts that sunk costs will not affect actors' behavior, as empirical evidence strongly suggests they do affect actors' behavior (Arkes and Blumer 1985); but behavioral economics is most naturally viewed as a complement to traditional economic analysis in thinking about the question of whether workers will demand fully compensating wage differentials for unsafe workplace conditions, given that both imperfect information (from traditional economic analysis) and optimism bias (from behavioral economics, as described more fully below) suggest that they may not demand fully compensating wage differentials.

The same pattern of complementing versus challenging traditional economic analysis is true within behavioral law and economics, which involves the application of behavioral economics insights to legal topics (Jolls, Sunstein, and Thaler 1998a). An important illustration of the pattern here involves the area of public law enforcement—how laws against behavior ranging from double parking (as in the excerpt above from Professor Polinsky's text) to employment discrimination should be enforced by public agents. If traditional economic analysis of public law enforcement had rested at the point described in the Polinsky excerpt—prescribing that few parking tickets be issued to double parkers and that a fine of $10,000 be assessed on those unfortunate enough to be ticketed—then bounded rationality would probably be understood as a challenge to traditional economic analysis of public law enforcement. But because traditional economic analysis of public law enforcement has produced a large literature (as described more fully below) by Professor Polinsky and others—a literature that pushes beyond the simple idea described in the excerpt from Polinsky's introductory text—bounded rationality is most sensibly understood, I want to suggest in this chapter, as a complement rather than a challenge to traditional economic analysis of public law enforcement.

Section 11.1 below sketches the basic conception of bounded rationality used in this chapter. Section 11.2 offers an account of public law enforcement with boundedly rational agents and relates this account to traditional economic analysis of public law enforcement. Section 11.3 briefly applies the bounded rationality analysis offered here to the specific area of public enforcement of employment discrimination laws.

A definitional comment is important at the outset. The relationship between the concept of bounded rationality emphasized in this chapter and the basic idea of "irrationality"—the term that appears in the title of the book containing this chapter—is a difficult and contested one. The goal of this chapter is not to weigh in on that definitional issue, but instead to explore the implications of some empirically important forms of human behavior (however they are termed, but I refer to them here as "bounded rationality") for the structure of public law enforcement. In invoking the idea of bounded rationality in this chapter, I mean to draw on the relatively well-established meaning of the term in the existing behavioral economics literature.[2]

## 11.1 A BRIEF ACCOUNT OF BOUNDED RATIONALITY

According to Gary Becker (1976, 14), "[A]ll human behavior can be viewed as involving participants who maximize their utility from a stable set of preferences and accumulate an optimal amount of information and other inputs in a variety of markets." Bounded rationality, in sharp contrast to this formulation, refers to "the obvious fact that human cognitive abilities are not infinite" (Jolls, Sunstein, and Thaler 1998a, 1477). Human behavior exhibits a variety of errors or inconsistencies. While such errors or inconsistencies may often be adaptive, they nonetheless mean that behavior will deviate systematically from that predicted by the standard economic model of unbounded rationality.

One central aspect of bounded rationality involves what are often called judgment errors. Many (though not all) judgment errors concern biases in the estimation of probabilities; these are a major emphasis of this chapter.

A widely studied example of a judgment error is optimism bias. As documented in over 250 studies, people exhibit a strong tendency to underestimate the probability that negative events will happen to them as opposed to others (Weinstein 1980, 1998). Elsewhere I discuss the important question of the distinction between estimates that are below the average person's probability of a negative event and estimates that are below the average probability of that event; a majority of people could in fact correctly estimate that their probability is below the average probability of an event, but the usual benchmark for comparison is the average person's probability of an event (Jolls 1998, 1659n24).

Examples of optimism bias range from estimates of the probability of getting a particular disease to estimates of the likelihood of getting fired from a job (Kirscht et al. 1966, 250–51; Weinstein 1980, 809–12). At least in some contexts, the empirical evidence makes clear that optimism bias reflects not only underestimation of the probability of a negative event relative to the average person's probability of that event, but also underestimation of the probability of a negative event relative to the actual probability of that event.[3]

Like other forms of bounded rationality, optimism bias may often be adaptive (even though it may harm people in particular instances) because by thinking that things will turn out well for them, people may increase the chance that things actually will turn out well for them. Indeed, there is evidence that optimism bias tends to correlate with happiness, contentment, and the ability to engage in productive, creative work (Taylor and Brown 1988).

A second well-known example of a judgment error is the way in which availability, or the ease with which a given event comes to individuals' minds, may affect probability estimates. In one experiment, for instance, individuals asked how many words in a four-page section of a novel end in *ing* gave much larger estimates than individuals asked how many words have *n* as the second-to-last letter, despite the fact that obviously there are more words satisfying the latter criterion than the former (Tversky and Kahneman 1983, 295). More generally, the perceptions of boundedly rational actors about probabilities of uncertain events are heavily influenced by how available other instances of the event in question are. Parallel to the case of optimism bias, availability is likely to be adaptive (here because it will often reflect optimizing behavior for people with limited information), but it can lead to systematic errors in probability assessment (Jolls, Sunstein, and Thaler 1998a, 1518).

While the first major component of bounded rationality involves judgment errors, the second major component involves departures of decision-making behavior from the precepts of expected utility theory. "[T]he axioms of expected utility theory characterize rational choice, [but] actual choices diverge in important ways from this model, as has been known since the early experiments by Allais and Ellsberg" (Jolls, Sunstein, and Thaler 1998a, 1478). In response to the limits of expected utility theory, more than two decades ago Daniel Kahneman and Amos Tversky (1979) pioneered an alternative decision-making model known as prospect theory. According to prospect theory, people evaluate outcomes based on the change they represent from an initial reference point rather than based on the nature of the outcome itself. Moreover, a given change produces less reaction the further a decision maker already is from the decision maker's reference point. Thus, for example, according to prospect theory the difference in value between losing $100 and losing $200 is greater than the difference in value between losing $1100 and losing $1200 (assuming a reference point of $0) (Kahneman and Tversky 1979, 278); this is precisely the opposite of what is implied by the concavity assumption routinely employed in expected utility theory.[4]

Bounded rationality—embracing judgment errors and departures from expected utility theory—is an enormously rich topic, one that could be approached and described in many different ways. The conception offered here is offered for its usefulness in analyzing the structure of public law enforcement, the focus of this chapter.[5] The next section puts the conception of bounded rationality just described to work in analyzing the question of public law enforcement from a behavioral economics perspective.

## 11.2 BOUNDED RATIONALITY AND PUBLIC LAW ENFORCEMENT

In traditional economic analysis of law, the essential problem of public law enforcement revolves around how to compel sometimes-recalcitrant actors to conform their behavior to legal rules at the lowest possible cost to the public fisc. Public agents in this picture should choose both efforts at detection and punishments imposed upon detected offenders with an eye toward inducing desired behavior at the lowest possible cost.

In the traditional economic model, potential offenders are assumed to compare the costs and benefits of a given behavior and to refrain from the behavior when costs exceed benefits (e.g., Polinsky and Shavell 2000, 47). It will not be surprising that, moving to a behavioral economics framework, both judgment errors and departures from expected utility theory can affect how potential offenders perform this cost-benefit comparison. Below I consider three specific ways that bounded rationality, in the form of both judgment errors and departures from expected utility theory, may come into play in actors' behavior, and the resulting implications for the structure of public law enforcement.

Before proceeding further, it is important to emphasize that I am not suggesting here that an approach to public law enforcement based upon the conception of bounded rationality described above captures everything or even close to everything that is relevant to how the law should be enforced by investigators, inspectors, prosecutors, and other public agents—any more than an approach based on the assumption of *un*bounded rationality would capture everything of relevance to that question. The behavior of potential offenders is likely to be strongly related to social factors that are not captured by bounded rationality.[6] In addition, psychological phenomena not emphasized by bounded rationality or other aspects of behavioral economics may play a role; this may be especially true in the case of public enforcement of laws regulating serious criminal conduct. My goal here is simply to suggest how bounded rationality as conceived above can complement traditional economic analysis of public law enforcement.

As just suggested, public enforcement of laws regulating serious criminal conduct may raise important issues distinct from those raised by public enforcement of other laws (such as the double-parking prohibition from the opening Polinsky excerpt). At the most basic level, the empirical evidence derived from the noncriminal population—the usual subjects in the experimental work on which behavioral economics is based—may fail to carry over to the criminal population; some tentative evidence to this effect is discussed at various points below. Because public enforcement of laws regulating serious criminal conduct seems to raise distinct and important issues, the public enforcement of such laws is not a focus of the analysis below.

## 11.2.1 Optimism Bias

As noted earlier, a highly robust feature of human behavior is that people underestimate the probability that negative events will happen to them as opposed to others. Given that detection of unlawful behavior by public agents is generally an undesirable event, an immediate implication of optimism bias in the public law enforcement context is that people will often underestimate the probability that their—as opposed to others'—unlawful behavior will be detected.

A study of drivers who consumed alcohol at least occasionally provides interesting empirical support for optimism bias in the public law enforcement context. (One might view laws prohibiting drunk driving as instances of laws prohibiting serious criminal behavior—which, as noted above, are not the laws on which I focus. Drunk driving obviously is an extremely serious offense, but, at the same time, the demographic group at issue for drunk driving seems likely—by comparison to the demographic group at issue for crimes such as homicide and armed robbery—to be relatively similar to the general population.) Drivers who consumed alcohol at least occasionally were found to attach a significantly lower probability to their being apprehended for drunk driving when driving with a blood-alcohol level over the legal limit than to the average driver's being apprehended for drunk driving when driving with a blood-alcohol level over the legal limit (Guppy 1993, 377–80). This was true not only for drivers who reported that they sometimes drove with blood-alcohol levels they believed to be over the legal limit, but also for drivers who said they did not engage in such behavior (although the magnitude of the optimism bias effect was smaller for the latter group). Thus, the results—suggesting significant optimism bias on the part of drivers—cannot be explained on the ground that some drivers (those who drive with blood-alcohol levels above the legal limit) underestimate the probability of apprehension while others overestimate it. Most alcohol-consuming drivers, whether or not they sometimes drove with blood-alcohol levels over the legal limit, said that their probability of being apprehended for drunk driving was below average; but this of course cannot be true.

*If* potential offenders not only underestimate their probability of detection relative to that of others but also underestimate their probability of detection relative to the actual probability, then a simple policy-relevant conclusion follows immediately for the public law enforcement context. Given any particular combination of a probability of detection and a sanction—in Professor Polinsky's example from the beginning of this chapter, a .001 probability of detection and a $10,000 fine— actors will tend to be less deterred from the behavior sought to be deterred than they would be in the absence of optimism bias; the bias leads them to underestimate in a systematic way the probability that they will be detected. If, to continue with the numbers from the Polinsky example, the actual probability of detection is .001 for each individual, but in fact people systematically think that their own probability is lower—say .0005—then deterrence obviously will suffer.

Of course, people may have no idea that the actual probability of detection is .001 (whatever they think it is for them personally); indeed, this point provides the jumping-off point for my discussion below of the role of availability in actors' estimation of the general probability of an uncertain event such as the detection of unlawful behavior. However, unless for some reason—contrary to the tenor of the discussion below as well as the evidence noted above[7]—people systematically *overestimate* the actual probability of detection, optimism bias will, as suggested above and as noted by Korobkin and Ulen (2000, 1092), lead to less deterrence than traditional economic analysis of public law enforcement would suggest.

As noted earlier, an important exception to the general discussion of optimism bias and public law enforcement may involve actors who contemplate engaging in serious criminal behavior (particularly violent crime). This is so because empirical evidence obtained from noncriminal subject populations may not carry over to the population at issue for serious criminal behavior. Indeed, there is empirical evidence that, among young males who have previously engaged in criminal behavior, the estimated probability of arrest for various crimes is *higher* than the actual probability observed in official arrest rates (Lochner 2001). This finding suggests that within the stated population actors do *not* underestimate the probability of detection.

Even in contexts in which optimism bias *does* lead actors to underestimate the probability of detection, it is important to note that optimism bias generally should not by itself alter the conclusion from the simple version of traditional economic analysis of public law enforcement—as reflected in the Polinsky excerpt at the beginning of this chapter—that minimizing the probability of detection and maximizing the punishment for offenders who are detected is the most cost-effective strategy for publicly enforcing the law.[8] Before noting how optimism bias generally should not alter this basic conclusion, it is useful to understand more fully the reasoning behind that conclusion within traditional economic analysis of public law enforcement.[9]

Within traditional economic analysis of public law enforcement, the prescription of minimal enforcement expenditures (meaning a low probability of detection) and large penalties for detected offenders stems from the trade-off between the benefits and costs to the enforcer of deterring unlawful behavior. As a first approximation, minimizing expenditures on enforcement and maximizing penalties on detected offenders allows society to achieve a desired level of deterrence at a lower cost than would the combination of higher enforcement expenditures and lower penalties. Thus, for instance, as between a .001 probability of detection and a $10,000 punishment, and a .002 probability of detection and a $5,000 punishment, the former course should be chosen, as both produce the same expected punishment, while the latter entails greater expenditures on enforcement. Taking the argument to its logical extreme, society should make expenditures on detection as low as possible and penalties for detected offenders as high as possible.

As discussed in Section 11.2.4 below, relaxing various assumptions made in the simple model of public law enforcement avoids—while remaining within the framework of traditional economic analysis of public law enforcement—the conclusion favoring $10,000 parking tickets. For now the important point is that an account emphasizing optimism bias among boundedly rational actors generally should not alter the basic prescription in favor of relatively small enforcement expenditures and large penalties for detected offenders. (As already noted, though, optimism bias may suggest that enforcement expenditures will need to increase, without any reduction in the penalties for detected offenders, if the level of deterrence anticipated under traditional economic analysis is to be achieved.) The basic reason that the simple prescription generally should not change with optimism bias is that even if potential offenders systematically underestimate the probability that they will be detected, the logic of achieving as much deterrence as possible through heavy punishment of detected offenders rather than through a higher probability of detection remains. As before, achieving deterrence through increasing the probability of detection is more costly for the enforcement agency than achieving deterrence through increasing the severity of the punishment. Although (assuming it is infeasible to raise the punishment further) the probability of detection may need to rise in response to optimism bias, in general there is no particular reason for the desired punishment level to decline. (A formal model, which I do not provide here, would be necessary to test the limits of this argument, but in simple algebraic terms, if $p$ is the actual probability of detection, $P(p)$ is the perceived probability of detection, and $S$ is the punishment, then under the assumptions stated above and as long as $P(p)$ is increasing in $p$, $S$ ought to be at its maximum, for otherwise $S$ could be raised and $p$ lowered so as to maintain the same level of deterrence at a lower cost for the enforcement agency.) Thus, at this juncture the prescription of $10,000 fines for those caught double parking remains essentially intact despite the introduction of optimism bias among boundedly rational actors.

## 11.2.2 Availability

Apart from optimism bias on the part of potential offenders regarding whether public law enforcement efforts will detect *their* unlawful behavior, there is the question of how potential offenders go about estimating the probability that *anyone* will be caught. Although traditional economic analysis of public law enforcement examines the possibility of mistaken predictions by potential offenders about the probability of detection, it focuses on the case in which, while individual actors may make mistakes, the group of actors covered by the enforcement activity is not wrong on average (Bebchuk and Kaplow 1992, 366). But for boundedly rational actors there may be a different and more systematic relationship between the perceived and actual probabilities of detection, given what bounded rationality teaches us about the way in which individuals perceive probabilistic events.

As described earlier, the perceptions of boundedly rational actors about probabilities of uncertain events are heavily influenced by the availability of the event in question, or how readily other instances of this event come to actors' minds. In the public law enforcement context, availability is likely to influence potential offenders' perceptions of the probability of detection through two central channels. The first concerns the salience of observed instances of detection, or how vivid and striking these instances are. The second concerns the actual frequency with which detection occurs.

### 11.2.2.1 The Role of Salience

An interesting context in which to consider salience in the public law enforcement setting is the context of parking enforcement discussed by Professor Polinsky in the passage quoted at the beginning of this chapter. Imagine two distinct methods of administering parking tickets: placing beige (unobtrusive) tickets under the windshield wiper on the curb side of the street (convenient for the parking officer to reach); and sticking large, bright orange tickets that read "VIOLATION" in oversize letters on the driver's-side window where they are clearly visible to other drivers passing by. In prior work, Cass Sunstein, Richard Thaler, and I suggested that the latter method (common in many cities) may be more likely to deter potential parking violators—holding constant the actual probability of getting a ticket—by making the risk of receiving a parking ticket more salient to potential offenders (Jolls, Sunstein, and Thaler 1998a, 1538).

Salience suggests, more generally, that the effects of public law enforcement activity will depend not merely on how frequently offenses are detected (the focus under traditional economic analysis of public law enforcement) but also on *how* they are detected—on the vividness of the enforcement activity. While the use of salient methods of detection, as in the example just given, would not play a role in traditional economic analysis of public law enforcement, an analysis of public law enforcement with boundedly rational actors suggests the importance of salience in shaping potential offenders' estimates of the probability of detection. Under traditional economic analysis of public law enforcement, by contrast, the costs of making enforcement activity more salient—for instance, by printing parking tickets on colorful, presumably more costly, paper—will be wasted because they do not change the actual probability of detection.

### 11.2.2.2 The Role of the Actual Probability of Detection

The ease with which events come to mind—how available they are—may be heavily influenced not only by their salience, but also by the actual frequency with which they occur and are observed. Events that are very rare—such as receipt of a parking ticket in the Polinsky excerpt from the beginning of this chapter—may not come easily to mind simply because of their infrequency, and thus the perceived probability of such events' occurrence for boundedly rational actors may tend to be less than their actual probability.

With regard to the effect of actual frequency of an event on boundedly rational actors' estimation of the probability of the event, the empirical evidence is mixed, with some evidence suggesting potential underestimation of the probability of infrequent events and other evidence pointing to overestimation of the probability of infrequent events (Kunreuther 1982, 209; Viscusi 1992, 150). Surely the salience of the event in question (holding constant its actual frequency) is likely to be a major factor, consistent with the discussion just above. At least in some cases, however, it is possible that the probability of infrequent events will be underestimated purely as a function of their infrequency; for instance, Howard Kunreuther (1976) has explored how people often fail to buy insurance against negative events such as floods and earthquakes despite massive federal subsidies and large-scale marketing efforts by insurers, and he suggests how underestimation of the probability of these relatively infrequent (though fairly salient) events may result simply from the lack of a friend, neighbor, or other contact who has experienced such an event in recent memory. Interestingly, there is again some evidence that the basic finding here does not carry over to the population of actors who contemplate engaging in serious criminal behavior; in a national sample of young males, many of whom had engaged in past criminal behavior, the subjects were not much influenced by the arrests of others in coming up with their own estimates of the probability of arrest—although it bears noting that the measure used for arrests of others in the study is quite noisy (Lochner 2001).[10] Moving back now to the context of offenders not engaged in serious criminal behavior, in Professor Polinsky's parking enforcement example at the beginning of this chapter, if the probability of getting a ticket is below some "critical threshold" (Kunreuther 1982, 209), it is possible that it will simply not show up on the radar screen of potential offenders. In cases such as this, potential offenders will systematically underestimate the probability of detection merely because that probability is below some threshold level.

Availability, then, differs from optimism bias in suggesting—albeit quite tentatively and with a need for further empirical inquiry—that bounded rationality may provide a systematic reason for questioning the simple prescription from traditional economic analysis that public law enforcement should involve minimal enforcement expenditures (meaning a small probability of detection) and large penalties for detected offenders. If, in a given context, the probability of detection is too small to make it onto the radar screens of potential offenders, then the large penalty specified for detected offenders will fail to achieve its intended deterrent effect. The case of optimism bias differs from the case of availability because optimism bias suggests people may underestimate the probability of detection *whatever* its actual level; by contrast, availability suggests—again, tentatively—that in certain contexts people will underestimate the probability of detection *if* that probability is below some critical level.

As already suggested, it is ultimately an empirical question whether there are important public law enforcement contexts in which the infrequent occurrence of detection may produce underestimation of the probability of detection. The basic empirical difficulty, however, is disentangling underestimation that results from the infrequency of actual incidents of detection from underestimation that results from optimism bias (which would span various levels of the actual detection frequency). More nuanced empirical designs would be necessary to shed light on the degree to which the infrequency of actual incidents of detection may, through the operation of availability, contribute to underestimation of the probability of detection.

### 11.2.3  Prospect Theory

As described in Section 11.1, bounded rationality results from both judgment errors—the focus of the discussion above of optimism bias and availability—and departures from expected utility theory. Prospect theory is the alternative to expected utility theory offered by behavioral economics. Prospect theory is concerned with how people process or evaluate the probability estimates they come up with (whatever those may be and whatever particular biases may shape them); the way in which people engage in this task has important implications for public law enforcement.

A first observation about prospect theory is that, under this theory, agents exaggerate the difference between a small probability of a particular event and a zero probability of that event (Kahneman and Tversky 1979, 265–67). This "certainty effect" reflects the Allais paradox noted in the earlier discussion of departures from expected utility theory. Under the Allais paradox—repeatedly confirmed across a range of studies—eliminating a given prospect for gain (say, a 50 percent chance of winning a given sum of money) has a greater effect when it alters what was previously a sure thing than when both the original and the revised situations involve some risk.[11]

The certainty effect under prospect theory might imply—at odds with Professor Kunreuther's suggestion from above with regard to flood and earthquake insurance—that people overweigh small probabilities; alternatively, it could imply that people weigh small probabilities accurately and a zero probability inaccurately. All we know from the empirical evidence is that they overweigh the difference between the two.[12] In the former but not the latter case, the certainty effect would mitigate the underestimation resulting from availability—if in fact there is underestimation resulting from availability—of the probability of relatively infrequent events.

More straightforward implications of prospect theory for public law enforcement arise from the fact that, under that theory, changes far from an individual's reference point matter relatively little. For instance, as noted above, the value difference between $100 and $200 is greater than the value difference between $1100 and $1200, assuming a reference point of $0. Also as noted above, prospect theory suggests that this is true both for gains and for losses, which in turn means that the value function will be convex rather than, as under the usual assumption, concave in losses (Kahneman and Tversky 1979, 278). Prospect theory thus implies that the deterrent effect of increasing the magnitude of penalties will have a strongly diminishing effect—the opposite of the case under the concavity assumption. Thus, for instance, the difference between a fine of $8,000 and a fine of $10,000 for a parking offender will be far less than the difference between a fine of $0 and a fine of $2,000—and the former difference may indeed be negligible.

## 11.2.4 Notes on Public Law Enforcement
## with Unboundedly Rational Actors

As described, several points about public law enforcement with boundedly rational actors point away from the basic prescription offered in Professor Polinsky's parking enforcement example described at the beginning of this chapter. In a very simple model, traditional economic analysis of public law enforcement suggested (in the context of that example) detecting only one out of every thousand parking offenders, but then imposing a fine of $10,000 on the detected offender. In suggesting reasons to question this prescription, bounded rationality complements, rather than challenges, traditional economic analysis because that analysis in its more refined form also rejects the broad prescription of minimal enforcement expenditures (meaning a small probability of detection) and large penalties for detected offenders.

The scholarly literature on traditional economic analysis of public law enforcement is sufficiently large and rich to prevent a full discussion of it here.[13] It is easy, however, to pinpoint from that literature several explanations for why very small probabilities of detection and very large penalties for detected offenders may be undesirable. Most obviously, risk aversion of potential offenders points away from this approach (Kaplow 1992; Polinsky 1989, 82–84; Polinsky and Shavell 1979). A second important argument against setting very small probabilities of detection and very large penalties for detected offenders is that if penalties were made as high as possible for all offenses, then marginal deterrence—the incentive to substitute less serious for more serious offenses—would be eliminated: "If robbery is punished as severely as murder, the robber might as well kill his victim to eliminate a witness" (Posner 1985, 1207). A third argument against very small probabilities of detection and very large penalties for detected offenders relies on the idea that individuals may be correct about the probability of detection only on average, rather than in individual cases; this makes the combination of small probabilities of detection and large penalties for detected offenders less desirable *if* (an important assumption) the degree of error in estimating the probability of detection falls with the actual magnitude of that probability (Bebchuk and Kaplow 1992, 366–67). (The degree of error would not fall with the actual magnitude of the probability of detection if, for instance, individuals' estimates were always off by 10 percent of the actual probability of detection.) Finally, a fourth argument in the same vein incorporates "general" as well as "specific" enforcement and again points away from the simple prescription of very small probabilities of detection and very large penalties for detected offenders (Shavell 1991).

These arguments (and others) suggest ways in which traditional economic analysis, like behavioral economic analysis, can go beyond the simple, stylized model and produce predictions that seem more plausible than $10,000 parking-ticket fines for rarely sanctioned double parkers. Thus, the public law enforcement context is one in which bounded rationality seems more to complement than to challenge traditional law and economics. Of course, as the discussion in the previous paragraph makes clear, going beyond the simple, stylized model—whether through traditional economic analysis or through bounded rationality—comes at the expense of spareness and parsimony; without any foray into bounded rationality, it seems fair to say that the substantial literature on traditional economic analysis of public law enforcement suggests that models can point in many different directions depending on the assumptions made. Thus, lack of parsimony, at least in the context of public law enforcement, does not seem to be a criticism specific to work in behavioral, as opposed to traditional, law and economics.[14]

## 11.3  PUBLIC ENFORCEMENT OF EMPLOYMENT DISCRIMINATION LAWS

This section briefly notes some applications of the ideas about bounded rationality and public law enforcement discussed above to the particular context of public enforcement of employment discrimination laws. A common rationale for public enforcement—the inability of victims to identify with ease the actor who caused their harm (Polinsky and Shavell 2000, 46)—is not present in this context, but, nonetheless, employment discrimination laws in the United States are enforced by public as well as private actors.

The analysis starts from a central empirical point—the persistence of significant discrimination in labor markets four decades after the enactment of Title VII of the Civil Rights Act of 1964. It asks whether bounded rationality might play a partial role in explaining the apparent limits on the effect of employment discrimination laws on the existence and persistence of employment discrimination.

As just noted, the basic empirical fact is that, notwithstanding the passage of four decades since the enactment of Title VII, discrimination appears to be alive and well in employment markets. As I have discussed in some detail elsewhere, several recent studies published in leading economics journals provide strong evidence of continued sex discrimination in labor markets (Jolls 2002, 3–11). To take just one example, Claudia Goldin and Cecelia Rouse (2000) have shown that female musicians auditioning for major symphony orchestras fare substantially better when auditions are conducted behind screens—so that the sex of the musician is not known to those making the selections—than when those doing the evaluations know the performer's sex.

Recent evidence suggests similar concerns with race discrimination. In "Are Emily and Brendan More Employable than Lakisha and Jamal? A Field Experiment on Labor Market Discrimination," Marianne Bertrand and Sendhil Mullainathan (2002) examine what happens when otherwise identical resumés are sent out either under a typically "white" name (such as Emily or Brendan) or under a typically "black" name (such as Lakisha or Jamal). They find that resumés with "white" names produced employer interview requests at a rate of one per ten resumés, while resumés with "black" names produced employer interview requests at a rate of one per fifteen resumés. Thus, "black-sounding" applicants had to send out about 50 percent more resumés for each interview than "white-sounding" applicants. This evidence complements earlier evidence from tester studies showing that black and Hispanic testers enjoyed significantly less success in getting interviews and jobs than otherwise-comparable white testers (Cross 1990; Kenney and Wissoker 1994; Turner, Fix, and Struyk 1991).

A simple aspect of bounded rationality that may provide part of the explanation for the persistence of employment discrimination, despite long-standing laws prohibiting such behavior, is optimism bias on the part of the potential offenders (employers). As discussed in Section 11.2.1 above, optimism bias suggests that, under any specified enforcement scheme, actors will tend to be less deterred from the prohibited behavior than they would be in the absence of optimism bias. This optimism bias account may usefully complement other important reasons—such as the unconscious nature of much modern employment discrimination (Krieger 1995)—for the limits Title VII faces in eradicating discrimination in labor markets.

An important qualification to the potential role of optimism bias in the persistence of employment discrimination is that the actors in question here are firms (although typically run by agents) rather than individuals acting in their personal capacities. Optimism bias may be less pronounced for firms because they may face competitive disadvantages if they make systematic errors (Jolls, Sunstein, and Thaler 1998a, 1525). Evidence on the failure of market pressures to curtail optimism bias in the context of entry into new industry (Tor 2002), however, provides some support for the view that optimism bias may be important even for firms (perhaps in part because of agency issues).

To the extent that optimism bias leads to a systematic reduction in the effectiveness of employment discrimination laws, other aspects of bounded rationality from the discussion above may provide hints of helpful responses the law might adopt. Most obviously, a high degree of salience in the enforcement of employment discrimination laws could harness availability and thereby increase the grip of public law enforcement. Intriguing suggestive evidence from the context of employment laws, although not employment discrimination laws, comes from the well-known work of Lauren Edelman, Steven E. Abraham, and Howard S. Erlanger (1992), who have suggested that personnel professionals significantly exaggerate the risk of liability under state wrongful discharge laws. Although Edelman, Abraham, and Erlanger primarily emphasize the role of status seeking by personnel professionals in producing these exaggerated estimates, they also note the grip of "horror stories" that "arouse . . . emotion" (Edelman, Abraham, and Erlanger 1992, 66, 74–78). Such "horror stories" may be nothing other than a method of harnessing, through salience, the availability phenomenon, and it might be helpful to employ similar strategies—or employ them to a greater degree than at present—in the context of public enforcement of employment discrimination laws.

## 11.4 CONCLUSION

Economic analysis of public law enforcement has been a central subfield of traditional economic analysis of law. It is also an area in which bounded rationality is best seen, I have suggested in this chapter, as a complement rather than a challenge to traditional economic analysis of law. As Professor Polinsky and Steven Shavell (1998, 186)—who have in general approached the public law enforcement topic from a traditional economic perspective—recently wrote: "The psychology and learning process . . . by which individuals assimilate and formulate perceived probabilities of sanctions and their magnitude are important . . . to determining how deterrence works and what optimal policy is." In other words, psychologically informed analysis both of how individuals estimate the probability of detection and of how they evaluate the consequences of detection is obviously important to the sensible structuring of public law enforcement. An important issue for bounded rationality—as well as other aspects of behavioral economics—going forward is the degree to which, in areas of legal analysis outside public law enforcement, behavioral economics is best seen as complementing rather than challenging traditional economic analysis.

1. Jolls, Sunstein, and Thaler (1998a, 1476) describe behavioral economics in terms of bounded rationality, bounded willpower, and bounded self-interest.

2. Jolls, Sunstein, and Thaler (1998b, 1594) urge an emphasis on "bounded rationality" over "irrationality."

3. Jolls (1998, 1660 – 61) discusses the relevant studies.

4. The concavity assumption implies that utility declines rapidly as losses mount.

5. Jolls, Sunstein, and Thaler (1998a, 1480 – 81) likewise emphasize aspects of bounded rationality that are useful for analysis of particular legal issues.

6. The discussion in Section 11.3 of the work by Lauren Edelman, Steven Abraham, and Howard Erlanger (1992) is a suggestive example.

7. Again, Jolls (1998, 1660 – 61) provides discussion of the relevant studies.

8. The statement in the text about the effect of optimism bias assumes a model that is similar in all respects—except optimism bias—to the simple model of traditional economic analysis of public law enforcement discussed in the Polinsky excerpt quoted at the beginning of this chapter. In particular, for simplicity the analysis assumes monetary penalties and risk neutrality. See Section 11.2.4 for discussion of more nuanced versions of the traditional economic analysis of public law enforcement.

9. For the basic explanation, see Polinsky (1989, 77–78). The text in the paragraph following this note reference summarizes his account.

10. The evidence noted in the text contradicts the idea that in the context of criminal law "increasing the frequency of punishment is likely to be more efficient [than increasing the severity of punishment], under the assumption that if a criminal knows or knows of someone who has been imprisoned for a particular crime, this information is likely to be available and to cause him to overestimate the likelihood that he will be arrested and convicted if he commits the same crime" (Korobkin and Ulen 2000, 1089).

11. Kahneman and Tversky (1979, 265 – 67) refer to several of the relevant studies.

12. For a description of Kahneman and Tversky's modeling approach with regard to the nature of the certainty effect, see Jolls (1998, 1667n50).

13. For a definitive survey of this literature, see Polinsky and Shavell (2000).

14. For a general discussion of the parsimony issue, see Jolls, Sunstein, and Thaler (1998a, 1487–89).

Arkes, H., and C. Blumer. 1985. The psychology of sunk cost. *Organizational Behavior and Human Decision Processes* 35:124–40.

Bebchuk, L., and L. Kaplow. 1992. Optimal sanctions when individuals are imperfectly informed about the probability of apprehension. *Journal of Legal Studies* 21:365–70.

Becker, G. 1976. *The economic approach to human behavior.* Chicago: University of Chicago Press.

Bertrand, M., and S. Mullainathan. 2002. Are Emily and Brendan more employable than Lakisha and Jamal? A field experiment on labor market discrimination. Working paper.

Cross, H. 1990. Employer hiring practices: Differential treatment of Hispanic and Anglo job seekers. *Urban Institute Report 90-4.* Washington, DC: The Urban Institute Press.

Edelman, L., S. Abraham, and H. Erlanger. 1992. Professional construction of law: The inflated threat of wrongful discharge. *Law and Society Review* 26: 47–83.

Goldin, C., and C. Rouse. 2000. Orchestrating impartiality: The impact of "blind" auditions on female musicians. *American Economic Review* 90:715–41.

Guppy, A. 1993. Subjective probability of accident and apprehension in relation to self-other bias, age, and reported behavior. *Accident Analysis and Prevention* 25:375–82.

Jolls, C. 1998. Behavioral economics analysis of redistributive legal rules. *Vanderbilt Law Review* 51:1653–77.

———. 2002. Is there a glass ceiling? *Harvard Women's Law Journal* 25:1–18.

Jolls, C., C. Sunstein, and R. Thaler. 1998a. A behavioral approach to law and economics. *Stanford Law Review* 50:1471–1550.

———. 1998b. Theories and tropes: A reply to Posner and Kelman. *Stanford Law Review* 50:1593–1608.

Kahneman, D., and A. Tversky. 1979. Prospect theory: An analysis of decision under risk. *Econometrica* 47:263–91.

Kaplow, L. 1992. The optimal probability and magnitude of fines for acts that definitely are undesirable. *International Review of Law and Economics* 12:3–11.

Kenney, G., and D. Wissoker. 1994. An analysis of the correlates of discrimination facing young Hispanic job-seekers. *American Economic Review* 84:674–83.

Kirscht, J., D. Haefner, S. Kegeles, and I. Rosenstock. 1966. A national study of health beliefs. *Journal of Health and Human Behavior* 7:248–54.

Korobkin, R., and T. Ulen. 2000. Law and behavioral science: Removing the rationality assumption from law and economics. *California Law Review* 88: 1051–1144.

Krieger, L. 1995. The content of our categories: A cognitive bias approach to discrimination and equal employment opportunity. *Stanford Law Review* 47:1161–1248.

Kunreuther, H. 1976. Limited knowledge and insurance protection. *Public Policy* 24:227–61.

———. 1982. The economics of protection against low probability events. In *Decision making: An interdisciplinary inquiry*, ed. G. Ungson and D. Braunstein, 195–215. Boston: Kent Publishing.

Lochner, L. 2001. A theoretical and empirical study of individual perceptions of the criminal justice system. Working paper.

Polinsky, A. 1989. *An introduction to law and economics*. 2nd ed. Boston: Little, Brown.

Polinsky, A., and S. Shavell. 1979. The optimal tradeoff between the probability and magnitude of fines. *American Economic Review* 69:880–91.

———. 1998. Public enforcement of law. In *The New Palgrave dictionary of economics and law*, ed. P. Newman, 178–88. Hampshire, UK: Macmillan Reference.

———. 2000. The economic theory of public enforcement of law. *Journal of Economic Literature* 38:45–76.

Posner, R. 1985. An economic theory of the criminal law. *Columbia Law Review* 85:1193–1231.

Shavell, S. 1991. Specific versus general enforcement of law. *Journal of Political Economy* 99:1088–1108.

Simon, H. 1955. A behavioral model of rational choice. *Quarterly Journal of Economics* 69:99–118.

Taylor, S., and J. Brown. 1988. Illusion and well-being: A social psychological perspective on mental health. *Psychological Bulletin* 103:193–210.

Tor, A. 2002. The fable of entry: Bounded rationality, market discipline, and legal policy. *Michigan Law Review* 101:482–568.

Turner, M., M. Fix, and R. Struyk. 1991. Opportunities denied, opportunities diminished: Racial discrimination in hiring. *Urban Institute Report 91-9*. Washington, DC: The Urban Institute Press.

Tversky, A., and D. Kahneman. 1983. Extensional versus intuitive reasoning: The conjunction fallacy in probability judgment. *Psychological Review* 90:293–315.

Viscusi, W. 1992. *Fatal tradeoffs: Public and private responsibilities for risk*. Oxford: Oxford University Press.

Weinstein, N. 1980. Unrealistic optimism about future life events. *Journal of Personality and Social Psychology* 39:806–20.

———. 1998. References on optimistic biases about risk, unrealistic optimism, and perceived invulnerability. Unpublished manuscript.

# 12 | THE BIOLOGY OF IRRATIONALITY: CRIME AND THE CONTINGENCY OF DETERRENCE

*Michael E. O'Neill*

> True!—nervous—very, very dreadfully nervous I had been and am; but why will you say that I am mad? The disease had sharpened my senses—not destroyed—not dulled them. Above all was the sense of hearing acute. I heard all things in the heavens and in the earth. I heard many things in hell. How, then, am I mad?
>
> *Edgar Allan Poe*

In Edgar Allan Poe's (1998) classic story "The Tell-Tale Heart," he explores the psyche of an individual who has committed murder. Poe writes this story from the perspective of the murderer, who continually stresses to the reader that he (or she, as the narrator is never identified by name or gender) is not mad and tries to convince readers of that fact by explaining how carefully his brutal crime was planned and executed: "Now this is the point. You fancy me mad. Madmen know nothing. But you should have seen me. You should have seen how wisely I proceeded—with what caution—with what foresight—with what dissimulation I went to work! I was never kinder to the old man than during the whole week before I killed him" (193).

The narrator explains that he carefully concealed the body to avoid detection and goes into painstaking detail about the premeditation of his plan—all the acts of a seemingly rational individual. Nevertheless, as the story progresses, we learn that something about the narrator is not quite "right." He explains that he killed the old man because of his "vulture eye." Little by little, the reader discovers that

I would like to thank Margaret O'Neill, Jeffrey Parker, Charles F. Stevens, and Todd Zywicki for their helpful comments in thinking through these rather difficult issues. This chapter is based upon my extended treatment of these same issues in *Irrationality and the Criminal Sanction*, a paper delivered at George Mason University as part of a symposium on irrationality and the law sponsored by the George Mason University Law and Psychiatry Center, which will appear in a forthcoming edition of the *Supreme Court Economic Review*. I would also like to thank Frank Buckley and the Law and Economics Center for such generous financial support, and Meghan Fatouros for her invaluable research assistance. Finally, by way of disclaimer, I would note that the opinions expressed within this article do not reflect the positions of the United States Sentencing Commission.

it is this irrational fear of the vulture eye that has consumed the narrator and plunged him into the madness that he had hoped to elude. The narrator continues to hear the old man's heart beating, long after he is dead, and in a final cataclysmic shriek, reveals the victim's body to the authorities.

Poe latched onto something interesting in his story; not the supernatural themes, for which he is often identified, but rather the disintegration process of the human mind. Poe's narrator appears rational at the outset. He has a motivation to commit an awful crime. Yet when we discover the roots of that motivation, we are quick to condemn it. Similarly, when we learn that the narrator continues to hear the dead man's heart beating, we recognize that something is amiss. The narrator's behavior would seem to be at odds with the standard neoclassical model of human behavior. That model posits that human behavior is innately self-directed and rational. Given the narrator's motivation for the killing (the old man's vulture eye) and his decision to reveal the body to the police (prompted by the heart's continuous beating), we must ask whether the narrator acted *rationally* in killing the old man or in revealing his crime to the police. Most of us would consider the narrator's behavior irrational, both in terms of the motivation for the deed's commission and the subsequent reasons for revealing it to the police.

Irrationality, however, save when it is used as an analogue for insanity, is not a particularly well-mined topic in the law (Jones 2001a; Morse 1998; White 1999). In part, this is due to the difficulty legal scholars have in understanding human behavior as the product of anything other than self-conscious choice. The assumption that human behavior is the product of willful choice undergirds the criminal law (O'Neill 2001; Rowe 2002). Although the literature contains scattered references to unconscious or internal compulsion, the law has remained remarkably resistant to the insights of psychiatry or biological causation generally and the study of irrationality in particular.[1]

The behavioral model posited by neoclassical economics assumes that the individual is a rational actor self-consciously choosing utility-maximizing behaviors. Rationality dominates, both as a descriptive model of human behavior and as a prescriptive norm for the development of legal rules. Today, the rational actor is a canonical figure in the law; indeed, policy makers craft legislation to further the aims of this mythical person, and legal scholars develop intricate theories to predict how this individual will behave in response to changes in legal norms (Cooter and Ulen 2000; Posner 1998a).

Rationality, however, is a notoriously difficult concept to understand.[2] The definition of rationality is ever shifting, changing to meet whatever demands the user may place upon it. Nevertheless, most often the term *rationality* is assumed to mean that individuals are "rational maximizers of personal utility" (Mercuro and

Medema 1997). Employing this assumption, scholars have modeled behavior under a variety of conditions, and legislators have attempted to craft public policy with an eye toward the assumption that individuals will behave in accordance with this understanding of rationality.

The rationality assumption has become so pervasive that some economists deny the existence of irrationality, claiming that all behavior is necessarily rational from the individual's perspective (Jolls, Sunstein, and Thaler 1998; Korobkin and Ulen 2000). If we understood the individual's subjective motivations, it is argued, we would realize that her behavior was rational. As a purely epistemological matter, however, it is difficult to label behavior as "rational" unless its converse can be acknowledged. In our everyday experience it is not uncommon to witness acts of seeming irrationality. Those who have dealt with children, substance abusers, or the chronically depressed doubtless have observed behavior that defies rationality. As a consequence, scholars complain that the neoclassical school's theoretical model of human behavior is overly simplistic and does not withstand rigorous empirical analysis (Hanson and Kysar 1999a, 1999b; Jolls, Sunstein, and Thaler 1998; Korobkin and Ulen 2000). Critics observe that real people often behave irrationally in that they are prone to become emotional, they accede to costly social norms, and they both make logical errors and base decisions on false (or incomplete) premises (Elster 1990; Jones 1999a; Mitchell 2002b). These criticisms may be particularly apt in the context of criminal law, where many offenders act on the basis of raw emotion or tend to be exceptional risk takers. Despite occasional attempts to demonstrate otherwise (Becker and Murphy 1986), for example, drug addiction often seems to defy rational explanation. Once-respectable people will sacrifice personal health, family, or employment to satisfy a drug habit. Similarly, the widely acknowledged age and gender components to criminality—that is, young men are consistently more likely to engage in violent criminal acts than women or the elderly (Ghiglieri 1999; Wilson and Hernstein 1985; Wrangham and Peterson 1996) —suggests that a traditional rationality model fails to account adequately for certain types of commonly observed behavior.

A cadre of scholars has thus started both to identify and to catalog seemingly irrational behavior and have examined whether such behavior may have implications for broader legal analysis (Arlen 1998; Eisenberg 1995; Jolls, Sunstein, and Thaler, 1998; Jones 2001b; Korobkin 1998; Korobkin and Ulen 2000; Kuran and Sunstein 1999; Langevoort 1998a; Posner 1998b; Rabin 1998; Rachlinski 2000; Sunstein 1997, 2000; Ulen 1989, 1998). This scholarship seeks to mesh empirical studies of human behavior with neoclassical economic modeling (Laibson and Zeckhauser 1998). As with much modern legal analysis, these efforts draw from both the social sciences and the hard sciences in an effort to better understand human behavior as it exists, not how we might wish it to exist. Unfortunately, social science–based initiatives are presently more suitable for describing irrationality and documenting individual cases of behavioral anomaly than they are at explaining *why* people exhibit such behavior and *under what conditions* such anomalous behaviors surface (Jones 2001a).[3]

Some are already dismissing the empirical observations of those working in the behavioral sciences as simple "noise" constituting merely random behavioral anomalies for which sound public policies could never be developed (Mitchell 2002a). Traditionalists assert that without an overarching and coherent explanatory framework for irrationality, such random insights can never be successfully incorporated into existing rational actor models (Kahneman, Knetsch, and Thaler 1986). The thrust of these criticisms is that mere empirical observation can have no predictive power and thus no realistic effect upon shaping legal policy.

To the extent such behavior may be linked to biological causes, however, it may well be predictive. Any theory seeking to explain human behavior, even the rational actor theory, is at bottom a theory about the brain, for behavior is a reflection of neurological activity.[4] In constructing any such theory, however, scholars must establish certain ground rules. For example, scholars need to construct operative definitions of *rationality* and *irrationality*. For purposes of this discussion, I offer two distinctive definitions of rationality: objective, or *social* rationality, and subjective, or *private* rationality. Social rationality consists of those behaviors that can be empirically verified as occurring in a wide spectrum of human behavior. In other words, ceteris paribus, human beings prefer eating chocolate to being punished. As a consequence, we can say that those individuals who avoid punishment and maximize their eating of chocolate are acting objectively rational. Other individuals, however, may exhibit the seemingly anomalous behavior of preferring corporal punishment to eating chocolate. Those individuals may be described as acting subjectively, or privately rational, if they eschew chocolate in favor of punishment but objectively *irrational* because their behavior does not lie within the mean of observed human activity.

This distinction is particularly important in criminal law in which policy makers inevitably craft punishments designed with social rationality in mind. This is the essence of deterrence. At a fundamental level, lawmakers assume that most people prefer freedom to prison. This assumption is the product of observing human behavior over time. If most people failed to respond to incentives (and disincentives), then it would be difficult to use law as a tool to shape behavior. The entire enterprise of deterrence would be futile if lawmakers did not believe that punishments could be fashioned to deter certain behaviors. Unfortunately, experience with criminal law demonstrates that such deterrence efforts, although in the main successful, are not *uniformly* successful.

For example, criminal law has long understood that some individuals are unable properly to care for themselves or have little ability to act in what we would consider a responsible fashion.[5] Those persons whom the law has labeled "insane"[6] often act in ways that are both predictable and seemingly irrational. Similarly, it is universally acknowledged that children lack adults' capacity for reasoned judgment.

Although anecdotal observations do not a theory make, they do provide a foundation for better understanding the complexities of human behavior and likely will enable us not only to identify patterns of irrationality but to predict them as well. I hope to demonstrate that a useful reservoir of biological knowledge exists about the manner in which the brain dictates behavior that may prove useful in reshaping the current legal and economic model's assumptions about behavior, particularly as it relates to questions of deterrence.

## 12.1 ECONOMICS AND CRIMINAL LAW

### 12.1.1 Understanding Mens Rea

The defining feature of criminal law is the concept of mens rea: the guilty mind (Dressler 1999). Under the American criminal justice system, for a crime to have been committed the defendant must have performed an *actus reus* (a socially undesirable act) and must have done so with the appropriate mens rea. Absent either requirement, even if a socially undesirable act may have been committed, no legal crime exists (Dressler 1999).

The linchpin of mens rea is the notion of rationality. To exhibit a guilty mind, one must be capable of reasoned and free choice. In other words, in order for an individual to be criminally responsible, he must have the capacity rationally to choose to engage in criminal conduct. The law's reach thus may extend only to creatures who are able to understand its requirements and to abide by its prescriptions.

The ancients understood and appreciated this concept. In Plato's (1892/2000) *Laws*, for example, the Stranger illustrates how Athenian law deals with rational motivation and the ability to understand the consequences of one's actions. He explains that individuals who choose to violate the law merit severe punishment (Plato 1892/2000). He notes, however, that not all who err are deserving of equal punishment, for some crimes may be committed "in a state of madness or when affected by disease, or under the influence of extreme old age, or in a fit of childish wantonness, himself no better than a child" (248). If the offender is suffering from such debilities in reasoning, the just state spares the uncomprehending offender from punishment.[7]

This notion of the reasoning malefactor was carried over into the early English legal tradition, where it was understood that criminal liability could be extended only to offenders who freely chose to undertake the proscribed conduct. By the time of Coke, the maxim "actus non facit reum nisi mens sit rea" (an act does not make one guilty unless his mind is guilty) (LaFave and Scott 1986) had become well ingrained in the common law (Coke 1817) and remains a central precept of Anglo-American criminal law today (Singer and Gardner 1989).[8]

Society permits legal fact finders to infer the defendant's intent from the act's commission. Society permits this inference to be drawn largely because it assumes that individuals are rational actors and any acts they commit are deemed the product of their intentional desire to bring about the proscribed conduct. The exemptions, namely, the young, the very old, and the outwardly demented, gain a special status presumably because their inability to act rationally is widely acknowledged within society. These broad intergenerational observations founded in personal experiences that are repeated over time are the virtual equivalent of modern empirical observation.

### 12.1.2 Rational Behavior

Max Weber (1978) was among the first to treat rationality as a mode of social interaction, identifying two distinct types of contextual rationality. The first, which forms the cornerstone of microeconomic rational choice theory, is the concept of *instrumental* rationality, which suggests that people seek to achieve their goals in an optimally efficient fashion. Such rationality is value neutral in that it describes only the means by which an end is reached and does not pass judgment upon the ends sought. The second, *values* rationality, is a judgment upon the selected end. Whereas instrumental rationality has little regard for preference content, values rationality does.

Economists modeling choice under conditions of scarcity assume that individuals will act rationally to maximize their own personal utility (Barnes and Stout 1992; Butler 1998; Cooter and Ulen 2000). The content of that utility, however, is given somewhat short shrift. Economists tend to assume that the end result of the rational deliberative process is best left up to the individual.[9] Economists do not assert that human beings *never* err; rather, the softer claim is merely that individuals adopt behavioral strategies that are optimal within the particular internal and external constraints that exist. Actual human beings have differing cognitive abilities and must function with limited knowledge and within limited time frames. Nevertheless, scholars argue that the suboptimal choices these limitations produce do not violate the premise of human rationality. Individuals still act rationally within their limited spheres of understanding.

If the rationality assumption reflects actual behavior, the law may serve as a tool to encourage certain types of socially desirable behavior and to discourage undesirable behavior. This has important consequences for criminal law. Penalty structures can be designed to deter activities society has chosen to label criminal or used to shape preferences by encouraging people to trade one form of conduct for another (Katyal 1997). A state might adopt the death penalty to deter premeditated murders or increase penalties for heroin in order to press addicts to substitute less harmful drugs. The selection of legal rules will therefore have real-world effects on human behavior.

As a result, the economic analysis of law is essentially a human behavioral theory. The entire discipline seeks to examine how individuals in a given legal system respond to incentives disguised as policy directives. However, in understanding how people respond to various policy directives, it is necessary to have an underlying theory of human behavior. One has to accept, for example, that human beings will respond to incentives. If human beings did not respond to incentives, then the entire project of classical economics would be hopelessly flawed. Similarly, in order to predict how individuals will respond to incentives, one has to assume certain characteristics of human behavior are commonly shared—the desire to avoid pain, for example. Without reliance upon such basic assumptions, it is impossible to accurately predict how individuals will respond to specific policy directives and incentives.

Rational choice may therefore be understood as action an agent chooses out of a belief that it will bring about a desired end (Coleman 1997; Harsanyi 1986). Behaviors or decisions are rational when they are consistent with the individual's broader system of beliefs and desires (Lear 1998). Nevertheless, moments of irrationality, when one's actions fail to fit within the larger context of one's beliefs and desires, are not only common but are an inescapable factor of human experience.

Criminal law has long treated two classes of persons as standing outside the working assumption of rationality: children and the demonstrably insane (Woodard 1994). The law treats children differently because common human experience demonstrates that they do not possess the same faculties of reason found in adults. Children doubtless respond to incentives and have the capacity to seek the satisfaction of their immediate needs, but they are poor at assessing risk or of comprehending fully the consequences of their actions. Similarly, criminal law has long refused to assign criminal responsibility to those persons who may suffer from a "mental disease or defect," which renders them "unable to appreciate the nature or quality" of their actions.[10] Such individuals are deemed "legally" insane, a shorthand way of saying that their actions are not the product of rational thought.

These are not the only two examples of situations in which people behave in ways that seem to belie their own properly considered interests. A growing body of scholarship empirically demonstrates that people frequently act in ways seemingly at odds with their own interests and do so in consistent and predictable ways (Langevoort 1998a; Sunstein 2000).

### 12.1.3 Rationality and Criminal Sanction

If behavior is a social modality, as Weber claimed, and rational, as economists assume, then certain behaviors may be labeled "antisocial," and the costs of indulging in that behavior may be increased so as to discourage it. In other words, if a legislator could know why an individual would choose to commit a crime, a law could be adopted to alter his or her decision.

Pursuant to standard deterrence theory, the rational calculus of the pain of legal punishment offsets the motivation for the crime, thereby deterring criminal activity. Classic rational choice theory, of course, takes no account of ends and thus assumes that one takes those actions, criminal or lawful, that maximize payoff and minimize costs (Jones 2001a).

This important link between deterrence and rational choice has become well established in the legal literature (Cornish and Clarke 1986; Klepper and Nagin 1989; Paternoster 1989a, 1989b; Pillavin et al. 1986; Williams and Hawkins 1989) and is the foundation of so-called optimal penalty theory (Becker 1968; Posner 1980). This theory posits that an appropriately constructed sanction will be no harsher than necessary to prevent the rational individual from engaging in criminal conduct. Individuals will thus be deterred from acting unlawfully when the sanction associated with the illegal behavior fully compensates society for the harm inflicted by the criminal behavior, while at the same time depriving the individual wrongdoer of the benefit of his illegal conduct (Nagin 1998).

Unfortunately, validating the effect deterrence-based punishment schemes have on behavior has been difficult to demonstrate. Research on *specific* deterrence, the effect of a sanction on the person who receives it, suggests that even sophisticated offenders whose penalties are ratcheted up are not appreciably deterred. Weisburd, Waring, and Chayet (1995), for example, have compared recidivism rates between federal white-collar offenders who were similar in many respects except that some received only probation and others received imprisonment.[11] They detected no difference in the recidivism rates between the two groups of offenders. The authors concluded that if a deterrent effect could not be found with this group of offenders, who are generally considered the most rational and calculating, finding such an effect for other types of crime is unlikely. But why is it that deterrence effects have been hard to demonstrate? If criminals act rationally, their behavior ought to be predictable and thus deterrable.

## 12.2 RATIONALITY, THE BRAIN, AND BEHAVIOR

Scholars have recently begun to acknowledge that neoclassical assumptions of rationality often fail as either a descriptive or a predictive model of individual behavior (Hurd 1998; Jolls, Sunstein, and Thaler 1998; Simon 1955). Turning to experimental work in cognitive psychology, researchers have borrowed the concept of bounded rationality to help explain seemingly nonrational behavior (Becker 1962). The theory of bounded rationality does this by identifying systematic, and therefore purportedly predictable, deviations from rational behavior (Conlisk 1996; Kahneman et al. 1990; Langevoort 1998b). The theory focuses on cognitive biases, heuristics, and limitations that lead individuals to depart from outcomes otherwise predicted by the rational choice model.[12] Bounded rationality is not a refutation of the rational actor model; rather, it seeks to recalibrate the neoclassical model to take account of predictable cognitive limitations and biases.[13]

The bounded rationality model seeks to ground abstract conceptions of human nature to empirically validated research (Jolls, Sunstein, and Thaler 1998; Simon 1955). Nevertheless, it may not go far enough in examining inherent biological limitations to rational thought processes (Eagle 1987; Simon 1955). The difficulty is that it fails to completely capitalize on this important insight by exploring fully the role neurological defects and abnormalities may play in decision making.

### 12.2.1 Rationality, Rightly Understood

A major difficulty with the rationality assumption is that people are often observed to behave seemingly at odds with their own articulated preferences and, even when they seek to attain those preferences, often employ inefficient means to pursue them. This differential between actual observed behavior and the theoretical behavior constructed by economic models may have contributed to the reluctance of social scientists to pay greater attention to economic behavioral constructs. Herbert Simon (1955) sought to bridge this gap. He borrowed from the empirical efforts of psychologists to conclude that people do not behave as true utility maximizers, but instead act as "satisficers." A satisficer neither acquires complete information about a decision nor uses a dispassionate decision-making process to arrive at an optimal decision. Instead, Simon explained that certain *internal* physiological limits (such as one's innate intelligence, defined as human computational and memory abilities), as well as the *external* costs of rational decision making (such as the cost of obtaining the proper information to make an optimal decision), restrict rational decision making. Simon suggested that in certain instances, given both internal and external limitations, it would be irrational to make the otherwise rational choice (see also Rachlinski and Farina 2002; Seidenfeld 2002; Simon 1972).

Simon's criticisms need not be assumed to be a refutation of instrumental rationality, but instead a refinement of it. Few scholars would be willing to completely abandon the idea that people act instrumentally rational on a variety of occasions. However, *striving* for rationality may be the most we can expect from human beings. Since Milton Friedman (1953) argued a version of this point, some economists have taken the position that people possess bounded rationality but that "they act as if unboundedly rational" (Conlisk 1996, 683). From a neurobiological perspective, however, this "as if" defense of rationality fails to acknowledge the ways in which acting "as if rational" can be used, defensively, to hinder expected utility maximization.

Taken together, the internal and external constraints individuals face create obstacles for yielding completely rational decisions (Conlisk 1996; Simon 1987, 1997). Although Simon (1957) acknowledged internal limitations that inhere in human beings, he perhaps did not push his analysis far enough to understand that internal limitations may not only be of the kind common to all people but also may include biological anomalies.

Rationality is based upon a conceptual distinction between a decision's rationality and its objective merits. It may occasionally be rational to engage in criminal conduct if all the available information happens to point to that decision. However, not every seemingly rational decision is "right" (a loaded term over which philosophers may disagree) (Korobkin and Ulen 2000; Mitchell 2002a), nor is every mistaken decision necessarily irrational. Oftentimes, when we talk about "rationality," we are referring to social, or objective rationality. By *social* rationality, I mean rationality that is exhibited by most human beings upon a spectrum of behavior. Those who adhere to traditional notions of deterrence within criminal law assume that most people prefer freedom to prison. For a more concrete example, it is safe to say that *most* human beings do not enjoy cutting or biting their own flesh. As a consequence, if we examine any given group of individuals, we will observe that the majority of them do not engage in self-destructive, physically harmful behavior of this type. Thus, we might say that it is *objectively* rational behavior not to maliciously injure one's self.

However, in any randomly selected group, there might be people who do enjoy self-mutilation. In fact, a clinically observable symptom of a disease known as Lesch-Nyhan syndrome is that the individual tears and bites uncontrollably at her own flesh.[14] If the person's hands are not bound, she will injure herself repeatedly. It can be assumed that the rational individual would not choose to harm herself in this way. Thus, from the perspective of social rationality, this person is acting deviantly, or irrationally, because she is acting contrary to the way in which most individuals behave.

One could argue, however, that this person was acting in accordance with her own *private*, or subjective rationality. For some reason, perhaps this particular individual places a high value on cutting or biting her own flesh. She therefore chooses to mutilate herself. To the extent this is willed behavior, then it is privately rational behavior. In my view, however, to accept this vision of subjective rationality is to render the concept of rationality devoid of any operational meaning. If an actor makes a decision that does not maximize net expected benefits to him, then he violates the behavioral predictions of the expected utility version of rational choice theory. One of the troubles of the microeconomic model is that ends are seldom taken into account. It is difficult to know, *ex ante*, which choices are optimal for a particular decision maker without knowing the profile of his utility function. Because individual utility functions are difficult to elicit, the behavioral predictions of expected utility theory often are not directly verifiable or falsifiable.

More salient versions of rational choice theory start from expected utility theory's predictions about the manner in which individuals will attempt to achieve their personal utility and then add predictions about the actors' goals and preferences (Smith 1869). If we can figure out which course of action will most profit the decision maker, we will be able to predict the individual's behavior. This intuition suggests falsifiable predictions about substantive behaviors, not just predictions about decision-making procedures. Most of these predictions will be based upon objective behavioral observations. Consider, for example, the simple prediction that if there is no punishment for overstaying one's time at a parking meter, people will monopolize parking spaces. This prediction implicitly relies on the assumption that individuals are concerned with punishments they might receive, not with the disutility others will suffer from not being able to find a parking space. Thus, the self-interested version of rational choice theory may lead to the creation of directly falsifiable behavioral predictions.

If, however, we simply define any expressed behavior as "freely chosen" behavior and the best evidence of personal utility, then "rational" action becomes little more than a tautology. Without accounting for social rationality as a baseline, however, there is no way to determine the content of any individual's utility function (Korobkin 2000). This has important consequences for legal policy. If society wishes to reduce crime, for example, assuming all other policy decisions are held constant, should it increase or decrease the length of prison sentences? Although the former appears to be the obvious answer, it is correct only if we assume that most people prefer to live outside prison than to be incarcerated. In order to make appropriate public policy determinations, it is thus necessary for the theory to include some predictions about the content of preferences.

## 12.2.2 The Neurobiological Roots of Rationality

Reason, like all human behavior, is a function of neurological activity. The brain is the product of evolution; thus, many seemingly anomalous behaviors may be traced to evolutionary forces (Jones 1997a, 1997b, 1999b, 2001b). Aggression, so often the concern of criminal sanction, may be an adaptive behavior that performed an important function for our ancestors. Nevertheless, just as the eye, also a product of evolution, can fail, so can the brain.

Although healthy individuals might be expected to follow behavioral patterns that reflect reasoned choice, individuals who suffer from neurological impairments may defy such expectations. Such impairments often yield predictable behavioral results. Neurologists have long understood that when a patient appears in the emergency room with partial paralysis and slurred speech, they can make a clinical diagnosis that this person has likely suffered a stroke (Berkow 1997). In fact, the entire *Diagnostic and Statistical Manual of Mental Disorders-IV* (American Psychiatric Association 1994), which is routinely employed by psychiatrists and psychologists as a means of guiding clinical diagnosis, is premised upon the examination of groupings of individuals who suffer from the same observable behaviors (Sharfstein 2002). Aberrant behavior may stem from causes as diverse as trauma, chemical dependency, environmental factors (such as exposure to lead paint), or developmental factors (as in the case of malnutrition) (Rowe 2002). Yet even these diverse causes may result in similar neurological deficiencies provided the same areas of the brain are affected.

### 12.2.2.1 Biology and Causation: A Cautionary Tale

Determining biological causation is quite a difficult undertaking. When we talk about rational action, we are really talking about a complicated and dynamic process originating in the brain. As an epistemological matter, of course, there can be no "rationality" *without* irrationality. We define rationality, in part, by reference to observable human behavior. Human beings lie upon a spectrum of mammals. When we examine animals, we observe certain instinctual behaviors that appear hardwired. My cat, whenever he takes a drink from his water dish, kneads the ground with his paws, a reflexive action that is a result of what he needed to do to obtain milk while he was a nursing kitten. This inbred characteristic is not the result of specific learning; rather, it is a part of the animal's internal hardwiring; it is instinctual behavior. Humans exhibit instinctual behavior as well. We act altruistically in circumstances that would seemingly belie predictions of self-interest, have evolved mechanisms for detecting dishonesty, and tend to be maximizers of individual utility.

However, deviations from such "normal" behaviors occasionally happen. My cat once suffered severe head trauma and, as a result, developed odd neurological problems. He could not smell food for a brief period of time and would have starved had he not been force-fed. When a certain area along his spinal column was touched, his hind legs would give way, and he would begin uncontrollably to lick himself. Much in the same way this cat suffered from neurological damage that "caused" him to act in a particular way, human actions may also be governed by neurological deficiencies.

Such deficiencies, although yielding predictable behavioral patterns, may nevertheless "cause" individuals to behave abnormally. If abnormal behavior may be defined as behavior that deviates from the norm, then we may be able to define "irrational" behavior as behavior that fails to conform to social norms. Although social irrationality could be nothing more than private rationality, if that private rationality is something more than mere atypical preference selection and violates deeply ingrained notions of social rationality, we could choose to label it "irrational."

Irrationality might thus be defined as behavior that falls outside the range of generally accepted social rationality or behavior that fails to enable the individual to obtain the self-selected ends. For example, someone who suffers from obsessive-compulsive disorder (OCD) may strongly desire *not* to wash her hands until they are raw and bleeding. Absent her disorder, she may freely choose not to wash. However, part of the diagnosis of OCD is that the individual is unable internally to control her ability to wash incessantly (American Psychiatric Association 1994). Thus, if she continues to wash her hands in the face of her desire to put an end to that behavior, we can say that she is acting irrationally.[15]

Social rationality is useful as a means of predicting group behavior. This is precisely why economic analysis works so well much of the time. Most of us do act as utility maximizers much of the time. Unfortunately, however, the assumptions underlying economic analysis do not consistently predict individual behavior. As a consequence, social systems that rely upon an understanding of objective rationality may not always work as predicted. Criminal sanctions, which are premised upon certain theories of human behavior, may thus act as a deterrent against most people, most of the time, but they may not deter all of the people all of the time. Although we cannot expect perfection in any human-engineered system, we can nevertheless make improvements upon such systems.

### 12.2.2.2 Neurological Damage and Behavior

Violence is certainly a human characteristic. Indeed, the ability to *be* violent may have helped to assure our survival as a species. Nevertheless, using violence to resolve conflict is not applicable to all situations. The basic model for how violence arises in the brain is that the initial impulses originate in deep regions of the limbic system. After that, the prefrontal cortex decides whether to act on these impulses (Abraham 2000; Berkow 1997; Gould 1996; Raine 2000; Rose 1998). The role of the prefrontal cortex is to engage in "executive function," that is, planning, integrating information, and generally serving as a mechanism to control emotional impulses that originate in deeper brain regions (Berkow 1997). If that region is damaged, predictable irrational behaviors will emerge.

Consider the example of ill-fated railway worker Phineas Gage, easily the most celebrated case of prefrontal lobe damage in the medical literature. In 1848, Gage accidentally sparked an explosion while using an iron rod to tamp blasting powder into place (Damasio et al. 1994; Field 2001). The explosion propelled the inch-thick, yard-long tamping iron directly through Gage's head. Although the iron caused catastrophic frontal lobe damage, it neither killed him nor even knocked him unconscious. Gage survived the severe head trauma and retained both memory and intelligence, as well as basic motor function. Interestingly, however, his personality changed dramatically after the accident. Gage became uncharacteristically vulgar and obstinate. He was unable to carry through planned activities and was subject to frequent temper outbursts (Damasio et al. 1994; Harlow 1868). In light of his prior history, Gage's sudden predilection to obdurate behavior appears less a rational decision and more a result of his head injury.

If Gage were the only individual to have experienced personality changes as the result of damage to the prefrontal cortex, we might be able to dismiss his conduct as mere happenstance and treat him as an outlier. After all, brain damage of the sort Gage suffered is doubtless uncommon. His survival was nothing short of miraculous. Evidence, however, continues to mount illustrating the importance of the prefrontal cortex to controlling behavior and influencing rational decision making.

At the National Institute of Neurological Disorders and Stroke, Dr. Jordan Grafman studied wounded Vietnam veterans and found that those with penetrating head injuries that caused damage to parts of the prefrontal cortex were at increased risk for violent behavior (Greenwood 2002). These individuals suffered from neurological deficits similar to the personality changes that plagued Phineas Gage.

Antonio Damasio has similarly illustrated a possible neurological underpinning for abnormal preference selection and behavior (Damasio, Tranel, and Damasio 1991; Damasio and van Hoesen 1983). In well-publicized research, Damasio (1994) studied two research subjects, one male and one female, who had suffered injuries to the prefrontal cortex during infancy. Although each of these individuals had grown up in stable, middle-class families with college-educated parents and otherwise normal biological siblings, neither had made a satisfactory transition into adulthood. Both lacked friends, were dependant upon parental support to survive, and had engaged in criminal behavior during adolescence. Interestingly, researchers tested both subjects on their ability to respond to the uncertainty of punishment and reward—vital to determining whether they could respond to classic deterrence efforts. Using a simple deck of cards, the subjects were instructed that rewards to the "bad" card deck were high and immediate, whereas payoffs to the "good" card deck were immediately low but substantially better in the long term. A control group of participants were easily able to determine that it was better to draw from the "good" deck for later and better payoffs. Neither research subject, however, was able to master the use of the long-term deck, suggesting that classic deterrence strategies might have little effect upon them. This provocative study demonstrates that although deterrence strategies may generally be effective, there may be people upon whom they simply will not work.

Adrian Raine, a clinical neuroscientist, has provided further support for a link between brain damage and violence (Raine et al. 2000). In an important study, Raine performed positron-emission tomography (PET) scans on forty-one murderers and forty-one control-group persons of similar ages.[16] In each group, thirty-nine of the forty-one people were male. The murderers consistently registered lower glucose metabolism in the prefrontal cortex, a sign that this region was not functioning as it should to inhibit aggressive impulses (Raine 2000; Raine et al. 2000). But murderers are clearly not all the same. Significantly, when Raine divided his subjects into those who had committed cold-blooded, premeditated murder and those who killed impulsively, the impulsive killers showed the poorest functioning in the prefrontal cortex. This suggests that premeditated killers, unlike their more impulsive cousins, might be amenable to deterrence efforts.

### 12.2.2.3 Genes and Behavior

A recent study reported that children who suffer abuse and who have a common variation in a gene linked to behavior are much more likely to become aggressive, antisocial adults than those who have similar environmental circumstances but lacked the genetic anomaly. This report was particularly important because it represented the first clear link between antisocial behavior and a specific interaction of genes and environment (Strokstad 2002).[17] This could explain why childhood mistreatment increases the risk of criminality by 50 percent, even though most abused children do not themselves become delinquents.

Similarly, researchers can point to the (in)famous Inmate X from Holland who has the only known gene linked directly to violent behavior in humans (Brunner et al. 1993a, 1993b). Based upon reports of consistent violent behavior among Inmate X's male relatives, Dr. Hans Brunner conducted a genetic analysis of the male members of the family to determine whether any identifiable genetic abnormalities existed. He discovered that each of the afflicted family members, all blood-related males, had an odd mutation in the monoamine oxidase A gene. This gene affects the production of an enzyme that normally regulates serotonin, a neurotransmitter implicated in governing behavior. Due to the mutation, this enzyme was rendered effectively nonfunctional. Brunner showed that Inmate X and his troubled male family members each had the same odd genetic mutation, but that the twelve healthy male family members did not. In light of the understanding that serotonin is a key to regulating impulse control, it was assumed that this genetic defect prevented Inmate X and his similarly afflicted male relatives from controlling their impulsive behavior.

Serotonin abnormalities have consistently been shown to play a role in violent, impulsive behavior. In a widely reported study, Dr. Frederick R. Goodwin examined U.S. marines receiving psychiatric discharges in an effort to determine whether any neurobiological anomalies existed (Hamer and Copeland 1998). Goodwin discovered that the discharged marines each displayed one significant feature in common; all had low levels of the neurotransmitter serotonin, a chemical neurobiologists had long suspected as being able to influence one's ability to control behavior. Researchers had discovered decreased levels of this same neurotransmitter in a broad range of other violent people, including prisoners convicted of committing aggressive, impulsive acts; children who had tortured animals; and men who had scored unusually high on psychological exams for aggression, hostility, or psychopathic deviance. Goodwin hypothesized that the low serotonin levels handicapped the marines' ability to control their impulsive tendencies. Once these intriguing patterns were noticed in humans, scientists began to manipulate serotonin levels in laboratory animals and found that decreased levels of serotonin apparently result in a tendency to be highly aggressive.[18] Of course, even though we may understand the function of serotonin in neurobiology, it is a major step to say that decreased levels of serotonin necessarily caused the behavior for which any of the former marines were discharged from service or that the decreased serotonin levels even predated the unbecoming behavior.[19]

### 12.2.2.4 Age, Gender, and the Link to Criminality

With some notable exceptions, violent behavior that results in homicide or injury is largely the province of young men (Miccio 2002). Across cultures, men kill men twenty to forty times more frequently than women kill women (Daly and Wilson 1988). In the United States alone, men are eight times more likely than women to commit murder, nine times more likely to commit armed robbery, and four to five times more likely to commit aggravated assault (Federal Bureau of Investigation 2001). Most of these male killers are *young* men, between the ages of fifteen and thirty (Wilson and Hernstein 1985). Interestingly, such violent behavior does not appear to be randomly distributed throughout this age range. According to at least one estimate, roughly 7 percent of young men commit some 79 percent of repeat, violent offenses (Wright 1995).[20]

Is this necessarily rationally chosen behavior, or could there be something else at work? One long-standing theory for this striking gender difference involves the hormone testosterone, which is more abundant in men than in women (Denno 1997; Kimura 2002). But precisely how testosterone may trigger violent impulses in the brain is a mystery. Research does show that male sex offenders who are castrated are less likely to repeat their crimes and that men who take body-building steroids, which are chemically close to testosterone, can become aggressive. Studies of prisoners, both male and female, also suggest that aggression is linked to high testosterone levels. Similarly, considerable data show that aggression in animals is linked to high testosterone and that castration, particularly before the onset of sexual maturation, decreases aggression (Bahrke and Wright 1990). If that is true, what implications does it hold for freely chosen, rational behavior?

## 12.3 IRRATIONALITY AND PUBLIC POLICY

Modern advances in neuroscience suggest that many behaviors we perceive as being socially irrational are the product of cognitive defects and neurological malfunctioning. These seemingly maladaptive behaviors are neither random nor entirely obscure, but rather appear consistently within populations. As brain-imaging devices become ever more sophisticated and our understanding of neurobiology more complete, it is likely that we will better be able to predict cognitive defects and socially irrational behavior in individuals. Although it is plausible that certain seemingly socially irrational behaviors were, in fact, rational from an evolutionary perspective (Owen 2001), it is equally likely that many observed irrational behaviors are the product of neurological defect. Such deficits in reason may not ultimately drive basic public policy, but they may be necessary to consider in refining the way in which we enact punishments and craft criminal law prohibitions.

To be useful for legal policy, behavioral theories need to predict the likely responses to legal rules of the particular classes of actors to whom the rules are geared. If individuals commit many more errors in their attempts to maximize utility than the rational choice model posits, and those errors are not the result of garden-variety market imperfections but rather the result of systematic, widespread cognitive imperfections, then our modeling of the relative efficiency of legal rules is flawed to the extent it fails to account for those imperfections (Ulen 1989). Legal policy makers rely upon those models when crafting legislative changes to modify incentive structures to influence human behavior. If policy makers, for instance, are considering revising penalties for violent offenders, they need a prediction of how such potential offenders will likely respond to competing sanctioning regimes. The struggle is that if a substantial number of violent offenders engage in such behavior because of the neurological or genetic defects discussed here, the traditional assumption that individuals will respond to increased sanctions may be inaccurate. New assumptions will be needed to more accurately reflect the reality of human behavior.

This is not to imply that the rational choice model as expressed in optimal penalty theory fails to predict socially rational behavior. This model has proven to be a powerful tool for conducting legal analysis. As with any tool, however, it may not be perfect for each intended application. Although public policy may often be based upon the assumptions employed by classical economics, it may need to take into account the fact that some individuals will not respond to utility maximization. That is not an indictment of the rationality assumption itself; rather, it is a refinement of that assumption to address the growing body of empirical and neuroscience literature that calls certain of its core assumptions into question.

Increasing the severity or frequency of punishment necessary to reduce or to increase the incidence of any human behavior will correlate positively or negatively, respectively, with the extent to which the predisposition underlying that behavior is either the product of evolutionary forces or the result of neurological defects. This is typified by behaviors that are motivated by addictions, which bear a strong resemblance to behaviors aroused by visceral cravings such as hunger, thirst, sleep, or sexual desire. Unlike addictions, such cravings are generally evolved traits rather than desires that stem directly from past individual behaviors. But much like harmful addictions, visceral cravings can overpower actors, causing them to act in ways that fail to maximize utility. Hunger can make the dieter overeat, even though he would rather lose weight than enjoy a fattening meal. Sexual desire may tempt an individual to abandon his family, even though the costs of doing so clearly outweigh the benefits.

Rational choice models can fail in predicting behavior in these situations because actors tend systematically to underestimate the power of such visceral cravings before they occur, hampering advanced planning. In an interesting example of the power of craving, experimental subjects were recruited and told they would be compensated if they agreed to complete a quiz that would test their knowledge of history (Korobkin and Ulen 2000). Some subjects were asked to choose, prior to completing the quiz, whether they would be compensated with a chocolate bar or a specified cash payment. Other subjects knew what their choice of compensation would be but were not required to make the choice until they had completed the quiz. Subjects in the latter group were significantly more likely to select the chocolate bar than subjects in the first group, demonstrating that people are often not very good at predicting the power of their cravings before a temptation is imminent. This insight may explain why government policies seeking to quell addiction are sometimes less successful than rational choice theory would predict.

In situations of addictions, where individuals are especially likely to act in ways contrary to their more considered, stable judgments as to how to maximize their utility, an argument can be made for more aggressive *ex ante* government regulation. If rational choice theory provided sufficient behavioral predictions, the government would need to do no more to combat heroin use than to ensure that information concerning the risks of heroin were made widely available to the general public. Plainly, such is not the case.

## 12.4 CONCLUSION

Economics teaches us about incentives (nurture), whereas biology tells us about limitations that inhere in our being human (nature). The law's resistance to consider irrationality reveals a serious flaw in its ability to account for, and to influence, human behavior. In the end, *any* theory of human behavior is only as good as the assumptions upon which it is based. To be useful as a means of constructing public policy, those assumptions must be based upon empirical foundations. Simply to claim that no competing theories of behavior exist that have the same elegance of the rational actor model does not mean that the assumptions underlying that theory should neither be reevaluated nor refined. A simple, elegant theory that systematically fails to account properly for human behavior is not a useful theory. Nor is a theory that refuses to permit modifications based upon empirical results of much more than decorative value.

We can understand social rationality by examining social statistics. It is for this reason that the insights provided by law and economics are so powerful. Economics, whether applied to law or not, is essentially a science of human behavior. It makes assumptions about how people will behave under given conditions. Although it is powerful in its predictive ability when applied to groups, or even sometimes to individuals, it is not always accurate. More complete models, especially in criminal law, where the focus is on socially aberrant behavior, will need to take into account recent advances in neuropsychiatry, genetics, and behavioral psychology in order to better shape public policy. To the extent researchers are able to posit theories that better explain, and predict, human behavior, they will be better able to assist policy makers.

# NOTES

1. The most important application of psychoanalytic ideas in the law was carried out by Frank (1930) in *Law and the Modern Mind*. A few prominent scholars attempted to integrate psychoanalysis into law earlier in this century (Goldstein 1968; Katz et al. 1967; Redmount 1973; Schoenfeld 1973; Stone 1972). One of the earliest discussions of psychoanalytic ideas in the legal literature appears to be that of Schroeder (1918).

2. The various rationality constructs are detailed in Frank (1997) and Korobkin and Ulen (2000).

3. "We have clear, causal, and experimental observations that indicate systematic deviations from the rational man paradigm. We look for models that will capture this evidence" (Rubenstein 1998).

4. Kandel (1991) has explained that "the central tenant of modern neural science is that all behavior is a reflection of brain function." See also Jones (2001a).

5. *Dusky v. United States*, 362 U.S. 402, 402 (1960), concluded that defendants must have sufficient present ability to consult with their lawyer with a reasonable degree of rational understanding and must have a rational as well as factual understanding of the proceedings against them.

6. *Kansas v. Hendricks*, 521 U.S. 346 (1997), held that potentially indefinite detention is permissible when a special justification, such as dangerous mental illness, outweighs the individual's constitutionally protected interest in avoiding physical restraint.

7. Under these special circumstances, the offender merits deferential treatment. For, "if this be made evident to the judges elected to try the cause, on the appeal of the criminal or his advocate, and he be judged to have been in this state when he committed the offense, he shall simply pay for the hurt which he may have done to another; but he shall be exempt from other penalties. . . ." (Plato 1892/2000, 248).

8. *Morissette v. United States*, 342 U.S. 246, 250–51 (1952), also commented on the persistence of mens rea requirement in modern law.

9. Becker (1976, 14), has identified the basic principles of standard economics as involving individuals who "(1) maximize their utility (2) from a stable set of preferences and (3) accumulate an optimal amount of information and other inputs in a variety of markets." Frank (1997) and Korobkin and Ulen (2000) provide useful distinctions between different kinds of rationality.

10. M'Naughten's Case, 8 Eng. Rep. 718 (1843), concluded that defendants

must establish that they either were not conscious of the nature of the act they were committing or that they were not aware that is was considered wrongful.

11. This research was conducted using offenders sentenced prior to implementation of the guidelines. The guidelines make this kind of matched-group design more difficult, because offenders who are similar now receive similar sentences.

12. For a useful listing of the cognitive biases, heuristics, and limitations discussed in the economic literature, refer to Langevoort (1996, 1998a) and Hanson and Kysar (1999a, 1999b, 1999c).

13. "These researchers claim not merely that we sometimes fail to abide by rules of logic, but that we fail to do so in predictable ways" (Hanson and Kysar 1999b). In the economics literature, the debate over rationality goes beyond cognitive biases to include alternative models of behavior such as learning theory and evolutionary psychology.

14. See generally, *The New England Journal of Medicine*, Massachusetts Medical Society (2002) at http://content.nejm.org.

15. See generally, *The New England Journal of Medicine*, Massachusetts Medical Society (2002) at http://content.nejm.org.

16. PET scans, which measure glucose uptake by brain cells, show which brain regions are most active.

17. The study of 1,037 males in New Zealand, now aged about thirty, revealed that the low-activity form of the gene alone is not linked to antisocial behavior. But those who had the gene variation and who had experienced moderate or severe mistreatment as children were much more likely to commit crimes. That group made up only 12 percent of the study group but were responsible for 44 percent of offenses.

18. The study of animal behavior has been a useful tool for understanding human behavior as well (Elliott 1997).

19. To substantiate this hypothesis of the effects of environmental manipulation on serotonin levels, Raleigh and McGuire (1991, 1994) subsequently tested college fraternity brothers, discovering that fraternity leaders had higher serotonin levels than recent pledges. This was a result that mirrored the studies involving monkeys, buttressing the notion that social hierarchy may itself have an effect on neurobiology. Thus, social experience, individual health, and developmental factors may each affect serotonin function.

20. Quoting Frederick R. Goodwin.

# REFERENCES

Abraham, C. 2000. Doctor pinpoints key to the criminal mind, research cites damage to brain's frontal lobes. *Globe and Mail*, March 22, A1.

American Psychiatric Association. 1994. Diagnostic and statistical manual of mental disorders. 4th ed. Washington, DC: American Psychiatric Association.

Arlen, J. 1998. Comment: The future of behavioral economic analysis of law. *Vanderbilt Law Review* 51:1765.

Bahrke, M., and J. Wright. 1990. Psychological behavioral effects of endogenous testosterone. *Sports Medicine International Ltd.* 10 (5): 303–37.

Barnes, D., and L. Stout. 1992. *Cases and materials on law and economics*. St. Paul, MN: West Wadsworth.

Becker, G. 1962. Irrational behavior and economic theory. *Journal of Political Economy* 70:1.

———. 1968. Crime and punishment: An economic approach. *Journal of Political Economy* 76:169.

———. 1976. *The economic approach to human behavior*. Chicago: University of Chicago Press.

Becker, G., and K. Murphy. 1986. A theory of rational addiction. Working paper no. 41. Chicago: University of Chicago Center for the Study of Economics and State.

Berkow, R. 1997. *The Merck manual of medical information*. New York: Pocket Books.

Brunner, H., M. Nelen, X. Breakefield, H. Ropers, and B. van Oost. 1993a. Abnormal behavior associated with a point mutation in the structural gene for monoamine oxidase A. *Science* 262:578–80.

———. 1993b. X-linked borderline mental retardation with prominent behavioral disturbance: Phenotype, genetic localization, and evidence for disturbed monoamine metabolism. *American Journal of Human Genetics* 52:1032–39.

Butler, H. 1998. *Economic analysis for lawyers*. Durham, NC: Carolina Academic Press.

Coke, E. 1817. *Institutes of the laws of England. Part 3*. London: Clarke.

Coleman, J. 1997. Rational choice and rational cognition. *Legal Theory* 3:183.

Conlisk, J. 1996. Why bounded rationality? *Journal of Economic Literature* 34:669.

Cooter, R., and T. Ulen. 2000. *Law and economics*. 3rd ed. Reading, MA: Addison-Wesley Longman.

Cornish, D., and R. Clarke, eds. 1986. *The reasoning criminal: Rational choice perspectives on offending*. Berlin: Springer Verlag.

Daly, M., and M. Wilson. 1988. *Homicide*. New York: Hawthorne.

Damasio, A. 1994. *Descartes' error: Emotion, reason and the human brain*. New York: Avon.

Damasio, A., D. Tranel, and H. Damasio. 1991. Somatic markers and the guidance of behavior. In *Frontal lobe function and dysfunction*, ed. H. Levin, H. Eisenberg, and A. Benton, 217–29. New York: Oxford University Press.

Damasio, A., and G. van Hoesen. 1983. Emotional disturbances associated with focal lesions of the limbic frontal lobe. In *Neuropsychology of human emotions*, ed. K. Heilman and P. Satz, 268–99. New York: Guilford.

Damasio, H., T. Grabowski, R. Frank, A. Galaburda, and A. Damasio. 1994. The return of Phineas Gage: Clues about the brain from the skull of a famous patient. *Science* 264:1102.

Denno, D. 1997. Gender differences in biological and sociological predictors of crime. *Vermont Law Review* 22:305.

Dressler, J. 1999. *Criminal law*. St. Paul, MN: Westgroup.

Eagle, L. 1987. The psychoanalytic and the cognitive unconscious. In *Theories of the unconscious and theories of the self*, ed. R. Stern, 155. Hillsdale, NJ: Academic Press.

Eisenberg, M. 1995. The limits of cognition and the limits of contract. *Stanford Law Review* 47:21.

Elliott, D. 1997. Law and biology: The new synthesis. *St. Louis University Law Journal* 41:595.

Elster, J. 1990. When rationality fails. In *The limits of rationality*, ed. K. Cook and M. Levi, 19. Chicago: University of Chicago Press.

Federal Bureau of Investigation. 2001. *Uniform crime reports*. Washington, DC: Federal Bureau of Investigation.

Field, A. 2001. *Altruistically inclined? The behavioral sciences, evolutionary theory, and the origins of reciprocity*. Ann Arbor: University of Michigan Press.

Frank, J. 1930. *Law and the modern mind*. Magnolia, MA: Smith.

———. 1997. *Microeconomics and behavior*. 3rd ed. Columbus: McGraw-Hill/ Irwin.

Friedman, M. 1953. *Essays in positive economics*. Chicago: University of Chicago Press.

Ghiglieri, M. 1999. *The dark side of man: Tracing the origins of male violence*. Boulder, CO: Perseus.

Goldstein, J. 1968. Psychoanalysis and jurisprudence. *Yale Law Journal* 77:1053.

Gould, S. 1996. *Mismeasure of man*. New York: Norton.

Greenwood, R. 2002. Head injury for neurologists. *Journal of Neurology, Neurosurgery and Psychiatry* 73 (8): 16.

Hamer, D., and P. Copeland. 1998. *Living with our genes*. New York: Anchor.

Hanson, J., and D. Kysar. 1999a. Taking behavioralism seriously: Some evidence of market manipulation. *Harvard Law Review* 112:1420.

———. 1999b. Taking behavioralism seriously: Some evidence of market manipulation. *New York University Law Review* 74:630.

———. 1999c. Taking behavioralism seriously: Some evidence of market manipulation. *Roger Williams University Law Review* 112:1420.

Harlow, J. 1868. Recovery from the passage of an iron bar through the head. *Publications of the Massachusetts Medical Society* 2:327–47.

Harsanyi, J. 1986. Advances in understanding rational behavior. In *Rational choice*, ed. J. Elster, 82–83. New York: New York University Press.

Hurd, S. 1998. Symposium: The legal implications of psychology: Human behavior, behavioral economics, and the law. *Vanderbilt Law Review* 51:1497.

Jolls, C., C. Sunstein, and R. Thaler. 1998. A behavioral approach to law and economics. *Stanford Law Review* 50:1471.

Jones, O. 1997a. Evolutionary analysis in law: An introduction and application to child abuse. *North Carolina Law Review* 75:1117.

———. 1997b. Law and biology: Toward an integrated model of human behavior. *Journal of Contemporary Legal Issues* 8:167.

———. 1999a. Law, biology and emotions. *Jurimetrics* 39:283.

———. 1999b. Sex, culture, and the biology of rape: Toward explanation and prevention. *California Law Review* 87:827.

———. 2001a. The evolution of irrationality. *Jurimetrics* 41:289, 291.

———. 2001b. Time-shifted rationality and the law of law's leverage: Behavioral economics meet behavioral biology. *Northwestern University Law Review* 95:1141.

Kahneman, D., D. Knetsch, L. Jack, and R. Thaler. 1990. Experimental tests of the endowment effect and the Coase theorem. *Journal of Political Economy* 98:1325.

Kahneman, D., J. Knetsch, and R. Thaler. 1986. Fairness and the assumptions of economics. *Journal of Business* 59:285–300.

Kandel, E., and J. Schwartz. 1991. Brain and behavior. In *Principles of neural science*, ed. E. Kandel et al., 5–17. Columbus: McGraw-Hill/Appleton and Lange.

Katyal, N. 1997. Deterrence's difficulty. *Michigan Law Review* 95:2385.

Katz, J., J. Goldstein, and A. M. Dershowitz. 1967. *Psychoanalysis, psychiatry and law*. New York: Free Press.

Kimura, D. 2002. Sex differences in the brain. *Scientific American*, September, 158.

Klepper, S., and D. Nagin. 1989. The deterrent effect of perceived certainty and severity of punishment revisited. *Criminology* 27:721.

Korobkin, R. 1998. The status quo bias and contract default rules. *Cornell Law Review* 83:608.

———. 2000. Behavioral analysis and legal form: Rules vs. standards revisited. *Oregon Law Review* 79:23, 44.

Korobkin, R., and T. Ulen. 2000. Law and behavioral science: Removing the rationality assumption from law economics. *California Law Review* 88:1051, 1060.

Kuran, T., and C. Sunstein. 1999. Availability cascades and risk regulation. *Stanford Law Review* 51:683.

LaFave, W., and A. Scott, Jr. 1986. *Criminal law*. 2nd ed. St. Paul, MN: Westgroup.

Laibson, D., and R. Zeckhauser. 1998. Amos Tversky and the ascent of behavioral economics. *Journal of Risk and Uncertainty* 16:7.

Langevoort, D. 1996. Selling hope, selling risk: Some lessons for law from behavioral economics about stockbrokers and sophisticated customers. *California Law Review* 84:627.

————. 1998a. Behavioral theories of judgment and decision making in legal scholarship: A literature review. *Vanderbilt Law Review* 51:1499.

————. 1998b. Behavioral theories of judgment and decision making in legal scholarship: A literature review. *Vanderbilt Law Review* 51:1499, 1502.

Lear, J. 1998. *Open minded: Working out the logic of the soul*. Cambridge, MA: Harvard University Press.

Mercuro, N., and S. Medema. 1997. *Economics and the law: From Posner to postmodernism*. Princeton, NJ: Princeton University Press.

Miccio, K. 2002. Male violence—state silence: These and other tragedies of the 20th century. *Journal of Gender, Race and Justice* 5:339.

Mitchell, G. 2002a. Taking behavioralism too seriously? The unwarranted pessimism of the new behavioral analysis of law. *William and Mary Law Review* 42:1907.

————. 2002b. Why law and economics' perfect rationality should not be traded for behavioral law and economics' equal incompetence. *Georgetown Law Journal* 91:67.

Morse, S. 1998. Excusing and the new excuse defenses: A legal and conceptual review. *Crime and Justice* 23:329.

Nagin, D. 1998. Criminal deterrence research at the outset of the twenty-first century. *Crime and Justice* 23:1.

O'Neill, M. 2001. Stalking and the mark of Cain. *Harvard Journal of Law and Public Policy* 25:31.

Owen, J. 2001. The evolution of irrationality. *Jurimetrics* 41:289, 291.

Paternoster, R. 1989a. Absolute and restrictive deterrence in a panel of youth: Explaining the onset, persistence/desistance and frequency of delinquent offending. *Social Problems* 36:289.

————. 1989b. Decisions to participate in and desist from four types of common delinquency: Deterrence and the rational choice perspective. *Law and Society Review* 23:7.

Pillavin, I., R. Thorton, C. Gartner, and R. Matsueda. 1986. Crime, deterrence and rational choice. *American Sociological Review* 51:101.

Plato. 1892/2000. *Laws, book IX*. Trans. B. Jowett. Repr. Amherst, NY: Amazon Press.

Poe, E. 1998. Tell-tale heart. In *Edgar Allen Poe selected tales*, ed. V. Leer, 193. New York: Oxford University Press.

Posner, R. 1980. Optimal sentences for white-collar criminals. *American Criminal Law Review* 17:409–10.

———. 1998a. *Economic analysis of law*. 5th ed. New York: Aspen.

———. 1998b. Rational choice, behavioral economics, and the law. *Stanford Law Review* 50:1551.

Rabin, M. 1998. Psychology and economics. *Journal of Economic Literature* 36:11.

Rachlinksi, J. 2000. The "new" law and psychology: A reply to critics, skeptics, and cautious supporters. *Cornell Law Review* 85:739.

Rachlinski, J., and C. Farina. 2002. Cognitive psychology and optimal government design. *Cornell Law Review* 87:549, 555.

Raine, A. 2000. Interview in *New Scientist* 166 (13 May): 43–45.

Raine, A., T. Lencz, S. Bihrle, L. LaCasse, and P. Colletti. 2000. Reduced prefrontal gray matter volume and reduced automatic activity in antisocial personality disorder. *Archives of General Psychiatry* 57:119–27.

Raleigh, M., and M. McGuire. 1991. Biodirectional relationships between tryptophan and social behavior in vervet monkeys. In *Advances in experimental medicine*. Amsterdam: Kluwer.

———. 1994. Serotonin, aggression, and violence in vervet monkeys. In *The neurotransmitter revolution: Serotonin, social behavior and the law*. Carbondale: Southern Illinois University Press.

Redmount, R. 1973. Law as a psychological phenomenon. *American Journal of Jurisprudence* 18:80.

Rose, S. 1998. *Lifelines*. Oxford: Oxford University Press.

Rowe, D. 2002. *Biology and crime*. Los Angeles: Roxbury.

Rubenstein, A. 1998. *Modeling bounded rationality*. Cambridge, MA: MIT Press.

Schoenfeld, C. 1973. *Psychoanalysis and the law*. Springfield, IL: Thomas.

Schroeder, T. 1918. The psychologic study of judicial opinions. *California Law Review* 6:89.

Seidenfeld, M. 2002. Cognitive loafing, social conformity, and judicial review of agency rulemaking. *Cornell Law Review* 87:486, 492.

Sharfstein, S. 2002. Values, mental disorders and the DSMS. *New England Journal of Medicine* 347:1289–90.

Simon, H. 1955. A behavioral model of rational choice. *Quarterly Journal of Economics* 69:99.

———. 1957. *Models of man*. New York: Wiley.

———. 1972. Theories of bounded rationality. In *Decision and organization*, ed. C. McGuire and R. Radner, 161, 165–71. Amsterdam: North-Holland.

———. 1987. Rationality in psychology and economics. In *Rational choice: The contract between psychology and economics*, ed. R. Hogarth and M. Reder, 25. Chicago: University of Chicago Press.

———. 1997. *Models of bounded rationality*. Cambridge, MA: MIT Press.

Singer, R., and M. Gardner. 1989. *Crimes and punishment: Cases, materials and readings in criminal law*. Dayton, OH: Lexis.

Smith, A. 1869. *An inquiry into the nature and causes of the wealth of nations*. Ed. J. Rogers. London: Clarendon Press.

Stone, A. 1972. Psychoanalysis and jurisprudence: Revisited. In *Moral values and the superego concept in psychoanalysis*, ed. S. Post. New York: International Universities Press, Library of Social Sciences.

Strokstad, E. 2002. Violent effects of abuse tied to gene. *Science* 297:752.

Sunstein, C. 1997. Behavioral analysis of law. *University of Chicago Law Review* 64:1175.

———, ed. 2000. *Behavioral law and economics*. Cambridge: Cambridge University Press.

Ulen, T. 1989. Cognitive imperfections in the economic analysis of law. *Hamline Law Review* 12:385.

———. 1998. The growing pains of behavioral law and economics. *Vanderbilt Law Review* 51:1747.

Weber, M. 1978. *Economy and society*. Ed. G. Roth and C. Wittich. Berkeley: University of California Press.

Weisburd, D., E. Waring, and E. Chayet. 1995. Specific deterrence in a sample of offenders convicted of white-collar crimes. *Criminology* 33:587.

White, A. 1999. Victims rights, rule of law, and the threat to liberal jurisprudence. *Kentucky Law Journal* 87:357.

Williams, K., and R. Hawkins. 1989. The meaning of arrest for wife assault. *Criminology* 27:721.

Wilson, J., and R. Hernstein. 1985. *Crime and human nature*. New York: Simon and Schuster.

Woodard, C. 1994. Listening to the mockingbird. *Alabama Law Review* 45:563, 584.

Wrangham, R., and D. Peterson. 1996. *Demonic males: Apes and the origins of human violence*. Boston: Houghton Mifflin.

Wright, R. 1995. The biology of violence. *New Yorker*, March 13, 70.

# 13

## ANALYZING ILLICIT DRUG MARKETS WHEN DEALERS ACT WITH LIMITED RATIONALITY

*Jonathan Caulkins and Robert MacCoun*

The United States spends more than $40 billion per year seeking to control illicit drugs, yet drugs create about $100 billion per year in quantifiable social costs (Harwood, Fountain, and Livermore 1998). An important policy lever, indeed the dominant lever in the United States, is law enforcement, notably incarceration, directed primarily at suppliers.[1] Constraining supply ought to drive up prices, and higher prices are historically associated with lower levels of drug use and use-related consequences, even for "hard" drugs such as cocaine and heroin (Caulkins 2001; Crane, Rivolo, and Comfort 1997). It appears that contrary to once popular perceptions, even addicted individuals respond to higher prices by reducing consumption (Chaloupka and Pacula 2000).

How well have supply-control efforts worked? On the one hand, drugs are much more expensive than they would be if they were legal (Caulkins and Reuter 1998). On the other hand, since 1980 cocaine and heroin prices have fallen sharply despite rapidly escalating enforcement. Between 1980 and 2001, drug arrests tripled from 471,000 to 1,380,000. Incarceration for drug law violations grew more than tenfold from 40,000 to 450,000, as has the federal drug control budget (Caulkins and Chandler, forthcoming). Yet prices have fallen sharply. The exact amount is subject to debate; data on illicit drugs are tricky to interpret for various reasons (Manski, Pepper, and Petrie 2001). However, the Office of National Drug

The authors thank Lori Bowes, Susan Everingham, Baruch Fischhoff, James Kahan, Mark Kleiman, Greg Pogarsky, and Peter Reuter for many helpful comments. This material is based upon work supported in part by the National Institute of Justice and the Office of National Drug Control Policy under Grant #98-IJ-CX-0040.

Control Policy (2001) reports that inflation-adjusted cocaine and heroin prices declined between 1981 and 2000 by 75 percent and 90 percent, respectively.[2]

This chapter explores the idea that one factor contributing to this paradox of prices falling despite increasing enforcement may be the way that drug sellers perceive and respond to enforcement risks.[3]

## 13.1 THE RISKS AND PRICES MODEL

Conventionally, criminal justice sanctions are thought of as working in three ways: deterrence, incapacitation, and rehabilitation. Replacement renders the last two largely irrelevant for suppliers of black-market services with "low barriers to entry" (Kleiman 1997a). That is, as long as there is demand, there will be opportunities for newcomers to replace sellers who are incarcerated or rehabilitated. Special skills or access is needed to supply some black-market goods (for example, fissile material), but it is not difficult to get into the business of supplying illicit drugs. Furthermore, for the important illicit drugs, markets are "dense" enough that true shortages are rare. Occasionally, unexpected enforcement successes create temporary conditions of scarcity (Crane, Rivolo, and Comfort 1997), but usually reduced supply translates into higher prices, not physical unavailability.

The benefit of committing some crimes is essentially some fixed level. If the perceived risk exceeds that level, one hopes the offender refrains. The benefits of drug selling, however, depend on the sales price or, more accurately, the markup. That is, a given intensity of enforcement deters people from selling drugs at prices that provide less than a certain monetary reward. Increasing enforcement risk reduces the range of prices at which drug dealing will be pursued, but one should not expect increasing enforcement risk to eradicate the market altogether. Rather, it raises the price and reduces the quantity of drugs sold.

The economic framework capturing these ideas is the "risks and prices" framework introduced by Reuter and Kleiman (1986). It can be summarized in the following equation:

$$
\begin{array}{c}
\text{Economic} \\
\text{return} \\
\text{from} \\
\text{dealing}
\end{array}
=
\begin{array}{c}
\text{Revenue} \\
\text{from} \\
\text{selling} \\
\text{drugs}
\end{array}
-
\begin{array}{c}
\text{Cost of} \\
\text{obtaining} \\
\text{the drugs} \\
\text{sold}
\end{array}
-
\begin{array}{c}
\text{Conventional} \\
\text{business} \\
\text{costs}
\end{array}
-
\begin{array}{c}
\text{Nonmonetary} \\
\text{costs}
\end{array}
.
$$

The economic return from dealing is assumed to be constant (governed by dealers' next best opportunity), and conventional business costs are negligible (Caulkins et al. 1999). Hence, markups (the difference between sales revenue and the cost of obtaining the drugs sold) are driven primarily by the nonmonetary costs, notably the risks of enforcement and violence. So one expects increasing enforcement to drive up nonmonetary costs and, hence, prices.

Less formally, the risks and prices framework views enforcement as similar to a tax that increases dealers' cost of doing business. Because drug dealers operate for profit, they are presumed to pass those higher costs along to consumers in the form of higher prices. Drug dealers are viewed as having made rational choices both before and after any increase in enforcement. They considered the risks. They considered the rewards (primarily monetary). And they chose the bundle of risks and rewards associated with dealing over whatever the alternative was. Expanding enforcement makes the drug-selling bundle less attractive: to preserve an equilibrium in which the marginal individual is indifferent between choosing the risky bundle and the less risky default alternative, rewards must rise when risks do.

This theory makes perfect sense assuming that dealers perceive and respond to risks the way an economic rational actor would, but the question we raise here is whether rational actor models describe drug dealers' behavior well enough for deterrence to work as is implied by the risks and prices theory.

A common defense of rational actor models for licit firms is that any firm that is not optimizing would quickly be driven out of business. When they can't meet payroll, they shut down. However, the dominant economic costs of drug dealing are nonmonetary. Hence, as Boyum (1992) notes, essentially every drug-selling individual or group, even badly managed ones, have positive cash flow. That cash flow may not be sufficient to compensate the principal for the objective risk of injury or incarceration, but there is no looming bankruptcy to force such people to stop selling.[4]

Like economic models, psychological models assume that actors are capable of responding to incentives, but they do not assume that actors are necessarily maximizing expected net revenues, utility, or any other objective function. This chapter raises the possibility that for the decision to sell drugs, deviations from a naive notion of rationality may be large, whether because of bounded rationality or even "less rational" behavior. In particular, they may be large enough to help explain why cocaine and heroin prices fell despite increasing enforcement intensity.

We cannot prove this conjecture but simply make a case for plausibility by pointing out that the structure of the decision to sell drugs parallels structures that the literature reports lead to perverse behavior, either in controlled experiments or in naturalistic settings. The case has an a fortiori character in the following sense. We strive to show that even modest departures from the classical model of decision making could be sufficient to break the link between drug enforcement and drug prices. To the extent that in reality the decision to sell drugs is even more spontaneous, emotional, and idiosyncratic than we describe, then the argument holds with even greater force.

Consistent with this a fortiori character, we consider how the decision to deal might look to someone who tries to look carefully and quantitatively at data concerning the benefits and costs of selling. This discussion is pursued in two parts. First we consider someone who has accurate and representative data concerning the probabilities and consequences of various outcomes. Then we consider reasons why these "inputs" to the decision process may be biased. We also distinguish between three stages of a dealing career: the decision to sell for the first time or first few times, the decision to escalate to regular selling, and the decision to continue selling even after being sanctioned.

## 13.2 OTHER FACTORS

Failures in judgment may *help* explain the paradox without explaining it entirely. That is, there may be other contributing factors that do not necessarily involve judgmental failure. We briefly mention some of these next. They do not make considering judgmental issues irrelevant, however, because they do not seem sufficient in and of themselves to explain all of what happened with prices.

A standard explanation for falling prices is declining demand. However, Everingham and Rydell (1994) estimate that the weighted sum of the number of light and heavy cocaine users, weighting by their relative propensities to consume, was stable during the 1980s; and Knoll and Zuba's (2002) update shows only very modest declines during the 1990s. Heroin demand is harder to estimate but, if anything, may have been increasing (ONDCP, 1999). So falling demand cannot explain the price declines for cocaine and heroin.

Conversely, one could argue that prices should be driven by the intensity of enforcement rather than its total magnitude. That is, it is sanctioning per market participant, not total sanctioning, that governs price. So growing demand could dilute enforcement risks—what Kleiman (1993) refers to as "enforcement swamping." However, stable demand also undermines this explanation for cocaine. It could possibly have played a role in declining heroin prices, but Reuter (1991) has argued that both the level and the intensity of drug enforcement generally increased between 1980 and 1990.

Drug prices may have fallen for the same reason computer prices did. The producers may have become more efficient at their craft (Cave and Reuter 1988; Kleiman 1989). This story seems more plausible for cocaine (whose prime markets were relatively new in America in 1980) than heroin (which had already been in widespread use for a decade). Furthermore, substantial efficiency gains could not stem primarily from reducing conventional business costs, because they are such a small part of the cost structure of distributing drugs. Rather, they must address the dominant cost drivers, namely, compensation for the risks of violence and incarceration. Hence, one potentially important efficiency innovation would be employing sellers who demand little compensation for these risks. If the lower demands stemmed from sellers not evaluating risks objectively, then those efficiency gains are really part and parcel of the central focus of this chapter.

A more pessimistic explanation is that enforcement triggers innovation that improves efficiency. Kleiman (1989) suggests that tougher marijuana enforcement encouraged smugglers, dealers, and users to substitute into cocaine because it was easier to conceal. The customary challenge to arguments for perverse effects is that if suppliers were able to cut costs under stiffer enforcement, why wouldn't they have done so already under standard enforcement to improve profits? One can generate hypotheses (cf. Rasmussen and Benson 1994). For example, in an atomized market with poor information flow, change may not occur until an exogenous force makes the status quo untenable. In general, however, these stories are compelling only in particular situations.

There are several reasons why enforcement's marginal effect on prices may diminish with increasing enforcement intensity. Reuter (1983) argues that structural consequences of product illegality mean that even a modest level of enforcement compels dealers to operate inefficiently; increments beyond that modest level induce limited further changes. Also, Caulkins et al. (1997) find that extending sentences is less cost-effective than imposing shorter sentences. However, by themselves such factors help explain only why prices didn't increase very much, not why prices actually fell.

Finally, the risks and prices argument applies to long-run equilibrium prices, but it is not clear how long one has to wait for long-run considerations to dominate. Cocaine as a mass-market phenomenon was relatively new in the United States in 1980. Perhaps prices in 1980 were "too high" in the sense of being out of equilibrium, and dealers then were reaping "supernormal" profits. If so, then the mystery is not why prices fell but rather why prices didn't fall faster. The answer may simply be that information flows very imperfectly in illicit markets, so it takes time for the equilibrium to be restored.

These factors may have contributed to the decline in cocaine and heroin prices, but even in total they do not offer a satisfactory explanation for why enforcement has been so singularly ineffective at driving up prices. So we now explore another possible explanation, namely, that enforcement may not deter drug dealers in quite the way the risks and prices paradigm would suggest.

## 13.3 THE INITIAL DECISION TO SELL DRUGS

We wish first to consider how human frailties might interfere even with a serious attempt to weigh carefully the benefits and costs of selling drugs. To do so, it is helpful to use specific numbers. The decision model described is by no means the most sophisticated or inclusive one we could devise. We keep it simple for expositional purposes and trust the reader to see that the points made are robust with respect to such elaborations.

Most applications of the risks and prices framework have assumed the decision to deal can be modeled as if it were made on an expected value basis (e.g., Caulkins et al. 1997; Rydell and Everingham 1994). That is, the marginal dealer is perceived as someone for whom the expected value of the benefits of dealing equals the expected value of the costs, including the opportunity cost of not dealing.

Expected value calculations "add up" surprisingly well given the quality of the data. Reuter, MacCoun, and Murphy (1990, 102–5) estimated relevant parameters for retail cocaine sellers in Washington, D.C., in the late 1980s. Deducting from net revenues of $27,000 per year compensation for the risk of injury (7 percent annual risk valued at $30,000 per injury), death (1.4 percent death risk valued at $7,500 per 1 percent chance of death), and incarceration (22 percent risk of serving an average of 1.5 years valued at the forgone earnings of $27,000 per year) leaves $5,500 per year. These individuals sold for an average of sixteen hours per week, which works out to about $6.65 per hour, net of risk compensation. By way of comparison, those that held legitimate jobs reported median earnings of $7 per hour. Caulkins and Reuter (1998) conducted a similar exercise at the industry level for the late 1990s.

Expected value is not, however, necessarily the most plausible utility function for a host of reasons, including, but not limited to, risk aversion. Note that with expected value calculations the duration of selling contemplated is almost irrelevant. The expected benefit of selling for a year is essentially fifty-two times the expected benefit of selling for a week. Likewise with the expected costs. If the expected benefits of selling for a week exceed the expected costs, so too will the expected benefits of selling for a year exceed the associated expected cost.[5]

However, if the seller's utility function is more complicated, it can matter what time horizon is contemplated, and for several reasons the decision to sell for the first time is not likely to be perceived as a decision to sell for a year.

Some of these reasons are psychological. With respect to probability judgment, people often fail to understand that activities with small per-transaction risks can have very large cumulative risks (Doyle 1997). With respect to the evaluation of outcomes, people tend to frame choices narrowly and locally rather than broadly and globally (see Kahneman and Tversky 2000). And it is likely that drug dealing (like other crimes) disproportionately attracts those high in impulsivity and low in self-control (Gottfredson and Hirschi 1990), implying short time horizons.

There are also structural factors that discourage long-term planning. Drug dealers have no employment contracts or union rules prohibiting part-time work, nor minimum time commitments as in the military. Part-time selling or "moonlighting" as a drug seller is common (Reuter, MacCoun, and Murphy 1990), and the more natural unit of commitment to selling is to carry out one cycle of buying drugs from a supplier, dividing the packages into smaller units, and selling those smaller units to customers. Suppliers will not accept returned merchandise or offer money-back guarantees, so abandoning dealing midcycle is costly, but cycles are short, typically ranging from a few hours to a few days or a week.

Thus, the decision to sell for the first time is probably better described as deciding to execute one drug-selling cycle, not deciding to commit to sell for a longer period of time, such as a year. Indeed, Reuter, MacCoun, and Murphy (1990, 82) found that relatively few adolescents (in a sample that included quite a few drug dealers) thought they would sell drugs after they left school, even though dealing was actually more prevalent among older cohorts in their neighborhoods.

Figures 13.1a and 13.1b use decision trees to illustrate how the "commit for a year" and "commit for a cycle" perspectives differ. In each case the choice is to sell drugs or not, and in each case the result of choosing to sell drugs is uncertain, with outcomes ranging from very bad ("death") to very good ("successfully selling the drugs while incurring no sanction"). The specific payoffs and probabilities differ, however. One is much more likely to evade sanction while selling one cycle as opposed to one year (99.3 percent chance vs. only a 64.1 percent chance), but the payoff for doing so is smaller ($450 vs. $27,000).

Caulkins and MacCoun (2003) explain the choice of decision tree parameters. They are based on national data, but are similar to those of Reuter, MacCoun, and Murphy (1990). They are plausible and the best available, but far from unassailable. For example, monetizing the risk of death and incarceration is speculative. What is important for present purposes, however, is not the derivation of the specific input parameters, such as the annual risk of injury, but rather the relationship between the parameter values in the two trees (for example, how the risk of injury per week relates to the annual risk).

We assume a regular dealer executes sixty selling cycles per year. The relationship between the per-cycle and per-year probabilities of adverse outcomes is that

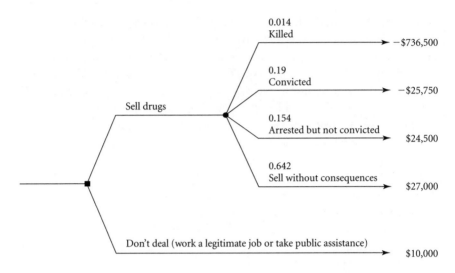

**Figure 13.1a** Tree for selling for one *year* with zero point being not making any money

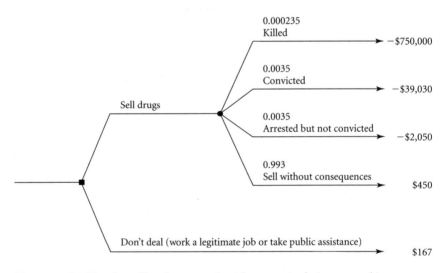

**Figure 13.1b** Tree for selling for one *cycle* with zero point being not making any money

implied by a "Bernoulli-process" or "coin-toss" model. For example, if the probability of being killed during one cycle is $p$, we assume the probability of being killed while attempting to execute sixty cycles is $1 - (1 - p)^{60}$. The Bernoulli model is not necessarily descriptively accurate, but we suppress issues such as discounting, diminishing returns, and skill increasing with experience in order to make the contrast between Figures 13.1a and 13.1b a function only of the time horizon.

We suspect that more people find the "deal" option appealing in Figure 13.1b, which takes a per-cycle perspective, than prefer the "deal" option in Figure 13.1a. Agreeing to sell drugs for a year is agreeing to a one-third chance of criminal sanction and a one-in-five chance of being incarcerated. A one-in-three chance of failure is sobering.

On the other hand, in Figure 13.1b there is a better than 99 percent chance of getting away without any adverse consequences.[6] One does not have to be Don Quixote to "give it a go" when the chance of suffering any adverse consequence is less than one in a hundred.

Indeed, some well-known psychological tendencies might lead individuals to choose to deal when looking at Figure 13.1b even if they would not do so in Figure 13.1a. In particular, prospect theory (Kahneman and Tversky 1979, 2000) suggests that people are risk averse with respect to gains and risk seeking with respect to losses, with gains and losses defined around some reference point. The reference point can depend on the framing of the decision; in Figures 13.1a and 13.1b we describe the reference point as the status quo if the individual neither sells drugs nor works in alternative employment. If one evaluates the choices in Figures 13.1a and 13.1b with utility functions of the form

$$U(x) = f(x) \qquad \text{for } x > 0$$
$$-f(-x) \quad \text{for } x < 0$$

for a variety of $f(x)$, selling is preferable when contemplating a single cycle, but not when contemplating a year-long commitment.[7]

Another aspect of prospect theory is that losses are perceived more poignantly than are gains, so there may be a "loss aversion multiplier" ($\lambda > 0$) such that

$$U(x) = f(x) \qquad \text{for } x > 0$$
$$-\lambda f(-x) \quad \text{for } x < 0.$$

When $\lambda = 2.25$ and $f(x) = x^{0.88}$ (typical values), selling is not the preferred option from a per-cycle or a per-year perspective, because losses are weighted so heavily.

But if one adopted more optimistic parameters (for example, profits per cycle were $650 instead of $450 or arrest and conviction probabilities were one-third as great), then the "deal" option becomes preferred under the per-cycle perspective but not the per-year perspective. Of course, if the parameters are optimistic enough (for example, a profit per cycle of $1,000), then the "deal" option becomes preferred with either framing. The point, though, is that a tendency to be risk averse with respect to gains and risk seeking with respect to losses can make the "deal" option relatively more appealing with the per-cycle perspective.

Another component of prospect theory, however, points in the opposite direction for an otherwise law-abiding person. There is evidence that people weigh outcomes not by their probabilities themselves but by a nonlinear function of those probabilities. In particular, "diminishing sensitivity" implies that the impact of a given change in probability diminishes as one moves away from either extreme of certainty (that is, for outcomes that occur with probability zero or one). Because deciding to deal for even one cycle moves the probability of arrest, incarceration, and death from zero to a positive number and these low probabilities get amplified by the decision-weighting function, this phenomenon would tend to discourage people from deciding to deal when considering the per-cycle perspective. Indeed, an actor applying prospect theory's nonlinear decision-weighting function would not choose to deal drugs over a no-risk baseline given any of the decision trees we examine in this chapter, even in cases where expected value theory predicts drug dealing.

How this nonlinear decision weighting plays out in practice is complicated by the fact that in reality the "don't deal" option involves some risk. For example, for a property criminal who has a baseline annual arrest risk of 0.2, the nonlinear decision weighting would tend to *reduce* rather than increase the weight placed on additional risk of arrest. Such arguments would seem less likely to apply to the incremental risk of death. Very few people have a baseline death risk of more than a few percent over their relevant planning horizon. However, it is perceptions that matter, and 62 percent of youth in one urban survey (Reuter, MacCoun, and Murphy 1990) believed that a dealer was "very likely" to be injured severely or killed.

Furthermore, Tversky and Kahneman (1992, 303) argue that this nonlinear function "is not well-behaved near the endpoints, and very small probabilities can be either greatly over-weighted or neglected altogether." Perhaps some people are repelled by the "per-cycle" framing (for example, because nonlinear weighting amplifies the death risk, and they never sell), but others view the probabilities of death as essentially zero and have high baseline risks of arrest, so they proceed. Because not everyone decides to sell drugs, we only need to understand why some people might not be deterred, not why none are deterred.

At any rate, the fundamental observation is that unlike expected value calculations, prospect theory suggests that the duration of dealing contemplated (one cycle or one year) can affect whether the "deal" or "don't deal" option seems more appealing. If the duration is one cycle and the tendency to be risk averse with respect to gains and risk seeking with respect to losses swamps the nonlinear weighting effect, then someone who would not agree to sell for a year might still decide to sell for a cycle.

## 13.4 THE DECISION TO CONTINUE SELLING DRUGS

The mechanism just described may help explain why some people decide to execute a drug-selling cycle once or, by extension, a few times, even if they would not commit initially to selling drugs for an entire year. Yet the phenomenon we seek to explain is not why some people dabble with dealing but why so many become regular dealers in the face of stiff enforcement. Is there something about having sold a moderate number of times that makes people more willing to commit to selling on an ongoing basis? In short, the answer is yes.

A key insight is that most people who execute a few selling cycles incur no sanction for that activity. With the parameters in Figure 13.1, fewer than four in a hundred people would experience any adverse outcome during their first month of regular selling (five cycles at a pace of sixty cycles per year). Nine out of ten sell for three months without incident.

Figure 13.1 assumed the decision makers assessed gains and losses relative to what they had before deciding to sell drugs, namely, nothing. Once someone has successfully sold drugs for a few cycles, the zero point might change to the outcome then being experienced, namely, selling drugs and not getting caught. That makes the per-year and per-cycle decision trees become those in Figures 13.2a and 13.2b.

This reframing, or shifting, of the zero point, could make dealing on an ongoing basis considerably more appealing relative to the alternative because "risk seeking is prevalent when people must choose between a sure loss and a substantial probability of a larger loss" (Tversky and Kahneman 1992). As Figure 13.2 shows, when selling successfully is the zero point, the decision to stop selling generates a guaranteed loss. If this tendency to be risk seeking with respect to losses is strong enough, then the reframing makes selling for a year more appealing than working for a year at another job, even if selling for a year would not be preferred

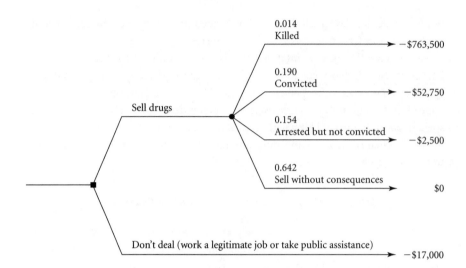

**Figure 13.2a** Tree for selling for one *year* with zero point being selling successfully

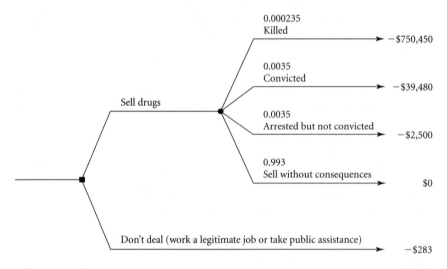

**Figure 13.2b** Tree for selling for one *cycle* with zero point being selling successfully

in Figure 13.1a. Indeed, that is the case with all of the simple utility functions mentioned previously.

## 13.5 JUDGMENTAL ERRORS AND BIASES

Even if dealers do integrate risk and outcome information in a completely rational manner, it is highly unlikely that they could accurately assemble the relevant *inputs* to the choice process. The most obvious problem is lack of relevant data. Drug policy analysts lack good estimates of the risks and rewards of drug selling, and there is little reason to believe individual citizens, through casual induction, could even approximate the relevant parameters. Furthermore, there are reasons why prospective dealers' estimation errors might not only be large but also be systematically biased in ways that undermine the ability of enforcement to deter dealing.

Some of these reasons are common to all risk-taking decisions. MacCoun (1993) suggests that drug users and sellers are likely to suffer from "optimism bias," the general tendency of people to have unrealistic optimism about their personal risk of experiencing negative events, even if they have an accurate sense of the risks incurred by people generally (see Svenson 1981; Weinstein 1980; Weinstein and Klein 1996).

Others are particular to the subpopulations prone to sell drugs. For example, there may be moments in the chaotic and cash-constrained life of a young adult when the desire for quick cash seems particularly urgent, whether the reasons are dramatic (for example, owing money to someone who will punish nonpayment with physical assault) or pedestrian (wanting to impress a date by spending lavishly).

Others are specific to the decision to sell drugs and bear elaboration. Perhaps the most obvious is that many drug sellers are active drug users. Street drugs tend to impair the same kind of frontal lobe "executive cognitive functions" that are necessary for rational deliberation and planning (Fishbein 2000).

More subtly, selling drugs involves a large number of actions, any one of which could go wrong from the dealer's perspective and lead to injury or arrest. The supplier might defraud the prospective seller. The seller might be robbed. Any of the seller's customers might turn out to be an informant. A sale might be observed by a police officer. In short, the failure modes are much more complex than those depicted in Figures 13.1 and 13.2, and people tend to ignore the full range of plausible causes of failure when assessing a course of action, which can lead to significant underestimation of the total probability of failure (Fischhoff, Slovic, and Lichtenstein 1978; Ofir 2000).

Also, aspects of the arrest and incarceration process tend to dilute casual observers' estimates of enforcement risks. There is no denying that arrests are often a dramatic, salient event. At the same time, arrests are fairly rare, and incarceration, by definition, reduces the visibility of the incarcerated. Moreover, arrests and incarceration are clustered because police target dealing organizations as well as individuals and they use information from arrestees to locate and arrest other dealers. Thus, for most people who have not been arrested, the fraction of drug-selling acquaintances who have been arrested will be smaller than the fraction of all sellers. If people estimate the probability of arrest based on the fraction of their friends who have been arrested, they will systematically underestimate their arrest risk.

Finally, the low risk per cycle creates opportunities for overgeneralization from early successes. Suppose that for whatever reason (per-cycle framing effects, intoxication, and so on) someone sells for a few cycles. As mentioned, the person probably would not suffer any adverse consequences. Given that experience, how should such "successful" sellers view the risks of continuing to sell?

In the spirit of Bayesian statistics, one's posterior probability estimate should combine one's prior estimate with the new information obtained by having sold without incident. Statistically, limited experience should provide limited confidence, but people are notoriously insensitive to sample size and tend to give much greater weight to salient personal experiences than to more abstract base-rate statistics (Kahneman and Tversky 1974). Perceptual deterrence studies on petty crimes such as marijuana smoking and shoplifting show that offenders who do not get arrested tend to revise downward their estimates of the probability of criminal sanctions (see Paternoster 1987). Similar "experiential effects" could occur for drug selling.

Moreover, several psychological and social mechanisms make selling the first time like "crossing the Rubicon." Psychologically, one has crossed a symbolic moral threshold; after someone has sold drugs once, the personal shame of selling a second time is greatly diminished (MacCoun 1993). There is likely to be a similarly diminishing marginal effect of the public stigma associated with being a drug seller, even if one is not arrested. Indeed, the labeling theory tradition in sociology and psychology would predict that this stigma will push the offender further from mainstream opportunities and relationships and further toward criminality.

## 13.6 THE DECISION TO CONTINUE SELLING DRUGS EVEN AFTER RECEIVING A SANCTION

Most people who sell full-time for a period of years will eventually get arrested. The risk per cycle is not very high, but the cumulative risk is substantial over hundreds of cycles. Even if enforcement is not very effective at preventing people from starting to sell drugs, why don't people stop selling when they get arrested? Empirically, recidivism is common, and at first blush that is hard to understand in an era of severe sanctions.

We suggest three classes of explanations. First, we are imagining people as choosing to sell drugs or seek income from some other source, such as a legitimate job. Conviction might reduce not only the perceived appeal of continuing to sell drugs but also the objective rewards of seeking legitimate employment (Freeman 1995). So too might extended periods of not working—because one was busy selling. Neither a blank space nor a criminal history looks good on an employment application.

Second, the average sanction following arrest for a drug law violation is quite severe, but the mode and median are not. Of those arrested for drug distribution, only about half are convicted.[8] So the modal and median sanction given arrest is nothing but the arrest itself. Of those convicted, 27 percent receive probation, 22 percent are sentenced to jail, and 51 percent are sentenced to prison (Maguire and Pastore 1998, 427). Furthermore, many sentencing statutes have enhanced sanctions for repeat offenders. Because the averages combine outcomes for first-time and subsequent convictions, the sanction following the first conviction is even less likely to involve incarceration. In some sense the criminal justice system currently gives drug sellers one or two relatively free bites of the apple (Caulkins and Heymann 2001).

Most drug sellers may initially fear the consequences of arrest. If they then experience no substantial consequence from an arrest, that arrest might lead them to revise down, not up, their assessment of overall enforcement risk. That is, even if they revised upward their estimate of the probability of arrest, they might revise downward their estimate of the severity of the consequences of arrest. This possibility is merely a conjecture, but there is evidence that the average person overestimates the probability of arrest and the severity of sanction (for a review, see MacCoun 1993). Kim et al. (1993) find that drug offenders who were given only probation upon (second) conviction had a very high propensity to recidivate. So arrest and conviction might lead the seller to see the criminal justice system as a paper tiger—until the conviction that sends the individual away for many years, at which point perceptions and deterrence are irrelevant.

Third, an adverse outcome after a string of successes might not change behavior as much as a naive behavioral model might suggest, for a variety of reasons— including status quo bias, confirmation bias, and people frequently showing a self-serving tendency to attribute their successes to skill and failures to bad luck (Zuckerman 1979)—so sellers may view the failures (arrests) as anomalous events. Finally, memories of incarceration could be less aversive than the actual experience. Due to both psychophysical adaptation and social coping, the early period of imprisonment is likely to be the most aversive (Petersilia 1990), but memories can be strongly influenced by a recency effect (Frederick and Loewenstein 1999).

## 13.7 DISCUSSION OF IMPLICATIONS FOR DETERRING OTHER TYPES OF ACTIVITIES

The research behind this chapter was motivated by a specific problem (explaining why drug enforcement has not been more effective at driving up drug prices), and we have tried to recognize and reflect on the contextual details of the decision to sell drugs or not. Nevertheless, an important part of our proposed answer revolves around the fundamental structure of the decision, not the specific context. Hence, if there is force to that conjecture in this context, it may also be relevant in other, parallel contexts.

The fundamental structure is the following. We observe that many people repeatedly engage in risky behaviors for which the probability of severe loss per "transaction" is modest but for which the cumulative probability of severe loss from ongoing participation is substantial. In particular, this occurs even when the cumulative risk, coupled with the magnitude of the loss, is so large that it is not easy to explain why so many people engage in the behavior so frequently. Activities with this structure include speeding, driving while intoxicated, using addictive drugs, engaging in unprotected risky sex, and participating in extreme sports.

In all these contexts, it is easy to imagine that the first time people undertake such an activity, they are only deciding to "take a chance just this once." They do not necessarily make a conscious decision to abandon their previous pattern of prudent behavior altogether and commit to participating in the risky activity for some number of years. That is, the decision to engage in the risky activity is done at first on a "per-transaction" basis.

There are a variety of reasons why someone who would not commit to a risky activity on an ongoing basis might do so for a transaction or two. We introduced one novel, structural explanation that stems from being risk averse with respect to gains and risk seeking with respect to losses relative to the status quo, which is the natural reference point (in the prospect theory sense of the word). There are also mathematically less interesting but probably more common reasons (intoxication, peer pressure, extreme moods or circumstances, and so on).

In all likelihood, an individual who decides to take the gamble on a half dozen or so occasions for whatever reasons will suffer no adverse consequences, because the probability of loss on any one transaction, or even any six or ten transactions, is not great. At this point various biases discussed previously may take effect (for example, the salience of the individual's own recent "success" relative to abstract statistics describing frequent failure and the tendency to move the reference point to be taking the gamble and winning as opposed to not gambling). A tendency to be risk seeking in the face of losses may then make the individual decide to persist in the activity.

Some of these other activities may also share another trait in common with drug selling, namely, a tendency for the punishment for being caught the first time to be less severe than originally anticipated. In such circumstances the "warnings" from being caught the first few times may lead people to reduce their estimate of the consequences of being caught by more than they increase their estimate of the likelihood of getting caught. That is certainly not relevant for the risk of contracting AIDS from unprotected sex. It may be relevant for various activities that are dismissed as youthful indiscretions and for various physical risks for which the most common punishment is much less severe than the one that is the real concern (for example, a significant but not life-threatening injury in an extreme sport).

## 13.8 CONCLUSIONS

### 13.8.1 The Limits of Deterrence

The risks and prices framework gives a clear and plausible argument for why increasing enforcement intensity should drive up drug prices. Historically, however, cocaine and heroin prices have fallen sharply over the last twenty years even though enforcement intensity has grown substantially.

The risks and prices image of individuals moving into and out of drug selling in a way that balances the expected return from selling and alternative activities makes strong assumptions about human decision making under uncertainty. In particular, it assumes that drug sellers perceive and estimate the relevant probabilities and consequences fairly accurately and that they make choices based on expected payoffs. Research on human decision making suggests that these conditions are not always, or perhaps not even often, satisfied in practice. If various cognitive biases and heuristics are prevalent among prospective and active drug sellers, they could help explain why enforcement has not been a more effective deterrent. If decisions to sell drugs are not just biased versions of careful calculations but are actually not well thought out at all, then our conclusion holds with even greater force.

We are not arguing that a psychologically more plausible model implies that enforcement causes prices to fall. Rather, the conjecture is that these factors so dilute the impact of enforcement on prices that other considerations (learning by doing, prices initially having been "too high," and so on) become more prominent. If the risks and prices model were accurate, one would have expected these to be trumped by increasing enforcement intensity. If, however, cognitive and perceptual limitations vitiate the price-raising effects of increased enforcement, then these otherwise second-order effects might become dominant.

So, all other things equal, increased enforcement might still be more likely to drive up price, but the linkage might be so weak that materially different outcomes can be observed. Also, enforcement imposes tangible costs on drug sellers in addition to nonmonetary costs—for example, having to post lookouts, refrain from selling to customers who look suspicious, and minimize their use of fixed locations and assets. Inasmuch as these costs are tangible, immediate, and/or monetary, they are less likely to be undervalued for the reasons discussed here.

Hence, we do not argue that drug enforcement has no value. But the previous discussion raises questions, particularly for the current highly punitive approaches to black-market suppliers operating in markets with low barriers to entry. On the other hand, recognizing that perceived risks can deviate from actuarial risks may suggest ways of making drug enforcement more effective than it has been. Raising the actuarial risks faced by drug sellers is expensive given the costs of prison to taxpayers (roughly twenty-five thousand dollars per cell-year) and the number of sellers (about a million Americans sold cocaine in the least twelve months). If there were ways to make perceived risk exceed actual risk in a sustained manner, that would be valuable. Kleiman (1997b, 1999, 2001) and Kennedy (1997) have offered suggestions along those lines, but there may be opportunities for other such innovations.

Some of the psychological and contextual factors considered are specific to drug selling, but many are not. So there may be exploitable parallels in the manipulation of risk perceptions for risky sex, speeding, and drug selling. Calls for taking a "public health" approach to preventing drug use are common, but there may be parallel opportunities for preventing drug selling (cf. Kleiman 1997c).

### 13.8.2 The Challenges of Policy Analysis in a World of Limited Rationality

Putting aside the details (and politics) of drug law enforcement, our analysis also highlights the challenges that psychologically realistic accounts of limited rationality pose for the professional policy analyst. Domains such as illicit drug policy are emotion laden and heavily ideological. From a normative perspective, economic analysis offers a powerful set of tools for conceptualizing social problems and thinking systematically about the consequences of pursuing various possible interventions. But the merits of economic policy analysis, as a prescriptive enterprise, hinge heavily on the validity of its description of actors and their likely responses to changes in their environment.

Current psychological models of limited rationality lack the rigor and clarity of economic models—they are more complex and less determinate. A particularly serious problem involves choice framing. For example, prospect theory provides a well-validated (and only slightly less parsimonious) formal model of choice, but it acknowledges in several ways the sensitivity of real-world choices to the way they are perceived. The value function is defined relative to a currently salient reference point, but reference points may change over time. The decision-weighting function describes responses to changes in perceived probabilities, but those probabilities are also psychologically volatile.

Until more rigorous and determinate models are available, analysts may need to proceed as we have here, using more traditional analyses as a starting point, then looking to psychology for likely counterarguments and, hopefully, insights into better policy choices. Presumably this approach will be most valuable in domains where behavior is least well approximated by traditional rational actor models. Decisions involving indeterminate risk of extreme adverse consequences, such as decisions to sell drugs, are one such example. Others might include long-range planning (such as social security and retirement policy), fairness (such as tax and entitlements policies), and paternalism (such as motorcycle helmet and consumer product regulation). Examining the implications of psychologically richer models of human judgment and decision making for welfare economics could be an important and interesting line of inquiry.

1. Many arrests and convictions are for drug possession, but most people in prison for drug law violations were involved in selling (e.g., because the possession charge was "possession with intent to distribute," they had a plea bargain down from a trafficking charge, or they were couriers transporting quantities beyond what is suitable for personal use). Possession purely for personal use is much less likely to lead to incarceration, particularly in prison (as opposed to jail). MacCoun (1993; MacCoun and Reuter 2001) examines deterrence against drug users using many of the same psychological principles considered here; that analysis also considers moral reasoning factors.

2. ONDCP presents two series. The declines cited here are for the second or "alternate" series, which we believe better accounts for variation in purity (see Caulkins 1994).

3. See Caulkins and MacCoun (2003) for a more detailed presentation of many of the arguments presented here.

4. That is, the zero long-run economic rents assumption underlying the risks and prices paradigm is a stronger assumption when applied to drug enterprises than it is when applied to more typical firms.

5. Whether benefits and costs literally scale proportionally depends on how one accounts for revenues when dealers are arrested or killed midway through a planned period of selling.

6. There are about 375,000 arrests for drug distribution each year and about 2 billion retail drug sales per year, suggesting an arrest risk per sale of about 1 in 5,000. Roughly half of arrests lead to conviction, so the conviction risk per sale is about 1 in 10,000. These figures are roughly comparable to the annual risk of dying in a car accident. A retail drug-selling cycle typically involves some thirty-five to forty sales, but the arrest and conviction risk per cycle are still below 1 percent.

7. Functions $f(x)$ for which this is true include $f(x) = \ln(x + 1)$, sqrt$(x)$, $1 - \exp(-xR)$ for $R$ less than about 30,000, and $x^{\beta}$ for $\beta$ less than about 0.9. Caulkins and MacCoun (2003) consider the newer, cumulative form of prospect theory (Tversky and Kahneman 1992) and find that it does not alter the conclusions presented here.

8. Drug sellers are also arrested for drug possession, but the conviction rate for possession arrests is even lower.

Boyum, D. 1992. Reflections on economic theory and drug enforcement. Ph.D. diss., Harvard University.

Caulkins, J. 1994. Developing price series for cocaine. MR-317-DPRC. Santa Monica, CA: Rand.

———. 2001. The relationship between prices and emergency department mentions for cocaine and heroin. *American Journal of Public Health* 91:1446–48.

Caulkins, J., and S. Chandler. Forthcoming. Long-run trends in incarceration of drug offenders in the US.

Caulkins, J., and P. Heymann. 2001. How should low-level drug dealers be punished? In *Drug addiction and drug policy: The struggle to control dependence*, ed. P. Heymann and W. Brownsberger, 206–38. Cambridge, MA: Harvard University Press.

Caulkins, J., B. Johnson, A. Taylor, and L. Taylor. 1999. What drug dealers tell us about their costs of doing business. *Journal of Drug Issues* 29:323–40.

Caulkins, J. P., and R. MacCoun. 2003. Limited rationality and the limits of supply reduction. *Journal of Drug Issues* 33:433–64.

Caulkins, J., and P. Reuter. 1998. What price data tell us about drug markets. *Journal of Drug Issues* 28:593–612.

Caulkins, J., C. Rydell, W. Schwabe, and J. Chiesa. 1997. *Mandatory minimum drug sentences: Throwing away the key or the taxpayers' money?* MR-827-DPRC. Santa Monica, CA: Rand.

Cave, J., and P. Reuter. 1988. *The interdictor's lot: A dynamic model of the market for drug smuggling services.* N-2632-USDP. Santa Monica, CA: Rand.

Chaloupka, F., and R. Pacula. 2000. Economics and anti-health behavior: The economic analysis of substance use and abuse. In *Reframing health behavior change with behavioral economics*, ed. W. Bickel and R. Vuchinich, 89–111. Hillsdale, NJ: Erlbaum.

Crane, B., A. Rivolo, and G. Comfort. 1997. *An empirical examination of counterdrug interdiction program effectiveness.* Alexandria, VA: Institute for Defense Analysis.

Doyle, J. 1997. Judging cumulative risk. *Journal of Applied Social Psychology* 276:500–524.

Everingham, S., and C. Rydell. 1994. *Modeling the demand for cocaine.* MR-332-ONDCP/A/DPRC. Santa Monica, CA: Rand.

Fischhoff, B., P. Slovic, and S. Lichtenstein. 1978. Fault trees: Sensitivity of estimated failure probabilities to problem representation. *Journal of Experimental Psychology: Human Perception and Performance* 42:330–44.

Fishbein, D. 2000. Neuropsychological function, drug abuse, and violence: A conceptual framework. *Criminal Justice and Behavior* 27:139–59.

Frederick, S., and G. Loewenstein. 1999. Hedonic adaptation. In *Well-being: The foundations of hedonic psychology*, ed. D. Kahneman, E. Diener, and N. Schwarz. New York: Sage.

Freeman, R. 1995. The labor market. In *Crime*, ed. J. Wilson and J. Petersilia. San Francisco: Institute for Contemporary Studies.

Gottfredson, M., and T. Hirschi. 1990. *A general theory of crime*. Stanford, CA: Stanford University Press.

Harwood, H., D. Fountain, and G. Livermore. 1998. *The economic costs of alcohol and drug abuse in the United States 1992*. NIH publication no. 98-4327. Bethesda, MD: National Institute on Drug Abuse.

Kahneman, D., and A. Tversky. 1974. Judgment under uncertainty: Heuristics and biases. *Science* 185:1124–31.

———. 1979. Prospect theory: An analysis of decision under risk. *Econometrica* 47:263–91.

———, eds. 2000. *Choices, values and frames*. New York: Cambridge University Press.

Kennedy, D. 1997. Pulling levers: Chronic offenders, high-crime settings, and a theory of prevention. *Valparaiso University Law Review* 31 (2): 449–83.

Kim, I., B. Benson, D. Rasmussen, and T. Zuehlke. 1993. An economic analysis of recidivism among drug offenders. *Southern Economic Journal* 60 (July): 169–83.

Kleiman, M. 1989. *Marijuana: Costs of abuse, costs of control*. New York: Greenwood Press.

———. 1993. Enforcement swamping: A positive-feedback mechanism in rates of illicit activity. *Mathematical and Computer Modeling* 17:65–75.

———. 1997a. The problem of replacement and the logic of drug law enforcement. *Drug Policy Analysis Bulletin* no. 3. http://www.fas.org/drugs/issue3 .htm#3.

———. 1997b. Coerced abstinence: A neo-paternalistic drug policy initiative. In *The new paternalism*, ed. J. Wilson and J. Petersilia, 182–219. Washington, DC: Brookings Institution Press.

———. 1997c. Reducing the prevalence of cocaine and heroin dealing among adolescents. *Valparaiso University Law Review* 31:551–61.

———. 1999. Getting deterrence right: Applying tipping models and behavioral economics to the problems of crime control. In *Perspectives on crime and justice: 1998–1999*. Washington, DC: National Institute of Justice.

———. 2001. Controlling drug use and crime among drug-involved offenders: Testing, sanctions and treatment. In *Drug addiction and drug policy*, ed. P. Heymann and W. Brownsberger, 168–92. Cambridge, MA: Harvard University Press.

Knoll, C., and D. Zuba. 2002. Modeling the U.S. cocaine epidemic: Dynamic trajectories of initiation and demand. Master's thesis, Department of Operations Research and Systems Theory, Vienna University of Technology.

MacCoun, R. 1993. Drugs and the law: A psychological analysis of drug prohibition. *Psychological Bulletin* 113:497–512.

MacCoun, R., and P. Reuter. 2001. *Drug war heresies: Learning from other vices, times, and places.* New York: Cambridge University Press.

Maguire, K., and A. Pastore. 1998. *Sourcebook of criminal justice statistics.* Washington, DC: U.S. Government Printing Office.

Manski, C., J. Pepper, and C. Petrie. 2001. *Informing America's policy on illegal drugs: What we don't know keeps hurting us.* Washington, DC: National Academy of Sciences.

Office of National Drug Control Policy (ONDCP). Various years. *The national drug control strategy.* Washington, DC: The White House.

———. 2001. *The price of illicit drugs: 1981 through the second quarter of 2000.* Washington, DC: The White House.

Ofir, C. 2000. Ease of recall vs. recalled evidence in judgment: Experts vs. laymen. *Organizational Behavior and Human Decision Processes* 81:28–42.

Paternoster, R. 1987. The deterrent effect of the perceived certainty and severity of punishment: A review of the evidence and issues. *Justice Quarterly* 4:173–217.

Petersilia, J. 1990. When probation becomes more dreaded than prison. *Federal Probation* 54:23–27.

Rasmussen, D., and B. Benson. 1994. *The economic anatomy of a drug war.* Lanham, MD: Rowman and Littlefield.

Reuter, P. 1983. *Disorganized crime: The economics of the visible hand.* Cambridge, MA: MIT Press.

———. 1991. On the consequences of toughness. In *The search for alternatives,* ed. M. Krauss and E. Lazear, 138–62. Stanford, CA: Hoover Institution Press.

Reuter, P., and M. Kleiman. 1986. Risks and prices: An economic analysis of drug enforcement. In *Crime and justice: An annual review of research, vol. 7,* ed. M. Tonry and N. Morris, 289–340. Chicago: University of Chicago Press.

Reuter, P., R. MacCoun, and P. Murphy. 1990. *Money from crime: A study of the economics of drug dealing in Washington, D.C.* Santa Monica, CA: Rand.

Rydell, C., and S. Everingham. 1994. *Controlling cocaine: Supply versus demand programs.* Santa Monica, CA: Rand.

Svenson, O. 1981. Are we all less risky and more skillful than our fellow drivers? *Acta Psychologica* 47:143–48.

Tversky, A., and D. Kahneman. 1992. Advances in prospect theory: Cumulative representation of uncertainty. *Journal of Risk and Uncertainty* 5:297–323.

Weinstein, N. 1980. Unrealistic optimism about future life events. *Journal of Personality and Social Psychology* 39:806–20.

Weinstein, N., and W. Klein. 1996. Unrealistic optimism: Present and future. *Journal of Social and Clinical Psychology* 15:1–8.

Zuckerman, M. 1979. Attribution of success and failure revisited: The motivational bias is alive and well in attribution theory. *Journal of Personality* 47: 245–87.

# 14 ON THE PSYCHOLOGY OF PUNISHMENT

*Cass R. Sunstein*

Judgments about punishment are typically a product of outrage about the underlying acts (Baron and Ritov 1993). Inside as well as outside of law, punitive acts
are undertaken when people have been wronged. When legislators penalize misconduct, they are typically responsive to the outrage of their constituents. And
when juries punish unlawful acts, either through sentencing or through punitive
damage awards, they are often motivated by outrage (Sunstein, Kahneman, and
Schkade 1998).

In this chapter I defend these points and use them to make two major claims
about the relationship between outrage and legal punishments. The first is that it
is extremely difficult to translate outrage into the terms that the legal system makes
relevant. Because of the difficulty of this task, the legal system risks incoherence in
the sense of erratic and unpredictable patterns. Precisely because of the unpredictability of particular awards, these patterns show a kind of irrationality. The second claim is that when people make one-shot judgments, as juries typically do,
they are likely to produce patterns that they themselves would repudiate. The result is another kind of incoherence—incoherence not in the sense of unpredictability but in the sense of patterns that are extremely hard to justify, and to that extent the patterns are irrational.

Taken together, these points help to support the Supreme Court's extraordinary

This chapter is a revised version of a paper presented at a conference, "The Law and Economics of Irrational Behavior," at George Mason University Law School on November 1, 2002. I am most grateful
to participants in the conference for their helpful reactions.

decision in *State Farm Mutual Insurance Co. v. Campbell* (123 S. Ct. 1513 (2002)), in which the Court attempted to discipline punitive awards by juries, in part by suggesting that the punitive award should ordinarily not be more than nine times higher than the compensatory award. The same concerns about unpredictability and incoherence clarify the argument for a number of legal institutions, including the United States Sentencing Commission and various bodies entrusted with producing workers' compensation awards.[1] The same points also raise questions about existing practice in many domains, including awards of punitive damages by juries, the system of civil penalties by administrative agencies, and compensatory awards in several areas of law, involving, for example, libel, intentional infliction of emotional distress, pain and suffering, and sexual harassment. I will urge that an understanding of the dynamics of outrage casts light on problems and potential reforms in a variety of areas of law.

In making these claims, I will draw on, and attempt to generalize, a series of experimental studies of punitive damage awards (Kahneman, Schkade, and Sunstein 1998; Schkade, Sunstein, and Kahneman 2000; Sunstein, Kahneman, and Schkade 1998, 2071; 2002; Sunstein, Schkade, and Kahneman 2000; Sunstein et al. 2002). The resulting work, much of it highly technical, seems to have broader implications for a range of issues in both law and politics. If punishment judgments are typically a function of outrage, the problems found in jury behavior might well have analogies in criminal sentencing and administrative fines. If outrage is difficult to translate into dollars or years, we might be able to understand seemingly unjustified disparities from both agencies and courts and also to see what might be done about those disparities. If people's outrage, when faced with an individual case, produces patterns that people cannot accept, we might be able to identify serious problems with both civil and criminal punishment. In investigating some of these issues, I draw throughout on empirical findings, but in a way that involves my own extrapolations, some of them admittedly speculative. One of my hopes is that the whole is larger than the sum of the parts. For purposes of the present discussion, I will speak broadly and in qualitative terms. Readers interested in numbers and statistical analysis might consult the papers from which I draw.

## 14.1 RETRIBUTION AND OUTRAGE: WHERE PUNISHMENT STARTS

Let us begin with the question of appropriate punishment. On the economic account the state's goal, when imposing penalties, is to ensure optimal deterrence (Landes and Posner 1993). To increase deterrence, the law might increase the severity of punishment or, instead, increase the likelihood of punishment. A government that lacks substantial enforcement resources might impose high penalties, thinking that it will produce the right deterrent signal in light of the fact that many people will escape punishment altogether. A government that has sufficient resources might impose a lower penalty but enforce the law against all or almost all violators.

## 14.1.1 Probability of Detection

In the context of punitive damages, all this leads to a simple theory: the major purpose of such damages is to make up for the shortfall in enforcement (Polinsky and Shavell 1998). If injured people are 100 percent likely to receive compensation, there is no need for punitive damages. If injured people are 50 percent likely to receive compensation, those who bring suit should receive a punitive award that is twice the amount of the compensatory award. The simple exercise in multiplication will ensure optimal deterrence. But do people actually want optimal deterrence? Do they accept or reject the economic theory of punishment?

Three simple experiments cast light on these questions (Sunstein, Schkade, and Kahneman 2000; Viscusi 2001). In the first, people were given cases of wrongdoing, arguably calling for punitive damages, and they were also provided with explicit information about the probability of detection. Different people saw the same case, with only one difference: varying probability of detection (by a factor of 20). People were asked about the amount of punitive damages that they would choose to award. The goal was to see if people would impose higher punishments when the probability of detection was low.

The basic finding was clear (Sunstein, Schkade, and Kahneman 2000). Varying the probability of detection had no effect on punitive awards. Even when people's attention was explicitly directed to the probability of detection, people were indifferent to it. In fact, there was a modest increase in awards when the probability of detection was high, though the difference was not statistically significant. Hence, people's decisions about appropriate punishment were largely unaffected by seeing a high or low probability of detection. The evident reason for this result is that people focus on the outrageousness of the defendant's actions, not on the likelihood that they will be detected.[2] Now it is possible that altering the likelihood of detection could increase or decrease outrage. If a corporate defendant was certain to be caught, but nonetheless dumped pollutants into drinking water, it might seem to be brazen and incorrigible, a kind of sadist, entirely deserving of serious punishment. And if a corporate defendant engaged in some act in an especially stealthy way, showing a real skill at evading the law, people might want to punish it especially severely, on the ground that stealth and skill are grounds for heightened outrage. But in either case, a high or low likelihood of detection is operating not in the economic fashion, as part of a deterrence calculus, but instead as a part of an inquiry into the egregiousness of the acts.

There was something indirect about the first experiment. It showed people the probability of detection, but it did not ask them to evaluate judgments that took probability into account. The second experiment filled that gap (Sunstein, Schkade, and Kahneman 2000). It asked people to evaluate judicial and executive decisions to reduce penalties when the probability of detection was high and to increase penalties when the probability of detection was low. People were asked to say whether they approved or disapproved of official decisions to vary the penalty with the probability of detection. Strikingly, strong majorities of respondents rejected judicial decisions to reduce penalties because of high probability of detection and also rejected executive decisions to increase penalties because of low probability of detection. In other words, people did not approve of an approach to punishment that would make the level of punishment vary with the probability of detection. What apparently concerned them was the extent of the wrongdoing and the right degree of moral outrage rather than optimal deterrence.

A third study was the most direct of all (Viscusi 2001). This study asked people to undertake a deterrence calculus, based squarely on the compensatory award and the probability of detection. All the necessary information was placed before jurors. The result was that people did not successfully perform the elementary calculations. Errors were pervasive. From this experiment, it is not entirely clear whether people erred because they were unable to do what they were asked or because they refused to do it, on the ground that it ran afoul of their moral convictions. But in either case, it is clear that people do not spontaneously think in terms of optimal deterrence, and indeed, they will fail to do so even if specifically requested to engage in that task.

The most general conclusion is that people are intuitive retributivists. Their moral intuitions are inconsistent with the economic theory of deterrence. Those intuitions are grounded in outrage.

### 14.1.2 Pointless Punishment?

Other studies support these findings. For example, Baron and Ritov (1993) studied people's judgments about penalties in tort cases involving harms resulting from the use of vaccines and birth control pills. In one case, subjects were told that the result of a higher penalty would be to make companies try harder to make safer products. In an adjacent case, subjects were told that the consequence of a higher penalty would be to make the company more likely to stop making the product, with the result that less safe products would be on the market. Most subjects, including a group of judges, gave the same penalties in both cases.

A related study found no reduction in penalty even when subjects were told that the amount of the penalty would have no effect on future behavior—because the penalty was secret, the company had insurance, and the company was about to go out of business (Baron and Ritov 1993). This study strongly suggests that punishment judgments are retributive in character, not tailored to consequentialist goals.

Another test of punishment judgments asked subjects, including both judges and legislators, to choose penalties for dumping hazardous waste (Baron, Gowda, and Kunreuther 1993). In one case, the penalty would make companies try harder to avoid waste. In another, the penalty would lead companies to cease making a beneficial product. Most people did not penalize companies differently in the two cases. Perhaps most striking, people preferred to require companies to clean up their own waste, even if the waste did not threaten anyone, instead of spending the same amount to clean up far more dangerous waste produced by another, now-defunct company. These studies indicate that when assessing punishment, people's judgments are rooted in outrage; they do not focus solely on social consequences, at least not in any simple way.

### 14.1.3 Cost-Benefit Analysis

A related test of punitive intuitions attempted to explore whether jurors would punish or reward companies that conducted a competent cost-benefit analysis before proceeding (Viscusi 2000). The test asked people to assess different scenarios involving safety precautions. In some of them, the company did no explicit cost-benefit analysis but simply concluded that the company "thought that there might be some risk from the current design but did not believe it would be significant." In other scenarios, companies engaged in cost-benefit analysis, with varying amounts used to value life (from $800,000 to $4 million). The key question is this: Will people reward or punish companies that have explicitly weighed costs against benefits?

The answer is that people do not react favorably to this kind of weighing (Viscusi 2000). A company that engages in cost-benefit balancing is very likely to face a punitive award, and the award that it faces is likely to be high. In fact, companies that place a high monetary value on human life are likely to face especially high awards. By contrast, people do not much punish companies that are willing to impose a risk on people (Tetlock 2000; Viscusi 2000).

There is a real oddity here: If the costs of precautions outweigh the benefits, then companies should not, under ordinary understandings, be deemed negligent at all. If jurors are punishing companies in such circumstances, it must be because of a kind of moral outrage that has little to do with either efficiency or law.[3] And why are awards especially high when companies place a high value on human life?

The most likely answer is that jurors have a difficult time in coming up with dollar amounts to punish misconduct and that a high value operates as an anchor, leading to high punitive judgments (Sunstein et al. 2002). This point directly bears on the problem of translating moral judgments into monetary terms, to which I will shortly turn.

Is it irrational to root punishment judgments in outrage? There is no simple answer. Many distinguished observers have argued in favor of retributive conceptions of punishment, and there is a clear connection between retribution and outrage (Galanter and Luban 1993; Hampton 1988; Owen 1989). To the extent that people are using a kind of "outrage heuristic," they cannot be shown to be making the sorts of errors to which ordinary heuristics sometimes lead them (Kahneman, Slovic, and Tversky 1982). On the other hand, it is possible to worry about the potentially harmful social consequences of a system of punishment that is rooted in outrage. I share that worry; but to those who believe in the rationality of outrage, or in retribution generally, the issue cannot be resolved without a complex normative argument. If we have irrationality here, it is not irrationality in any simple sense. But for the legal system, the use of outrage does lead to serious problems, as we shall now see.

## 14.2 THE TRANSLATION PROBLEM

Punitive judgments are rooted in outrage, but do people agree about the appropriate level of outrage? Imagine that diverse Americans are confronted with a case of clear wrongdoing. Should we expect a sharp divergence if they are asked to answer, on a bounded numerical scale, "How bad was the underlying conduct?" I now offer evidence suggesting that people's outrage is widely shared but that the consensus breaks down when people are asked to translate their outrage into dollars. The Supreme Court's evident concern about arbitrary punitive awards has a sound basis in the psychology of punishment, as we shall now see (*State Farm Mutual Insurance Co. v. Campbell*, 123 S. Ct. 1513 (2002)).

### 14.2.1 Shared Outrage

A series of studies of citizen judgments demonstrates that at least in some domains, people agree about the degree of outrage that appropriately fits social misconduct (Sunstein, Kahneman, and Schkade 1998). At least if people use a bounded scale (of, say, 0 to 6 or 0 to 8) with accompanying verbal descriptions ("not at all outrageous" for 0 and "extremely outrageous" for 6 or 8), a high degree of social agreement is likely. In personal injury cases, the judgment of any particular group of six is likely to provide a good prediction of the judgment of any other group of six. In this sense, a "moral judgment" jury is indeed able to serve as the conscience of the community.

In one study, people were asked to assess the outrageousness of the defendant's conduct on a bounded scale and separately to say how much the defendant should be punished on that scale. Two striking facts emerged. The first was an extraordinary degree of correlation between judgments of outrageousness and judgments about appropriate punishment—a finding that confirms the previous suggestion that punishment judgments are rooted in outrage (Sunstein, Kahneman, and Schkade 1998). The second was a high degree of regularity in both sets of judgments so that people tend to rank and rate diverse cases in essentially the same way. At least in a set of highly varying personal injury cases, people's punishment judgments do not significantly diverge, and the assessment of one jury is a good predictor of the assessment of another.

Indeed we can go further. Members of different demographic groups show considerable agreement about how to rank and rate personal injury cases (Sunstein, Kahneman, and Schkade 1998). Thousands of people were asked to rank and rate cases. Information was elicited about the demographic characteristics of all of those people. As a result, it is possible, with the help of the computer, to put individuals together, so as to assemble all-male juries, all-female juries, all-white juries, all–African American juries, all-poor juries, all-rich juries, all-educated juries, all–less educated juries, and so forth. When "statistical juries" were created in this way, there were no substantial disagreements, in terms of rating or ranking, within any group. In personal injury cases, people largely agree with one another.

Subsequent work has broadened this finding, showing that people agree on how to rank tax violations, environmental violations, and occupational safety and health violations (Sunstein 2001). From this evidence, it seems reasonable to hypothesize that in a wide range of domains, people will agree how to rank and rate cases. The moral norms within a heterogeneous culture are, to that extent, widely shared, and strikingly so. Now this does not mean that people will agree on how to rank cases from different categories (a point to which I will return). Nor does it mean that small groups will always agree on how to do the ranking. Nor does it mean that demographically diverse groups will agree about how to rate cases in contentious areas of the law—consider sexual harassment or racial discrimination. But the findings do suggest that within category, disagreement about both outrage and punishment is the exception, not the rule.

## 14.2.2 Erratic Dollar Awards

There is a consensus about the appropriate level of outrage. But even when that consensus exists, there is no consensus about appropriate punishment in terms of dollars. As we shall see, the reason for the lack of consensus lies in particular properties of the dollar scale. The scale of years in jail, used for criminal punishment, suffers from similar problems.

With respect to dollars, both individuals and jury-size groups are all over the map (Schkade, Kahneman, and Sunstein 2000; Sunstein, Kahneman, and Schkade 1998). Even when moral rankings are shared—as they generally are—dollar awards are extremely variable. A group that awards a "5" for defendant's misconduct might give a dollar award of $500,000 or $2 million or $10 million. A group that awards a "7" might award $1 million or $10 million or $100 million. In fact, there is so much noise, in the dollar awards, that differences cannot be connected with demographic characteristics. It is not as if one group—say, whites—give predictably different awards from another—say African Americans or Hispanics. We cannot show systematic differences between young and old, men and women, well educated and less well educated. The real problem is that dollar awards are quite unruly, from one individual to another and from one small group to another.

### 14.2.3 Why Are Awards Erratic?

These findings raise an obvious question: Why are erratic dollar awards found amid shared moral judgments? The best answer involves the problem of translating outrage into dollars. More particularly, the answer is that the effort to "map" moral judgments onto dollars is an exercise in "scaling without a modulus" (Kahneman, Schkade, and Sunstein 1998). In psychology, it is well known that serious problems will emerge when people are asked to engage in a rating exercise on a scale that is bounded at the bottom but not at the top and when they are not given a "modulus" by which to make sense of various points along the scale. For example, when people are asked to rate the brightness of lights or the loudness of noises, they will not be able to agree if no modulus is supplied and if the scale lacks an upper bound. But once a modulus is supplied, agreement is substantially improved. Or if the scale is given an upper bound and if verbal descriptions accompany some of the relevant points, people will come into accord with one another.

The upshot is that much of the observed variability with punitive damage awards—and in all likelihood with other damage awards too—does not come from differences in levels of outrage. It comes from variable and, inevitably, somewhat arbitrary, "moduli" selected by individual jurors and judges. If the legal system wants to reduce the problem of different treatment of the similarly situated, it would do well to begin by appreciating this aspect of the problem. The point applies to many legal problems, including criminal sentences; pain and suffering awards; administrative penalties; and damages for libel, sexual harassment, and intentional infliction of emotional distress. In these areas as well, those entrusted with the task of "mapping" lack a modulus with which to discipline their decisions. An empirical study of pain and suffering awards finds that no less than 40 percent of the variance cannot be explained by differences in case characteristics (Leebron 1989). A legal system that does not give guidance for "mapping" is bound to create similar problems in other areas. Indeed, the rise of guidelines for criminal sentencing can be understood as responsive, at least in part, to exactly this problem.

### 14.2.4 The Effects of Deliberation

The study just described involved individual judgments, aggregated, with the aid of the computer, so as to produce statistical jurors. A subsequent study tested the effects of deliberation on both punitive intentions and dollar judgments (Schkade, Kahneman, and Sunstein 2000). The study involved about three thousand jury-eligible citizens; its major purpose was to determine how individuals would be influenced by seeing and discussing the punitive intentions of others. To test the effects of deliberation on punitive intentions, people were asked to record their individual judgments privately, on a bounded scale, and then to join six-member groups to generate unanimous "punishment verdicts." Hence, subjects were asked to record, in advance of deliberation, a "punishment judgment" on a scale of 0 to 8, where 0 indicated that the defendant should not be punished at all and 8 indicated that the defendant should be punished extremely severely. After the individual judgments were recorded, jurors were asked to deliberate to a unanimous "punishment verdict."

Two findings are especially important. First, deliberation made the lower punishment ratings decrease, when compared to the median of predeliberation judgments of individuals, whereas deliberation made the higher punishments ratings increase, when compared to that same median. When the individual jurors favored little punishment, the group showed a "leniency shift," meaning a rating that was systematically lower than the median predeliberation rating of individual members. But when individual jurors favored strong punishment, the group as a whole produced a "severity shift," meaning a rating that was systematically higher than the median predeliberation rating of individual members. But when the median juror judgment was less than 4, the jury's verdict was below the median judgment of individuals (Schkade, Kahneman, and Sunstein 2000).

The second important finding is that dollar awards of groups were systematically higher than the median judgment of individual group members—so much so that in 27 percent of the cases, the dollar verdict was as high as, or higher than, that of the highest individual judgment, predeliberation. The basic result is that deliberation causes awards to increase, and it causes high awards to increase a great deal. The effect of deliberation, in increasing dollar awards, was most pronounced in the case of high awards. For example, the median individual judgment, in one case involving reckless misconduct, was $450,000, whereas the median jury judgment, in that same case, was $1 million. But awards shifted upward for low awards as well (Schkade, Kahneman, and Sunstein 2000).

These findings create many puzzles. For present purposes, the key point is that the translation problem is not cured by deliberating bodies. On the contrary, the problem of unpredictability is increased, not decreased, by the existence of deliberation. If we are seeking an explanation for the movements that are observed, the best answer lies in the phenomenon of group polarization (Brown 1990). This is the pervasive process by which group members end up in a more extreme position in line with the predeliberation tendencies of group members. It is predicted, according to group polarization, that high levels of outrage will be increased by deliberation and that low levels of outrage will be decreased by deliberation. Nor do such movements present any real puzzles for rationality. A central reason for group polarization involves the exchange of information within the group. In a group that favors a high punishment rating, group members will make many arguments in that direction and relatively few the other way. Speaking purely descriptively, the group's "argument pool" will be skewed in the direction of severity. Group members, listening to the various arguments, will naturally move in that direction.

In the context of actual dollar awards by juries, a particular finding deserves emphasis (Schkade, Kahneman, and Sunstein 2000, 1149–51). As I have noted, the highest awards increased by the largest amount, but all awards increased. This might appear to be a surprise. An understanding of group polarization might suggest that low awards would drop and high awards would be raised, with the difference pivoting around some neutral point, say, $60,000. But this is not what was observed. Why did dollar awards systematically increase? A possible explanation, consistent with group polarization, is that any positive median award suggests a predeliberation tendency to punish, and deliberation aggravates that tendency by increasing awards. But even if correct, this explanation seems insufficiently specific. The striking fact is that those arguing for higher awards seem to have an automatic "rhetorical advantage" over those arguing for lower awards. A subsequent study supported this finding, suggesting that given prevailing social norms, people find it much easier to defend higher awards against corporate defendants than the opposite (Schkade, Kahneman, and Sunstein 2000, 1161–62). If this is so, then processes of deliberation will naturally lead to jury awards that are systematically higher than the award of the median individual member in advance of deliberation.

My major goal here, however, is not to investigate the sources of movements in awards but to suggest that group deliberation does not solve the translation problem. Deliberating juries, no less than statistical juries, show a high degree of consensus about appropriate punishment (and hence outrage). Deliberating juries, even more than statistical juries, show a high degree of variability in terms of appropriate dollar awards.

## 14.3 OUTRAGE, PUNISHMENT, AND CONTEXT

I now turn to the largest puzzles of all. Thus far, it has seemed that people's moral judgments are quite stable. But that proposition was established only by looking at a set of personal injury cases. Here the relevant level of outrage is both predictable and coherent, in the sense that people's judgments are not much affected by whether they are seeing cases in isolation or simultaneously and in the context of other cases from the same category. But is this coherence maintained when people look at cases from different categories? Suppose, for example, that people are evaluating personal injury cases involving commercial fraud and that similar people are evaluating personal injury cases involving rape and murder. Would the judgments about personal injury cases remain stable across these various contexts? Are judgments about cases different, depending on whether those cases are seen in isolation or in the context of cases from other categories?

We do not have full answers to these questions, but suggestive evidence has started to emerge (Sunstein, Kahneman, and Schkade 2002). It appears that people agree on how to rank cases within categories and that their judgments about particular cases are not affected by seeing them in isolation or alongside other cases within the same categories (Sunstein, Kahneman, and Schkade 1998). It also appears that people have a kind of implicit ranking of categories themselves; they think that murder is worse than rape, that rape is worse than assault, and that assault is worse than libel. But when people are trying to rank cases from different categories, they have far more difficulty, in the sense that they are unsure exactly what to do. They are not certain, for example, whether a relatively bad income tax violation is worse than a relatively not-so-bad occupational safety and health violation (Sunstein 2001). This lack of certainty translates into a lack of consensus. People agree much more on how to rank cases within a category than how to rank cases across categories. Note that I am putting aside the evident difficulties in deciding what counts as a "category." It is easy to design experiments in which people will simply disagree about whether, for example, a comparatively serious tax violation is worse, or less bad, than a lawless act that harms the environment. Hence, the social norms that govern cross-category comparisons are not as widely shared as the social norms that govern within-category comparisons. It follows that judgments about outrage, and about appropriate punishment, are more variable across categories than within categories.

Perhaps this is not big news. A more striking finding is that people's judgments about cases, taken one at a time, are very different from their judgments about the same cases, taken in the context of a problem from another category (Sunstein, Kahneman, and Schkade 2002, 1173–78). For example, people were asked to assess a case involving a personal injury, on a bounded punishment scale and also on a dollar scale. People were also asked to assess a case involving financial injury, on a bounded punishment scale and also on a dollar scale. The financial injury involved relatively egregious misconduct, such as a violation of trust by a trustee, for the benefit of a favored client; the personal injuries were relatively less egregious, such as an injury caused to a driver when a steering system failed. The basic goal was to ask people to assess, in isolation but then in comparison, a financial injury case that would seem outrageous for its type and a personal injury case that would seem less outrageous for its type.

When each of the two cases is judged in isolation, the financial injury case receives a more severe punishment rating and a higher dollar award. But when the two cases are seen together, there is a significant judgment shift, in which people try to ensure that the financial award is not much higher, and for many respondents is lower, than the personal injury award. The upshot is that people's decisions about the two cases are very different, depending on whether they see the case alone or in the context of a case from another category (Sunstein, Kahneman, and Schkade 2002).

Exactly the same kind of shift was observed for judgments about two problems calling for government regulation and expenditures: research on bone marrow cancer among the elderly and protection of coral reefs by banning of cyanide fishing (Sunstein, Kahneman, and Schkade 2002, 1176–77). Looking at the two cases in isolation, people are willing to pay about the same to protect coral reefs and register more satisfaction, on a bounded scale, from doing that. But looking at the two cases together, people will be quite disturbed at this pattern and will want to pay significantly more to protect elderly people from cancer and will also register more satisfaction from doing that. Here, too, there is a significant shift in judgment.

In these findings, the translation problem is not the source of the difficulty. People's evaluations shift depending on whether they see cases in isolation or in the context of cases from other categories. What accounts for these shifts? Let me offer a preliminary account. When people see a case in isolation, they naturally normalize it by comparing it to a set of comparison cases that it readily calls up. If people are asked whether a German shepherd is big or small, they are likely to respond that it is big; if they are asked whether a Volkswagen Beetle is big or small, they are likely to respond that it is small. But people are well aware that a German shepherd is smaller than a Volkswagen Beetle. People answer as they do because a German shepherd is compared with dogs, whereas a Volkswagen Beetle is compared with cars. So far, so good; in these cases, everyone knows what everyone else means. We easily normalize judgments about size, and the normalization is mutually understood. Another example is John Stockton, who is about six feet tall, and hence a small basketball player. What happens, in ordinary communication, is innocuous. It does not breed error or confusion.

In the context of legally relevant moral judgments, something similar happens, but it is far from innocuous. When evaluating a case involving financial injury, people apparently normalize the defendant's conduct by comparing it with conduct in other cases from the same category. They do not easily or naturally compare that defendant's conduct with conduct from other categories. Because of the natural comparison set, people are likely to be quite outraged by the misconduct if it is far worse than what springs naturally to mind. The same kind of thing happens with the problem of bone marrow cancer among the elderly. People compare that problem with other similar problems and conclude that it is not so serious, within the category of health-related or cancer-related problems. The same is true with personal injury cases (normalized against other personal injury cases) and problems involving damage to coral reefs (normalized against other cases of ecological harm).

When a case from another category is introduced, this natural process of comparison is disrupted. Rather than compare a cancer case involving the elderly with other cancers or other human health risks, people see that it must be compared with ecological problems, which (in most people's view) have a lesser claim to public resources. Rather than compare a financial injury case to other cases of business misconduct, people now compare it to a personal injury case, which (in most people's view) involves more serious wrongdoing. As a result of the wider view screen, judgments shift, often dramatically. It follows that if people's informed judgments are taken to be the criterion, punitive damage awards are likely to be too high in financial injury cases and too low in personal injury cases. Some data support this suggestion (Karpoff and Lott 1999). Similar shifts could be produced with many other pairs of categories. For example, punitive damage awards involving libel might well be higher, in isolation, than punitive damage awards involving racial discrimination; but there is likely to be a reversal if the two cases are put together.

It is reasonable to hypothesize that the comparative situation may alter judgments in another way, by reducing the anchoring effects of compensatory damages on punitive awards. In the real world of punitive damages, unlike our experiment, compensatory awards are generally much larger in financial cases than in cases of physical injury.[4] As a consequence, a case of financial damage with a large compensatory anchor (say, $10 million) is expected to receive a higher punitive damage award than a case of physical injury with a smaller anchor (say, $500,000) when the two are judged in isolation. When cases of the two kinds are directly compared, many people will be more strongly influenced by the relative prominence of the harms than by the relative size of the anchors. Preliminary evidence supports this hypothesis, which suggests that two distinct mechanisms may cause punitive awards for financial cases to be higher in the current system than they would be if jurors were given a richer context: anchoring on high dollar numbers and masking of the low prominence of the category through the effect of normalization (Sunstein, Kahneman, and Schkade 1998).

I believe that this uncovers a serious problem with current practice in many domains of law. The problem is that when people assess cases in isolation, their view screen is usually narrow, indeed often limited to the category to which the case belongs, and that as a result, people produce a pattern of outcomes that makes no sense in their own light. In other words, the overall set of outcomes is one that people would not endorse if they were only to see it as a whole. Their considered judgments reflect the very pattern that they have produced because of a predictable feature of human cognition. The result is a form of incoherence.

We can find that incoherence not only in jury verdicts but also in administrative fines and in criminal sentencing, where no serious effort has been made to ensure that the overall pattern of outcomes makes the slightest sense (Sunstein, Kahneman, and Schkade 2002, 1189–96). Indeed, there is reason to believe that the pattern, in many domains, is quite senseless. And it may not be too much of a stretch to suggest that the same is true of reactions, some of the time, by both individuals and institutions. People are quite outraged about behavior that in a broader or different comparison set would outrage them little or not at all.

What should be done by way of legal reform? I cannot answer that question here. If outrage is the appropriate basis for punishment, then steps should be taken to ensure that outrage reflects a wide view screen rather than a narrow one, so as to reduce the risk that the legal system will produce punishment patterns that people reject. Perhaps the United States Sentencing Commission can be understood partly in this light; and perhaps an emphasis on incoherence suggests directions in which the commission might go in the future. To date, the commission has made little effort to ensure that penalties cohere across categories.

In the context of punitive damages, the claims I have made suggest that judges might take a stronger role in overseeing jury awards, in part to ensure that those awards cohere with what has been done in other areas of the law. The natural implication is that judges should decrease unjustifiably high awards and increase unjustifiably low ones; and indeed the Supreme Court's unexpectedly ambitious ruling in the *State Farm* case is a clear step in the direction of imposing discipline in jury awards. It might be tempting to reject this suggestion by emphasizing the populist credentials of the jury and by fearing judicial usurpation of the jury's functions. But the translation problem, and the risk of incoherence from one-shot judgments, demonstrates that this concern is misplaced, because the decisions of any particular jury do not produce community sentiment about what patterns of punishment make sense.

Outside the domain of punitive awards, it would make sense to try to systematize civil fines in general to ensure that the penalties imposed by, for example, the Environmental Protection Agency, fit well with the penalties imposed by, say, the Internal Revenue Service, the Fish and Wildlife Service, and the Occupational Safety and Health Administration. The discussion thus far suggests that any effort at systematization would present a daunting task. But incoherent judgments are extremely likely in the administrative arena as well, and at least it would be worthwhile to attempt to correct the most egregious anomalies.

## 14.4 CONCLUSION

In this chapter I have argued that punishment judgments are rooted in outrage and that people do not naturally think in terms of optimal deterrence. With respect to punishment, people are intuitive retributivists, and their outrage is, in an important respect, stable across individuals or at least small groups. But for purposes of operating a legal system, punishments that are based on outrage present two key problems. The first is that the legal system does not attempt to measure outrage directly but instead requires people to translate their moral opprobrium into the unbounded scale of dollars. This act of translation produces unpredictable and arbitrary awards. The second problem is that outrage is category specific. People's level of outrage is a function of comparison cases. When they confront a case in isolation, they evaluate it by comparing it not to the full universe of cases but to a natural set of similar cases. When cases from other categories are introduced, then people's outrage is shifted. The result is that when making decisions in isolation, people produce patterns of outcomes that they themselves repudiate once those decisions are seen together.

These findings raise a number of problems. Economically oriented observers reject the idea that punishment should be rooted in outrage, which could easily result in too much and too little deterrence. For those who believe that punishments should not be an outgrowth of outrage, it is wrong to base civil and criminal punishments on ordinary intuitions. In addition, the translation problem ensures a high degree of unexplained noise in punishments, resulting in unclear signals to possible defendants and also ensuring that similarly situated plaintiffs and defendants will not be treated similarly. And for those who would like to take outrage seriously and who believe in retributive goals, the existence of incoherence raises serious problems of its own, above all because it suggests that one-shot judgments by juries will not reflect the levels of outrage that would come from a wider view screen.

For many purposes, outrage is highly desirable from the social point of view. But when operationalized into legal terms, it tends to produce punishments that are both unpredictable and incoherent and to result in systems that fall far short of rationality. I do not suggest that an understanding of the psychology of punishment clearly supports any particular set of legal reforms. But such an understanding helps explain many problems with existing institutions and offers a number of clues about how those problems might be solved.

1. A helpful overview is in Fishback and Kantor (1999).
2. We will see further evidence of this in Section 14.2.
3. What underlies these judgments? I cannot fully answer that question here. But a careful look raises the possibility that people are outraged by any explicit decision to trade money for risks. They are generalizing from a set of moral principles that are generally sound, and even useful, but that work poorly in some cases. Consider the following moral principle: Do not knowingly cause a human death. People disapprove of companies that fail to improve safety when they are fully aware that deaths will result. But people do not disapprove of those who fail to improve safety while appearing not to know, for certain, that deaths will ensue. When people object to risky action taken after cost-benefit analysis, it seems to be partly because that very analysis puts the number of expected deaths squarely "on-screen." Companies that fail to do such analysis, but that are aware that a risk exists, do not make clear, to themselves or to jurors, that they caused deaths with full knowledge that this was what they were going to do. People disapprove, above all, of companies that cause death knowingly. I suggest, then, that a genuine heuristic is at work, one that imposes moral condemnation on those who knowingly engage in acts that will result in human deaths. The problem is that it is not always unacceptable to cause death knowingly, at least if the deaths are relatively few and an unintended by-product of generally desirable activity. If government allows new highways to be built, it will know that people will die on those highways; if government allows new power plants to be built, it will know that some people will die from the resulting pollution; if companies produce tobacco products, and if government does not ban those products, hundreds of thousands of people will die; the same is true for alcohol. Much of what is done, by both industry and government, is likely to result in one or more deaths. Of course, it would make sense in most or all of these domains to take extra steps to reduce risks. But that proposition does not support the implausible claim that we should disapprove, from the moral point of view, of any action taken when deaths are foreseeable.
4. Karpoff and Lott (1999) show mean awards of $14.8 million in fraud cases and $20.6 million in business negligence cases, but $6.2 million in product liability cases, $1.6 million in malpractice cases, and $991,000 in motor vehicle accident cases.

# REFERENCES

Baron, J., R. Gowda, and H. Kunreuther. 1993. Attitudes toward managing hazardous waste: What should be cleaned up and who should pay for it? *Risk Analysis* 13:183.

Baron, J., and I. Ritov. 1993. Intuitions about penalties and compensation in the context of tort law. *Journal of Risk and Uncertainty* 7:17.

Brown, R. 1990. *Social psychology*. 2nd ed. New York: Simon and Schuster.

Fishback, P., and S. Kantor. 1999. *A prelude to the welfare state: The origins of workers compensation*. Chicago: University of Chicago Press.

Galanter, M,. and D. Lubtan. 1993. Poetic justice. *American University Law Review* 42:1393.

Hampton, J. 1988. The retributive idea. In *Forgiveness and mercy*, ed. J. Hampton and J. Murphy, 111. Cambridge: Cambridge University Press.

Kahneman, D., D. Schkade, and C. Sunstein. 1998. Shared outrage and unpredictable awards. *Journal of Risk and Uncertainty* 16:47.

Kahneman, D., P. Slovic, and A. Tversky, eds. 1982. *Judgment under uncertainty: Heuristics and biases*. Cambridge: Cambridge University Press.

Karpoff, J., and J. Lott. 1999. On the determinants and importance of punitive damage awards. *Journal of Law and Economics* 42:527, 539.

Landes, W., and R. Posner. 1993. *The economic structure of tort law*. Cambridge, MA: Harvard University Press.

Leebron, D. 1989. Final moments: Damages for pain and suffering prior to death. *New York University Law Review* 64:246.

Owen, D. 1989. The moral foundations of punitive damages. *Alabama Law Review* 40:705.

Polinsky, A., and S. Shavell. 1998. Punitive damages: An economic analysis. *Harvard Law Review* 111:869, 870–76.

Schkade, D., C. Sunstein, and D. Kahneman. 2000. Deliberating about dollars: The severity shift. *Columbia Law Review* 100:1139.

Sunstein, C. 2001. Legal coherence and incoherence. Unpublished manuscript.

Sunstein, C., R. Hastie, J. Payne, D. Schkade, and W. Viscusi. 2002. *Punitive damages: How juries decide*. Chicago: University of Chicago Press.

Sunstein, C., D. Kahneman, and D. Schkade. 1998. Assessing punitive damages. *Yale Law Journal* 107:2071.

———. 2002. Predictably incoherent judgments. *Stanford Law Review* 54:1153.

Sunstein, C., D. Schkade, and D. Kahneman. 2000. Do people want optimal deterrence? *Journal of Legal Studies* 29:237.

Tetlock, P. 2000. *Copying with tradeoffs, in elements of reason: Cognition, choice, and the bounds of rationality.* Cambridge: Cambridge University Press.

Viscusi, W. 2000. Corporate risk analysis: A reckless act? *Stanford Law Review* 52:547.

———. 2001. The challenge of punitive damages mathematics. *Journal of Legal Studies* 30:313.

# 15 | SOME WELL-AGED WINES FOR THE "NEW NORMS" BOTTLES: IMPLICATIONS OF SOCIAL PSYCHOLOGY FOR LAW AND ECONOMICS

*Yuval Feldman and Robert MacCoun*

---

Following Ellickson's (1991) book, *Order Without Law*, law and economics scholars have taken the leading role in the legal scholarship of social norms. Dozens of papers have been written on a variety of topics, showing the importance of taking norms into account when studying the effect of legislation on people's behavior (Symposium 1996, 1998, 2000).[1] Given the amount of review papers and symposiums, which have analyzed the current and potential contribution of the new norm scholarship on legal scholarship, we will not attempt to conduct a full review of the various ideas developed by scholars working in this scholarship.

Scholars of the law and economics of norms (henceforth, "LEN scholars") have proposed various theoretical mechanisms. Bernstein (1992) has relied on the concept of reciprocity and reputation, citing it as the main reason that people engage in norms, hence arguing that norms could govern efficiently in close-knit groups or in situations in which reputations could be monitored (Axelrod 1984; Bernstein 1992). Following the reputation rationale, Posner (2000) has argued that norms allow actors to signal a low discount rate, enhancing their attractiveness as business partners. Moving to a less instrumental and materialistic account of norms, McAdams argues that people's primary motivation for following norms stems from their need for others' approval to maintain their self-esteem (Baumeister and Leary 1995; McAdams 1997). Cooter (2000) goes even further, arguing that, ultimately, self-enforcing mechanisms are ensured only when people internalize the norm.

The motivation for writing this chapter thus sprang from the fact that in many cases, this emerging literature is tackling questions very similar to those that have been discussed by social psychologists for the past seventy years (Meares 2002; Tushnet 1998). Most LEN scholars appear to recognize that social norms have been analyzed by other social scientists (especially by sociologists), but such analyses are rarely examined explicitly, and earlier noneconomic efforts are often dismissed in passing as primitive or at least prescientific. As a result, this new literature has almost completely ignored decades of systematic theory, experimentation, and field research on normative processes by social psychologists.[2] We find this omission to be especially puzzling when considering the great visibility of cognitive psychology in the economic analysis of law, an area known as behavioral law and economics (Kahneman and Tversky 1984; Tversky and Kahneman 1981).

Of course, historical precedence does not give one discipline sufficient justification to criticize or patronize models developed by other disciplines. We do not contend that economic psychological models should replace economic models—indeed, existing psychological accounts have important limitations—but that recent law and economics accounts of social norms would benefit from taking into account relevant principles and findings from social psychology. We will show that psychologists have already developed elaborate and empirically based answers for many of the questions that law and economics scholars are dealing with today.

Our discussion of relevant findings will be organized around three questions. First, *how* do norms operate? Some LEN scholars have recognized a few basic normative influence processes, but we will show that social psychology has detailed numerous normative mechanisms in detail. Second, *when* do norms operate? We will identify a number of robust generalizations about classes of situational and dispositional (individual-difference) factors that moderate the norm-behavior relationship.[3] Third, *how* does internalization occur? LEN scholars have treated this question as a complete enigma, but we will identify several well-understood processes by which actors internalize normative messages.

Of course, we acknowledge at the outset that LEN scholars are concerned with important questions that social psychologists have largely ignored. For example, can a rational choice model of human behavior explain why people would follow social norms (Mansbridge 1998; Sugden 1998)? Under what circumstances could norms govern efficiently, and when would state intervention be required? To what extent do norms mediate the effect of legislation on people's behavior? And what is the interaction between formal and informal enforcement of laws (MacCoun 1993; MacCoun and Reuter 2001; Robinson and Darley 1995; Tyler 1990)?

The general theme of the chapters in this volume is the law and economics of irrational behavior. Many norms do appear irrational, but many do not, and of course the mere fact that people often follow social norms is not irrational. Norms can provide a powerful coordination mechanism, and adherence to norms is often dictated by simple cost-benefit calculations. Our interest is less in the irrationality of normative content than in the frequent *arationality* of the normative influence process—the ways in which norms can shape behavior absent any explicit deliberative calculation by the actor (Tetlock 2002). We see little value in further debates about whether norm compliance is instrumental or not, or whether people are egoist or altruistic (Sunstein 1996); such debates often boil down to semantics. Instead, we will simply assert that it is often clarifying and parsimonious to label certain behavior as normatively influenced, and we will identify a number of robust generalizations about such influence. Our hope is to improve the predictive and explanatory power of current LEN models by drawing attention to well-understood phenomena they oversimplify or obscure.

Economists sometimes criticize psychology for treating all social phenomena as context dependent, producing a chaotic, falsifiable, and nonapplicable view of reality. Scott (2000, 1607–8) argues that "a preference-shaping analysis provides a richer explanation for commonly observed interactions among legal rules, norms, and values, but at a considerable price. The introduction of nonfalsifiable hypotheses produces an analysis that is rich in content but also speculative and context-dependent." Although we acknowledge that the picture we portray is considerably more complex than the pithy and stylized models of the LEN literature, a wealth of evidence from both controlled experiments and field studies shows that the complexity is a property of reality rather than a shortcoming of psychological analysis. The moderators and theoretical distinctions we will focus on are well established, testable, and fairly easy to recognize *ex ante*, even from a legal-policy perspective.[4] We fail to see how these concepts are any less falsifiable than the key factors in LEN accounts, and it is clear that social psychologists have gone far further than the LEN community in actually devising and conducting rigorous tests.

## 15.1 RECENT CRITICISM OF SOCIAL NORMS

Our argument for the failure of law and economics to recognize the important contribution that social psychology could make becomes even clearer and more appealing when one considers the criticism this new literature has received. We will show that, at least to some extent, the proposed modifications in the models we advocate could reduce some of the criticism of this new literature.

Mitchell argues that the new norms models offer an oversimplified account of the functioning of norms.[5] Elster stipulates that it is simply impossible to explain norms only on grounds of rationality.[6] Other scholars who discuss these trends in law and economics argue that current models of law and economics are either not backed by empirical research (Rachlinski 2000) or cannot be backed by future research because they are just not falsifiable.[7] Similarly, Griffith and Goldfarb (1991) discuss the methodological complexities required of incorporating norms into positive economic models. More recently, Rostain (2000) has criticized both the "law and behavioral and economics" and the "law and economic of social norms" for lacking the required empirical foundations.[8] More specifically, she recognizes that there is almost no field research backing the generalization made by game theorists regarding fairness and social norms.

The criticism of the current interests of law and economics in social norms is not limited only to social scientists, however. Legal scholars who are themselves identified with the new approaches to law and economics argue that some of the models used in this literature suffer from significant limitations.

Kahan (2002), discussing rational choice models of social norms, says,

> A theory can be said to be over determined when it furnishes a menu of opposing behavioral mechanisms that are sufficiently abundant to account for essentially any phenomena as well as its negation. In that circumstance, the theory does not generate "explanations" at all; it merely supplies a convenient set of story-telling templates that allow the theorist to rationalize ex post whatever existing facts she encounters and to justify whatever policy prescriptions she chooses ex ante. Rational choice theories are notoriously vulnerable to this defect.

McAdams (2001), himself a leading scholar in this tradition, focusing on models developed by Posner, argues that the signaling model is nonfalsifiable and gives no prediction as to when given norms will succeed and when they are likely to fail. A very similar critique is suggested by Rachlinski (2000, 1539): "[T]he law and social norms scholarship is merely a post hoc effort to accommodate some anomalous phenomena [that] might not generalize to new situations, making them useless to policy-makers." And even Ellickson (2001, 44), the founding father of the LEN approach, admits in his evaluation of the area that he co-created that "law and economic scholars while eager to draw on *others'* studies of norms governing smoking, dwelling, footbinding, and so on, themselves rarely take primary research on norms."

It is evident from the short review that we have conducted that the LEN approach has drawn a lot of fire from critics from different and sometimes even opposing directions. In our view the criticisms aren't unwarranted, but we think that the integration of informal social controls into law and economics scholarship is an important advance that should not be dismissed prematurely. Moreover, recent changes in law and economics have enabled the use of psychological literature in legal areas that were traditionally off-limits for psychology. Traditionally, psychology was employed both in legal practice and in legal theory to areas such as insanity defense, child custody, and jury research. Prior to the interest of law and economics scholars in psychology, there were limited interactions between psychological theories and substantive legal questions in such areas as contracts, property, and corporate law. In the last ten years, however, coinciding with the increasing interest in social norms and in behavioral decision making, reference to psychological theories is a common practice in more and more areas of legal research. Hence, the new LEN scholarship has created a "portal" for psychology to access legal doctrines to which it was never before considered relevant. Thus, in our view psychology should be seen as *complementary* to economics rather than a substitute for it.

We think that it is important for scholars from other disciplines to recognize the benefits of an economic treatment of social norms. Relative to psychology, we see three important advantages. First, economics has a metatheory about the conditions under which the norm will be efficient (Ellickson 1991). A legal policy maker that focuses on norms must take into account not only how norms operate but what the likely content of the norms will be and how the content of the norms might be affected by the legal regulation.

Second, the economic analysis has an explicit account of social equilibrium and stability in the development of norms (Sugden 1998). The focus on equilibrium is especially important for legal policy making, which is naturally interested in understanding not only how norms affect behavior in a given situation but also how the dynamics of change and stability are expressed in social forces over time.

Third, there is a clear connection between positive and normative economics. Although the connection is less important from the perspective of pure social science, when the interest is in using social science to enhance social welfare, the normative orientation of economics as well as the existence of a metatheory of efficiency enables it to advocate more forcefully for a legal policy making that will be sensitive to the functioning of social norms. Psychology, in contrast, largely lacks an explicit normative framework that is clearly linked to its descriptive theory and research.

We should also acknowledge two impediments to the incorporation of psychological theories into law and economics models: the fact that most theories in psychology are not formalized and the proliferation of jargon.

Because theories in psychology aren't always formalized, it can be hard for economists to take advantage of those theories.[9] Some argue, for example, that the relative success of the theories of Kahneman and Tversky in the context of decision making among economists is due to their theories being formalized in a way that makes the incorporation of their theories into economics relatively painless (Kahneman and Tversky 1984; MacCoun 2002b; Tversky and Kahneman 1981).

Social psychology is also plagued by a proliferation of jargon, which makes it difficult to understand what the "bottom line" is within psychological theories regarding policy questions. This fact is especially problematic given the general lack of mathematical formalization that could otherwise be used to avoid redundancy. Hence, sometimes-identical phenomena received different names by different scholars, creating needless complexities and uncertainties about the existence of bottom lines. Also frustrating for the LEN scholar is the fact that the term *norm* is rarely used. Instead, there is a bewildering array of related concepts—conformity pressure, group identification, public self, and so forth. We will attempt to clear much of this conceptual underbrush in the sections that follow.

## 15.2 HOW DO NORMS OPERATE?

Social psychology offers several overlapping taxonomies of social influence. Whereas a single comprehensive taxonomy might be preferred, attempts to integrate the taxonomies into a grand scheme have been more cumbersome than useful, losing much of their heuristic focus for explanation and prediction.[10] Table 15.1 presents a rough depiction of the overlapping categories of these taxonomies.

### 15.2.1 Compliance, Identification, and Internalization

The most well known model is that developed by Kelman (1958), which distinguishes compliance, identification, and internalization.[11] Kelman discusses "compliance," which focuses on the fear of societal reaction, also known as the "rule" perspective; "identification," which focuses on the maintenance of a relationship with the social source, also known as the "role" perspective; and "internalization," which focuses on the change in "values." In compliance the individual changes his or her opinion only externally simply to get rewarded or to avoid being punished. The change will hold only as long as the behavior is being scrutinized by the source of authority.

### 15.2.2 Sources of Social Power

French and Raven (1959) suggest a different classification that consists of five bases of social power. In other words, their focus was not on different processes of social influence but instead on the factors that give the influencing source its social power. The first two bases, reward and coercive power, seem to be central to the deterrence-compliance model. The next base of social power, reference power, seems to be essential to the identification model. The last two bases, expert power and legitimate power, seem to be most important in the internalization model.

The potential value that could emerge from a comparison of the psychological and the economic models is clear when we consider the functions of the

## TABLE 15.1

*Approximate overlap among five different social influence taxonomies*

| Kelman | Compliance | | Identification | Internalization[a] | | |
|---|---|---|---|---|---|---|
| French and Raven | Coercive power | Reward power | Reference power | Legitimate power | Expert Power | (Argument strength)[b] |
| Cialdini | Descriptive norms | | Injunctive norms | | | |
| SDS literature; ELM model[c] | Strength in numbers; strength of other peripheral persuasion cues | | | | Strength in arguments | |

NOTE: This table reflects our interpretation and not necessarily that of the authors of these taxonomies. The integration of Kelman with French and Raven was suggested by Shaver (1987).

[a] This is Shaver's placement and corresponds to Kelman's own treatment, but as noted later in the text, we believe that internalization can result from any social influence process via dissonance, self-perception, or constraint satisfaction mechanisms.

[b] French and Raven treated argument strength as a property of expert power, but research by Petty and Cacioppo, discussed in the text, suggests that these should be disentangled.

[c] SDS = social decision scheme; ELM = elaboration likelihood model.

identification versus the expressive model. According to McAdams's (2000a) expressive model of attitudinal change, local government-enacted law might be better equipped from an expressive perspective because local governments can better reveal the preferences of people in the relevant community. The identification model, focusing on the importance of the relationship between the source and its reference power, might suggest that the local government could do better from the expressive perspective because people's group identity may be stronger and more salient on the local level than on the state or federal levels.[12]

### 15.2.3 Descriptive and Injunctive Norms

Another very important distinction is Cialdini and colleagues' distinction between descriptive norms and injunctive norms (Cialdini, Reno, and Kallgren 1990; Kallgren, Reno, and Cialdini 2000). An injunctive norm is a person's perception of what other people think the person should be doing, whereas a descriptive norm is a person's perception of what other people are themselves doing (Troyer and Younts 1997). According to Cialdini's focus theory, the saliency of the normative source (descriptive-injunctive) will determine the influence of norms on behavior, a prediction he has supported in numerous field experiments involving littering of public spaces. Cialdini and colleagues argue that injunctive norms tend to have a more robust and enduring effect and tend to be more easily generalized to different situations (Cialdini, Bator, and Guadagno 1999).

LEN scholars are naturally aware of this distinction, and yet it does not really get any treatment by them. As Cooter puts it, "I use 'social norm' . . . to mean an effective consensus of obligation. By this definition, norm exists when almost every one in a community agrees that they *ought to* behave in a particular way in specific circumstances, and this agreement affects what people actually *do*." In other words, although Cooter recognizes the difference between "ought" (injunctive) and "do" (descriptive), he assumes that these two concepts are going to follow the same path and that, therefore, a distinction between them is not required (Cooter 1998, 587).

This distinction is also not maintained with regard to the expressive function of the law. According to Cooter (1998, 595),[13] enacting law increases the perceived number of people who obey the law (in Cialdini's terms, "descriptive"), leading to a shift in equilibrium.[14] According to Scott, law signals to people that the majority of people in the community believe in the content of the law and will disapprove of any violation (in Cialdini's terms, "injunctive").[15] Others treat the law as a focal point in a coordination game (McAdams 2000b), which implies a focus on descriptive norms: what people would do in specific circumstances rather than what they would approve.[16]

We would argue that greater notice should be given to this distinction, as norm management could backfire if it is neglected. For example, Cialdini argues that antilittering ads have an injunctive message ("don't litter") that is undermined by a covert descriptive message ("look at all this littering here").

Another example comes from Dishion, McCord, and Poulin (1999), who argue that interventions for juvenile delinquency inadvertently reinforce problem behavior. Several long-term studies show negative effects when high-risk kids meet with counselors about their problems. The leading hypothesis is that peer influence is stronger than any other message that they receive from those counselors. Thus, while the kids who were invited to the intervention group were exposed to injunctive norms disapproving criminal activity, they engaged in a process of "deviancy training."

A final example of this sort of backfiring is described in the work of Kahan (2001). Although Kahan's analysis of the decrease in the amount of trust in the tax system doesn't overtly discuss the differences between descriptive and injunctive norms, his policy conclusion does seem to target the tension between injunctive norm and descriptive norms:

> [I]f the state says that it will enforce it, it is basically signaling to other people that many other people evade the law. . . . When the IRS engages in dramatic gestures to make individuals aware that it is redoubling its efforts to catch and punish tax evaders, it also causes individuals to infer that more taxpayers than they thought are choosing to cheat. . . . This inference in turn triggers a reciprocal motive to evade, which dominates the greater material incentive to comply associated with the higher than expected penalty. (Kahan 2001, 342)

### 15.2.4 Diminishing Marginal Social Impact

Latane's social impact theory posits that the social influence of a set of sources is a power function of faction size, $i = sN^t$. The exponent $t$ is hypothesized to be smaller than 1, which means that there is marginally decreasing impact of the additional sources (Campbell and Fairey 1989; Latane 1981; Mullen 1983; Nowak, Szamrej, and Latane 1990; Tanford and Penrod 1984; Tindale et al. 1990). Across a wide variety of field studies involving different settings, samples, and behaviors, the exponent is usually in the .35 to .55 range. In the reverse direction, when the individual stands with others in the target, there is an inverse function of the strength, immediacy, and number of the others who share the positions ($I = SN^t$). Given that many LEN scholars assume that an increase in the number of people who follow the law affects others' willingness to do the same (Cooter 1997; Scott 2000), the social impact theory could be an important addition to the understanding of how much change could really be expected from an announcement of the law.[17]

The social impact of others is also influenced by their configuration in social, and sometimes physical, space. For example, dynamic cellular automata models of social influence processes show that under a variety of plausible assumptions, social influence processes will result in a "clustering" of opinion members across social space, a pattern long established empirically (Axelrod 1997; Epstein and Axtell 1996; Festinger, Schachter, and Back 1950; Latane 1996; Latane and L'Herrou 1996). If so, "interior" members will have less opportunity to "group" with members of out-groups than predicted by random sampling; only "border" members may end up in overlapping groups. Latane (1995) argues that social impact falls off as the inverse square of physical distance, but his results may be artifactual (Knowles 1999). A recent simulation shows that under certain conditions, geographic proximity is not important for the emergence of cooperation among agents (Axelrod, Riolo, and Cohen 2002).

The models share a simplifying assumption that sources can be cleanly assigned to one of a small number of discrete opinion groups—usually two. In real life, of course, opinions vary in multidimensional space, though social categorization research suggests that perceivers do strive to "lump" sources together for cognitive simplicity. Wilder (1990) found that a faction's influence exceeded what might be predicted from its size and position when efforts were made to individuate or distinguish faction members. But this finding may be the exception that proves the rule, in the sense that redundancy—in an information-theoretic sense—may help to explain diminishing marginal sensitivity to sources.

## 15.2.5 Strength in Arguments Versus Strength in Numbers

Latane's work on social impact theory, like that of Cialdini on norms, has drawn heavily on data from information that perceivers glean from casual interaction with others, mere observation of others, or observation of the traces of others' behaviors. The social decision scheme literature has systematically examined faction-size effects in the context of deliberating experimental groups, where faction size, discussion content, and task factors can be disentangled using experimental manipulation (Strasser, Kerr, and Davis 1989). This literature has tested the relative fit of a wide variety of "social decision schemes"—roughly, transition probability matrices mapping the relationship between the distribution of initial individual opinions and either postdiscussion individual opinions or postdiscussion group decisions. Across dozens of experiments, two classes of decision schemes appear to describe the bulk of group processes.

One class involves "strength in numbers" schemes in which majority factions have drawing power disproportionately larger than would be expected from their relative size alone. When such schemes are operative, groups appear to be operating under a "majority-rule" scheme, even when they are assigned a unanimity rule (at one extreme) or given no explicit instructions to reach consensus (at the other).

A second class of schemes is asymmetrical, such that certain opinions or positions hold disproportionate drawing power, even when initially endorsed by only a minority of those present. The most extreme case is the "truth-wins" scheme, in which such a position will prevail if at least one person present endorses it.

A simple majority scheme or slight variants have been shown to do a good job of summarizing group judgments under a very broad array of decision tasks, settings, and populations, particularly in judgmental situations in which there is no normative algorithm for defining or deriving a correct answer (for example, poetry, art, faculty hires). But when there is a shared scheme for identifying correct option (for example, math, fastest runner), small factions with strong arguments are much more likely to prevail (Wood 1994). But even here, the extreme "truth wins" model does a poor job of describing actual group behavior. At best, "truth-supported wins"—that is, the member finding the solution needs at least some initial social support or the group will often fail to adopt the correct solution.[18] Mac-Coun and Kerr (1988) have demonstrated that the reasonable doubt standard promotes such an asymmetric influence function in criminal juries; when mock criminal juries are assigned a preponderance of evidence instruction, influence becomes symmetrical. Kerr, MacCoun, and their colleagues have shown that because of such influence processes, group deliberation can either attenuate or amplify biases in individual judgment, depending on whether there is a shared conceptual scheme by which a minority can call attention to the bias (Kerr, MacCoun, and Kramer 1996; MacCoun 2002a).

### 15.2.6 Norms as Biased Samples

A challenge for the application of a norms analysis is that norms are formed from samples of social information, and those samples arise through processes that are statistically biased. Except perhaps in the (increasingly common) influence of publicized polling results, actors usually encounter normative information in a piecemeal fashion. The geographic features of social space, noted previously, make it likely that physically and temporally proximate information will have a disproportionate weight in normative judgment (Latane 1981).

Ceteris paribus, the analyst might cope with this fact through a simple scheme of distance weighting, as in Latane's hypothesis that impact falls off via an inverse square rule (Latane 1981). But this adjustment will often be inadequate because normative information sampling is an active, selective perceptual process. Sociologists have long recognized that actors are disproportionately influenced by "reference groups"—loosely, groups of special salience or interest to the perceiver. Social psychologists have identified various forms of selection.

One dimension is *horizontal*—we can make comparisons across individuals (me versus her) or across groups (us versus them). For example, actors tend to experience greater anger, and are more likely to engage in political action, when they perceive that their group is treated unjustly than when they perceive personal injustice (Tyler et al. 1997). And as discussed later, people apply different evaluative standards to the outcomes and actions of "in-group" versus "out-group" members (Messe, Hymes, and MacCoun 1986; Tyler 1990).

A second dimension is *vertical*—psychologists distinguish upward, lateral, and downward comparisons, referring, respectively, to those superior, comparable, or inferior to us on the dimension of interest (Festinger 1954; Goethals and Klein 2000). A vast number of experiments and field studies have shown that vertical comparisons influence important judgments and behaviors, but the literature is still inconclusive about the underlying principles determining the direction of vertical choice. People tend to look upward when their goal is to improve their own abilities or to verify the correctness of their beliefs. People tend to compare themselves with similar individuals when their goal is to appraise their own abilities, preferences, and outcomes. Evidence is mixed for the proposition that people look downward—to those less able or less fortunate—when their goal is promote their own self-esteem (Forsyth 1959; Suls, Martin, and Wheeler 2002).

Most LEN scholars that discuss norms focus on the concept of consensus. In fact, in many business contexts, different groups might hold different views about the nature of the norm.[19] When those views are in conflict, it is very important to be able to predict which the chosen reference group will be in every situation. By knowing which the likely reference group is, one could both predict better the behavior of the individual and target any policy effort on this specific target group. Along those lines Feldman (2003) has demonstrated, using experimental techniques, that employees were giving the approval of their previous employer different weight in different contexts when deciding whether or not to share information. In most cases employees gave less weight to the likelihood of approval by their previous employer while giving much greater weight to their current employer's approval. However, in some cases (when they were told that the confidential information was downloaded while they were working for their previous employer), the approval of their previous employer was significant, whereas the approval of their current employer was not. Given the differing interests of the previous and the current employer with regard to the use of confidential knowhow sharing, the importance of the choice of reference group carries policy implications for the optimization of nonformal enforcement. This finding demonstrates our argument that the norm-management literature might be better off taking a more detailed view of the most likely reference group instead of defining norms only when they are shared by the consensus among the general community.

### 15.2.7 True and Pseudo "False Consensus"

In many areas of law and economics scholarship it has become almost mainstream to draw on the psychological literature on heuristics and biases in discussions of risk assessment and the evaluation of economic goods. Curiously, the new norms literature has largely ignored such work; people are expected to accurately estimate public views and to be as sensitive to changes in consensus as they would to changes in the price of an economic good.[20] But it is likely that a variety of cognitive and motivational factors produce systematic distortions in consensus judgments. For example, Ross, Greene, and House (1977) proposed that perceivers are susceptible to a "false consensus bias" such that people who favor position A estimate more support for that position than people who don't favor A (Krueger 2000).

That such a bias might produce a normative failure follows from economic models of the expressive function of the law (for example, Cooter 1998; McAdams 2000b). According to these models, one of the basic mechanisms that leads people to follow the law is a perceived consensus in one's relevant community. Nonetheless, according to the false consensus effect, sometimes the causal relationship will go the other way around. Thus, people who are unable to really know what most people in their community think about a certain law might infer what most people do from what they themselves would do in a similar situation. According to this bias, the ability of the law to use consensus as a tool for social change might be slowed by people's inability to realize that their behavior is inconsistent with the changing consensus.

Along those lines, Feldman (2003) has shown that employees who were very likely to share confidential information estimated that 95 percent of employees in Silicon Valley would have done that the same.[21] However those who were unlikely to share information gave a much lower estimate of approximately 40 percent.[22] Thus, whereas recent LEN expressive law theorists claim that people will correct their views about what they should and should not do based on a perceived consensus, in reality they might correct their views of the consensus based on their own beliefs (Cooter 1998). Thus, it might take people a much longer time to realize that their behavior is inconsistent with that of the consensus. The existence of multiple equilibria (when one's own dominant strategy is contingent upon the behavior of others) might suggest that such biases could be hard to fix by relying solely on market evolution.

It is important to recognize that the false consensus effect has received considerable criticism. The most vocal opponent of this view is Dawes (Dawes and Mulford 1996), who argues that the effect may be a rational Bayesian calculation based on one's own knowledge (that is, a sample of $n = 1$).

On the normative level, it may not matter whether the false consensus effect is a rational heuristic or a bias. From a policy perspective, there can be a normative failure if people's ability to update their beliefs about the consensus is not independent of the views of the individual. Even if we accept Dawes's arguments, people with undesirable views will think that more people in society hold undesirable views than hold desirable views.[23] This fact in itself is a normative failure.[24]

The second objection to Dawes's critique is more positive, focusing on the work of Krueger (2000) regarding the "truly false consensus effect". They show that the consensus bias is actually much larger than assumed in a Bayesian calculation in which information is received about the first chip. Moreover, Dunning and Cohen (1992) found no difference in the consensus judgments of people who did or did not receive true consensus information.[25] (This, even though they were specifically told that the target student was in the 50th percentile. This shows strong egocentric bias even when information about the consensus was available.

## 15.2.8 Pluralistic Ignorance

A related—and seemingly contradictory—perceptual principle is pluralistic ignorance, a concept at least one LEN scholar has recently deployed (Kuran 1995).[26] According to Prentice and Miller (1996, 244), the state is "characterized by the belief that one's private attitudes and judgments are different from those of others, even though one's public behavior is identical." It tends to occur in situations that preclude the expression of private views (for example, strangers on sidewalks) or that encourage the active concealment or even misrepresentation of public views (for example, discussions of politically sensitive or emotionally charged topics). In such settings, "people's tendency to rely on the public behavior of others to identify the norm leads them astray. . . . Their own behavior may be driven by social pressure, but they assume that other people's identical behavior is an accurate reflection of their true feelings" (244). The discovery that one has misread social consensus can lead to sudden and dramatic "nonlinear" shifts in public support.[27]

On the surface, the pluralistic ignorance phenomenon seems to directly contradict the false consensus phenomenon, but they can be reconciled. Prentice and Miller (1996, 253) note that "[pluralistic ignorance] is most appropriately operationalized as a mean difference between the actual group norm and the perceived group norm . . . false consensus, on the other hand, is most appropriately operationalized as a positive correlation between ratings of the self and ratings of others." They cite at least two studies where both patterns occurred together.

### 15.2.9 Relationship-Specific Norms

A further complication is that both the content of norms and the implicit rules of social influence (whose inputs matter, and when) vary as a function of the interaction of setting and relationship.

The importance of relationship is not unanticipated for LEN scholars studying social norms. One of the basic distinctions in the functioning of norms in game theory literature about norms is related to the difference between repeated players and one-shot players[28] and its implications for reputation, reciprocity, and so on.[29] Leading LEN scholars, such as Ellickson (1991) and Bernstein (2001), cite reciprocity and tit for tat as key factors in the maintenance of social norms among repeated players in a specific community.

However, psychologists have offered a richer and more nuanced account of the influence of relationships. In the early 1970s, Foa (1971) showed that the implicit rules of social exchange varied depending on the nature of the social resource being exchanged—for example, money versus love versus esteem or prestige. Later, Clark and Mills (1993) distinguished exchange relationships from communal relationships. In essence, exchange relationships are those in which participants "keep score," a tendency that is corrosive to the long-term stability of more communal, nurturance-based relationships. Clark, Mills, and Powell (1986) have shown that the tendency to reciprocate significantly varied with the nature of the relationship.[30] When the participants were manipulated to think that the other partner desired an exchange relationship, they were willing to help only when there was an opportunity for reciprocity.[31] However, when the participants were manipulated to think that the other partner desired a communal relationship, they were equally willing to help, whether there was opportunity for the other party to reciprocate or not.[32]

Fiske (1992) has recently merged these two perspectives with foundational ideas from sociology into a fourfold taxonomy of fundamental social relational schemas: communal sharing, authority ranking, equality matching, and market pricing (MacCoun 2000). Fiske's theory contends that social relations in all societies are governed by various combinations of four fundamental psychological templates: We sometimes categorize individuals and treat category members identically (communal sharing), we sometimes treat individuals by their rank within a group (authority ranking), we sometimes keep score of outcomes and strive to equalize them (equality matching), and we sometimes value outcomes on an absolute metric and make trade-offs among them (market pricing). Each template has its own rules of appropriate conduct, its own norms of distributive fairness, and most crucially, its own consensually agreed upon domains of operation in a community's life (Fiske 1992, 693–708). Fiske's model fits a considerable body of sociological and anthropological evidence, and it has fared well in more exacting psychometric analyses and social-cognitive laboratory experiments (Fiske 1992, 693–708).

The activation of different schemas is posited to have numerous effects with regard to decision making, moral judgment, and the exchange of goods and services (Robbennolt, Darley, and MacCoun, forthcoming). But of special relevance to the present discussion is the argument that the four schemas are associated with distinct social influence processes. Communal sharing involves a desire to promote similarity and maintain unanimity; thus, the individual will change attitudes to maintain a certain harmony in the group. In authority ranking, there is obedience to authority or prestigious leaders, irrespective of the content of the norm. In equality matching, the focus is on reciprocity and turn taking. Finally, in market pricing, influence flows from incentives and a weighing of the costs and benefits of compliance with a request or demand.

The fact that different processes of social influence are more dominant in one schema than another indicates that a single account of the interaction between laws and norms might fail to capture important differences across domains of law, such as family law, employment law, or administrative law. For example, a model of social norms that is likely to predict the function of social norms in a family context could not be applied, as is, to the social norms of corporate directors. Because people are likely to comply with the social norms through different behavioral mechanisms across these different schemas, factors such as reciprocity, monetary incentives, ability for monitoring, and the like will carry differing weights with regard to the efficiency of legal decentralization and the policy maker's ability to rely on social norms in each legal doctrine.

## 15.3 *WHEN* DO NORMS OPERATE?

### 15.3.1 Norms Versus Attitudes

Psychologists tend to measure attitudes fairly rigorously but to define them fairly loosely. Most definitions involve a relatively stable evaluative judgment reflecting the desirability of various outcomes associated with an object or behavior, weighted by the likelihood that those outcomes will occur. In this sense, attitudes roughly correspond to the expected utilities of rational choice theories, but without the (unsupported) expectation that these evaluations and expectations are formed and combined in a mathematically coherent and rationally defensible way.

In the 1960s and 1970s, there was growing skepticism about the predictive power of public opinion polls and other attitudinal measures. In recent decades, there have been considerable advances in understanding the conditions under which attitudes do or do not predict and influence behavior (Eagly and Chaiken 1993). Much of this work has been organized under the rubric of Ajzen and Fishbein's (1980) "theory of reasoned action" and its successor, Ajzen's (1991) "theory of planned behavior."[33] Three principles from these theories are relevant to the present discussion.

First, to be predictive, attitudes and behaviors need to be matched at the same level of specificity. Because most behaviors are specific (for example, voting for a particular ballot proposition), abstract attitudes ("I abhor guns") are far less predictive than highly specific attitudes ("This gun control proposition is a hopeless and meaningless compromise"). These more specific attitudes are less intriguing than the lofty abstractions at issue in many sociolegal analyses, but they are often more relevant in particular settings.

Second, attitudes are only one determinant of the intention to engage in a behavior. A second determinant is the actor's perceived capability of performing the act—what Bandura (1997) calls "self-efficacy beliefs" and Ajzen (1991) calls "control beliefs." Two actors can share identical attitudes toward an action, yet only the actor with high perceived control will follow through with the action, reducing the attitude-behavior correlation.

More relevant for the present essay, Ajzen and Fishbein (1980) identify subjective norms as a third major determinant of behavioral intentions.[34] Across dozens of field studies involving many different classes of behavior (diet, drug use, exercise, voting, energy conservation, military enlistment), investigators have assessed both attitudes and perceived injunctive norms, allowing a comparison of their relative associations with behavior. In an examination of thirty different types of behavior, Trafimow and Finlay (1996) found that overall, behavioral intentions were better predicted by attitudes than by subjective norms (median correlations = .68 versus .40). As might be expected from our earlier discussions of consensus and social clustering, attitudes and norms were reliably correlated (median correlation = .37). But for most behaviors, perceived norms significantly increased the predictability of intentions above and beyond attitudes (Finlay, Trafimow, and Villareal 2002). Behaviors varied in the degree to which they were under attitudinal versus normative control. For example, "eat vegetables regularly" was almost entirely under attitudinal control, but "go into debt on my credit card" was primarily influenced by perceived norms, and "use condoms if I have sex" was influenced about equally by both factors.

Trafimow and Finlay (1996, 823–25) also found strong individual differences in the relative weight given to attitudes versus norms across behaviors (Miller and Grush 1986). The behavior of one-fifth of the people in their study was mainly under normative control, whereas the remaining four-fifths were mainly under attitudinal control. Later, we identify some empirical correlates of these individual differences.

### 15.3.2 Habit and Automaticity

An acknowledged boundary condition on the "planned behavior" framework described previously is that behavior itself is only partly intentional, at least in the sense of consciously formed plans. The notion of intentional choice is becoming increasingly problematic as psychologists discover the considerable extent to which behavior is mediated by factors outside conscious awareness (Bargh and Ferguson 2000; Wegner 2002; Wilson 2002). But that question is probably orthogonal to debates about rationality; it is quite possible for the brain to make coherent, incentive-based choices without conscious deliberation.

Though behaviors cannot be neatly parsed into "conscious" and "unconscious" categories, it is both meaningful and useful to distinguish relatively habitual or "scripted" behaviors from more novel behaviors and choices. Thus, a meta-analytic path analysis of sixty-four separate studies by Ouellette and Wood (1998) found that past behavior was a stronger predictor of present behavior for actions that tend to occur routinely (for example, once or more a week; weighted path coefficient = .45) than for actions occurring less frequently or in varying contexts (weighted path coefficient = .12). Conversely, self-reported intentions were a weaker predictor of behavior for routine actions (weighted path coefficient = .27) than for actions performed less frequently or in highly variable settings (weighted path coefficient = .62). Of special interest to the present discussion, perceived norms were stronger predictors of behavior for fairly novel actions than for routine actions. We suspect the latter finding is more general; because highly routinized behaviors become increasingly automaticized and "mindless," any external source of information seems more likely to influence novel choices than routine choices (Bargh and Ferguson 2000).

### 15.3.3 Ambiguity of Situational Cues

Norms are particularly likely to influence behavior in highly ambiguous situations. In an early demonstration, Sherif (1966) showed that strangers quickly formed an arbitrary consensus about the "size" of an illusory movement of light produced by an optical illusion. Festinger (1954) later argued that people engage in social comparison in order to reduce uncertainty by learning about the behavior of others.

Feldman (2003) has found suggestive evidence that the perceived clarity of trade-secret law.[35]

Ambiguity may be sufficient to promote reliance on norms, but it is not necessary. In the famous conformity paradigm created by Solomon Asch (1951), a large fraction of participants were willing to endorse patently false beliefs if enough experimental confederates first endorsed them. This is a clear-cut case of Kelman's compliance factor; no identification or internalization was involved. What is interesting is that no explicit social sanctions were involved other than the vague possibility of peer disapproval; the parties were strangers with nothing at stake and no expectation of future interaction.

### 15.3.4 Public and Private Selves

Contemporary psychology tends to view "the self" not as a unitary agent but rather as a complex of currently activated memories and goal states, emerging through processes of spreading activation and competition for limited cognitive resources. It is convenient to classify these various complexes in terms of multiple selves, though no implication of discrete cognitive or neurological modules is intended.

Carver and Scheier (1981, 1998) distinguish behavior under private versus public self-regulation. The fundamental distinction is that private self-awareness focuses on matching one's conduct to personal goals and standards, whereas public self-awareness strives to match one's conduct to the perceived goals and standards of other people. Extremely subtle situational factors can promote increased private versus public self-focus. For example, the presence of a mirror significantly increases private self-focus (as measured in various ways), and relative to a control condition, this private focus in turn leads to greater self-comparison to personal standards and behavior that is more consistent with prior attitude survey responses. On the other hand, the presence of a patently nonoperational camera stimulates attention to broader social standards and greater conformity to the behaviors of others (Gibbons 1990).

Private and public self-focus varies dispositionally as well as situationally; that is, there are stable individual differences in chronic attention to private standards versus public standards, as assessed by Snyder's (1974) self-monitoring inventory, which identifies the extent to which individuals strategically cultivate public appearances. High self-monitors engage in expressive control, based on sensitivity to social cues and the tendency to be influenced by the expectations of others. Low self-monitors put more weight on their own attitudes. Self-monitoring has been shown to moderate or qualify many bivariate relationships in the personality and social psychology literatures. Of particular relevance here, high self-monitors show greater conformity to the behavior of others; low self-monitors show significantly stronger attitude-behavior correlations (Carver and Scheier 1981, 1998; Kraus 1995; Miller and Grush 1986).

Interestingly, scores on the self-monitoring scale are bimodal rather than the bell-shaped distribution typical of many traits (Gangestad and Snyder 2000). This is problematic for the "representative individual" assumption that is implicit, if not explicit, in most economic models and indeed in much of social psychology prior to the "interactionist" trend that began in the mid-1980s (Kirman 1992).

For example, the paradigm of self-monitoring is an important model to consider for Cooter's (1998) conception of Pareto self-improvement and the signaling theory of Posner (2000), because it basically discusses the extent to which people engage in expressive control. Both accounts seem to better describe chronic high self-monitors than low self-monitors.

### 15.3.5 Individual Differences in Moral Reasoning

Another individual-differences moderator of normative influence is moral reasoning style. Kohlberg's (1984) well-known theory of moral development proposes a developmental sequence of six stages, divided into three levels: preconventional, conventional, and postconventional.[36] In the preconventional orientation characteristic of younger children, compliance is primarily motivated by the desire to avoid punishment. At the conventional level, individuals are more likely to be affected by perceived injunctive norms—what they think is expected of them by their family or other reference groups. People in the postconventional level are more likely to be influenced by more abstract and universal principles of justice and morality. The framework suggests a complex pattern of attitude-behavior relations, with pre- and postconventional individuals more influenced by "attitudes" (perceived sanctions in the former case and perceived impact on others in the latter) and conventional individuals more influenced by norms.

Tapp and Kohlberg (1971, 1977) have applied this framework to legal compliance in a manner that closely parallels the three-tier approaches of Kelman as well as Cooter, although from an individual-difference perspective rather than a multiprocesses approach (Kelman and Hamilton 1989). They distinguish rule-obeying, rule-maintaining, and rule-making orientations. The first type is most sensitive to the magnitude of risk and obeys the law mainly out of fear of punishment, without any respect for the rules. This type seems to be best described by deterrence models (MacCoun 1993). The second type is most sensitive to the legality of the act and tends to obey the law mainly out of a law-and-order perspective: "If the lawmaker says I should do it, it is probably good." This type seems to be those most aligned with the expressive model because they are most likely to care about the announcement of the law, disregarding its sanctions or its alignment with morality.[37] The last type is exemplified by one who thinks about the law, using abstract principles of justice that are independent of society, and who is more concerned about the legitimacy of the law. This individual will naturally be most likely to obey the law in a similar way to those who engage in the processes of internalization.

## 15.4 HOW AND WHEN DO WE INTERNALIZE NORMS?

A basic question in the new norms literature is whether the effect of a norm is external-exogenous or internal-endogenous. In previous sections of this chapter, we have discussed the mix of attitudes and norms as if these factors are independent. Nonetheless, in many cases, this independence will cease to exist, and the attitudes and norms of the individual will merge.[38] In neoclassical economic theory, preference change was long off-limits as an area of research. Despite the fact that the internalization of social norms captures much attention from LEN scholars, the behavioral mechanism underlying this "internalization" is still far from clear.[39] Although a full analysis of the endogenous-exogenous nature of preferences is beyond the scope of this chapter, we would like to clarify the concept of internalization, to the extent that this process is being treated by LEN scholars of social norms as being relevant to psychology.

Some LEN scholars have suggested that psychology cannot explain the mechanism of internalization. Scott (2000, 1637), for example, maintains, "The fact is that behavioral science does not yet understand the mechanism of internalization." A similar argument is that internalization is a mysterious and, to some extent, nonreversible process that requires depth psychology (Cooter 1996).

We find such arguments puzzling. It is true that psychologists lack a complete and comprehensive "final theory" of internalization, but the gap is far from cavernous. Psychologists actually know a great deal about internalization, but the topic is so large that it encompasses many rubrics. There is vast literature on the principles of inductive learning (Gilovich, Griffin, and Kahneman 2002; Holland et al. 1986), vicarious social learning (Bandura 1986), and moral socialization by parents (Kochanska 2002; Ruble and Goodnow 1998), each of which involves robust empirical generalizations based on literally thousands of laboratory and field studies. Rather than attempt to do justice to such vast literatures, we will simply focus on two explanatory paradigms that seem readily applicable to internalization by adults following an exposure to new norms.

### 15.4.1 Central Versus Peripheral Routes to Persuasion

Applied work by psychologists for the military in World War II launched an enormous postwar effort to identify the systematic principles of persuasion. By the mid-1970s, there was an enormous and unwieldy catalog of findings involving specific source, audience, and message factors, alone or in combination. In the late 1970s and early 1980s, it was discovered that most of this literature could be integrated using a few straightforward organizing principles that yield clear, testable a priori predictions.[40]

Petty and Cacioppo's (1986) elaboration likelihood model distinguishes between two basic routes to persuasion, corresponding to two distinct types of information processing. The "central route" involves active, conscious deliberation: an assessment of arguments and the attempt to generate plausible counterarguments. The central route is activated only when two conditions are met: the individual is motivated to think about a message, and the individual is able to cognitively process information. When those two conditions are met, the primary determinant of persuasion is the perceived strength of the presented arguments. Argument change generated by the central route tends to be durable and resistant to all but the strongest counterinfluence attempts.

When individuals are disinterested in the topic (low motivation), distracted (low ability), or unable to comprehend the message (low ability), at best they will be influenced by a quick and superficial reliance on currently salient "cues to persuasion"—for example, "the majority favors this"; "there are a lot of arguments here, so it must be right"; "she's the expert, so I'll take her word for it"; "he's the NBA's leading scorer, and he buys Nikes." Petty and Cacioppo call this the "peripheral" route to persuasion. Attitudes and beliefs formed via peripheral persuasion are fragile and transitory, easily "knocked out" when alternative peripheral cues become more salient.

This framework has obvious relevance for the influence taxonomies of Kelman (1958), French and Raven (1959), and Cialdini (1990) (see Table 15.1). For example, in the Petty-Cacioppo framework, French and Raven's "expert power" may be correlated with strong arguments, but only if the audience is motivated and able to reflect on those arguments. If not, expertise serves as a mere, and transitory, peripheral cue. The central route—persuasion based on thoughtful deliberation—is a key path toward internalization, but it is only one such path. Peripheral persuasion, on the other hand, can produce mere public compliance, identification, or (as we shall see) even internalization.

## 15.4.2 Self-Reinforcing Peripheral Beliefs

The central route is not the only path to internalization. Peripherally formed beliefs are ephemeral when they fail to produce action, but under the right conditions, positions adopted expediently or superficially via the peripheral route to persuasion can become self-reinforcing and stable.

This can occur through the sort of path dependency that has long interested economists (Arthur 1988). Actions based on transitory views ("whims") can expose the actor to new settings and a new mix of social contacts, which can in turn place the individual under new compliance pressures but also under new cognitive pressures.

Festinger's (1957) work on cognitive dissonance and Bem's (1967) work on self-perception suggest two similar, but still distinctive, mechanisms by which a change in behavior can produce a change in attitudes, but they differ in their view of which mechanism is being employed. According to Festinger, the gap between one's attitudes and behavior creates a mental dissonance associated with an unpleasant feeling that could potentially be reduced by a change in one's attitudes. According to Bem, the processes are more straightforward. The individual simply infers from his or her behavior what his or her attitudes are. Empirically, Festinger's theory is most applicable to attitudes that the actor cares about; Bem's account mostly applies to more trivial or casually considered views (Eagly and Chaiken 1993).

A related process is parallel constraint satisfaction, as represented using connectionist models (Read and Miller 1998; Robbennolt, Darley, and MacCoun, forthcoming; Thagard 2000). Constraint satisfaction algorithms are used to model the cognitive processes by which actors integrate numerous interrelated elements (for example, concepts, propositions, or goals), which may or may not be consistent, into a coherent whole (Read and Miller 1998). There is some evidence that the processes described by dissonance theory and other cognitive consistency theories are simply special cases of the operation of more general constraint satisfaction mechanisms (Read, Vanman, and Miller 1997; Simon and Holyoak 2002).

We recognize that these theories both clarify and complicate the LEN analysis. They clarify it in the sense that they make internalization less mysterious, but they also identify conditions for internalization—strong arguments, motivated and able perceivers, pressures toward self-consistency—that are difficult to incorporate into stylized formal analyses. These accounts also make internalization somewhat less of a legal panacea. The law's normative messages are not the only norms that can get internalized; processes of persuasion, dissonance reduction, and constraint satisfaction can solidify all sorts of views that the government would wish to discourage. Nor can economists assume that all types of internalization are permanent and irreversible. The law's messages will have to compete in a marketplace of ideas—both good and bad, serious and trivial.

## 15.5 CONCLUSION

In this chapter we have reviewed and organized into three themes some of the main theories of social norms in the psychological literature. The choice of theories was conducted not according to their importance within psychology but according to their relevancy to the new norms literature in law and economics. The first theme that we have discussed is the multiplicity of normative processes. We have argued that taking these distinctions into account could refine and improve the current vague definition of *norm* used by LEN scholars. Our second theme is the multiplicity of normative moderators—factors that strengthen or attenuate the influence of norms relative to attitudes, prices, and other factors. We have argued that any policy maker who is interested in decentralizing legal enforcement must be aware of factors that mitigate the effect of norms on behavior, because the widespread existence of a norm is insufficient to guarantee its influence on behavior. Our third theme is that internalization is neither as simple as suggested by some LEN accounts nor as mysterious as suggested by others.

In all, we realize that the theories we have reviewed and their implication to the current law and economics models of social norms create considerable complexity and heterogeneity. We don't contend that theorists need to construct a grand theory that accounts for the full depth and breadth of the social psychology literature—if psychologists haven't, why should economists? Rather, we think the challenge is for LEN theorists to draw upon social psychology selectively in a manner that increases the validity and realism of the models while striving to maintain their formal tractability and heuristic value. Taking this challenge into account in our review, we have focused mainly on the types of theories that once incorporated into the current models, seem to be worth the cost. We believe that by taking these moderators and theoretical distinctions into account, LEN scholars will be able to analyze in much greater clarity and predictability when norms are likely to govern efficiently and what the nature of interaction is between norms and law. At the same time, we are aware of the fact that not all theories reviewed here will have equally practical implications for the "norm-management" project. Nonetheless, we think that even in these cases a theoretical value emerges from the comparison of newer economic models with older psychological models that aim to answer exactly the same questions from different, and sometime richer, perspectives.

1. "The demonstrated importance of social norms to law and the availability of analytical techniques from economics have caused a renaissance in legal scholarship on social norms."

2. As a matter of fact, although arguing that psychologists have studied norms for longer periods than economists have, it is appropriate to admit that the sociologists' interest in social norms preceded that of social psychologists (e.g., Durkheim, about the creation of norms and customs by groups). Psycho-social experimental research goes back to the experiments conducted by Sherif (1966) in 1936, as well as to the field research conducted by Newcomb at Bennington College in 1943. These studies are the most well known early works of social psychologists in the area of social norms. Naturally, the focus of psychologists (unlike that of sociologists) was more focused on understanding the behavioral processes underlying the effects of norms rather than exploring the content or areas in which norms are created. Even critical scholars of the new law and economics approach to social norms do not tend to find the lack of psychology to be problematic. For example, Mitchell (1999, 247) argues that "formally the province of anthropologists, sociologists, economists and philosophers, lawyers have begun to attempt to understand the norms play in ordering society and social groups outside the sphere of the norms promulgated by the state."

3. A moderator is a variable that determines the magnitude or valence of a relationship between two other variables, amplifying, attenuating, reversing, or placing boundary conditions on more simplistic theoretical principles (Baron and Kenny 1986).

4. The main exception to this can be found in our discussion of individual differences, which are naturally harder to predict *ex ante*. Nonetheless, we will argue that awareness of the existence of individual differences is required in order to predict the likely effect of norms, even if the identity of the specific individual could not be known in advance.

5. "[T]he new norms jurisprudence suffers from the same failing that led to the diminishing influence of the strict Chicago-style neoclassical law and economics—the oversimplification of a complex world" (Mitchell 1999).

6. "[S]ocial norms provide an important kind of motivation for action that is irreducible to rationality or indeed to any other form of optimizing mechanism" (Elster 1991).

7. See also Scott (2000, 1603).

8. Interestingly enough, the work of law and economics scholars who do field research is for the most part based on interviews and is more qualitative

in nature, which makes it harder to generalize from their case studies to other contexts (Bernstein 1992, 2001; Cooter 1991).

9. It is easy to overstate this point. There are many formal mathematical theories in social psychology, including the social impact, social decision scheme, and constraint satisfaction models discussed later. Curiously, social psychology was actually more mathematical, and more closely linked to decision theory and game theory, in the 1950s and 1960s. However, those early models were used for the formal deduction of new hypotheses. We believe such formalizations became less common in part because they became too cumbersome to accommodate empirical advances in the field.

10. One scheme offers sixteen different forms of influence, including such curiosities as "anticonversion," "disinhibitory contagion," "anticontagion," and "paradoxical anticompliance" (Nail, MacDonald, and Levy 2000).

11. For a more developed discussion of the theoretical justification to see those models as separated and their relationship with other models, see Kelman (1961) and Kelman and Hamilton (1989); see Feldman (2003) for a comparison of these distinctions and the LEN approaches (e.g., Cooter (1998)) to deterrence, expression, and internalization functions of the law.

12. Nonetheless, our discussions of the "central route to persuasion" and of internalization that follow suggest that internalization is preferable.

13. Enacting law might increase the number of right-doers to a point in which more and more people will obey the law even when no sanctions are presented.

14. What Cooter refers to as the "tipping point model" (Cooter 1997).

15. "Why might the Smiths revise their estimate of the probabilities of sanction without experiencing a change in their preferences or in the underlying norms? The Smiths, as all of us, recognize that statutes are enacted only if (1) a substantial majority of the community has at least a weak preference for the new rule" (Scott 2000, 1603).

16. For an empirical demonstration of the differences in the relationship between injunctive norms, descriptive norms, and announcement of the illegality of an act (know-how sharing), see Feldman (2003).

17. The models discussed by Cooter (1997) don't seem to assume linearity; however, there is no attempt to realistically predict what the ratio is other than suggesting that the law and the norm move in the same direction.

18. This generalization largely stems from the research program of Laughlin (1996). Note that the notion of tasks with a "shared conceptual scheme" is neither circular nor ad hoc; it is fairly easy to identify such tasks a priori and quite straightforward to validate using individual-level pretesting in the population of interest.

19. Hardin (1998, 428) recognizes the idea that different subgroups within an organization could have conflicting interests and will compete to increase their influence over members of that organization.

20. Following up on this puzzling omission, Feldman (2003) has demon-

strated empirically some of the normative failures that could emerge from people's systematic errors in estimating what the consensus in their relevant community is, focusing on engineers' estimates of the proportion of their coworkers that engage in disclosure of trade secrets when they move from one company to another.

21. Overall, the average estimate was that just under 70 percent of Silicon Valley employees share confidential know-how information. (The sample was not fully random.)

22. Because both measures were self-reported, the direction of causality could not be inferred. However, one can say with confidence that the deviation of the participants from the actual consensus was strongly correlated with their own reported behavior.

23. These are exactly the people whose views the policy maker is most interested in changing.

24. Along those lines, there is now a new focus in prevention research: challenging exaggerated views of the popularity of drug use (Brown 1974) and alcohol use (Miller and Prentice 1994). In the context of trade secrets, Feldman (2003) has found the following results when using the same sample in which the false consensus effect was salient: in the self-reported, only about 40 percent of subjects said that they would divulge trade secrets; the estimate grew to 55 percent when questions were focused on one's coworkers; and the estimate grew to almost 70 percent when the target group was the general population of Silicon Valley employees. Even when taking into account that the sample was not completely random and that people are more likely to lie about their own intentions (e.g., social desirability), these results emphasize the possibility of exaggeration of undesirable norms.

25. Coefficient of .25 between estimation of consensus and own behavior for those with knowledge about the consensus, and .27 for those with no knowledge about the consensus.

26. A classic early source is Latane and Darley (1968); a more recent review is in Miller and Prentice (1994); a related source in the political science literature is Noelle-Neumann (1993).

27. For examples, see Kuran (1995); MacCoun and Reuter (2001, 401–4); Miller and Prentice (1994). Sudden nonlinear shifts in opinion can arise, even in the absence of any self-censorship, because of the lability of views on unfamiliar or complex topics; for a book-length analysis and many examples, see Jones (1994).

28. Game theory has been an active area of research in social psychology for many decades. Mathematical psychologist Anatol Rappoport submitted the "tit-for-tat" strategy used in Axelrod's famous computer tournaments (Axelrod 1984).

29. Bernstein (2001, 1764) states the following:

> In general, in order for cooperation to emerge in a particular market, transactors must each adopt strategies of cooperating at the beginning of each contracting

relationship and thereafter responding to cooperative behavior with cooperation and responding to uncooperative behavior (defection) with punishment (such strategies are called "tit-for-tat" strategies). Each transactor must also be able to obtain information about the reputations of other market participants, and reputation must be at least partially dependent on how a transactor behaved in previous transactions. In addition, each transactor must be able to observe whether the person he is dealing with has cooperated or defected.

30. Some argue that the distinction between exchange and communal relationships was exaggerated and that, in fact, some reciprocity also exists in communal relationships (Batson 1993).

31. Thus, for participants in this group, reciprocity significantly predicted the help that participants were offering. It should be noted that there were also strong individual differences with regard to the role of reciprocity in humans (Perugini and Gallucci 2001).

32. The distinction between communal and exchange relationships was shown to moderate related activities as well. Clark (1984) has found that people keep track of inputs in exchange relationships but not in communal relationships.

33. Charles Manski (1995) correctly points out that much of the research motivated by these theories suffers from serious statistical identification problems, but his critique greatly overstates the problem. First, such identification problems are in fact endemic in correlational research, including most econometric tests of economic theory. Second, he ignores the many experimental and quasi-experimental studies that use random assignment, temporal sequence, or other features to strengthen causal inferences. Without discounting the contribution of these theories, it should be noted that they are used most widely as organizing frameworks for empirical work in applied settings, being too general and open ended to play an important directive role in most theory-testing efforts in social psychology.

34. They focus primarily on injunctive norms, beliefs about what others think a person should do. They acknowledge that one might subsume these beliefs under "attitude" as anticipated consequences of the action but note that doing so leads the analyst to underemphasize the importance of these beliefs and begs the interesting question regarding the relative influence of external and internal influences on behavior.

35. Legal certainty in that context was operationalized by asking the participants in the study about the clarity and perceived certainty with which they felt they could specify the types of information that could be defined as trade secrets.

For those who had a clearer view about the meaning of trade-secrets laws the relationship between perceived norms and morality, fairness and career effect were much weaker than for those who were not clear about the actual meaning of trade-secrets laws. The existence of interaction was conducted by creating a product term interaction factor of centering factors of descriptive norms and certainty.

36. Kohlberg's theory has been controversial, in part because of his Rawlsian normative stance and in part because of unsupported claims that his findings mostly describe males rather than females (Hyde and Shibley 2000).

37. This also appears to be very similar to the identification process because conventional people tend to see the system of rules as responsible for the maintenance of society and social order. Thus, although the relationship with the lawmaker is less emphasized according to this model, these people do care dearly about their relationship with society as a whole.

38. Of course, attitudes and norms are dependent in a second sense, because a person's expressed attitudes may help constitute someone else's perceived norms.

39. Another overlooked aspect of the relationship between the expressive and internalization aspects of social norms is whether these aspects are supposed to come one after the other or to function in tandem. Such a discussion could be seen with regard to the development of trust in different types of relationships (Lewicki and Bunker 1996). One of the early accounts by leading LEN scholars of the sociobiology of internal norms is that in Landes and Posner (1978).

40. These principles were independently proposed in 1979 doctoral theses by Shelly Chaiken and by Richard Petty. Chaiken's heuristic-systematic model is described in detail in Eagly and Chaiken (1993); we will focus instead on Petty's model (developed with John Cacioppo) (Petty and Cacioppo 1986), which is more transparent for present purposes.

REFERENCES

Ajzen, I. 1991. The theory of planned behavior. *Organizational Behavior and Human Decision Processes* 50:179.

Ajzen, I., and M. Fishbein. 1980. *Understanding attitudes and predicting social behavior.* Upper Saddle River, NJ: Prentice Hall.

Arthur, W. 1988. Competing technologies, increasing returns, and lock-in by historical events. *Economics Journal* 99:116.

Asch, S. 1951. Effects of group pressure upon the modification and distortion of judgments. In *Groups, leadership and men,* ed. H. Guetzkow, 177–90. Pittsburgh: Carnegie Press.

Axelrod, R. 1984. *The evolution of cooperation.* New York: Basic Books.

———. 1997. *The complexity of cooperation.* Princeton, NJ: Princeton University Press.

Axelrod, R., R. Riolo, and M. Cohen. 2002. Beyond geography: Cooperation with persistent links in the absence of clustered neighborhoods. *Personality and Social Psychology Review* 6:341.

Bandura, A. 1986. *Social foundations of thought and action: A social cognitive theory.* Upper Saddle River, NJ: Prentice Hall.

———. 1997. *Self efficacy: The exercise of control.* Stanford, CA: Stanford University Press.

Bargh, J., and M. Ferguson. 2000. Beyond behaviorism: On the automaticity of higher mental processes. *Psychology Bulletin* 126 (6): 925.

Baron, R., and D. Kenny. 1986. The moderator-mediator variable distinction in social psychological research: Conceptual, strategic, and statistical considerations. *Journal of Personality and Social Psychology* 51 (6): 1173.

Batson, D. 1993. Communal and exchange relationships: What is the difference? *European Journal of Personality* 15 (1): 19.

Baumeister, R., and M. Leary. 1995. The need to belong: Desire for interpersonal attachments as a fundamental human motivation. *Psychological Bulletin* 117 (3): 497–529.

Bem, D. 1967. Self-perception: An alternative interpretation of cognitive dissonance phenomena. *Psychology Review* 74 (3): 183.

Bernstein, L. 1992. Opting out of the legal system: Extralegal contractual relations in the diamond industry. *Journal of Legal Studies* 21 (1): 115.

———. 2001. Private commercial law in the cotton industry: Creating cooperation through rules, norms, and institutions. *Michigan Law Review* 99 (7): 1724.

Brown, J. 1974. Turning off: Cessation of marijuana use after college. *Social Problems* 21 (4): 527.

Campbell, J., and P. Fairey. 1989. Informational and normative routes to conformity. *Journal of Personality and Social Psychology* 57:456.

Carver, C., and M. Scheier. 1981. *Attention and self-regulation: A control-theory approach to human behavior*. Heidelberg, Germany: Springer-Verlag.

———. 1998. *On the self-regulation of behavior*. Cambridge: Cambridge University Press.

Cialdini, R., R. Bator, and R. Guadagno. 1999. Normative influences in organizations. In *Shared cognition in organizations: The management of knowledge*, ed. L. Thompson and J. Levine, 195. Mahwah, NJ: Erlbaum.

Cialdini, R., R. Reno, and C. Kallgren. 1990. A focus theory of normative conduct: Recycling the concept of norms to reduce littering in public places. *Journal of Personality and Social Psychology* 58 (6): 1015.

Clark, M. 1984. Record keeping in two types of relationships. *Journal of Personality and Social Psychology* 47 (3): 549.

Clark, M., and J. Mills. 1993. The difference between communal and exchange relationships. *Journal of Personality and Social Psychology* 51 (2): 333.

Clark, M. S., J. Mills, and M. Powell. 1986. Keeping track of needs in communal and exchange relationships. *Journal of Personality and Social Psychology* 51: 333–38.

Cooter, R. 1991. Inventing market property: The land courts of Papua New Guinea. *Law and Society Review* 25 (4): 759.

———. 1996. Decentralized law for a complex economy: The structural approach to adjudicating the new law merchant. *University of Pennsylvania Law Review* 144:1643, 1661–62.

———. 1997. Symposium: Normative failure theory of law. *Cornell Law Review* 82:947, 963.

———. 1998. Expressive law and economics. *Journal of Legal Studies* 27:585, 587.

———. 2000. Do good laws make good citizens? An economic analysis of internalized norms. *Virginia Law Review* 86 (8): 1577.

Dawes, R., and M. Mulford. 1996. The false consensus effect and overconfidence: Flaws in judgment or flaw in how we study judgment? *Organizational Behavior and Human Decision Processes* 65 (3): 201.

Dishion, T., J. McCord, and F. Poulin. 1999. When interventions harm: Peer groups and problem behavior. *American Psychology* 54 (9): 755.

Dunning, D., and G. Cohen. 1992. Egocentric definitions of traits and abilities in social judgment. *Journal of Personality and Social Psychology* 63:341.

Eagly, A., and S. Chaiken. 1993. *The psychology of attitudes*. Orlando, FL: Harcourt Brace Jovanovich.

Ellickson, R. 1991. *Order without law: How neighbors settle disputes*. Cambridge, MA: Harvard University Press.

———. 2001. The market for social norms. *American Law and Economics Review* 3 (1): 1–49.

Elster, J. 1991. *The cement of society: Studies in rationality and social change.* Cambridge: Cambridge University Press.

Epstein, J., and R. Axtell. 1996. *Growing artificial societies.* Washington, DC: Brookings Institution Press.

Feldman, Y. 2003. An experimental approach to the study of normative failures: Divulging of trade secrets by Silicon Valley employees. *Journal of Law, Technology and Policy* 105 (1).

———. 2004. The behavioral foundations of the expressive function of trade-secret laws: Legality, cost, intrinsic motivation and consensus. http://ssrn .com /abstract=562242.

Festinger, L. 1954. A theory of social comparison processes. *Human Relations* 7:117.

———. 1957. *A theory of cognitive dissonance.* Stanford, CA: Stanford University Press.

Festinger, L., S. Schachter, and K. Back. 1950. *Social pressures in informal groups: A study of human factors in housing.* New York: Harper and Row.

Finlay, K., D. Trafimow, and A. Villareal. 2002. Predicting exercise and health behavioral intentions: Attitudes, subjective norms, and other behavioral determinants. *Journal of Applied Social Psychology* 32 (2): 342.

Fiske, A. 1992. The four elementary forms of sociality: Framework for a unified theory of social relations. *Psychology Review* 99:689, 693–708.

Foa, U. 1971. Interpersonal and economic resources. *Science* 177:344.

Forsyth, D. 1959. Social comparison and influence in groups. In *Handbook of social comparison*, ed. J. Suls and L. Wheeler, 81. Amsterdam: Kluwer.

French, J., and B. Raven. 1959. The bases of social power. In *Studies in social power*, ed. D. Cartwright, 150. Oxford: Oxford University Press.

Gangestad, S., and M. Snyder. 2000. Self-monitoring appraisal and reappraisal. *Psychology Bulletin* 126 (4): 530.

Gibbons, F. 1990. Self-attention and behavior: A review and theoretical update. In *23 advances in experimental social psychology*, ed. M. Zanna, 249. Amsterdam: Academic Press.

Gilovich, T., D. Griffin, and D. Kahneman, eds. 2002. *Heuristics and biases: The psychology of intuitive judgment.* Cambridge: Cambridge University Press.

Goethals, G., and W. Klein. 2000. Interpreting and inventing social reality: Attributional and constructive elements in social comparison. In *Handbook of social comparison*, ed. J. Suls and L. Wheeler, 23. Amsterdam: Kluwer.

Griffith, W., and R. Goldfarb. 1991. Amending the economist's "rational egoist" model to include moral values and norms. In *Social norms and economic institutions*, ed. K. Koford and J. Miller, 39. Ann Arbor: University of Michigan Press.

Hardin, R. 1998. Institutional commitment: Values or incentives? In *Economics, values and organizations*, ed. A. Ben-Ner and L. Puterman, 428. Cambridge: Cambridge University Press.

Holland, J., K. J. Holyoak, R. E. Nisbet, and P. R. Thagard. 1986. *Induction: Processes of inference, learning and discovery.* Cambridge, MA: MIT Press.

Hyde, S., and J. Shibley. 2000. Gender differences in moral orientation: A meta-analysis. *Psychology Bulletin* 126 (5): 703.

Jones, B. 1994. *Reconceiving decision-making in democratic politics.* Chicago: University of Chicago Press.

Kahan, D. 2001. Trust, collective action and law. *Boston University Law Review* 81:333.

———. 2002. Commentaries on Eric Posner's "Law and social norms: Signaling or reciprocating?" A response to Eric Posner's "Law and social norms." *University of Richmond Law Review* 36:367, 371.

Kahneman, D., and A. Tversky. 1984. Choices, values and frames. *American Psychology* 39 (4): 341.

Kallgren, C., R. Reno, and R. Cialdini. 2000. A focus theory of normative conduct: When norms do and do not affect behavior. *Personality and Social Psychology Bulletin* 26 (8): 1002.

Kelman, H. 1958. Compliance, identification and internalization: Three processes of attitude change. *Journal of Conflict Resolution* 2:51.

———. 1961. Process of attitude change. *Public Opinion Quarterly* 25 (1): 57.

Kelman, H., and L. Hamilton. 1989. *Crimes of obedience.* New Haven, CT: Yale University Press.

Kerr, N., R. MacCoun, and G. Kramer. 1996. Bias in judgment: Comparing individuals and groups. *Psychology Review* 103:687.

Kirman, A. 1992. Whom or what does the representative individual represent? *Journal of Economic Perspectives* 6 (2): 117.

Knowles, Eric S. 1999. Distance matters more than you think! An artifact clouds interpretation of Latane, Liu, Nowak, Bonevento, and Zheng's results. *Personality and Social Psychology Bulletin* 25 (8): 1045.

Kochanska, G. 2002. Mutually responsive orientation between mothers and their young children: A context for the early development of the conscience. *Current Directions in Psychological Science* 11:191.

Kohlberg, L. 1984. *The psychology of moral development: The nature and validity of moral stages.* New York: Harper and Row.

Kraus, S. 1995. Attitudes and the prediction of behavior: A meta-analysis of the empirical literature. *Personality and Social Psychology Bulletin* 21:58–75.

Krueger, J. 2000. The projective perception of the social world. In *Handbook of social comparison*, ed. J. Suls and L. Wheeler, 323, 328–31. Amsterdam: Kluwer.

Kuran, T. 1995. *Private truths, public lies: The social consequences of preference falsification.* Cambridge, MA: Harvard University Press.

Landes, W., and R. Posner. 1978. Altruisms in law and economics. *American Economic Review* 68:417.

Latane, B. 1981. The psychology of social impact. *American Psychology* 36:343.

———. 1995. Distance matters: Physical space and social impact. *Personality and Social Psychology Bulletin* 21 (8): 795.

———. 1996. Strength from weakness: The fate of opinion minorities in spatially distributed groups. In *Understanding group behavior: Consensual action by small groups*, ed. E. Witte and J. H. Davis, 194. Mahwah, NJ: Erlbaum.

Latane, B., and J. Darley. 1968. *The unresponsive bystander: Why doesn't he help?* New York: Appleton-Century-Crofts.

Latane, B., and T. L'Herrou. 1996. Spatial clustering the conformity game: Dynamic social impact in electronic groups. *Journal of Personality and Social Psychology* 70 (6): 1218.

Laughlin, P. 1996. Group decision-making and collective induction. In *Understanding group behavior*, vol. 1, ed. E. Witte and J. Davis, 61. Mahwah, NJ: Erlbaum.

Lewicki, R., and B. Bunker. 1996. Developing and maintaining trust in work relationships. In *Trust in organizations: Frontiers of theory and research*, ed. R. Kramer and T. Tyler, 114. Thousand Oaks, CA: Sage.

Maas, A., and C. Volpato. 1996. Social influence and the verifiability of the issue under discussion: Attitudinal versus objective items. *British Journal of Social Psychology* 35 (1): 15.

MacCoun, R. 1993. Drugs and the law: A psychological analysis of drug prohibition. *Psychological Bulletin* 113:497.

———. 2000. The costs and benefits of letting juries punish corporations: Comment on Viscusi. *Stanford Law Review* 52:1821.

———. 2002a. Comparing micro and macro rationality. In *Judgments, decisions and public policy*, ed. R. Gowda and J. Fox, 116. Cambridge: Cambridge University Press.

———. 2002b. Why a psychologist won the Nobel Prize in economics. *American Psychological Society Observer* 15:1.

MacCoun, R., and N. Kerr. 1988. Asymmetric influence in mock jury deliberation: Juror's bias for leniency. *Journal of Personality and Social Psychology* 54:21.

MacCoun, R., and P. Reuter. 2001. *Drug war heresies: Learning from other vices, times, and places*. Cambridge: Cambridge University Press.

Mansbridge, Jane. 1998. Starting with nothing: On the impossibility of grounding norms solely in self-interest. In *Economics, values and organizations*, ed. A. Ben-Ner and L. Puterman, 73. Cambridge: Cambridge University Press.

Manski, C. 1995. *Identification problems in social sciences*. Cambridge, MA: Harvard University Press.

McAdams, R. 1997. The origin, development and regulation of norms. *Michigan Law Review* 96 (2): 338.

———. 2000a. An attitudinal theory of expressive law (new and critical approaches to law and economics). *Oregon Law Review* 79 (2): 339.

———. 2000b. A focal point theory of expressive law. *Virginia Law Review* 86:1649.

———. 2001. Signaling discount rates: Law, norms, and economic methodology law and social norms. *Yale Law Journal* 110:625, 633.

Meares, T. 2002. Commentaries on Eric Posner's "Law and social norms: Signaling, legitimacy and compliance": A comment on Posner's "Law and social norms and criminal law policy." *University of Richmond Law Review* 36:407, 408.

Messe, L., R. Hymes, and R. MacCoun. 1986. Group categorization and distributive justice decisions. In *Justice in social relations*, ed. R. Cohen and J. Greenberg. New York: Plenum Press.

Miller, L., and J. Grush. 1986. Individual differences in attitudinal vs. normative determination of behavior. *Journal of Experimental Social Psychology* 22:190.

Miller, D., and D. Prentice. 1994. Collective errors and errors about the collective. *Personality and Social Psychology Bulletin* 20:541.

Mitchell, L. 1999. Understanding norms. *University of Toronto Law Journal* 49: 177, 247.

Mullen, B. 1983. Operationalizing the effect of the group on the individual: A self-attention perspective. *Journal of Experimental Social Psychology* 19 (4): 295.

Nail, P., G. MacDonald, and D. Levy. 2000. Proposal of a four-dimensional model of social response. *Psychological Bulletin* 126:454.

Newcomb, T. 1943. Personality and social change: Attitude formation in a student community. Stamford, CT: Dryden.

Noelle-Neumann, E. 1993. *The spiral of silence*. Chicago: University of Chicago Press.

Nowak, A., J. Szamrej, and B. Latane. 1990. From private attitude to public opinion: A dynamic theory of social impact. *Psychology Review* 97:362.

Ouellette, J., and W. Wood. 1998. Habit and intention in everyday life: The multiple processes by which past behavior predicts future behavior. *Psychology Bulletin* 124 (1): 54.

Perugini, M., and M. Gallucci. 2001. Individual differences and social norms: The distinction between reciprocators and prosocials. *European Journal of Personality* 15:S19–S35.

Petty, R., and J. Cacioppo. 1986. The elaboration likelihood model of persuasion. *Advances in Experimental Social Psychology* 19:123.

Posner, E. 2000. *Law and social norms*. Cambridge, MA: Harvard University Press.

Prentice, D., and D. Miller. 1996. Pluralistic ignorance and alcohol use on campus: Some consequences of misperceiving the social norm. *Journal of Personality and Social Psychology* 64 (2): 243–56.

Rachlinksi, J. 2000. Symposium on law, psychology and emotions: The limits of social norms. *Chicago-Kent Law Review* 74:1537.

Read, S., and L. Miller, eds. 1998. *Connectionist models of social reasoning and social behavior.* Mahwah, NJ: Erlbaum.

Read, S., E. Vanman, and L. Miller. 1997. Connectionism, parallel constraint satisfaction processes, and Gestalt principles: (Re)introducing cognitive dynamics to social psychology. *Personality and Social Psychology Review* 1:26.

Robbennolt, J., J. Darley, and R. MacCoun. Forthcoming. Symbolism and incommensurability in civil sanctioning: Decision-makers as goal managers. *Brooklyn Law Review.*

Robinson, P., and J. Darley. 1995. *Justice, liability, and blame: Community views and the criminal law.* Nashville, TN: Westview.

Ross, L., D. Greene, and P. House. 1977. The false consensus effect: An egocentric bias in social perception and attributional processes. *Journal of Experimental Social Psychology* 13:279.

Rostain, T. 2000. Educating *homo economicus*: Cautionary notes on the new behavioral laws and economics movement. *Law and Society Review* 34:973.

Ruble, D., and J. Goodnow. 1998. Social development in childhood and adulthood. In *Handbook of social psychology*, vol. 1, ed. S. Fiske and L. Gardner, chap. 16. New York: McGraw-Hill.

Scott, R. 2000. The limits of behavioral theories of social norms. *Virginia Law Review* 86 (8): 1603, 1637.

Shaver, K. G. 1987. *Principles of social psychology.* 3rd ed. Hillsdale, NJ: Erlbaum.

Sherif, M. 1966. *The psychology of social norms.* New York: Harper and Row.

Simon, D., and K. Holyoak. 2002. Structural dynamics of cognition: From consistency theories to constraint satisfaction. *Personality and Social Psychology Review* 26:283.

Snyder, M. 1974. Self-monitoring of expressive behavior. *Journal of Personality and Social Psychology* 30:526.

Strasser, G., N. Kerr, and J. Davis. 1989. Influence processes and consensus models in decision-making groups. In *Psychology of group influence*, ed. P. Paulus, 279. Mahwah, NJ: Erlbaum.

Sugden, R. 1998. Normative expectations: The simultaneous evolution of institutions and norms. In *Economics, values and organizations*, ed. A. Ben-Ner and L. Puterman, 73. Cambridge: Cambridge University Press.

Suls, J., R. Martin, and L. Wheeler. 2002. Social comparison: Why, with whom, and with what effect? *Current Directions in Psychological Science* 11:159.

Sunstein, C. 1996. Social norms and social roles. *Columbia Law Review* 96: 903, 945.

Symposium. 1996. Law, economics, and norms. *University of Pennsylvania Law Review* 144:1643.

———. 1998. Social norms, social meaning, and the economic analysis of law. *Journal of Legal Studies* 27:537.

———. 2000. The legal construction of norms. *Virginia Law Review* 86:1577.

Tanford, S., and S. Penrod. 1984. Social influence model: A formal integration of research on majority and minority influence processes. *Psychology Bulletin* 95:189.

Tapp, J., and L. Kohlberg. 1971. Developing senses of law and legal justice. *Journal of Social Issues* 27 (2).

———. 1977. Developing sense of law and legal justice. In *Law, justice, and the individual in society*, ed. J. Tapp and F. Levine, 89. Austin, TX: Holt, Rinehart and Winston.

Tetlock, P. 2002. Social functionalist frameworks for judgment and choice: Intuitive politicians, theologians, and prosecutors. *Psychological Bulletin* 109 (3): 451.

Thagard, P. 2000. *Coherence in thought and action*. Cambridge, MA: MIT Press.

Tindale, R. S., J. H. Davis, D. A. Vollrath, D. H. Nagao, and V. B. Hinsz. 1990. Asymmetrical social influence in freely interacting groups: A test of three models. *Journal of Personality and Social Psychology* 58 (3): 438.

Trafimow, D., and K. Finlay. 1996. The importance of subjective norms for a minority of the people. *Personality and Social Psychology Bulletin* 22:820, 823–25.

Troyer, L., and W. Younts. 1997. Whose expectations matter? The relative power of first-and-second-order expectations in determining social influence. *American Journal of Sociology* 103 (3): 692.

Tushnet, M. 1998. "Everything old is new again": Early reflections on the "New Chicago school." *Wisconsin Law Review* 1998:579, 584.

Tversky, A., and D. Kahneman. 1981. The framing of decisions and the psychology of choice. *Science* 211:453.

Tyler, T. 1990. *Why people obey the law*. New Haven, CT: Yale University Press.

Tyler, T., R. J. Boeckmann, H. J. Smith, and Y. J. Huo. 1997. *Social justice in a diverse society*. Nashville, TN: Westview.

Wegner, D. 2002. *The illusion of conscious will*. Cambridge, MA: MIT Press.

Wilder, D. 1990. Some determinants of the persuasive power of in-groups and out-groups: Organization of information and attribution of independence. *Journal of Personality and Social Psychology* 59 (6): 1202.

Wilson, T. 2002. *Strangers to ourselves: Discovering the adaptive unconscious*. Cambridge, MA: Belknap.

Wood, W. 1994. Minority influence: A meta-analytic review of social influence processes. *Psychology Review* 115:323.

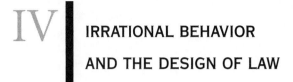

# IV

## IRRATIONAL BEHAVIOR
## AND THE DESIGN OF LAW

# 16 HUMAN FALLIBILITY AND THE FORMS OF LAW: THE CASE OF TRAFFIC SAFETY

*Thomas S. Ulen*

In the United States automobile accidents exact a large toll. Approximately forty thousand people die in automobile accidents each year, there are more than 3 million injuries, and the annual financial losses arising from traffic accidents exceed $130 billion (National Highway Traffic Safety Administration [NHTSA] 1998). In the European Union, which has a comparable population, the figures are similar. Compounding these figures is the widely remarked fact that the number of automobiles in use in society is increasing dramatically. Because the carrying capacity of highways has not increased at the same pace, the increasing number of cars is creating significant costs for society (Seabrook 2002).[1] Those costs are most evident in the number and duration of traffic jams that occur around major cities in Europe and North America. But they also include an increase in the social costs from automobile accidents. Although the safety of cars and the skill of traffic management have increased significantly so that the number of accidents per mile driven in almost all the developed countries has fallen, the social costs of accidents are still extremely high.[2] Clearly, traffic safety is a significant area in which public policy can seek to improve matters.

In this chapter I want to speak of how public policy—in which I want to in-

I would like to thank Professors Hubert Bocken and Boudwijn Bouckaert of the Faculty of Law, University of Ghent, for their invitation to spend a delightful period at Ghent that proved helpful in writing this paper; Professor Giuseppe Dari Mattiacci of the University of Utrecht; Ben Depoorter of the Faculty of Law, University of Ghent; and Professor Francesco Parisi of George Mason University School of Law for their comments on an earlier draft. I would also like to thank Megan Rudd, University of Illinois College of Law, class of 2005, for her invaluable research assistance.

clude legal policy—can further reduce the social costs of traffic accidents. I do so by looking at the recent literature on rational decision making and the economic analysis of law. I first briefly review rational choice theory and show how an application of that theory to decision making regarding automobile safety will suggest certain legal and other public policies designed to minimize the social costs of traffic accidents. Then I turn to a brief review of the so-called behavioral economics literature that is critical of some aspects of rational choice theory. Finally, I show how the incorporation of that behavioral literature into the conclusions on legal and public policy designed to reduce the costs of traffic accidents might lead to significant alteration in those policies.

My central claim is that there is little reason to hope that better or deeper exposure to legal liability can be expected to cause any significant increase in traffic safety. Rather, a recognition of the limited rationality of individual drivers and, therefore, of the necessarily limited efficacy of other legal and regulatory policies may lead us to put far more faith in technological fixes to the problems of traffic safety and mandatory regulations of automobile manufacturers than we might otherwise do. Society can adopt various policies, which I outline here, in order to hasten and make more complete these technological improvements in automobiles, roads, traffic signals, and other aspects of traffic safety.

## 16.1 RATIONAL CHOICE THEORY AND TRAFFIC SAFETY

Law and economics has had a remarkable impact on law and on legal scholarship through the application of rational choice theory to the analysis of legal rules and institutions. The reason is that law seeks to channel behavior into socially constructive behaviors. Because rational choice theory offers the most proven and comprehensive method of predicting how people respond to explicit and implicit incentives, this theory has served as the principal tool for predicting how people will respond to legal sanctions (Cooter and Ulen 2003).

### 16.1.1 Rational Choice Theory Generally and Its Application to Law

There is no widely accepted definition of *rational choice theory*, but we can distinguish two broad senses in which the term is used. The first is an informal sense: choice is said to be rational when it is deliberative and consistent. The decision maker has thought about what he or she will do and can give a reasoned justification for the choice. But this definition is not really very useful; at best it only distinguishes thoughtful from impulsive decisions. Every nonimpulsive action would seem to be the result of some deliberation and to be justifiable *ex post*.

The second sense is the formal sense in which economists speak of "rational choice": it is the result of the process whereby consumers with transitive preferences maximize their utility or well-being, subject to various constraints.[3]

There are critics of the more formal definition, too. For instance, some have said that the formal notion of rational choice is as tautological as the informal sense. That is, there is no, or almost no, behavior that refutes the formal sense of rationality. All behavior may be said to be directed at utility maximization (who would ever do otherwise?), and all preferences can be said to be transitive. But let us set these and other objections aside and focus on how economists use rational choice theory to explain behavior.

Economists use rational choice theory to explain and predict every individual choice. In routine circumstances, the use of the theory seems easy to accept. A particular consumer may choose to forgo a vacation and instead to continue working. Why? Rational choice theory might explain that the consumer's employer offered a bonus for continuing to work, so the opportunity cost of not working exceeded the anticipated utility of the vacation. A different decision maker purchased bonds rather than stocks because he anticipated the return to bondholding to be greater than the return to stockholding (whether or not that decision proved correct). Yet another decision maker chose to underpay her income taxes because she believed that the probability of her underpayment's being detected and punished by the tax authorities was less that the money saved from not paying the taxes.

My last example illustrates an application of rational choice theory that may stretch the application of the theory beyond what noneconomists are willing to accept. But law and economics—and the other disciplines, such as political science, international relations, sociology, and even biology, that have adopted rational choice theory—routinely apply rational choice theory to the explanation and prediction of noneconomic decisions. For instance, Gary Becker (1968), in one of the most famous applications of rational choice theory, sought to explain the decision to commit a crime. Assume that criminals are, as everyone else is, rational. In deciding whether to be lawful, they compare the expected costs and benefits of crime. They count the benefits of crime as being the monetary gain they anticipate or the increase in utility or well-being that they expect to enjoy from completion of the crime. They count as the expected costs of crime the probability of their crime's being detected, of their being arrested and convicted, multiplied by the value of the punishment—for example, a fine or term of imprisonment—and, perhaps, the loss of reputation or standing in their community that they may suffer if they are caught. If the expected benefits of committing the crime exceed the expected costs, then the rational criminal commits the crime. If the expected costs exceed the benefits, then the rational criminal does not commit the crime.

The decision makers of rational choice theory generally know what they are doing: they are capable of calculating costs and benefits, of assessing alternatives, and of recognizing when they need more information and when they have enough information to make a decision. They invariably take action well suited to helping them achieve their ends—namely, the maximization of utility. They are not necessarily selfish or self-centered people, because it is perfectly consistent with rational choice theory that they derive utility or well-being from the pleasure of others. But these rational choice decision makers do not make mistakes (unless they are the victims of fraud or misrepresentation); they do not have the foibles and fallibilities with which you and I are burdened. This does not mean that rational choice theory is unhelpful, because the theory is doing only what all scientific theories do: simplifying and abstracting away from real-world complexities.

## 16.1.2 The Application of Rational Choice Theory to Issues of Traffic Safety

Law and public policy seek to improve traffic safety through a number of different means. Here I want to concentrate on two of those means and show how a standard rational choice analysis of them might proceed. I begin with an examination of how exposure to tort liability might be thought to induce greater precaution by both manufacturers and individual drivers. Then I turn to a brief investigation of more direct regulation—administrative regulation of automobile manufacturers, for example, and enforcement of traffic regulations. At the end of this section I also note some possible synergies between those two different sets of policies.

### 16.1.2.1 Greater Precaution and Fewer Accidents
### Through Exposure to Tort Liability

Law and economics explains tort law as that body of rules designed to minimize the social costs of accidents, defined as the sum of prevention, accident, and administrative costs (Cooter and Ulen 2003). By holding out the possibility of imposing liability on a party for the costs of accidents, tort law seeks to get both potential injurers and potential victims to internalize the costs that their actions or failures to act may impose on others. This possibility induces rational parties to take all cost-justified care—that is, to purchase precaution up to the point at which the marginal benefit of that precaution (in terms of the reduced probability and severity of an accident) equals the marginal cost.[4] Doing so minimizes the social costs of accidents.

Consider this view as applied to the economic analysis of negligence. Negligence is the more efficient tort liability standard in situations of bilateral precaution (situations in which both the potential injurer and the potential victim can take precaution to reduce the probability and severity of an accident).[5] Imagine a situation in which it is not clear beforehand who will be a victim and who will be an injurer—automobile accidents, for example. Because anyone who is driving might be a victim or an injurer, there needs to be some method of inducing *every* driver to take care. Negligence does just that. A rational driver recognizes that he might be an injurer or a victim. He calculates that, if he should be an injurer, he will be liable under the negligence standard if he fails to take cost-justified precaution (as interpreted by, for example, the modern formulation of the Hand Rule). Therefore, being a rational cost minimizer or utility maximizer, he will take all cost-justified precaution and thereby escape liability as an injurer.

Now consider how that same rational driver decides how to behave if he should happen to be a victim. He reasons that if someone should injure him in an accident, that person will be rational and will have reasoned that he should take all cost-justified precaution so as to escape liability to the victim. As a result, the accident costs will be visited upon the *victim*. This potential victim will further reason that he must take all cost-justified precaution himself because he will have to bear the financial burden of any accident losses that arise.

In sum, negligence induces socially optimal care by both potential victims and injurers, both presumed to be rational actors, in situations of bilateral precaution.[6]

Note an important implication of this account of rational decision making regarding liability: automobile manufacturers have an incentive to introduce optional innovations to their cars that improve safety, and rational consumers have an incentive to purchase cost-effective safety options. I elaborate on this matter shortly.

### 16.1.2.2 Regulation of Suppliers and Enforcement of Traffic Regulations as a Means of Achieving Traffic Safety

Society can also seek to minimize the social costs of accidents by means of several forms of direct regulation, what is commonly called "command and control" regulation or, in this instance, "safety regulation." For example, rather than rely on automobile manufacturers to produce safer cars (as a means of reducing their exposure to tort liability for, perhaps, the production and marketing of defective products), society may seek to induce safer automobiles by mandating their production. The United States, for instance, has, through the NHTSA and other agencies, required that automobiles be equipped with safety features, such as front seat air bags, padded dashboards, crashworthy bumpers, collapsible steering columns, and the like.[7]

Manufacturers originally resisted these regulations, principally on two grounds: first, they would significantly increase the price of their automobiles—air bags are said to raise the retail price of an automobile by between five hundred dollars and one thousand dollars—perhaps leading consumers to cut their expenditures on other, nonmandated options for which the profit rate to manufacturers was, presumably, greater than that on mandated items; and second, these regulations might be the thin edge of a widening wedge of production requirements to come. The initial reluctance on the part of automobile manufacturers to mandated safety regulations appears to have waned (Mashaw and Harfst 1990). Perhaps the manufacturers have found that the safety features are cost-effective, in the sense that they have reduced the likelihood and severity of automobile accidents by a greater dollar amount than the required features cost to produce. At any rate, the manufacturers' complaints about direct regulation appear to have abated.[8]

Other direct regulations seek to increase traffic safety through providing rules of good driving behavior. These regulations include speed limits, lane markings, yield signs, stoplights, and the requirement that drivers take tests in order to receive a driver's license. They also include laws requiring drivers to wear seat belts and not to drive under the influence of alcohol or other drugs. Recently, there has been some concern that the use of cellular phones while driving has led to a decrease in traffic safety. In response, some states in the United States and many European Union countries have made the use of cellular phones by a driver in a moving automobile illegal.[9]

The theory of these legal policies—the exposure to tort liability for automobile manufacturers and drivers and to direct regulations for manufacturers and drivers—is that rational decision makers will seek to conform their behavior to the law. To do so will minimize their expected liability. Because policy makers believe most decision makers to be rational and to be seeking to maximize their utility while minimizing their costs, including their exposure to legal sanctions, policy makers believe that this range of legal policies will minimize the social costs of traffic accidents.

How does this model explain changes in rules and regulations (and the mix between tort liability and safety regulation) designed to achieve traffic safety? New technologies, changing preferences, and alterations in patterns and practices of automobile use may all necessitate change. So, for example, as cellular phones have become more popular, traffic regulations had to take account of their use on safety. As sports utility vehicles have become increasingly popular, traffic regulations might alter to take account of the fact that these vehicles, being much larger and higher than the usual car, may create special risks of harm. It is almost certain that in the future there will be significant changes in the design of cars; in the availability of devices within the automobile, such as televisions and Internet connectivity; in the speed and handling capabilities of cars; and so on that will necessitate alterations in traffic regulations. Still, the general point remains that if decision makers (automobile manufacturers, individual drivers, and public administrators) are rational, these adjustments can be made and can establish a new equilibrium at which the social costs of traffic accidents are minimized.[10]

Naturally, the question arises whether the actual fact that there are traffic accidents and traffic deaths means that rational choice theory is an inappropriate guide to public policy with respect to traffic safety. I address this matter more completely in the following section. Here I want to address the extent to which rational choice theory can explain the fact that people do not apparently fully conform their behavior to the requirements of law.

Rational choice theory is not incompatible with human fallibility. For example, rational people clearly engage in risky behavior: they may drive too fast, both for the prevailing conditions and in violation of the speed limit. One could say that such behavior is not a violation of rational choice theory in that a speeder has rationally computed the expected benefit of driving fast, discounted by the likelihood of meeting unforeseen circumstances and the likelihood of being detected by the police. This account of the decision to violate the traffic safety laws is just as rational as a decision to purchase a lottery ticket. Risks, even those of low probability, sometimes materialize, leading to an accident or a traffic ticket for speeding—just as a rationally purchased lottery ticket may turn out not to be a winning ticket.

In addition, there are lapses in concentration that every human being, even the hyperrational, experience. Very, very few people can pay such close attention to their driving as to avoid children unexpectedly darting out between parked cars. Even a rational decision maker may not be able to slow down sufficiently on ice or when suddenly entering a bank of fog. And an otherwise perfectly rational person may decide not to buckle her seat belt when she decides to drive a few blocks to pick something up at the local grocery store.

Finally, rational decision makers may not fully understand the tort laws and direct regulations with which they are to comply. They may mistakenly believe that the law urges them to wear seat belts but does not require it. They may mistakenly infer from a recent series of accidents in which air-bag explosions caused severe harm to children in car seats that it is wiser not to put their small children in the front seat or that their children should not be placed in their car seats at all. Information—and particularly asymmetric information—is a notoriously difficult commodity or service for markets to handle. No matter how rational decision makers may be, they still have problems in generating or disseminating the socially optimal amount of information or in knowing what information to believe.[11]

## 16.2 BEHAVIORALISM AND TRAFFIC SAFETY

Contrary to the argument of the prior sections, there is an increasing amount of evidence suggesting that decision makers are not fully rational.[12] Indeed, Daniel

Kahneman, a psychologist, won the Nobel Prize in economics in October 2002 for his work showing the limitations of rational choice theory. The serious literature on this topic does not conclude that human beings are irrational. Rather, it suggests that they make predictable mistakes in the exercise of judgment and in decision making. These mistakes are deviations from the predictions of rational choice theory. There is not yet a comprehensive theory of human decision making that incorporates these deviations with the view that there are many circumstances in which and many decisions about which human beings make perfectly rational decisions. We are at an early stage of a more nuanced or textured view of human decision making in which rationality and predictable deviations from rationality are explainable.

Nonetheless, there is an emerging consensus about some of the most common deviations from rational choice theory. For our purposes, what is most important about these deviations is how they ought to cause us to alter our views of the appropriate policies for achieving traffic safety. If manufacturers and drivers are not as rational as we assumed in the previous section, then policies that make that assumption need to be reexamined.

I begin that reexamination in this section. First, I give a very brief summary of the literature on behavioralism (as this literature critical of rational choice theory is known). Then, I show how those findings might alter our policies designed to achieve the minimization of the social costs of traffic accidents.

## 16.2.1 Behavioral Science and Law

Economists place great stock in the scientific method, as does, increasingly, law (Ulen 2002). As a result, they believe that empirical work is a necessary supplement to theoretical work. With respect to rational choice theory, that belief has given rise to a great deal of empirical work that seeks to confirm or refute the predictions of rational choice theory. And somewhat surprisingly, there is significant empirical work to suggest that actual human behavior does not always conform to the predictions of rational choice theory. Following, I briefly describe several examples of the literature that are critical of rational choice theory and that have particular relevance to the issues of traffic safety.

### 16.2.1.1 Reluctance to Bargain

Imagine a game, called the "ultimatum bargaining game," that is to be played between two players. The object of the game is to divide a sum of money—say, twenty dollars—according to the following rules. The players will not be allowed to speak to or see one another. (They will communicate only by means of, say, a computer connection.) The experimenter will designate one of the players as player 1 and the other as player 2. Player 1 is to make a proposal for the division of the twenty dollars; once she or he receives that proposed division, player 2 can accept the proposal, in which case each player gets the division proposed by player 1 and accepted by player 2, or player 2 can reject the proposal, in which case neither of the players receives any money.[13]

Rational choice theory makes no particular prediction about how rational actors will play this game, but there is one possible suggestion that sounds a chord for rational choice theorists: player 1 will reason that he or she can propose a strongly one-sided division of the stakes—say, nineteen dollars for him and one dollar for player 2—and that player 2, being a rational actor, will reason that one dollar is better than nothing and will accept the division. Perhaps that proposed division is too extreme; the more general point is that rational parties may reason that they can get more than half of the twenty dollars (and maybe much more) and that the other player will accept that division.

This game has been played in the form of an experiment, supervised by economists and others, in many different countries and with thousands and thousands of participants of all ages and from diverse backgrounds. In almost every playing of the game there is a modal outcome: an even division of the twenty dollars. There is also another common outcome: most player 2s will refuse to accept the proposed division if the proposal gives more than 70 percent of the stakes to player 1.

What to conclude from these experiments? There is no suggestion that the experiment threatens rational choice theory; after all, the common outcomes are perfectly consistent with the assumptions of that theory. However, the results of the ultimatum bargaining game experiments do seem to suggest that there is a much stronger taste for fairness than rational choice theory might have suspected and that the taste may lead people to behave in ways that rational choice theory might not have predicted. In particular, the second result (that parties will walk away from a gain if they perceive the division of the surplus as unfair) seems to be at odds with a widespread prediction of rational choice theory—namely, that whenever there is a cooperative surplus, there will be a bargain, if transaction costs are low. Apparently there is more to the story than that—there will be a bargain when there is a cooperative surplus, low transaction costs, and an equitable division of that surplus.[14]

### 16.2.1.2 *The Availability and Representativeness Heuristics*

The accurate prediction of the probability of future events demands that actors consider the statistical probability of an event's occurring and "update" (adjust) this "base rate" with any available particularized information about a specific situation.[15] There is significant evidence, however, that actors systematically underuse or ignore altogether base rates when making probability predictions. Related phenomena—the "representativeness heuristic" and the "availability heuristic"—describe two ways that actors often err in making such predictions.[16]

The "representativeness heuristic" refers to the tendency of actors to ignore base rates and, therefore, to overestimate the correlation between what something appears to be and what something actually is (Tversky and Kahneman 1982b). As an example of this tendency, consider the now-famous "bank teller" problem used by Tversky and Kahneman (1982b). Experimental subjects were given a description of a woman, Linda, with a number of characteristics that appeared representative of someone who is a feminist. Subjects were then asked whether it was more likely that Linda was a bank teller (choice *a*) or a bank teller active in the feminist movement (choice *b*). Nearly 90 percent of respondents chose *b*, a choice that is logically impossible because every person described by choice *b* is also described by choice *a*, but the reverse is not true.[17] Subjects ignored the base rate (there are more bank tellers than feminist bank tellers) because the description of Linda appeared more "representative" of the latter than of the former.

The pervasiveness of the representativeness heuristic can help justify a set of rules of evidence law frustrating to rational choice theory. The *Federal Rules of Evidence* 404 (1998) provide that "character evidence" is inadmissible in a trial to prove the truth of the matter asserted, unless one of a series of exceptions to the rule applies. For example, a prosecutor may not introduce evidence that a criminal defendant charged with murder has a previous record of conviction for armed robbery.[18] In most circumstances, a prosecutor cannot even introduce evidence that a defendant charged with murder has a previous murder conviction (Muller and Kirkpatrick 1994).

Assuming that jurors seek to maximize the positive relationship between their verdict and a criminal defendant's guilt, this type of character evidence is quite useful in enabling jurors to maximize their utility. Armed robbers are more likely than the average person to commit a murder, so the character evidence is quite relevant. The rational juror should consider the base rate of murderers in the population (quite small) and update that probability with the information that the particular defendant has been convicted of armed robbery. Preventing the presentation of the character evidence reduces the likelihood that a rational juror will reach the appropriate conclusion about the defendant's guilt.

The law correctly excludes character evidence from consideration, however, if jurors are likely to ignore the base rate—that is, to ignore the fact that most armed robbers are *not* murderers—and base their conclusion about the defendant's guilt on whether specific features about him look like stereotypical features of a murderer. Using the representativeness heuristic, many jurors are likely to conclude that because the defendant has the appearance of a criminal (in that he has a felony conviction), he therefore must have committed the crime for which he is charged.

When actors overestimate the relevance of salient or memorable incidents at the expense of base rates, they employ the "availability heuristic."[19] This mental shortcut can often lead to estimates that approximate statistical probabilities, as memorable events can be memorable precisely because they are common.[20] Unfortunately for the sake of precision, however, memorable events can also be memorable for reasons having nothing to do with their general prevalence—for example, because they are vivid, well publicized, or more prevalent among a particular actor's friends and acquaintances. Actors often estimate these available events as being much more common than they actually are.

For example, most people believe that words beginning with the letter $k$ are more prevalent than words in which $k$ is the third letter, although the latter set of words is actually twice as large as the former (Tversky and Kahneman 1982a). Presumably, the reason is that it is easier to bring to mind words that begin with the letter $k$ than those that have $k$ as their third letter (such as *ark* and *ankle*). Similarly, most people believe that homicides and car accidents kill more Americans than diabetes and stomach cancer—presumably because of the greater media coverage provided to the former—although the two diseases kill far more people (Plous 1993). McCaffery (1994) hypothesizes that most states favor sales taxes over income and property taxes even though income and property taxes have a lower net cost to residents (they are deductible from federal income tax, whereas sales taxes are not), in part because the latter taxes are more prominent to taxpayers than are the former.

That people are biased by availability can have a widespread impact on legal policy in a variety of specific situations. Consider the potential impact of the availability heuristic on the policy prescriptions that rational choice theory provides for deterring crime. According to conventional rational choice analysis, potential criminals maximize their utility by committing crimes only if the expected benefits exceed the expected costs. If criminals are rational utility maximizers, society can deter crime by raising these expected costs above the expected benefits of crime. And society can achieve this end equally successfully by increasing the severity of punishment or the frequency of arrest, conviction, and punishment. Because increasing severity (for example, by lengthening jail terms or imposing monetary fines) is generally thought to be cheaper than increasing frequency (for example, by increasing the number of police, prosecutors, and judges), it is generally assumed that increasing severity is the more efficient deterrence strategy (Kahan 1997).

If criminals are biased by availability when calculating (no doubt in an informal sort of way) the anticipated costs of crime, this analysis could change radically, depending on what types of events are more salient to potential criminals. In order to determine which deterrence mechanism will be most efficient, policy makers need to understand whether criminals are likely to over- or underestimate the frequency and the severity of punishment that is actually meted out. If punishments are so severe that some sentences become shocking and well publicized, increasing severity could be the more efficient deterrence strategy. Otherwise, increasing the frequency of punishment is likely to be more efficient, under the assumption that if criminals know or know of someone who has been imprisoned for a particular crime, this information is likely to be available and cause them to overestimate the likelihood that they will be arrested and convicted if they commit the same crime.

Finally, an understanding of the availability heuristic can provide a caution to policy makers tempted to enact new regulatory regimes in response to highly available information concerning health or safety risks. Jolls, Sunstein, and Thaler (1998) argue persuasively that the enactment of "Superfund" legislation in 1980 was largely a result of publicity concerning the coverage of environmental contamination in Love Canal, New York, beginning in 1978. It is at least arguable that the legislation's attempt to solve the problem of toxic waste dumps diverted scarce public and congressional attention from far more dangerous and pervasive environmental health risks.[21]

### 16.2.1.3 Overconfidence and Self-Serving Biases

Even when actors know the actual probability distribution of a particular event, their predictions as to the likelihood that the event will happen to them are prone to the "overconfidence bias": the belief that good things are more likely than average to happen to us and bad things are less likely than average to happen to us (Jolls 1998). Demonstrating that a particular individual is overconfident is difficult to do, because the individual might well differ from the statistically average person in positive ways. For example, a student who believes he will score above the mean on an exam might be overconfident of his ability. On the other hand, he might be smarter or a more diligent studier than his peers, making the prediction quite reasonable. But the pervasiveness of the overconfidence bias has been demonstrated persuasively in experiments that elicit opinions from all members of a group about how they are likely to compare to other members of the group (Weinstein 1980).

Weinstein (1987) has demonstrated the overconfidence bias by asking a sample of students at Rutgers University to estimate whether each of a series of events was more or less likely (and how much more or less likely) to happen to them than to their classmates. For eighteen positive events, ranging from owning their own home to avoiding a hospital stay for five years, the mean respondent estimated her chances at greater than the average for her peers—for example, the other survey respondents—in fifteen of the events. In contrast, subjects on average believed that negative events, ranging from suffering a divorce to losing a job to contracting lung cancer, were less likely to happen to them than to their average peer in twenty-two of twenty-four events. Similarly, in a survey of Virginia residents who applied for a marriage license, Baker and Emery (1993) found that although most respondents knew that close to half of all marriages end in divorce, when asked to predict the likelihood that their marriage would end in divorce, the median response was zero!

The overconfidence bias could have a wide-ranging impact on deterrence policy in a variety of areas of law. Policy makers rarely wish to deter 100 percent of even undesirable conduct, because the costs of doing so would likely be too great. For any type of conduct that the state wishes to discourage, from criminal behavior to carelessness likely to lead to a tort, rational choice theory advises policy makers to set the penalty for the undesirable conduct such that the desired fraction of the population—say, potential injurers—will calculate that the expected costs of the conduct exceed the expected benefits to them. Where the targets of such policies exhibit overconfidence, however, policy makers will have to set the penalties higher—sometimes substantially so—than they would in a world of utility-maximizing actors who are not systematically overconfident. If bank robbers believe that they are less likely to be apprehended than their peers, if absentminded drivers believe they are less likely to cause an accident than other drivers, or if physicians believe they are less likely to be found liable for malpractice than other physicians, penalties for the undesirable behavior will have to be higher than policy makers would otherwise think necessary to achieve the desired level of deterrence (Gawande 1999).

For policy makers to be able to make effective use of the insights provided by the overconfidence bias, more empirical research needs to be done on which groups and in what situations overconfidence is likely to be most severe.[22] Currently, one useful conclusion can be drawn from the literature: at least for events perceived to be negative, actors apparently tend to be more overconfident when the event in question is perceived to be controllable than when it is perceived not to be controllable.[23] This finding suggests that an understanding of the overconfidence bias is, in fact, particularly necessary to develop optimal deterrence policies, because such policies are targeted at controllable events.

Related to the overconfidence bias is the "confirmatory" or "self-serving" bias, the description given to the observation that actors often interpret information in ways that serve their interests or preconceived notions. For example, Lord, Ross, and Lepper (1979) found that when experimental subjects were given factual evidence about the effects of the death penalty, subjects identified as proponents of capital punishment said the evidence reinforced their prior beliefs, whereas subjects identified as opponents of capital punishment said that the information reinforced their prior beliefs.

In a series of papers, Loewenstein et al. (1993) and Babcock et al. (1995, 1996) found a similar effect of information in the litigation context. A group of law student subjects were provided with factual information about a dispute in litigation. Despite being given identical information, subjects who were told to imagine that they were the attorney representing the plaintiff interpreted the facts as favorable to the plaintiff, whereas subjects told to imagine that they were the attorney representing the defendant interpreted the facts as favorable to the defendant.[24]

The conventional law and economics approach to trial and settlement, based on rational choice theory, predicts that because trials are more costly than out-of-court settlement, lawsuits will settle out of court unless the parties have substantially different predictions about the likely results of trial (Cooter and Rubenfeld 1989; Cooter and Ulen 2003; Priest and Klein 1984). Plaintiffs and defendants may reach different predictions about the likely outcome of a trial, but differences in predictions are presumed to be in both directions—that is, where the predictions of plaintiffs and defendants diverge, half of the time plaintiffs will believe their prospects are worse than defendants anticipate (Babcock et al. 1995; Priest and Klein 1984). An implication of this conventional account is that because litigation will be less likely when the parties have more accurate estimates of the likelihood of prevailing, anything that improves those estimates—such as expanded pretrial discovery or better legal representation—is to be favored.

Evidence of the self-serving bias in the analysis of lawsuits suggests, in contrast, that plaintiffs will systematically anticipate their trial prospects as being better than defendants believe. The consequence of this is more trials than would be predicted by the rational choice model, unless steps are taken to mitigate the parties' evaluative biases. More information—provided, perhaps, in the form of expanded pretrial discovery—is unlikely to be effective because, as we have seen in the experiments cited previously concerning the death penalty controversy, people seem to use more evidence to solidify their views rather than to alter them.

### 16.2.1.4 Hindsight Bias

Perhaps the most studied shortcoming in probabilistic assessment is the "hindsight bias," the term that describes the tendency of actors to overestimate the *ex ante* prediction that they had concerning the likelihood of an event's occurring after learning that it actually did occur.[25] In what is arguably the most famous of the many hindsight bias studies, Fischhoff (1975) gave five groups of subjects a passage to read describing the events leading up to a military confrontation between the British army and the Gurkhas in Nepal in the nineteenth century and asked them, on the basis of that information alone, to specify the likelihood that four specified military outcomes would have resulted. Each of four groups was told that a different outcome of the four specified outcomes actually occurred, whereas the fifth group (the control group) was given no information on the actual outcome. Subjects in each of the groups to whom the investigators gave an outcome reported an *ex ante* prediction of that outcome that was considerably higher than the prediction for that outcome made by the subjects in the control group.[26] In other words, information about what actually occurred apparently influences our judgments concerning what we thought would occur before we knew the outcome. Events that have actually occurred seem, through the lens of hindsight, to have been almost inevitable.

Kamin and Rachlinski (1995) demonstrated the effect that the hindsight bias can have on the assignment of tort liability (see also Labine and Labine 1996). Using a fact pattern based on the famous case *Petition of Kinsman Transit Company*, 338 F.2d 708 (2d Cir. 1964); cert. denied, 85 S. Ct. 1026 (1965), the experimenters asked a group of subjects to play the role of jurors and to determine whether a company operating a bridge had been negligent in its failure to take precautions that would have prevented flood damage to third parties. They instructed subjects to use the Hand Rule to determine whether an act was negligent—that is, to assess liability only if the costs of precaution to the bridge company would have been less than the expected costs of flood damage to third parties (given the uncertainty of a flood occurring) of not taking the precaution (Kamin and Rachlinski 1995). Although 57 percent of the juror subjects would have found the bridge company negligent under this standard, only 24 percent of subjects in a control condition, who had the same information except that they did not know that the flood had in fact occurred, believed that the cost of precaution would have been justified by the risks of not taking the precautions. Law and economics suggests that precaution is efficient when its benefits outweigh its costs and that tort law should impose liability for negligence when an actor fails to take efficient precaution but not when the actor fails to take inefficient precaution. But if jurors are subject to the hindsight bias, defendants will be found negligent in situations in which they acted in a socially efficient manner (failed to take inefficient precautions) but were struck by bad luck. This, in turn, could provide actors with a private incentive to take an inefficiently high amount of precaution.

As is true with many of the deviations from the predictions of rational choice theory, the legal implications of the behavioral phenomenon are not clear cut. If jury instructions could obviate the hindsight bias, such a strategy would clearly be appropriate in a variety of situations in which efficient deterrence requires jurors to impose liability based on *ex ante* judgments about the likelihood of certain events occurring. Unfortunately, psychologists have yet to find a method of eliminating the hindsight bias, and even reducing its effect has proven quite difficult (Rachlinski 1998).

Some analysts have suggested that the bias might be countered by raising the standard of proof necessary to find a defendant negligent—for example, from the existing "preponderance of the evidence" standard to one of "clear and convincing evidence" (Jolls, Sunstein, and Thaler 1998; Rachlinski 1998). Rachlinski (1998) has argued that this is one way to understand the business judgment rule in corporate law: corporate officers and directors are held liable for, in effect, "negligently" operating their companies only when there is evidence of "gross negligence."[27] The problem with this approach, of course, is its lack of precision. If the hindsight bias is strong, raising the standard of proof might not eliminate overdeterrence. On the other hand, raising the standard of proof could swamp the bias, leading to underdeterrence. This might happen if the hindsight bias effect, in the event of litigation, is not terribly strong so that liability is difficult to establish under the "clear and convincing evidence" standard and, as a result, potential injurers take less precaution than they ought to because the likelihood of being held liable has fallen significantly.

Jolls, Sunstein, and Thaler (1998) have suggested that the bias might be avoided by shielding juries from evidence concerning what action the defendant actually took until after jurors have determined what decision would have been reasonable *ex ante*. To illustrate how this might work, the authors give the example of a food-processing company that might have subjected its customers to contaminated food if it chose *not to use* a certain preservative and might subject them to carcinogenic chemicals if it chose *to use* the preservative. Jurors would then be asked to assess the costs and benefits of using and not using the preservative, *not knowing which choice the defendant made or the consequences of that choice*.

This is a creative solution, but it can work only in the limited number of cases in which it is plausible that both acting and not acting could subject the defendant to a lawsuit. In most litigation situations, it is clear from the fact that a lawsuit has been filed and a jury impaneled that a particular type of accident occurred (or allegedly occurred). Therefore, as creative as the proposal is, it does not seem practicable as a general solution to the problem the hindsight bias creates.

Instead, we believe that the presence of the hindsight bias argues for two other reforms of accident regulation, one within the realm of private tort law, the other within public law. The first is the wider use of strict liability and, consequently, a more restricted scope for negligence liability. The hindsight bias casts doubt on the ability of juries to reach proper negligence determinations because juries are likely to believe precautions that could have been taken would have been more cost-effective than they actually appeared to be *ex ante*. But the bias presents no similar impediments to the ability of juries to reach proper liability determinations under a strict liability regime, in which the jury need only determine that the alleged accident occurred and was caused by the defendant in order for liability to attach.

The second reform designed to overcome the problems of hindsight bias in adjudication is to downplay *ex post* adjudication as a method of minimizing the social costs of accidents in favor of broader *ex ante* administrative agency regulation of safety. Administrative regulation has, of course, a host of problems of its own: inflexibility, political pressures from well-organized interest groups, bureaucratic bumbling, and the like (Breyer 1982; Farber and Frickey 1991). But holding all other things constant, evidence of the hindsight bias strengthens the argument for protecting public safety prospectively through administrative regulation as opposed to retrospectively through private tort actions.

## 16.2.2 Behavioral Implications for Legal and Public Policy for Traffic Safety

The implications of the behavioral literature for issues of traffic safety are profound. Consider the impacts of three of the findings about human decision-making imperfections noted in the previous section on traffic safety.

First, the availability and representativeness heuristics may suggest that individual drivers will not do a very good job of estimating the probabilities of being involved in an accident or the value of precautionary behavior and equipment. Rather than rely on objective estimates of probability or of other information relevant to safety decisions, most individuals will rely on potentially misleading information that is readily available or that they deem to be representative of the issue at hand. If, to take one example, the issue is whether to wear a seat belt, individuals may make that decision on the basis of whether they or someone they know has recently had an accident and been spared serious injury as a result of wearing a seat belt. If they have no such readily available information or if their experience is that they have not routinely worn a seat belt and have never been in an accident, then they may be led not to take precaution because, in their experience, it is unnecessary. They may not rely on objective estimates of the value of seat belts. Nor is it probable that fear of paying a fine for not wearing a seat belt will induce safer conduct.

These (and the following) heuristics may also play an important part in explaining the likelihood that private safety innovation will make itself attractive to automobile purchasers. Here is the issue. One might argue, following rational choice theory, that there is no particular need for government intrusion into private decision making regarding auto safety because inventors, manufacturers, and consumers all face socially appropriate incentives. First, an innovator has an incentive, through the intellectual property system and other legal and market devices, to invest in the discovery and marketing of a device that greatly improves the safety of those in an automobile in the event of an accident. Suppose that the innovation reduces the expected costs (the probability times the severity) of an accident by more than it costs to produce and market. Surely then, automobile manufacturers have the appropriate incentive to purchase or license the use of the innovation from the inventor and to sell the innovation to consumers. To be concrete, suppose that the innovation costs five hundred dollars to license, produce, and market and that it reduces expected accident costs by one thousand dollars. Consumers ought to be willing to pay between five hundred and one thousand dollars additional for each automobile that includes the superior innovation. Everyone—innovator, manufacturer, automobile purchaser, and potential victims—will be better off.

Even if the innovator and the auto manufacturer respond appropriately to the incentives to improve safety, the fact that consumers may not place the right value on an innovation—because, for example, they systematically underestimate the likelihood of being in an accident, either because the right information is not readily available or because they are overoptimistic about their abilities as careful drivers—could mean that the incentives to develop and market safety innovations may not lead to the socially appropriate amount of traffic safety invention and purchase.

Second, overconfidence or overoptimism suggests that all drivers believe themselves to be above average in their driving abilities. As a result, they may well not take sufficient precaution in the belief that their skills will protect them from being involved in an accident. Importantly, there does not seem to be any straightforward method of using exposure to tort liability or direct regulation to correct for this bias in human decision making. Making the imposition of liability more likely or more severe is unlikely to dampen overoptimism or to correct the self-serving bias. Nor is there much in the way of alteration of direct regulation that can take due account of these biases in human decision making. Lowering speed limits to induce overconfident drivers to drive more slowly might possibly have an effect, but that effect is likely to be both small, if it can be realized, and extremely difficult to implement.[28] Nor will overconfident individuals take adequate account of the fact that they have had too much alcohol to drink and ought not to drive or that they are overly tired and unable to react quickly to danger.[29]

Finally, the presence of the hindsight bias suggests that tort law may not work as well as rational choice theory had hoped to create incentives to take care.[30] If, as Jolls, Sunstein, and Thaler (1998) argue, juries and even judges are likely to find defendants liable on the ground that if an accident actually occurred, someone must have done something wrong, then there is little that manufacturers, for instance, can do to avoid liability if there happens to be an accident. The only method that they have for limiting their liability for failing to produce crashworthy cars is to build expensive and perhaps absurd levels of safety into them or to lobby the relevant federal decision makers to protect them from litigation.

### 16.2.3 Technological Improvements for Traffic Safety

In light of these issues, I believe that we should be doubtful that any further exposure to tort liability (by, for example, tightening tort law's bite or making private litigation cheaper) will induce any further improvements in traffic safety. Similarly, it is probably the case, because of the decision-making shortcomings highlighted earlier, that the ability of private manufacturers to induce private individuals to purchase more safety is limited. These are the central claims of this chapter.

How then can traffic safety be improved? The answer probably lies in government-sponsored technological improvements in automobile and road safety. I have in mind the sort of government-mandated safety devices—such as air bags—that have, in the past, caused such consternation among economists and private-sector interests. If, as I have argued, we cannot count on individual drivers to drive carefully or to purchase the socially optimal amount of safety equipment, then society must require them to do so.

Consider what is widely considered to be one of the next important innovations in automobile safety—the Collision Warning System (CWS). NHTSA believes that driver inattention and following too closely account for 88 percent of rear-end collisions. The CWS, if installed on automobiles, could warn drivers that they are following too closely and even apply brakes to prevent a collision. NHTSA estimates that a CWS could "theoretically prevent 37 percent to 74 percent of all police-reported rear-end crashes." [31]

The key to this proposal is the governmental funding of research into mandatory safety—in the U.S. case, this means "federal governmental," although the state governments would certainly not be precluded from sponsoring such research—and ultimately the requirement that certain of those innovations be mandatory for auto manufacturers to install. I recognize that there are serious practical problems in specifying the procedures for determining which innovations to fund. The government has in the past done a reasonably good job of identifying some innovations to back—such as the Internet—and a reasonably good job in identifying those that ought to be left to the market—such as the standards for high-definition television. There will be powerful academic and private interests involved in government-sponsored research into automobile safety, but there always are those interests to contend with. There will also be difficult issues of deciding when the safety innovations have matured to the point that they are reasonably priced and effective enough to warrant being mandatorily included in all new automobiles. Perhaps those issues will prove so troubling as to make the system of governmental technology forcing in traffic safety a failure. At the moment, I see no realistic alternative to further improvements other than the proposal I am here putting forward.

No one should be deluded into believing that taking decisions about auto safety out of the hands of manufacturers and consumers and placing them in the hands of public and private organizations will be a perfect solution. There will be different problems under this alternative regime for achieving traffic safety, but with due attention these new problems will be open, correctible, and less damaging than those I have sought to identify previously.

We can anticipate two particular kinds of problems with placing the burden for developing safer automobiles and highways on government and private suppliers. First, group decision-making processes are subject to their own biases (Langevoort 1997, 2001). For example, there is extensive evidence that if there is a range of opinions within a group and the group must express a single opinion, the group's opinion will tend to polarize toward one of the extreme positions within the group rather than settle on the average or median opinion (Sunstein 2000). Second, there are the forces of public choice with which to contend. Politicians and private profit-making enterprises are symbiotic. Government agencies may well trim their regulations to accommodate the wishes of well-organized industry lobbying groups, whereas the general public interest in safety may be underrepresented. There are myriad examples of public policy being made not for the broad social interest but rather for the interests of the small, well-organized interest group. That could happen with respect to technology-forcing traffic safety regulations, too, and a prudent public policy should be on the lookout for undue private interference in the design of administrative policy.

## 16.3 CONCLUSION

In this chapter I have tried to show that predictable shortcomings of private decision making make it difficult for two traditional tools designed to achieve traffic safety—exposure to tort liability and privately generated safety innovations—to achieve their goals. Rather, further improvements in the safety of automobiles are likely to come only from technological innovations that manufacturers adopt at the urging, even the insistence, of government regulators.

1. The estimate in Seabrook's article is that the number of automobiles in the United States has increased by 400 percent since the early 1970s and that the carrying capacity of roads has increased by, at most, 50 percent. The European Union has experienced a roughly similar pattern of car ownership and road building in the last thirty years.

2. The improved lighting, signage, and traffic control measures (such as putting stop signs at all rural intersections and crossing barriers at the intersection of railroads and highways) have had an important positive effect on traffic safety. So, too, have technological improvements in automobiles, such as passive-restraint systems, child-care seating, air bags, shatter-proof glass, reinforced crash-zone protection, neck rests, collapsible steering columns, exterior lighting improvements, and the like. The result has been that "the fatality rate per hundred million vehicle miles traveled [in the United States] has fallen from 5.5 to 1.7 in the period from the mid-1960s to 1994" (NHTSA 1998; http://www.nhtsa .dot.gov/people/injury/research /pub/ACAS/ACAS_index.htm).

3. Transitive preferences are those for which, if some good or bundle of goods denoted $A$ is preferred to another good or bundle of goods denoted $B$ and $B$ is preferred to a third good or bundle of goods denoted $C$, then it must be the case that $A$ is preferred to $C$. By contrast, if it were the case that $A$ were preferred to $B$, $B$ were preferred to $C$, and $C$ were preferred to $A$, we would find that distinctly odd—indeed, irrational.

4. This is the modern law and economics formulation of the famous Hand Rule. For the original formulation, see *U.S. v. Carroll Towing Co.*, 159 F.2d 169 (2d Cir. 1947). For an elaboration of the modern formulation, see Cooter and Ulen (2003).

5. Strict liability is the more efficient liability standard in situations of unilateral precaution (in which only the potential injurer can realistically take precaution to reduce the probability or severity of an accident).

6. I have, of course, left out much of the nuance of the theory. One important oversight is the analysis of how different liability standards might affect the activity levels of potential injurers. For a summary, see Landes and Posner (1987). The original statement of the activity level argument was by Shavell (1980).

7. The regulations apparently establish a minimum acceptable level of safety in automobiles. Manufacturers are free, of course, to include additional features for which they believe that consumers will be willing to pay. And manufacturers may still be held liable in a private tort action even though they have complied with all relevant safety regulations.

8. I am not strictly certain that this has occurred. It is possible that complaints are constant or that manufacturers have gained control of the relevant political processes so that they need fear no further safety regulation.

9. There is no controlling federal statute on the use of cellular phones while driving; this is exclusively, so far, a matter of state law. And the default rule appears to be that drivers may use cell phones while driving. There is only one state that strictly prohibits the use of cellular telephones while operating a motor vehicle: New York (N.Y. Veh. & Traf. Law § 1225-c. 2003). The few states that impose restrictions short of complete bans do so in idiosyncratic ways. Maine prohibits minors and those on learner driving licenses from using a cellular telephone while driving (Act of May 23, 2003, 2003 Me. Legis. Serv. 286 (West)) (to be codified at Me. Rev. Stat. Ann. tit. 29-A, § 1304). New Jersey prohibits persons driving on learner's permits from using a cellular telephone while driving (N.J. Stat. Ann. § 39:3-13.2(a) (2003)). Massachusetts permits cellular phone use so long as it does not interfere with the operation of the vehicle and one hand remains on the steering wheel at all times (Mass. Gen. Laws Ann. ch. 90, § 13 (2003)). There are two states that have adopted the curious policy of not only not regulating use at the state level but also prohibiting local jurisdictions from imposing any regulations: Oklahoma (Okl. St. Ann. 47 § 15-102.1 (2003)) and Oregon (Or. Rev. Stat. § 801.038 (2001)). Three states ban bus drivers from using cellular telephones while operating the bus: Illinois (625 Ill. Comp. Stat. Ann. 5/12-813.1 (2003)); New Jersey (N.J. Stat. Ann. § 39:3B-25 (2003)); and Rhode Island (R.I. Gen. Laws § 31-22-11.8 (2002)).

Internationally, about forty-four countries, including Australia, Belgium, Denmark, Germany, Italy, Poland, Spain, and India, banned the use of cellular phones while driving. Information about international and U.S. state regulations of cell phone use while driving is available at http://www.cellular-news.com/car_bans/.

10. I mention later very briefly the possibility that law need not take some of these changes into account in seeking to achieve traffic safety. There may be strong incentives on private manufacturers to introduce and market cost-justified safety innovations.

11. Governmental policies can correct for some of these problems—for example, by sponsoring research and by subsidizing the distribution of information.

12. For an extensive treatment of this empirical work, see Korobkin and Ulen (2000). Much of this section of the chapter draws on that longer piece.

13. The twenty dollars may be characterized as a "cooperative surplus." That is the term of art that is used to describe the new value that arises from mutually beneficial voluntary exchange. The general presumption in bargaining theory and economics is that if there is a cooperative surplus to be had and transaction costs are not too high, then the parties will find a way to cooperate so as to realize a portion of that surplus.

14. See Korobkin and Ulen (2000) for some elaborations on the ultimatum bargaining game literature. An example of an elaboration is one in which the experimenter selects player 1, not according to chance but rather according to some seemingly meritorious criterion, such as the ability to answer a question. Where that method is used to select the player who makes the initial proposal about the division of the cooperative surplus, there appears to be a greater willingness on the part of player 2s to accept a more one-sided division of that surplus.

15. This method of calculating probabilities is known as "Bayes's law." Hogg and Craig (1970) show that in application of the law, one "updates" a prior probability assessment with new information, in a manner defined by the law, in order to get a posterior probability estimate.

16. For a more detailed (but still brief) discussion of the representativeness and availability heuristics, see Plous (1993). See Tversky and Kahneman (1982a, 1982b) for more detailed treatments.

17. More specifically, this is an example of the conjunction fallacy. The Conjunction Rule states, "The probability of some event A occurring cannot be less than the probability of A and some other event B both occurring" (Stein 1996). As a further example, suppose that I tell you that there is a 50 percent chance that it will rain and be at least 70 degrees Fahrenheit tomorrow. What is the probability that it will rain tomorrow? It cannot be less than 50 percent.

18. "[T]he basic rule of exclusion is of fundamental importance. It implements the philosophy that a defendant should not be convicted because he is an unsavory person, nor because of past misdeeds, but only because of his guilt of the particular crime charged" (Muller and Kirkpatrick 1994).

19. "A person is said to employ the availability heuristic whenever he estimates frequency or probability by the ease with which instances or associations could be brought to mind" (Tversky and Kahneman 1982a).

20. Note that so long as available incidents are representative of base rates, relying on available anecdotes rather than statistical probabilities will not lead to suboptimal decision making. "It is entirely rational for people to rely on anecdotal evidence in the absence of better evidence" (Posner 1998).

21. Consider another famous example of how individuals often fail to adequately consider base rates when making probability predictions, provided by Kahneman and Tversky (1982a). Suppose that 85 percent of the cabs in town are green and 15 percent are blue. A cab is involved in a hit-and-run accident, but the victim did not see the color of the cab. An eyewitness says that the offending cab was blue. How much credence should we give to the eyewitness's account? Suppose that the court, in an attempt to probe the worthiness of the eyewitness, creates an experiment in which she is shown a number of cabs under exactly the same conditions as those prevailing at the time of the accident and that she gets the color of the cab correct 80 percent of the time. When asked, "What is the

likelihood of the offending cab's being blue, given that the eyewitness said it was blue?" most people estimate it to be 80 percent likely. But that is wildly wrong. In point of fact, the probability that the cab is blue, given that the witness says that it is blue, is only about 40 percent. To see why, suppose that the eyewitness had been shown 100 cabs of which 85 were green and 15 were blue. Of the 85 green cabs, she would have correctly identified 80 percent of them, or 68, as being green but would have incorrectly identified 17 of the green cabs as being blue. Of the 15 blue cabs, she would have correctly identified 12 of them as blue but would have incorrectly identified 3 of the blue cabs as being green. In total, she said that 29 of the cabs that she saw were blue (17 green cabs mistakenly identified as blue plus 12 blue cabs correctly identified). Of those 29, only 12 were actually blue. The probability that the offending cab was blue, given that the eyewitness said that it was blue, is 12/29 or approximately 40 percent. Because most people do not take account of the base rate in making probability estimates, they are prone to the sort of error of this example: here, they give twice as much credence to the eyewitness as they ought to.

22. One plausible—but as yet unproven—hypothesis is that older people are less overconfident than younger people (Posner 1995). Available data do suggest, however, that the bias is not limited to the young, who disproportionately serve as subjects in psychology experiments (Guppy 1993; Weinstein 1987).

23. Weinstein (1980) concluded that when subjects perceived an event to be controllable, they tended to compare themselves with the stereotypical victim of the negative event, leading to overconfident predictions. In contrast, when events were perceived as uncontrollable, subjects did not perceive a stereotype of a victim with whom to compare themselves.

24. Investigators have identified a closely related effect called "cognitive dissonance," which is a form of selective perception in which actors give greater weight to evidence that confirms beliefs they already hold and lesser weight to contradictory evidence (Festinger 1957; Plous 1993).

25. For a review of well over one hundred studies of the hindsight bias, see Christensen-Szalanski and Willham (1991).

26. The experiment is discussed, among other places, in Rabin (1998) and Rachlinski (1998).

27. See, e.g., *Aronson v. Lewis*, 473 A.2d 805 (Del. 1984) (stating the "gross negligence" standard). Of course, there are other ways of justifying that rule. For instance, a standard argument is that shareholders would want managers to have wide discretion to run the company without having to face repeated challenges to their decisions on a close standard such as "preponderance of the evidence."

28. I am referring to the political difficulties in passing legislation to reduce speed limits. Such legislation would be difficult to pass in any state in the United States, partly because it would be widely unpopular but also because it might disadvantage the state that passed such legislation if its neighbors did not follow

its lead. There may be, that is, a collective action problem in seeking to achieve a further reduction in traffic accidents by means of lowering speed limits: it is unlikely to be done by individual states and may, therefore, necessitate federal action, which strikes me as politically very unlikely.

29. Alcohol use is still the leading cause of serious and fatal traffic accidents in the United States. However, the NHTSA is so concerned about the effects of drowsiness on traffic safety that it has convened a task force to discuss the problem and to recommend polices to combat the increasing social costs of drowsy drivers. See www.nhtsa.gov.

30. This is a theme of De Geest and Mattiacci (2003).

31. *ACAS, Final Report* (NHTSA 1998, 9). The system can also warn of forward, side, and rear impending collisions by means of both long-range and short-range radar, optical sensors, and a lane detection system. To speak to the practicability of this system, it is worth noting that the *ACAS Final Report* appeared in 1998 and that no regulatory or other action has been taken on its recommendations in the last five years. In large part this inaction is attributable to the high cost of the system and in part to political factors that may make it difficult or inappropriate for the federal government to finance further development of the system.

REFERENCES

Babcock, L., G. Loewenstein, S. Issacharoff, and C. Camerer. 1995. Biased judgments of fairness in bargaining. *American Economic Review* 85:1337.

———. 1996. Choosing the wrong pond: Social comparisons in negotiations that reflect a self-serving bias. *Quarterly Journal of Economics* 111:1.

Baker, L., and R. Emery. 1993. When every relationship is above average: Perceptions and expectations of divorce at the time of marriage. *Law and Human Behavior* 17:439.

Becker, G. 1968. Crime and punishment: An economic approach. *Journal of Political Economy* 76 (2): 169–217.

Breyer, S. 1982. *Regulation and its reform.* Cambridge, MA: Harvard University Press.

Christensen-Szalanski, J., and C. Willham. 1991. The hindsight bias: A meta-analysis. *Journal of Organizational Behavior and Human Decision Processes* 48:147.

Cooter, R., and D. Rubenfeld. 1989. Economic analysis of legal disputes and their resolution. *Journal of Economic Literature* 3:1067.

Cooter, R., and T. Ulen. 2003. *Law and economics.* 4th ed. Boston: Addison-Wesley.

De Geest, G., and G. Mattiacci. 2003. On the intrinsic superiority of regulation and insurance to tort law. Paper presented at the DWTC Conference on Economic Analysis of Traffic Safety, February 26.

Farber, D., and P. Frickey. 1991. *Law and public choice: A critical introduction.* Chicago: University of Chicago Press.

Festinger, L. 1957. *A theory of cognitive dissonance.* Stanford, CA: Stanford University Press.

Fischhoff, B. 1975. Hindsight is not equal to foresight: The effect of outcome knowledge on judgment under uncertainty. *Journal of Experimental Psychology: Human Perception and Performance* 1:288–90.

Gawande, A. 1999. Why doctors make mistakes. *New Yorker,* February 1, 40–52.

Guppy, A. 1993. Subjective probability of accident and apprehension in relation to self-other bias, age, and reported behavior. *Accident Analysis and Prevention* 25:375, 377–78.

Hogg, R., and A. Craig. 1970. *Introduction to mathematical statistics.* 3rd ed. Upper Saddle River, NJ: Prentice Hall.

Jolls, C. 1998. Behavioral economics analysis of redistributive legal rules. *Vanderbilt Law Review* 51:1653, 1659.

Jolls, C., C. Sunstein, and R. Thaler. 1998. A behavioral approach to law and economics. *Stanford Law Review* 50:1471.

Kahan, D. 1997. Social influence, social meaning, and deterrence. *Virginia Law Review* 83:349, 351–52, 378.

Kamin, K., and J. Rachlinski. 1995. Ex post ≠ ex ante: Determining liability in hindsight. *Journal of Law and Human Behavior* 19:89.

Korobkin R., and T. Ulen. 2000. Law and behavioral science: Removing the rationality assumption from law and economics. *California Law Review* 88:1051.

Labine, S., and G. Labine. 1996. Determinations of negligence and the hindsight bias. *Journal of Law and Human Behavior* 20:501.

Landes, W., and R. Posner 1987. *The economic structure of tort law.* Cambridge, MA: Harvard University Press.

Langevoort, D. 1997. Organized illusions: A behavioral theory of why corporations mislead stock market investors (and cause other social harms). *University of Pennsylvania Law Review* 146:101.

———. 2001. The human nature of corporate boards: Law, norms, and the unintended consequences of independence and accountability. *Georgetown Law Journal* 89:797.

Loewenstein, G., S. Issacharoff, C. Camerer, and L. Babcock. 1993. Self-serving assessments of fairness and pretrial bargaining. *Journal of Legal Studies* 22:135.

Lord, C., L. Ross, and M. Lepper. 1979. Biased assimilation and attitude polarization: The effects of prior theories on subsequently considered evidence. *Journal of Personality and Social Psychology* 37:2098, 2102.

Mashaw, J., and D. Harfst. 1990. *The struggle for auto safety.* Cambridge, MA: Harvard University Press.

McCaffery, E. 1994. Cognitive theory and tax. *University of California Law Review* 41:1861, 1901–04.

Muller, C., and L. Kirkpatrick. 1994. *Federal evidence.* 2nd ed. New York: Aspen.

National Highway Traffic Safety Administration (NHTSA). 1998. *Automobile Collision Avoidance System (ACAS) program, final report.* Washington, DC: NHTSA.

Plous, S. 1993. *The psychology of judgment and decision making.* New York: McGraw-Hill.

Posner, R. 1995. *Aging and old age.* Chicago: University of Chicago Press.

———. 1998. Rational choice, behavioral economics, and the law. *Stanford Law Review* 50:1551.

Priest, G., and B. Klein. 1984. The selection of disputes for litigation. *Journal of Legal Studies* 13:1, 12.

Rabin, Matthew. 1998. Psychology and economics. *Journal of Economic Literature* 36(1): 11–46.

Rachlinski, J. 1998. A positive psychological theory of judging in hindsight. *University of Chicago Law Review* 65:571, 576.

Seabrook, J. 2002. The slow lane. *The New Yorker*, September 2, 120–29.

Shavell, S. 1980. Negligence versus strict liability. *Journal of Legal Studies* 9:1.

Stein, E. 1996. *Without good reason*. Cambridge: Cambridge University Press.

Sunstein, C. 2000. Deliberative trouble? Why groups go to extremes. *Yale Law Journal* 110:71.

Tversky, A., and D. Kahneman. 1982a. Availability: A heuristic for judging frequency and probability. In *Judgment under uncertainty: Heuristics and biases*, ed. D. Kahneman, P. Slovic, and A. Tversky, 163. Cambridge: Cambridge University Press.

———. 1982b. Judgments of and by representativeness. In *Judgment under uncertainty: Heuristics and biases*, ed. D. Kahneman, P. Slovic, and A. Tversky, 84. Cambridge: Cambridge University Press.

Ulen, T. 2002. A Nobel Prize in legal science: Theory, empirical work, and the scientific method in the study of law. *University of Illinois Law Review* 2002:875.

Weinstein, N. 1980. Unrealistic optimism about future life events. *Journal of Personality and Social Psychology* 39:806.

———. 1987. Unrealistic optimism about susceptibility to health problems: Conclusions from a community-wide sample. *Journal of Behavioral Medicine* 10:481, 487–89.

# 17 | THE FREE RADICALS OF TORT

*Mark F. Grady*

Tort law contains an intriguing but unexplored puzzle. Courts hold that irrational actors, even actors with severe mental illness, are liable for their torts in exactly the same way that rational people would be. Nevertheless, courts also hold rational actors liable for encouraging or provoking irrational actors, under the same circumstances in which they would cut off a defendant's liability if the defendant had instead provoked a rational actor. Why do courts fail in the first situation to make a distinction that they observe in the second situation?

Here is a case example that illustrates the puzzle. In *Satcher v. James H. Drew Shows, Inc.*, 177 S.E.2d 846 (Ga. Ct. App. 1970), the plaintiff's wife, Mrs. Satcher, went to an amusement park and bought a ticket to ride on the bumper cars. The defendant, James H. Drew Shows, Inc., operated this ride. Bumper cars run on an oval metal floor and are propelled by electricity, which each car receives from an aerial that rubs against the metal roof. Each car has its own steering wheel and accelerator pedal and can travel anywhere on the metal floor of the ride. Bumper car drivers frequently try to bump into other drivers; those who are being assaulted frequently try to dodge their assailants.

The plaintiff's wife paid her admission and took a seat in a bumper car. Then, a group of mental patients was led up to the ride. The patients were on an excursion to the amusement park. When the attendant turned on the electricity to start the ride, the mental patients began to converge on the plaintiff's wife and to crash into her from different angles. After the ride was over, her neck was permanently injured. The plaintiff alleged that the defendant had been negligent by allowing the mental patients to converge on his wife and to injure her. The appellate court held that the trial court erred in dismissing the plaintiff's complaint.

The case illustrates two striking aspects of tort law. First, if the plaintiff had sued the mental patients for battery, she probably would have won. Their mental illness would not have been a defense. The plaintiff did not sue them, because they lacked the assets to pay a judgment. Second, the assailants' status as mental patients was critical to the defendant's liability for negligence. As will be shown later, if the bumper car drivers were instead well-known bankers, it is unlikely that the defendant would have been liable.

To some analysts both sides of this puzzle will seem odd. Many believe that persons with mental illness should not be liable in the same way as other people are. The same analysts might be equally troubled when they see that the courts hold actors responsible only if a subsequent actor was irresponsible. This rule seems to make irresponsible people less accountable than others. Their bad acts count for less. Under current legal doctrine, it would not be a defense for the *Satcher* defendant to show that the mental patients knew that ganging up on the plaintiff's wife was wrong; similarly irrelevant would be whether the mental patients had moral faculties sufficient to weigh whether it was right to gang up on Mrs. Satcher. The *Satcher* defendant was liable simply because it encouraged mental patients instead of bankers. Indeed, the only circumstance that would destroy the defendant's liability is if the group led up to the bumper cars only looked like mental patients when in reality they were well-known bankers. In that bizarre case, the *Satcher* defendant would probably escape negligence liability.[1]

We can solve this puzzle by seeing that tort law is not concerned with corrective justice in its usual moral sense but instead focuses liability where it will do most good—that is, on responsible people. This point will be further developed.

Economists and others could argue about whether persons with mental illness, children, criminals, riotous groups, and so forth are or are not rational and on what level. It is a standard economic conclusion that apparently irrational behavior often turns out to be rational when viewed in a slightly different frame. As already noted, however, the negligence doctrines of duty and proximate cause embed a surprising legal distinction between responsible and irresponsible people. Responsible people who encourage irresponsible people are often liable, whereas responsible people who encourage other responsible people are usually immune (unless they are liable as principals for their agents). In real life, most of the irresponsible people (whose encouragement leads to liability) are not fully rational in the everyday way of speaking. They are children, young adults, persons with mental illness, criminals, anonymous members of crowds, and the like.

A good name for these irresponsible people is "free radicals." Children, young adults, mental patients, crowds of unidentifiable people, and so forth frequently behave in radical, tortious ways, and their lack of assets frees them from tort sanctions.[2]

Liability for encouraging free radicals—the EFR doctrine—is interesting both because it is a significant part of tort law and because it seems to treat free radicals differently in two different contexts, and each treatment is the opposite of what most people would predict from common sense.

## 17.1 EVERYONE IS EQUAL BEFORE TORT LAW

Similar to the proverbial laws entitling rich and poor to sleep under bridges, tort law allows both the rational and the irrational to commit torts and does not pay much attention to their special challenges and disabilities. The extremes of this doctrine continue to startle beginning law students and become the first set of examples for Holmes's view that the law of tort, for all of its stress on fault, has little to do with morality.[3]

In *McGuire v. Almy*, 8 N.E.2d 760 (Mass. 1937), the defendant was a person with mental illness who still lived in her own home with her relatives who had moved in with her. They hired a nurse to care for her. One day the defendant was in an ugly mood that her live-in relatives had seen before, and she grabbed a leg from a piece of furniture and began to threaten those around her. The relatives drafted the nurse to disarm her, and the defendant struck her with the furniture leg. The nurse sued for battery.

The issue arose whether it was a defense that the defendant was insane, and the court held that it was not.[4] The court said that the proper rule was whether the defendant was capable of the intent that would make a normal person liable for battery. *Vosburg v. Putney*, 50 N.W. 403 (Wis. 1891), held that a normal person is liable for a battery if the person desires to create the unlawful contact—in *Vosburg* a kick to the plaintiff's shin; in *McGuire* a blow to the plaintiff's body. Liability in *McGuire* therefore depended only on whether the defendant wished to strike the plaintiff, which she obviously did. The court stressed a practical reason for its strict rule. Making the concededly irrational defendant liable would render the people possessing an interest in her estate more cautious about watching her.[5]

The courts have applied the *McGuire* principle to an astounding range of cases. In *Polmatier v. Russ*, 537 A.2d 468 (Conn. 1988), the defendant was a paranoid schizophrenic and had the delusion that his father-in-law was a Chinese spy trying to kill him. He therefore shot him first. At the trial a psychiatrist testified that the defendant was legally insane and could not form a rational choice but that he could make a schizophrenic or crazy choice. This diagnosis made no difference. The defendant was liable because he desired to shoot his father-in-law and did so.

Children are also liable for their intentional torts as if they were fully responsible adults. The only qualification is that they must possess the maturity to form the intent required for the tort in question. Usually it does not require much maturity to form the needed intent. For battery, the only intent they need is the desire to commit the unlawful touching or just the ability to know that the contact will result from their act. Indeed, a lesser intent will often suffice.

In *Ellis v. D'Angelo*, 253 P.2d 675 (Cal. Ct. App. 1953), a four-year-old child was liable for pushing his babysitter down even upon the objection that the child lacked the moral capacity to know that his act was wrongful. Also, in the famous case of *Garratt v. Dailey*, 279 P.2d 1091 (Wash. 1955), a five-year-old child pulled a chair away after a neighbor got up. The neighbor fell to the ground when she tried to sit down in the same place where the chair had been before. The court held that the child would be liable even if he was not trying to play a prank on the plaintiff. All that was needed to make him liable was the ability to predict that the plaintiff would try to sit down in the same place without looking. In other words, the issue had nothing to do with moral responsibility.

Similarly, children are strictly liable for their trespasses to land, whether or not they are morally culpable. In *Huchting v. Engel*, 17 Wis. 230 (1863), a six-year-old child defendant was liable for destroying the plaintiff's shrubs, and in *Seaburg v. Williams*, 148 N.E.2d 49 (Ill. App. Ct. 1958), a five-year-eleven-month-old child was liable for starting a fire in his neighbor's garage.

The situation is similar when we move to negligence law, though here children get more of a break than do persons with mental illness. When children are engaged in juvenile activities, the courts hold them to a standard that takes their youth into account. Nevertheless, children and youths are held fully to the adult standard when they engage in many adult activities, such as driving a boat or driving a car.

Persons with mental illness are usually held to the standard of normal people, even when they could not have achieved that standard. In *Breunig v. American Family Insurance Co.*, 173 N.W.2d 619 (Wis. 1970), the plaintiff began having dangerous delusions and continued to drive her car. As the court reasoned—and its reasoning was typical—if a normal person would have realized that the delusions were a danger signal, then it was negligent for the defendant to have continued to drive. In other words, the court imputed a normal person's insight to the mentally ill defendant and then asked whether she was negligent given that she possessed this fictitious insight.

All of these cases reveal a kind of strict liability that inheres in the negligence rule. The courts seem much less concerned with moral culpability than with avoiding accidents. Holmes (1881) famously glossed the legal doctrine in this area by saying that the courts cut slack for people with "distinct defects," what we would today call "obvious disabilities." Thus, children riding bicycles, blind people walking with white canes, and persons with mental illness on the hospital grounds would all get dispensation from the courts. The reason could be that unless the standard for them drops, it is difficult to increase the standard for others who can use more precaution because of what their eyesight tells them, namely, that they are about to interact with someone who will not be using the normal amount of precaution. On the other hand, youths or persons with mental illness driving cars are held to the same standard as everyone else. It is difficult or impossible for those interacting with them to realize that they need to use more precaution, so we might as well hold the youthful drivers to the same standard as everyone else. Perhaps the justification is similar to the one stated by the *McGuire v. Almy* court. If youths or persons with mental illness have valuable assets and want to drive cars, probably some more responsible person will have an incentive to preserve these assets and will more likely do so if the courts do not give challenged people a break.

## 17.2 SOME ARE LESS EQUAL THAN OTHERS

### 17.2.1 Controversial Applications of the EFR Doctrine

Perhaps because of the failed common-law experiments of the 1960s and 1970s, many legal scholars are wary of novel liability. The EFR doctrine is actually old, but some think it is new. Modern legal analysts have generally failed to recognize the importance and extension of the EFR doctrine in tort law. Also, many have argued that intentional wrongdoing should cut off liability for mere negligence.[6] The EFR doctrine, as evolved over the centuries, is totally inconsistent with this idea. It imposes liability when intentional, even criminal, behavior intervenes.

Let us then start with an EFR case that many modern analysts have criticized. In *Weirum v. RKO General, Inc.*, 539 P.2d 36 (Cal. 1975), the defendant was a popular Los Angeles radio station that broadcast to a teenage audience. In order to increase the number of its listeners, the station started a promotion called the Super Summer Spectacular in which one of its disk jockeys drove a red muscle car to various locations in the L.A. area; another disk jockey back at the station announced his changing destinations. Under the rules of the contest, the first listener who caught up with the traveling disk jockey won a small cash prize and a minute or two of fame. The contest was enormously successful. The Real Don Steele later testified that he knew that teenagers were racing to catch up with him.

On the day in question, the station announced that he was going to be at the Holiday Theater in the San Fernando Valley. Seventeen-year-old Robert Sentner and nineteen-year-old Marsha Baime independently drove their cars to the theater only to find that they were too late. They then independently decided to follow Steele to his next stop. For the next few miles the Sentner and Baime cars jockeyed for position closest to the Steele vehicle, reaching speeds up to eighty miles an hour. About a mile and a half from Thousand Oaks, the two teenagers heard a broadcast saying that Steele might stop there.[7]

Then, confirming the prediction, the Steele vehicle left the freeway at a Thousand Oaks off-ramp. Either Baime or Sentner, in attempting to follow, forced the decedent's car onto the center divider, where it overturned. Baime stopped to report the accident. Sentner, after pausing momentarily to relate the accident to a passing peace officer, continued to pursue Steele, successfully located him, and collected a cash prize. The jury returned a verdict against the two free radicals and the radio station as joint tortfeasors. The radio station appealed to the California Supreme Court, which affirmed the judgment.

Many have criticized this decision as failing to recognize the undivided responsibility of the teens in producing this tragedy. To them, the court's decision represents a wrongheaded wish to take the truly culpable parties off the hook and blame a corporation. Of course, the teens remained liable to the extent that they had assets to pay the judgment, and the plaintiff was free to try to execute the entire judgment against either or both. Nevertheless, the radio station was certainly a deeper pocket, and it ended up paying most of the judgment. The rule prevents accidents because tort can operate only against people who can be found and who have the assets to pay tort judgments. When the encouraged people predictably lack exposure to tort law deterrence, the courts have concluded that more responsible people should be deterred from encouraging them.[8] In many cases, imposing liability on the irresponsible people is a futile act because they will often lack the resources to pay the judgment.

*Weirum* is not as novel as many people think.[9] The EFR doctrine hails back to a case decided in 1822 and even to a dictum from 1773.[10] In any event, *Weirum*'s critics have failed to stress that the California Supreme Court relied on a similar 1925 case from Utah, a jurisdiction unrenowned for common-law experiments. In *Shafer v. Keeley Ice Cream Co.*, 234 P. 300 (Utah 1925), the defendant was a local business that operated a float in a commercial parade in Salt Lake City. The main feature was young women who threw candy to the crowd as the float passed down the parade line. Whenever the young women threw candy, boys scrambled to get it. During one of these cascades, the boys knocked over the plaintiff, who was an older woman, standing with her family to watch the parade. The court again made the defendant liable. As in so many EFR cases, it probably would have been difficult to find the boys and sue them and probably fruitless to try. They were free radicals both because they were boys and because they were members of a crowd.

Moreover, *Weirum* and *Shafer*, far from being modern innovations, are indistinguishable from *Guille v. Swan*, a case decided by the New York Supreme Court in 1822. The defendant ascended in a balloon over New York City near the plaintiff's garden. Somehow he got into trouble and descended, body hanging out of the car, right into the garden. He called to one of the plaintiff's field workers to help him, in a voice audible to a pursuing crowd. After the balloon descended, it dragged along over potatoes and radishes, about thirty feet, until the defendant was taken out. Soon afterward, more than two hundred people broke into the plaintiff's garden through the fences and came on his premises, beating down his vegetables and flowers. The damage done by the defendant with his balloon was about fifteen dollars, but the crowd did much more. The plaintiff's total damages were ninety dollars.

The defendant maintained at trial that he was responsible only for the damage done by his balloon and not for the damage done by the crowd, but the trial judge instructed the jury that the defendant was responsible for all the damages. The New York Supreme Court affirmed the plaintiff's judgment and stressed that it did not matter whether the crowd was attracted by a wish to help the defendant or just out of curiosity.[11] They were free radicals. As we will see, courts are especially sensitive to the fact that people behave differently in crowds. One reason must be that being part of a crowd creates anonymity and makes it difficult for an injured plaintiff to assign fault. Thus, a responsible person becomes a free radical by joining an unruly crowd.

Each of these three cases presents basically the same scenario. A responsible person has encouraged irresponsible people to engage in negligent behavior and becomes liable for the harm they have done. In all cases, the free-radical behavior was predictable to the defendant and could have been avoided at reasonable cost. This pattern extends backward almost two hundred years and maybe a little more. The next section will briefly review the early history of the EFR doctrine. However, let us first look at another case that almost always comes up in this context—the famous case of *Ross v. Hartman*, 139 F.2d 14 (D.C. Cir. 1943). The defendant violated a statute that required drivers to take their keys with them when they parked their motor vehicles. This defendant left his keys in his truck outside a parking garage without telling anyone he wanted it parked, and a thief stole it. The thief then collided with the plaintiff, who sued the defendant and cited the statutory duty. The D.C. Circuit, overruling its own prior precedent, found the defendant liable and based its decision on three New York cases in which children had hurt themselves or others when they started a car or truck whose owners had left the keys in the ignition and had parked in streets thronged with children.[12] The weakness of *Ross v. Hartman* comes from the fact that car thieves have a greater incentive than others to drive carefully so they will not attract the attention of the police. The main loser from leaving the key in the ignition is the one who has done so.

Most courts have refused to follow *Ross v. Hartman* on indistinguishable facts.[13] In *Richards v. Stanley*, 271 P.2d 23, 27 (Cal. 1954), a case whose facts were identical to *Ross* right down to the San Francisco statute that made it a misdemeanor to park a car without removing the ignition key, the California Supreme Court held that the defendant was not liable. As Justice Traynor said, "By leaving the key in her car [the defendant] at most increased the risk that it might be stolen. Even if she should have foreseen the theft, she had no reason to believe that the thief would be an incompetent driver."

The evolved California rule is typical of that of most jurisdictions. Leaving the keys in unusually dangerous or difficult-to-manage vehicles will yield liability if they are parked under circumstances that make theft or meddling probable.[14] *Richardson v. Ham*, 285 P.2d 269 (Cal. 1955), decided the year after *Stanley*, made a construction company liable for leaving its bulldozer parked overnight, unlocked, on top of a mesa in a built-up area of San Diego. The bulldozer was easy to start but hard to shut off. The free radicals in that case, aged seventeen, eighteen, and twenty, fortified with alcohol, started the bulldozer and then could not stop it. After they abandoned it, still moving, the bulldozer went off the edge of the mesa, down the hill, and across a freeway and traveled for about a mile before a retaining wall and utility pole finally halted it. During its random journey, it traveled through a house, seriously injuring the occupants, and then collided with a mobile home and an automobile, causing further property damage and personal injuries. In this case, which prefigured *Weirum* and was scarcely distinguishable from it, the California Supreme Court made the bulldozer owners liable to those injured. *Richardson* was distinct from *Ross v. Hartman* because practically any variety of free radical (child, teenager, drunk, thief) would be an extreme hazard to himself or herself and others once the bulldozer started moving.

*Weirum* and *Ross v. Hartman* are a good introduction to the EFR doctrine. *Weirum* is a good and reliable expression of the EFR doctrine as it has evolved throughout the United States though its facts are more dramatic than is typical; *Ross v. Hartman* appears to have been a mistake that does not reflect the more general doctrine in the United States. We can now turn to a brief history of the early development of the EFR doctrine.

## 17.2.2 Early EFR Cases

The first case in which a court considered the EFR problem is *Scott v. Shepherd*, 96 Eng. Rep. 525 (K.B. 1773). On the evening of fair day in Milbourne Port, England, October 28, 1770, the defendant threw a lighted squib, made of gunpowder, from the street into the market house, which was a covered building supported by arches and enclosed at one end but open at the other and both sides. A large crowd of people was assembled there. The lighted squib originally fell next to Yates's gingerbread stand. One Willis picked it up and threw it across the market house, where it fell next to Ryal's stand, who also sold baked goods. Ryal quickly picked up the lighted squib and threw it to another part of the market house where it struck the plaintiff in the face, exploded, and put out one of his eyes.

The plaintiff brought his case for trespass *vi et armis*, and the jury returned a verdict for him. The defendant appealed on the ground that the evidence was insufficient to support this action. In that procedurally unreformed era, a plaintiff had to choose between trespass *vi et armis* and trespass on the case; the former writ was for direct harms, and the latter was for consequential (indirect) harms. *Scott v. Shepherd* presented a famous writ problem because it was unclear whether the intermediate throwers destroyed the directness of the defendant's original throw in producing the harm.

At the trial, it had never become totally clear whether the intermediate throwers were acting out of panicked self-defense or, as Justice Blackstone believed, "to continue the sport" as true free radicals would behave in a crowd.[15] Three of the four judges thought that the intermediate throwers were acting out of self-defense or necessity and that for this reason the harm was direct from the defendant's first throw of the squib.[16] Blackstone, on the other hand, thought they were continuing a game that the defendant had started. On that view of the facts, the harm was merely consequential from the defendant's act, and the proper writ was trespass on the case (which the plaintiff had not selected). Going further, Blackstone cautiously opined that trespass on the case would lie against the original thrower on these facts, though that issue was not raised because the plaintiff had elected to stand or fall on trespass *vi et armis*, which required a direct harm.[17] There is hardly a greater expert on the common law of this era than William Blackstone. If his dictum was correct, something like the EFR doctrine existed in 1773.[18]

*Guille v. Swan*, the 1822 balloonist case already discussed, was probably the original EFR case in this country. Not all two hundred members of the crowd that trampled the plaintiff's crops were needed to rescue the defendant. Moreover, Chief Justice Spencer broadly stated his *ratio decidendi*, "Now, if his [the defendant's] descent, under such circumstances, would, ordinarily and naturally, draw a crowd of people about him, either from curiosity, or for the purpose of rescuing him from a perilous situation; all this he ought to have foreseen, and must be responsible for." This is a classic description of the EFR doctrine.

Meanwhile in 1816, the English Court of King's Bench had already decided the first indisputable EFR case, which was *Dixon v. Bell*, 105 Eng. Rep. 1023 (K.B. 1816). The defendant kept a loaded gun in his apartment. One day when he was away from it, he sent his thirteen-year-old servant to his landlord to have him get the gun, unload it, and give it to the servant so that she could bring it back to him. Of course, it was difficult to tell whether the muzzle-loading guns of that era were in fact unloaded. The landlord got the gun, took the priming out, told the girl that he had done so, and then gave the gun to the girl. She put it down in the kitchen but later picked it up to play with the plaintiff's eight-year-old son, saying she was going to shoot him. She pointed the gun at him, pulled the trigger, and the gun went off, injuring the plaintiff's son. The plaintiff's declaration basically alleged that the defendant was liable because he had encouraged a free radical.[19] The King's Bench upheld the jury verdict for the plaintiff.

In 1841, again in England, the first case occurred that looked very similar to a swarm of modern EFR cases that began roughly with the full development of the Industrial Revolution. Recall that the *Ross v. Hartman* court had relied on New York precedents, never overruled and since extended, making someone liable for leaving an unlocked automobile or truck in a crowded neighborhood where children could start it up and hurt themselves or other people. The first case of this type was *Lynch v. Nurdin*, 113 Eng. Rep. 1041 (Q.B. 1841), in which the defendant's driver had left the defendant's horse and cart in Compton Street for a half an hour while the driver was inside an adjoining house. Compton Street was normally thronged, and on this day it was busier than usual, because an adjoining street was blocked. The defendant's driver knew that groups of children would be coming down Compton Street and that they would be interested in his horse and cart. Nevertheless, he dawdled in the house while his cart and horse were sitting in the street. The plaintiff, who was a child between six and seven years old, had his leg crushed beneath the wheels of the cart when another boy, who was playing on the cart, caused it to move, the plaintiff to fall off, and the wheels accidentally to run across the plaintiff's leg. The Queen's Bench held the defendant liable for encouraging free radicals.

In *Lane v. Atlantic Works*, 111 Mass. 136 (1872), the defendant parked its truck in Boston with loose iron bars carelessly laid on the flat bed so that they would easily fall off. A twelve-year-old boy got up on the truck and jostled the bars so that they fell off and hurt the eight-year-old plaintiff, who was innocently standing on the sidewalk. The Massachusetts Supreme Court held that the defendant was liable.

As the Industrial Revolution progressed, EFR cases became more common, as did negligence cases more generally. Attractive nuisance is a branch of the EFR doctrine, and an early case was *Travell v. Bannerman*, 75 N.Y.S. 866 (App. Div. 1902), in which the plaintiff sued the defendant for injuries that he suffered when ammunition factory refuse material that the defendant had negligently discarded into a vacant lot exploded.[20] The defendant operated a gun and ammunition factory in Brooklyn, which then as now was full of children. The factory premises were enclosed by a fence, but the adjoining lot, also owned by the defendant and casually used as a temporary dumping place for ashes and other refuse material from the factory, was unfenced and crisscrossed by paths worn by people of the neighborhood. For a long time the fourteen-year-old plaintiff and other boys had used this open lot as a playground. On September 14, 1900, the plaintiff was standing in the street just outside this vacant lot, when two younger boys approached him with a mass of black, asphaltlike material composed of caked gunpowder and old cannon primers. The boys had found this mass, which was about a foot long, among the rubbish on the vacant lot; and, after joining back up with the plaintiff, they proceeded to extract the pieces of brass that it contained. They could sell these brass pieces to a scrap metal dealer. One of the boys, not the plaintiff, pounded the lump with a rock, and an explosion resulted. The New York Appellate Division affirmed the plaintiff's verdict.

The EFR doctrine has a long history; it is by no means a modern innovation. Throughout the nineteenth century free-radical cases developed mass and number as negligence cases did more generally. The following discussion will give more examples of old and new EFR cases and will analyze the pattern of courts' decisions. The most important element is that a free radical is indeed needed. If the encouraged person does not belong to a free-radical class, and if the defendant's encouragement stops short of making him or her a co-actor with the immediate wrongdoer, the defendant is immune. This basic part of the EFR doctrine is the topic of the following section.

## 17.3  A NON—FREE RADICAL LETS THE DEFENDANT OFF

If the intervening person—the person encouraged by the defendant—belongs to a typically responsible class of persons, the defendant's liability is eliminated. In *Seith v. Commonwealth Electric Co.*, 89 N.E. 425 (Ill. 1909), the defendant maintained an electrical grid strung overhead in Chicago. Because of the defendant's negligent maintenance, a wire broke and fell down to a sidewalk. Two nine-year-old girls saw the wire just after it broke, while it was still moving on the ground. Recognizing the danger to passersby, they immediately went to a nearby saloon and told the saloon keeper that a live electrical wire had fallen to the ground. Two police officers who were in the saloon came out to investigate, and one of them walked over to where the wire was lying. At the same time, the plaintiff, who knew nothing of what had happened, came down the back stairs of his nearby apartment. The investigating police officer took his police club and flipped the wire toward the plaintiff. The plaintiff instinctively caught it and suffered a severe electrical shock. Luckily, passersby were able to take a wooden plank and knock the wire from the plaintiff's hands before he was killed. The Illinois Supreme Court reversed the trial court's judgment for the plaintiff and stressed that no one would ever anticipate that a police officer would behave the way this one did.[21] He was a non–free radical. If the girls, instead of the police officer, had flipped the wire toward the plaintiff, the defendant would have been liable by analogy to many EFR cases, for instance, *Travell v. Bannerman*, just discussed in the prior section.

Although the *Seith* intervenor belonged to a responsible class—police officers—the defendant had no way of predicting that he would belong to a responsible class. Hence, the defendant's liability depended on a fact knowable only after the accident occurred, namely, that it was a police officer who intervened and not children or some other free radical who might have been tempted by the downed wire. In *Satcher*, it was probably knowable to the defendant before the accident that most of the bumper car drivers were mental patients or the equivalent.

In *Snyder v. Colorado Springs & Cripple Creek District Ry.*, 85 P. 686 (Colo. 1906), the defendant had overcrowded its interurban railroad cars. On the night of December 20, 1900, the plaintiff was a passenger on the defendant's one-car electric commuter train, going from Cripple Creek, Colorado, to Midway, Colorado. He had paid his fare. The car was crowded, and the plaintiff was standing near the door with his hand resting on the door jamb. There were people between the plaintiff and the door, some upon the steps. The head of the man upon the lower step reached to about the thigh of the plaintiff. The conductor, in pushing his way through the crowd, pressed the plaintiff against a man who was sitting in a seat on the side of the car. This man became angry, said that he was "getting tired of playing cushion for the electric line," and lifted himself up against the plaintiff and gave a surge by the force of which the plaintiff was literally thrown out of the moving car. The passenger's "surge" must have been fairly substantial, because the plaintiff was flung over the head of the passenger who stood upon the lower step.

The trial court directed a verdict for the defendant, and the Colorado Supreme Court affirmed. The court stressed that the man who threw the defendant out of the railcar was an ordinary passenger; again, he was a non–free radical.[22] He wasn't really part of the same type of impromptu crowd that preserved the *Guille v. Swan* defendant's liability, but was more identifiable.

In *Rubio v. Swiridoff*, 211 Cal. Rptr. 338 (Cal. Ct. App. 1985), the defendant Rudolph Swiridoff and his friend Linda Karcie had been dating each other for about a year and a half, but the relationship had fallen on hard times. When the two met at a bar, they fought and the defendant peeled out of the restaurant parking lot, burning rubber. Karcie took the shriek of Swiridoff's tires as an insult and challenge. She followed at high speed and collided with and killed the plaintiff's decedent.

Both Karcie and Swiridoff denied participating in any type of race, and the plaintiff did not assert that the two young adults were racing with each other at the time of the accident. The trial court entered summary judgment for the defendant Swiridoff, holding that under the circumstances he did not owe the plaintiff's decedent a duty of care. The plaintiff appealed, and the appellate court affirmed. Karcie's age is not revealed in the opinion, but it seems clear that she was older than a teenager, because she was in the bar with Swiridoff. Again, she was a non–free radical, so the result was different than in *Weirum*.

Finally, in *Marenghi v. New York City Transit Authority*, 542 N.Y.S.2d 542 (App. Div. 1989), the plaintiff brought suit to recover damages for personal injuries sustained by the plaintiff on October 16, 1981, at approximately 10:30 A.M., after she had alighted from a subway train operated by the defendant at the Chambers Street subway station in lower Manhattan. According to the plaintiff's trial testimony, she emerged from the train and had taken a few steps. The doors had closed behind her. Just then she observed an unidentified passenger rushing down a flight of steps that led to the platform, shouting, "Hold the train!" The steps were to her right, although the distance between the plaintiff and this passenger, when she observed him, was unclear from the record. The plaintiff looked backward and to her left, observing about nine feet away the head of the conductor extended through the train's open window. The train doors opened and then immediately began to close. The unidentified passenger knocked the plaintiff over, injuring her, and jumped over her body and through the closing doors. The train then left the station, leaving the plaintiff injured on the platform. The jury awarded the plaintiff substantial damages, but the New York Appellate Division reversed. The court stressed that nothing about the man suggested that he was a free radical.[23] Opening the doors for a football crowd under similar circumstances would probably lead to liability.

The lesson of these cases, and many like them, is that a defendant can encourage a non–free radical and still face no liability.

## 17.4 EFR FACTORS

Here are seven factors that seem to influence courts in holding a defendant liable for harm immediately caused by free radicals:

1. The defendant's encouragement of the free radical was substantial.

2. The defendant created a scarce opportunity for free-radical depredations (similar to the first factor).

3. The free radical acted predictably when judged by a free-radical standard.

4. The free radical harmed a third party as opposed to himself or herself.

5. The predictable harm was serious.

6. The defendant's encouraging behavior was deliberate as opposed to inadvertent (important in some cases).

7. The defendant had a special relationship with the free radical, with the victim, or with both (important in some otherwise marginal cases).

### 17.4.1 Substantial Encouragement

When the defendant has only slightly encouraged free radicals, he or she is not liable. A good example is *Donehue v. Duvall*, 243 N.E.2d 222 (Ill. 1968), in which the five-year-old plaintiff sued for an injury to his eye. Another child had thrown a dirt clod that struck him. The plaintiff's complaint alleged, four days before he was attacked, that the defendants had had some loads of dirt hauled into their backyard and it lay there in a large pile. The defendants knew that neighborhood children had frequented the pile, throwing clods of dirt at each other, and that the defendants should have known that the large clods on the pile created a hazard. The trial court dismissed the complaint, and the Illinois Supreme Court affirmed.[24] Similar cases have held that no liability exists for leaving a stake at a construction site (*Cole v. Housing Authority*, 385 N.E.2d 382 (Ill. 1979)) or for leaving a screwdriver out in a yard (*Dennis Evans v. Timmons*, 437 S.E.2d 138 (S.C. Ct. App. 1993)). In all of these cases the defendant's encouragement was too slight.

A similar case is *Segerman v. Jones*, 259 A.2d 794 (Md. 1969), in which the defendant teacher started the calisthenics song "Chicken Fat" on the classroom record player and then left the classroom. The Maryland Supreme Court held that she was not liable when one student kicked out another student's teeth in the course of the calisthenics after she had left. In order to be liable, she would have had to do something more encouraging of mayhem than just leave the classroom for a few minutes. Again, her encouragement of free radicals was too slight.

One situation exists in which at least in some jurisdictions do not require that the defendant substantially encouraged the free radical. It is a modern principle of proximate cause that if a defendant's negligence makes the plaintiff especially vulnerable to someone else's inadvertent negligence, the defendant remains a joint tortfeasor with the second actor (Grady 2002). A good example of this doctrine is *Derdiarian v. Felix Contracting Corp.*, 414 N.E.2d 666 (N.Y. 1980), in which a worker sued a construction company for failing to provide him a sturdier barrier against errant traffic. The defendant main contractor was installing an underground gas main and subcontracted with the plaintiff's employer to seal the pipes. For this work, the plaintiff and his crew used molten enamel that was kept in a vat at four hundred degrees. At this same time, a second defendant was driving through town and suffered an epileptic seizure, because he had negligently forgotten to take his antiseizure pills. This second defendant lost consciousness, and his car crashed through the flimsy horse-type barricade that was set up on the street side of the excavation, struck the vat, and hurt the plaintiff.

The first defendant had negligently failed to guard the worksite from invading traffic, and the second defendant had negligently lost consciousness. Obviously, the most likely reason that a car would breach the work area would be that the car's driver had been negligent. Both the trial court and the New York Court of Appeals held both defendants liable, as almost all courts do.[25] In the classic cases, such as this one, the last wrongdoer was both a responsible individual and inadvertently negligent.

*Derdiarian* was not a case in which the defendant had encouraged free radicals, because having a flimsy barrier around a worksite did not really qualify as an encouragement to free radicals. This was a different kind of case in which the defendant has set the stage for a subsequent act of inadvertent negligence—probably by a non–free radical. Suppose, however, that the second actor turns out to be a free radical whose wrongdoing is deliberate.

Probably the leading case here is *Bigbee v. Pacific Telephone and Telegraph Co.*, 665 P.2d 947 (Cal. 1983), which has become famous. The plaintiff's complaint alleged that on the night of the accident, at approximately 12:20 A.M., the plaintiff was standing in the defendant's telephone booth located in a parking lot of a liquor store on Century Boulevard in Inglewood, California. A second defendant, Roberts, was driving, intoxicated, east along Century Boulevard. Because she was driving under the influence, it seems reasonable to see Roberts as a free radical. Probably because of her intoxication, she lost control of her car and veered off the street into the parking lot, crashing into the telephone booth in which the plaintiff was standing.

The plaintiff saw Roberts's car coming toward him and realized that it would hit the telephone booth. He attempted to escape but was unable to do so because the door had jammed. The plaintiff alleged that the defendant telephone company's failure to maintain its booth was a breach of duty and a cause in fact of his injury. Had the door operated freely, he would have been able to escape and would have suffered no harm. The plaintiff also alleged, as a second untaken precaution, that the defendant negligently located its booth "too close to Century Boulevard, where 'traffic . . . traveling easterly, generally and habitually speeded in excess of the posted speed limit,' thereby creating an unreasonable risk of harm to anyone who used the booth."

The California Supreme Court held that the plaintiff's complaint stated a good cause of action, a result that outraged many. If the defendant would have been liable for a driver who had inadvertently (though negligently) crashed into the booth, perhaps it is not so different if a free radical has done so.

A more extreme California case of the same type has extended *Bigbee*. In *Wiener v. Southcoast Childcare Centers, Inc.*, 132 Cal. Rptr. 2d 883 (Cal. Ct. App. 2003), the plaintiffs' complaint alleged that the defendant's child-care center was situated on a busy street and that the playground was located immediately adjacent to that street. The playground was enclosed by only a four-foot-high chain-link fence, which was inadequate to protect the children from errant automobile traffic coming off the street. The plaintiffs further alleged that the defendants were aware the fence was inadequate and that the owner of the child-care center had previously requested the church landlord to provide funds to erect a sturdier barrier. When the church refused, the owner did nothing further to remedy the problem. Although the children might have been injured by a negligently errant driver, they were not. Instead, a criminal intentionally smashed through the fence with the intent to kill children. He killed two, who were the plaintiff's deceased. The California Court of Appeal upheld the complaint, analogizing the case to *Bigbee*.

Again, in both this case and *Bigbee* the respective defendants' negligence did not substantially encourage a free radical. Someone intent on killing children is not significantly encouraged by an inadequate fence; many other opportunities exist. The main argument in favor of both cases is that the injured parties could have been hurt just as easily by an inadvertently negligent driver. Nevertheless, both are extreme cases, and *Wiener* is more extreme than *Bigbee*. If either defendant had been inadvertently negligent, it would be difficult to square these cases with other cases. Normally, courts do not like to extend the liability of people who may have made an innocent mistake. Nevertheless, the *Bigbee* defendant intentionally located its telephone booth in a dangerous place, and the *Wiener* court stressed that the defendant's owner knew that its fence was inadequate.[26] In this type of situation, there is less concern that liability will induce counterproductive substitutions or inefficient reductions in activity levels. Also, the respective defendants both had special relationships with the victims, so they were in a position to indemnify themselves *ex ante*, which is another circumstance that tends to make courts more willing to extend liability. It will be interesting to see whether these two cases will be followed in other jurisdictions.[27]

In order for a defendant to be liable for encouraging free radicals, the encouragement must be substantial. *Bigbee* and *Wiener* are two cases in which the defendant was liable for free-radical harm, but neither defendant really encouraged free radicals at all. These cases are exceptional in that they seem to fall under a related but different doctrine that holds defendants liable for setting the stage for subsequent negligence.

### 17.4.2 Scarce Opportunity for Wrongdoing

Often the best way to see whether a defendant has encouraged free radicals is to look at the world from their perspective. Has the defendant created some tempting opportunity that does not normally exist for them?

In *Stansbie v. Troman*, 2 K.B. 48 (1948), the defendant was an interior decorator who was left alone in his client's house. The defendant left to purchase some wallpaper in the homeowner's absence and failed to lock the door. A thief came through the open door and stole the plaintiff's diamond bracelet, and the court made the defendant liable. Viewed from the perspective of thieves, the defendant made available to them an opportunity that does not normally exist.[28]

*Russo v. Grace Institute*, 546 N.Y.S.2d 509 (Sup. Ct.1989), was similar. There the defendant erected a scaffold next to the building in which the plaintiff rented an apartment. The complaint alleged that armed robbers used the scaffold to gain entry onto the terrace of the plaintiff's apartment and from thence into the apartment itself. Once there they stole the plaintiff's goods. The New York Supreme Court held that the defendant was not entitled to summary judgment. The defendant encouraged free radicals because it made available a scarce and tempting opportunity.

A contrasting case was *Gonzalez v. Derrington*, 363 P.2d 1 (Cal. 1961), in which the defendant sold free radicals five gallons of gasoline into their open pail, which was a violation of a municipal ordinance that required gasoline to be pumped into closed containers and in quantities not to exceed two gallons. The free radicals then took the gasoline to a bar, spread it around, and lighted it, thus burning the plaintiffs. The defendant was not liable. Although the free radicals in question did need gasoline, it would not have been difficult to siphon this quantity from a car.[29]

Children find many more tempting opportunities for mischief than, for instance, adult thieves. Hence, a defendant who left a gun accessible to children was liable in *Hall v. Watson*, 2002 W.L. 1396763 (Ohio App.).[30] The gun was something that children might be expected to investigate because it was not in their normal environment. In a contrasting case, however, when someone leaves a screwdriver out in the yard and one child throws it at another, putting out the child's eye, the defendant is not liable (*Dennis Evans v. Timmons*, 437 S.E.2d 138 (S.C. Ct. App. 1993)). A child who wants to throw sharp objects at another child usually does not have to look far in order to find such an object. On the other hand, when a child has been shooting a bow and arrow in an enclosed porch and his father takes it away and hides it, the child's grandmother is liable for giving it back to him when the child then shoots out the eye of a nine-month-old child (*Carmona v. Padilla*, 163 N.Y.S.2d 741 (App. Div. 1957), aff'd without op, 149 N.E.2d 337 (N.Y. 1958)). The grandmother controlled a scarce opportunity for her free-radical grandson.

An opportunity is scarce or not depending on the predictable preferences and tastes for mischief of the local free radicals, which may change over time. For instance, *Lynch v. Nurdin*, the old English case mentioned earlier, seems based on the plausible assumption that the children of that era were interested in unguarded horses and carts and that they could not easily find them. Cases from the early twentieth century seem based on the similar idea that the children of that era were fascinated by automobiles or trucks with keys left in the ignition.[31] Nevertheless, between the extremes of leaving a screwdriver for children (no liability) and leaving a gun (liability), there are many intermediate cases that courts decide based on how tempting to children and how scarce to them was the opportunity that the defendant made available.[32]

### 17.4.3 Predictable Free-Radical Behavior

Most free radicals will behave exactly how a reasonable person in the shoes of the encourager would have predicted. This was the situation in each of the EFR cases of liability just mentioned. For instance, if a radio station encourages teens to race to catch a roving disk jockey, they will race, and the radio station is liable. Suppose, however, to be first, one of the teens had shot the other teen. It seems highly doubtful that the radio station would be liable in that case.

If an encouraged free radical goes too far, the defendant will escape liability. A good example is *Cole v. German Savings & Loan Society*, 124 F. 113 (8th Cir. 1903), in which the defendant owned an office building with an elevator. A boy, unconnected with the defendant's business, came into the defendant's building and became fascinated with the elevator, which was at the time of this case a new invention. The "strange boy," as the court called him, befriended the elevator attendant, who was also a boy. By watching the regular elevator boy, the strange boy learned how to impersonate him. Perhaps the defendant was negligent in failing to keep the boy out of the lobby, because it should have been obvious that he had no business there.

On the day in question the strange boy was hanging around the lobby as usual, standing next to the elevator. A woman walked up to the elevator. The strange boy decided to play a practical joke on the woman. The boy knew the elevator was on an upper floor, but he nevertheless opened the door to the elevator shaft and beckoned toward it. The woman walked through the open door and fell down the empty shaft. She sued the defendant, which as noted earlier, owned the building and the elevator. On appeal the court upheld the defendant's verdict. Assuming that this defendant was negligent in failing to exclude the strange boy from its lobby, the strange boy's negligence went beyond the encouragement provided by the defendant. In *Weirum* the teenagers behaved exactly the way one would have expected; the strange boy did not.

A similar but more modern case was *Bansasine v. Bodell*, 927 P.2d 675 (Utah App. 1996), in which the defendant and his passenger, the plaintiff's deceased, both provoked a driver who had demonstrated that he was highly aggressive. Nevertheless, when the provoked driver shot the deceased, the defendant was not liable. The court stressed the unpredictability of his behavior.[33]

### 17.4.4 Third Parties Threatened

Being a free radical and encouraging free radicals are often their own punishment. The principal reason for tort liability occurs when the free radicals injure third parties, as in *Weirum v. RKO General, Inc.* and most of the other cases mentioned previously. The main exception is children, whom the doctrine protects against themselves. The attractive nuisance doctrine is the main branch, but liability for EFR extends beyond dangerous attractions on the land.

Except in the cases where the victims are very small children, the courts do not readily allow the free radicals themselves to recover for injuries they have caused themselves through their free-radical behavior. In *Gilmore v. Shell Oil Co.*, 613 S.2d 1272 (Ala. 1993), the defendant's employee left a loaded revolver behind the counter of the defendant's convenience store. The deceased, who was seventeen years old, took the gun, placed it on his temple, and pulled the trigger, killing himself. Although he intentionally shot himself, the evidence made it unlikely that he really wanted to do so. Clearly, if the gun had not been left behind the counter, he would not have killed himself. The trial court entered summary judgment for the defense, and the Alabama Supreme Court affirmed.[34] Tort law is not needed to deter this behavior.[35]

### 17.4.5 Serious Harm

A defendant is likely to be liable if the harm that he or she has encouraged the free radical to inflict is serious. This is another reason why someone who has left explosives for children to play with (*Travell v. Bannerman*, 75 N.Y.S. 866 (App. Div. 1902)) is more likely to face liability than someone who has left a screwdriver (*Dennis ex rel. Evans v. Timmons*, 313 S.C. 338, 437 S.E.2d 138 (1993)). Similarly, a camp that has issued campers book bags is not liable if one of them uses the book bag as a weapon (*Hennen v. Terwey*, 1994 W.L. 1111 (Minn. App. 1994)). The predictable harm was not sufficiently serious.[36]

### 17.4.6 Deliberate Encouragement

A battery depends on a defendant's purpose to create an unlawful touching or the defendant's knowledge with substantial certainty that this unlawful touching will follow from the act. In negligence law, an actor can either deliberately fail to use a reasonable precaution or can inadvertently omit reasonable precaution.

Some battery cases exist in which the defendant has encouraged a free radical to such an extent that the defendant becomes a co-actor with the person who physically does the deed. In these cases, usually both parties are free radicals, and they are jointly liable for the battery or other intentional tort that results.[37]

Co-actor liability can also arise under negligence law, as the case of *Michael R. v. Jeffrey B.*, 205 Cal. Rptr. 312 (Cal. Ct. App. 1984), illustrates. The plaintiff Michael R., while walking home from a school banquet, was struck in the eye with a marble and, as a result, was blinded in that eye. The plaintiff brought a negligence action against Jeffrey B., the minor who shot the marble at him, and also against Bruno N., who said, "Hey shoot him; go for it," just before Jeffrey B. shot the plaintiff. Jeffrey B. and Bruno N. had previously been shooting marbles at cars. The trial court granted summary judgment to Bruno N. (the encourager), and the appellate court reversed. This is not the typical case because the two boys were both free radicals. Still, it illustrates an important principle.

A more common EFR situation, as we have seen, occurs when a responsible party has encouraged a free radical. The easier cases of liability occur when the defendant has behaved deliberately. Such was the case in *Weirum v. RKO General, Inc.*, in which the radio station deliberately designed and broadcast the dangerous contest. The defendant certainly did not wish the plaintiff's deceased to die, but it did behave deliberately as opposed to inadvertently. Sometimes the line between encouragement and co-action is murky. In a recent case that recapitulates *Scott v. Shepherd*,[38] the defendant's bartender, in a dimly lit bar, handed the plaintiff a powerful firecracker, and an unknown free radical, who was never identified, lit it (*Bodkin v. 5401 S.P., Inc.*, 768 N.E.2d 194 (Ill. App. 2002)). The defendant was liable. The court treated the case as one in which the defendant encouraged a free radical. There was evidence that many of the bar's patrons were intoxicated.

A more difficult kind of EFR case, and a rarer case of liability, occurs when the defendant has inadvertently encouraged free radicals. Early examples are the torpedo cases.[39] In *Mills v. Central of Georgia Ry.*, 78 S.E. 816 (Ga. 1913), the plaintiff sued for the wrongful death of one of his sons.

The defendant railroad had left a signal torpedo on its tracks just outside the town of Eden. A signal torpedo, although a pleasing and attractive-looking object, was an explosive device. Before electrical signaling equipment became common, railroad workers would place torpedoes on top of the tracks in order to give warnings to the engineers of approaching trains. For instance, when a train stalled unexpectedly, the stalled train's crew would run back and set a torpedo to warn oncoming trains to slow down. When an oncoming train blew up the torpedo, it would get the attention of the oncoming train's crew, and they would know to slow down. If a torpedo was not detonated, a railroad employee was supposed to pick it up. According to the plaintiff's complaint, the torpedo in question was not in use but had been left on the tracks carelessly, that is, inadvertently. The plaintiff's two sons, one fifteen years old and the other eight years old, found the torpedo in question, and the fifteen-year-old hit it with an iron nut or hammer to open it and to see what was inside. The torpedo exploded, and a piece of shrapnel hit his brother and killed him.

The defendant demurred to the plaintiff's complaint, and the Georgia Supreme Court ultimately held that the complaint was good. Some of the key-in-the-ignition cases also seem to be situations in which the defendant acted inadvertently as opposed to deliberately. When the harm threatened is sufficiently serious and probable, even the inadvertent creation of an opportunity will yield liability.

## 17.4.7 Special Relationship

Consistent with more general principles of negligence law, when the defendant had a special relationship with the victim, the free radical, or both, liability is more likely. In *Cobb v. Indian Springs, Inc.*, 522 S.W.2d 383 (Ark. 1975), the defendant's security guard, who was supposed to protect the young people living in the mobile home park, instead encouraged one of them to show the security guard how fast his car would go. When the boy lost control of his speeding vehicle and struck another resident, the defendant was liable.

Similarly, a hotel or a common carrier has an especially great duty not to encourage free radicals who might attack customers. In *Stagl v. Delta Airlines, Inc.*, 52 F.3d 463 (2d Cir. 1995) (per Calabresi, J.), the defendant maintained a highly disorderly baggage claim area for its passengers. The plaintiff, who was seventy-seven years old, described it as bedlam. The space was so constricted and order so poor that passengers jostled each other constantly to get their bags. The plaintiff was jostled to the ground by another passenger. The court held the defendant liable. The case is similar to *Shafer v. Keeley Ice Cream Co.*, 234 P. 300 (Utah 1925), the Utah precedent for *Weirum*, in which a float owner was liable to an older woman for creating disorder along a parade route.

One final limitation is that normally a defendant who has encouraged free radicals through a nonfeasance as opposed to a misfeasance will not be liable; a special relationship will be required in this case, as in the rest of negligence law more generally.[40]

## 17.5 CONCLUSION

Tort sanctions operate only because people are concerned that they will forfeit their assets if they do not use care to protect their neighbors. Nevertheless, tort sanctions are largely ineffective against people who lack assets. For this reason, the courts have created duties to avoid encouraging these people. These duties are old—they are certainly not novel—and they are important. Moreover, the duties that we have to avoid encouraging free radicals amount to the law's main strategy for controlling the behavior of apparently irrational individuals.

1. See *Seith v. Commonwealth Edison Co.*, 89 N.E. 425 (Ill. 1909); see text accompanying note 21 for discussion. The line is somewhat fine, however, because a defendant who encourages Jaycees to wreak havoc will face liability. See *Connolly v. Nicollet Hotel*, 95 N.W.2d 657 (Minn. 1959) (hotel liable for failing to shut down out-of-control Jaycee convention).

2. I am grateful to my colleague John Witherspoon, who found the following definition in the *Condensed Chemical Dictionary*: "[F]ree radicals are always materials with high reactivity and high energy, and can be collected and stored only with special precautions such as collection in solution or at very low temperatures and in the absence of all but inert solvents or diluents. Some efforts have been made to devise means of collecting free radicals for subsequent use to generate power" (Rose and Ross 1961).

3. Holmes (1897) wrote,

The law is full of phraseology drawn from morals, and by the mere force of language continually invites us to pass from one domain to the other without perceiving it, as we are sure to do unless we have the boundary constantly before our minds. The law talks about rights, and duties, and malice, and intent, and negligence, and so forth, and nothing is easier, or, I may say, more common in legal reasoning, than to take these words in their moral sense, at some stage of the argument, and so to drop into fallacy.

4. The *McGuire* court said,

[W]here an insane person by his act does intentional damage to the person or property of another he is liable for that damage in the same circumstances in which a normal person would be liable. This means that in so far as a particular intent would be necessary in order to render a normal person liable, the insane person, in order to be liable, must have been capable of entertaining that same intent and must have entertained it in fact. (*McGuire v. Almy*, 8 N.E.2d 760, 763 (Mass. 1937))

5. The *McGuire* court said, "[A] rule imposing liability tends to make more watchful those persons who have charge of the defendant and who may be supposed to have some interest in preserving his property" (*McGuire v. Almy*, 8 N.E.2d 760, 762 (Mass. 1937)).

6. For instance, Shavell (1980) has written, "Criminal or intentional acts of

parties other than the defendant would seem more important to discourage than those involving uncomplicated negligence, and the former but not the latter tend to exclude the defendant from the scope of liability."

7. The broadcast announced,

11:13 — The Real Don Steele with bread is heading for Thousand Oaks to give it away. Keep listening to KHJ. . . . The Real Don Steele out on the highway — with bread to give away — be on the lookout; he may stop in Thousand Oaks and may stop along the way. . . . Looks like it may be a good stop Steele — drop some bread to those folks. (*Weirum v. RKO General, Inc.*, 539 P.2d 36, 39 (Cal. 1975))

8. The *Weirum* case slightly preceded modern systems of relative fault in which the jury apportions among joint tortfeasors. See *American Motorcycle Association v. Superior Court (Gregos)*, 146 Cal. Rptr. 182 (1978) (holding that juries should be instructed to apportion fault between joint tortfeasors and that solvent tortfeasors should make up the share of insolvent tortfeasors according to jury's apportionment). If the case were to arise under such a system, most juries would probably assess most of the fault to the two teenagers. Nevertheless, if the free radicals were insolvent, the responsible person who has encouraged them would have to pay for their share, assuming the jurisdiction has retained joint liability. If the jurisdiction has adopted several liability, the responsible person would not have to make up the unpaid share of the free radicals' apportioned share of the judgment.

9. The *Weirum* court came close to imposing liability on First Amendment–protected speech. Nevertheless, the court concluded that the Super Summer Spectacular was either unprotected commercial speech or else unprotected conduct. The issue has arisen in other cases in which the courts have carved out an exception to the EFR doctrine when the defendant encouraged free radicals with First Amendment–protected speech; in these cases, the defendant is immune. See *Olivia N. v. NBC*, 178 Cal. Rptr. 888 (Cal. Ct. App. 1981) (defendant not liable when children sexually abused plaintiff following model provided by the defendant's television show); *Shannon v. Walt Disney Productions*, 281 S.E.2d 648 (1981) (defendant not liable to child who put out his eye while following, somewhat imperfectly, defendant's instructions on its Mickey Mouse Club Show about how to produce a particular sound effect); *DeFilippo v. NBC*, 446 A.2d 1036 (R.I.1982) (defendant not liable to parents of child who hanged himself following stunt performed on the Johnny Carson Show). Most critics of *Weirum* stress not the First Amendment aspect of the case but that the parties most at fault were the teens and that the court's decision made a corporation liable for their behavior.

10. *Guille v. Swan*, 19 Johns 381 (N.Y. 1822); for discussion, see text accompanying note 11. *Scott v. Shepherd*, 96 Eng. Rep. 525 (K.B. 1773); for discussion,

see text accompanying notes 15–17. Another early EFR case is *Dixon v. Bell*, 105 Eng. Rep. 1023 (K.B. 1816); for discussion, see text accompanying note 19.

11. Chief Justice Spencer said,

> I will not say that ascending in a balloon is an unlawful act, for it is not so; but, it is certain, that the *Aeronaut* has no control over its motion horizontally; he is at the sport of the winds, and is to descend when and how he can; his reaching the earth is a matter of hazard. He did descend on the premises of the plaintiff below, at a short distance from the place where he ascended. Now, if his descent, under such circumstances, would, ordinarily and naturally, draw a crowd of people about him, either from curiosity, or for the purpose of rescuing him from a perilous situation; all this he ought to have foreseen, and must be responsible for. (*Guille v. Swan*, 19 Johns 381 (N.Y. 1822))

12. *Squires v. Brooks*, 44 App. D.C. 320 (1916) (defendant not liable for leaving car unlocked in violation of municipal ordinance after thief negligently collided with plaintiff). *Connell v. Berland*, 228 N.Y.S. 20 (App. Div. 1928) (defendant left car parked in street with doors unlocked and key in ignition; one boy started it and crushed another boy). *Lee v. Van Beuren*, 180 N.Y.S. 295 (App. Div. 1920) (defendant liable for parking its electric truck with power switch in on position after a neighborhood boy started it up, and it crushed the five-year-old plaintiff who was sitting on front bumper); *Gumbrell v. Clausen Flanagan Brewery*, 192 N.Y.S. 451 (App. Div. 1922) (basically same fact as previous case).

13. See William H. Danne Jr., *Liability of Motorist Who Left Key in Ignition for Damage or Injury Caused by Stranger Operating the Vehicle*, 45 A.L.R. 3d 787 (1972).

14. Compare *Hergenrether v. East*, 393 P.2d 164 (Cal. 1964) (holding the defendant, whose employee left a partially loaded two-ton truck overnight in a dangerous section of city, liable to the plaintiff struck by a thief), with *Avis Rent a Car Sys., Inc. v. Superior Court*, 15 Cal. Rptr. 2d 711 (Cal. 1993) (holding that defendant Avis, which maintained poor security in its rental lot, was nevertheless immune from suit from someone with whom a car thief collided).

15. Blackstone, J., took the view that the necessity of the subsequent throws was a lot less than the plaintiff claimed. He said, "The throwing it across the market-house, instead of brushing it down, or throwing it out of the open sides into the street, (if it was not meant to continue the sport, as it is called), was at least an unnecessary and incautious act" (*Scott v. Shepherd*, 96 Eng. Rep. 525, 527 (K.B. 1773)).

16. Justices Nares and Gould and Chief Justice DeGrey took this position. In casting his decisive vote for trespass *vi et armis*, Chief Justice DeGrey said, "It has been urged, that the intervention of a free agent will make a difference: but I do not consider Willis and Ryal as free agents in the present case, but acting under a

compulsive necessity for their own safety and self-preservation. On these reasons I concur with Brothers Gould and Nares, that the present action is maintainable" (*Scott v. Shepherd*, 96 Eng. Rep. 525, 529 (K.B. 1773)).

17. Blackstone, J., said, "I give no opinion whether case would lie against Shepherd for the consequential damage; though, as at present advised, I think, upon the circumstances, it would" (*Scott v. Shepherd*, 96 Eng. Rep. 525, 527 (K.B. 1773)).

18. It would not be a classic EFR case because the intermediate throwers, except as members of a crowd, were not classic free radicals. They were trades-people, and the case shows that they were clearly identifiable, thus unlike the members of the *Guille v. Swan* crowd. Blackstone's analysis suggests that if the defendant would be liable for trespass on the case, it would be similar to a situation in which the parties were co-actors, as in *Keel v. Hainline*, 331 P.2d 397 (Okla. 1958) (defendant liable for battery for participating in game of throw-the-eraser, even though he did not personally make throw that hit plaintiff).

Recently in Illinois, something like the famous case has arisen again. See *Bodkin v. 5401 S.P., Inc.*, 768 N.E.2d 194 (Ill. App. 2002) (defendant's bartender handed plaintiff a firecracker and unknown patron, presumably drunk, lit it).

19. The plaintiff's declaration alleged that the defendant had "wrongfully and injuriously sent a female servant . . . to fetch away the gun so loaded, he well knowing that the said servant was too young, and an unfit and improper person to be sent for the gun, and to be entrusted with the care or custody of it" (*Dixon v. Bell*, 105 Eng. Rep. 1023 (K.B. 1816)). Besides being the first EFR case, it was also the first negligent entrustment case. Negligent entrustment is a subset of the EFR doctrine.

20. The case goes a little beyond the standard attractive nuisance case because the harm took place off the defendant's land.

21. The *Seith* court said,

> The defendant would be liable, although there was some intervening cause, if it were such as would naturally be anticipated as the result of the wire falling to the ground; but it seems inconceivable that the defendant ought to have anticipated that a policeman would throw the wire upon the plaintiff by striking it with his club when it was lying where no injury would be done by it either to a person on the sidewalk or the roadway. There is no evidence tending in the slightest degree to prove that policeman struck the wire for the purpose of removing it as a source of danger. He testified that he did not touch it, and told the plaintiff to get away from it; but assuming, as we are bound to do, that the testimony of the children was true, and that he struck the wire and knocked it toward the sidewalk, that testimony did not even remotely tend to prove that he was attempting to remove the wire so as to prevent injurious consequences. The injury to the plaintiff followed as a direct and immediate consequence of the independent act of the policeman, and

but for such act any negligence of the defendant would have caused no injury to the plaintiff. (*Seith v. Commonwealth Electric Co.*, 89 N.E. 425, 429 (Ill. 1909))

22. The court said,

There is nothing to show that such a consequence as happened was liable to occur. It was of course possible that some extremely nervous or irritable person would become angry because of his being inconvenienced on account of the crowded condition of the car; but it is not in accordance with the usual and ordinary course of events to anticipate that a seated passenger would so far lose control of himself on account of having a standing passenger crowded against him that he would eject the standing passenger from the car with such force as to throw him over the head of one who was standing upon the step below the party so ejected. It is apparent from the record in this case that the proximate cause of the injury to plaintiff was the action of the irritated passenger, and that this cause could not be anticipated by defendant or its agents. (*Snyder v. Colorado Springs & Cripple Creek District Ry.*, 85 P. 686, 687 (Colo. 1906))

23. The appellate court said, "It simply could not be expected that because the doors were re-opened the unidentified passenger would run directly into the plaintiff. [The court referenced *Palsgraf v. Long Is. R.R. Co.*, 248 N.Y. 339, 162 N.E. 99 (N.Y. 1928).] There was no evidence that the station was overcrowded, or that the only path to the open doors was through the spot on which plaintiff was standing" (*Marenghi v. New York City Transit Authority*, 542 N.Y.S.2d 542, 543 (App. Div. 1989)).

24. The Illinois Supreme Court also held that an amended complaint alleging that the defendants' dirt and the dirt clod contained glass also failed to state a cause of action.

25. See, e.g., *Hairston v. Alexander Tank & Equipment Co*, 311 S.E.2d 559 (N.C. 1984) (defendant auto dealer liable for not tightening deceased's wheel, which fell off stranding him next to a busy highway where he was struck by a negligently driven automobile).

26. A somewhat similar case cited by the *Wiener* court was *Robison v. Six Flags Theme Parks, Inc.*, 75 Cal. Rptr. 2d 838 (Cal. Ct. App. 1998), in which the defendant maintained an inadequate barrier between its picnic area and parking lot. An incompetent driver crashed through the barrier and hurt the plaintiffs. The court held the amusement park liable even though the negligence of the intervening actors was not totally inadvertent.

27. *Bigbee* and *Wiener* are exceptionally extreme when viewed against the history of the proximate cause doctrine. According to early cases, even inadvertent negligence by a responsible person would cut off liability for negligence that was deliberate or bordered on deliberate. See *Stone v. Boston & Albany Railroad*, 171 Mass. 536 (1898) (defendant negligently storing oil barrels on railroad platform

not liable to plaintiff when the most immediate cause of fire was a businessman's dropping a lighted match on it). The modern doctrine that makes people liable for setting the stage for negligence seems to have come from courts' growing recognition that negligence is common, especially inadvertent negligence. If inadvertent negligence is common, it can make good sense to impose liability on those who negligently set the stage for it.

*Wiener* also seems inconsistent with classic cases such as *Alexander v. Town of New Castle*, 115 Ind. 51 (1888). The plaintiff had himself deputized as a special policeman in order to arrest Mr. Heavenridge, who was operating a gambling device in town. After he had taken Heavenridge before a judge and got him convicted, the plaintiff was escorting Heavenridge to jail. The pair passed a large excavation that the defendant city had negligently failed to fill in. Seeing his chance, Heavenridge, who was clearly a free radical, threw the plaintiff into the excavation, thus injuring the plaintiff and accomplishing his own escape. The court held this defendant immune. As in *Wiener*, there was a large risk from inadvertently caused injury, as when someone accidentally fell into the hole, and not a particularly attractive opportunity for most free radicals. A possible distinction between the two cases is that a special relationship between the parties existed in *Wiener* but not in *Alexander*.

28. A more obvious English case is *Home Office v. Dorset Yacht Co.*, [1970] A.C. 1004 (H.L.), in which the plaintiffs sued the British Home Office for its negligence in allowing seven juvenile offenders to escape from an island where they had been taken for a work detail. Contrary to the defendant's own regulations, instead of posting a guard at night, the defendant's employees simply went to sleep. This was a tempting opportunity that did not normally exist for the incarcerated youths. Trying to escape the vicinity, the seven got on board a yacht moored off the island and set it in motion. They collided with the plaintiffs' yacht and damaged it. Again, the defendant's encouragement was substantial because the defendant controlled and made available to the free radicals a scarce opportunity for wrongdoing. Allowing a prisoner to escape does not normally lead to liability, especially when the harm caused happens some time after the escape. See *Buchler v. State*, 853 P.2d 798 (Ore. 1993) (defendant negligently allowed prisoner to escape, and some time later he shot the plaintiff's deceased).

29. A close but distinguishable case is *Daggett v. Keshner*, 134 N.Y.S.2d 524 (App. Div. 1954), in which the defendant sold the arsonists' accomplices thirty-three gallons and fifty-five gallons of gasoline into containers, well in excess of a statute's one-gallon limit. The purpose of the statute was to prevent arson, and the plaintiffs, two police officers, were hurt after they entered the premises about to be torched and were met with an explosion of the gasoline that the defendants had spread around in pails. The purpose was to collect the insurance on the burned building. Although the arsonists could have acquired the gasoline in some other way, the defendant made it easy for them. It would have been more

difficult to siphon it from four or five cars. See also *Watson v. Kentucky & Indiana Bridge & RR*, 126 S.W. 146 (Ky. 1910) (defendant not liable for spilling gasoline that exploded if intervenor was arsonist as opposed to someone who inadvertently dropped a match into it).

30. A contrasting case is *Kingrey v. Hill*, 425 S.E.2d 798 (Va. 1993), in which the defendant wife made available to her husband a gun that he was not allowed to own because of a prior conviction. Although he was not permitted to own a gun, there were many other ways in which he could have acquired one.

31. *Connell v. Berland*, 228 N.Y.S. 20 (App. Div. 1928) (defendant left car parked in street with doors unlocked and key in ignition; one boy started it and crushed another boy). *Lee v. Van Beuren*, 180 N.Y.S. 295 (App. Div. 1920) (defendant liable for parking its electric truck with power switch in on position after a neighborhood boy started it up and crushed the five-year-old plaintiff who was sitting on front bumper); *Gumbrell v. Clausen Flanagan Brewery*, 192 N.Y.S. 451 (App. Div. 1922) (basically same facts as previous case).

32. In *Loftus v. Dehail*, 65 P. 379 (Cal. 1901), the defendants owned a vacant lot in Los Angeles from which a house had been removed. The plaintiff's brother, who was four years old, pushed the plaintiff, who was seven, into the abandoned cellar. The court held that the evidence was insufficient to support the jury's verdict for the plaintiff. Heights from which playmates can be pushed are not as scarce to children as guns.

For the defendant in *Lane v. Atlantic Works*, 111 Mass. 136 (1872), simply leaving a horse-drawn truck on a city street, as in *Lynch v. Nurdin*, was a sufficiently tempting opportunity to create liability. Nevertheless, in *Glassey v. Worcester Consol S. Ry.*, 70 N.E. 199 (Mass. 1904), the defendant left a large reel on its side on the side of a road, outside the traveled portion. Boys turned the reel on its edge and pushed it down the road, ultimately ramming it into the plaintiff's carriage. The court found that the defendant was not liable.

In *Perri v. Furama Restaurant, Inc.*, 781 N.E.2d 631 (Ill. App. 2002), the defendant's server put a hot teapot on the lazy Susan, and a four-year-old child spun it, injuring a two-year-old child. The court held the restaurant liable.

33. The court said, "We agree that a reasonable juror could not find that defendant should foresee that another driver on the road would fire a gun into his car simply because he shined his high beams on that person, passed him, then sped up as the driver tried to approach. If such a response were so common as to make it foreseeable, the streets and highways of this country would be empty" (*Bansasine v. Bodell*, 927 P.2d 675, 677 (Utah App. 1996)).

34. Accord *Ordonez v. Long Island RR*, 492 N.Y.S.2d 442 (App. Div. 1985) (ten-year-old deceased intentionally placed iron bar on third rail, knowing that it was electrified); *Gaines v. Providence Apartments*, 750 P.2d 125 (Okla. 1987) (defendant not liable to fourteen-year-old who built ramp from defendant's trash and broke neck riding a bicycle over it).

35. In *Yania v. Bigan*, 155 A.2d 343 (Pa. 1959), the defendant encouraged the plaintiff's deceased to jump into a pit, and then, when he did, allowed him to drown without trying to assist him. The case resulted in no liability for the defendant. First, the deceased was not a free radical; instead, he seems to have been a responsible citizen. Also, the harm resulted to the plaintiff himself, not to a third party.

36. See also *Brewster v. Rankins*, 600 N.E.2d 154 (Ind. App. 1992) (defendant school district not liable when it allowed elementary school student to take home golf club to practice and he accidentally struck plaintiff's three-year-old).

37. *Keel v. Hainline*, 331 P.2d 397 (Okla. 1958) (defendant participated in game of throw-the-eraser and was liable to the person hit even though he did not actually throw the eraser that struck her).

38. See text accompanying notes 15–17.

39. See *Mills v. Central of Georgia Ry*, 78 S.E. 816 (Ga. 1913); *Harriman v. Railway Co.*, 12 N.E. 451 (Ohio 1887); *Penso v. McCormick*, 25 N.E. 156 (Ind. 1890).

40. See *Jarboe v. Edwards*, 223 A.2d 402 (Conn. Super. Ct. 1966) (defendant parents failed to hide matches from their pyromaniac son, and he lighted a playmate's pants on fire).

## REFERENCES

Grady, M. 2002. Proximate cause decoded. *UCLA Law Review* 50:293, 312–15.
Holmes, O. 1881. *The common law*. Mineola, NY: Dover.
———. 1897. The path of law. *Harvard Law Review* 10:457, 459–60.
Rose, A., and E. Ross. 1961. *The condensed chemical dictionary*. 6th ed. New York: Reinhold.
Shavell, S. 1980. An analysis of causation and the scope of liability in the law of torts. *Journal of Legal Studies* 9:463, 497.

# 18 PROBABILITY ERRORS: SOME POSITIVE AND NORMATIVE IMPLICATIONS FOR TORT AND CONTRACT LAW

*Eric A. Posner*

Evidence from experiments and empirical studies suggests that people make systematic errors when they estimate probabilities. The exact nature of these errors remains controversial, but two themes are that people discount low probability events, treating them as though they occur with a probability of zero, and that more generally, people are insensitive to small differences between probabilities. The first bias might cause a homeowner to treat the probability of a remote event such as an earthquake as though it were equal to zero; the second bias might cause a person to divide potential accidents into a small number of categories—high, medium, and low. I will follow the literature and call the first problem one of "optimism," though, as we shall see, this term is imprecise; and I will call the second problem one of "insensitivity." [1]

Legal scholars think that optimism and probability insensitivity justify additional regulation because optimists will take too little care. If the driver of an automobile believes that the risk of an accident is zero, he will drive too quickly. But the truth turns out to be more complex. A person who discounts remote risks might take too much care rather than too little. By increasing his level of care incrementally, the person can reduce his perceived probability of an accident nonincrementally, from some positive amount to zero. If the perceived reduction in expected accident costs exceeds the cost of the additional care, the person will use

Thanks to Oren Bar-Gill, Omri Ben-Shahar, Bill Landes, Doug Lichtman, Anup Malani, Francesco Parisi, John Pfaff, Steve Shavell, Al Sykes, David Weisbach, and participants in the George Mason conference and at a seminar at the University of Virginia Law School, for comments; and to the Sarah Scaife Foundation Fund and the Lynde and Harry Bradley Foundation Fund, for financial support.

more care than is efficient, which remains true regardless of whether the legal rule is strict liability or negligence.

This result holds as well for people who suffer from probability insensitivity. Even if they do not treat low probability events as though they would occur with probability of zero, they will enjoy large perceived benefits when they can take a small amount of additional care in order to move the risk of an accident from the "high" category to "medium," or from "medium" to "low." The existence of discontinuities or inflexion points in probability functions plays havoc with intuitions about the relationship between the law and decisions about care level.

This chapter explores these and other implications of optimism and insensitivity for the law.[2] Section 18.1 focuses on optimism and tort law. My other main result is that sufficiently optimistic agents engage in the same level of activity under strict liability and negligence; by contrast, rational agents engage in more activity under strict liability than under negligence. The reason for this difference is that the optimistic agent under strict liability and the rational agent under negligence do not internalize accident costs when they take due care (or what they think is due care). I also discuss the difference between harm-sensitive and harm-insensitive optimism; the relationship between optimism and probability insensitivity; and the implications of optimism for bilateral accidents. Section 18.2 briefly discusses optimism and contract law, and Section 18.3 contains some general comments about the treatment of probability errors in normative law and economics.

## 18.1 PROBABILITY ERRORS AND TORT LAW

### 18.1.1 Summary of Analysis

Suppose that agents are rational except that they are optimistic about low probability accidents. When they engage in some behavior like driving, they know that their behavior creates a risk of harm. When choosing the level of care, agents know the actual probability of harm associated with each level of care when the probability is above some threshold; below that threshold the probability of harm, which is low but positive, is treated as though it were zero.

Intuition tells us that such an agent would take too little care, whether the tort regime is strict liability or negligence. The analysis will show that for sufficiently high levels of optimism, the agent might take too much or too little care. The effect that causes too little care is the discounting of harms: the agent underestimates expected liability for a high level of care and so will take less care. The effect that causes too much care is that the agent can cause a (subjective, that is, error-driven) reduction of expected liability by taking a small amount of additional care. If the agent takes some level of care that causes a perceived positive probability of harm, and if a small additional amount of care would cause that probability to drop from the threshold amount to zero, then the agent will think that he is, in effect, taking a small extra precaution that will eliminate all potential liability. Which of the effects dominates depends on the relationship between the probability distribution, the level of harm, and the care function. Optimism could cause an agent to think that a bad event will not occur or that a little extra care will have a dramatic effect on the probability of a bad event occurring.

In addition, for sufficiently low levels of optimism, the agent will take the optimal care, and this amount of care is invariant with respect to the amount of optimism below a threshold. The agent does not take too much care because the amount of care necessary to create zero perceived expected harm is greater than the sum of the cost of optimal care and the correctly perceived expected harm. The agent does not take too little care because at the optimal level of care an accident is risky enough to be accurately anticipated by the low-optimism agent.

A well-known result in the literature is that for unilateral accidents, strict liability and negligence have the same effect on care but different effects on the level of activity. Strict liability causes the efficient level of activity; negligence causes too much activity. However, the difference between the two rules nearly disappears when the agent is optimistic. Both rules cause too much activity; indeed, unless the risk is sufficiently remote, the two rules cause the same level of inefficient activity. The reason is that under both regimes the optimistic agent will treat remote events as though they do not occur, so the main difference between strict liability and negligence—namely, that under negligence the agent is not liable if he takes due care—disappears in the agent's mind.

Next, I show informally that the results can hold even under less extreme assumptions about probability misestimation. The factor that drives the results is not the possibility that people could treat certain probabilities as though they were zero, but the possibility that people have trouble thinking of probability distributions as smooth or continuous functions and divide lower and higher probability events into discrete groups.

Finally, I argue that for bilateral accidents the different effects of strict liability and negligence on rational individuals carry over to the case of optimism: both rules cause the injurer to take care, but only negligence causes the victim to take care. However, under both rules the level of care taken by injurer and victim will not be optimal. As for activity level, the different effects of strict liability with contributory negligence, and negligence, on rational individuals do not carry over to the case of optimism. Strict liability with contributory negligence encourages rational victims but not rational injurers to engage in too much activity; negligence encourages rational injurers but not rational victims to engage in too much activity. By contrast, the two rules have the same effect on optimistic injurers and victims, encouraging both groups to engage in too much activity.

## 18.1.2 Analysis

### 18.1.2.1 Level of Care

Let $x$ = level of care (normalized, so $x$ is also the cost of care); $p(x)$ = the probability of an accident, as a function of the level of care $[p'(x) < 0; p''(x) > 0]$; and $h$ = harm. For illustrative purposes, we assume that $p(x) = x^{-2}$. For simplicity harm is a constant: the agent controls only the probability of the harm occurring.

The total (that is, social) cost function, $TC = x + x^{-2}h$. The optimal level of care $x^* = (2h)^{1/3}$.

Strict liability will cause the agent to choose $x^*$; negligence will cause the agent to choose $x^*$ if, for example, the agent must pay $h$ if $x < x^*$. Figure 18.1 illustrates these standard results (Brown 1973; Landes and Posner 1987; Shavell 1987).

Now we want to ask what happens if the agent has an irrational probability function $p^i(x)$, where

$$p^i(x) = x^{-2} \quad \text{if } p(x) > \overline{p}$$
$$= 0 \quad \text{otherwise.}$$

The value of $\overline{p}$ refers to the floor below which the probability of the accident is so small that the agent treats it as if it were 0.

Corresponding to $\overline{p}$ is a level of care, $x'$, which is the threshold between levels of care associated with accurate probability assessments and levels of care associated with optimistic probability assessment. To determine the value of $x'$, we must first make an additional assumption about whether the agent's optimism is sensitive to the level of harm or not. Consider the driver of an ordinary truck and the driver of a tanker truck filled with gasoline. One could imagine that each driver is equally insensitive to a low probability accident for a given level of care $x$, where $p(x) < \overline{p}$, but one could also imagine that the driver of the tanker is *more* sensitive. In the first (harm-insensitive) case, $p^i(x) = x^{-2}$ if $p(x) > \overline{p}$, so $x' = (1/\overline{p})^{1/2}$. In the second (harm-sensitive) case, $p^i(x) = x^{-2}$ if $p(x) > \overline{p}/h$, so $x' = (h/\overline{p})^{1/2}$. I will assume that optimism is harm sensitive, which seems more realistic, but will briefly discuss the harm-insensitive case later in Section 18.1.2.3.

The agent will minimize $TC^i = x + p^i(x)h$. There are two separate cases to consider. First, if $\overline{p}$ is sufficiently low, and thus $x'$ is sufficiently high, the agent will choose $x^i = x^*$. The reason is that the level of care necessary to reach $x'$ is higher than the combined care and accident costs for $x^*$. Think of a driver who believes

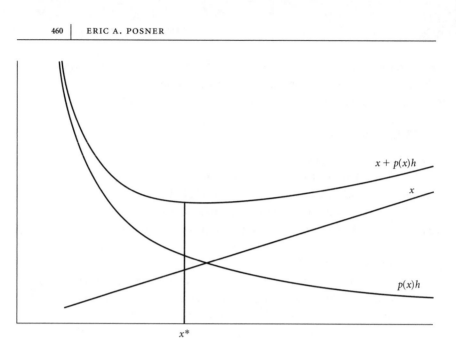

**Figure 18.1**  The standard model

SOURCE: *Supreme Court Economic Review*, University of Chicago Press, 2003.

that he can reduce the probability of an injury to zero only by driving a Volvo, but the ownership cost of a Volvo is greater than the joint cost of owning a Honda and expected liability from an accident. The driver will not buy the Volvo but will buy the Honda and take efficient care.

Second, if $\bar{p}$ is not too low, and thus $x'$ is not too high, $x^i = x'$. This is the case where the ownership cost of the Volvo, and thus the illusory sense of never being liable, is less than the combined ownership and expected accident costs of the Honda.

To find the dividing line between the two cases, one sets the cost of the "irrational" level of care that generates illusory expected zero liability (Volvo) equal to the joint care and accident costs for rational care (Honda): $TC(x') = TC(x^*)$. Because $TC(x') = x'$ (the expected accident cost is zero), we have $x' = (h/\bar{p})^{1/2} = TC(x^*) = (3h)^{1/3}/2^{2/3}$. Simplifying,

$$x^i = x^* \quad \text{if } \bar{p} \leq 2^{4/3}h^{1/3}/9 \approx 0.27h^{1/3}$$

$$x' \quad \text{otherwise.}$$

If we limit ourselves to the second case, where $x^i = x'$, then we can ask whether $x^i$ is greater than or less than $x^*$. Setting $x^i = x^*$, we get $\bar{p} = h^{1/3}/2^{2/3} \approx 0.63h^{1/3}$. It turns out that it could be either.

TABLE 18.1

*Relationship between optimism and care*

| Low optimism | Moderate optimism | High optimism |
|---|---|---|
| $\bar{p} \leq 0.27h^{1/3}$ | $0.27h^{1/3} < \bar{p} < 0.63h^{1/3}$ | $0.63h^{1/3} \leq \bar{p}$ |
| $x^i = x^*$ | $x^i = x' > x^*$ | $x^i = x' \leq x^*$ |
| Optimal care | Too much care | Too little care |

SOURCE: *Supreme Court Economic Review*, University of Chicago Press, 2003.

If $\bar{p} < 0.63h^{1/3}$, then $x^i > x^*$.

If $\bar{p} \geq 0.63h^{1/3}$, then $x^i \leq x^*$.

Thus, there are three regions. (See Table 18.1.) In the first region, the probability threshold (where the agent treats the probability of the event as though it were zero) is so remote that the agent would need to incur a lot of care in order to reach it. Because the cost of care is so high, the agent would prefer choosing the level of care that minimizes the "rational" total cost function. This is the example where the agent buys the Honda rather than the Volvo.

In the second region, the probability threshold is not so remote, so the agent finds it worthwhile to take extra care in order to reduce expected accident cost from a positive amount to an amount perceived as 0 (see Figure 18.2). The optimal level of care while driving is, let us suppose, a good night's sleep and driving during the day; but the agent thinks that if he does these things *and* buys antilock breaks, he will never have an accident. He takes too much care because the extra precaution creates the illusory sense of no expected liability.

In the third region, an inefficiently low level of care is sufficient to reach the probability threshold, and the agent has no incentive to take additional care (see Figure 18.3). The agent thinks that a good night's sleep is sufficient to reduce the probability of an accident to zero; therefore, he does not bother confining his driving to the day.

Figure 18.4 shows care as a function of optimism. For low levels of optimism, care is $x^*$. Above $\bar{p} = 0.27h^{1/3}$, care is a declining function of optimism.

*18.1.2.1.1 Negligence.* We have assumed strict liability, but what about negligence? If the agent assumes that courts will set the level of due care at $x^i$ rather than $x^*$, then the results remain the same. The agent will take too little care or too much care, depending on $\bar{p}$ and $h$. Thus, the agent has the same care incentives under strict liability and negligence.

But there is another possibility. If the agent believes that the court (irrationally!) will insist on setting the due care level at $x^*$, then the agent's behavior under

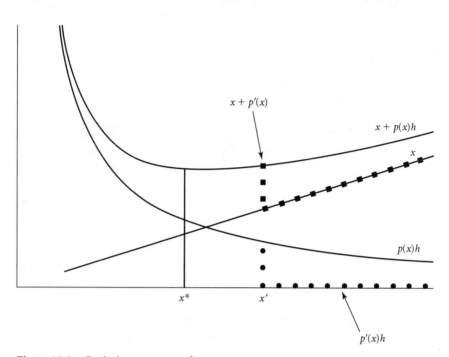

**Figure 18.2** Optimism—too much care

SOURCE: *Supreme Court Economic Review*, University of Chicago Press, 2003.

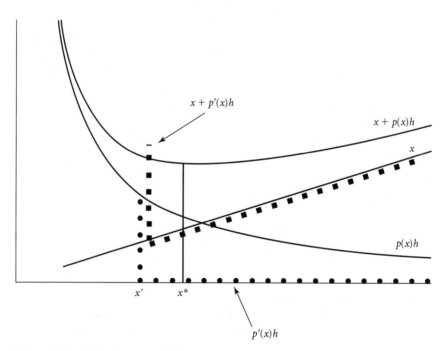

**Figure 18.3** Optimism—too little care

SOURCE: *Supreme Court Economic Review*, University of Chicago Press, 2003.

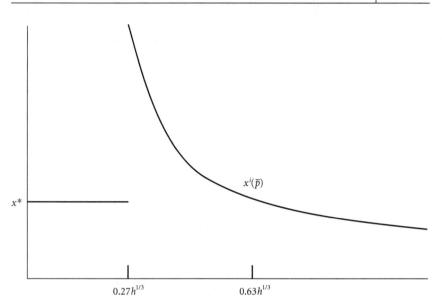

**Figure 18.4**  Care as a function of optimism

SOURCE: *Supreme Court Economic Review*, University of Chicago Press, 2003.

negligence and strict liability will differ but only in the midlevel optimism case. In the latter case, the agent will prefer to incur the cost of optimal care, $x^*$, rather than too much care, $x'$, because $x^* < x'$. Under negligence, the agent does not bear expected accident costs if he takes level of care $x^*$, so he gains nothing by increasing the level of care to $x'$.

### 18.1.2.2 Activity Level

Now suppose that the agent can choose his level of activity. Let $s$ = level of activity and $u(s)$ = the agent's level of utility from engaging in a certain level of activity [$u'(s) > 0$, $u''(s) < 0$]. Then the utility function is $u(s) - sx - sp(x)h = u(s) - s[x + p(x)h]$. The agent maximizes utility by minimizing the value of the negative expression, which means choosing optimal care $x^*$, and then by choosing an activity level $s^*$ that maximizes utility given the per-unit joint cost of care and expected liability (Shavell 1987).

Using our earlier probability function, $p(x) = x^{-2}$, it follows that utility is maximized if $x^* = (2h)^{1/3}$ (minimizing the negative expression) and if $s^*$ is such that $u'(s) = (2h)^{1/3} + [(2h)^{1/3}]^{-2}h = (3h)^{1/3}/2^{2/3}$.

Now let us look at the agent's incentives if optimistic probability estimates are used.

**18.1.2.2.1  Strict liability.** The agent will choose $s$ and $x$ to maximize $u(s, x) = u(s) - sx - sp^i(x)h$. Recall that if $\bar{p}$ is low enough, the agent will choose $x^i = x^*$. Otherwise, the agent will choose $x^i = x'$. Let us consider the two cases separately.

In the first case, where the agent chooses $x^i = x^*$, the agent internalizes the expected harm and thus acts the same as the rational agent. Thus, the agent chooses $s^i = s^*$.

In the second case, where the agent chooses $x^i = x'$, the agent's utility function is, in effect, $u(s) - sx^i$. The reason is that at $x^i = x'$, the agent treats the probability of the accident, and thus the expected accident cost, as though it were zero. Thus, the agent will choose $s^i$ such that $u'(s) = x^i = x' = (h/\bar{p})^{1/2}$. Intuitively, the agent will choose $s^i \geq s^*$, because the only internalized cost of the agent's activity is the level of care and not the expected accident cost.

**18.1.2.2.2  Proof.** In the second case, the agent chooses $x^i = x'$ because he has more than low optimism: $\bar{p} \geq 0.27h^{1/3}$. Manipulating the inequality, we get $(h/\bar{p})^{1/2} \leq (3h)^{1/3}/2^{2/3}$. The left side of the inequality is $u'(s^i)$, and the right side is $u'(s^*)$, as we saw previously. Thus $u'(s^i) \leq u'(s^*)$. Because $u''(s) < 0, s^i \geq s^*$.

This shows that the optimistic agent will engage in too much activity as long as $\bar{p}$ is not too low. The reason is that he will simply not take account of some of the cost (low probability harms) that he inflicts on others. For arbitrarily low values of $\bar{p}$, the agent will engage in the optimal level of activity. Thus, for a sufficiently broad distribution of $\bar{p}$, strict liability results in too much activity.

**18.1.2.2.3  Negligence.** Under negligence, the rational agent will choose $s$ and $x$ to maximize $u(s) - sx$. Thus, he will choose $s^*$ to maximize $u'(s) - x^*$. Because the agent does not internalize the expected cost of accidents if he takes due care, he will engage in too much activity (Shavell 1987).

The optimistic agent will choose $s$ and $x$ to maximize $u(s) - sx^i$, where, as before, we assume that the agent believes that the court will apply $x^i$ as the standard of care. In the low-optimism case, where $x^i = x^*$, the agent will act the same as the rational agent and choose $s^i = s^*$.

In the second case, where $x^i = x'$, the agent will choose $s^i$ to maximize $u(s) - \bar{p}^{-1/2}$. Thus, the agent will choose the same high level of activity as under strict liability.[3]

We can summarize the results as follows: (1) When the agent is sufficiently optimistic, strict liability and negligence will have the same effect on activity. When the agent's optimism is at a low level, strict liability produces efficient activity and negligence produces too much activity, just as they do for the rational agent. (2) Under strict liability and negligence, the sufficiently optimistic agent might engage in too much care as well as too little care ($x^i$ could be greater, less than, or

TABLE 18.2
*Harm-insensitive optimism*

| Low optimism | Moderate optimism | High optimism |
|---|---|---|
| $\bar{p} \leq 0.27h^{-2/3}$ | $0.27h^{-2/3} < \bar{p} < 0.63h^{-2/3}$ | $0.63h^{-2/3} \leq \bar{p}$ |
| $x^i = x^*$ | $x^i = x' > x^*$ | $x^i = x' \leq x^*$ |
| Optimal care | Too much care | Too little care |

SOURCE: *Supreme Court Economic Review*, University of Chicago Press, 2003.

equal to $x^*$) and will engage in too much activity ($s^i > s^*$). The point is that if the agent treats low probability events as though they will not occur, the agent will (usually) act like a rational agent under a negligence regime in which no liability is attached to careful behavior that causes expected harms.

### 18.1.2.3 Level of Harm

It is clear from Table 18.1 that the level of harm will affect the chances that the agent will take the optimal level of care, or too much or too little. As harm increases, the agent is more likely to take the optimal level of care, more likely to take too much care, and less likely to take too little care. It is worth mentioning that one would get a different result if one assumed harm-insensitive optimism. Thus, in the analogous table (see Table 18.2), as harm increases, the agent is less likely to take the optimal level of care; more likely to take too much care; and more likely to take too little care.

The optimal level of care increases with harm. The harm-insensitive optimist will not internalize the increase in harm, whereas the harm-sensitive optimist will internalize it partially. For this reason, an increase in harm will cause the harm-sensitive optimist to act more efficiently than the harm-insensitive optimist.

Figure 18.5 shows care as a function of harm. The curve labeled $x^*(h)$ depicts optimal care rising at a declining rate with the level of harm. The curve labeled $x^i(h)$ depicts irrational care. Note that it matches $x^*(h)$ at high levels of harm; otherwise, it is too low or too high except when the curves cross. The curve labeled $x^{ii}(h)$ shows harm-insensitive care, which of course is a horizontal line, invariant with respect to $h$, except at high levels of harm.

Figure 18.5 also shows how courts, in theory, could adjust awards in order to give efficient incentives to optimists. Focusing on the harm-sensitive case (the court cannot affect the behavior of the harm-insensitive agent except at high levels of harm), in which the level of harm is roughly in the middle of the $x$-axis, the court could provide efficient incentives either by reducing the award or by increasing the award. If the award is reduced, the agent will take a level of care that

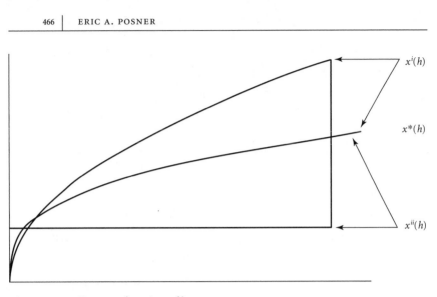

**Figure 18.5** Care as a function of harm

SOURCE: *Supreme Court Economic Review*, University of Chicago Press, 2003.

is optimal for a rational agent but below optimal for the optimist. If the award is increased enough, the agent will be thrust into the region of the midlevel optimist and act as though he were rational. This result holds in the region of midlevel optimism, where $x^i(h)$ and $x^*(h)$ cross on the left and join on the right. At a higher level of optimism, the court should increase the award; at a lower level of optimism, the court does not need to adjust the award.

### 18.1.2.4 Generality: Alternative Probability Distributions

One objection to the analysis so far is that the assumed probability distribution (or class of probability distributions) is implausible. It does not seem likely that when people drive a car, they accurately estimate the probability of an accident as long as they take little care, but when care exceeds a threshold, they then inaccurately think that the probability of an accident is zero. Indeed, the evidence for optimism is mixed, and other evidence suggests that in some settings people overestimate the probability of a small harm.

However, my results do not depend on people believing that low probabilities are zero or even that they optimistically underestimate probabilities. My results can hold even if people are pessimistic and overestimate the probability of a small harm. The necessary assumption is only that people are insufficiently sensitive to probabilities.

One might think, for example, that the agent's subjective probability could be a step function. The agent thinks that for a range of lower care behavior the probability of an accident is the same high number; for a range of medium care behavior the probability of an accident is the same middle number; and for a range of low care behavior the probability of an accident is low, though not necessarily zero. It remains the case that the agent could take too much or too little care. Too little care is easy to understand. Too much care will occur as long as the perceived drop in probability occurs soon enough after the optimal level of care, that the decline in expected accident liability is greater than the increase in the cost of care. Thus, the result does not depend on a discontinuous probability function, just on the function having at least one inflection point and a sufficiently steep slope soon after the optimal level of care. Nor does the result depend on optimism; the tail of the step function, for example, could be higher than the tail of $p(x)$.

One other possibility is that people are optimistic but that the optimism does not affect the slope of the objective probability function. Formally, $p^{i\prime}(x) = p\prime(x)$ and $p^i(x) < p(x)$ for all $x$. If $p(x)$ is a linear function, for example, then $p^i(x)$ would be just a parallel line that is below $p(x)$. This assumption might seem to be the most natural, but it is inconsistent with the literature, which suggests that people are more likely to be wrong about low probability events than about high probability events. But even if we accepted this assumption, it has an interesting and unintuitive result, namely, that the agent would take the optimal level of care (neither too much nor too little) under both strict liability and negligence. The reason is that the marginal benefit of care remains the same if the slope does not change. Thus, the current tort system provides the correct incentives for care (although not for activity level) even if agents are optimistic.

### 18.1.2.5  Bilateral Accidents

Suppose that the victim as well as the injurer can reduce the probability of an accident by taking care; thus $p(x, y)$. If both agents estimate probabilities correctly, then strict liability produces less efficient levels of care than negligence does. Both rules cause the injurer to take optimal care; but full compensation under strict liability gives the victim no incentive to take care. Negligence, by contrast, makes the victim bear the cost of personal carelessness when the injurer takes due care but the accident occurs anyway (Brown 1973; Landes and Posner 1987; Shavell 1987).

Now suppose that both parties are optimistic. As we saw before, the injurer will take the same level of care under both rules. If we put aside for the moment the level of care, the first thing to see is that the effect of the two rules on the victim remains the same: the victim will have no incentive to take care under strict liability and will have such an incentive under negligence. Now returning to the question of level of care, the injurer could take too much or too little care; the victim under the negligence regime will also take too much or too little care, both because the victim is optimistic and because the victim's choice will be affected by the inefficient level of care chosen by the injurer.[4]

As to the question of activity level, for rational agents strict liability with a defense of contributory negligence causes victims to engage in too much activity; negligence causes injurers to engage in too much activity (Shavell 1987). For sufficiently (midlevel or high level) optimistic agents, under both rules victims and injurers will engage in too much activity. For strict liability with contributory negligence, injurers will act as though they were governed by a negligence rule and not internalize accident costs above $x^i$. For negligence, victims will act as though they will not incur accident costs above $y^i$. Thus, the two rules have the same behavioral effects, and the choice between the rules no longer matters.

### 18.1.3 Insurance and Redistribution

The argument so far illustrates some of the complex implications of probability estimation error for care and activity level. Here, I will briefly point out its implications for insurance and redistribution, focusing on optimism.

If people underestimate low probability events, they will buy too little insurance. But if they are optimistic, they might take too much, rather than too little, care. For example, rather than put in too few smoke detectors because she is heavily insured, a homeowner might put in too many smoke detectors in order to reduce her perceived probability of a serious fire to zero. An insured optimist, then, might face less risk of fire than an insured person who is rational.

Jolls (1998) argues in a different context that optimism can justify redistributing wealth through the tort system.[5] Because people underestimate low probability events, redistributive tort awards will distort neither their care nor their labor-leisure choice and so will have a less negative effect than high taxes, which people can anticipate more easily and which distort their labor-leisure choice. In terms of the model, Jolls argues that the award should be $h + t$, where $t$ is the transfer, when the defendant is wealthy.

The problem is that increasing the award from $h$ to $h + t$ will distort behavior. To see why, look at Figure 18.5 and imagine that $h$ is the midpoint of the $x$-axis. The optimist's level of care, $x^i(h)$ is already too high, and $x^i(h + t)$ would be even worse. The court could produce optimal care by *reducing* the award by some amount, $r$, such that $x^i(h - r) = x^*(h)$. Although there are cases in which a positive transfer, $t$, would also reduce the distortion, Figure 18.5 provides no reason to think that awarding $t$ is anything but arbitrary and, in any event, shows that redistributive tort awards can distort the care behavior of optimists.[6]

## 18.2 SOME COMMENTS ON PROBABILITY ERRORS
## AND CONTRACT LAW

The argument so far has implications outside tort law. Consider the following model of contract law. At time 1, seller and buyer enter an incomplete contract for the delivery of a good. Buyer has valuation, $v$. At time 2, seller chooses a level of care, $x$. At time 3, seller either performs or pays damages, $d$. Seller's cost is either 0 or, with probability $p(x)$, a high amount, $c$, where $c > v$. We suppose that the market is competitive and buyer pays a price $\pi$ equal to seller's expected cost.

If transaction costs were zero and the parties could enter a complete contract, they would agree that seller will take a level of care $x^*$ that minimizes the joint cost of care and loss to buyer ($v - \pi$) that results if seller does not perform. That is, $x^*$ solves min $p(x)v + x$. Buyer pays price $\pi = x^*$ and earns a return of $v - x^*$. Seller obtains a return of 0. If transaction costs are positive and the parties cannot enter a complete contract that specifies $x^*$, then the optimal level of damages is $v - \pi$, that is, expectation damages, which causes seller to choose $x^*$ (Cooter and Ulen 2000).

Suppose now that both buyer and seller are irrationally optimistic and think that the probability distribution is $p^i(x)$. The analysis is the same as in the tort case. A complete contract would specify $x^i$, which could be greater or less than $x^*$; if the contract is incomplete and expectation damages are the remedy, the same result will be achieved. In addition, people will enter too many contracts because they will discount losses caused by low probability events (as before).

Suppose instead that seller is rational at the time that she enters the contract but expects that she will be optimistic when she chooses $x$. If a complete contract is possible, she will want to include a provision requiring her to choose $x^*$ (and will hope that renegotiation is not possible at time 2). But verifiability problems will often prevent such a course of action: a court might not be able to determine $x^*$. Another possibility is to agree to liquidated damages. If the seller expects to choose $x^i < x^*$, then she will want low liquidated damages; if she expects to choose $x^i > x^*$, then she will want high liquidated damages. The reason is that liquidated damages can be used to shift the $p^i(x)h$ curve up or down, in such a way as to cause the optimistic seller at time 2 to choose $x^*$. This shows, contrary to much of the literature, that the existence of cognitive biases is not necessarily an argument for the penalty doctrine.[7] Parties might agree to high liquidated damages in order to blunt the effects of optimism (Rachlinski 2000).

## 18.3 WELFARE

In welfare economics, it is conventional to assume that the goal of the state is to maximize social welfare, which is some aggregation of the individual utility functions of all citizens. Suppose that an agent prefers driving a car to taking a bus, but only because he underestimates the probability of a car crash. Should the state tax car driving in order to make the agent act the same way as he would if he knew the correct probability of the car crash? The legal literature answers this question positively, and a positive answer was implicitly assumed in the analysis in Sections 18.1 and 18.2 of this chapter.

But the problem is more complex. To see why, consider the simplest case. Suppose that an agent engages in some activity that can injure only herself, and no one else. She is an optimist and ignores the small chance that the activity will injure her. Suppose the government now mandates a precaution that reduces the low probability of an injury to zero. The agent will perceive this mandate as a cost, with no offsetting benefits. Therefore, her utility will decline, and so will the social welfare function. A welfare-maximizing government would therefore not impose what otherwise would seem to be a sensible mandate.

The problem also occurs in the more general tort case, whenever victims are optimistic. High tort awards designed to counter the wrongdoer's carelessness will not be experienced as an *ex ante* gain by the victim and will not affect the victim's behavior. The insights of cognitive psychology, especially those relating to biases in perception and risk estimation, are not easily reconcilable with welfare economics and thus cannot be straightforwardly imported into normative law and economics. Many normative proposals made by authors writing within "behavioral law and economics" fail to address this problem.

This is not to say that the problem is insoluble. But solving it requires a conception of welfare different from the conception used by economics. One could imagine that welfare is objective in the sense that regardless of one's preferences one has less welfare if one unknowingly takes high risks than if one does not. Or welfare could involve not just having any preference but the right kind of preferences, and when a person's preference for driving is not sufficiently informed, that preference does not fully count in the person's welfare. But these are difficult and complex problems that have not been resolved by economists and philosophers.

## 18.4 CONCLUSION

The most important methodological point I want to make is that when one tries to operationalize the insights of cognitive psychology and make them usable for law and economics, one must make certain specific assumptions about the shape of probability functions, and terms such as *optimism* are too vague to be of help. A person who underestimates low probability events might be called an optimist but might also be called a pessimist (in certain ranges) about the likelihood that more care will avoid accidents. The pessimist about care might act the same as the optimist about liability. The chapter has explored various ways that probability errors can be formalized and their implications for tort and contract law.

The chapter also has some testable empirical implications. One might use psychological exams to test for optimism and then see whether optimistic people take the same level of care under strict liability and under negligence, or whether optimistic people are more likely to take too much care under both rules than nonoptimistic people are. The model also allows for indirect tests of optimism: if people are harm sensitive, then they should take the optimal level of care when harm is low, higher levels of care when harm is moderate, and lower levels of care when harm is high. Indirect tests such as these would be difficult, and open to multiple interpretations, but they might be a useful way for avoiding the problem of measuring optimism.

1. I am aware that the evidence is ambiguous, that these phenomena might be sensitive to context and limited by offsetting biases or cognitive strategies, and so forth, but I set aside these questions for the purposes of analysis.

2. The law and economics literature does address error and misperception, but in a different context. For discussions of error by courts, see Craswell and Calfee (1986) or Shavell (1987); of the effect of care on expected liability, see Diamond (1974); of the use by courts of information about products that was not available to the producer, see Ben-Shahar (1998); of the effect of judgment-proofness and causation requirements on incentives, see Landes and Posner (1987). There is also a related literature on consumer protection and misperception (Hynes and Posner 2002).

3. This assumes that the agent believes the court will choose $x^i$ as due care; if not, the moderate-optimism case becomes the same as the low-optimism case, as explained earlier.

4. There are interesting variations that one could consider: suppose that victims are rational and mistakenly think that injurers will choose $x^*$ rather than $x^i$ or that the victims are rational but understand that injurers will choose $x^i$. One could also assume that the injurer is rational but the victim is optimistic, and so on.

5. Jolls's argument, as she acknowledges and discusses, depends on some assumptions that are in my view questionable: that the stochastic loss will not be converted into a certain (small) loss through insurance and that a "tax lottery" is not politically feasible.

6. These problems can also complicate the analysis of transitions. For example, Kaplow (1986) assumes that if people underestimate the risks of a natural disaster such as a flood, government-supplied insurance would not distort incentives.

7. The result is sensitive to the assumption that the probability function is discontinuous or has an inflexion point. Under more conventional assumptions (a smooth probability function), we get the opposite result: if $x^i < x^*$, seller will choose high liquidated damages, and vice versa. But the basic point—that the existence of cognitive biases is not necessarily an argument for the penalty doctrine—remains valid. Rationally anticipating optimism, parties will sometimes choose high liquidated damages provisions. I thank Oren Bar-Gill for this point.

## REFERENCES

Ben-Shahar, O. 1998. Should products liability be based on hindsight? *Journal of Law, Economics, and Organization* 14:325.

Brown, J. 1973. Toward an economic theory of liability. *Journal of Legal Studies* 2:323.

Cooter, R., and T. Ulen. 2000. *Law and economics*. New York: Addison Wesley Longman.

Craswell, R., and J. Calfee. 1986. Deterrence and uncertain legal standards. *Journal of Law, Economics, and Organization* 2:279.

Diamond, P. 1974. Single activity accidents. *Journal of Legal Studies* 3:107.

Hynes, R., and E. Posner. 2002. The law and economics of consumer finance. *American Law and Economics Review* 4:162.

Jolls, C. 1998. Behavioral economics analysis of redistributive legal rules. *Vanderbilt Law Review* 51:1653.

Kaplow, L. 1986. An economic analysis of legal transitions. *Harvard Law Review* 99:509, 548.

Landes, W., and R. Posner. 1987. *The economic structure of tort law*. Cambridge, MA: Harvard University Press.

Rachlinski, J. 2000. The "new" law and psychology: A reply to critics, skeptics, and cautious supporters. *Cornell Law Review* 85:739.

Shavell, S. 1987. *Economic analysis of accident law*. Cambridge, MA: Harvard University Press.

# 19 THREATENING AN "IRRATIONAL" BREACH OF CONTRACT

*Oren Bar-Gill and Omri Ben-Shahar*

> A person who is known to "dislike" an unfair bargain can credibly threaten
> to walk away from one, even when it is in her narrow interest to accept it. By
> virtue of being known to have this preference she becomes a more effective
> negotiator.
>
> *Robert H. Frank*

When circumstances surrounding a contract change, a party might consider breach a more attractive option than performance. His incentive to breach, often manifested by an explicit modification demand backed by a threat to cease performance, may convince the other party to modify the original agreement. The contract law doctrine of modification determines whether and when these modifications, reached under explicit threats to breach, are enforceable.

It has been recognized, by courts and scholars, that one of the factors that should affect the decision to enforce the modification is the "reasonableness" of the threat to breach. If the new circumstances are such that performance under the original terms would come to involve a loss for one party, his demand for better terms is viewed more favorably, and the resulting modification is more likely to be enforced.[1] This reasonableness-of-threat test is not, however, the only—or even the main—criterion for enforcing modification agreements. A second test is often applied, focusing instead on the perspective of the *threatened party*, examining whether her acquiescence to the modified terms was extracted in a coercive manner. Under this test, it matters whether the threatened party had reasonable alternatives or adequate resort to remedies. If she had not, the modification agreement is deemed coercive and is governed under the doctrine of "duress," rendering it voidable.[2]

Financial assistance from the John M. Olin Centers for Law and Economics at the University of Michigan and Harvard Law School and from the William F. Milton Fund of Harvard University is gratefully acknowledged.

The two tests—one focusing on the motivation of the threatening party and the other on the alternatives available to the threatened party—may be in conflict. It is not uncommon for a modification demand-threat to be motivated by unanticipated losses and nevertheless leave the threatened party no choice but to concede. When these conflicts arise, the duress perspective is often the primary one endorsed by courts, rendering the modification unenforceable (Corbin 1964).[3] We have argued elsewhere against this hierarchy among the normative criteria. We demonstrated that enforcement of modifications should turn on one, and only one, factor: whether the threat to breach, which led to the modification, was credible (Bar-Gill and Ben-Shahar 2004). In this chapter, we turn to examine more systematically the factors that can render the threat to breach credible. In doing so, we hope to complement our previous work with a more robust descriptive account of the bargaining environment.

Accordingly, the analysis in this chapter addresses the contract modification problem from the perspective of the threatening party. It examines the credibility of his modification threat, namely, his motivation to breach the original contract in case his modification demand is turned down.

Economic analysis provides a standard tool to evaluate the issue of threat credibility. It assesses the payoff to the threatening party from carrying out the threat, which usually equals his breach liability, and compares it to his payoff from retracting the threat and performing the agreement under the original terms. It is only when the pecuniary loss from performance exceeds the pecuniary cost of breach that the threat is deemed credible. Otherwise, the threat to breach is "cheap talk," as game theorists would put it, or a "bluff," and may well be disregarded.

This chapter develops an additional perspective to supplement the standard economic account of the credibility of threats to breach. This perspective suggests that the breach-or-perform decision can be motivated by factors that are not captured by standard pecuniary calculus. In particular, the decision can be motivated by sentiments toward the *fairness of the division* of the surplus between the parties. A party whose share in the surplus is reduced in a manner that violates the party's notions of fairness may have a credible threat to breach, even if the absolute payoff from performance is still positive and greater than the payoff from breach.

Building on previous literature that identified the general prevalence of "fairness" sentiments in economic decisions, the chapter explores the patterns by which such fairness concerns affect the credibility of threats to breach existing contracts. It demonstrates that the threat to breach can be credible while "irrational": the threatening party may carry it out even if doing so, and bearing liability for breach, is more costly than performance under the original terms.[4] The chapter then studies the normative implications of this descriptive insight. It shows that in order to protect the interests of the *threatened party*, modifications ought to be enforceable in a larger set of circumstances than previously perceived.

To illustrate, consider a seller who experiences an unexpected increase in his cost of performance (due to forces outside the seller's control). Assume that the increased cost is such that the seller would suffer a small net loss if he performs the contract but would suffer a greater loss if he breaches and is ordered to pay damages. The seller demands a modification—one that would allow the seller to cover his cost but would still leave the buyer with a positive profit. Imagine that the buyer refuses to modify the contract, requiring the seller to bear the entire burden of the unanticipated cost increase. Traditional notions of credibility suggest that if the buyer refuses to modify the contract, the seller would simply perform it. The seller is better off bearing the cost increase than liability for breach. However, the seller may also deem performance under the original terms to be unfair. It provides him with a smaller share of the *ex post* surplus than he "deserves," violating his desire to be treated fairly by his opponent, stirring sentiments of anger, insult, and the like. Such sentiments provide an additional reason for the seller to prefer breach to performance under the original terms. If these fairness concerns are sufficiently strong, they can render the seller's seemingly noncredible threat to breach sufficiently credible to be taken seriously. It might be in the interest of the buyer to acquiesce to such a threat and concede better terms to the seller, thereby avoiding the risk of stirring a hostile action on the part of the seller. The only way the buyer can make such a commitment and avoid breach is by making an enforceable modification.

The analysis in this chapter is organized as follows. Section 19.1 begins with a brief introduction to the law of contract modification. Section 19.2 describes the "credibility principle," namely, the idea that enforcement of modifications should turn *solely* on the issue of the credibility of the threat to breach. Section 19.3 is the core of the chapter. It develops a model of decision making motivated (in part) by fairness concerns. It distinguishes several sources of fairness sentiments and identifies their effect on the credibility of the threat to breach. Section 19.4 then derives the normative implications for modification doctrine and applies these lessons to some leading cases, and Section 19.5 concludes.

## 19.1 THE LAW OF CONTRACT MODIFICATION

The law of contract modification has long outgrown its early premise that modifications are promises lacking consideration and thus unenforceable (Williston 1992). In the old days, this premise forced courts to recite two false observations. First, it was commonly stated that the acquiescing party—usually a creditor who is asked to waive some of the debt—is receiving nothing in return for his acquiescence. "Payment of a lesser sum on the day cannot be a satisfaction of a greater sum" was the instructive statement by Lord Coke in *Pinnel's Case*, 77 Eng. Rep. 237 (C.P. 1602). Even in following this directive, courts acknowledged its fallacy: "[I]t may be much more advantageous to the creditor to obtain immediate payment of part of his debt than to wait to enforce payment" (*Foakes v. Beer*, 9 App. Cas. 605 (1884)). Accordingly, courts have invented an "offsetting" fiction, also evidently false, that modification involves consideration in the form of rescission of the original contract.[5]

The notion that a modification's fate ought to be determined by the doctrine of consideration has been reformed, both judicially and legislatively.[6] Instead, courts are instructed to verify that the modification demand was made in good faith and that it was "fair and equitable" in view of the changed circumstances. These instructions direct courts to examine the perspectives of both parties. They have to look at the reasons why a party made the modification demand in the first place, namely, were there "reasonable commercial reasons" such as "a market-shift which makes performance come to involve a loss."[7] But courts also look at the position of the other party, whether her surrender to the modification demand exhibits coercion and duress.[8]

Much of the modification jurisprudence has focused on the issue of duress. Both the Restatement and the Code agree that if duress was present, the modified agreement is voidable (Chirelstein 2001). And both Code and common-law court decisions tend to find duress whenever the threatened party has no effective resort to remedies or to substitute deals and must surrender to the threat.[9] Although there is occasional adherence to the idea that the enforceability of modification should turn on the issue of the credibility of the threat to breach,[10] court decisions have by and large conformed to the duress principle.[11]

Finally, in those cases that do apply the credibility principle, namely, enforce a modification only if the modification demand was reasonable or credible, the main factor that courts investigate is whether the original contract came to involve a loss. In such circumstances, where the party suffering a pecuniary loss is likely to breach rather than perform under the original terms, some courts have reasoned that in the absence of a modification, breach would likely occur, to the detriment of both parties.[12] Still, even in these cases, in evaluating the credibility of the modification demand, courts have looked strictly at the pecuniary comparison between the cost of performance under the original terms and the cost of breach.

It is fair to say, then, that the law of contract modification has generally been subsumed by the doctrine of duress. What determines if a modification is enforceable is the threatened party's free assent (Hillman 1979). In the next section, we examine the desirability of this approach. We develop the "credibility principle," which suggests that the threatened party's free assent should *not* be the determining issue. Instead, the sole enforceability criterion should be the credibility of the threat to breach.

## 19.2 THE CREDIBILITY PRINCIPLE

### 19.2.1 Informal Analysis

When a party makes a demand for modification of a contract, backed by a threat to breach if the demand is rejected, will the threatened party acquiesce and accept less favorable terms? In analyzing this question, we have to consider what will be the result of a rejection of the modification demand.

For the threatened party to accommodate the modification demand and surrender to less favorable terms, she must first perceive the threat to breach to be credible (or that there is a positive probability that it is credible). If she deemed the threat to be a bluff, there would be no cost for her in rejecting the threat: the threatening party will not carry his threat out but rather will perform the contract under the original agreed-upon terms. Thus, a necessary condition for modification to occur is the credibility of the threat to breach.

Credibility is a necessary, but not sufficient, condition for modification. Even if the threat is credible, the threatened party may prefer to reject it. Because she already acquired a contractual right for performance under the original terms, she expects that a rejection of the threat would result in breach, which in turn would entitle her to expectation damages. Thus, the threatened party compares the value of the remedy to the value that she will be left with under a modified contract. Note that when the threat to breach is credible, her choices no longer include a third alternative, namely, the value of performance under the original terms; the other party, having a credible threat to breach, will not perform the contract under the original terms. Accordingly, the threatened party's remaining choice is between performance under the modified, less favorable, terms, and breach remedies.[13]

For modification to occur, then, it is necessary that the threat to breach would be credible and that the threatened party would prefer the modified terms to remedies for breach. Further, modification will only be agreed upon if the parties can, at the renegotiation stage, find terms that would make them *both* better off relative to nonagreement and breach. One obvious case in which no such "bargaining range" exists is one in which performance came to involve costs exceeding its value (the case of "efficient breach"). But a bargaining range may not exist at the renegotiation stage even if performance is still efficient. If the burden of remedies on the breaching party is less than the value of remedies to the breached-against party, such a "bargaining range" may not exist, and an inefficient breach—rather than modification—would occur.

This analysis suggests that in order to understand (and predict) when a modification would occur, we need to examine the motivations of both the threatening party and the threatened party. Accordingly, it might be conjectured, in determining when a modification should be *enforced*, courts would need to examine both parties' positions. In particular, courts would need to check whether the threatening party had a credible threat to breach *and* whether the threatened party had reasonable alternatives or adequate resort to remedies. Indeed, this is what courts often do (Farnsworth 1999).

As we showed elsewhere (Bar-Gill and Ben-Shahar 2004), however, this conclusion is misguided. In deciding whether to enforce a modification that was obtained by threat to breach, the court should focus *solely* on the threatening party's perspective and enforce the modification any time the threat that led to it was credible. In particular, the court should *not* focus on the motivation of the threatened party. Whether this party had adequate resort to remedies or not should have no bearing on the normative decision whether to enforce a modification.

The reason why enforcement should *not* turn on the issue of the adequacy of remedies is the following. When the threatened party's effective choice is between the modified terms and remedies for breach, her acquiescence to the modification demand indicates that she herself deemed remedies for breach to be inferior to the modified terms. Otherwise, if remedies were deemed adequate, why would she concede to the threat and accept less favorable terms? Thus, from the perspective of the threatened party, her acquiescence indicates she would unambiguously be better off if the modification were enforced than having to settle for remedies. Put differently, if a court faces a case in which a modification occurred, it must infer that the threatened party deemed her remedies to be inadequate. Thus, there is no reason to condition enforcement on the question of the adequacy of remedies. This inadequacy-of-remedies test is equivalent to a regime of nonenforcement of modifications.

Moreover, the tendency of courts to examine the threatened party's situation and to invalidate the modification whenever it was extracted by duress, namely, whenever the threatened party had no reasonable alternatives or adequate remedies, is harmful to the *threatened party* herself (even though she is the one who, *ex post*, is seeking this invalidation). It means that she cannot make a credible commitment *ex ante* to modify the original contract. In such situations, the other party will not bother to extract a modification (anticipating that the modification will be struck down anyway). That is, precisely in those cases in which the threatened party would want to make a commitment and avoid the outcome of breach, courts' reluctance to enforce the modification makes this goal impossible to achieve.

This analysis suggests that the only factor that should bear on the decision to enforce a modified contract is the credibility of the threat that led to the modification. In particular, to the extent that the threatened party may have difficulty distinguishing between credible threats and bluffs and may thus be unable to acquiesce "selectively" only to credible threats, courts can promote the optimal outcome by inquiring into the credibility of the threat and enforcing modifications only when the threats that led to them were credible.

Once it is established that the sole relevant criterion for enforceability of deals reached under a threat is the credibility of the threat, it is worth exploring the various factors that bear on the issue of credibility. For example, it would be important to understand which categories of unanticipated cost increases are more likely to enhance the credibility of the threat to breach. In addition, it would be important to examine the modification jurisprudence and check the extent to which court decisions conform to the credibility condition. We began this exploration elsewhere (Bar-Gill and Ben-Shahar 2004).[14] However, in that work we restricted our attention to factors that would affect the credibility of a *rational* threatening party. We did not explore factors that might make an *irrational* threat credible nevertheless. It is this direction that we pursue here. We argue that a threat to breach can be credible even if it is against the pecuniary interest of the threatening party to carry it out. However, before turning to the analysis of such "irrational credibility," let us briefly restate the previous discussion in more formal terms and thus develop a framework for the subsequent irrationality analysis.

## 19.2.2 Formal Analysis

Consider a seller (he) and a buyer (she) contracting over the sale of one indivisible asset. The following timing summarizes the interaction. At period 0, the two parties sign the original contract, specifying the delivery of the asset by the seller to the buyer in exchange for a payment, $p$.[15] The value of the asset to the buyer is $v$. The seller's cost of creating the asset (or parting with the asset, namely, the value of the asset to the seller) is thought to be $c$, at this period.

Before period 1, an "unanticipated" change of circumstances might increase the cost of performance for the seller from $c$ to $C > c$. It is assumed that performance is efficient, even with the higher price $C$, namely, $v > C$. Whereas the seller observes the actual cost realization, $c$ or $C$, the buyer can only observe the distribution from which this cost is drawn. For simplicity, assume that there is a probability $\pi$ that the seller's cost will be $C > c$, and a probability $(1 - \pi)$ that the seller's cost will remain $c$.

As a result of the cost increase, at period 1 the seller may demand to renegotiate the contract price. It is assumed that if renegotiation is successful, the parties agree on a new price, $P > p$. The conditions under which such a modification will occur and the precise value of $P$ are analyzed in the following discussion. Then, at period 2, the seller decides whether to deliver the asset to the buyer, that is, whether to perform or breach the original or modified contract (depending on the success or failure of the period 1 renegotiation).

Finally, at period 3, litigation may occur. If a modification was agreed upon at period 1, the buyer may seek to invalidate it and the seller may seek to enforce it. The court's decision will depend on the legal rule of enforceability, and the analysis will consider possible legal regimes. If, instead, a modification was not negotiated and the seller breached, the buyer will seek damages for breach, $d$, and it is assumed that she can secure a judgment for monetary damages equal to her expectation loss, namely, $d = v - p$.

One begins by looking at the seller's incentive. If the seller's attempt at modification fails, will he perform or breach the initial contract? The seller's decision is based on a comparison between his performance payoff and his breach payoff. If the seller performs, he nets $p - \hat{c}$, where $\hat{c} \in \{c, C\}$. If he breaches, a court will ideally order him to pay damages of $d = v - p$ at period 3. Generally, however, the burden imposed on the seller by these prospective damages is different from $d$ and may be either higher or lower. Denote this burden by $D_S$. Comparing the seller's performance payoff and breach payoff, following a rejection by the buyer of the modification demand, the seller will decide to breach *if and only if*

$$\hat{c} - p > D_S. \tag{1}$$

If condition (1) holds, the seller will decide to breach at period 3. Otherwise, he will perform.

When condition (1) is satisfied, the seller has a *credible threat to breach*.[16] Accordingly, we refer to condition (1) as the "credibility condition." We assume that when $\hat{c} = c$, the credibility condition is not satisfied, but when the cost of performance turns out to be unexpectedly high, that is, when $\hat{c} = C$, the credibility condition may be satisfied and the seller may have a credible modification demand.

Turn now to period 1, when the parties may renegotiate the original contract. These renegotiations are influenced by the informational asymmetry between the two parties. In particular, the buyer does not observe the seller's actual performance cost and therefore does not know whether the seller has a credible modification demand.[17] However, the buyer knows how much she can recover if a breach occurs. Although the court will ideally award the buyer damages of $d = v - p$, the actual value of the remedial right will generally be different from $d$. Denote this value by $D_B$. The buyer will refuse to negotiate any modification and will resort to damages whenever $D_B \geq v - p \ (= d)$. If, however, $D_B < v - p$, namely, if the buyer is inadequately protected by remedies, she may agree to a new, higher price, $P$. What this price will be depends on her bargaining power, the informational structure of the bargaining, and the legal regime concerning enforceability of modifications.

In particular, it can be shown that if courts apply a selective enforcement regime, under which a modification is enforceable only when the threat that led to it was credible, the buyer will concede a price increase of $\Delta p \in [C - p - D_S, v - p - D_B]$,[18] and a modification will be demanded (and agreed upon) only when the seller has a credible threat (Bar-Gill and Ben-Shahar 2004). It can also be shown that such a regime is superior, from the buyer's perspective as well as from a social perspective, to either an unconditional enforcement regime, a no-enforcement regime, or a "duress" regime that conditions enforcement on the absence of buyer's alternatives (Bar-Gill and Ben-Shahar 2004).

## 19.3 FAIRNESS

We have seen that a modification ought to be enforced any time it results from a credible threat to breach. The credibility of a seller's threat to breach is determined by condition (1):

$$\hat{c} - p > D_S. \tag{1}$$

We focus initially on the cost element in condition (1). Recall that absent an unanticipated change of circumstances, the cost of performance is $c$ and condition (1) does not hold. Now, consider an unanticipated event that raises the cost of performance to $C$, such that the seller now faces a losing contract, that is, $C > p$. Assume, however, that this loss is still smaller than the cost of breach, that is, $C - p < D_S$. From a perfect rationality perspective, the seller does not have a credible threat to breach.

By assumption, the cost of breach is greater than the material cost of performance. But the material cost may not be the only relevant cost associated with performance. In particular, the seller might incur a "fairness cost" when performing the contract. After all, why should the seller bear the entire burden imposed by an unanticipated cost increase, the occurrence of which was beyond his control? Why should he lose from the transaction, while the buyer profits? Moreover, the transaction can be readily modified by adjusting the contract price such that the seller's loss will be prevented, and still the buyer will make a positive profit. Why not insist on such a modification? Any other outcome would simply be unfair. Accordingly, we turn to examine the patterns by which such notions of unfairness would affect the seller's willingness to breach.

## 19.3.1 Preferences for Fairness

Recent experimental studies have reported that in important economic settings individuals' behavior cannot be described solely on the basis of the maximization of absolute monetary payoffs. In particular, fairness concerns have been shown to play a role in describing individuals' assessment of their well-being. Observed patterns of decision making appear, in these instances, to be at odds with the assumption of maximization of absolute monetary payoff.

In the labor market context, workers, when treated unfairly, often react and respond by reducing the effort they invest (Akerlof and Yellen 1990). Fairness considerations have also been invoked to explain why many employers do not cut wages during periods of high unemployment despite the potential offered by the supply-demand levels (Akerlof 1979; Frank 1988; Kahneman, Knetsch, and Thaler 1986a, 1986b; Neale and Bazerman 1991; Solow 1980). The significant impact of fairness concerns on behavior has been demonstrated in other economic contexts as well. Arthur Okun (1981, 170) observed that "firms in the sports and entertainment industries offer their customers tickets at standard prices for events that clearly generate excess demand. Popular new models of automobiles may have waiting lists that extend for months. Similarly, manufacturers in a number of industries operate with backlogs in booms and allocate shipments when they obviously could raise prices and reduce the queue." The failure of these markets to clear has been attributed to "the hostile reaction of customers to price increases that are not justified by increased costs and are therefore viewed as unfair" (Kahneman, Knetsch, and Thaler 1986b, 728; see also Frank 1988; Kahneman, Knetsch, and Thaler 1986a).

Most relevant to the contract modification problem, fairness clearly affects behavior in bargaining contexts (Bazerman and Neale 1995; Huck and Oechssler 1999; Rabin 1993). The most striking example concerns the simplest form of bargaining, the take-it-or-leave-it offer, also known as the ultimatum game. To give a concrete example, assume that A and B must decide how to allocate one hundred dollars between them. A proposes a certain allocation. B can either accept or reject A's proposal. If B accepts, the money is divided according to A's proposal. If B rejects, both parties get nothing. The perfect rationality game theoretic equilibrium in this game is straightforward. A offers an allocation in which B gets a penny, and B accepts A's proposal, because a penny is better than nothing. Any implicit or explicit threat by B to reject offers that give her less than some larger share is not credible, will not affect A's offer, and will not be carried out by B. This prediction, based on the assumption of individual maximization of absolute monetary payoffs, might be straightforward, but it is also patently unrealistic. Robust empirical results demonstrate that responding parties in one-shot ultimatum games consistently reject "unfair" offers even at the expense of reducing their own payoffs significantly. Consequently, proposing parties offer "fair" allocations with substantial sums awarded to the respondent (Camerer and Thaler 1995; Guth, Schmittberger, and Schwartz 1982; Jolls, Sunstein, and Thaler 1998; Kahneman, Knetsch, and Thaler 1986a; Korobkin and Ulen 2000).[19]

One intuition explaining this result is that people would like to be treated fairly and that this fairness concern may affect their behavior. As Richard Thaler (1992, 23) puts it, when a party declines a positive offer, "he signals that his utility function has non-monetary arguments. (In English, this means he is insulted.) [He] says: 'I would rather sacrifice 1¢ than accept what I consider to be an unfair allocation of the stake.'" Another way to view this phenomenon is as one manifestation of an internalized social norm, usually applied in repeated interactions, which prescribes retaliatory actions toward selfish behavior (Binmore 1998; Gibbard 1990).

Irrespective of their underpinning, fairness concerns clearly play a role in describing individual behavior. To better understand this role, we attempt to impose some structure onto these preferences for fairness. In doing so, we begin with the concept of a "fair outcome" in the modification problem. We then develop a notion of an "unfairness cost" that a seller bears when performing an unfair contract.

### 19.3.2 What Is Fair? Identifying the Fair Outcome in the Modification Context

The first step in incorporating fairness concerns into an individual's preferences is the introduction of a concept of a "fair outcome." A "fair outcome" or a concept of "fairness" is not an objective term. The perception of fairness depends on the social environment (for example, on "what other people get") or on the history of the interaction. Players do not necessarily agree on the concept of fairness, as it may depend on the role they play in the game. Consequently, fairness is in the eye of the beholder.[20]

Fairness concerns at the modification stage are triggered by the unanticipated increase in the seller's cost of performance. But the cost of performance is not a uniform concept. Various changes can affect different elements making up the seller's cost of performance. And changes in different types of costs may have a different impact on the relevant fairness concept. The question is therefore, what types of cost increase trigger a fairness claim supporting the seller's attempt to pass on (at least) part of the cost increase to the buyer?

The central distinction is between actual costs and alternative costs. An increase in the seller's actual costs is exemplified by an unexpected rise in factor prices. This type of cost increase will often invoke fairness concerns that may assist the seller in extracting a modification. But economic costs are not limited to such actual costs.

Economists have long recognized the importance of alternative costs. The alternative cost of a given action equals the forgone opportunities that this action entails. Therefore, the alternative cost of performance equals the value of the best alternative use the seller has for the same resources he must devote to performance. In particular, if a new buyer offers the seller a much higher price for the said performance, the seller's alternative cost would increase. Empirical evidence suggests that compared to an increase in actual costs, an increase in the seller's alternative costs will have a much smaller effect on the seller's ability to extract a modification. Okun (1981) documents the hostile reaction of customers to price increases triggered by excess demand, as opposed to price increases induced by increased actual costs. Kahneman, Knetsch, and Thaler (1986b) presented subjects with a hypothetical concerning a hardware store that raises the price of snow shovels after a large snowstorm. Eighty two percent of the subjects considered such a price increase, driven by access demand, namely, by the increase in alternative costs, to be unfair. A similar price increase driven by a rise in the wholesale price of shovels would not have garnered such hostile reactions.

To ascertain the effect of fairness on credibility, we focus on the seller's perspective. We identify three considerations that may affect the seller's perception of a fair outcome at the modification stage: (1) equal division of the actual *ex post* surplus, (2) sharing the burden of an unexpected cost increase, and (3) guaranteeing the *ex ante* division of surplus.[21]

### 19.3.2.1 The Equal Split

The first consideration that may affect the seller's concept of fairness relies on a notion of *ex post* equality. According to this notion, fairness requires an equal division of the actual surplus between the two parties. If the cost of performance turns out to be $C$, the contract price should be increased to $\frac{1}{2}(v + C)$ in order to achieve a fair allocation. The fair outcome, from the seller's perspective, is defined by the fair price $\frac{1}{2}(v + C)$.

Numerous studies have demonstrated that the equal split is considered by many to be the fair outcome (Guth, Schmittberger, and Schwartz 1982; Kahneman, Knetsch, and Thaler 1986a; Ochs and Roth 1989).[22] Note, however, that the equal-split notion of fairness is by no means unique to the modification context. It is prevalent in general bargaining problems. As Gibbard (1990, 262–63) puts it, individuals "latch onto symmetries, favoring equal division or proportionality," and this judgment is "deeply ingrained by early acculturation."

In particular, this notion of fairness would arguably affect also the first-stage bargaining between the seller and the buyer. At this first stage, when both parties believe that the seller's cost of performance is $c$, the equal-split norm advocates a contract price of $\frac{1}{2}(v + C)$. Obviously, this does not mean that the original contract price will always be $\frac{1}{2}(v + C)$. Disparate bargaining power and other factors also play an important role in determining the stage 1 price. It does mean, however, that other things equal, a deviation from this benchmark of equality reduces the willingness of a party to enter into the deal. Likewise, at the renegotiation stage, a deviation from the adjusted benchmark of equality will affect the willingness of a party to remain in the deal.

It should be noted that the existence of an original agreement between the parties, which often deviates from the equal-split notion, suggests that pecuniary interests might override parties' fairness concerns. It may well be, however, that the intensity of the fairness sentiments under the original contract—the deviation of the original price from the benchmark of $\frac{1}{2}(v + C)$—is sufficiently increased under the new circumstances, once the original price is compared to the revised equal-split benchmark of $\frac{1}{2}(v + C)$, to override the rational pecuniary calculus. The framework for formalizing the intensity of fairness concerns will be developed in Section 19.3.3.

### 19.3.2.2 Sharing Unexpected Burdens

The second consideration that may affect the seller's concept of fairness also relies on a notion of equality or sharing, but to a lesser degree. According to this sharing notion, fairness does not require an equal split of the overall surplus but only of the unanticipated increase in the seller's cost of performance. By assumption the seller was not responsible for this change of circumstances and thus should not bear the burden alone. In contrast to the equal-split consideration, the sharing principle applies only where the original contract is silent, namely, it applies only to the unanticipated cost increase and not to the overall surplus.

Charles Fried (1981) in his seminal book *Contract as Promise* advocates this sharing approach with respect to what he calls "contractual accidents."[23] A "contractual accident" occurs when an unanticipated contingency arises on which agreement is absent. In such cases,

> there may be no basis for holding the parties responsible or accountable to one another. Rather, persons in some relation, perhaps engaged in some common enterprise, suffer an unexpected loss. . . . The sharing principle comes into play where no agreement obtains, [and] no one in the relationship is at fault. . . . Sharing applies where there are no rights to respect. . . . It is peculiarly appropriate to filling the gaps in agreements, to picking up after contractual accidents. (Fried 1981, 70–71)

Although Fried advocates a normative principle, it is based on intuitive notions of justice that may often motivate individuals, and to that extent it would have a positive, or descriptive, validity. Accordingly, if an anticipated increase in the seller's cost from $c$ to $C$ is viewed as a contractual accident, the sharing principle will be triggered. According to the sharing principle, the loss of $(C - c)$ should be split between the parties such that each party should bear $\frac{1}{2}(C - c)$. Therefore, the contract price should be increased by $\frac{1}{2}(C - c)$.

### 19.3.2.3 Guaranteeing the Ex Ante Division of Surplus

The third consideration that may affect the seller's perception of a fair outcome places greater weight on the *ex ante* division of surplus as determined by the original contract price. Specifically, if the stage 1 price is $p$, then the original contract allotted a fraction $(p - c)/(v - c)$ of the surplus to the seller and a fraction $(v - p)/(v - c)$ of the surplus to the buyer. Fairness requires respect for this *ex ante* division. This division was the true product of the parties' mutual assent. That is, under this view what the parties fundamentally agree upon when they enter a contract is a certain division of the surplus: what the relative fraction is that each gets. They dress this agreement in a set of ad hoc terms, but only because these terms achieve the intended split. Accordingly, when circumstances change, the basic agreement concerning the division of surplus should be maintained, and the terms of the agreement should be adjusted.

When the seller experiences an unexpected cost increase, this alters (specifically, reduces) the *magnitude* of the surplus. According to the seller's fairness perception, these changed circumstances should not affect the agreed upon *division* of the (new) surplus. Therefore, if the seller is to receive a fraction $(p - c)/(v - c)$ of the actual surplus, the modified contract price should satisfy: $(P - C)/(v - C) = (p - c)/(v - c)$, or $P = C + (v - C) \cdot (p - c)/(v - c)$, implying $P > p$.

The notion that the fair price at the modification stage depends on the original transaction relates to the empirical findings regarding the strong influence of the "reference transaction" on people's conception of fairness.[24] Moreover, these findings suggest that exogenous shocks, leading to an increase in the cost of performance, justify an increased price that maintains the "reference profit" (Kahneman, Knetsch, and Thaler 1986b).

### 19.3.2.4 The Three Concepts of Fairness Compared

We have presented three distinct concepts of fairness that may influence the seller's behavior in the modification stage. Before proceeding further, it is useful to compare these three concepts and identify the relationships between them.

Consider the following example. Assume that $c = 0$, $v = 100$, and $C = 60$. According to the equal-split (ES) concept, the fair price should now be $P^{ES} =$

$\frac{1}{2}(100 + 60) = 80$. According to the sharing-of-burdens (SB) concept, the fair price should be $P^{SB} = p + \frac{1}{2}(60 - 0) = p + 30$. And according to the *ex ante* division of surplus (ED) concept, the fair price should be $P^{ED} = 60 + (100 - 60) \cdot (p - 0)/(100 - 0) = 60 + 0.4 \cdot p$.

Using the preceding example, we can now state the relationship between the three fairness concepts.

Claim:

1. When the original contract price, $p$, implements an equal split of the *ex ante* surplus, $v - c$, all three fairness concepts imply the same modification, that is, $P^{ES} = P^{SB} = P^{ED}$. In the example, $p = \frac{1}{2}(100 - 0) = 50$ implies $P^{ES} = P^{SB} = P^{ED} = 80$.

2. When the original contract price, $p$, allocates a larger share of the *ex ante* surplus, $v - c$, to the seller, $P^{ES} < P^{ED} < P^{SB}$. For instance, in the example, if $p = 55$, then $P^{ES} = 80$, $P^{SB} = 55 + 30 = 85$, and $P^{ED} = 60 + 0.4 \cdot 55 = 82$.

3. When the original contract price, $p$, allocates a larger share of the *ex ante* surplus, $v - c$, to the buyer, $P^{SB} < P^{ED} < P^{ES}$. For instance, in the example, if $p = 45$, then $P^{ES} = 80$, $P^{SB} = 45 + 30 = 75$, and $P^{ED} = 60 + 0.4 \cdot 45 = 78$.[25]

The relative importance of the three fairness concepts can affect the credibility of the seller's threat to breach. When fairness requires a more substantial modification of the original contract, namely, a larger increase of the contract price, the credibility-bolstering effect of fairness will likely be greater. Therefore, if the original contract price, $p$, allocates a larger share of the *ex ante* surplus, $v - c$, to the seller, the SB concept of fairness will provide most credibility, the ED concept will provide less credibility, and the ES concept will provide least credibility. Conversely, if the original contract price, $p$, allocates a larger share of the *ex ante* surplus, $v - c$, to the buyer, the ES concept of fairness will provide most credibility, the ED concept will provide less credibility, and the SB concept will provide least credibility. Finally, if the original contract price, $p$, implements an equal split of the *ex ante* surplus, $v - c$, all three fairness concepts will have the same effect on the credibility of the seller's threat to breach.

After discussing the possible concepts of a fair outcome, we now turn to analyze the influence of fairness concerns on the seller's bargaining behavior at the modification stage. For this purpose, we do not distinguish between the three fairness concepts and the three "fair" prices implied by them, $P^{ES}$, $P^{SB}$, and $P^{ED}$, and rather refer to a generic fair price, $P^{F}$.

### 19.3.3 "Unfairness Costs" and Credibility

Acknowledging the potentially important impact of fairness concerns does not mean that the seller will invariably insist on the fair outcome (specifically, on the fair price $P^F$).[26] Even when a seller cares about fairness, he will generally still care about his material payoffs as well. Thus, behavior will be the result of a balance between a party's material interests and his fairness concerns. Such a balance requires the definition of a measure of unfairness and a quantification of the cost of unfairness.

In the present context, fairness is not an all-or-nothing concept. For instance, if the fair price is $P^F = 100$, an actual price of 90 will be considered more fair, and an actual price of 50 will be considered less fair. For simplicity, let $P^F - P$ measure the degree of unfairness of the price $P$. Accordingly, we can say that a seller, who performs in exchange for a price $P$, bears a fairness cost of $\sigma \cdot [P^F - P]$, where $\sigma \in [0, \infty)$ represents the level of the seller's fairness concern.[27]

As noted previously, the seller will balance material interests with fairness concerns to determine his bargaining behavior.[28] In particular, the balance of these two considerations will determine the seller's reservation price at the renegotiation stage:[29]

$$\Delta p_S = \frac{1}{1 + \sigma} \cdot [C - p - D_S] + \frac{\sigma}{1 + \sigma} \cdot [P^F - p].$$

Consider first a seller with no fairness concerns, that is, $\sigma = 0$, who is guided by material interests alone. At the renegotiation stage, whenever $C - p < D_S$, this seller will have a zero reservation price and there will be no modification. At the other extreme, a seller with very strong fairness concerns, that is, $\sigma \to \infty$, will insist on the fair price, and his reservation price would be $\Delta p = P^F - p$.

Between these two extremes, a stronger fairness concern increases the seller's reservation price, $\Delta p_S / \partial \sigma > 0$. In particular, there exists a threshold value $\hat{\sigma} = \dfrac{D_S - C + p}{P^F - p}$ such that sellers with weaker fairness concerns, $\sigma < \hat{\sigma}$, will not have a credible threat to breach (that is, their reservation price will be zero), and sellers with stronger fairness concerns, $\sigma > \hat{\sigma}$, will have a credible threat to breach (that is, their reservation price will be positive).

A seller's preference for fairness transforms empty words into a credible threat to breach.[30] In his book, *Passions Within Reason: The Strategic Role of the Emotions*, Robert Frank (1988, 5) notes that "a person who is known to 'dislike' an unfair bargain can credibly threaten to walk away from one, even when it is in her narrow interest to accept it. By virtue of being known to have this preference she becomes a more effective negotiator."[31]

## 19.4 IRRATIONALITY IN MODIFICATION DOCTRINE— CASE DISCUSSION

Recognizing the credibility of "irrational" threats can shed different light on some of the prominent cases in the law of contract modification. These are cases in which courts decided not to enforce the modification agreement, decisions that most commentators and subsequent courts have endorsed. The analysis in this chapter suggests that nonenforcement may have been an undesirable result.

Consider first the classic casebook favorite *Alaska Packers v. Domenico*, 117 F. 99 (9th Cir. 1902). A group of seamen aboard a fishing vessel, hired under a contract that entitled them to a wage of fifty dollars for the season and two cents for each fish they caught, went on strike soon after the season had begun, demanding a wage increase. Unable to find substitute workers and expecting large losses if work did not resume (such that could not be recovered from the judgment-proof seamen), their employer agreed to modify the contract and increase the fixed component of the wage to one hundred dollars. At the end of the season, after the seamen completed their obligations satisfactorily, the employer refused to pay the modified wage. The seamen sued to recover this increment.

The Court of Appeals reversed the decision of the Court of Admiralty and decided not to enforce the modification. It explained that the employer's consent to the wage increase was coerced, being extracted at a time in which the employer was most vulnerable, having no adequate remedies or substitutes. Indeed, contract law commentary in the hundred years since has branded this case as the prototype gun-to-the-head case, suggesting that the seamen timed their threat opportunistically so as to maximize the employer's vulnerability (Chirelstein 2001). The result seems logical and desirable (Posner 1997).

The decision in *Domenico* was reached under the duress principle. Would a different result be mandated had the court utilized the credibility principle? Although the analysis would have to focus on the incentives of the threatening employees rather than on the perspective of the threatened employer, it has been suggested that the result would not change. Under the view that the seamen's threat was strictly opportunistic, it is clear that they would not have carried it out. Had the employer rejected their demand, they would have been better off returning to work than breaching the contract and losing the entire season's worth of wages. Accordingly, the reluctance of the law to enforce the modification provides the desirable effect of deterring similarly situated parties from making their noncredible hold-up threats in the first place.[32]

But a different account has also been suggested. In their complaint, the seamen argued that their modification demand came as a result of their realization that the fishing equipment was in poor shape, thereby reducing the expected volume of the catch and their corresponding per-catch compensation. In fact, a careful study of the circumstances of this case shows that the seamen had many reasons to be upset (Threedy 2000). For one, the entire fixed component of their wage (fifty dollars) was deducted as a "recruitment fee." Being dependent solely on the per-fish bonus, they realized, as they arrived in Alaska, that more employees than they anticipated would share these bonuses, reducing their income. In fact, the eighty-two seamen who were part of the strike were all new to this particular cannery, and they discovered that the veteran fishermen—all of different ethnic background—were earning higher salaries for equivalent tasks. Further, whereas there was genuine dispute whether the recycled fishing nets supplied to the seamen were of inferior quality, it is quite clear that the seamen genuinely thought they were and had difficulty utilizing those nets effectively.

Thus, learning that their overall income would be less than anticipated, because of what they perceived as the fault of their employer, and realizing that they were treated less favorably than their co-employees, the seamen may have come to regard the terms of their contract as unfair. From this perspective, it might well be that the seamen were willing to forgo whatever remaining wage they would earn in order to avoid what they considered an exploitative and unfair compensation, one that falls short of what they initially expected to get and what others get for identical effort.

In its decision, the trial court rejected offhand this possible motivation. It held that the seamen's claim that the equipment was defective is "highly improbable," but it did so solely on the "self-evident" grounds that it was against the employer's interest to provide equipment that would diminish his own profits.[33] The trial court nevertheless decided to enforce the modified contract, reasoning that the modification was necessary to avoid the even less desirable result for the employer, of uncompensated breach. Apparently, the trial court too was under the impression that but for the modification the seamen would have remained on strike. In other words, the court considered the seamen's threat, although irrational, credible.[34] On the basis of the underlying circumstances, and recognizing the seamen's state of mind, this impression is quite plausible.

Another illustration of the implications of fairness concerns for the credibility of the threat to breach is the famous case of *Lingenfelder v. Wainwright Brewery Co.*,

15 S.W. 844 (Mo. 1891). In that case, an architect who was hired to oversee the construction of a brewery threatened to cease work unless his fee was increased. Here, unlike the typical modification of a construction contract, the reason for the demand was not an unexpected increase in the actual cost of performance but rather the architect's disappointment from not being awarded the second and highly profitable phase of the project: installation of the refrigeration plant in the brewery. The court, in accordance with the consideration doctrine that governed the problem of modification at the time, held that no new consideration was provided by the architect to justify his increased pay: "[U]nder the new promise, he was not to do any more or anything different" (848). The court highlighted the coercion under which the brewery's acquiescence was extracted, given the loss of time and money that would be involved in finding a replacement.

Although this case appears as another prototype hold-up example, in which the threat to breach is opportunistic and noncredible, a careful reading may suggest otherwise. The referee who adjudicated the case and who ruled against the architect found that when the architect learned that one of his competitors was picked for the profitable refrigeration project, "he felt disappointed, aggrieved, angry." Indeed, we are told that the threat to breach was not mere words; immediately after being notified of the brewery's decision to pass him over, the architect "took away his plans, called off his superintendent on the ground, and notified Mr. Wainwright that he would have nothing more to do with the brewery" (846). This action was not a strategic display of false emotions, a bluff. The testimony offered in this case suggests that for a period of two months, the architect refused to return to the site, did not respond to daily telephone and mail communications, and eventually returned only upon the intervention of an intermediary—his close friend Adolphus Busch.[35] It appears that the architect made significant efforts to secure the refrigeration project. In terms of the previous analysis, the architect's profit declined unexpectedly when he was overlooked for the second phase of the project. He deemed this to be unfair and was willing to forgo the small profit under the original agreement in order to avoid working for a client that treated him in this manner.

We can only speculate whether the threats in *Domenico* and in *Lingenfelder* were credible. Accordingly, it would be an overstatement to suggest that the decisions in these cases were wrong. Recognizing the role of fairness motivations, our analysis of these cases yields at least a tentative claim: to the extent that the threats were motivated by an emotional reaction to what the threatening parties considered an unfair deal, and that this emotional reaction was sufficiently intense to render credible the threats to breach, the decisions in these cases are detrimental to the interests of the *threatened parties*. If indeed the threats were credible, the legal restriction on the ability to extract a modification will only induce the threatening parties, and parties similarly situated, to breach the contract.

Finally, it should be emphasized that the analysis in this chapter is *normative*. It addresses the question, when should modifications be enforced? It is not a positive analysis, for it does not suggest that case decisions conform to the enforcement principle developed here. In fact, the two leading cases just examined, as well as our companion study of contract modifications (Bar-Gill and Ben-Shahar 2004), convinced us that courts more often than not overlook the credibility condition. Nevertheless, modification doctrine can be interpreted to incorporate the type of fairness motivations studied here. For example, Section 89 of the Restatement provides that a modification should be binding if it is "fair and equitable in view of circumstances not anticipated by the parties when the contract was made." Even though the current application of the "fair and equitable" requirement has not been linked to the credibility of the threat to breach, Section 89 could be interpreted to support such a link. That is, when the fairness concerns rise to the magnitude that would induce the threatening party to breach the unmodified contract, the modification ought to be enforceable. A similar reinterpretation could be proposed for the "good faith" requirement in U.C.C. § 2-209.

## 19.5 CONCLUSION

Whether a threat to breach is rendered credible as a result of the fairness and emotional motivations of the kind identified in this chapter might be a difficult determination to make. It requires the decision maker to trace the emotions and the state of mind of the threatening party, not merely the threatening party's objectively verifiable pecuniary interests. These are variables that do not lend themselves to straightforward quantification and comparison; thus, it is not always clear whether they exist and—if they exist—whether they are sufficiently intense to overcome the rational, strictly pecuniary, calculus. Moreover, in light of the difficulty in verifying the authenticity of such behavioral reactions, parties might be tempted to bluff, to appear angrier and more insulted than they really are, and thus convince their counterparts (and courts) that their threats are credible. As Frank (1988) recognized, there may be a strategic advantage to an emotional facade.[36] Further, as with many emotional responses, what initially, at the time of the threat, may well have been an authentic display of a fairness-based sentiment may subside over time. In particular, when the time comes to carry out the threat, the irrational considerations that supported it at the outset may diminish. That is, the credibility characteristic of the threat may wear away.

Indeed, it would be plausible to conclude that fairness-based concerns cannot provide a threat with the same dependable and verifiable basis of credibility as "hard" pecuniary concerns. It is tempting, then, to ignore this set of motivations in designing legal policy. But the fact that transactors' fairness considerations are difficult to verify does not mean that they are nonexistent. Ignoring them will not make them go away. To the extent that these motivations nevertheless exist, failing to account for them may give rise to undesirable legal policy. The fact that transactors do not have a rational basis for their threat to breach does not mean that they also do not have an irrational basis for their threat.

Hence, the conclusion proposed is tentative: If it is evident that a threat to breach a contract was motivated by an irrational yet credible drive, the resulting modification ought to be enforceable. Failure of the law to enforce the modification will not serve to uproot such irrational conduct.[37] It will merely hamper the ability of the threatened party to commit to a modification, confining this party to the less desirable outcome of breach.

As with any tentative conclusion, its importance depends on the empirical validity of the underlying premise. It remains for future work to explore, both experimentally and by case analysis, the extent to which threats to breach are motivated by "irrational," fairness-oriented concerns.

1. U.C.C. § 2-209, cmt. 2.

2. The Restatement (Second) of Contracts § 175 (1981) states, "If a party's manifestation of assent is induced by an improper threat by the other party that leaves the victim no reasonable alternative, the contract is voidable by the victim." The Restatement at cmt. b, Ill. 5 states, "A, who has contracted to sell goods to B, makes an improper threat to refuse to deliver the goods to B unless B modifies the contract to increase the price. B attempts to buy substitute goods elsewhere but is unable to do so. Being in urgent need of the goods, he makes the modification. [. . .] B has no reasonable alternative, A's threat amounts to duress, and the modification is voidable by B."

3. Farnsworth (1999, 282) writes, "In fashioning a solution to the problem of the enforceability of modifications, the drafters of the Code discarded the trappings of the doctrine of consideration to bare the real abuse of the bargaining process—coercion. The result is remarkably consistent with the liberalized rules on duress."

4. Throughout the discussion we do not take a position on the question of whether emotional responses, such as anger and insult, are necessarily in conflict with the predictions of rational choice theory. For recent contributions to this debate, see Binmore (1998) and Ridley (1997).

5. See, e.g., *Schwartzreich v. Bauman-Basch, Inc.*, 131 N.E. 887 (N.Y. 1921).

6. Refer to The Restatement (Second) of Contracts § 89 (1981). Also, U.C.C. § 2-209 (1) states, "An Agreement modifying a contract within this Article needs no consideration to be binding."

7. U.C.C. § 2-209, cmt. 2.

8. See, e.g., *Austin Instrument, Inc. v. Loral Corp.*, 272 N.E.2d 533 (N.Y. 1971).

9. *Austin Instrument, Inc. v. Loral Corp.*, 272 N.E.2d 533, 535 (N.Y. 1971) states that duress exists only when "the threatened party could not obtain the goods from another source of supply and the ordinary remedy of an action for breach of contract would not be adequate."

10. *Gobel v. Linn*, 11 N.W. 284 (Mich. 1882); *Angel v. Murray*, 322 A.2d 630 (R.I. 1974).

11. Corbin (1964, 57) states, "A modification coerced by a wrongful threat to breach under circumstances in which the coerced party has no reasonable alternative should prima facie be voidable. . . . In such circumstances, *it should be immaterial that the party exercising coercion has a good business reason for its wrongful demands.*"

12. See, e.g., *Jaffray v. Greenbaum*, 20 N.W. 775, 778 (Ia. 1884): High rent originally agreed upon may be less valuable to the landlord than the modified lower rent, which guarantees that the tenant should remain in business and in occupancy.

13. Many courts have taken the position that the threatened party should be entitled to the value of the performed contract under the *original*, premodification terms, and have pursued this policy by refusing to enforce the conceded modification. However, under this prevalent nonenforcement approach, the threatening party will realize that any renegotiated concession he extracted is valueless and will not bother offering the modification. If he has a credible threat to breach, he will prefer to breach. In other words, courts' perception that the premodification terms can be enforced is misguided.

14. There, we argue that much of the modification jurisprudence does *not* conform to the credibility principle. We identified prominent examples in which modifications were voided even though the threats under which they were made were credible. See, e.g., *Kelsey-Hayes Co v. Galtaco Redlaw Casting Corp*, 749 F. Supp. 794 (E. D. Mich. 1990).

15. This is clearly an incomplete contract. For similar accounts of contractual incompleteness and subsequent renegotiation see, e.g., Harris and Holmstrom (1987), Dye (1985), and Shavell (1984).

16. Note that condition (1) implies $D_S < d$.

17. Assume for now that $C$ is sufficiently large so that $C - p > D_S$.

18. Depending on the parties' relative bargaining power. Note that there will be no modification unless $C - p - D_S \leq v - p - D_B$ or $v - C \geq D_B - D_S$.

19. It should be noted that the experiments mentioned in the text were carefully designed to preclude any reputation effects by staging the game as a one-shot interaction between strangers.

20. Neale and Bazerman (1991, 158) state, "[F]airness is not an objective state. Rather, a social environment is cognitively transformed, and a state of (un)fairness is perceived." Also see Babcock et al. (1995); Babcock and Loewenstein (1997); and Raiffa (1985, 345), who writes that "you want your just share, and what you think is a 'just share' may not agree with your adversaries' assessments."

21. A fourth consideration may place greater weight on the original contract, arguing that the parties' initial agreement must be honored regardless of any changed circumstances. However, this concept of fairness will most likely be adopted by the buyer and not by the seller. See the sources cited in Note 20 of this chapter for a discussion of the subjectivity and self-serving nature of fairness concerns. Moreover, such a concept of fairness, if adopted by the seller, will not bolster the credibility of the threat to breach.

22. Frank (1988, 165) has proposed the following definition of a fair transaction: "A fair transaction is one in which the surplus is divided (approximately)

equally. The transaction becomes increasingly unfair as the division increasingly deviates from equality." It has also been argued that the fifty-fifty split is the evolutionary stable convention in bargaining (Young 1993).

23. Fried focuses on excuse cases (mistake, frustration of purpose, impossibility, and impracticability), but the logic of his argument applies to the modification context as well.

24. Kahneman, Knetsch, and Thaler (1986b, 730) write that "when the reference profit of a firm is threatened . . . it may set new terms that protect its profit at the transactor's expense."

25. More generally, recall that $P^{ES} = \frac{1}{2}(v + C)$, $P^{SB} = p + \frac{1}{2}(C - c)$, and $P^{ED} = C + (v - C) \cdot (p - c)/(v - c)$, and note that $p = \frac{1}{2}(v + c)$ implies an equal division of the *ex ante* surplus. Hence, the results stated in the claim can be derived as follows. Comparing $P^{ES}$ and $P^{SB}$, it can be readily shown that $P^{ES} \geq P^{SB}$ *if and only if* $p \leq \frac{1}{2}(v + c)$. Comparing $P^{ES}$ and $P^{ED}$, it can be readily shown that $P^{ES} \geq P^{ED}$ *if and only if* $p \leq \frac{1}{2}(v + c)$. And comparing $P^{SB}$ and $P^{ED}$, it can be readily shown that $P^{ED} \geq P^{SB}$ *if and only if* $p \leq \frac{1}{2}(v + c)$.

26. This subsection borrows from Bar-Gill and Fershtman (2004).

27. The $\sigma$ parameter can also represent the intensity of the emotional response to an unfair deal. As Frank (1988, 157) notes, "Standards evoke an emotional response, and specifically breach of fairness standards can trigger emotions in the modification context." More generally, Frank observes that "[t]he rationalists speak of tastes, not emotions, but for analytical purposes, the two play exactly parallel roles. Thus, for example, a person who is motivated to avoid the emotion of guilt may be equivalently described as someone with a 'taste' for honest behavior" (15). Emotions and "tastes" (i.e., preferences for fairness) are often used interchangeably in these contexts (Hirshleifer 1987; Rabin 1993).

Generally, our account of fairness assumes that an individual wishes to be treated fairly and suffers if not treated fairly. This "individualistic" account of fairness is supported by empirical findings (Bolton 1991; Huck and Oechssler 1999; Neale and Bazerman 1991; Ochs and Roth 1989).

28. Our formulation of the "unfairness cost" relates to the following observation by Frank (1988, 6–7): "A behavioral predisposition, in economic terms, is thus much like a tax on not behaving in a particular way."

29. The seller's reservation price is formally derived as follows. If a price increase of $\Delta p$ is agreed upon, the seller's utility from performing the modified contract is given by, where $y_S$ is the seller's income. On the other hand, if the seller breaches the contract, his utility will be. Comparing the seller's performance utility and breach utility, we can derive the seller's reservation price at the renegotiation stage. (The expression for the seller's reservation price provided in the text assumes $P^F > p + \Delta p$.)

30. Compare to Schelling's (1960) description of the power of principles:

A threat based on a "principle" is more powerful or credible. In the modification context, the seller's threat, when based on fairness principles, gains credibility.

31. For this reason preferences for fairness can be expected to evolve endogenously (Bar-Gill and Fershtman 2004; Huck and Oechssler 1999). As noted by Hirshleifer (1987), "The economist must go beyond the assumption of 'economic man' precisely because of the economic advantage of not behaving like economic man—an advantage that presumably explains why the world is not populated solely by economic men." Some of those opposed to the view that emotions can serve as commitment devices agree nevertheless that emotions, which are "hardwired" to preserve norms of cooperation, may occasionally be invoked outside their rational realm (Binmore 1998).

32. Posner (1977, 423) states, "[*Alaska Packers*] is a clear case of where the motive for the modification was simply to exploit a monopoly position conferred on the [fishermen] by the circumstances of the contract." Also see Chirelstein (2001).

33. *Domenico v. Alaska Packers*, 112 F. 554, 556 (9th Cir. 1901). Under Threedy's (2000) account, however, the seamen's claim appears more plausible. In that particular season, because of the abundance of salmon, the employer's interest may well have been to limit the volume of the catch, as it already exceeded the capacity of the cannery. The seamen were needed primarily as sailors, not fishermen.

34. *Domenico*, 112 F. at 559 stating,

> The reason why the defendant did not choose to rely upon the original agreement, and bring an action for the damages occasioned by its breach, may have been, and probably was, because of the inability of the libellants to respond in damages. Under such circumstances it would be strange, indeed, if the law would not permit the defendant to . . . enter into [a] contract mutually beneficial to all the parties thereto, in that it gave to the libellants reasonable compensation for their labor, and enabled the defendant to employ to advantage the large capital it had invested in its canning and fishing plant.

35. Transcript of testimony of Ellis Wainwright, *Lingenfelder v. Wainwright Brewery* at 158–59 (unpublished, St. Louis Cir. Ct., October Term 1885).

36. Frank also notes the problem of mimicry, where a party might pretend to have credibility-enhancing emotions or fairness concerns. Frank argues, however, that genuine emotions and fairness concerns often have observable symptoms, such as involuntary body language. Therefore, for instance, it is easier for a truly angry person to appear angry. But see Binmore (1998).

37. It should be noted, as a theoretical possibility, that failure of the law to enforce modifications that result from fairness-driven threats might reduce the prevalence of such fairness motivations. A transactor's sense of unfairness can be reinforced under a regime that gives recognition to such sentiments and—conversely—can be mitigated under a regime that denies their existence.

## REFERENCES

Akerlof, G. 1979. The case against conservative macroeconomics: An inaugural lecture. *Economica* 46:219–37.

Akerlof, G., and J. Yellen. 1990. The fair wage-effort hypothesis and unemployment. *Quarterly Journal of Economics* 105:255–83.

Babcock, L., and G. Loewenstein. 1997. Explaining bargaining impasse: The role of self-serving biases. *Journal of Economic Perspectives* 11:109.

Babcock, L., G. Loewenstein, S. Issacharoff, and C. F. Camerer. 1995. Biased judgments of fairness in bargaining. *American Economic Review* 85:1337–43.

Bar-Gill, O., and O. Ben-Shahar. 2004. The law of duress and the economics of credible threats. *Journal of Legal Studies* 33:391–430.

Bar-Gill, O., and C. Fershtman. 2004. Law and preferences. *Journal of Law, Economics, and Organization* 20:331–52.

Bazerman, M., and M. Neale. 1995. The role of fairness considerations and relationships in a judgmental perspective of negotiation. In *Barriers to conflict resolution*, ed. K. Arrow, 86–106. New York: Norton.

Binmore, K. 1998. *Game theory and the social contract.* Vol. 2, *Just playing.* Cambridge, MA: MIT Press.

Bolton, G. 1991. A comparative model of bargaining: Theory and evidence. *American Economic Review* 81:1096–1110.

Camerer, C., and R. Thaler. 1995. Ultimatums, dictators, and manners. *Journal of Economic Perspective* 9:209.

Chirelstein, M. 2001. *Concepts and case analysis in the law of contracts.* New York: Foundation Press.

Corbin, A. 1964. *Corbin on contracts.* Eagan, MN: West.

Dye, R. 1985. Optimal length of labor contracts. *International Economic Review* 26:251–70.

Farnsworth, E. 1999. *Contracts.* 3rd ed. Boston: Little, Brown.

Frank, R. 1988. *Passions within reason: The strategic role of the emotions.* New York: Norton.

Fried, C. 1981. *Contract as promise.* Cambridge, MA: Harvard University Press.

Gibbard, A. 1990. *Wise choices, apt feelings.* Cambridge, MA: Harvard University Press.

Guth, W., R. Schmittberger, and B. Schwartz. 1982. An experimental analysis of ultimatum bargaining. *Journal of Economic Behavior and Organization* 3:367.

Harris, M., and B. Holmstrom. 1987. On the duration of agreements. *International Economic Review* 28:389–405.

Hillman, R. 1979. Policing contract modifications under the UCC: Good faith and the doctrine of economic duress. *Iowa Law Review* 849:880–84.

Hirshleifer, J. 1987. On the emotions as guarantors of threats and promises. In *The latest on the best: Essays on evolution and optimality*. Cambridge, MA: MIT Press.

Huck, S., and J. Oechssler. 1999. The indirect evolutionary approach to explaining fair allocations. *Games and Economic Behavior* 28:13–24.

Jolls, C., C. Sunstein, and R. Thaler. 1998. A behavioral approach to law and economics. *Stanford Law Review* 50:1471–89.

Kahneman, D., J. Knetsch, and R. Thaler. 1986a. Fairness and the assumptions of economics. *Journal of Business* 59:S285–S300.

———. 1986b. Fairness as a constraint on profit seeking: Entitlements in the market. *American Economic Review* 76:728–41.

Korobkin, R., and T. Ulen. 2000. Law and behavioral science: Removing the rationality assumption from law and economics. *California Law Review* 88:1051–1154.

Neale, M., and M. Bazerman. 1991. *Cognition and rationality in negotiation*. New York: Free Press.

Ochs, J., and A. Roth. 1989. An experimental study of sequential bargaining. *American Economic Review* 79:335.

Okun, A. 1981. *Prices and quantities: A macroeconomic analysis*. Washington, DC: Brookings Institution.

Posner, R. 1977. Gratuitous promises in economics and law. *Journal of Legal Studies* 6:411.

———. 1997. *Economic analysis of law*. 5th ed. New York: Aspen Law and Business.

Rabin, M. 1993. Incorporating fairness into game theory and economics. *American Economic Review* 83:1281–1302.

Raiffa, H. 1985. *The art and science of negotiation*. Cambridge, MA: Harvard University Press.

Ridley, M. 1997. *The origins of virtue*. New York: Viking Penguin.

Schelling, T. 1960. *The strategy of conflict*. Cambridge, MA: Harvard University Press.

Shavell, S. 1984. The design of contracts and remedies for breach. *Quarterly Journal of Economics* 99:121–48.

Solow, R. 1980. On theories of unemployment. *American Economic Review* 70:1–11.

Thaler, R. 1992. *The winner's curse: Paradoxes and anomalies of economic life*. Princeton, NJ: Princeton University Press.

Threedy, D. 2000. A fish story: *Alaska Packers v. Domenico*. *Utah Law Review* 2000:185.

Williston, S. 1992. *A treatise on the law of contracts*. 4th ed. Rochester, NY: Cooperative.

Young, H. 1993. An evolutionary model of bargaining. *Journal of Economic Theory* 59:145–68.

# 20 | REGULATING IRRATIONAL EXUBERANCE AND ANXIETY IN SECURITIES MARKETS

*Peter H. Huang*

Investing, especially by institutions, can increasingly take advantage of artificial intelligence, nonlinear chaotic models, genetic algorithms, neural network time series forecasting, pattern recognition software, and sophisticated quantitative computer valuation models (Wilmott 2000, 2001). Thus, it seems that investing could become progressively more like the behavior described by the rational actor model of law and economics. But even for institutions, humans are ultimately responsible for investing, and they feel emotions during the investing process. Yet the rational actor model postulates that humans unemotionally maximize expected utility functions (von Neumann and Morgenstern 2004).

Behavioral economics advances an alternative to expected utility theory, namely,

Thanks to Anita Allen-Castellitto, Jennifer Arlen, Ken Arrow, Howard Chang, Stephen Choi, Lloyd Cohen, Rachel Croson, Shari Diamond, Phoebe Ellsworth, Claire Hill, Rebecca Huss, Bruce Johnsen, Michael Knoll, Donald Langevoort, Clarisa Long, Kristin Madison, Julia Mahoney, Gideon Parchomovsky, Francesco Parisi, Frank Partnoy, Hillary Sale, Chris Sanchirico, Bobbie Spellman, Lynn Stout, Steph Tai, Fred Tung, Laura Underkuffler, and the audience members in faculty workshops at the University of Minnesota Law School; the Wharton Decision Processes Colloquium; the American Psychology-Law Society 2004 Conference; the Gruter Institute for Law and Behavioral Research Conference on Law, Behavior, the Brain; the Gruter Institute for Law and Behavioral Research Symposium on Behavioral Building Blocks of Free Enterprise; the University of Cincinnati Law School; Rutgers School of Law-Camden; the Society for the Advancement of Behavioral Economics 2003 meetings; the University of Virginia Law School; George Mason University Law School; the University of Iowa Law School; Duke University Law School; and Fordham University Law School for their helpful comments, questions, and suggestions on earlier versions of this chapter. Thanks to Bill Draper and the University of Virginia Law School reference librarians Taylor Fitchett, Mandana Hyder, Micheal T. Klepper, Kent Olson, Cathy Palombi, Barbie Selby, and Joseph J. Wynne for their extraordinary bibliographic assistance. Finally, special thanks to my fiancée for our many discussions concerning her patients' emotional reactions to disclosures involving the various risks of alternative medical procedures.

prospect theory (Guthrie 2003; Kahneman and Tversky 1979). The fact that Kahneman was the corecipient of the 2002 Nobel Prize in economic sciences is the latest example of the ascendancy of behavioral economics (Hilsenrath 2002). Behavioral economics has gained much popularity and prestige in recent years.[1] Recently, some legal scholars have applied behavioral economics to analyze legal rules and institutions (Jolls 1998; Jolls, Sunstein, and Thaler 1998). These legal scholars consider the policy and regulatory implications of cognitive limitations by drawing on a literature about information processing errors (Hanson and Kysar 1999; Lipman 2000). But the scope and normative implications of such legal applications remain the subject of continuing debate.[2]

In addition, although prospect theory provides an alternative model of choice under risk to expected utility theory, prospect theory, expected utility theory, and "virtually all current theories of choice under risk or uncertainty are cognitive and consequentialist" (Loewenstein et al. 2001, 267). But human behavior is both cognitive and emotional (Camerer and Loewenstein 2003; Camerer, Loewenstein, and Prelec, forthcoming; Loewenstein and Lerner 2003). Moreover, cognition and emotion are interrelated (Charland 1998; Hanoch 2002; Williams et al. 1997). For example, investors may be overconfident due to hubris. Yet "research from clinical, physiological, and other subfields of psychology . . . show that emotional reactions to risky situations often diverge from cognitive assessments of those risks. When such divergence occurs, emotional reactions often drive behavior" (Loewenstein et al. 2001, 267).

Behavioral finance, which is behavioral economics over time and under conditions of risk, has revolutionized academic finance (Barberis and Thaler 2003; De-Bondt and Thaler 1995; Shefrin 2001; Shiller 2003). Although behavioral finance sometimes refers to such emotions as greed and fear, behavioral finance considers only emotions to explain why some investors utilize cognitive biases and heuristics (Nofsinger 2002b; Shefrin 2000). The main focus of behavioral finance is to demonstrate how investing driven by cognitive limitations explains observed anomalies in asset pricing and impacts asset pricing (Barberis, Huang, and Santos 2001; Barberis and Thaler 2003; Benartzi and Thaler 1995; Daniel, Hirshleifer, and Teoh 2002; Hirshleifer 2001; Nofsinger 2002a).

For example, many individuals (and even some financial practitioners) overreact to information as well as to what they believe others will do (Daniel, Hirshleifer, and Subrahmanyam 1998). Some behavioral finance models assume there are noise traders who are unable to differentiate between payoff-irrelevant information (noise) and payoff-relevant information, usually because of cognitive biases in processing information (Shleifer 2000). Recently, scholars have begun to consider the implications of cognitive biases for securities regulation (Choi and

Pritchard 2003; Cunningham 2002a; Hodder, Koonce, and McAnally 2001; Langevoort 2002; Prentice 2002; Thompson 1997). This chapter builds upon the legal scholarship that focuses primarily on cognitive biases and heuristics by focusing instead on emotional investing.

Most U.S. federal securities laws focus on the cognitive form and content of certain information.[3] In contrast, many investors respond emotionally to both the form and content of information and while investing experience a series of "successive emotional states of hope, joy, craving and euphoria" (Goldberg and von Nitzsch 1999). This is sometimes followed by anxiety and fear. It is thus not surprising that a moment of introspection reveals that people usually feel many emotions before, during, and after they invest. In fact, certain emotions might exemplify visceral factors that short-circuit or trump normal logical reasoning (Adler, Rosen, and Silverstein 1998; Elster 1999; Loewenstein 1996, 2000). For example, an investor feeling exuberant may optimistically misperceive, or even ignore completely, the risk factors associated with a particular security during the investment decision process. Similarly, an investor who feels anxious over a string of accounting scandals and instances of corporate malfeasance may pessimistically misperceive, or even ignore completely, any sound fundamentals associated with a particular security during the investment decision process. This chapter analyzes the regulatory implications of irrational exuberance and anxiety in securities markets.

People usually answer the question, What is emotion? with these synonyms: affect, feelings, or mood (Damasio 2003). Even today, the precise definition of an emotion remains contested among researchers (Evans 2001). But there is a consensus that emotions involve a number of related characteristics, namely, great intensity, instability, relative brevity, and a partial perspective (Ben-Ze'ev 2000). Before proceeding further, we should distinguish among these three related but distinct concepts: emotions, affect, and mood. Emotions describe particular states, such as fear, anger, or happiness, that are "intense, short-lived, and usually have a definite cause and clear cognitive content" (Forgas 1992). Affect refers to "a feeling state that people experience, such as happiness or sadness. It may also be viewed as a quality (e.g. goodness or badness) associated with a stimulus" (Finucane et al. 2000). Mood refers to "a feeling (such as having the blues) that is low in intensity, can last for a few minutes or several weeks, has no object or has fleeting objects, and does not have to have a specific antecedent cause or cognitive content" (Finucane, Peters, and Slovic 2003). Scholars often describe the stock market as experiencing (bipolar) mood swings (Cunningham 2001, 2002b). There is experimental evidence that happy and sad moods have large and consistent effects on estimating subjective probabilities of positive and negative events (Wright and Bower 1992).

There are (at least) two principal alternative ways to conceive of emotions. First, there is a tradition dating back to Aristotle, Socrates, and Plato that conceives of emotions as factors that disturb rational deliberation, thought, and reflection. Second, there is a more recent view informed by cognitive neuroscience that conceives of emotions as factors that complement rationality in effective decision making (Gazzaniga, Ivry, and Mangun 2002). Naturally, these different conceptions of emotions have diametrically opposed implications for whether and, if so, how the law can or should respond to emotional human behavior. The first viewpoint implies that law should be designed to protect us from our emotions,[4] whereas the second viewpoint implies that law should take a more laissez-faire attitude toward our emotions.

Asking whether emotional decision making is socially desirable is akin to asking whether self-interested decision making is socially desirable. Under certain strong conditions, including but not limited to complete markets and perfect competition, the pursuit of self-interest can lead to socially desirable results in the sense of Pareto efficient outcomes. In other situations, including but not limited to the presence of externalities or public goods and in certain strategic interactions, the pursuit of self-interest can lead to socially undesirable results in the sense of Pareto inefficient outcomes.

Existing legal doctrines provide numerous examples of both conceptions of emotions. Criminal law considers excuses based upon extreme emotional disturbance, such as the battered woman syndrome, and posttraumatic stress disorder; but it also encourages compassion, mercy, and sympathy. Tort law recognizes some but not all forms of emotional harm and suffering. Contract law recognizes the formation defense of procedural unconscionability, which can be due to distress, transactional incapacity, or unfair persuasion (Eisenberg 1982). The Federal Trade Commission promulgated a rule granting consumers a three-day "cooling-off period" during which buyers can rescind their contracts with door-to-door salespeople (16 C.F.R. § 429.1(a) (2002)). There is a similar three-day cooling-off period for home equity loans providing buyers with a limited right to rescind certain credit transactions involving their principal dwelling as a security interest (15 U.S.C. § 1635(a) (2000)). Congress imposed a seven-day waiting period on any employee waiver of rights under the Age Discrimination in Employment Act (ADEA) (29 U.S.C. § 626(f)(1)(G) (2000)). The family law statutes of many states require that couples must wait awhile after the issuance of a marriage certificate before they can marry.[5] Some of these states also require that a couple may not divorce until after the passage of a mandatory waiting period, which usually exceeds the mandatory prenuptial waiting period.[6]

Asking whether emotions are good or bad for decision making is analogous to asking if heuristics are good or bad for decision making. Sometimes heuristics are good for making decisions, and at other times they are bad. Similarly, sometimes emotions are good for making decisions, whereas at other times they are not beneficial. The reason for this mixed or nuanced answer is the same in the case of both emotions and heuristics, namely, emotions and heuristics act faster than rational deliberation, but precisely because of their speed, emotions and heuristics can mislead us into systematic errors in making decisions.

This chapter focuses on emotions before or during investing and therefore complements my previous work on anticipated emotions, which are fully and correctly anticipated before or during the decision-making process (Huang, 1998, 1999, 2000, 2002, 2003; Huang and Wu 1992, 1994). A difficulty with anticipated emotions is that people may systematically make prediction errors regarding their future interim or *ex post* feelings (Blumenthal 2004; Gilbert et al. 1998, 2002; Gilbert and Wilson 2000; Loewenstein, Nagin, and Paternoster 1997; Loewenstein, O'Donoghue, and Rabin 2003; Loewenstein and Schkade 1999; Wilson 2002). Because irrational exuberance and anxiety occur before or during the process of decision making, there are no such difficulties with irrational exuberance and anxiety.

The rest of this chapter is organized as follows. Section 20.1 provides empirical and experimental evidence, a case study, and theoretical models of irrational exuberance and anxiety in securities markets. Section 20.2 contributes to the debate over mandatory securities disclosures by examining the implications of irrational exuberance and anxiety for such disclosures. Section 20.2 also develops implications of the fact that securities regulators, including but not limited to the Securities and Exchange Commission (SEC), juries, and private litigants themselves, may experience irrational exuberance and anxiety. Section 20.3 provides conclusions.

## 20.1 IRRATIONAL EXUBERANCE AND ANXIETY IN SECURITIES MARKETS

The chairman of the Federal Reserve Board in Washington, D.C., Alan Greenspan, described stock market investor behavior with the phrase "irrational exuberance" in his now-infamous December 5, 1996, speech. Those two words resonated with many commentators in the media and with the public worldwide. The publication of a book titled *Irrational Exuberance* cemented the permanence of that phrase in the popular lexicon about securities markets (Shiller 2000). What exactly, though, does irrational exuberance mean, as opposed to rational exuberance or irrational anxiety? In this chapter, the phrase "irrational exuberance" refers to exuberance that is not justified by merely cognitive processing of the available information about securities markets. Thus, rational exuberance refers to exuberance that is warranted by merely cognitive processing of securities disclosures and risks. "Irrational anxiety" refers to anxiety that is unwarranted by merely cognitive analyses of fundamentals of securities markets. "Rational anxiety" refers to anxiety that is supported by merely cognitive assessments of the costs and benefits of securities investing.

Most people at some point during investing experience fear or hope over their investments. People often make investments motivated by fears. There is the fear of losing money.[7] There is the fear of not keeping up with others or being left out of a bull market (Gilovich and Medvec 1995). The fear of regret also partially explains why investors often select conventional stock choices, use full-commission brokers rather than discount brokers (the former may give useless advice but provide easy scapegoats), and hold onto losing stocks too long (Shefrin 2000, 222–24; Shefrin and Statman 1986). People often avoid purchasing such volatile securities as those of biotech or Internet companies to minimize anxiety.[8] On the other hand, some investors, such as day traders, might engage in risky portfolio strategies partly for the excitement. One legal scholar likens euphoric financial market transactions to gambling (Gabaldon 2001). That same legal scholar believes that laws may reduce the irrational exuberance of securities markets (Gabaldon 2000; 2001, 278–84). Arguably, certain policies of the SEC and the Federal Reserve facilitate investor enthusiasm about stocks (Hu 2000). Not only financial rewards but also excitement and general optimism often motivate the issuers of securities, original investors in initial public offerings (IPOs), and subsequent early investors.[9]

Irrational exuberance and anxiety raise a couple of questions, namely, how and why does irrational exuberance and anxiety persist in light of so-called learning effects and selection effects? Learning effects occur if people learn from their own personal investing experience or that of others and get better at investing over time, as they discover that relying on irrational exuberance and anxiety can yield investment returns that they subsequently realize are financially suboptimal. As with Bill Murray's character, Phil, in the movie *Groundhog Day* (Columbia Pictures Corporation 1993), noiseless feedback and stationary environments promote learning effects. But investing yields very noisy feedback because people can quite naturally (and perhaps even subconsciously) confuse their investment successes with financial insight and confuse their investment failures with bad luck. In addition, empirical evidence suggests that securities markets are highly nonstationary environments. It might seem that institutional and organizational structures can foster learning effects and thus dampen irrational exuberance and anxiety in a manner analogous to how corporate agency contexts dampen endowment effects (Arlen, Talley, and Spitzer 2002). But irrational exuberance and anxiety are not really biases to be unlearned.

Selection effects occur if securities market pressures weed out irrational exuberance and anxiety. Even when some investors continue to feel irrational exuberance and anxiety over time, perhaps the overall impact of irrational exuberance and anxiety on securities markets in the aggregate may decrease over time due to arbitrage. It might seem that arbitrage is a powerful force that selects for (more) rational investing decision making and weeds out irrational exuberance and anxiety. However, as is well known by now, there are costs and limits to arbitrage (Shleifer and Vishny 1997). Also, arbitrage is a strong engine of information transfer that travels in two directions. In other words, just as those investors who do not feel irrational exuberance and anxiety can arbitrage away the impact of those investors who do feel irrational exuberance and anxiety, the reverse is true as well. The often-cited observation that securities markets are the archetypal model of perfectly competitive markets is true but is a moot point if institutional, professional, or sophisticated investors also feel irrational exuberance and anxiety. In fact, there is anthropological, economic, ethnographic, and sociological evidence that documents how the corporate cultures of many institutional investors foster irrational exuberance and anxiety (Abolafia 1996). Recent empirical evidence finds that securities market professionals feel the same emotions as individual investors do (Lo and Repin 2002). Finally, there is anecdotal evidence that even institutional investors feel strong emotions over their investments (Lowenstein 2000).

Although securities markets are highly competitive, valuation in securities markets is an extremely subjective process. Emotional factors often influence the assessment of securities values across investors, just as emotions often affect subjective appraisals of the value of residential properties across home buyers and home owners. In fact, because securities, unlike consumer durables and real estate, are never consumed, securities markets, even more than other durable goods markets, involve subjective, often ephemeral and potentially very emotional anticipations of the future. Whereas reasonable people may agree on the past and the present (although there is reason to be skeptical of even these propositions as evidenced by the well-known fallibility of eyewitness testimony and memory), reasonable people often disagree on the future, both in terms of the set of contemplated outcomes and their various relative likelihoods. People are repeatedly caught off guard upon the realization of previously subjectively unforeseen contingencies.

It would not be surprising to note that many emotional factors have affected investor behavior even before the Securities Act of 1933 and the Securities Exchange Act of 1934 were enacted, and certainly they have done so since then. The legislative history of both acts that are the centerpiece of U.S. federal securities regulation contains numerous horror stories. Many of the cognitive psychological insights of behavioral finance were already an accepted part of the folk wisdom that formed the basis and rationale for our federal system of securities regulation. U.S. securities laws can be understood as an attempt to alter the manner in which investors make decisions by helping, or forcing, them to make better decisions. For example, the Securities Act of 1933 goes to extremely great lengths to try to structure the investment process into a hyperrational process in which a reasonable investor, sitting in the calm of a study, reviews only the prospectus of the registration statement without being influenced unduly by pushy stockbrokers, high-pressure scare tactics, glossy ads, promotional materials, or anything else. The puffery defense attempts to minimize the distortions that puffery can cause by placing investors on legal notice that they should ignore it, assuming that they can do so. The quiet period, the prohibitions against "conditioning" securities markets by engaging in so-called gun jumping during the period before the filing of a registration statement with the SEC (Securities and Exchange Commission 1971), and the mandatory disclosures required of a securities registration statement are all designed to improve investor decision making by limiting the influence of distortions on the rational investment process.

In light of not only the persistence of but also the recent growth in irrational exuberance and anxiety, existing federal securities regulations have clearly failed to sufficiently protect investors from their emotional selves or from emotional others. This chapter thus critiques our current federal securities laws on two accounts. First, U.S. federal securities laws fail to incorporate the best model of decision making, namely, one that incorporates the realities and robustness of human emotions. Second, U.S. federal securities laws fail to incorporate the best techniques for teaching investors how to improve their decision-making skills. (For example, the law should be teaching investors to make decisions based on different factors, such as more forward-looking rather than backward-looking information.)

The next section of the chapter analyzes the recent experimental and empirical evidence of, and theoretical models about, irrational exuberance and anxiety in securities markets. A recent, comprehensive synthesis of the research on how feelings influence stock pricing also suggests future directions of research, proposes richer hypotheses, and raises open questions about how investors' feelings impact securities prices (Dowling and Lucey 2003).

## 20.1.1 Empirical Evidence

An important finding of research on the perception of risk is that "[r]isk is multi-attribute in nature. It involves such elements as feelings of control, dread, and knowledge. . . . Risk always contains an emotional or affective dimension" (Olsen 2001). Investing is clearly risky. Survey evidence indicates that such emotional factors as catastrophic potential, control, and dread figure prominently in the perception of financial risks (Holtgrave and Weber 1993); and "emotional dimensions such as dread are important in the perceived risk of financial gambles" (Holtgrave and Weber 1993, 558). Studies demonstrate that moods induced by reading brief newspaper stories reporting on tragic or happy incidents produce large and pervasive changes in estimates on the frequency of risks, independent of whether the stories and risks are similar (Johnson and Tversky 1983). Evidence of the prevalence of affect in forming risk perceptions occurs in many diverse settings (Slovic 2000a).

Emotional investing exemplifies Damasio's (1994) theory of the role of emotion in decision making. Damasio believes that "[t]he factual knowledge required for reasoning and decision making comes to the mind in the form of images" (96). His somatic marker hypothesis is that with experience, these images become "marked" by positive and negative feelings linked directly or indirectly to somatic or bodily states (173–75, 179–80). Damasio's research documents clinical evidence of patients with damage to the ventromedial frontal cortices of their brains having trouble feeling emotions, associating those feelings with the anticipated consequences of their actions, and making decisions in spite of retaining their basic intelligence, memory, and capabilities for analytical reasoning and for logical thought (53–54; Damasio, Tranel, and Damasio 1990). Neurobiological and psychological research demonstrates that people recall new facts better if certain emotions are present during learning than if they are not (Damasio 1999; Lerner, forthcoming). The next section of the chapter analyzes the empirical evidence of emotional investing in experiments, by securities professionals and in response to online brokerage ads.

### 20.1.1.1 Experimental Evidence

The fact that Smith was the corecipient of the 2002 Nobel Prize in economic sciences is the latest example of the ascendancy of experimental economics (Hilsenrath 2002). There is both an increasing appreciation for and application of empirical and experimental methodology to study legal rules and institutions (Symposium 2002). A particular laboratory experiment investigated the behavior of investors when they face what is known as global risk, namely, a risk independent of their decisions (Bosman and van Winden 2001). Political risk that is not country specific is an example of global risk. The study found that global risk significantly and substantially decreases average investment. This finding is not consistent with such theories of rational decision making in the presence of risk as expected utility theory (von Neumann and Morgenstern 2004), prospect theory (Kahneman and Tversky 1979), disappointment theory (Bell 1985), and regret theory (Loomes and Sugden 1982). But this experimental result is consistent with the notion that experienced acute emotions affect behavior (Loewenstein et al. 2001) and with psychological evidence that anxious people make pessimistic probability estimates, are biased in terms of the amounts and types of information they utilize, and are thus motivated to reduce the level of risks they face (Lerner and Keltner 2001; Raghunathan and Pham 1999; Tiedens and Linton 2001).

### 20.1.1.2 Empirical Evidence Involving Securities Professionals

A recent study of professional derivative securities traders documents the importance of emotional responses in their decision-making processes (Lo and Repin 2002). The study measured physiological characteristics, such as body temperature, cardiovascular data, electromyographical signals, respiration rate, and skin conductance response, during actual trading sessions. The study found significant correlation between electrodermal responses and transient market events, and between changes in cardiovascular variables and market volatility. This data suggest that an important factor in the success of some derivative securities traders is their ability to utilize their emotions to make very rapid trading decisions. In addition, there is anecdotal evidence that even professional traders react emotionally to financial decisions, information, and outcomes (Lewis 1989).[10]

A number of empirical studies document a statistically significant effect of weather on stock market prices (Hulbert 2001). For example, local cloud cover in New York City from 1927 to 1989 was significantly correlated with low daily returns on three U.S. stock indices (the Dow Jones Industrial Average, a New York Stock Exchange (NYSE)–American Stock Exchange (AMEX) equal-weighted index, and a NYSE–AMEX value-weighted index) (Kramer and Runde 1997; Saunders 1993; Trombley 1997). In fact, there was a strong positive correlation between morning sunshine at a country's leading stock exchange and the market index stock returns that day at twenty-six stock exchanges internationally from 1982 to 1997 (Hirshleifer and Shumway 2003). In addition, seasonal variations in biorhythms and disruptions in sleep caused by changing from and to daylight saving time affect stock returns internationally (Dowling and Lucey 2002; Kamstra, Kramer, and Levi 2000). Furthermore, returns on international stock exchanges are correlated with fluctuations in the amount of daylight over the year (Kamstra, Kramer, and Levi 2003). But some people question whether this means that seasonal changes in depression cause changes in risk aversion and hence stock prices (Kelly and Meschke 2004). A different approach studies the relationship between stock returns and temperature (Cao and Wei 2002). Another study finds that, on average, morning stock returns exceed afternoon returns (Kramer 2001). All of these studies imply that the moods of individual investors or professional market makers affect stock prices (Goetzmann and Zhu 2003). In addition, there is empirical evidence that unusually high levels of geomagnetic storms (GMS) have a statistically and economically significant negative impact on world and country-specific stock returns, even after controlling for behavioral, environmental, and well-known market seasonal factors (Krivelyova and Robotti 2003). Finally, other studies speculate that there is a lunar cycle effect in stock prices whereby stock returns are significantly higher on days near a new moon than on days near a full moon (Dichev and James 2001; Yuan, Zheng, and Zhu 2001).

### 20.1.1.3 A Case Study of Irrational Exuberance: Online Brokerage Ads

A case study of irrational exuberance is provided by emotional online investing advertisements that present visceral and powerful images of online investors getting rich quickly. Some individuals exposed to such emotionally appealing online brokerage television commercials and billboards are likely to ignore, or be insensitive to, variations in the probability of striking it rich. Some online traders will focus instead on the outcome of becoming rich. Television commercials by online securities brokerages not only emphasized the personal control, ease, and profitability of such trading, but also were rich in emotional imagery.

Barber, Elsbach, and Odean (2001) performed a content analysis of five hundred television commercials from thirteen brokerages. They found that 28 percent of all commercials between 1990 and 2000 depicted images and messages likely to induce good or positive moods in viewers, and the percentage of such commercials more than doubled from 12.39 percent during 1990–95 to 32.98 percent during 1996–2000 (Barber, Elsbach, and Odean 2001, 16). This empirical finding is consistent with and understandable in light of recent psychological experiments demonstrating that people in moderately good or positive moods tend to be less thorough and less vigilant decision makers, are more subject to cognitive biases, and rely more on heuristics than people in moderately negative moods (Bliss, Schwarz, and Kemmelmeier 1996; Elsbach and Barr 1999; Schwarz, Bliss, and Bohner 1991). Online brokerages voluntarily ceased the broadcasting of positive emotional commercials due to changes in financial market conditions and moods.

A Discover Brokerage Direct television commercial about online trading depicted a conversation between a passenger and a stock-trading tow-truck driver, who states, "That's my home. Looks more like an island. Technically, it's a country" (Spitzer 1999). Another television commercial included a stock-trading teenager, who owned his own helicopter (J. Kahn 1999). A series of Schwab commercials featured such celebrities as former teenage Russian tennis star Anna Kournikova (J. Kahn 1999). An E*TRADE advertisement claimed "that on-line investing is 'A cinch. A snap. A piece of cake'" (Nofsinger 2001).

A commentator noted,

The years prior to 2000 featured a collection of e-trading commercials that could be viewed as hilarious by the seasoned professional and convincing by the novice trader. A typical commercial began by showing a teen-age boy or an elderly woman who appear to be very ordinary, and are treated as such. In the next scene, the other characters, and no doubt the viewers, are surprised to find out that this person is being thanked for bailing out a country, for example. The strong suggestion is that anyone who has a modest savings account can acquire a fortune, and be treated accordingly, if only they start trading on the Internet. For any skeptical viewers having their doubts, a resumption of the news, particularly the business news cable stations, would often turn to factual stories of the day's new IPO billionaires. (Caginalp 2001, 4)

These commercials clearly conjured up mental images of becoming rich quickly and easily. Former SEC Chairman Arthur Levitt said, "Quite frankly, some advertisements more closely resemble commercials for the lottery than anything else. When firms, again and again, tell investors that on-line investing can make them rich, it creates unrealistic expectations. . . . [M]any investors are susceptible to quixotic euphoria" (Levitt 1999). New York Attorney General Eliot Spitzer observed that an online brokerage ad "conveys a message of convenience, speed, easy wealth, and the risk of 'being left behind' in the on-line era" (Spitzer 1999).

Like much advertising, these advertisements do not provide information for viewers to process cognitively as much as they appeal to viewers' emotions (Edell and Burke 1987). These commercials were directed at evoking strong positive mental imagery and favorable emotional reactions to online investing risks. Such online brokerage ads decreased significantly after the bull market ended, further suggesting that the goals of such commercials were primarily to complement an overall mood of irrational exuberance and euphoria that prevailed then in securities markets and to stir up such emotions as hope and greed (Singhania 2001). In a January 26, 2001, report about online trading, the SEC expressed concerns that certain types of aggressive online brokerage ads may cause investors to possess unrealistic expectations over the risks and rewards of investing (Securities and Exchange Commission Office of Compliance Inspections and Examinations 2001). In that report, the SEC noted that "[a]dvertising that contains misrepresentations or omissions of material fact may violate the antifraud provisions of the federal securities laws" (14). In 2000 and 2001, the SEC and National Association of Securities Dealers (NASD) formally investigated the advertising practices of E*TRADE Group (On-line Investor Complaint Center 2001). However, both lengthy investigations resulted in the SEC dropping its fair disclosure case and the NASD settling with E*TRADE (CNNfn 2001; Schroeder 2001). The SEC did not publicly state the reasons for its decision to drop the case. Although there is little concern over such types of advertisements in the current anxious securities market environment, similar advertisements may return when an exuberant securities market environment does. In addition, there may be cause for concern over advertisements that exploit investor anxiety in a bear market (Hanson and Kysar 1999; Levere 2003). Furthermore, SEC releases already express concern over the advertising of such complex financial instruments as collateralized mortgage obligations. For example,

> (c)(2) Advertisements concerning collateralized mortgage obligations, advertisements concerning security futures, and advertisements and sales literature concerning registered investment companies (including mutual funds, variable contracts and unit investment trusts) that include or incorporate rankings or comparisons of the investment company with other investment companies where the ranking or comparison category is not generally published or is the creation, either directly or indirectly, of the investment company, its underwriter or an affiliate, shall be filed with the Department for review at least 10 days prior to use (or such shorter period as the Department may allow in particular circumstances) for approval and, if changed by the Association, shall be withheld from publication or circulation until any changes specified by the Association have been made or, if expressly disapproved, until the advertisement has been refiled for, and has received, Association approval. The member must provide with each filing the actual or anticipated date of first use. Any member filing any investment company advertisement or sales literature pursuant to this paragraph shall include a copy of the data, ranking or comparison on which the ranking or comparison is based. (Securities and Exchange Commission 2002)

SROs (self-regulating organizations), such as the NASD, also have approval and record-keeping rules related to complex financial instruments. Also relevant for whether and how the SEC should regulate such advertisements are Federal Trade Commission (FTC) deceptive advertising cases and the FTC's Policy Statement on Deception.[11] Finally, of relevance are the literature on consumer psychology in general (Hanson and Kysar 1999, 1428–1528; Jacoby 2000) and the marketing power of emotions in particular (O'Shaughnessy and O'Shaughnessy 2002).

There are many other securities areas where investing is more likely to be driven by emotional reactions to rather than cognitive processing of financial risks and information. The analysis of this chapter applies to such areas for drawing legal policy implications that differ from those based on unemotional investing. One such area is day trading (Buckman 1999; Buckman and Simon 1999; Thomas and Gregax 1999) and emotional advertisements for day trading (Arora and Reno 1999; Craig 2001). Financial scams by con artists are another such area (Cunningham 2002b, 166–78). Examples of such financial scams are so-called prime bank programs, which promise incredible returns from investing in "prime bank" securities (Securities and Exchange Commission 2003). Another example of such a financial scam, the so-called affinity fraud, is targeted at members of identifiable groups, such as ethnic minorities and religious groups (Securities and Exchange Commission 2001).

## 20.1.2 Theoretical Models

Neoclassical economic theory already incorporates certain emotions in several ways. First, love or hate can be treated as part of an individual's tastes or non-monetary utility in the sense of interdependent individual preferences (Becker 1996). Second, certain emotional reactions function as commitment devices in multiperson decision environments (Frank 1988; Hirshleifer 1987; Romer 2000). Third, game theory can accommodate emotions that depend on probability beliefs about strategic behavior (Geanakoplos, Pearce, and Stacchetti 1989; Kolpin 1992). Recently, several economists have urged their fellow economists to include more studies of emotions in their models (Romer 2000, 439–43; Thaler 2000). Discussions about emotions in several recent surveys of economic research illustrate this renewed interest (Camerer and Loewenstein 2003; Camerer, Loewenstein, and Prelec, forthcoming; Elster 1998). One survey, however, criticized the interpretation of emotions as psychic benefits and costs or as merely a source of preferences because such interpretations ignore how emotions affect the ability to make rational choices (Elster 1998, 73). This chapter addresses this criticism by explicitly analyzing irrational exuberance and anxiety in securities investing.

### 20.1.2.1 Psychological Expected Utility Theory and Anticipatory Feelings

A new economic framework introduces a general psychological expected utility model that includes anticipatory feelings prior to the resolution of risk. This model extends the neoclassical expected utility model to incorporate a general class of anticipatory feelings, such as anxiety and suspense (Caplin and Leahy 2001). This model shows how anticipatory feelings can result in time inconsistency because as time passes, anticipatory feelings and preferences may change. This model has applications to anticipatory pleasure or savoring and implies a resulting preference for commitment devices to facilitate planning and overcome intertemporal inconsistency (Caplin and Leahy 2001, 72–73). Applying this model to suspense and gambling yields the empirically supported prediction that people will bet on their emotional favorites in a sporting event (Caplin and Leahy 2001, 73). This model is also rich enough to analyze preferences over illusions and the dilemma that a doctor faces about whether to give a patient (more than legally required) detailed information concerning an upcoming medically benign, but subjectively threatening diagnostic surgical procedure (Caplin and Leahy 2001, 76; Miller and Mangan 1983).[12] Furthermore, this model has policy implications for the provision to the public of payoff-relevant information by the Federal Reserve and other government agencies (Caplin and Leahy 2001, 76–77). Finally, this model supports recommendations for "psychologically-appropriate" formats of disseminating medical information to the general population and providing medical advice to specific patients at risk of diabetes or breast cancer (Caplin and Leahy 2001, 77; Dube, Belanger, and Trudeau 1996; Fries 1998; Kahn and Luce 2003; M. Kahn 1999; Kash et al. 1992; Klusman 1975).

Caplin and Leahy (2001) found that applying this model to focus on the portfolio decisions of anxious investors demonstrates that a security producing anxiety on the part of its owners commands a lower price and a higher required rate of return than if that security did not cause its owners to experience anxiety (68). This model also formally demonstrates that the price of a riskless security is greater than it would be in a world in which investors do not experience anxiety because riskless securities provide the benefit of anxiety reduction. This model proves that "anxiety will reduce the price of stocks and increase their return relative to the standard [unemotional] model" and that "stock ownership entails psychic costs [because stockholders have] to live with the anxiety that accompanies the holding of a risky portfolio" (1, 69). Finally, this model explains how the desire to avoid the stress and anxiety associated with retirement planning can result in people avoiding thinking about, let alone planning for, their retirement until it is too late to avoid anymore (72). Such irrational anxiety has very disturbing implications for the social desirability of recent proposals to privatize social security and retirement investment decisions.

Finally, Mehra and Sah (2002) construct a general equilibrium model that provides theoretical support for the proposition that feelings affect securities prices. This model argues that investors' feelings have an effect on stock prices if three conditions are satisfied (870). First, investors do not realize their investment decisions are influenced by fluctuations in their moods. Second, investors' subjective parameters, such as their judgments of the appropriate discount factor or their levels of relative risk aversion, fluctuate in response to fluctuations in their moods over time. Third, investors uniformly and widely experience the impacts of such fluctuations in their moods on their subjective parameters. This model has closed-form solutions for equilibrium stock prices (873–76). The model predicts that a 0.10 percent fluctuation in the beliefs of investors regarding the discount factor can alone generate a 3–4 percent standard deviation in stock prices (878). The model also finds a similarly important, but smaller effect on the standard deviation of stock prices due to a fluctuation in risk attitudes (881).

### 20.1.2.2  The Risk-as-Feelings Hypothesis

A new theory about decision making under risk, namely the risk-as-feelings hypothesis, focuses on the role of emotions that decision makers experience leading up to and including the moment of decision making (Loewenstein et al. 2001, 267). The risk-as-feelings hypothesis is based upon four well-supported premises: emotions can arise without any cognitive antecedents, there are emotional reactions to cognitive evaluations, emotions inform cognitive evaluations, and emotions play a crucial role in affecting behavior.

Emotional reactions to and cognitive evaluations of risk and information differ for two reasons. First, emotions and cognitive evaluations of risk respond in different ways to probabilities and outcomes. A fundamental difference between emotional reactions to risk and cognitive evaluations of risk is that anticipatory emotions are insensitive to changes in probability for a wide range of probability values (Sunstein 2002b). Expected utility depends linearly and symmetrically on the probabilities and utilities of outcomes. Variations in probability generate corresponding variations in expected utility, holding the utility of outcomes constant. Under prospect theory, cognitive evaluations of risk depend linearly and symmetrically on the probability weighting functions and subjective valuations of outcomes. Variations in probability generate corresponding variations in probability weighting functions, holding the subjective valuations of outcomes constant. In contrast, probability plays a relatively minor role in such anticipatory emotions as irrational exuberance and anxiety.

If potential outcomes have a lot of emotional resonance, such as (perhaps) kisses from your favorite movie star or electric shocks, then their attractiveness or unattractiveness is extremely insensitive to changes in the probability of that outcome, even if that probability drops from 99 percent to 1 percent (Rottenstreich and Hsee 2001). For positive outcomes, any departure from certainty induces fear, whereas any deviation from impossibility produces hope. For negative outcomes, any departure from certainty produces hope, whereas any deviation from impossibility induces fear.

Second, other causal factors besides probabilities and outcomes influence anticipatory emotions. The risk-as-feelings hypothesis focuses on several emotional factors as having a predictable influence on decision making. These factors include the vividness of the associations that risks evoke, the time path of the decision process, and how evolutionarily prepared individuals are for certain emotional reactions. For the purposes of understanding irrational exuberance and anxiety in securities investing, there are two such important determinants, namely, imagery and misattribution. The following section on the related affect heuristic analyzes the phenomenon of misattribution.

Another account of why anticipatory emotions display probability neglect is that anticipatory emotions are primarily due to mental images of the outcome of a decision. Such images are discrete and so are not much affected by probabilities. Thus, anticipatory emotions that arise from such images will be insensitive to changes in probability. An investor's mental image of what it will be like to participate in an IPO of stock is likely to be approximately the same whether the probability of that stock skyrocketing is 1 in 100,000 or 1 in 100 million. In contrast, an investor's mental image of what it will be like to participate in a stock IPO that skyrockets will likely be very different from that investor's mental image of what it will be like to participate in a stock IPO that has only a very modest increase.

### 20.1.2.3 The "How-Do-I-Feel-About-It" Heuristic

Experimental results and clinical phenomena demonstrate that emotional reactions are fairly independent of, often impervious to, and precede in time, cognitive judgments (Zajonc 1980, 1984, 2000). Evolutionary forces may explain why affect precedes cognition (Cohen and Dickens 2002; Olsen 2000). A recent study found that "affective processes play a critical role in determining choices and that these affective processes may sometimes influence choice without the decision maker's awareness" (Peters and Slovic 2000). A large body of empirical psychological research finds that affective impressions attach to images, and those affective impressions influence judgments and decisions (Finucane, Peters, and Slovic 2003).

A recent theoretical framework emphasizes the importance of an affect, or "how-do-I-feel-about-it" heuristic, in guiding decisions and judgments (Finucane, Peters, and Slovic 2003; Slovic et al. 2002; Sunstein 2003). People utilize this heuristic when they come to have an emotional, all-things-considered reaction to make judgments. People utilizing this heuristic essentially ask, "How do I feel about something?" They utilize their answer as the basis for making their judgment (Schwarz and Clore 1983).

The affect, or "how-do-I-feel-about-it" heuristic, is related to the mood-as-information hypothesis. This hypothesis argues that people's moods inform their decisions, even when the causes of those moods are unrelated to their decisions. This phenomenon is known as misattribution. It explains how and why nominally irrelevant feelings, or what the famous macroeconomist Keynes (1936) called "animal spirits," influence securities investing (see also Marchionatti 1999).

The "how-do-I-feel-about-it" heuristic explains public concerns about health and environmental risks, high punitive damage awards, and people's reactions to contested political events (Sunstein 2002a). This heuristic is related to the dual process theory that people process information via two parallel, interactive modes (Epstein 1994). The first is a rational, deliberative, and analytical system employing such rules of logic and evidence as probability theory. The second is an experiential system that encodes reality in terms of images, metaphors, and narratives that are imbued with affect and feelings. There is much experimental evidence that a person's mood influences which of these two information-processing strategies is utilized (Schwarz 2002a, 2002b).

The affect infusion model (AIM) argues that the extent to which people rely on their feelings to make decisions depends on how abstract, risky, and uncertain those decisions are (Forgas 1995). Usually, people who are rational utilize high affect infusion strategies (HAIS) in highly complex decisions, such as securities investing. Emotions form a major input of decisions made via HAIS. People usually employ low affect infusion strategies (LAIS) in decisions requiring "little generative constructive processing" (Forgas 1995, 40). Thus, LAIS are more appropriate for decisions that are familiar and low in complexity than for decisions that are infrequent and high in complexity.

## 20.2 MANDATORY SECURITIES DISCLOSURES

"Mandatory disclosure is a—if not the—defining characteristic of U.S. securities regulation" (Bainbridge 2000, 1023). The Supreme Court in *SEC v. Capital Gains Research Bureau, Inc.*, 375 U.S. 180, 186 (1963), stated that the "fundamental purpose" of federal securities regulations "was to substitute a philosophy of full disclosure for the philosophy of caveat emptor." In another famous case, *SEC v. Ralston Purina Co.*, 346 U.S. 119, 124 (1953), the Supreme Court stated that the Securities Act of 1933 and its mandatory disclosure requirements were designed "to protect investors by promoting full disclosure of information thought necessary to informed investment decisions." Investor protection is clearly a fundamental goal of U.S. securities regulation. In fact, upon clicking on "What We Do" under the heading "About the SEC" on the SEC's home page on the Internet, one learns that "[t]he primary mission of the U.S. Securities and Exchange Commission (SEC) is to protect investors" (Securities and Exchange Commission 1999).

There is a long-standing debate over the purpose and effectiveness of mandatory securities disclosure (Coffee 1984; Easterbrook and Fischel 1984; Schwarcz 2004). An often-cited purpose is to improve the informational efficiency of securities prices (Gilson and Kraakman 1984; Gordon and Kornhauser 1985; Jarrell 1981; Kahan 1992).[13] Critics of this accuracy-enhancement efficiency justification argue that mandatory securities disclosure has not achieved this purpose (Benston 1973; Kitch 1995; Kripke 1979). Mahoney (1995a) proposes reducing the agency costs that arise between investors and promoters and between corporate managers and their shareholders as an alternative justification for mandatory securities disclosure. Both of these justifications of mandatory securities disclosures focus on the cognitive impacts of increased disclosures.

Mandatory disclosures generate not only information but also such emotions as perhaps anxiety, embarrassment, euphoria, exuberance, feeling stupid, relief, or shame. For example, mandating disclosure of the realistically very low odds of winning a lottery and the present discounted value of the after-tax prize winnings produces no benefits if such disclosures fail to reduce the number of lottery ticket buyers, but instead causes lottery players to feel dumb or foolish and reduces their pleasure from daydreaming about possible future riches. Such emotional consequences of mandatory disclosure can alter behavior. For example, the display by retailers of detailed facts about food content mandated by food labeling acts may result in the so-called Snackwell effect, named for the fat-free cookie that appears to lead to greater consumption (Shemo 1997).

Emotional reactions to securities risks imply emotional reactions to securities information, because information is in essence the negative of risk, as information involves the reduction of risk. Analogous to fear in the investment context, evaluating strategies for combating terrorism depends on how much fear involves misperception about risk, whether fear is a hedonic loss that should count as being a cost or harm under a cost-benefit analysis, and to what extent fear is contagious (Posner 2002). The fact that people feel emotions and would like to minimize anxiety also has novel implications for health and medical regulatory policy (Katz 1984, 1993; Schuck 1994; Slovic 2000b).

Questions about how much and precisely what disclosures federal securities laws should require are analogous to recent questions about how much and precisely what disclosures the federal government should issue about possible terrorist attacks. Although nonspecific disclosures provide information, they also produce anxiety, fear, and general uneasiness. There is the danger that over time people become desensitized to many nonspecific disclosures, so a more specific disclosure may fall on deaf ears. Broad and general disclosures lack the vividness of more specific and narrowly focused disclosures.

Securities disclosures function not only as information and marketing documents but also as protection from civil liability for securities fraud. Even though there is no analogous marketing role for disclosures about possible terrorist attacks, after September 11, 2001, the U.S. government has become concerned with a severe public relations penalty for nondisclosures about possible terrorist attacks that is analogous to liability for fraudulent securities nondisclosures. Another difference between securities disclosures and disclosures about potential terrorist attacks is their actual or intended audience. Some legal scholars believe and argue that the investing public is neither the actual nor intended audience for the disclosures that federal securities laws mandate (Langevoort 2002, 173–75). Instead, these commentators feel that professional analysts are the intended audience for much of the accounting and financial disclosures that federal securities regulations mandate. Professional analysts filter that information to the investing public.[14] Because analysts are professionals who have repeated experience at interpreting such disclosures, they may seem less likely than inexperienced and unsophisticated individuals to feel irrational exuberance and anxiety as the result of securities disclosures.[15] But precisely because of their experience with other similar securities in the past, professional analysts may have more vivid reactions to securities disclosures than laypersons lacking any personal or direct knowledge of similar cases. Because of their compensation, there may also be serious conflicts of interest between professional analysts and the investing public, which means that analysts could routinely make unjustifiably optimistic or irrationally exuberant securities recommendations (Fisch and Sale 2003; Hovanesian 2002; Vickers and France 2002).

The debate over mandatory disclosure in federal securities regulation ignores the emotional benefits or costs of such disclosures, in particular, irrational exuberance and anxiety that potential and existing investors may feel due to disclosures or the absence of disclosures. Such emotional benefits or costs affect individuals in terms of increased or reduced social utility and affect issuers of securities in terms of a lower or higher cost of capital due to such emotional reactions. The heterogeneity of people's emotional reactions to mandatory securities disclosures complicates if and how securities regulations should take irrational exuberance and anxiety into account. The extent to which different people feel irrational exuberance and anxiety from securities disclosures affects the socially optimal amount of those disclosures. Even holding the content of disclosed information fixed, anxiety has implications for the form or presentation of that information.

Because irrational exuberance and anxiety depend more on the possibility than on the probability of certain outcomes, some people may overreact in their securities investments to disclosures about material events with positive, but small, probabilities of occurrence. Irrational exuberance and anxiety may also cause individuals to avoid acquiring or processing material information and to avoid thinking carefully about certain financial outcomes. Even if the apocryphal widows and orphans feel irrational exuberance and anxiety, some financial and legal scholars believe that equilibrium securities market prices may accurately reflect all relevant material information if analysts and institutional investors do not experience irrational exuberance and anxiety (Malkiel 2003; Rubinstein 2001). Even if securities professionals and institutions were to be immune from irrational exuberance and anxiety, limited arbitrage prevents them from eliminating the impact of those investors who do feel irrational exuberance and anxiety on securities prices.

On the other hand, just as disclosure of information may trigger irrational exuberance and anxiety, lack of disclosure may also trigger fear of the unknown (or a false sense of contentment from limited knowledge) and fear over imagined worst-case scenarios (or joy over imagined best-case scenarios). Lack of mandated disclosures does not mean lack of irrational exuberance and anxiety, because there are many other sources of information or noise besides mandated disclosures, including security analysts, friends, family members, colleagues, investment clubs, and Internet chat rooms (Langevoort 2002, 154–63). Thus, there is a countervailing emotional benefit from disclosure, namely, the prevention of irrational exuberance and anxiety that would result from lack of disclosure.[16]

The previous observation helps explain why some people react with irrational anxiety over companies' not expensing stock options utilized to compensate and provide incentives for their executives (Norris 2002; Saporito 2002). Not knowing how much those stock options actually cost a company may lead both existing and potential investors to overestimate the cost of granting such executive stock options and experience irrational anxiety from such overestimates or from just not knowing. On the other side of the emotional spectrum from irrational anxiety due to lack of disclosure is possible irrational exuberance or unjustified excitement. In the case of the bull market of the late 1990s, many investors evaluated companies in the so-called new economy based more on irrational exuberance and irrational euphoria than on fundamental analysis.

The key legal policy questions thus involve what can and should we do about irrational exuberance and anxiety (Partnoy 2000). The Brady Commission formed to examine the 1987 stock market crash advocated circuit breakers to "cushion the impact of market movements, which would otherwise damage market infrastructures" (Presidential Task Force on Market Mechanisms 1998). In 1988, U.S. securities exchanges adopted trading halts to essentially provide investors a cooling-off period if the Dow Jones Industrial Average index fell too much too fast (Cunningham 2002b, 233–46). Symmetrically, reverse circuit breakers could mandate trading halts for overall securities markets or individual securities if securities price indices or individual securities prices rise too quickly (Gabaldon 2000, 127; 2001, 283). But experimental studies find that circuit breakers are ineffectual and mandated market closures accelerate trading activity (Ackert, Church, and Jayaraman 1999). Another experiment finds that circuit breakers do not work to retard bubbles but actually somewhat exacerbate bubbles for inexperienced subjects (King et al. 1993).

Instead of using circuit breakers, the SEC can require greater firm-specific disclosures that detail how a particular firm's securities differ from the overall securities markets. Section 13(a) of the Securities Exchange Act (15 U.S.C. § 78m(a)

(2002)) provides the SEC with authority to require companies registered under the Securities Exchange Act to file such information and documents as it deems to be in the public interest. Such additional firm-specific disclosures could be provided in the form of "public reports explicitly addressing the relationship between their earnings, dividends, and prevailing stock prices and perhaps containing management commentary upon the wisdom of this relationship and how long it might be expected to be sustained" (Gabaldon 2000, 128). However, such mandatory disclosures presume that individuals can and will cognitively evaluate such disclosures as opposed to increase noise trading (Mahoney 1995b). If one believes that individuals should be holding broadly diversified portfolios instead of engaging in dubious individual stock picking, then individuals do not require firm-specific information. If one believes that irrational exuberance and anxiety dominate securities investing, then mandatory disclosure, which is the linchpin of U.S. federal securities regulation, may have unexpected emotional effects, and little or no cognitive effects, upon investing.

Answering the questions of whether, what, and how much of mandatory securities disclosures are socially desirable requires comparing the unemotional and emotional consequences of such disclosures with the unemotional and emotional consequences of voluntary securities market disclosures. An emotional cost-benefit analysis differs from the unemotional considerations raised in the past and current debate over mandatory securities disclosures. The relative size of the emotional costs and benefits of mandatory securities disclosures versus the emotional costs and benefits of voluntary securities disclosures will vary depending on the precise nature of the specific disclosures involved.

Finally, there is another set of actors in securities regulation who are subject to irrational exuberance and anxiety, namely, the securities regulators themselves, be they SEC Commissioners; SEC staff; lawyers and other professionals at SROs, such as the NYSE or the NASD; members of Congress and their staff; state attorney generals and their staff; private litigants and plaintiffs' attorneys; issuers and their counsel; judges; or juries. Certainly, investors do not have a monopoly on feeling irrational exuberance and anxiety. A central message of this chapter is that emotions are ubiquitous and not always necessarily defects in or flaws of human decision making. Just as (securities) regulators are no less prone to cognitive biases and heuristics than investors are (Choi and Pritchard 2003), so too (securities) regulators are no less prone to irrational exuberance and anxiety than investors are prone to irrational exuberance and anxiety. Just as behavioral explanations of securities regulations complement and enrich public choice accounts (Choi and Pritchard 2003; Macey 1994; Mahoney 2001), so too for emotional regulatory stories.

It is perhaps no surprise that emotional regulating not only happens but also systematically differs from unemotional regulating. The social desirability of emotional regulating, including but not limited to zealous advocates, passionate public servants, possibly envious or sympathetic regulators, and ideologically fanatical prosecutors, is a difficult question. But whether or not emotional regulating is socially desirable, it exists and is likely to continue. In light of the realities of emotional regulating, the SEC in general and its mandatory disclosure regime in particular might do more harm than good and yet persist due to emotional appeal, rationales, and considerations. The history of U.S. federal securities regulation from its very inception in the aftermath of the Great Depression to its most recent Sarbanes-Oxley Act of 2002 in the aftermath of Enron, Arthur Anderson, Rite Aid, Worldcom, Tyco, Adelphia, Merck, and Global Crossing is that of (possibly benign) neglect of securities markets interrupted by legislation in response to political and public pressure arising from highly visceral and public episodes of banking, corporate, or securities fraud and scandals (Grundfest 2002; Seligman 1995). Mandatory disclosure might be, at best, an impotent and, at worst, a socially harmful regulatory policy if the majority of investors experience cognitive biases and utilize heuristics in the processing of information and/or feel irrational exuberance and anxiety before and during their investing process. But the SEC's obsession with mandatory disclosure may be due to its emotional resonance with the metaphor of a "level playing field" and the rationale of protecting investors from others and possibly themselves.

## 20.3 CONCLUSIONS

This chapter analyzed a still growing but already large body of empirical and experimental evidence of and theoretical economic and psychological models supporting the prevalence of irrational exuberance and anxiety. Because the financial and legal implications of irrational exuberance and anxiety differ significantly and systematically from those of unemotional rational investing, further empirical, psychological, experimental, and theoretical financial economic research concerning the applicability, generality, and robustness of irrational exuberance and anxiety is crucial.

An important question for legal policy is to what extent education or experience mitigates irrational exuberance and anxiety. After all, many individual and novice investors lost money by investing heavily in high-technology and Internet stocks during the 1990s, but so did many hedge funds and mutual funds managed by financially sophisticated and experienced investors (Brunnermeier and Nagel 2004). To the extent that individuals are more evolutionarily prepared for certain emotions than others, it may be neither easy nor socially desirable to alter irrational exuberance and anxiety in response to securities disclosures (Cohen and Dickens 2002; Henderson and Rachlinski 2000; Loewenstein et al. 2001, 279; Olsen 2000).

Whether more paternalistic securities regulations than our current federal system of mandatory disclosure is socially desirable depends on to what extent and how others can improve upon the behavior and performance resulting from irrational exuberance and anxiety.[17] Indeed, if we suspect that most investing is driven by irrational exuberance and anxiety, then securities regulation should focus primarily on emotional reactions to, instead of unemotional processing of, the form and content of mandatory disclosures. If we believe that short of explicit and outright cognitive fraud judges, juries, and the SEC are not well equipped to evaluate the likely emotional reactions to securities disclosures, then perhaps the SEC should not base federal securities regulation upon a philosophy of mandatory disclosure. But experts can assist both the SEC *ex ante* and courts *ex post* in determining the likely emotional reactions to securities disclosures or marketing hype by conducting empirical surveys of actual people.

An intermediate regulatory strategy is to adopt cautiously paternalistic or asymmetrically paternalistic regulations, namely, regulations that greatly benefit people who are prone to mistakes but only slightly (or not at all) hurt people who are not prone to mistakes (Camerer et al. 2003; O'Donoghue and Rabin 1999; Thaler and Sunstein 2003). It is important here as elsewhere to not view all emotional investing as being synonymous with making investing errors. A fundamental lesson of recent economic, neurobiological, and psychological research (and hopefully, this chapter) is that emotions sometimes are superior to, sometimes reinforce, but sometimes work in the opposite direction of unemotional reasoning (Etzioni 1998). In particular, there are many varieties of emotional investing and some complement, whereas others substitute for unemotional investing. Determining how much of emotional investing is "rational" or "reasonable" is difficult, both for any particular investor and for others, such as counterparties (of derivative securities), the SEC, and SROs (such as the NASD, NYSE, and AMEX).

A recent argument proposes not protecting so-called irrational investors from themselves in order to reap the public good provided by having equilibrium securities market prices reflect the private information of those "irrational" investors (La Blanc and Rachlinksi, this volume). However, under a general equilibrium analysis, the price impact and survival of irrational investors are two related, yet quite distinct and independent concepts (Blume and Easley 2001; Hirshleifer, Subrahmanyam, and Titman 2004; Kogan et al. 2004; Sandroni 2000). In other words, in a long-run equilibrium, irrational investors can have a significant impact on prices whether or not they survive. Moreover, even if irrational investors survive, they may have no price impact. In addition, such a proposal assumes the private information of irrational investors has high signal-to-noise ratios. Although the signal-to-noise ratio for emotional investing is difficult to determine in general, there are clearly situations where the ratio is low. For example, emotional investing caused by the online brokerage ads described in this chapter is likely to have a low signal-to-noise ratio, and therefore regulating such ads is likely not to have any deleterious effect on the informational efficiency of securities prices.

1. Akerlof (2002, 424) argued in a revised version of the lecture he presented upon receiving the 2001 Nobel Prize in economic sciences (December 8, 2001) that macroeconomics should be behavioral and that John Maynard Keynes (1936) "was the progenitor of the modern behavioral finance view of asset markets." Also see Loewenstein (2000) and Uchitelle (2001).

2. For a discussion of the possible scope and legal implications, see Arlen (1998); Hanson and Kysar (2000); Henderson and Rachlinski (2000); Hillman (2000); Issacharoff (1998); Mitchell (2002, 2003). For an opposing point of view, see Rachlinski (2000, 2003).

3. For example, *A. C. Frost & Co. v. Coeur D'Alene Mines Corporation*, 312 U.S. 38, 43, n. 2 (1941), states that the fundamental purpose of the Securities Act is to protect investors by mandating full disclosure of the information that is thought necessary for investors to make informed investment decisions; *Feit v. Leasco Data Processing Equipment Corp.*, 332 F. Supp. 544, 563 (E.D. N.Y. 1971) states "that without complete, accurate and intelligible information about a company, investors cannot make intelligent investment decisions with regard to its securities."

4. "Where a majority is included in a faction, the form of popular government . . . enables it to sacrifice to its ruling passion or interest both the public good and the rights of other citizens" (Madison1787/1999).

5. New York, for example, provides that "[a] marriage shall not be solemnized within twenty-four hours after the issuance of the marriage license" (N.Y. Dom. Rel. Law § 13-b (McKinney 1999)).

6. Connecticut, for example, requires married couples to wait ninety days after filing a complaint for dissolution or legal separation before the court may proceed (Conn. Gen. Stat. Ann. § 46b-67(a) (West 1995)).

7. The robust experimental findings that people can be very loss averse and treat out-of-pocket losses differently from opportunity costs have clear implications for the way that people actually invest.

8. It is crucial to distinguish anxiety from risk aversion. Anxiety is a dynamic notion that arises because some decision makers may prefer not to live with a feeling of uncertainty across time periods. Risk aversion is a static notion related to how curved a decision maker's utility function over wealth is within a fixed period of time (Weber and Hsee 1998).

9. The original investors in IPOs are typically not individual investors but institutional investors. Sale (2000, 441) observes that the class of "first buyers of

the securities issued (original shareholders) . . . is usually very limited, including only institutional investors, members of Congress, and those with connections to underwriters."

10. Lewis (1989, 15) assesses the founder and head of Salomon's legendary bond trading Arbitrage Group by saying, "He had, I think, a profound ability to control the two emotions that commonly destroy traders—fear and greed—and it made him as noble as a man who pursues his self-interest so fiercely can be." Also refer to Lowenstein 2000, 76–77.

11. Included in the deceptive advertising cases is *Florence Mfg. Co. v. J. C. Dowd & Co.*, 178 F. 73, 75 (C.A.2 1910), which states that "[t]he law is not made for experts but to protect the public,—that vast multitude which includes the ignorant, the unthinking and the credulous, who, in making purchases, do not stop to analyze but too often are governed by appearances and general impressions." *Aronberg v. FTC*, 132 F.2d 165, 167 (7th Cir. 1942), states that "the buying public does not ordinarily carefully study or weigh each word in an advertisement" and that "[a]dvertisements are intended not 'to be carefully dissected with a dictionary at hand, but rather to produce an impression upon' prospective purchasers" (quoting *Newton Tea & Spice Co. v. United States*, 288 F. 475, 479 (6th Cir. 1923)). *Standard Oil Co. of California v. FTC*, 577 F.2d 653, 659 (9th Cir. 1978), states "that commercial messages might lead the average viewer, in his anxiety . . . , to overreact even though upon careful reflection he might see for himself the limitations inherent in the advertiser's claim."

According to Policy Statement on Deception, 4 Trade Reg. Rep. (CCH) ¶13, 205 at 20, 917 (FTC Oct. 14, 1983), an advertisement is deceptive when there is "a misrepresentation, omission or other practice, that misleads the consumer acting reasonably in the circumstances, to the consumer's detriment." In determining if an advertisement deceives consumers, the FTC asks what does the advertisement say or imply, and does the advertisement have a reasonable basis for its claims?

12. Miller and Mangan report on a study exploring the interaction between the amount of information provided and personal coping styles of forty gynecologic patients scheduled for colposcopy.

13. See also Kitch (1995, 838–74).

14. *Dirks v. SEC*, 463 U.S. 646, 658–59, n.17 (1983), discusses the importance of market analysts who "ferret out and analyze information." Choi (2002) discusses the benefits and harms of selective disclosures to analysts; Goshen and Parchomovsky (2001) discuss the positive externalities that analysts' research provides all investors; and Talley and Choi (2002) discuss the costs and benefits of selective disclosures to analysts.

15. Similar arguments have been made concerning the relative cognitive competence of judges versus juries (Viscusi 2001; see also Meadow and Sunstein 2001; Sale 2002).

16. An analogy is to a patient's fears and behavior in the medical disclosure context. A patient may imagine and fear the worst if a physician does not disclose certain information about medical risks in a timely fashion. In other words, in both financial and medical contexts, people may infer or imagine bad news from silence and experience fear or anxiety from not having enough information.

17. For empirical evidence concerning a similar question about consumption decisions, see Waldfogel (2002).

## REFERENCES

Abolafia, M. 1996. *Making markets: Opportunism and restraint on Wall Street.* Cambridge, MA: Harvard University Press.

Ackert, L., B. Church, and N. Jayaraman. 1999. An experimental study of circuit breakers: The effects of mandated market closures and temporary halts on market behavior. Working paper 99-1, Federal Reserve Bank of Atlanta.

Adler, R., B. Rosen, and E. Silverstein. 1998. Emotions in negotiation: How to manage fear and anger. *Negotiation Journal* (April): 161, 168–74.

Akerlof, G. 2002. Behavioral macroeconomics and macroeconomic behavior. *American Economic Review* 92:411, 424–28.

Arlen, J. 1998. Comment: The future of behavioral economic analysis of law. *Vanderbilt Law Review* 51:1765.

Arlen, J., E. Talley, and M. Spitzer. 2002. Endowment effects with corporate agency relationships. *Journal of Legal Studies* 31:1.

Arora, A., and J. Reno. 1999. Rolling the dice with a click of the mouse: Day trading is a seductive but tricky game, a subculture in which traders find that risks are high and profits elusive. *Newsweek*, August 30, 9.

Bainbridge, S. 2000. Mandatory disclosure: A behavioral analysis. *University of Cincinnati Law Review* 68:1023.

Barber, B., K. Elsbach, and T. Odean. 2001. Investing advice from television commercials. Document prepared for the AARP Public Policy Institute.

Barberis, N., M. Huang, and T. Santos. 2001. Prospect theory and asset prices. *Quarterly Journal of Economics* 116:1.

Barberis, N., and R. Thaler. 2003. A survey of behavioral finance. In *Handbook of the economics of finance: Financial markets and asset pricing*, ed. G. Constantinides, M. Harris, and R. Stulz, 1053, 1054, 1065–75. Amsterdam: North-Holland.

Becker, G. 1996. Spouses and beggars: Love and sympathy. In *Accounting for tastes*, 231–37. Cambridge, MA: Harvard University Press.

Bell, D. 1985. Disappointment in decision making under uncertainty. *Operations Research* 33:1.

Benartzi, S., and R. Thaler. 1995. Myopic loss aversion and the equity premium puzzle. *Quantitative Journal of Economics* 110:73.

Benston, G. 1973. Required disclosure and the stock market: An evaluation of the Securities Exchange Act of 1934. *American Economic Review* 63:132.

Ben-Ze'ev, A. 2000. *The subtlety of emotions.* Cambridge, MA: MIT Press.

Bliss, H., N. Schwarz, and M. Kemmelmeier. 1996. Mood and stereotyping:

Affective states and the use of general knowledge structures. *European Review of Social Psychology* 7:63, 67–74.

Blume, L., and D. Easley. 2001. If you're so smart, why aren't you rich? Belief selection in complete and incomplete markets. Discussion paper 1319, Yale University Cowles Foundation. http:www.ssrn.com.

Blumenthal, J. 2004. Law and the emotions: The problems of affective forecasting. *Indiana Law Journal* 80:1.

Bosman, R., and F. van Winden. 2001. Anticipated and experienced emotions in an investment experiment. Tinbergen Institute Discussion Paper 01-058/1. http://www.tinbergen.nl/discussionpapers/01058.pdf.

Brunnermeier, M., and S. Nagel. 2004. Hedge funds and the technology bubble. *Journal of Finance* 59:2013.

Buckman, R. 1999. Gambling man: Stock losses roiled a volatile personality, and slaughter ensued. *Wall Street Journal*, August 2, A1.

Buckman, R., and R. Simon. 1999. Day trading can breed perilous illusions. *Wall Street Journal*, August 2, C1.

Caginalp, G. 2001. The real year 2000 problem: Investor psychology. *Journal of Psychology and Financial Markets* 2:2–4.

Camerer, C., S. Issacharoff, G. Loewenstein, T. O'Donoghue, and M. Rabin. 2003. Regulation for conservatives: Behavioral economics and the case for "asymmetric paternalism." *University of Pennsylvania Law Review* 151:1211.

Camerer, C., and G. Loewenstein. 2003. Behavioral economics: Past, present and future. In *Behavioral economics*, ed. C. Camerer, G. Loewenstein, and M. Rabin, 1–52. Princeton, NJ: Princeton University Press.

Camerer, C., G. Loewenstein, and D. Prelec. Forthcoming. Neuroeconomics: Why economics needs brains. *Scandinavian Journal of Economics*.

Cao, M., and J. Wei. 2002. Stock market returns: A note on temperature anomaly. *Journal of Banking and Finance*.

Caplin, A., and J. Leahy. 2001. Psychological expected utility theory and anticipatory feelings. *Quarterly Journal of Economics* 116:55, 60–66.

Charland, L. 1998. Is Mr. Spock mentally competent? Competence to consent and emotion. *Philosophy, Psychiatry, and Psychology* 5:67, 71–72.

Choi, S. 2002. Selective disclosures in the public capital markets. *University of California Law Review* 35:533, 540–52.

Choi, S., and A. Pritchard. 2003. Behavioral economics and the SEC. *Stanford Law Review* 56:1.

CNNfn. 2001. E*trade ad probe near end. http://money.cnn.com/2001/06/27/companies/etrade/.

Coffee, J. 1984. Market failure and the economic case for a mandatory disclosure system. *Virginia Law Review* 70:717.

Cohen, J., and W. Dickens. 2002. A foundation for behavioral economics. *American Economic Review* 92:335–38.

Craig, S. 2001. Regulators zap day-trading guru Houtkin and All-tech. *Wall Street Journal*, June 14, C1.

Cunningham, L. 2001. How to think like Benjamin Graham and invest like Warren Buffet. New York: McGraw-Hill.

———. 2002a. Behavioral finance and investor governance. *Washington and Lee Law Review* 59:767, 786–837.

———. 2002b. *Outsmarting the smart money: Understand how markets really work and win the wealth game.* New York: McGraw-Hill.

Damasio, A. 1994. *Descartes' error: Emotion, reason, and the human brain.* New York: Avon.

———. 1999. *The feeling of what happens: Body and emotion in the making of consciousness.* Orlando, FL: Harcourt.

———. 2003. *Looking for Spinoza: Joy, sorrow and the feeling brain.* Orlando, FL: Harcourt.

Damasio, A., D. Tranel, and H. Damasio. 1990. Individuals with sociopathic behavior caused by frontal damage fail to respond autonomically to social stimuli. *Behavioral Brain Research* 41:81.

Daniel, K., D. Hirshleifer, and A. Subrahmanyam. 1998. Investor psychology and security market under- and over-reactions. *Journal of Finance* 53:1839.

Daniel, K., D. Hirshleifer, and S. Teoh. 2002. Investor psychology in capital markets: Evidence and policy implications. *Journal of Monetary Economics* 49:139.

DeBondt, W., and R. Thaler. 1995. Financial decision-making in markets and firms: A behavioral perspective. In *Finance, handbooks in operations research and management science*, ed. R. Jarrow, V. Maksimovic, and W. Ziemba, 385. Amsterdam: Elsevier.

Dichev, I., and T. James. 2001. Lunar cycle effects in stock returns. Unpublished manuscript. http://www.ssrn.com.

Dowling, M., and B. Lucey. 2002. Weather, biorhythms and stock returns: Some preliminary Irish evidence. Unpublished manuscript. http://www.ssrn.com.

———. 2003. The role of feelings in investor decision-making. Unpublished manuscript. http://www.ssrn.com.

Dube, L., M. Belanger, and E. Trudeau. 1996. The role of emotions in health care satisfaction. *Journal of Health Care Marketing* 16:45, 47–51.

Easterbrook, F., and D. Fischel. 1984. Mandatory disclosure and the protection of investors. *Virginia Law Review* 70:669.

Edell, J., and M. Burke. 1987. The power of feelings in understanding advertising effects. *Journal of Consumer Research* 14:421, 431.

Eisenberg, M. 1982. The bargain principle and its limits. *Harvard Law Review* 95:741.

Elsbach, K., and P. Barr. 1999. The effects of mood on individual's use of structured decision protocols. *Organizational Science* 10:181, 185–94.

Elster, J. 1998. Emotions and economic theory. *Journal of Economic Literature* 36:47.

———. 1999. *Strong feelings: Emotion, addiction, and human behavior.* Cambridge, MA: MIT Press.

Epstein, S. 1994. Integration of the cognitive and psychodynamic unconscious. *American Psychology* 49:709, 717–19.

Etzioni, A. 1998. Normative-affective factors: Toward a new decision-making model. *Journal of Economic Psychology* 9:125, 128–40, 144–47.

Evans, D. 2001. *The science of sentiment.* Oxford: Oxford University Press.

Finucane, M., A. Alhakami, P. Slovic, and S. Johnson. 2000. The affect heuristic in judgments of risks and benefits. *Journal of Behavioral Decision Making* 13:1, 2n1.

Finucane, M., E. Peters, and P. Slovic. 2003. Judgment and decision making: The dance of affect and reason. In *Emerging perspectives on decision research,* ed. S. Schneider and J. Shanteau, 327. Cambridge: Cambridge University Press.

Fisch, J., and H. Sale. 2003. The securities analyst as agent: Rethinking the regulation of analysts. *Iowa Law Review* 88:1035.

Forgas, J. 1992. Affect in social judgments and decisions: A multiprocess model. In *Advances in experimental social psychology,* ed. M. Zanna, 227, 230. San Diego, CA: Academic Press.

———. 1995. Mood and judgment: The affect infusion model (AIM). *Psychology Bulletin* 117:39.

Frank, R. 1988. *Passions within reason: The strategic role of the emotions.* New York: Norton.

Fries, J. 1998. Reducing the need and demand for medical services. *Psychosomatic Medicine* 40:140.

Gabaldon, T. 2000. The role of law in managing market moods: The whole story of Jason who bought high. *George Washington Law Review* 69:111, 123–34.

———. 2001. John Law, with a tulip, in the South Seas: Gambling and the regulation of euphoric market transactions. *Journal of Corporate Law* 26:225, 227.

Gazzaniga, M., R. Ivry, and G. Mangun. 2002. *Cognitive neuroscience: The biology of the mind.* 2nd ed. New York: Norton.

Geanakoplos, J., D. Pearce, and E. Stacchetti. 1989. Psychological games and sequential rationality. *Games and Economic Behavior* 1:60, 65.

Gigerenzer, G. 1999. *Simple heuristics that make us smart.* Oxford: Oxford University Press.

———. 2000. *Adaptive thinking: Rationality in the real world.* Oxford: Oxford University Press.

Gilbert, D., E. Pinel, T. Wilson, S. Blumberg, and T. Wheatley. 1998. Immune neglect: A source of durability bias in affective forecasting. *Journal of Personality and Social Psychology* 75:617, 620–36.

———. 2002. Durability bias in affective forecasting. In *Heuristics and biases: The psychology of intuitive judgment*, ed. T. Gilovich, 292, 297–312. Cambridge: Cambridge University Press.

Gilbert, D., and T. Wilson. 2000. Miswanting: Some problems in forecasting of future affective states. In *Feeling and thinking: The role of affect in social cognition*, ed. J. Forgas, 178, 185–94. Cambridge: Cambridge University Press.

Gilovich, T., and V. Medvec. 1995. The experience of regret: What, when and why. *Psychology Review* 102:379.

Gilson, R., and R. Kraakman. 1984. The mechanisms of market efficiency. *Virginia Law Review* 70:549, 601.

Goetzmann, W., and N. Zhu. 2003. Rain or shine: Where is the weather effect? Working paper no. 9465, National Bureau of Economic Research. Unpublished manuscript. http://www.ssrn.com.

Goldberg, J., and R. von Nitzsch. 1999. *Behavioral finance*. Trans. A. Morris. New York: Wiley.

Gordon, J., and L. Kornhauser. 1985. Efficient markets, costly information and securities research. *New York University Law Review* 60:761, 802.

Goshen, Z., and G. Parchomovsky. 2001. On insider trading, markets and "negative" property rights in information. *Virginia Law Review* 87:1229, 1234, 1246, 1262–67.

Grundfest, J. 2002. Punctuated equilibria in the evolution of the United States securities regulation. *Stanford Journal of Law, Business and Finance* 8:1–2.

Guthrie, C. 2003. Prospect theory, risk preference and the law. *Northwestern University Law Review* 97:1115.

Hanoch, Y. 2002. "Neither an angel nor an ant": Emotion as an aid to bounded rationality. *Journal of Economic Psychology* 23:1, 3.

Hanson, J., and D. Kysar. 1999. Taking behavioralism seriously: The problem of market manipulation. *Harvard Law Review* 112:1420, 1462–66.

———. 2000. Taking behavioralism seriously: A response to market manipulation. *Roger Williams University Law Review* 6:259.

Henderson, J., and J. Rachlinski. 2000. Product-related risk and cognitive biases: The shortcomings of enterprise liability. *Roger Williams University Law Review* 6:213, 218–58.

Hillman, R. 2000. The limits of behavioral decision theory in legal analysis: The case of liquidated damages. *Cornell Law Review* 85:717, 738.

Hilsenrath, J. 2002. Nobel winners for economics are new breed. *Wall Street Journal*, October 10, B1.

Hirshleifer, D. 2001. Investor psychology and asset prices. *Journal of Finance* 56:1533.

Hirshleifer, D., and T. Shumway. 2003. Good day sunshine: Stock returns and the weather. *Journal of Finance* 58:1009.

Hirshleifer, D., A. Subrahmanyam, and S. Titman. 2004. Feedback and the success of irrational investors. Charles A. Dice Center for Research in Financial

Economics Working Paper. http://www.cob.ohio-state.edu/fin/dice/papers/2004/2004-8.htm.

Hirshleifer, J. 1987. On the emotions as guarantors of threats and promises. In *The latest on the best: Essays in evolution and optimality*, ed. J. Dupre, 307, 311–21. Cambridge, MA: MIT Press.

Hodder, L., L. Koonce, and M. McAnally. 2001. SEC market risk disclosures: Implications for judgment and decision making. *Accounting Horizons* 15:49.

Holtgrave, D., and E. Weber. 1993. Dimensions of risk perception for financial and health risks. *Risk Analysis* 13:553, 556–58.

Hovanesian, M. 2002. How analysts' pay packets got so fat. *Business Week*, May 13, 40.

Hu, H. 2000. Faith and magic: Investor beliefs and government neutrality. *Texas Law Review* 78:777, 837–84.

Huang, P. 1998. Dangers of monetary incommensurability: A psychological game model of contagion. *University of Pennsylvania Law Review* 146:1701.

———. 1999. Herd behavior in designer games. *Wake Forest Law Review* 34:639.

———. 2000. Reasons within passions: Emotions and intentions in property rights bargaining. *Oregon Law Review* 79:43.

———. 2002. International environmental law and emotional rational choice. *Journal of Legal Studies* 31:S237.

———. 2003. Trust, guilt and securities regulation. *University of Pennsylvania Law Review* 151:1059.

Huang, P., and H. Wu. 1992. Emotional responses in litigation. *International Review of Law and Economics* 12:31.

———. 1994. More order without more law: A theory of social norms and organizational cultures. *Journal of Law, Economics and Organization* 10:390.

Hulbert, M. 2001. Forget about efficient markets, let the sun shine in. *New York Times*, June 17, C7.

Issacharoff, S. 1998. Can there be a behavioral law and economics? *Vanderbilt Law Review* 51:1729.

Jacoby, J. 2000. Is it rational to assume consumer rationality? Some consumer psychological perspectives on rational choice theory. *Roger Williams University Law Review* 6:81n1.

Jarrell, G. 1981. The economic effects of federal regulation on the market for new security issues. *Journal of Law and Economics* 24:613.

Johnson, E., and A. Tversky. 1983. Affect, generalization, and the perception of risk. *Journal of Personality and Social Psychology* 45:20, 23–30.

Jolls, C. 1998. Behavioral economic analysis of redistributive legal rules. *Vanderbilt Law Review* 51:1653.

Jolls, C., C. Sunstein, and R. Thaler. 1998. A behavioral approach to law and economics. *Stanford Law Review* 50:1471.

Kahan, M. 1992. Securities laws and the social costs of "inaccurate" stock prices. *Duke Law Journal* 41:977, 979.

Kahn, B., and M. Luce. 2003. Understanding high-stakes consumer decisions: Mammography adherence following false alarm tests. *Marketing Science* 22:393.

Kahn, J. 1999. On-line brokerages use advertising in a battle for new customers. *New York Times*, October 4. http://www.nytimes.com/library/tech/99/10/biztech/articles/04trad.html.

Kahn, M. 1999. Diabetic risk taking: The role of information, education, and medication. *Journal of Risk and Uncertainty* 18:147, 155–58.

Kahneman, D., and A. Tversky. 1979. Prospect theory: An analysis of decision under risk. *Econometrica* 47:263.

Kamstra, M., L. Kramer, and M. Levi. 2000. Losing sleep at the market: The daylight savings anomaly. *American Economic Review* 90:1005.

———. 2003. Winter blues: A SAD stock market cycle. *American Economic Review* 93:324.

Kash, K., J. Holland, M. Halper, and D. Miller. 1992. Psychological distress and surveillance behaviors of women with a family history of breast cancer. *Journal of the National Cancer Institute* 84:24.

Katz, J. 1984. *The silent world of doctor and patient*. Baltimore, MD: Johns Hopkins University Press.

———. 1993. Informed consent—must it remain a fairy tale? *Journal of Contemporary Health Law and Policy* 10:69, 87.

Kelly, P., and J. Meschke. 2004. The link between depression and stock returns: A reexamination. Unpublished manuscript. http://www.ssrn.com.

Keynes, J. 1936. *The general theory of employment, interest and money*. Amherst, NY: Prometheus Books.

King, R., V. Smith, A. Williams, and M. Van Boening. 1993. The robustness of bubbles and crashes in experimental stock markets. In *Nonlinear dynamics and evolutionary economics*, ed. R. Day and P. Chen, 183, 194–95, 199. Oxford: Oxford University Press.

Kitch, E. 1995. The theory and practice of securities disclosures. *Brooklyn Law Review* 61:763, 838–74.

Klusman, L. 1975. Reduction of pain in childbirth by the alleviation of anxiety during pregnancy. *Consulting and Clinical Psychology* 43:162.

Kogan, L., S. Ross, J. Wang, and M. Westerfield. 2004. The price impact and survival of irrational traders. Working paper no. 9434, National Bureau of Economic Research. http://web.mit.edu/lkogan2/www/KRWW2002.pdf.

Kolpin, V. 1992. Equilibrium refinement in psychological games. *Games and Economics* 4:218, 220–21.

Kramer, L. 2001. Intraday stock returns, time-varying risk premia, and diurnal mood variation. Unpublished manuscript. http://www.ssrn.com.

Kramer, W., and R. Runde. 1997. Stocks and the weather: An exercise in data mining or yet another capital market anomaly. *Empirical Economics* 22:637.

Kripke, H. 1979. *The SEC and corporate disclosure: Regulation in search of a purpose.* Orlando, FL: Harcourt.

Krivelyova, A., and C. Robotti. 2003. Playing the field: Geomagnetic storms and the stock market. Working paper 2003-5b, Federal Reserve Bank of Atlanta. http://www.ssrn.com.

Langevoort, D. 2002. Taming the animal spirits of the stock markets: A behavioral approach to securities regulation. *Northwestern University Law Review* 97:135.

Lerner, A. Forthcoming. Using our brains: What cognitive science tells us about teaching problem solving and professional responsibility. *Clinical Law Review.*

Lerner, J., and D. Keltner. 2001. Fear, anger and risk. *Journal of Personality and Social Psychology* 81:146–51.

Levere, J. 2003. An online bank has a message for skittish investors: Consider a savings account. *New York Times,* January 30, C7.

Levitt, A. 1999. Plain talk about on-line investing. Speech at the National Press Club, Washington, DC, May 4. http://www.sec.gov/news/speech/speecharchive/1999/spch274.htm.

Lewis, M. 1989. *Liar's poker.* London: Penguin.

Lipman, B. 2000. Information processing and bounded rationality: A survey. *Canadian Journal of Economics* 28:42.

Lo, A., and D. Repin. 2002. The psychophysiology of real-time financial risk processing. *Journal of Cognitive Neuroscience* 14:323.

Loewenstein, G. 1996. Out of control: Visceral influences on behavior. *Organizational Behavior and Human Decision Processes* 65:272, 288.

———. 2000. Emotions in economic theory and economic behavior. *American Economic Review* 90:426–31.

Loewenstein, G., and J. Lerner. 2003. The role of affect in decision making. In *Handbook of affective science,* ed. R. Davidson, 619. Oxford: Oxford University Press.

Loewenstein, G., D. Nagin, and R. Paternoster. 1997. The effect of sexual arousal on expectations of sexual forcefulness. *Journal of Research in Crime and Delinquency* 34:443, 445–47.

Loewenstein, G., T. O'Donoghue, and M. Rabin. 2003. Projection bias in predicting future utility. *Quarterly Journal of Economics* 118:1209.

Loewenstein, G., and D. Schkade. 1999. Wouldn't it be nice? Predicting future feelings. In *Well-being: The foundations of hedonic psychology,* ed. D. Kahneman, 85, 88–100. New York: Russell Sage.

Loewenstein, G., E. Weber, C. Hsee, and N. Welch. 2001. Risk-as-feelings. *Psychology Bulletin* 127:267.

Loomes, G., and R. Sugden. 1982. Regret theory: An alternative theory of rational choice under uncertainty. *Economic Theory* 92:805.

Lowenstein, R. 2000. *When genius failed: The rise and fall of long-term capital management*. New York: Random House.

———. 2001. Exuberance is rational or at least human. *New York Times*, February 11, sec. 6, 66–71.

Macey, J. 1994. Administrative agency obsolescence and interest group formation: A case study of the SEC at sixty. *Cardozo Law Review* 15:909.

Madison, J. 1787/1999. The federalist no. 10. In *The federalist papers*, ed. Clinton Rossiter. New York: Mentor.

Mahoney, P. 1995a. Mandatory disclosure as a solution to agency problems. *University of Chicago Law Review* 62:1047.

———. 1995b. Is there a cure for "excessive" trading? *Virginia Law Review* 81: 713, 742.

———. 2001. The political economy of the Securities Act of 1933. *Journal of Legal Studies* 30:1.

Malkiel, B. 2003. The efficient markets hypothesis and its critics. *Journal of Economic Perspectives* 17:59–72.

Marchionatti, R. 1999. On Keynes' animal spirits. *Kyklos* 52:415, 431.

Meadow, W., and C. Sunstein. 2001. Statistics, not experts. *Duke Law Journal* 51:629, 633–35.

Mehra, R., and R. Sah. 2002. Mood fluctuations, projection bias, and volatility of equity prices. *Journal of Economic Dynamics and Control* 26:869.

Miller, S., and C. Mangan. 1983. Interacting effects of information and coping style in adapting to gynecologic stress: Should the doctor tell all? *Journal of Personality and Social Psychology* 45:223, 225–35.

Mitchell, G. 2002. Why law and economics' perfect rationality should not be traded for behavioral law and economics' equal incompetence. *Georgetown Law Journal* 91:67.

———. 2003. Tendencies versus boundaries: Levels of generality in behavioral law and economics. *Vanderbilt Law Review* 56:1781.

Nofsinger, J. 2001. *Investment madness: How psychology affects your investing . . . and what to do about it*. New York: Prentice Hall.

———. 2002a. *Investment blunders of the rich and famous . . . and what you can learn from them*. New York: Prentice Hall.

———. 2002b. *The psychology of investing*. New York: Prentice Hall.

Norris, F. 2002. Accounting board proposes a new rule on a hot topic: Opinions. *New York Times*, August 15, C5.

O'Donoghue, T., and M. Rabin. 1999. Procrastination in preparing for retirement. In *Behavioral dimensions of retirement economics*, ed. H. Aaron, 125, 150. Washington, DC: Brookings Institution.

Olsen, R. 2000. The instinctive mind on Wall Street: Evolution and investment decision making. *Journal of Investing* 9:47, 50.

———. 2001. Behavioral finance as science: Implications from the research of Paul Slovic. *Journal of Psychology and Financial Markets* 2:157, 159.

On-line Investor Complaint Center. 2001. U.S. securities regulators criticize, war on-line brokers—yet again. http://www.investingcomplaints.com /secreport .html and http://www.investingcomplaints.com /.

O'Shaughnessy, J., and N. O'Shaughnessy. 2002. *The marketing power of emotion.* Oxford: Oxford University Press.

Partnoy, F. 2000. Why markets crash and what law can do about it. *University of Pittsburgh Law Review* 61:741, 762–817.

Peters, E., and P. Slovic. 2000. The springs of action: Affective and analytical information processing in choice. *Personality and Social Psychology Bulletin* 26:1465, 1473.

Posner, E. 2002. Fear and the regulatory model of counterterrorism. *Harvard Journal of Law and Public Policy* 25:681, 684–89.

Prentice, R. 2002. Whither securities regulation? Some behavioral observations regarding proposals for its future. *Duke Law Journal* 51:1397, 1450–89.

Presidential Task Force on Market Mechanisms. 1998. The report of the presidential task force on market mechanisms (Brady report). Federal Register page and date: 52 FR 49341; December 31, 1987.

Rachlinski, J. 2000. The "new" law and psychology: A reply to critics, skeptics, and cautious supporters. *Cornell Law Review* 85:739.

———. 2003. The uncertain psychological case for paternalism.. *Northwestern University Law Review* 97:1165.

Raghunathan, R., and M. Pham. 1999. All negative moods are not equal: Motivational influences of anxiety and sadness in decision making. *Organizational Behavior and Human Decision Processes* 79:56, 63–65.

Romer, P. 2000. Thinking and feeling. *American Economic Review* 90:439, 441–43.

Rottenstreich, Y., and C. Hsee. 2001. Money, kisses, and electric shocks: On the affective psychology of risk. *Psychological Science* 12:185, 186–88.

Rubinstein, M. 2001. Rational markets: Yes or no? The affirmative case. *Financial Analysts Journal* 57:15.

Sale, H. 2000. Disappearing without a trace: Sections 11 and 12(a)(2) of the 1833 Securities Act. *Washington Law Review* 75:429, 441.

———. 2002. Judging heuristics. *University of California Law Review* 35:903, 905–6.

Sandroni, A. 2000. Do markets favor agents able to make accurate predictions? *Econometrica* 68:1303–4, 1306, 1319–21.

Saporito, B. 2002. Wall Street's verdict: While Washington dithers on reform, investors are pushing the stock market down, down, down. *Time,* July 29, 18, 23–24.

Saunders, E. 1993. Losing stock prices and Wall Street weather. *American Economic Review* 83:1337.

Schleifer, A. 2000. *Inefficient markets: An introduction to behavioral finance.* Oxford: Oxford University Press.

Schroeder, M. 2001. NASD to settle its ad dispute with E*trade. *Wall Street Journal*, June 27, C1.

Schuck, P. 1994. Rethinking informed consent. *Yale Law Journal* 103:899, 903, 926–27, 942.

Schwarcz, S. 2004. Rethinking the disclosure paradigm in a world of complexity. *University of Illinois Law Review* 2004:1.

Schwarz, N. 2002a. Feelings as information: Moods influence judgments and processing strategies. In *Heuristics and biases: The psychology of intuitive judgment*, ed. T. Gilovich, 534, 536–47. Cambridge: Cambridge University Press.

———. 2002b. Situated cognition and the wisdom of feelings: Cognitive tuning. In *The wisdom of feelings*, ed. L. Barrett and P. Salovey, 144–66. New York: Guilford.

Schwarz, N., H. Bliss, and G. Bohner. 1991. Mood and persuasion: Affective states influence the processing of persuasive communications. *Advances in Experimental Social Psychology* 24:161, 187.

Schwarz, N., and G. Clore. 1983. Mood, misattribution, and judgments of well-being: Informative and directive functions of affective states. *Journal of Personality and Social Psychology* 45:513.

Securities and Exchange Commission. 1971. Guidelines for the release of information by issuers whose securities are in registrations. SEC release no. 5180. *Federal Security Law Reporter* 1:3056.

———. 1999. The investor's advocate: How the SEC protects investors and maintains market integrity. http://www.sec.gov/about/whatwedo.shtml.

———. 2001. Investor alert: Affinity fraud: How to avoid investment scams that target groups. http://www.sec.gov/investor/pubs/affinity.htm.

———. 2003. How prime bank fraud works. http://www.sec.gov/divisions/enforce/primebank/howtheywork.shtml.

Securities and Exchange Commission Office of Compliance Inspections and Examinations. 2001. Examinations of broker-dealers offering on-line trading: Summary of findings and recommendations. http://www.sec.gov/news/studies/online.htm.

Seligman, J. 1995. *The transformation of Wall Street: A history of the Securities and Exchange Commission and modern corporate finance*. Rev. ed. Boston: Northeastern University Press.

Shefrin, H. 2000. *Beyond greed and fear: Understanding behavioral finance and the psychology of investing*. Oxford: Oxford University Press.

———. 2001. *Behavioral finance (The international library of critical writings in financial economics)*. Cheltenham, UK: Elgar.

Shefrin, H., and M. Statman. 1986. How not to make money in the stock market. *Psychology Today*, February, 52, 56–57.

Shemo, C. 1997. Fake fats, real threat. *Vegetarian Times*, February, 20.

Shiller, R. 2000. *Irrational exuberance*. New York: Broadway Books.

———. 2003. From efficient markets theory to behavioral finance. *Journal of Economic Perspectives* 17:73, 90–91.

Shleifer, A. 2000. *Inefficient markets: An introduction to behavioral finance.* Oxford: Oxford University Press.

Shleifer, A., and R. Vishny. 1997. The limits of arbitrage. *Journal of Finance* 52:35.

Singhania, L. 2001. Downturn brings changes to on-line brokerage sector: Firms cut back on pricey ads; expand services. *Chicago Tribune*, February 25, 9.

Slovic, P. 2000a. *The perception of risk.* London: Earthscan.

———. 2000b. Rational actors and rational fools: The influence of affect on judgment and decision making. *Roger Williams University Law Review* 6:163, 166–200.

Slovic, P., M. Finucane, E. Peters, and D. MacGregor. 2002. The affect heuristic. In *Heuristics and biases: The psychology of intuitive judgment*, ed. T. Gilovich, D. Griffin, and D. Kahneman, 397, 400–20. Cambridge: Cambridge University Press.

Spitzer, E. 1999. From Wall Street to Web Street: A report on the problems and promise of the on-line brokerage industry. Prepared by Investor Internet Bureau and Securities Bureau, 1189 PLI/Corp. 355. http://www.oag.state.ny.us/investors/1999_online_brokers/brokers.html.

Sunstein, C. 2002a. The laws of fear. *Harvard Law Review* 115:1119, 1137–40.

———. 2002b. Probability neglect: Emotions, worst cases, and law. *Yale Law Journal* 112:61, 95–97.

———. 2003. Hazardous heuristics. *University of Chicago Law Review* 70:751.

Symposium. 2002. Empirical and experimental methods in law. *University of Illinois Law Review* 2002:791.

Talley, E., and S. Choi. 2002. Playing favorites with shareholders. *Southern California Law Review* 75:271, 310.

Thaler, R. 2000. From *homo economicus* to *homo sapiens. Journal of Economic Perspectives* 14:133, 139–40.

Thaler, R., and C. Sunstein. 2003. Libertarian paternalism. *American Economic Review* 93:175.

Thomas, E., and T. Gregas. 1999. It's a bad trading day . . . and it's about to get worse. *Newsweek*, August 22, 9.

Thompson, R. 1997. Securities regulation in an electronic age: The impact of cognitive psychology. *Washington University Law Quarterly* 75:779–89.

Tiedens, L., and S. Linton. 2001. Judgment under emotional certainty and uncertainty: The effects of specific emotions on information processing. *Journal of Personality and Social Psychology* 81:973, 978–81.

Trombley, M. 1997. Stock prices and Wall Street weather: Additional evidence. *Quarterly Journal of Business and Economics* 36:11.

Uchitelle, L. 2001. Following the money, but also the mind: Some economists call behavior a key. *New York Times*, February 11, sec. 3, 1, 11.

Vickers, M., and M. France. 2002. How corrupt is Wall Street?: New revelations have investors baying for blood and the scandal is widening. *Business Week*, May 13, 36.

Viscusi, W. 2001. Jurors, judges and the mistreatment of risk by the courts. *Journal of Legal Studies* 30:107.

von Neumann, J., and O. Morgenstern. 2004. The theory of games and economic behavior: sixtieth anniversary ed. Princeton, NJ: Princeton University Press.

Waldfogel, J. 2002. Does consumer irrationality trump consumer sovereignty? Evidence from gifts and own purchases. Unpublished manuscript. http://rider.wharton.upenn.edu/~waldfogj/trump.pdf.

Weber, E., and C. Hsee. 1998. Cross-cultural differences in risk perception, but cross-cultural similarities in attitudes towards perceived risk. *Management Science* 44:1205.

Williams, J., F. Watts, C. MacLeod, and A. Mathews. 1997. *Cognitive psychology and emotional disorders*. 2nd ed. New York: Wiley.

Wilmott, P. 2000. *Paul Wilmott on quantitative finance*. New York: Wiley.

———. 2001. *Paul Wilmott introduces quantitative finance*. New York: Wiley.

Wilson, T. 2002. *Strangers to ourselves: Discovering the adaptive unconscious*. Cambridge, MA: Belknap Press.

Wright, W., and G. Bower. 1992. Mood effects on subjective probability assessment. *Organizational Behavior and Human Decision Processes* 52:276, 280–88.

Yuan, K., L. Zheng, and Q. Zhu. 2001. Are investors moonstruck? Lunar phases and stock returns. Unpublished manuscript. http://www.ssrn.com.

Zajonc, R. 1980. Feeling and thinking: Preferences need no inferences. *American Psychology* 35:151, 158–65.

———. 1984. On the primacy of affect. *American Psychology* 35:117–20.

———. 2000. Feeling and thinking: Closing the debate over the independence of affect. In *Feeling and thinking: The role of affect in social cognition*, ed. J. Forgas, 25–55. Cambridge: Cambridge University Press.

# 21 IN PRAISE OF INVESTOR IRRATIONALITY

*Gregory La Blanc and Jeffrey J. Rachlinski*

Thank goodness for the optimism of restaurateurs. It is widely understood that the majority of new restaurants fail, and yet new restaurants open all the time. Often enough the same location houses one new eatery after another, as people repeatedly undertake a venture in the precise location that bankrupted their predecessors. That people devote their energy and savings to new restaurants in the face of such poor odds is remarkable—some might say irrational. Some small number of restaurants do succeed, however, to the benefit of both their owners and their patrons. For the owners, the risks hardly seem worth the rewards, but restaurant patrons experience only the rewards of an interesting parade of new dining opportunities. Without an excess of optimism on the part of potential restaurateurs, this parade would quickly end.

This story is not limited to restaurants. Many businesses begin with little more than cockeyed optimism that causes entrepreneurs to undertake foolishly risky ventures. Although undertaking such risk is potentially extremely costly to investors, society benefits greatly from this optimism. Unwarranted optimism underlies many of the successful businesses that generate economic growth (Langevoort 1997). Fear of optimistic entry by newcomers might even discipline existing businesses, forcing them to behave as if they exist in an environment that is more competitive than is really the case (Tor 2002). Although overoptimism in some cases can lead to wasteful overinvestment (Camerer and Lovallo 1999), it may invigorate competition leading to a substantial reduction in monopoly rents. In a perfectly competitive world with zero long-run profits, the illusory prospect of profit might be a key factor in encouraging a dynamically efficient investment pattern (Brenner 2000).

Even if an excess of optimism is essential to encouraging new businesses, it might be a destructive force in the financial markets. A well-functioning capital market must produce accurate asset pricing to allocate capital efficiently. Mispricing of securities would lead society to invest its productive capital in wasteful ventures that cannot ultimately produce economic growth (Barberis and Thaler 2003). The same cognitive processes that affect restaurateurs might also affect investors, leading to psychologically irrational beliefs about the true value of securities. If such cognitive processes are widespread, then they could affect the value of securities. Thus, in addition to suffering from erroneous prices that arise from fraud or bad information, the securities market might suffer from "cognitive mispricing."

Unlike the broader market for business entrants, however, irrationality might not persist in a fluid capital market. Even though reality and market forces would eventually either teach excessively optimistic entrepreneurs the error of their ways or drive them into bankruptcy, either process would be slow (Alchian 1950). If a small number of people each engage in one costly business venture in their lifetime, the economy as a whole will witness a great many entrepreneurial ventures (Langevoort 1997). But in a fluid, fast-moving capital market, irrational investors seem like sitting ducks. People and institutions who search for arbitrage opportunities will quickly pick them off, driving them out of the market (Friedman 1953). Thus, even if some investors are irrational, they might quickly lose their money and be driven out of the market. Cognitive mispricing might be a myth.

Therein lie the conventional stories of the role of irrationality in an efficient market. Either irrationality among investors is so chronic and persistent that it causes assets to be mispriced or it induces individual investors to make such bad choices that they are driven out of the market. In either case, irrationality is costly and should be curbed, if possible. If it affects prices, it is causing capital to be allocated inefficiently. If it does not affect prices but does consume individual investors, then individuals are hurting themselves—possibly risking their retirement savings as a result of their irrationality. If so, then possibly individuals should be saved from themselves.

Regulations to curb irrational investment could be accomplished in several ways (Huang 2002; Langevoort 2002; Prentice 2002). Incentives to save money for retirement could be structured so as to favor collective pools of investments rather than individual accounts. Additionally, regulations could encourage individual investors to make investment choices through a professional adviser rather than on their own. The rise of Internet investing, in which individuals can quickly transfer their investments on an irrational whim, might be a disastrous development that should be curtailed (Barber and Odean 1999; Schiller 2000; Shefrin 2001).[1] Investor education programs could also reduce the degree of erroneous beliefs about the markets. Finally, advertisements that play into the irrationality of individual investors might get closer scrutiny (Huang 2002). Widespread irrationality among investors might be hard to remedy completely, but steps such as these can be taken to curb its adverse effects.

Efforts to reduce the adverse consequences of irrationality should not be adopted without comparing the costs of these regulations with their potential benefits (Mahoney 1995a). In addition to the ordinary costs associated with regulating private behavior, steps to reduce the effect of investor irrationality would eliminate *benefits* that investor irrationality creates. Just as irrational optimism creates a positive externality in entrepreneurial activities, it also creates a positive externality in financial markets. Namely, several cognitive errors investors commonly make encourage them to make investment choices in situations in which a rational decision maker would refrain. Cognitive errors common among investors give them an excess of confidence in their knowledge, thereby encouraging investors to allocate their investments based only upon a modicum of private information. Just as most entrepreneurs should probably refrain from sinking their time and fortunes into new businesses, so too should most investors refrain from trading on their own beliefs. The individual investor can hardly distinguish useful from useless information and well-founded beliefs from foolish ones. And yet, if individual investors consistently refrained from trading on their beliefs, they would, collectively, withhold a great deal of valuable information from the market. Efforts to discourage individual investors from trading on irrational beliefs would deprive the market of valuable pricing information.

Even if individual investment decisions reflect little real private information and are merely noise produced from a reliance on misleading cognitive processes, regulatory efforts to reduce the influence of cognitive errors might be a mistake. Increased regulation of relatively open capital markets would funnel equity investment through institutions and make equity financing more expensive, thereby making debt financing a more attractive option. The sophisticated institutions that make decisions about debt financing might avoid many of the mistakes individuals commit, but such institutions are prone to their own set of cognitive errors (Fanto 2001; Langevoort 1996). Individual decision makers working within institutions are still subject to cognitive errors, and institutional structures create new sources of errors (Langevoort 1997). An increased institutional influence on the financial markets thus leaves open the possibility that securities will be mispriced and that cognitive errors among institutional investors in a market dominated by debt will have a bigger effect on securities pricing than cognitive biases by individuals in an open equities market. The cognitive errors ordinary individuals make will often be a somewhat unique product of their own perspective. Consequently, such errors are less likely to affect the overall price of a security than are mistakes made by institutional investors financing through the debt market. Favoring debt over equity thus raises the prospect for less accurate pricing of securities than an open market produces.

Thus, even if cognitive errors cloud individual investor decisions, efforts to save individuals from their erroneous investment decisions should be approached with grave caution, for two reasons. First, the excess confidence investors have in their beliefs leads them to provide private information to the markets. If reforms of the securities markets reduced or eliminated this confidence, then this private information would be lost. Second, the alternative system, institutional financing, could produce even less accurate prices than a fluid securities market fraught with individually erroneous decisions. The multiple perspectives individual investors adopt may be more likely to offset one another and be more easily corrected, whereas institutions may produce errors that lack corrective mechanisms and could have a greater impact on pricing.

This chapter defends this thesis. First, we present two competing visions of investor behavior. One vision assumes investor rationality, and the other assumes cognitive error. Both theories lead to different regulatory approaches and perspective on cognitive error, but both are incomplete. We then present a third approach, that of behavioral finance, which presents a more integrated and complete portrait of investor rationality and what it means for regulation of securities markets. A behavioral finance perspective, we contend, supports our view that the irrationality of individual investors is a valuable component to the capital financing structure upon which our economy depends. We conclude by discussing implications of this perspective to regulatory efforts to manage investor error.

## 21.1 THEORIES OF INVESTOR RATIONALITY

The model of the individual investor among finance theorists has changed dramatically in just the last five years (Shefrin 2001; Shleifer 2000). Decades ago, economists and finance theorists developed a model of market behavior known as the efficient markets hypothesis (EMH) (Fama 1970). These theorists contend that if investors are rational, then the market price for all securities will reflect fundamental values, that is, future cash flows discounted by a rate of return that accounts for risk. Behavioral economists began to attack the EMH by providing examples of circumstances in which people make choices that are inconsistent with rational choice models of behavior (Barberis and Thaler 2003; Kahneman and Riepe 1998). Behavioral economists argue that the market is populated with irrational investors—a theory one might term the deficient markets hypothesis (DMH) (Hirshleifer 2001). Relying in part on the teachings and the methods of psychologists who study judgment and choice, proponents of the DMH have provided evidence of the disastrous choices individual investors can make (Belsky and Gilovich 1999). The debate has been fierce. Behavioral economists lambasted finance theorists for their seemingly dogmatic worship of a model that seemed, from their perspective, to be so obviously wrong (Barberis and Thaler 2003); finance theorists, for their part, ridiculed the behavioral economists for their lack of rigor, unqualified acceptance of psychology, and seeming inability to generate a competing theory (Fama 1991). The debate is largely over now, and one can pass judgment: It is a stalemate that has led to a compromise in the birth of a new field, behavioral finance (Shleifer 2000).

Both sides of the debate are right. The market seems, at least across reasonably lengthy periods of time, to be quite rational. Firms that make money have high stock prices; firms that do not eventually lose out (Jensen 1978). At the same time, the individual investors who produce these historically rational prices are hopelessly disastrous decision makers.[2] They trade too often, trade at the wrong time, buy too many risky investments, save too little, use the wrong vehicles for what they do save, fail to consult experts, retire with too little money, and retire with too much money (Barberis and Thaler 2003; Hirshleifer 2001; Shleifer 2000). Individuals embrace ludicrous theories about the operation of the stock market, retirement plans, and savings vehicles, and even more foolishly, they seem more than willing to act on these theories (Barberis and Thaler 2003). Institutional investors seem to avoid some obvious problems, but they hardly seem immune from irrational theories and choices (Barberis and Thaler 2003). Reconciling how such chaotic behavior of individuals can produce such a rational system has been the fundamental mission of behavioral finance. The EMH and DMH each have implications for how markets should (or should not) be regulated. The implications of the synthesis of these models into behavioral finance have their own set of implications that are only beginning to be explored. Determining what behavioral finance says about sensible regulatory policy requires understanding what the implications of each of the two competing theories of the marketplace are and how the two conflicting positions have been reconciled into a unified approach.

### 21.1.1  The Efficient Markets Hypothesis

For decades, economists have assumed that rational behavior dominates investment choices in securities markets (Shleifer 2000). Rational investors would base their investment decisions on fundamentals, such as the cash flow a company was expected to produce and the variability associated with that cash flow. The higher the cash flow associated with a given security, the more a rational investor would pay for it. Investors would also insist upon a risk premium for investments that pose greater nondiversifiable risk. Differences in investment strategies among rational investors would depend only upon individual differences in liquidity needs, investment time horizons, and risk preferences. A need for liquidity and a short investment horizon would dictate a risk-averse strategy for an individual investor, for example. Otherwise, every investor, being rational, would behave similarly, seeking out a portfolio that offered the highest rate of return at any given risk.

### 21.1.1.1 What Is the EMH?

A collection of perfectly rational investors would produce a particular kind of market. Recognizing that unless they have some private information that is known only to them and not to anyone else in the market, rational investors would not attempt to beat the market. Private information would create an arbitrage opportunity, but these opportunities would be scarce or nonexistent. Investors would not find opportunities to take advantage of a mispriced security; all securities in a rational market would be priced accurately (Shleifer 2000).

In an efficient market, securities prices would move, of course. Prices would react immediately and efficiently to the dissemination of news that implicates the fundamentals underlying the security (Shleifer 2000). Public events would cause all investors to react immediately and in the same direction, quickly adjusting the value of the security to reflect this new information. Because all information is public, however, information would not create arbitrage opportunities. All investors would know the information, and hence the market price of a security would jump quickly to the new value. To be sure, information not known to the general public would create an opportunity to obtain supernormal profits. Advocates of the EMH disagree somewhat on the extent to which such private information exists and creates such opportunities, but most scholars agree that efficient markets contain some limited arbitrage opportunities based on private information (Shleifer 2000).

The value of pursuing private information that creates arbitrage opportunities, however, is elusive. Gathering private information is costly. In a perfectly rational market, investors would recognize that their own efforts to gather information can be matched by other investors' efforts to gather the same information. Hence, if it is valuable for one investor to gather private information, it is valuable for others to do the same. Investors who have larger portfolios might be able to take greater advantage of private information and hence might find the production of private information more valuable. Rational investors can pool their wealth with others, however, in common investment funds. The managers of such funds can then direct the collective resources of many investors in the production of private information to match the efforts of the wealthier investors. Knowing that the competition for private information can be matched, in turn, suggests that such competition is foolish. Rational investors recognize that their efforts to create private information can be so closely matched by others that it can produce no benefit. Only in rare circumstances in which an investor knows that he or she has a superior ability to gather valuable private information is a strategy of collecting private information apt to produce superior rates of return on investments. Rational investors should recognize the futility of trying to beat the market with private information and should purchase an index of the market.

If the EMH accurately describes the operation of the securities markets, then a particular regulatory style is appropriate (Gilson and Kraakman 1984). Regulatory efforts should be directed at the two particular problems that an efficient market creates: an efficient market is a target of opportunity for fraud and is potentially a market for lemons. In an efficient market, investors are not investing in efforts to create any kind of private information, including information that could reveal fraud. Insiders thus have the opportunity to mislead the public. Even without fraud, insiders would sell interest only in securities in which they have an informational advantage that creates an arbitrage opportunity for them. Rational outside investors, realizing the advantages of the insiders, would resist purchasing any security if they believed that their trade was apt to be with an insider. Such a problem would make it difficult for any firm to use the equities markets to raise capital. Furthermore, no individual firm, acting alone, would solve this problem by disclosure, because their disclosures would not be credible (Mahoney 1995b).

The regulatory remedies for the problems that can affect an efficient market thus reflect efforts to combat these problems. EMH theorists support both scrupulous policing against fraud and broad mandatory dissemination of information (Mahoney 1995b). Policing against fraud is the necessary remedy to the general unwillingness of rational investors to search for private information that would discredit fraudulent statements. Monitoring the accuracy of financial reports is a public good and will be underprovided in the absence of some governmental role. Centralized enforcement supplemented by governmentally imposed sanctions is necessary to encourage the optimum amount of information dissemination (Easterbrook and Fischel 1991).

Similarly, disclosure requirements enable honest firms to provide information without raising suspicion as to the extent or purpose of their disclosure. Creation and enforcement of a uniform, all-encompassing set of disclosure requirements allow firms to credibly disclose information relevant to their fundamental value. It also allows investors to trust the information, knowing that misleading or incomplete disclosures expose the firm's officials to civil and criminal liability. Mandatory disclosure, by ensuring the credibility of corporate financial reporting, benefits the corporate issuers of securities as much as it does the investors in those securities.

### 21.1.1.2 Regulatory Implications of the EMH

Faith that the EMH accurately describes the operation of the securities markets identifies a regulatory approach that emphasizes consistent, uniform disclosure with serious efforts to combat fraud. Firms may be unable to coordinate their disclosure standards and may lack the incentive to reveal adequate amounts of information absent such regulatory interventions. Without these regulations, investors would be reluctant to purchase securities, and indeed, the lemons-market problem alone guarantees that investors would be foolish to do so. Likewise, in the absence of prohibitions, fraud could become commonplace, driving investors out of the market. Adherents of the EMH thus see the prospects of fraud and need for uniform disclosures as the prime source of market inefficiency. Hence, they advocate directing all regulatory efforts at remedying these problems.

The presence of some number of clearly irrational investors need not shake faith in the accuracy of the EMH. Irrationality on the part of some investors (so-called noise traders) will not have much effect on the overall functioning of the market, so long as most of the investors are rational (Black 1986). According to the EMH, one of two things happens to irrational investors, depending upon how many irrational investors there are. If the market includes only a small number of irrational investors, then the presence of these investors will have little effect on the market price (Black 1986). Interestingly, the consequences of irrationality to these investors will be much less than one might expect. In an efficient market, all securities are accurately priced, which prevents irrational investors from overpaying for securities. Erratic and irrational investors might undertake more risk than their investment time horizon would suggest is appropriate, but the irrational investors will be rewarded with higher returns for undertaking this risk (DeLong et al. 1990). Whatever investors' irrational beliefs and preferences might lead them to be willing to pay for securities, the price the market will offer them is an efficient price that reflects the security's true value. Irrational investors simply feel as if they are constantly getting bargains.

For irrational investors, there is no safety in numbers, however. If enough investors adopt erroneous beliefs, then these beliefs *will* affect the market price in the short run, thereby allowing investors to express their costly preferences (Jamal and Sunder 1996). The pressures that fundamental forces exert on securities will ultimately be irresistible in the long run. Eventually, enough investors will come to realize their mistake and abandon their beliefs, and the market price will return to the inexorable balance of risk and return. When the market price does stabilize, many of the irrational investors will realize losses. In fact, any imbalance that irrationality creates will likely be corrected quite quickly. The mispricing that the irrational beliefs cause creates an arbitrage opportunity for investors who are not afflicted with the irrationality (Friedman 1953). Although arbitrage opportunities might sometimes be hard to realize, the inevitable presence of arbitrageurs hastens the correction process. A true inaccuracy in a stock price will create such a lucrative arbitrage opportunity that it will attract a great deal of capital quickly, thereby making it impossible that the opportunity will persist.

Thus, for adherents of the EMH, irrationality among investors does not present a serious problem. If the number of irrational investors is small, then they cannot affect the market price and cannot create a misallocation of capital. Irrational investors will not even suffer much inasmuch as they essentially are randomly purchasing securities at reasonable prices. If the number of irrational investors is large, then their effect on the market price will be so short lived that it will still not cause capital to be misallocated. Even with irrational investors in the market, firms' ability to raise capital will depend solely on their stream of cash flow and its risk— which is exactly what society as a whole wants it to depend upon. Valuable investment opportunities will attract capital, and useless ones will not.

The only worrisome aspect of irrationality under the EMH is its destructive effect on the irrational investors in those cases in which there are enough irrational investors to affect the price of a security. In these cases, the investors can lose a great deal of money as arbitrageurs convert them into money pumps that correct the market price. Adherents of the EMH might sympathize with these investors, but they do not advocate regulation to stop them from losing. Indeed, arguably the existing regulations encourage the creation of such irrationality by allowing firms to engage in "puffery" that might take advantage of cognitive biases (Huang 2002; Langevoort 2002). For adherents of the EMH, however, this is the price to be paid for efficient capital markets. Arbitrageurs must take money from irrational investors in order to correct market prices. Efficiency demands that the irrational investors be sacrificed. Over time, investors who repeatedly chase mispriced securities either will learn better or will run out of money.

For purposes of the EMH, irrationality is not a justification for regulatory intervention in the markets. Proponents of the EMH believe that most investors are rational and that their efforts produce a highly efficient means of raising capital. Regulations designed to restrain arbitrageurs from taking advantage of the irrational investors would be counterproductive—they would only interfere with the corrective process that arbitrage creates. Regulations that keep investors from making irrational decisions might be useful but might be extremely difficult to implement, absent some *ex ante* ability to identify irrationality. Those who believe that the EMH accurately describes the operation of the securities markets therefore believe that regulation should be directed exclusively at producing broad and accurate disclosure of company information.

### 21.1.1.3 Skepticism About the EMH

Naturally, even though a sizable body of empirical research supports the proposition that market prices reflect fundamentals, the EMH has attracted critics and skeptics. Recent flameouts among Fortune 500 companies such as Worldcom, Enron, Tyco, and Adelphia, have made many academics and investors alike suspicious of the market's inherent rationality. For adherents of the EMH, these recent disasters merely constitute evidence of a greater need for detailed disclosure requirements and greater enforcement of antifraud provisions. But for skeptics, the length of time that insolvent or Potemkin companies maintained market capitalizations in the billions of dollars suggests that prices in the markets can substantially deviate from fundamental values.

Another reason to be suspicious of the efficient market hypothesis is that it predicts aggregate behavior that is inconsistent with what we observe in practice. If markets were fully efficient and investors entirely rational, there would be no returns to private information. The joke is that an adherent of the EMH who encounters a twenty-dollar bill on the sidewalk should let it be—if it were really a twenty-dollar bill, someone else would have already picked it up. And yet we observe enormous sums being spent on research and analysis as part of an effort to beat the market. To be sure, much of this seems wasted, as professional investors generally fail to beat the index (Elton et al. 1993; Lakonishok, Shleifer, and Vishny 1992; Malkiel 1995). But rationality must also be eluding them, as almost all financial academics, whether proponents or critics of the efficient markets hypothesis, advise individuals to avoid individual stocks and invest the equity portion of their portfolio exclusively in some form of index fund (Fox 2002).

Opponents of the EMH have also identified other anomalies in the market that are hard for the EMH to explain. The massive run-up in and subsequent crash of tech-sector stocks defy most conventional explanations within the EMH framework (Shleifer 2000). Explanations for several other puzzles are also elusive under the EMH: equity markets have generated excess returns to risk for a great many years—the so-called equity premium puzzle (Fama 1998; Mehra and Prescott 1985). In an efficient market, this could not be so—such gains would quickly be dissipated by other investors who would drive the prices of equities down. Also, closed-end funds typically do not trade at the market value of the securities that they hold, thereby presenting a wealth of unexploited arbitrage opportunities (Lee, Shleifer, and Thaler 1991). Finally, some securities hold subsets of other securities and yet do not trade at prices that reflect this ownership structure (Lamont and Thaler 2003; Shefrin 2001). These instances create what look like clear arbitrage opportunities and yet they persist. Although proponents of the EMH have at-

tempted to devise explanations for these anomalies, the persistence and ubiqui-
tousness of these anomalies at least raise doubts about the degree of efficiency in
the markets.

## 21.1.2 The Deficient Markets Hypothesis

The EMH is not without competitors who have a different vision of how investors behave. Psychologists, experimental economists, and behavioral finance theorists propose that the markets are not populated by rational investors whose collective efforts produce well-behaved securities prices (Barberis and Thaler 2003;
Hirshleifer 2001). Rather, they propose that investors, like all human beings, make
choices that are inconsistent with the rational choice model. Borrowing mostly
from psychological research, these scholars argue that people rely on mental shortcuts, known as heuristics, to make choices (Tversky and Kahneman 1974). These
heuristics serve us well in many circumstances but can lead to systematic errors
in judgment, or biases. If in all aspects of our lives we make good choices but are
also prone to systematic mistakes in judgment, it is hard to believe that the same is
not true of our investment decisions. This insight inspires the deficient markets
hypothesis.

### 21.1.2.1 What Is the DMH?

According to the DMH, the market is populated by investors who often make
systematic errors in their assessments that will affect market prices. Because irrational choices pervade the market, securities prices might fail to reflect fundamentals (Odean 1998). Cognitive errors commonly lead to mispriced securities. In
turn, cognitive mispricings undermine the proper functioning of securities markets. They cause a misallocation of capital and have adverse consequences to the
individual investors.

Although some psychologists and others have disputed the notion that human
choice is riddled with errors (Gigerenzer 1991; Scott 2000), investment choices
have characteristics that make investors particularly vulnerable to error (Barberis
and Thaler 2003). Basic human intuition that would otherwise promote sensible
choice will instead lead investors astray. Assessment of market information requires
an attention to statistical information that has, in other contexts, eluded people's
inferential abilities. As a prominent example, people have difficulty in many contexts with incorporating base rate, or background statistics (such as a firm's historic performance or the historic volatility of a particular industry), with individuating information (such as a firm's most recent quarterly earnings report or the
vague puffery contained in its communications with shareholders) (Koehler 1996).
An excess of attention to the individuating information would lead people to pay

too much attention to the most recent information and not enough to the long-term trends (Shleifer 2000).

Furthermore, accurate assessment of the market value of a security requires that an investor not only understand how the available information relates to a security's value but also how other investors react to the same information. That is, a belief that a security is undervalued implies that one has information about a security's value that the rest of the market either does not know or has failed to appreciate. If even a small number of other investors share the same belief, then the market will quickly adjust to correct the ostensible mispricing. Indeed, it is likely to have done so long before most investors can react. Identifying situations in which the market has somehow failed to react properly to the available information is an extremely difficult task.

In other contexts, people seem particularly unable to understand how others react to information (Ross and Ward 1995). As the aphorism about how difficult it is to see the world through other people's eyes suggests, the task seems to exceed our cognitive abilities (Ross and Nisbett 1991). People tend to assume either that others see the world in exactly the same way that they do (naive realism) or that their view is completely unique (naive cynicism) (Kruger and Gilovich 1999). Although naive realism and naive cynicism make opposite predictions, researchers have observed both phenomena and attributed them to the same basic cognitive failure to understand how others process similar events (Kruger and Gilovich 1999).

The difficulty people experience with understanding others' perspectives produces a strong self-serving bias. In many studies, upward of 80–90 percent of people rate themselves as being better than 50 percent of their peers at some desirable ability (Camerer 1995). Couples about to get married demonstrate this tendency to a staggering degree—99 percent rate themselves as less likely than the average couple to get divorced (Baker and Emery 1993). Results such as these demonstrate a profound inability to understand how other people react to the same information (Camerer 1995). A couple about to get married might rate themselves as less likely than the average couple to get divorced in part because they would see themselves as being "really in love" or "willing to work out problems," whereas at the same time couples fail to recognize that other couples will see themselves in the same way (Gilovich, Kruger, and Savitsky 1999). To answer a question about relative ability, a couple must know how the strength of their own devotion compares to that of all of the other couples, who also feel themselves to be "really in love." Likewise, couples fail to appreciate that all of the other couples they compare themselves to also feel that they are willing to work out their problems, and again, the issue the couples need to understand is whether they are more willing (or able) to work out their problems than other couples are. Even a couple who knows their own proclivities well does not necessarily know the relationship of their own proclivities to those of other couples.

With regard to valuing securities, this gap in cognitive abilities makes it difficult for individuals to appreciate what, if any, private information they have (Shefrin and Statman 1994). Knowing when to trade on information that one possesses requires that one both understand how this information relates to the security's value and also how many other investors also have that information and how others will react to it. Just as couples about to get married feel themselves to be deeply in love, investors fail to appreciate that a large number of other investors know what they know. For example, an investor who makes investment decisions based on corporate cash flow forecasts seen on CNN fails to appreciate that by the time such information makes it to CNN, it has almost certainly already been incorporated into the market price. The EMH's notion that all information is immediately incorporated into the share price seems to be a particularly elusive concept for individual investors. Investors are apt to treat the information that they possess as more unique than is actually the case (Barberis and Thaler 2003).

This naive overconfidence in one's information might, despite its costs, seem to be prevalent and widespread among investors (Barberis and Thaler 2003). Evidence suggests that investors are indeed overconfident about many aspects of their investment strategies. They overestimate the value of their private information and their abilities to beat the market (Huck and Oechssler 2000; Hung and Plott 2001). Indeed, even after investors lose money, they adopt an attribution strategy that protects their overconfidence in their abilities; they attribute success to themselves and failure to unforeseeable market shifts (Daniel, Hirshleifer, and Subramanyam 1998). In a portfolio of investments in which some do well and some do poorly, this biased attributional style will invariably lead to overconfidence in abilities. Small wonder then that investors also underestimate the riskiness of their portfolios (Barberis and Thaler 2003).

Overconfidence is not the only problem that afflicts the individual investor. Investors also seem to be particularly sensitive to whether their investment is creating gains or losses—which psychologists term framing effects (Kahneman and Tversky 1984). Rational investors would look for overall return on a portfolio, looking to maximize total wealth within a certain risk perspective related to their investment goals. This means ignoring arbitrary reference points such as whether a security has risen or fallen from a purchase price, or from any other reference point. It is the total package and total wealth that matter to the rational investor.

In many contexts, however, psychologists have found that people are sensitive to deviations from the status quo and somewhat insensitive to the total wealth at stake. People seem to weigh losses more heavily than gains, and their risk preferences vary with whether a choice involves a loss or a gain. People make risk-averse choices when facing potential gains and risk-seeking when facing potential losses (Kahneman and Tversky 1984; Thaler and Johnson 1991). Overall, this package of risk preferences supports taking gambles that produce returns that lead to a slow but steady increase in portfolio value. Although that seems a sensible enough policy, its emphasis on uniformly positive returns can lead to costly decisions. In particular, people seem to so value avoiding any negative outcomes that they will risk sizable losses for the prospect of avoiding small losses (Shleifer 2000). The risk-seeking choices that this attitude produces can be extremely costly and is inconsistent with a sensible approach to investing, which necessarily incurs the risk of some small losses.

In the context of investing, investors face several natural frames that might affect their choices (Barberis and Thaler 2003). Perhaps most powerfully, investors know whether they have gained or lost from their purchase price on a security. If they have gained, then they might adopt a risk-averse perspective, being too willing to sell and cash out, rather than incur the risks of holding it longer.[3]

Of course, in an efficient market, the risks of holding a security that has increased in value are not necessarily any greater than the risks associated with holding a security that has recently declined in value. The market price reflects all information at all times and hence cannot be affected by recent gains or losses. Yet, if investors see a sale of stock as involving gains, they will likely act in a risk-averse fashion with respect to that stock and be more likely to sell. Conversely, for a stock that has declined in value, investors might be apt to see a sale as incurring a loss. Of course, once the security has declined, the loss has already been incurred. The sale of the stock after a decline has no affect on value (holding aside tax implications, for the moment). Once again, in an efficient market, the decline in value implicates nothing for the future of a security because any bad news that caused it to decline has already occurred. But if selling means incurring a loss, then investors are apt to adopt a risk-seeking approach. That is, they are more apt to hold on to a security until it can be sold without incurring a loss.

The data support this theory (Barberis and Thaler 2003). Investors are more apt to sell securities that are trading for an amount greater than what they paid and are less apt to sell a security trading at an amount less than they paid. This result is particularly surprising in light of the tax treatment of sales of securities. Investors incur no tax gains or losses from fluctuations in the value of securities until they trade them. Attention to tax treatment would, therefore, produce the opposite effect (Shleifer 2000). That is, investors should hang on to winners, because a sale will result in a taxable event. A loss is also a taxable event, but a beneficial one for the taxpayer. Taxpayers will be able to charge the loss against their income, thereby reducing their tax liability. These incentives make the effect even more difficult to reconcile with the position that the market is filled with rational investors. Other irrational beliefs might also feed into this tendency. A misplaced reliance on the representativeness heuristic would have similar consequences to framing effects (Shleifer 2000). Many investors believe that recent increases in the price of a security indicates a tendency for the security to increase more in the future.

Some investors seem to use a more nuanced version of the representativeness heuristic in which they believe that recent revenue reports will accurately predict future revenue forecasts (Barberis and Thaler 2003). Although this belief might sometimes be correct, it is nevertheless a mistake to trade on the basis of recent revenue reports alone. The reason is simple—in an efficient market, a recent revenue report is old news. Its projected effect on a company's future revenue stream is already incorporated into the market price of the security. An individual who trades on such information must be trading on the belief that she or he has a better ability to assess the meaning of the future revenue stream than the market does. As noted previously, this is a kind of naive cynicism, in which the investor fails to appreciate that the entire market has already seen and already reacted to the information that she is seeing and to which she is reacting. It is also similar to the notion of the mistaken belief in the hot hand; that is, the belief that recent success predicts future success, even in the face of good evidence to the contrary (Gilovich, Valone, and Tversky 1985).

Many investors also hold erroneous beliefs that are directly opposite to the hot-hand phenomenon. They believe in what has been called the gambler's fallacy—which is the tendency to believe in quick correction to long-term statistical trends (Hirshleifer 2001). Even though proponents of the EMH have documented that the daily price of a stock is unrelated to recent performance, some investors have interpreted this information to mean that after a few days of increases (or decreases), the price of a security will likely decrease (or increase). Even though the hot-hand and the gambler's fallacies contradict each other, investors seem to pursue both, with slightly different time frames (Hirshleifer 2001). Investors believe in the hot hand after a single day (meaning they believe that a positive performance on one day will likely be followed by another) but believe in the gambler's fallacy after several days (after several positive days, a downturn will occur) (Shleifer 2000).

Individual investors also engage in somewhat irrational thinking about how to allocate their money. They tend to segregate their money, even if only mentally, into different accounts (Shefrin 1999). They have some money that they set aside for safe investing and some for risky investment strategies. Although that might seem to make sense as a diversification strategy, it is actually somewhat foolish. Given their investment time horizon, investors should adopt a particular attitude toward risk for all of their wealth. It makes little sense to have separate accounts for which people adopt different risk preferences unless this combination perfectly creates a portfolio with the appropriate level of risk. As a result of this mental accounting, investors undertake an excess of risk. Mental accounting does restrict the excess of risk to a segregated portion of an investor's assets, but the error is no less a mistake just because it is confined to a fraction of an investor's wealth.

Similarly, investors seem to make choices about when to buy and when to sell that reflects an asymmetry in the regret people feel in choice (Barberis and Thaler 2003; Shleifer 2000). People tend to regret actions more than inaction (Gilovich and Medvec 1995). This tendency might make investors more reluctant to sell a security than to purchase a security. Although this might be an adaptive response both to the temptation to trade too much and the efforts of brokers to induce people to trade too much, it can also lead to an unwillingness to update a portfolio to reflect changes in one's investment time horizon or changes in the risk that the securities present.

People also adopt naive diversification strategies (Benartzi and Thaler 2001; Patel, Zeckhauser, and Hendricks 1991). That is, when offered a menu of securities, perhaps through a pension plan, they tend to allocate their securities equally among the options offered. Increasing the number of options increases the number that people choose. Although this might sound like a sensible diversification plan, its wisdom depends upon the options offered. Selecting uniformly from a number, range, and type of options that an employer or broker creates might not present sensible investment strategy. An investor who allocates equally among eight equities funds and one bond fund, for example, might, if he is approaching retirement, be incurring an excess of risk. Furthermore, if the eight equities funds invest in similar collections of stocks, then spreading one's wealth across them will create only the illusion of diversification.

As a general matter, most of the cognitive errors individual investors commit seem to encourage them to trade. In general, overconfidence among investors as to the value of their private information would lead them to trade. Misplaced reliance on the importance of trends and recent news about a company can also lead individual investors to trade when they should not. Among the cognitive processes, only regret aversion seems to deter trading. Because investors are vulnerable to excess trading, brokers and other entities have incentives to engage in advertising campaigns that play into the cognitive processes that encourage trade. Thus, under the DMH view, the market is filled with investors who adopt overconfident investment strategies that lead them to trade excessively.

### 21.1.2.2 Regulatory Implications of the DMH

Unlike the EMH, the DMH suggests that irrationality is a serious concern. Proponents of the DMH worry that individual investors will constantly lose significant sums by following unwise investment strategies. For adherents of the DMH, the prevalence of irrationality raises the specter of individual investors losing their life savings in the securities markets. Furthermore, if securities are as chronically mispriced as the DMH suggests, then cognitive errors could be creating a serious misallocation of capital. If cognitive mispricing is the norm in the equities markets, then firms have incentives to engage in business strategies that play into investors' cognitive errors rather than engage in strategies designed to improve the firm's fundamentals.

Despite the potential individual and social costs of mispricing, the regulatory implications of the DMH are somewhat murky. If investors make bad choices, then the sensible option would seem to be to keep them from making these choices (Langevoort 2002). Overt and extensive paternalism that would prevent individual investors from entering the market is unappealing, however. Less intrusive reforms might be more constructive. Incentives for individual investors to rely more on institutional intermediaries in investments might reduce the prevalence and costs of irrationality. That is, if investors gained some obvious and compelling advantage to investing through an institution, rather than on their own, they would be more likely to use professionals and collective mechanisms that might reduce the likelihood that they would make a naive mistake.

Other minimally intrusive efforts to save individual investors from irrational beliefs are also feasible (Langevoort 2002). Investor education programs could correct some problems. Many of the deficiencies that the DMH identifies in investors arise because people rely on their intuition as a source of beliefs about the likely functioning of the market. An educated investor need not rely on her intuition for a sense of how the market functions, thereby reducing the role that the misleading heuristics would play. Some undesirable phenomena might persist, however, even among educated investors. For example, framing effects, regret aversion, and the artificial segregation of accounts might depend on emotional reactions rather than cognitive misunderstanding (Huang 2002). Likewise, overconfidence effects might arise from motivated inference processes rather than from the cold cognitive process described previously.

Reforms designed to remedy cognitive errors might also target the behavior of brokers and firms who sell securities to individual investors. Even if these entities refrain from disclosures and statements that fall short of fraud, they might still present assertions that appeal to the mistaken cognitive processes (Langevoort 2002). Companies might rely on assertions that leave the impression that they will do well in the future, even as they make honest statements. They might describe their firm's immediate future in graphic terms that sound like puffery but appeal to an emotional side of investors. Similarly, brokerages run advertisements to the general public designed to imbue individual investors with a misplaced sense of confidence (Spitzer 1999). For example, at the height of the stock market boom, the online investment company E*TRADE ran advertisements indicating that ordinary people could become fabulously wealthy by engaging in online trading (Huang 2002). These advertisements were clearly designed to get people to invest through the Internet and tapped into the overconfidence that individual investors possess. Through these efforts, the advertisements might also have encouraged the overconfidence.

The DMH also points regulators toward greater attention to the format in which information is presented. In other contexts, for example, banking regulations require specific formats for disclosure of interest rates to make them more comprehensible (Fair Credit Reporting Act 2002). Presumably, securities regulations could also restrict advertising and dictate the disclosure format of investment information. More-aggressive regulations might restrict the use of investment devices that feed directly into cognitive errors such as overconfidence. In particular, the instant access to investments on the Internet, unmediated by a broker, might be troublesome. The Internet has made it essentially costless for brokers to communicate seemingly benign information to trades that might induce an excess of trading. Constant reminders of account balances might encourage investors to trade more than they should (Barberis and Thaler 2003).

As a general matter, all of the reforms that this cognitive error story suggests would reduce the influence of the individual investor on market prices (Langevoort 1997). Obviously, extreme reforms that limit individual access to the markets would reduce individual presence, but the more plausible reforms would also reduce their influence on market prices. Some of the reforms would reduce individual access to the markets by requiring or strongly encouraging the reliance on intermediaries. Intermediaries provide expertise, but at a price, thereby increasing the cost of investment. Even investor education is designed to curtail individual investors' effect on market prices. Education would inevitably be designed to school individual investors in the EMH, which, in turn, teaches individuals to buy the index and not individual securities. The more individuals followed such advice, the more they would be taken out of the pricing structure of securities.

It follows logically from the DMH that individual investors should be constrained in a way that restricts their ability to affect market prices. The reason is that the source of the deficiency is individual judgment. The only way to rid the market of its influence and protect individuals is either to keep them out or get them to buy index funds.

## 21.2 BEHAVIORAL FINANCE: A NEW SYNTHESIS

The DMH is, in many ways, as unsatisfying as the EMH. Even as the EMH seems to fail to incorporate the cognitive and judgmental limitations of individual investors, the DMH fails to address basic objections that EMH proponents argue about (Fama 1998). First, much of the cognitive error story is static; it does not assess the role that arbitrage might have in moderating the impact of cognitive errors on prices. Second, it is unclear what the policy implications of the DMH are. Given the costs of regulation, does it really make sense to adopt any of the regulations that its insights seem to support? In addition to the obvious costs of creating and implementing a regulatory regime, the effect of driving out the influence of individual investors might not be beneficial. If individual investors truly followed the EMH, market liquidity might suffer. Also, by investing only in index funds, individual investors would deprive the market of any private information that they had been providing. The new synthesis of the EMH and the DMH into the field of behavioral finance addresses many of these concerns. The implications of behavioral finance for regulation of the securities markets, however, have yet to be fully addressed.

### 21.2.1 Combining the EMH and the DMH

The phenomena underlying the DMH are interesting by themselves but somewhat trivial if they represent only transient quirks among investors. After all, economics is notoriously bad at predicting short-term movements and individual choice; the field's most robust claims arise from describing equilibrium tendencies. The recent work on behavioral finance has made efforts to use the best of both the EMH and the DMH. Behavioral finance attempts to determine how it is that empirical evidence shows that investors are often irrational while at the same time the basic tenets of the EMH attract widespread empirical support.

Rather than reject one of the two lines of empirical research as methodologically inappropriate or misleading, behavioral finance takes both seriously. Behavioral finance theorists start with the empirically supported premise that many investors rely on cognitive processes that will lead them to assign mistaken values to securities. They also believe that in many circumstances, a significant number of investors will rely on the same cognitive processes, such that they put pressure on a security to be mispriced. In effect, they do not assume that cognitive errors simply cancel each other out. At the same time, behavioral finance theorists worry about how arbitrage in a dynamic market will interact with misleading cognitive processes. They acknowledge that arbitrage places pressure on securities prices back toward fundamental values and try to incorporate such pressure into their models. At the same time, behavioral finance theorists recognize that arbitrage is a limited tool for correcting cognitive mispricing. Behavioral finance is thus an effort to describe how the fundamental tension between cognitive mispricing documented by the DMH and arbitrage pressures on securities documented by the EMH produces securities prices.

This fundamental insight is perhaps best illustrated by so-called beauty contest studies. In one such study, a group of subjects (investors) were asked to pick a number from 0 to 100 (Ho, Camerer, and Weigelt 1998).[4] They are told that the winner will be the person who chooses a number that is two-thirds the mean of all the guesses. If all of the subjects are rational and know that all the subjects are rational, they will all choose 0, and then they all win (and either share a prize or get a $1/n$ chance of getting the prize if it is not split). This result is analogous to the EMH's description of the market, in which all investors select the index. But the efficient result is never observed in such studies, and 0 is never a winning answer. Subjects adopt all manner of theories as to how to approach the problem, all of which incorporate some simple belief or heuristic about how to win the contest.[5] As Keynes noted long ago, knowing what a rational market would produce is far less useful than knowing what others' reactions will be.[6] Doing well in the securities markets thus requires knowing not what the fundamentals are but knowing how others will invest.

Even with an understanding of the cognitive processes investors rely upon, identifying how investors think can be extraordinarily difficult. Behavioral finance researchers have documented both overreaction and underreaction to news, in somewhat different contexts, and have been able to attribute both to reliance on misleading cognitive heuristics by investors (De Bondt and Thaler 1986, 1990). Cognitive processes that cause large numbers of investors to overreact or underreact to news can thus produce market pressure to misprice securities. Given the contextual nature of how people think about risk, it is not surprising that psychological processes produce conflicting phenomena. Consequently, in order to exploit arbitrage opportunities that arise from perceived cognitive mispricing, an arbitrageur has to be able to predict whether the market is overreacting or underreacting. A would-be arbitrageur who misidentifies a cognitive trend risks extreme losses.

Several factors limit the ability of arbitrageurs to take advantage of cognitive mispricing of securities, even among would-be arbitrageurs who know how a security is mispriced. Because not all investors in the market are perfectly rational and not all investors are investing as if all investors are rational, an investment strategy based on superior information about fundamentals may turn out to be costly. This is particularly true when the investment strategy involves selling a security short. If an investor knows that the ultimate valuation of a security will be zero, he can still lose his entire stake by selling short if the security increases in value, even briefly, on its way to being worthless (Shleifer and Summers 1990). This risk is especially great when stock is difficult to borrow due to a limited float (Ofek and Richardson 2001). Arbitrage opportunities arising from cognitive mispricing are effectively limited by the investor's wealth and investment time horizon.

Investors who hold irrational beliefs might be rewarded in the short run because they take on riskier investments (Barber and Odean 2000) or because professionals who trade "against" investor irrationality are net losers in the short run (DeLong et al. 1990). Either of these events would provide positive feedback to irrational investment strategies, reinforcing any divergence in price from what would be the long-run equilibrium. In effect, the essential arbitrage strategy—betting that securities will return to fundamental values—might lead to such dramatic short-run losses among would-be arbitrageurs that cognitive mispricing can persist.

Dynamic modeling techniques have demonstrated the limits of arbitrage against irrationality. In one famous computer modeling experiment, researchers at the Santa Fe Institute created a simulated market that included intelligent agents with various investment strategies (Arthur et al. 1997). After an initial distribution of random strategies, some market conditions led to the rapid diffusion of momentum trading strategies in which many agents simply bought into winners and bailed out of losers. The presence of these momentum traders exaggerates perturbances in prices. For their part momentum traders tended to dominate the market for substantial periods until their ranks were ultimately decimated in some kind of correction. The experiment demonstrated that fluid markets can tolerate, and even reward, irrational traders for long periods of time and that the presence of these irrational traders will substantially affect prices.

The results of this simulation are consistent with findings about irrationality among real investors. In a study of day traders, researchers found that individuals who traded most often had higher mean returns, but only because they took on more risk (De Bondt and Thaler 1995). Although this suggests that the traders were behaving perfectly rationally, they continually misattributed their success to trading skill, underestimating the risk that they were assuming. Eventually, traders who exhibit this profile are destined to be wiped out. So long as overconfident investors misattribute their investment success to their skill at evaluating and trading on private information, they will fail to recognize this ultimate risk. In the meantime, they can remain in the market for substantial periods of time because the market rewards them for bearing risk (Barber and Odean 2000).

Understanding the timing of how a cognitive mispricing will play out is thus critical to arbitraging against cognitive mispricing. Investors who trade solely on momentum aggravate this problem further. Thus, one observes situations in which the market begins reacting to news and tends to overreact because of cognitive errors, and the trend is exaggerated by those investors who believe in the hot hand. Even if an arbitrageur understood the extent of the overreaction due to the initial news, he might fail to appreciate the influence of momentum traders. Indeed, some arbitrageurs become momentum traders themselves, riding the wave of sentiment and exacerbating the overreaction. The general unpredictability of the strength of market reactions and of the power of momentum traders converts seemingly riskless arbitrage opportunities into incredibly risky ventures.

Instead of arbitrage opportunities that arise from betting against market trends, the influence of investor irrationality makes it possible for momentum traders who bet on market trends to be successful, at least some of the time (DeLong et al. 1990). Contrary to both the EMH and the DMH, cognitive errors in the market can create an opportunity for people who fall prey to other cognitive errors to make supernormal profits. Consider the following example. Suppose a firm announces some bit of unexpected good news. Suppose further that owing to some cognitive error, the market overreacts to the good news, driving the stock price well up beyond the point that could be rationally justified by the news early in a trading session. Two investors react differently to this event: an arbitrageur sells the stock short (and hedges with the purchase of a comparable security that has not experienced the good news); a momentum trader buys the security, even at seemingly inflated prices (and hedges with a short position on a comparable security); a third, more naive momentum trader just buys the stock, even at inflated prices (with no hedge position to guard against industrywide risks unrelated to the individual stock). The market might then react either with the gambler's fallacy or the hot hand. If the market adopts a gambler's fallacy approach to the recent run-up in share price, then the price will fall, and the arbitrageur will do well. If the market adopts a hot-hand approach, then the price will run up further, and both momentum traders will do well. If the market relies on some misguided version of the representativeness heuristic or halo effect that inspires a buying spree for both the firm and the industry, then only the naive momentum trader will do well (DeLong et al. 1990).

For cognitive mispricing to create an arbitrage opportunity, the arbitrageur must also be able to identify the magnitude of the cognitive phenomena creating the mispricing. For example, closed-end funds would appear to create arbitrage opportunities that arise from cognitive error. Closed-end funds arguably recast investment decisions for individual investors. When choosing whether to purchase a closed-end fund, investors look at the underlying information in a different way, which might inspire different mental shortcuts and hence different valuations. Many psychologists have found that gambles can be presented in different ways that create a different way of thinking and thereby produce different choices. For example, consider the following gambles:

A. $500 for sure, then a gamble involving a 50 percent chance to win either $100 or $0 or $50 for sure

B. $600 for sure, then a gamble involving a 50 percent chance of losing either $100 or $0 or a $50 loss for sure

Even though these gambles are economically identical, people value them differently. The choice in option A involves gambles among gains, suggesting people will tend to make risk-averse choices. Most people would prefer the sure $50, and knowing this, would value option A at $550. By contrast, the choice in option B involves losses, suggesting people will make risk-seeking choices. They will prefer the gamble and will value the security at something greater than $550 (discounting somewhat the likelihood of losing). Likewise, a bundle of securities will produce a different set of gambles than the individual securities will. Indeed, just as the psychological research suggests, closed-end funds rarely trade at the combined market value of their underlying securities (Barberis and Thaler 2003).

An arbitrageur hoping to cash in on misevaluation in a closed-end fund, however, faces a considerable challenge. Even if the arbitrageur recognizes a cognitive mispricing, unless the arbitrageur also understands when the market will correct itself, the mere fact of the misevaluation does not create a clear arbitrage opportunity. For example, suppose an arbitrageur recognizes that two separate securities create the equivalent of option B when bundled together. Separately, the securities are worth $550, but together, investors value them bundled at slightly greater than $550, say, $560. This discrepancy suggests that the arbitrageur can purchase the combined securities separately and sell the bundled security short (assuming that position is available) at $560. Indeed, the EMH suggests that an arbitrageur should put all of his money into this combined position to maximize the benefits of the arbitrage opportunity. Although this arbitrageur seems sure to earn $10 per share, he may not. If the cognitive mispricing persists beyond the settlement period for the short sale, then he will earn nothing. Worse, if the mispricing intensifies before his short position closes, then he may face liquidity constraints that bankrupt him before he can realize the benefits of his position. Only an investor with infinite wealth could be certain to profit from this opportunity. For everyone else, the inability to predict how the erroneous belief will unfold will make such opportunities risky. Successful arbitrage of a cognitive mispricing requires not only that the arbitrageur identify the mispricing but also that the arbitrageur understand the magnitude of the anticipated mispricing. Otherwise, the would-be arbitrageur risks bankruptcy.

Finally, cognitive mispricing might arise from such widespread and fundamental processes among investors that the market will never correct itself. For example, some behavioral economists believe that an analysis of cognitive errors in investment can solve the equity premium puzzle (Benartzi and Thaler 1995). Behavioral finance theorists argue that individual investors are myopically focused on averting losses from individual investments within their portfolio. Investors who frequently examine their portfolio (and hence commonly observe downturns) view their securities as more risky than those who infrequently examine their portfolios (and hence rarely observe downturns). In order to be induced to hold securities that seem so risky, individual investors consistently insist on higher rates of return. Arguably, this premium shows that there is little overall confidence in the securities markets.[7] This belief is so chronic that it cannot be arbitraged away (DeLong et al. 1990). Arbitrageurs cash in only when the markets correct, which never really happens when beliefs are so fundamental that the correction never occurs. Potential arbitrageurs would long ago have gone bankrupt waiting for the market to correct itself against the equity premium.

Thus, absent a complete theory of how irrationality works, a partial theory can lead only to disaster. Inasmuch as arbitrageurs either learn this or go bankrupt, then irrationality does not create arbitrage opportunities. Because irrationality does not create arbitrage opportunities, it will persist. Although it is an interesting theoretical exercise to construct apparently riskless arbitrage strategies, arbitrage in the real world is fraught with dangers. In the absence of an unlimited credit line and infinite patience, arbitrageurs lead very risky lives, as illustrated by the collapse of Long Term Capital Management (LTCM) and efforts to arbitrage against the recent run-up in technology stocks. LTCM may have had a deep reservoir of Nobel prize–winning brain power, but it lacked a correspondingly deep reserve of credit (Lowenstein 2000; Shleifer 2000). Although their bets turned out to be correct for the most part in the long run, to paraphrase Keynes, in the long run we are all dead, and so too was the patience of LTCM's lenders. Likewise, several efforts to hedge against a perceived bubble in the technology sector also went bankrupt before the bubble burst.[8]

Behavioral finance is thus a combination of two theories. It has rational components and borrows heavily from the dynamic models of the EMH. The behavioral finance approach recognizes that investors can adopt irrational beliefs but, at the same time, these irrationalities affect prices. Behavioral finance suggests that arbitrage pressures will generally push markets toward efficiency, but that assessing when efficiency obtains is a function of the depth and timing of the cognitive process of investors.

### 21.2.2 The Value of Irrationality in a Largely Efficient Market

Concluding that because irrational beliefs can affect market prices they are an undesirable presence in the market would be a mistake. Behavioral finance reveals hidden benefits of irrationality. Efficient markets persist in spite of individual investor irrationality, and indeed may even be served by investor irrationality. We make three observations that support this thesis: (1) investor irrationality might be critical for liquidity, (2) investor overconfidence encourages investors to provide information to the market that would otherwise be withheld, and (3) the collective set of errors that individuals bring to the market leads to a more efficient price than a market run by institutional investors.

### 21.2.2.1 *"Noise Traders" Provide Liquidity*

In a fully efficient market filled with rational traders, all trading would be motivated solely by liquidity needs. That is, purchases would be made by investors who were accumulating wealth, and sales would be made by those drawing down their wealth, whether for major purposes or for life-cycle reasons. In this world, there would be no way to acquire an informational advantage, so all investment in the acquisition of such information would dry up. The EMH in its most extreme form runs up against this problem: if markets are efficient because of the pervasiveness of information, where does the information come from if no one is digging it up? It presupposes that information is created and disseminated without cost, if not by magic (Bernstein 1999).

Of course, this vision of the market exists only as a theoretical exercise (Grossman and Stiglitz 1980). We know that there are professional investors who spend a great deal of time and money accumulating information and expertise about companies so as to trade on their informational advantage. Thousands of investment professionals pore over financial reports; interview managers, clients, and employees of companies; draft sophisticated discounted cash flow models; and attempt to predict the effect of different economic variables on corporate performance. This value-added research has a positive economic payoff and has been the basis for quite a few modern fortunes. Even efficient markets theorists have gotten into the game, starting funds on the basis of what they believe to be superior access to information, or at least a superior ability to analyze this information.

If the acquisition of superior information about assets is to lead to positive returns, it must come at the expense of those with inferior information. If investors followed the advice of financial academics, they would purchase the index and avoid losing out in trades against those with superior information. In some sense, it is hard to see how individuals fail to miss this point. As Akerlof (1970) points out, anyone who knows himself to be in possession of inferior information will be wary of trading with the professionals. Any price that the professional is willing to ask must be too high, and any price she is willing to bid is too low. When information is unevenly distributed, trading (except for liquidity purposes) should dry up. Thus, a robust efficient market could not exist regardless of the distribution of information. If information is uniformly distributed, there is no way to make money trading because there will be no predictable price movements; and if information is unequally distributed, there is no way to make money trading because there will be no one willing to trade.

Because we do observe active trading and because investment professionals are here to stay, there must be some investors who are systematic losers. It is these "noise traders," as Black (1986) calls them, who create market liquidity. In the simplest version of this model, all investors can be divided into two camps: those who trade on genuine information and those who trade on bogus information, or noise. Investors are continually bombarded with signals that may have relevance to asset valuation. Investment professionals can filter out the noise and use what remains as the basis for their investment decisions. Nonprofessionals are unable to filter out the noise and so use it as the basis for their investment decisions. The existence of these uninformed investors is what allows the investment professionals to earn a return on their superior information processing. In order for this model to work, it must be the case that the noise traders do not view themselves as such. They honestly believe that they are trading on relevant information.

Noise traders, then, are nothing more than overconfident investors. Each of them believes himself to be in possession of some private information that is relevant to the future price of the security, but this belief is erroneous (Hilary and Menzly 2001). On average, noise traders will do worse than the market and professional investors will beat it. If the only effect of noise trading in the market were to furnish a money pump, channeling savings away from these naive, overconfident investors into the hands of the more rational professionals, it would be hard to argue with paternalistic regulations that put a stop to this flow. But by providing professionals with a return on their information acquisition, noise traders effectively subsidize the process by which asset prices approach their appropriate value. Noise traders are essential to the price setting that leads to the efficient allocation of capital. Any policies that curtailed their willingness to continue with their subsidies might jeopardize the functioning of the capital market.

This is, admittedly, a fairly weak argument in opposition to protecting irrational investors. If investment professionals need to be subsidized, surely there are more equitable ways to do so. In the basic noise trader model, those individual investors who are the most risk seeking and the most overconfident, that is, the most irrational, will be disproportionately hurt by this process. Why not have the government subsidize the financial markets directly? Perhaps the government could actively trade stocks at random. This would provide the market with adequate liquidity without imposing the cost exclusively on the more irrational members of the investing public. This policy would provide adequate liquidity while providing paternalistic protection against the worst consequences of poor judgment.

### 21.2.2.2 Overconfident Investing Strategies
### Promote Accurate Pricing of Securities
If overconfident noise traders did nothing more than serve as the gullible counterparts to informed investors, providing the necessary lubrication to a well-

functioning capital market, it would be difficult to justify a policy that sacrificed their financial well-being. Irrational investors, however, are valuable in other ways. Random trading by the government would be no substitute for noise traders, because the liquidity that it would provide would come with no corresponding informational content—it would be pure noise to create liquidity. By contrast, most private investors probably trade on both information and noise. Even those who are professional investors may be trading on information that turns out *ex post* to be irrelevant or misguided. In other words, all traders are noise traders, to a degree. As a corollary, almost all investors also inject some relevant information into the market.

A standard demonstration, used in most introductory classes in decision theory or finance, illustrates the point. Students are asked to estimate the total value of a large number of coins in a jar and to provide a 50 percent confidence interval around their guesses.[9] Although individual guesses can be wildly off the mark and the true value is more often than not outside individual confidence intervals, it is almost always the case that the average guess lies somewhere close to the underlying value. This serves as an instructive analogy to the process by which securities are traded on a liquid market. In spite of the limited knowledge and overconfidence of those making the guesses, the larger the number of guesses, the more accurate is the average guess. Nevertheless, most investors would be well advised to avoid betting on their guesses. If those submitting guesses were cured of their overconfidence and discouraged from submitting guesses, the quality of the average would suffer. A securities market that is open to all comers, which solicits investment decisions from a wide range of people, may do a much better job of pricing securities than one that relies on a small number of trained individuals.

Rational investors would, in most cases, likely refrain from betting on their beliefs. Risk aversion makes the easily available alternative of investing in a market index too attractive. As proponents of the DMH note, investors rely on cognitive processes that make trading on their beliefs seem like a good idea. Although the DMH suggests this is a disastrous strategy that should be curbed, if possible, curbing the strategy potentially eliminates a great deal of information from the market.

To see this, consider the phenomenon known as the "home bias"—which is the tendency to overinvest in familiar securities (Chorvat 2002; Huberman 2001). For example, after the breakup of ATT into the regional Bell operating companies (RBOCs), ATT stockholders received pro rata shares in all of the RBOCs. If investors were perfectly rational, subsequent trades in RBOC stocks should be unrelated to geographic location. Nevertheless, investors exhibit a correlation between an individual's RBOC stockholdings and the person's telecom service provider. Similarly, investors tend to accumulate shares in other companies with whom they do business or whose products they admire (Lewis 1999). Home bias can explain why investors are wary of stocks in foreign companies (French and Poterba 1991). Investors systematically underestimate the rates of return on foreign stocks relative to domestic ones. Home bias can also explain why employees tend to invest a disproportionate amount of their wealth in the retirement savings plans sponsored by their companies (Benartzi 1999). The bias arguably keeps investors from adequately diversifying; in other words, investors buy familiar stocks instead of just an index.

At the same time, the home bias might be an example of the "quick and dirty" familiarity heuristic that can produce superior decisions (Borges et al. 1999). "Invest in what you know" might be a rough proxy for having some superior information (Levy and Livingston 1995). Employees, for example, are often in a superior position to evaluate firm performance even without access to illegal insider information. Telephone customers might have more insight into the performance of their local RBOC than distant RBOCs, through personal contacts with employees or personal experience with the local RBOC's business practices. Home bias generally encourages investors to act on even the appearance of superior information. Whether it is sensible for them to do so or not, by acting on this rough heuristic, investors feed their information into the market.

Acknowledging the benefits of the home bias creates a different perspective on the role that many public financial advisers play in the markets. If most investors are foolishly pursuing erroneous beliefs, then investment advisers seem to encourage overconfidence in investment by pandering to cognitive errors. For example, consider Peter Lynch (1989), who made his name as a manager of the Fidelity Magellan Fund, which sustained supernormal returns during his tenure. He became well known also as a financial guru to the investing public by arguing that individual investors could outperform the market by investing in what they knew. He argued that ordinary individuals possess information that is relevant to the value of securities long before it becomes common knowledge among investment professionals. If an individual enjoys a product or finds that a company provides exceptional service, or if she observes herself or others switching their loyalty from one company to another, this may say something about the future value of the company. In other words, anecdotal evidence may be relevant. Lynch's advice might sell well in part because it plays into strategies that investors are prone to follow. Even though Lynch's arguments appeal to investors' cognitive vulnerabilities and encourage the kind of overconfident investment strategies that inspire calls for regulatory intervention (Huang 2002), Lynch also encourages investors to provide information to the markets.

Also consider the problem that individual investors seem to treat stocks the way that they would other commodities. That is, investors sometimes buy and sell based on feeling and anecdote (Huang 2002). In part, this is the reason that advertising campaigns by brokerages and electronic trading companies rely so heavily on emotional and anecdotal appeals. Such appeals might well be effective in getting people to invest when they perhaps should not. Once again, the potential effectiveness of these appeals has triggered alarms and concern for regulatory intervention to save individual investors (Huang 2002). Investing on a story, however, might have effects similar to those of the home bias. People tend to base most of their decisions on stories and anecdotal support and yet organize their lives pretty well (Koehler and Tversky 1994; Pennington and Hastie 1993). Perhaps these appeals induce people to overcome a natural risk aversion and interject their understanding of a firm's economic future into the market. Individually, such a strategy might cause an investor to undertake too much risk, but it might also produce a collectively accurate estimate of firm value.

Investing on the basis of anecdote or personal experience might well be characterized as falling prey to a misleading heuristic. At the same time, most of the heuristics that produce overconfident investment strategies are driven by some kernel of reality. The only way to get these kernels of truth into the market is to induce investors to act on them. Open securities markets allow overconfident investors to contribute their kernel to the market price. Although it is true that all bets placed by those with limited information will inject noise into the pricing process, embedded in that noise is some important information of relevance. The noise is a necessary cost of information revelation. A noisy signal is better than no signal at all (Sunder 2004).

In a world of overconfident investors who rely on heuristics and stories that can be misleading, Lynch's advice is most likely misguided. So too are advertising campaigns designed to encourage excessive trading misguided. The actual amount of relevant private information that any individual investor possesses is undoubtedly of less importance than the investor takes it for. But by encouraging individual investors to put trust in their own observations, market cheerleaders such as Peter Lynch and E*TRADE induce investors to perform a public service.

### 21.2.2.3 Individual Versus Institutional Investors

Corporate finance abhors a vacuum; any effort to drive the choice of individual investors out of the market implicitly replaces open-market equities funding with institutional debt-based finance. Even if the DMH were compelling enough to inspire policy changes that would diminish the role of individual investors, capital would then be allocated by investment professionals, by large institutional investors, or within large conglomerates. Individuals would continue to be the source of investment capital, but they would delegate to others the major investment decisions. They would hold shares in mutual funds, bank deposits, insurance policies, and claims on pension assets, but the actual allocation of those funds to companies or investment projects would be done by employees of those institutions. Unless institutional choice is somehow free of cognitive error, such a move would replace the cognitive errors of individual investors with those produced by professionals within institutions. It would seem to be the case that institutions have a major advantage over individuals when it comes to rationality. The decisions of an institution can be rational without any of the individuals that make up the institutions being rational (Heath, Larrick, and Klayman 1998). Institutions can design decision processes whereby individual preferences are aggregated and individual biases canceled out. Of course this is also true of a market, which is also an institution in the broad sense. In the finance literature, however, institution typically refers to a large investment entity such as an investment bank.

Financial institutions are not free from cognitive error. Their perspective is different from that of individual investors, and they see investment choices through a different lens, but they still rely on the same kinds of cognitive processes that affect individuals. This means that financial institutions will produce different choices about capital allocation than an open securities market will but that these choices will not necessarily be more accurate ones.

One of the principal differences between individual and institutional investors is the greater reliance of the former on experts to make choices. Expert decisions differ in several ways from lay decisions. First, experts might be better calibrated in their confidence than ordinary people (Fischoff, Slovic, and Liechtenstein 1977). For example, weather forecasters seem to be aware of the limited value of their predictions about the weather. But this is not always the case. Experts frequently exhibit overconfidence in their area of expertise precisely because they are experts. It is said that experts are "often wrong, but rarely in doubt" (Griffin and Tversky 1992). The manner in which expertise affects overconfidence has to do with the difficulty of the task and the predictability of the subject matter. When they are both relatively high, experts are better calibrated than ordinary people. Bookmakers and professional cardplayers tend to be well calibrated. When dealing with subject matter that is inherently more complicated, such as psychological diagnoses and financial markets, experts may be more susceptible to overconfidence. Weather forecasters may be the exception to this rule. The more complicated the experts' model, the more faith they have in it (Yates 1990). Holding probabilities constant, they will overestimate their competence and be willing to bet on vague beliefs concerning subjects of relevance to their skill (Heath and Tversky 1991).

In financial markets, the overconfidence that the individual investor has about private informational signals and about recent news items seems to be matched by the institutional investor's overconfidence in its model (Gervais and Odean 2001; Hilary and Menzly 2001; Nelson, Krische, and Bloomfield 2000). In other words, when a new piece of information is released, individual investors immediately rush to trade on it, whereas institutional investors will discount its relevance. Individual investors tend to overreact to news, whereas institutional investors underreact to news (Grinblatt, Titman, and Wermers 1995; Trueman 1994). Investment professionals are too conservative: they are reluctant to revise their models and so are frequently surprised (Shefrin 1999). Neither bias can be evaluated in terms of its impact on capital allocation in isolation. Elimination of one bias may allow the other free reign. If these biases offset one another, any policy that is designed to minimize the impact of the one would need to account for its impact on the other.

Expertise itself can produce both overconfidence and a biased way of evaluating choice. Experts tend to pay greater attention to things that may allow them to make use of their expertise. In the financial community, sell-side analysts tend to always be bullish about companies in their industry, consistently overestimating the future earnings of companies that they follow.[10] At the same time short sellers tend to be far more skeptical (Shefrin 1999). Even within a single investment firm, an equity analyst may be bullish about a stock while the debt analyst on another floor is advising clients to bail out of the bonds. This is puzzling, because presumably all of these people were trained in the same kinds of valuation techniques. When analysts use those techniques to analyze discounted cash flow, a company's assets should be expected to have a single value, which is either above or below the current market price. Whether you are in the business of buying shares long or selling them short should not influence your valuation. Here, too, these biases may serve as necessary correctives of one another. Policies aimed at making markets work better might do better to focus not on the elimination of these biases but rather on making sure that there is an optimal mix.

Although much of the evidence for this phenomenon is still anecdotal, it seems to illustrate the effect of "enrichment." When subjects are asked to evaluate job candidates, their evaluations will depend in part on whether they are asked to find reasons to accept candidates or reject candidates. Frequently, the same candidates who are selected to be accepted in one case are selected to be rejected in the other. When experts develop a skill, which is based on continually looking for reasons to carry out some action, they will tend to find more cases in which to do so. In other words, these experts overestimate the legitimate scope of application of their skill (Shafir, Simonson, and Tversky 1993).

Another reason to be skeptical about the ability of financial market professionals to calibrate their overconfidence is that overconfidence frequently increases with exposure to more information (Heath and Tversky 1991; Stewart and Lusk 1994). Although there is some evidence that more information makes a decision maker discount the relevance of any one piece of information, it tends to lead to greater confidence about the whole package of information, even if the increase is a product of totally irrelevant information (Oskamp 1965).

Another key difference between individual investors and institutions is the widespread reliance on group decision making in institutions. Although groups have several advantages over individuals (they know more, they can aggregate different views, and so on), a group setting can exacerbate some biases and create new ones. Groups are subject to their own dynamics that lead to systematic biases.[11] Just as within a jury, certain biases are amplified. In many cases the biases of each of the individuals in the group are mutually offset, but there are other cases in which they are not. For instance, in a competitive auction setting, high bidders in the group frequently drive the outcome (Cox and Hayne 2002). Communication at close quarters can lead to a rapid dissemination of information but can also lead to rapid dissemination of sentiment (Banerjee and Fudenberg 1999). Enthusiasm can be infectious at close proximity.

In a financial system organized around institutions, the increased communication and frequent interaction between the corporate managers receiving funding and the agents of the institutions making investment decisions can lead to reinforcing beliefs. Although it might be thought that proximity allows one to see the warts, it also allows one to catch the fevers. The more time an investor spends with overoptimistic entrepreneurs, the more likely the investor is to "drink the Kool-Aid" (Schultz and Zirman 2001).

Furthermore, small groups exhibit a conformity bias (Asch 1956; Janis 1982; Moscovici 1985). Although initial impressions may differ, once impressions are disclosed, individual group members tend to coalesce in their impressions, frequently around the most charismatic or authoritative individual. Japanese culture is frequently seen as more conformist than American culture, and this is seen by some as the cause of their investment institutions, but it may well be the case that it is the structure of the institutions that drives this cultural bias (Rajan and Zingales 1998).

Small groups tend to take on more risk in their collective decisions than each of the individuals would if left to his or her own devices.[12] In part, this is an agency problem. If a risk-averse individual is held accountable for the outcome of her decisions, she will tend to play it safe. When blame can be diffused within a group, risky choices look more attractive. But it is also a cognitive process. When others seem comfortable with taking a risk, individual inhibitions are weakened. This "risky shift" would suggest that overconfidence and the possibility of irrational exuberance might be greater in small groups. Of course, individual investors in a liquid market will frequently be subject to the same effects, especially when they frequently discuss their investment decisions with coworkers and friends.

Groups also seem to exacerbate some biases, notably the sunk cost fallacy. Just as individual investors are reluctant to realize their losses, so too are professional investors and managers making investment decisions. Instead of terminating a loss-making project, managers will pour more money into it, thereby escalating their commitment (Staw 1997). In one study, identical descriptions of two projects were presented to individuals and to groups. Both were unattractive projects, but one project was described as having a sunk cost. In both cases, the existence of the sunk cost increased the number of subjects who recommended further investment, but the increase was significantly greater with group subjects (Whyte 1993).

If institutions as well as individuals are subject to biases, then the case for reducing the impact of biases by expanding the role of institutions is less than overwhelming. If cognitive biases are a problem and lead to systematic mispricings, a thorough examination of the effect and magnitude of the different biases would be in order. In either case, whatever system we chose would be second best—a world without biases is impossible. It may well be the case that some of the biases offset one another; if this is so, then a case could be made for making sure that we had an appropriate mix of the two. Even though both institutions and individuals may be subject to overconfidence, the sources of their overconfidence are different.

## 21.2.3 Comparing Financial Systems from a Behavioral Finance Perspective

The role that the behavioral finance perspective should play in the regulation of securities thus reduces to a choice between finance methods: institutional investors versus open markets. In assessing the merits, it is worth noting that a comparative literature on this choice already exists. The individual investor is, in fact, largely a creature of the Anglo-American financial markets. Although other countries have made strides toward expanding the scope of their shareholding public in recent years, in most countries financial institutions play a much greater role in capital allocation. In Germany and Japan, financial institutions play a much larger role than individual investors do (La Porta 1999). In these countries, commercial banks, merchant banks, insurance companies, and pension funds provide capital through debt financing or through large stockholdings. Rather than engage in frequent short-term transactions, they tend to develop long-term relationships with their clients. As a result the equity markets are less important, and there is less active trading of securities. In an extreme form, all capital allocation decisions are made administratively within a large enterprise, such as a Japanese keiretsu (Aoki 1990).

A large literature has developed on the relative merits of each system (Allen and Gale 2000; Chew 1997; Roe 1998). On the one hand, institutional investors accumulate large stocks of company-specific expertise and have an active say in management. This would seem to overcome any asymmetric information: the institutions are in constant contact with active management, frequently holding board memberships, and so it is less likely that the managers will be able to deceive their investors (Diamond 1984; Hoshi, Kashyap, and Scharfstein 1991). This close contact also comes with a great deal of control. The problems of opportunistic managers who engage in empire building and hoard free cash flow are substantially reduced (Jensen 1986).

The drawback to this institutional finance system is a lack of liquidity. Buyers and sellers of these large holdings can be difficult to find. This difficulty arises not just because of the small number of potential investors but also because of the uneven distribution of information about the company and expertise necessary to evaluate it. Highly concentrated ownership may reduce the information asymmetry between the company and its current investors, but it exacerbates the asymmetries among current and prospective investors in that company (Bhide 1993). Any current investor is thus essentially an insider, and any decision to sell is a signal of the investor's lack of confidence. It is less likely in such a system for the ownership in the company to make its way into the hands of the investor who might value it the most and be able to maximize its value.

Because ownership is relatively stagnant, there is relatively little feedback about major business decisions. Whereas the institutional investors may have superior expertise in many cases about how to run the enterprise, it is often the case that they do not possess all of the necessary information. It is difficult to extract that information from outsiders without some way to reward them, by for example, allowing them to trade on that information, by betting on it in a liquid market. This suggests that there may be some companies that stand to benefit more from the accumulated wisdom of their small group of long-term investors than they could from the aggregate wisdom of a large number of small investors. These companies may be in industries that are relatively nondynamic: where there is little relevant information provided by outsiders that would need to be quickly incorporated. But if a company is in a dynamic industry, where continual feedback is necessary, a lack of liquidity in claims on the company could be crippling (Allen 1993).

Proponents of the DMH point to the propensity toward bubbles in liquid securities markets as one of its major weaknesses. Markets dominated by professionals, however, might be equally vulnerable (Shiller and Pound 1989). Japan has yet to recover from the bubble that it experienced in the 1980s, a bubble that arose in a system largely devoid of individual investors (Kashyap 2002). The continued existence of "zombie firms" in Japan is testimony to the lack of resilience of such a system (Krugman 1998). It is arguable that the Internet bubble in the United States in the late 1990s left behind far more of value in the form of physical and human capital than was left behind by the Japanese bubble (DeLong 2001).[13] Japan's lack of liquidity lengthens the time necessary before feedback is received by investors, resulting in a perpetuation of overconfidence in underlying trends.

Although the behavioral finance perspective on finance choice is only a part of the picture, it raises a clear red flag against efforts to regulate the open-access securities markets in an effort to reduce cognitive errors among individual investors. Such efforts would inevitably increase the role of institutional players—and indeed, this is the purpose of such regulation. This change would magnify the impact of erroneous investment choices, concentrating these choices in institutions responsible for large amounts of money. Also, this change would reduce the arbitrage pressures that discipline some of the cognitive errors in the open market.

## 21.3 CONCLUSION AND COMMENTS

The regulatory implications of behavioral finance are somewhat uncertain. On the one hand, efforts to reduce the irrational beliefs investors adopt will have much more effect on the operation of the market than the EMH might predict. Recall that according to the EMH, irrationality is an ephemeral phenomena that has little real impact on the market and therefore should not inspire regulatory intervention. Research in behavioral finance shows how cognitive errors can lead to the persistent mispricing of securities. This result suggests that the case for regulation is strong; cognitive mispricing could lead to misallocation of capital. On the other hand, unlike the DMH, behavioral finance emphasizes the dynamic interaction of cognitive processes and economic pressures toward efficiency. Regulatory interference with this complex system might have unintended deleterious effects on the markets' struggle toward efficiency.

Irrespective of its actual merits as an explanatory tool, the belief in efficient markets is a two-edged sword. George Soros (1994, 2002) has blamed the efficient markets hypothesis for the recent, prolonged irrational exuberance in the equities market. His reasoning was this: Even if you believed that a company's stock price was completely divorced from its fundamentals, a rational investor would also be skeptical of his own private evaluation. After all, how could so many people be wrong? If information is instantaneously incorporated in stock prices, then any private valuation that differs must be incorrect, so there is no point in trading (Bernstein 1999). On the other hand, if information were highly asymmetric, there would be no way to justify trading, because of the danger that you are in possession of inferior information. Faith in the securities market requires that its participants believe that markets are moderately efficient. That is, there are no severe asymmetries of information, but there is enough asymmetry to allow for advantageous trading. Because we can't all be winners in the latter world, we must all believe ourselves to be the ones in possession of the relevant information. Our collective delusion must be that of a Lake Wobegon market, where we are all above average. The policy implication is that the purpose of the SEC may have less to do with ensuring the allocation of information and more to do with promoting beliefs about the allocation of information. The (relatively) efficient markets hypothesis may be the Noble Lie of a successful securities market.

A corollary to the Noble Lie of efficient markets is the Noble Lie of fundamental valuation. There is no reason to believe that the value of a security must always regress to its underlying fundamental valuation in terms of discounted cash flow or dividends. Rational investors may forgo research into fundamental values if they believe that the costs of this investigation exceed the benefits. This is most famously illustrated in models of rational bubbles. If all investors have access to some private signals that are uncorrelated in their errors but of equal reliability, and if all investors can observe the trading behavior of other investors, then it is perfectly rational in many cases to give more weight to the observed trading behavior of others than to rely on a private signal that may be in conflict. If these signals are relatively accurate on the whole, the equilibrium price will be become accurate after just a few trades. If signals are costly, then it would be suboptimal to have subsequent traders invest in the acquisition of information that they would ignore in any case. In a minority of cases, however, there may arise an equilibrium price that diverges from the underlying value, even if the signals are relatively accurate on the whole. The reason is that the actions of the first few traders will dictate the outcome. If those first few traders receive inaccurate signals, there would be no rational reason for subsequent investors to solicit additional signals, even if the majority of them would point toward a different price. This reduces the informational value of subsequent trades. In this model, prices can be divorced from fundamental valuations indefinitely, until some new round of signaling occurs, leading to an information "cascade" (Bikhchandani, Hirshleifer, and Welch 1998). Availability of information about the trading activity of others can lead to a lower amount of information overall.

If investors in this model overweigh the relevance of their private signals, they will continue to solicit them, even after their expected value is negative. If investors believe that prices divorced from fundamental valuation cannot persist, then they will attach a greater weight to their private valuations based on fundamentals and less to the trading behavior of others.

In the words of Thomas Schelling (1960), the belief in fundamental valuation may serve as "convergence equilibrium." In Schelling's famous model, travelers know that they are to meet in New York but have no other information about the location of their meeting. Rather than go to the place that seems most sensible individually, each traveler will try to infer what the other would believe would be most sensible and so on. A common meeting place will be arrived at only if there is some convergence about perceptions of sensibility. Schelling, conducting his experiments in the 1950s, suggested Grand Central Terminal. Even if one traveler thinks that the ice rink at Rockefeller Center or the top of the Empire State Building is a more sensible or convenient place to meet, she would be foolish to act on it if she thought the other traveler might have different ideas.

If investors were to pay greater attention to the insights of behavioral economists and to downplay the importance of fundamental valuation in their investment decisions, this could have a destabilizing effect. If investors were to pay more attention to the trading behavior of others and to speculate about the psychological factors that underlie them, we might see a world in which there is no convergence equilibrium. Thus, the empirical accuracy of both the EMH and the DMH may depend to some extent on the degree to which they are accepted by the investing public. Beliefs about how the market operates influence the way it actually operates. Investors behave differently over time for various reasons: they have access to different kinds of information, there are changes to their underlying cognitive mechanisms, or they incorporate different theories about how the market works. It is unclear how developments in behavioral finance will ultimately influence the behavior of arbitrageurs, investment professionals, and individual investors. Any attempts to incorporate the insights of behavioral economics into regulatory policy will also need to consider the ways in which those same insights have been incorporated by market participants.

1. There is evidence to suggest that access to Internet trading leads to a greater volume of trading and has a substantial negative effect on an investor's portfolio performance (Barber and Odean 1999). The apparently harmful effects of Internet trading led the former SEC chairman to refer to it as a "narcotic" (Shefrin 1999).

2. "Many individual investors are virtually beyond redemption with respect to probabilistic and financial illiteracy" (Hu 1996, 2371).

3. See Barberis and Thaler (2003), Locke and Mann (2000, 2001), Shefrin and Statman (1985), and Shleifer (2000).

4. A recent demonstration of this result was obtained by a contest run by the *Financial Times* and open to all readers. At stake were two round-trip transatlantic business-class tickets. The winning number turned out to be 13 (Thaler 1997).

5. For this reason, irrational trades might still affect the market price, even if they are weeded out (Kogan and Uppal 2002).

6. Keynes's observations about the fallibility of an arbitrage pricing strategy based on fundamental valuations were illustrated by actual examples of beauty contests. In his account, a newspaper ran a survey asking its readers to guess which of a number of faces would be considered most beautiful by the largest numbers of its readers. In the contest, however, no one was asked to provide an individual assessment of the faces' beauty, but rather only guesses about the other readers' guesses. It is easy to see how a winning strategy can become divorced from any independent criteria of beauty.

7. It could be argued that this thesis is inconsistent with the overall view that investors are overconfident. It must be noted, however, that the finding is that investors are overconfident in their judgment and investment abilities, not overconfident that the market will produce high returns.

8. Rather than bet against the boom, most hedge funds rode the trend and bailed out right before the peak. Hedge funds that bet against the boom, such as Julian Robertson's Tiger Management, went belly-up while waiting for the bubble to burst (Brunnermeier and Nagel 2002).

9. Average guesses have been shown to have superior results in weather forecasting (Armstrong 1985; Von Holstein 1971).

10. This seems to be an example of wishful thinking. In other studies, supporters of soccer teams and political candidates were shown to overestimate the probability of their team or candidate winning games or elections (Bahad 1987; Uhlaner and Grofman 1986).

11. Results of survey available (Gigone and Hastie 1997; Kerr, MacCoun, and Kramer 1996).

12. Actually, they tend to be more extreme, not just more risky (Sunstein 2002).

13. Alan Blinder, former governor of the Federal Reserve and author of *The Fabulous Decade* (2000), continues to believe that irrational exuberance was a small price to pay for the productivity increases that went along with it (Blinder 2002).

REFERENCES

Akerlof, G. 1970. The market for "lemons": Qualitative uncertainty and the market mechanism. *Quarterly Journal of Economics* 97:488.

Alchian, A. 1950. Uncertainty, evolution and economic theory. *Journal of Political Economy* 58:211.

Allen, F. 1993. Strategic management and financial markets. *Journal of Strategic Management* 34:31.

Allen, F., and D. Gale. 2000. *Comparing financial systems.* Cambridge, MA: MIT Press.

Aoki, M. 1990. Toward an economic model of the Japanese firm. *Journal of Economic Literature* 28:2.

Armstrong, J. 1985. *Long range forecasting.* New York: Wiley.

Arthur, W., J. Holland, B. Le Baron, R. Palmer, and P. Tayler. 1997. Asset pricing under endogenous expectations in an artificial stock market. In *The economy as a complex adaptive system II: Proceedings (Santa Fe Institute Studies in the Science of Complexity)*, ed. W. Arthur, S. Durlauf, and D. Lane, 15–44. Boulder, CO: Westview.

Asch, S. 1956. Studies of independence and submission to group pressure. *Psychological Monographs* 70:1.

Bahad, F. 1987. Wishful thinking and objectivity among sport fans. *Social Behavior* 4:231.

Baker, L., and R. Emery. 1993. When every relationship is above average: Perceptions and expectations of divorce at the time of marriage. *Law and Human Behavior* 17:439.

Banerjee, A., and D. Fudenberg. 1999. "Word of mouth" learning. Working paper, Harvard University.

Barber, B., and T. Odean. 1999. Online investors: Do the slow die first? Unpublished manuscript, University of California, Davis.

———. 2000. Trading is hazardous to your wealth: The common stock investment performance of individual investors. *Journal of Finance* 55:773.

Barberis, N., and R. Thaler. 2003. A survey of behavioral finance. In *Handbook of the economics of finance*, ed. G. Constantinides, M. Harris, and R. Stulz, 1051–1144. Amsterdam: North-Holland.

Belsky, G., and T. Gilovich. 1999. *Why smart people make big money mistakes—and how to correct them: Lessons from the new science of behavioral economics.* New York: Simon and Schuster.

Benartzi, S. 1999. Why do employees invest their retirement savings in company stock? Working paper, University of California, Los Angeles.

Benartzi, S., and R. Thaler. 1995. Myopic loss aversion and the equity premium puzzle. *Quarterly Journal of Economics* 110:73.

———. 2001. Naïve diversification strategies in retirement savings plans. *American Economic Review* 91:79.

Bernstein, P. 1999. Why the efficient market offers hope to active management. *Journal of Applied Corporate Finance* 12:129.

Bhide, A. 1993. The hidden costs of stock market liquidity. *Journal of Financial Economics* 34:31.

Bikhchandani, S., D. Hirshleifer, and I. Welch. 1998. Learning from the behavior of others: Conformity, fads and information cascades. *Journal of Economic Perspective* 12:151.

Black, F. 1986. Noise. *Journal of Finance* 41:529.

Blinder, A. 2000. *The fabulous decade.* New York: Twentieth Century Fund.

———. 2002. "The bubble has burst, but strength remains." *New York Times,* September 22, sec. 3, 4.

Borges, B., D. Goldstein, A. Ortmann, and G. Gigerenzer. 1999. Can ignorance beat the stock market? In *Simple heuristics that make us smart,* ed. G. Gigerenzer and P. Todd, 59–73. New York: Oxford University Press.

Brenner, R. 2000. Why society needs irrational exuberance—and what this means for valuations and monetary policy. *Journal of Applied Corporate Finance* 13:112.

Brunnermeier, M., and S. Nagel. 2002. Arbitrage at its limits: Hedge funds and the technology bubble. Working paper, Princeton University.

Camerer, C. 1995. Individual decision-making. In *Handbook of experimental economics,* ed. J. Kagel and A. Roth, 587–704. Princeton, NJ: Princeton University Press.

Camerer, C., and D. Lovallo. 1999. Overconfidence and excess entry: An experimental approach. *American Economic Review* 89 (1): 306.

Chew, D. 1997. *Studies in international corporate finance and governance systems: A comparison of the U.S., Japan, and Europe.* Oxford: Oxford University Press.

Chorvat, T. 2002. Ambiguity and income taxation. *Cardozo Law Review* 23:617.

Cox, J., and S. Hayne. 2002. Barking up the right tree: Are small groups rational agents? Working paper, University of Arizona, Tucson.

Daniel, K., D. Hirshleifer, and A. Subramanyam. 1998. A theory of over-confidence, self-attribution, and security market under- and over-reactions. *Journal of Finance* 53:1839.

De Bondt, W., and R. Thaler. 1986. Does the market overreact? *Journal of Finance* 40:793.

———. 1990. Do securities analysts overreact? *American Economic Review* 80:52.

———. 1995. Financial decision-making in markets and firms: A behavioral perspective. In *Finance, handbooks in operations research and management science*, ed. R. Jarrow, V. Maksimovic, and W. Ziemba, 385. Amsterdam: Elsevier.

DeLong, B. 2001. The macroeconomy and the new economy. *Worldlink* (May/June).

DeLong, B., A. Shleifer, L. Summers, and R. Waldmann. 1990. Noise trader risk in financial markets. *Journal of Political Economics* 98:703.

Diamond, D. 1984. Financial intermediation and delegated monitoring. *Review of Economic Studies* 51:393.

Easterbrook, F., and D. Fischel. 1991. *The economic structure of corporate law.* Cambridge, MA: Harvard University Press.

Elton, E., M. Gruber, S. Dias, and M. Hlavka. 1993. Efficiency with costly information: A reinterpretation of evidence from managed portfolios. *Review of Financial Studies* 6:1.

Fair Credit Reporting Act. 2002. 15 U.S.C. § 1681–1681(u).

Fama, E. 1970. Efficient capital markets: A review of theory and empirical work. *Journal of Finance* 25:383.

———. 1991. Efficient capital markets II. *Journal of Finance* 46:1575.

———. 1998. Efficiency, long-term returns and behavioral finance. *Journal of Financial Economics* 49:283.

Fama, E., and K. French. 2001. The equity risk premium. Working paper 522, Center for Research in Securities Prices, University of Chicago School of Business. http://equity-premium.behaviouralfinance.net/FaFr01.pdf.

Fanto, J. 2001. Braking the merger momentum: Reforming corporate law governing mega-mergers. *Buffalo Law Review* 49:249, 288–89.

Fischoff, B., and P. Slovic. 1980. A little learning . . . confidence in multicue judgment. In *Attention and performance VIII*, ed. R. Nickerson. Cambridge, MA: MIT Press.

Fischoff, B., P. Slovic, and S. Liechtenstein. 1977. Knowing with uncertainty: The appropriateness of extreme confidence. *Journal of Experimental Psychology: Human Perception and Performance* 3:522.

Fox, J. 2002. Is the market rational? *Fortune*, December 9.

French, K., and J. Poterba. 1991. Investor diversification and international equity markets. *American Economic Review* 81:222.

Friedman, M. 1953. The case for flexible exchange rates. In *Essays in positive economics*, 157. Chicago: University of Chicago Press.

Gervais, S., and T. Odean. 2001. Learning to be overconfident. *Review of Financial Studies* 14:1.

Gigerenzer, G. 1991. How to make cognitive illusions disappear: Beyond "Heuristics and biases." *European Review of Social Psychology* 2:83.

Gigone, D., and R. Hastie. 1997. The impact of information on small group choice. *Journal of Personality and Social Psychology* 72:132.

Gilovich, T., J. Kruger, and K. Savitsky. 1999. Everyday egocentrism and everyday interpersonal problems. In *The social psychology of emotional and behavioral problems: Interfaces of social and clinical psychology*, ed. R. Leary and M. Leary, 69. Washington, DC: American Psychological Association.

Gilovich, T., and V. Medvec. 1995. The experience of regret: What, when and why. *Psychological Review* 102:379.

Gilovich, T., R. Valone, and A. Tversky. 1985. The hot hand in basketball: On the misperception of random sequences. *Cognitive Psychology* 17:295.

Gilson, R., and R. Kraakman. 1984. The mechanisms of market efficiency. *Virginia Law Review* 70:549.

Griffin, D., and A. Tversky. 1992. The weighing of evidence and the determinants of confidence. *Cognitive Psychology* 24:411, 412.

Grinblatt, M., S. Titman, and R. Wermers. 1995. Momentum investment strategies, portfolio performance and herding: A study of mutual fund behavior. *American Economic Review* 85:1008.

Grossman, S., and J. Stiglitz. 1980. On the impossibility of informationally efficient markets. *American Economic Review* 70:393.

Heath, C., R. Larrick, and J. Klayman. 1998. Cognitive repairs: How organizational practices can compensate for individual shortcomings. *Research in Organizational Behavior* 20:1.

Heath, C., and A. Tversky. 1991. Preference and belief: Ambiguity and competence in choice under uncertainty. *Risk and Uncertainty* 4:5.

Hilary, G., and L. Menzly. 2001. Does past success lead analysts to become overconfident? Working paper draft, University of Chicago.

Hirshleifer, D. 2001. Investor psychology and asset pricing. *Journal of Finance* 56:1533.

Ho, T., C. Camerer, and K. Weigelt. 1998. Iterated dominance and iterated best response in experimental "p-beauty contests." *American Economic Review* 88:947.

Hoshi, T., A. Kashyap, and D. Scharfstein. 1991. Corporate structure, liquidity and investment: Evidence from Japanese industrial groups. *Quarterly Journal of Economics* 106:33.

Hu, H. 1996. Illiteracy and intervention: Wholesale derivatives, retail mutual funds, and the matter of asset class. *Georgetown Law Journal* 84:2319.

Huang, P. 2002. Affective investing and effective securities regulation: Regulating anxiety and euphoria in securities markets. Draft, University of Pennsylvania (on file with authors).

Huberman, G. 2001. Familiarity breeds investment. *Review of Financial Studies* 14:659.

Huck, S., and J. Oechssler. 2000. Information cascades in the laboratory: Do they occur for the right reasons? *Journal of Political Economics* 21:661.

Hung, A., and C. Plott. 2001. Information cascades: Replication and an extension to majority rule and conformity rewarding institutions. *American Economic Review* 91:1508.

Jamal, K., and S. Sunder. 1996. Bayesian equilibrium in double auctions populated by biased traders. *Journal of Economic Behavior and Organizations* 31:273.

Janis, I. 1982. *Groupthink*. Indianapolis, IN: Houghton Mifflin College.

Jensen, M. 1978. Some anomalous evidence regarding market efficiency. *Journal of Financial Economics* 6:95.

————. 1986. Agency costs of free cash flow, corporate finance, and takeovers. *American Economic Review* 76:323.

Kahneman, D., and M. Riepe. 1998. Aspects of investor psychology. *Journal of Portfolio Management* 24:52.

Kahneman, D., and A. Tversky. 1984. Choices, values and frames. *American Psychologist* 39:341.

Kashyap, A. 2002. Sorting out Japan's financial crisis. Working paper, University of Chicago.

Kerr, N., R. MacCoun, and G. Kramer. 1996. Bias in judgment: Comparing individuals and groups. *Psychology Review* 103:687.

Koehler, D., and A. Tversky. 1994. Support theory: A nonextensional representation of subjective probability. *Psychological Review* 101:547.

Koehler, J. 1996. The base rate fallacy reconsidered: Descriptive, normative, and methodological challenges. *Behavioral and Brain Science* 19:1.

Kogan, L., and R. Uppal. 2002. Asset prices in a heterogeneous-agent economy with portfolio constraints. Working paper, MIT.

Kruger, J., and T. Gilovich. 1999. "Naïve cynicism" in everyday theories of responsibility assessment: On biased assumption of bias. *Journal of Personality and Social Psychology* 76:742.

Krugman, P. 1998. It's baaack! Japan's slump and the return of the liquidity trap. *Brookings Papers on Economic Activity* 1998:137.

Lakonishok, J., A. Shleifer, and R. Vishny. 1992. The structure and performance of the money management industry. *Brookings Papers on Economic Activity: Microeconomics* 1992:339.

Lamont, O., and R. Thaler. 2003. Can the market add and subtract? *Journal of Political Economy* 111:227.

Langevoort, D. 1996. Selling hope, selling risk: Some lessons for law from behavioral economics about stockbrokers and sophisticated customers. *California Law Review* 84:627.

————. 1997. A behavioral theory of why corporations mislead stock market investors (and cause other social harms). *Pennsylvania Law Review* 146:101, 149–56.

————. 2002. Taming the animal spirits of the stock markets: A behavioral approach to securities regulation. *Northwestern University Law Review* 97:135.

La Porta, R. 1999. Corporate ownership around the world. *Journal of Finance* 54:471.

Lee, J., A. Shleifer, and R. Thaler. 1991. Investor sentiment and the closed-end puzzle. *Journal of Finance* 46:79–109.

Levy, A., and M. Livingston. 1995. The gains from diversification reconsidered: Transaction costs and superior information. *Financial Markets, Institutions and Instruments* 4:1.

Lewis, K. 1999. Trying to explain home bias in equities and consumption. *Journal of Economic Literature* 37:571.

Locke, P., and S. Mann. 2000. Professional traders exhibit loss realization aversion. Draft. www.ssrn.com.

———. 2001. House money and overconfidence on the trading floor. Draft. www.ssrn.com.

Lowenstein, R. 2000. *When genius failed: The rise and fall of long-term capital management.* New York: Random House

Lynch, P. 1989. *One up on Wall Street.* New York: Simon and Schuster.

Mahoney, P. 1995a. Is there a cure for "excessive" trading? *Virginia Law Review* 81:713.

———. 1995b. Mandatory disclosure as a solution to agency problems. *University of Chicago Law Review* 62:1047.

Malkiel, B. 1995. Returns from investing in equity mutual funds 1971 to 1991. *Journal of Finance* 50:549.

Mehra, R., and E. Prescott. 1985. The equity premium puzzle. *Journal of Monetary Economics* 40:145.

Moscovici, S. 1985. Social influence and conformity. In *The handbook of social psychology*, vol. 2, ed. G. Linzey and E. Aronson, 347–412. Mahwah, NJ: Erlbaum.

Nelson, M., S. Krische, and R. Bloomfield. 2000. Confidence and investor's reliance on disciplined trading strategies. Draft.

Odean, T. 1998. Volume, volatility, price and profit when all traders are above average. *Journal of Finance* 8:1887.

Ofek, E., and M. Richardson. 2001. Dot-com mania: Market inefficiency in the internet sector. Working paper, New York University.

Oskamp, S. 1965. Overconfidence in case study judgments. *Journal of Consulting Psychology* 29:261.

Patel, J., R. Zeckhauser, and D. Hendricks. 1991. The rationality struggle: Illustrations from financial markets. *American Economic Review* 81:232.

Pennington, N., and R. Hastie. 1993. A theory of explanation-based decision making. In *Decision making in action: Models and methods*, ed. G. Klein and J. Orasanu, 188. Norwood, NJ: Ablex.

Prentice, R. 2002. Whither securities regulation? Some behavioral observations regarding proposals for its future. *Duke Law Journal* 51:239.

Rajan, R., and L. Zingales. 1998. Which capitalism? Lessons from the East Asian crisis. *Journal of Applied Corporate Finance* 11:40.

Roe, Mark J., ed. 1998. Corporate governance today: The Sloan Project on Corporate Governance at Columbia Law School.

Ross, L., and R. Nisbett. 1991. *The person and the situation: Perspectives of social psychology*. Philadelphia: Temple University Press.

Ross, L., and A. Ward. 1995. Psychological barriers to dispute resolution. In *Advances in experimental social psychology*, vol. 27, ed. M. Zanna, 255. San Diego, CA: Academic Press.

Schelling, T. 1960. *The strategy of conflict*. Cambridge, MA: Harvard University Press.

Schiller, Robert. 2000. *Irrational exuberance*. Princeton, NJ: Princeton University Press.

Schultz, P., and M. Zirman. 2001. Do the individuals closest to Internet firms believe they are overvalued? *Journal of Financial Economics* 59:347.

Scott, R. 2000. The limits of behavioral theories of law and social norms. *Virginia Law Review* 86:1603.

Shafir, E., I. Simonson, and A. Tversky. 1993. Reason-based choice. *Cognition* 49:11.

Shefrin, H. 1999. *Beyond greed and fear: Understanding behavioral finance and the psychology of investing*. Boston: Harvard University Press.

———. 2001. Behavioral corporate finance. *Journal of Applied Corporate Finance* 14:3.

Shefrin, H., and M. Statman. 1985. The disposition to sell winners too soon and ride losers too long: Theory and evidence. *Journal of Finance* 40:777.

———. 1994. Behavioral capital asset pricing theory. *Journal of Finance and Quantitative Analysis* 29:323.

Shiller, R., and J. Pound. 1989. Survey evidence of diffusion of interest among institutional investors. *Journal of Economic Behavior and Organization* 12:47.

Shleifer, A. 2000. *Inefficient markets: An introduction to behavioral finance*. Oxford: Oxford University Press.

Shleifer, A., and L. Summers. 1990. The noise trader approach to finance. *Journal of Economic Perspective* 4:19.

Soros, G. 1994. *Alchemy of finance: Reading the mind of the market*. New York: Wiley.

———. 2002. Busted: Why the markets can't fix themselves. *New Republic*, September 2, 18.

Spitzer, E. 1999. From Wall Street to Web Street: A report on the problems and promise of the on-line brokerage industry. Prepared by Investor Internet Bureau and Securities Bureau, 1189 PLI/Corp. 355. www.oag.state.ny.us/investors/1999_online_brokers/brokers.html.

Staw, B. 1997. Escalation of commitment: An update and appraisal. In *Organizational decision making*, ed. Z. Shapira, 191. Cambridge: Cambridge University Press.

Stewart, T., and C. Lusk. 1994. Seven components of judgmental forecasting skill: Implications for research and the improvement of forecasts. *Journal of Forecasting* 13:579.

Sunder, S. 2004. Market as artifact: Aggregate efficiency from zero-intelligence traders. In *Models of a Man: Essays in Memory of Herbert A. Simon*, ed. M. E. Augier and J. G. March, 501–519. Cambridge, MA: MIT Press.

Sunstein, C. 2002. The law of group polarization. *Journal of Political Philosophy* 10:175.

Thaler, R. 1997. Contest. *Financial Times*, Mastering Finance section, 29. May 9.

Thaler, R., and E. Johnson. 1991. Gambling with house money and trying to break even: The effects of prior outcomes on risky choice. In *Quasi-rational economics*, ed. R. Thaler, 48. New York: Russell Sage.

Tor, A. 2002. Fable of entry: Bounded rationality, market discipline, and legal policies. *Michigan Law Review* 101:482.

Trueman, B. 1994. Analyst forecasts and herding behavior. *Review of Financial Studies* 7:97.

Tversky, A., and D. Kahneman. 1974. Judgment under uncertainty: Heuristics and biases. *Science* 185:1124.

Uhlaner, C., and B. Grofman. 1986. The race may be close but my horse is going to win: Wish fulfillment in the 1980 presidential election. *Journal of Policy Behavior* 8:101.

Von Holstein, C. 1971. An experiment in probabilistic weather forecasting. *Journal of Applied Meteorology* 10:635.

Whyte, G. 1993. Escalating commitment in individuals and decision making: A prospect theory approach. *Organization Behavior and Human Decision Processes* 54:430.

Yates, J. F. 1990. *Judgment and decision making*. Englewood Cliffs, NJ: Prentice Hall.

# INDEX

*Italic page numbers indicate material in tables or figures.*